WORLD of
FORENSIC SCIENCE

WORLD of FORENSIC SCIENCE

VOLUME **2**
M-Z

THOMSON

GALE

Detroit • New York • San Francisco • San Diego • New Haven, Conn. • Waterville, Maine • London • Munich

World of Forensic Science

K. Lee Lerner and Brenda Wilmoth Lerner, Editors

Project Editor
Elizabeth Manar

Editorial
Luann Brennan, Meggin M. Condino, Kathleen J. Edgar, Madeline Harris, Melissa Hill, Kristine Krapp, Paul Lewon, Kimberley A. McGrath, Heather Price, Lemma Shomali, Jennifer York Stock

Editorial Support Services
Andrea Lopeman

Indexing
Synapse, The Knowledge Link Corporation

Rights and Acquisitions
Margaret Abendroth

Imaging and Multimedia
Emma Hull, Lezlie Light, Denay Wilding

Product Design
Michelle DiMercurio

Composition
Evi Seoud, Mary Beth Trimper

Manufacturing
Wendy Blurton, Dorothy Maki

LIBRARY OF CONGRESS CATALOGING-IN-PUBLICATION DATA

World of forensic science / K. Lee Lerner and Brenda Wilmoth Lerner, editors.
    p. cm.
      Includes bibliographical references and index.
      ISBN 1-4144-0294-5 (set : hardcover : alk. paper) —
      ISBN 1-4144-0295-3 (v. 1) — ISBN 1-4144-0296-1 (v. 2)
      1. Forensic sciences—Encyclopedias.
      2. Criminal investigation—Encyclopedias.
      I. Lerner, K. Lee. II. Lerner, Brenda Wilmoth. III. Title.
  HV8073.W674 2005
  363.25'03—dc22
                                         2005006921

This title is also available as an e-book.
ISBN: 1414406118 (set)
Contact your Gale sales representative for ordering information.

Printed in the United States of America
10 9 8 7 6 5 4 3 2 1

CONTENTS

ACKNOWLEDGMENTS

In compiling this edition, we have been fortunate in being able to rely upon the expertise and contributions of the following scholars who served as academic and contributing advisors for *World of Forensic Science*, and to them we would like to express our sincere appreciation for their efforts to ensure that *World of Forensic Science* contains the most accurate and timely information possible.

Contributing Advisors

Susan Aldridge, Ph.D.
London, United Kingdom

Brian Cobb, Ph.D.
Institute for Molecular and Human Genetics
Georgetown University, Washington, D.C.

Nicolas Dittert, Dr. rer. Nat.
University of Bremen
Bremen, Germany

Brian D. Hoyle, Ph.D.
Microbiologist
Nova Scotia, Canada

Alexandr Ioffe, Ph.D.
Russian Academy of Sciences
Moscow, Russia

Pamela V. Michaels, M.S.
Forensic Psychologist

Eric Stauffer, MS, F-ABC, CFEI
Senior Forensic Scientist
MME Forensic Services
Suwanee, GA

Because they are actively working in criminal investigations, some advisors, contributors, and biographical subjects requested the release or inclusion of a minimum of personal information.

Special Thanks

In addition to our academic and contributing advisors, it has been our privilege and honor to work with the following contributing writers, and scientists: Janet Alred, William Arthur Atkins, Juli Berwald, Ph.D., Robert G. Best, Ph.D., Sandra Galeotti, M.S., William Haneberg, Ph.D., Agnieszka Lichanska, Ph.D., Adrienne Wilmoth Lerner, Eric v.d. Luft, Ph.D., M.L.S., Holly F. McBain, Caryn Neumann, Ph.D., Michael J. O'Neal, Ph.D., Mark H. Phillips, Ph.D., and Jennifer M. Rossi, Ph.D.

Many of the advisors or contributors to *World of Forensic Science* authored specially commissioned articles within their fields of expertise. The editors would like to specifically acknowledge the following contributing advisors for their special contributions:

Ed Friedlander, M.D.
Autopsy

Antonio Farina, M.D., Ph.D.
Gestational age, forensic determination

Nancy Masters
Friction Ridge Skin and Personal Identification: A History of Latent Fingerprint Analysis

The editors would like to extend special thanks to Connie Clyde for her assistance in copyediting. The editors also wish to specially acknowledge Jenny Long for her diligent and extensive research related to the preparation of sensitive biographical entries.

The editors gratefully acknowledge the assistance of many at Thomson Gale for their help in preparing *World of Forensic Science*. The editors wish to specifically thank Ms. Meggin Condino for her help and keen insights while launching this project. Special thanks are also offered to Gale Senior Editor Kim

McGrath for her timely and friendly guidance through various project complexities. Most directly, the editors wish to acknowledge and offer both professional and personal thanks to our Project Manager, Ms. Elizabeth Manar, for her thoughtful and insightful sculpting of *World of Forensic Science*. Her good nature and keen eye kept *World of Forensic Science* on course throughout a hectic production schedule.

INTRODUCTION

World of Forensic Science portrays the vast scope and influence of modern forensic science. From its origins in pre-scientific human fascination with the causes, manner, and circumstances of death, to the increasingly vital role of forensic science in law, security, and global economic and health issues, *World of Forensic Science* contains articles dedicated to providing insight into the science, applications, and importance of forensics.

To cover a topic of such scope and impact as forensic science is a daunting task. Interest in forensics spans human history, impacts philosophical and religious thoughts about death, and now, fueled by television and movies, is reflected in popular culture. Human interest in forensics dates to our earliest recorded histories. Egyptian Pharaohs first appointed officials to make inquiries into questionable deaths as early as ca. 3000 B.C., and accounts of ancient Roman law include references to the use of forensic experts in legal proceedings. Medieval English Common law, upon which portions of modern United States law is based, called for forensic determinations in the handling of estates.

Forensic science also has played—and in some cases continues to play—an important part in philosophical and religious thoughts about death. In some religions, for example, the determination of the manner of death may impact whether a body is fit for burial in certain grounds. Religious beliefs can also impact forensics, as there are still areas of the world and groups that consider autopsies as desecration.

As a formal science, forensics grew lockstep with advances in many branches of science during the nineteenth and twentieth centuries. The interval from scientific invention to forensic application narrowed as forensic scientists borrowed from the latest innovations of virtually every field of science to solve mysteries. However, just as advances in microscopes and atomic science allowed forensic applications to aid in the investigation of crimes at the most minute molecular and cellular level, the breadth of applications of forensic science underwent exponential expansion. In modern times, in addition to solving local crime, the next global pandemic or bioterrorist attack might well be first detected by a forensic scientist initially investigating a mysterious death.

World of Forensic Science is a collection of nearly 600 entries that evidence the wide diversity of forensic science. Articles on topics such as art forgery and wine authenticity indicate the far-reaching economic impact of forensic science. Heart-wrenching applications of forensic science, from uncovering the mindsets, methods, and motives of modern terrorists to discovering the far-reaching extent of natural disasters, are discussed in articles ranging from the "Identification of Beslan victims in Russia" to "Identification of tsunami victims"

Articles on a number of topics related to genetics, DNA fingerprinting, and microbiology show how recent advances in research quickly find their way into forensic application. A range of articles related to basic science reflects the fact that modern forensic investigators must be able to understand and properly apply tools from virtually every scientific discipline.

Nature is often innately tricky enough to confound scientists seeking to uncover its mysteries, but forensic scientists must also pit their skills against those deliberately trying to conceal or mislead. The importance of skill and experience to the forensic investigator is evidenced in the authoritative writing of many articles, including Ed Friedlander's article on autopsy procedures and Nancy Master's article on latent fingerprint analysis. (Friedlander serves as chairman, Dept. of Pathology, Kansas City University of Medicine and Biosciences, is board-certified in anatomic and clinical pathology, and has conducted an estimated 700 autopsies. Masters is the 2004 Dondero Award winner for identification in forensics.)

While selected topics acknowledge the relationship of forensic science to history and culture, and others describe the brutal realities of sensational crimes involving serial murders, ritual killers, or bombers, it was our intent to keep *World of Forensic Science* focused on science. The editors hope that *World of Forensic Science* serves to inspire a new generation of forensic scientists and investigators. It is also our modest wish that this book provide valuable information to students and readers regarding topics often in the news or the subject of civic debate.

K. Lee Lerner & Brenda Wilmoth Lerner
Editors
Santa Rosa Island, Pensacola, FL, and London, U.K.
April 2005

How to Use This Book

The articles in the book are meant to be understandable by anyone with a curiosity about topics in forensic science. Cross-references to related articles, definitions, and biographies in this collection are indicated by **bold-faced type**, and these cross-references will help explain and expand the individual entries. *World of Forensic Science* carries specifically selected fundamental topics in genetics, anatomy, physiology, microbiology, and immunology that provide a basis for understanding forensic science applications.

This first edition of *World of Forensic Science* has been designed with ready reference in mind:

- **Entries are arranged alphabetically**, rather than by chronology or scientific field.
- **Bold-faced terms** direct the reader to related entries.
- **"See also" references** at the end of entries alert the reader to related entries not specifically mentioned in the body of the text.
- A **sources consulted** section lists the most worthwhile print material and web sites we encountered in the compilation of this volume. It is there for the inspired reader who wants more information on the people and discoveries covered in this volume.
- The **historical chronology** includes many of the significant events in the advancement of forensic science.
- A **comprehensive general index** guides the reader to topics and persons mentioned in the book. Bolded page references refer the reader to the term's full entry.

Although there is an important and fundamental link between the composition and shape of biological molecules and their detection by forensic testing, a detailed understanding of chemistry is neither assumed or required for *World of Forensic Science*. Accordingly, students and other readers should not be intimidated or deterred by the complex names of chemical molecules. Where necessary, sufficient information regarding chemical structure is provided. If desired, more information can easily be obtained from any basic chemistry or biochemistry reference.

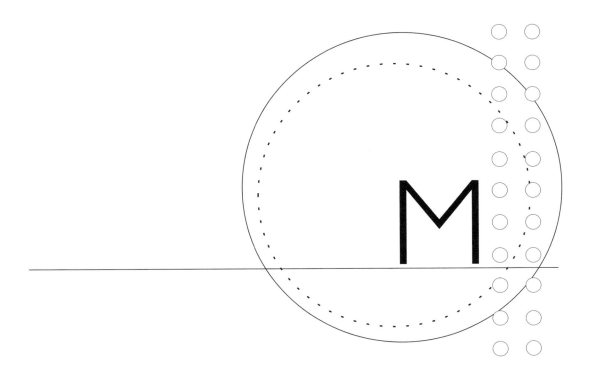

Herbert Leon MacDonell

AMERICAN
FORENSIC SCIENTIST

Herbert L. MacDonell has conducted important research and investigation in the field of **forensic science** for over forty years. MacDonell is the inventor of the MAGNA Brush **fingerprint** device, and is considered an expert in **blood** splatter analysis. MacDonell has written and lectured about a wide range of forensic science topics, and has consulted on several high-profile criminal cases.

MacDonell attended the University of Rhode Island, earning his M.S. degree in 1956. He soon went into the field of forensic science, and in 1960 invented the MAGNA Brush fingerprint device. The brush, which changed the way fingerprint **evidence** was processed, uses a magnet and metallic powder to identify a latent print. Because the MAGNA Brush has no bristles, it reduces the likelihood of damaging the ridge detail of the print. He also began extensive research and experimentation with blood splatter analysis. In 1971, he wrote the booklet *Flight Characteristics and Stain Patterns of Human Blood*, published by the U.S. Department of Justice. It contains MacDonell's findings and instructs crime scene investigators on how to interpret blood spatters.

MacDonell continued his successful career by taking the position of director of the Laboratory for Forensic Science in Corning, New York. Because of his breadth of experience, he has consulted on criminal cases across the country and around the world.

He testified in the O.J. Simpson case on blood evidence matters, and was involved in the investigations of the assassinations of Senator Robert F. Kennedy and Dr. Martin Luther King Jr. He has also appeared on a number of news television programs, including *Good Morning America*, *20/20*, and *Dateline NBC*.

Along with author Alfred Allan Lewis, MacDonell wrote the 1984 book *The Evidence Never Lies: The Casebook of a Modern Sherlock Holmes*. MacDonell serves as the subject of the book, and profiles a number of cases that he worked on and solved. He has also written numerous articles for a variety of **professional publications**. In addition, MacDonell has shared his expertise in academic settings, as a lecturer at various conferences and universities. He also serves as the director of the Bloodstain Evidence Institute, which runs a study program for forensic science students. MacDonell was the 1974 winner of the John A. Dondero Award from the **International Association for Identification**.

SEE ALSO Bloodstain evidence; Simpson (O. J.) murder trial.

Mad cow disease investigation

Bovine spongiform encephalopathy (BSE, also popularly known as mad cow disease) and Creutzfeldt-Jakob disease (CJD, which occurs in humans) are ailments in which the functioning of the brain is progressively impaired.

Beginning in the 1980s in the United Kingdom, mad cow disease has been a sporadic concern in that country and others. By 1992, three cows in every 1,000 in Britain were estimated to have the disease. Then in the winter of 1997, another outbreak led to the slaughter of 100,000 cattle as a measure to stop the spread of the disease. In more recent incidents, detection of the disease in the Canadian province of Alberta in 2003 led to a ban on imports of Canadian beef to the United States. As of mid-2005, the ban is still in effect, although it is anticipated to be lifted before year's end.

The detection of mad cow disease and the determination of the extent of the disease involved a large, coordinated epidemiological (disease-tracking) and **forensic science** investigation.

Initially, a cow may be suspected of being infected because of behavioral changes, including loss of coordination, clumsy gait, and even the appearance of foam at the mouth (hence the origin of the mad cow moniker). Typically, the suspect cow will be removed from the herd and slaughtered. Then, examination of tissues and **fluids** commences. These examinations can involve microscopy of tissue sample and the use of antibodies to identify the causative agent.

Mad cow disease is associated with visually abnormal pinpoints (or plaques) in the brain, and in a changed texture of the brain tissue. These alterations are detected when the brain tissue is microscopically examined as part of an **autopsy** of a cow suspected of having the disease. The brain tissue, particularly in the cortex and cerebellum, becomes filled with large open spaces (vacuoles) and becomes spongy in texture. The "spongiform" part of the BSE descriptor comes from this texture characteristic.

In Canada, cattle have been tagged with an identifying code since 2001. The identifier enables the movement of cattle to be tracked from the herd (and from herd to herd) to the slaughterhouse. This enables the pattern of an illness outbreak, including mad cow disease, to be better investigated.

Mad cow disease, CJD, and maybe even other diseases such as scrapie, transmissible mink encephalopathy, fatal familial insomnia, and kuru, are thought to have a common cause, namely **prions**. Prions are particles that are made solely of protein. Even though they lack genetic material, they are infectious.

Mad cow disease causes a progressive neurological deterioration in cattle that is similar to the course of CJD in humans. Infected cattle are more temperamental, have problems with their posture and coordination, have progressively greater difficulty in rising off the ground and walking, produce less milk, have severe twitching of muscles, and lose weight even though their appetite is undiminished. The suspected incubation period, the time from when the animal is first infected until symptoms appear, ranges from two to eight years. After appearance of symptoms, deterioration is rapid and the animal dies or is destroyed within six months. The disease is one of a group of related diseases called transmissible spongiform encephalopathies (TSEs) in animals.

Bovine spongiform encephalopathy was confirmed as a disease of cattle in November 1996. Since then, with the exception of cases in Canada and a single case in the United States in 2004, almost all reported cases have been in cattle born in the United Kingdom. Other countries in Europe and Asia have reported BSE, but in far fewer numbers than in the U.K. As of November 2001, the total number of confirmed cases of BSE in U.K. cattle was just over 181,000. In 1993, a BSE epidemic in the U.K. peaked at almost 1,000 new cases per week. While the cause of this near-exclusivity has yet to be conclusively determined, a common practice in the United Kingdom was to feed cattle "offal," the ground up waste from the slaughter process. Cattle feed was also prepared from the ground bones and tissues of sheep, cattle, and other animals, providing a means of delivering prions from infected animals to healthy ones. The exact origin of the prions is not known. Sheep, susceptible to a similar disease called scrapie, known for many years, are considered a likely source.

Until the 1900s, scientists thought that the transmission of the BSE agent to humans did not occur. However, several post-mortem, forensic studies (autopsies and brain tissue examination) conducted in the 1990s debunked this assumption. In 1994, cases of young people (median age was 26 years) with a CJD-type disease began appearing in the U.K., often in related geographical areas. As CJD affects mostly people over age 65, and symptoms differed slightly and developed more slowly in those affected in the new outbreak, the disease was given the distinct name of variant CJD, or vCJD. An intensive investigation was launched that eventually revealed vCJD as most likely caused by eating beef from cattle infected with BSE. As of 2005, 105 cases of vCJD have been identified in young adults mostly in the U.K., with three cases occurring in France and one in Ireland. The largest number of cases occurred during 1999 (27), and has decreased to less than five cases per year afterward, suggesting that the outbreak of the disease is waning. Chances of contracting vCJD by eating beef in the U.K. are very small as of 2005, due to measures implemented more than a decade earlier (longer than the usual vCJD incubation period) to protect the **food supply** from BSE-infected beef.

As well, studies on mice published in 2004 have cast doubt on the previous view that the infectious agent of mad cow disease is localized exclusively in only the brain, spleen, spinal cord, and lymph tissue. Prions were additionally detected in the kidney, pancreas, and liver tissues of infected mice. This finding has profound forensic implications, since typically an investigation of mad cow disease focuses on examining samples from the brain and the other traditional locations. The presence of prions elsewhere would be overlooked. As there is no conclusive diagnostic test for variant CJD while an affected person is alive, other than a costly and invasive brain biopsy that will offer no benefit for the outcome of the disease, forensic examination of brain tissue at autopsy is the usual method of providing a definitive diagnosis of CJD and variant CJD in humans, and BSE in cattle.

SEE ALSO Animal evidence; Autopsy; Prions.

Mail sanitization

Forensic investigations sometimes require the analysis of substances found in contaminated mail. Identifying **toxins** or harmful residues present in mail, along with their concentrations, provides **evidence** in criminal cases and information necessary to decontaminate the mail. Mail sanitization is the process in which mail is decontaminated. The possible methods for mail sanitization work by exposing mail to radiation, high pressure, or gases. Microorganisms, such as the bacterium that causes **anthrax**, cannot survive these conditions. The process of mail sanitization can be applied as a precautionary measure to kill microorganisms that may be contained in the mail or to sterilize mail that is known to be contaminated with dangerous microorganisms.

Shortly after the September 11, 2001, terrorist attacks, the United States Postal Service (USPS) was the vehicle for **bioterrorism** attacks on Americans. Mail containing the anthrax bacterium was detected. Five persons who were infected by the anthrax bacterium died from the disease. As a direct result of this, the USPS developed an Emergency Preparedness Plan with the goal of protecting USPS employees and customers from future bioterrorism attacks. The Plan is composed of six initiatives:

- Prevention—reducing the risk that the mail could be used as a vehicle for bioterrorism.
- Protection and health-risk reduction—reducing the risk that USPS employees and customers could be exposed to biological weapons and preventing contaminated mail from contaminating other mail.
- Detection and identification—detection and **identification** of biological weapons as early in the mail stream as possible.
- Intervention—routine decontamination of mail as a precautionary measure.
- Decontamination—elimination of known biological weapons in the mail.
- Investigation—enhancement of criminal investigation methods.

Mail sanitization applies to the intervention and decontamination initiatives. Achieving mail safety is no small undertaking when one considers the complexity of the USPS system and volume of mail that is processed. The postal service handles nearly 680 million pieces of mail each day. This mail primarily consists of letters, "flats" such as catalogs and magazines, and packages. Mail enters the USPS system in many different ways, including street collection boxes, post offices, personal mailboxes, and business mail entry units. The USPS has about 300 processing and distribution centers that manage outgoing mail. The computer-controlled sorting equipment and data processing systems located at these centers distribute mail to its destination. Mail is moved from processing and distribution centers to final destination processing centers by ground, rail, or air transportation. Once at a final destination processing center, mail is then sorted and distributed to the recipients.

The USPS is studying several different methods of decontamination to find one (or more) that can effectively sanitize mail. To be useful in mail sanitization, the decontamination method must thoroughly penetrate letters, flats, and packages but not damage the mail in any way. Irradiation has been found to be the only acceptable method for decontaminating mail. The addition of a sanitization step to the USPS mail system may slow down the mail delivery rate.

Ionizing radiation kills bacteria. The energy from ionizing radiation is transferred to molecules which, when absorbed by the molecules, breaks chemical bonds and destroys chemical structures. Reactive chemicals (ions and free radicals) that are produced by this process cause even further damage. This results in significant damage to the **DNA** and proteins of bacteria, causing the bacteria to die.

The USPS is considering three sources of ionizing radiation as candidates for mail sanitization: x rays, gamma rays, and electron beams. All three are used to sterilize medical equipment and to kill microorganisms in food to prevent spoilage. They each can kill the anthrax bacteria. Radiation can easily penetrate and sanitize most types of mail, however, it may damage film, electronics, and live objects such as seeds.

X rays are a type of high-energy electromagnetic radiation. X-ray particles, or photons, are generated when electron-dense materials are bombarded by high-energy electrons. X rays have a high-energy content and can penetrate most objects.

Gamma rays are another type of high-energy electromagnetic radiation. Gamma rays are released by decaying radioactive compounds such as cesium 137 or cobalt 60.

An electron beam, or e-beam, is a stream of electrons that is propelled by a high accelerating voltage. The energy content of the e-beam is determined by the accelerating voltage and is lower than both x rays and gamma rays.

Of the three ionizing radiation sources, e-beam technology is the safest and most readily adaptable system for mail sanitization. In 2001, the USPS bought eight e-beam machines and planned to install them in Washington, D.C., and the New York and New Jersey areas. The e-beam machine requires high power and chilled water and must be contained by a structure with 10 to 15 foot-thick concrete walls and a six foot-thick concrete ceiling. E-beam technology has been used to sanitize incoming federal government mail only.

Types of non-ionizing radiation that have been used for sterilization are ultraviolet (UV) light irradiation and microwave irradiation. Both are effective at killing microorganisms, but by different ways.

UV light radiation damages DNA by causing DNA strand breaks and binding DNA bases together (thymine dimers). Bacteria with damaged DNA cannot reproduce or survive. UV light radiation cannot penetrate objects and is used to sterilize surfaces and air only. In addition, some microorganisms are resistant to the effects of UV radiation. Therefore, UV radiation is an unacceptable method to sanitize mail.

Microwave radiation is a low-energy non-ionizing radiation. The energy in microwaves is transferred to water molecules in microorganisms. The water molecules heat up and the heat is transferred to surround-

ing molecules, thereby damaging and ultimately killing the microorganism. Microwave radiation sanitization has shortcomings. Most importantly, it is difficult to control the heating effects and it is common to have "hot spots" and "cold spots." Also, the water content of dormant bacterial cells (**spores**) is low, so microwave radiation may not destroy them. Microwave radiation would be ineffective for mail sanitization.

Ultra-high-pressure (UHP) sterilization is accomplished by applying a pressure of almost 100,000 psi, which causes physical changes to DNA and proteins. The resulting cellular damage kills the microorganisms. Without added heat, UHP sterilization techniques may be less effective against bacterial spores than against growing bacterial cells.

UHP sterilization is being developed for the food industry and has been shown to be effective on both solid and liquid foods. The UHP sterilization cycle time can be less than 30 minutes and the process is non-destructive to the object being sterilized. This method could be applied to mail as a sanitization method, however, a UHP sterilization system for mail will not be available for several years.

Certain gases have anti-microbial properties and are used for disinfection and sterilization. Large amounts of gas would be needed to sterilize mail and it is not evident that gases can kill microorganisms within sealed letters, flats, and packages. Gaseous sterilization of mail is not currently a viable option for mail sanitization, though the USPS has identified several possible candidates for gaseous sanitization:

- Chlorine dioxide—an oxidizer that disrupts proteins and protein synthesis. It was used to disinfect an office building that was contaminated with anthrax spores.
- Ethylene oxide—an alkylating agent that damages proteins, leading to bacterial or viral death. It is used to sterilize medical equipment.
- Methyl bromide—a toxic pesticide that has been used to fumigate large buildings. It is an ozone-depleting chemical and will not be used after 2006.
- Ozone—an oxidizing agent used to disinfect water and decontaminate unoccupied spaces. Its effect on spores is variable depending upon the specific bacterial strain.

SEE ALSO Anthrax; Biological weapons, genetic identification; Decontamination methods; Toxicological analysis; Toxicology; Toxins.

Malicious data

A forensic examination such as **forensic accounting** often involves tracing an electronic data trail. Roadblocks can be deliberately introduced to obscure the trail and thwart those attempting to uncover the wrongdoing. As well, data can be deliberately introduced with the aim of compromising or destroying the quality of the information housed in a database or computer file. Forensic accounting and criminal investigations both attempt to identify so-called malicious data.

Malicious data is data that, when introduced to a computer—sometimes by an operator unaware that he or she is doing so—will cause the computer to perform actions undesirable to the computer's owner. It often takes the form of input to a computer application such as a word-processing or data spreadsheet program. It is thus distinguished from a malicious program such as a **computer virus**, compared to which malicious data is perhaps even more stealthy.

An example of malicious data at work is the Melissa "virus," which spread through the e-mail systems of the world on March 26, 1999. Though the media called Melissa a virus, this was a misnomer; rather, it was a case of malicious data wedded to a macro virus, or a virus that works by setting in motion an automatic sequence of actions within a software application. Melissa did not damage computers themselves, yet it produced a result undesirable to anyone but its creator. By taking advantage of a feature built into the Microsoft Word program, it sent itself to the first 50 addresses in the user's Outlook Express, an e-mail program also produced by Microsoft. Melissa, for which computer programmer David L. Smith was eventually charged, caused $80 million worth of damage, primarily in the form of lost productivity resulting from the shutdown of overloaded mailboxes.

In practice, malicious data is much like a malicious program, yet it is difficult to protect against malicious data using the methods typically used to circumvent malicious programs, such as file access control, firewalls, and the like. Malicious data has been used, not simply for pranks such as Smith's, but to transfer funds out of the operator's financial accounts, and into those of the perpetrator. In this crime, the operator is a participant, albeit an unwitting and unwilling one.

SEE ALSO Computer forensics; Computer hackers; Computer security and computer crime investigation.

Marcello Malpighi

3/10/1628–8/29/1694
ITALIAN
PHYSICIAN

In the second half of the seventeenth century, Marcello Malpighi used the newly invented microscope to make a number of important discoveries about living tissues and structures, earning himself enduring recognition as a founder of scientific microscopy, histology (the study of tissues), embryology, and the science of plant anatomy.

Malpighi was born at Crevalcore, just outside Bologna, Italy. The son of the owners of a small plot of land, Malpighi studied **medicine** and philosophy at the University of Bologna. While at Bologna, Malpighi was part of a small anatomical society headed by the teacher Bartolomeo Massari, in whose home the group met to conduct dissections and vivisections. Malpighi later married Massari's sister.

In 1655 Malpighi became a lecturer in logic at the University of Bologna. One year later, he assumed the chair of theoretical medicine at the University of Pisa. In 1659 he returned to Bologna as lecturer in theoretical, then practical, medicine. From 1662 to 1666 he held the principal chair in medicine at the University of Messina. Finally, in 1666, he returned again to Bologna, where he remained for the rest of his teaching and research career. In 1691, at the age of sixty-three, Malpighi was called by his friend Pope Innocent XII to serve as the pontiff's personal physician. Reluctantly, Malpighi agreed and moved to Rome, where he died on November 29, 1694, in his room in the Quirinal Palace.

Early in his medical career, Malpighi became absorbed in using the microscope to study a wide range of living tissue—animal, insect, and plant. At the time, this was an entirely new field of scientific investigation. Malpighi soon made a profoundly important discovery. Microscopically examining a frog's lungs, he was able for the first time to describe the lung's structure accurately—thin air sacs surrounded by a network of tiny blood vessels. This explained how air (oxygen) is able to diffuse into the blood vessels, a key to understanding the process of respiration. It also provided the one missing piece of **evidence** to confirm William Harvey's revolutionary theory of the blood circulation: Malpighi had discovered the capillaries, the microscopic connecting link between the veins and arteries that Harvey—with no microscope available—had only been able to postulate. Malpighi published his findings about the lungs in 1661.

Malpighi used the microscope to make an impressive number of other important observations, all "firsts." He observed a "host of red atoms" in the blood—the red blood corpuscles. He described the papillae of the tongue and skin—the receptors of the senses of taste and touch. He identified the rete mucosum, the Malpighian layer, of the skin. He found that the nerves and spinal column both consisted of bundles of fibers. He clearly described the structure of the kidney and suggested its function as a urine producer. He identified the spleen as an organ, not a gland; structures in both the kidney and spleen are named after him. He demonstrated that bile is secreted in the liver, not the gall bladder. In showing bile to be a uniform color, he disproved a 2,000-year-old idea that the bile was yellow and black. He described glandular adenopathy, a syndrome rediscovered by Thomas Hodgkin (1798–1866) and given that man's name 200 years later.

Malpighi also conducted groundbreaking research in plant and insect microscopy. His extensive studies of the silkworm were the first full examination of insect structure. His detailed observations of chick embryos laid the foundation for microscopic embryology. His botanical investigations established the science of plant anatomy. The variety of Malpighi's microscopic discoveries piqued the interest of countless other researchers and firmly established microscopy as a science.

SEE ALSO Microscope, comparison; Microscopes.

Manslaughter SEE Murder vs. manslaughter

Markov (Georgi) murder investigation

The 1978 **murder** of Bulgarian dissident playwright and broadcaster Georgi Markov is one of the most unusual events of the Cold War. While walking on a busy London street, Markov was struck by a poison pellet fired from an umbrella. After his death, it took British authorities weeks to discover that Markov had been poisoned by **ricin**.

Born in 1929 to an army officer, Markov witnessed the Communist takeover of Bulgaria in 1944. Subsequently, as a student at Sofia's Polytechnic University, Markov was imprisoned for his anti-communist beliefs in 1950 and 1951. He became a chemical engineer and briefly ran a metallurgy factory. During his career as

an engineer, Markov wrote newspaper articles and short stories. In 1962, he became a literary star with the publication of the novel *Men*, and he began to socialize with the Bulgarian elite.

Markov defected to the West in 1969. Within ten days of his defection, an article appeared in a Communist party newspaper criticizing Markov's works. Within two months, all of his plays had been taken off the stage. Within the year, the Bulgarian press was describing Markov as a traitor. In 1973, a special court in Sofia sentenced Markov in absentia to six and a half years imprisonment and the confiscation of his property.

In 1975, Markov began to share his stories of life in Bulgaria on Radio Free Europe and the British Broadcasting (BBC) radio. He was particularly known for his harsh criticism of the autocratic rule of the communist leader, Todor Zhivkov. Markov's shows were broadcast into Bulgaria and he was seen as providing inspiration to the Bulgarian dissident movement.

Markov had been warned that the Bulgarian government was planning to kill him, but he believed that his enemies would attempt to administer poison orally. On September 7, 1978, Markov left his BBC office at Bush House in London to take the train home to Clapham in southwest London. As he passed a bus stop on Waterloo Bridge in the middle of the day, Markov felt a sudden, stinging pain in the back of his right thigh. Turning sharply, he saw a man behind him bending down to retrieve an umbrella. The man murmured, "I'm sorry" and then immediately hailed a taxi. Though in pain, Markov continued home. Only in the early morning hours of September 8, when his temperature rose suddenly did Markov go to the hospital. He lingered for four days and then died on September 11.

Physicians were unsuccessful in diagnosing Markov's illness. However, the circumstances of the attack and Markov's political leanings prompted the British government to order an **autopsy**. A post mortem, conducted with the help of scientists from Britain's germ warfare center at Porton Down, established that he had been killed by a tiny pellet containing a 0.2 milligram dose of the poison ricin. The platinum and iridium pellet, smaller than a pinhead, was detected only because it had not dissolved as expected.

Ricin is derived from the castor oil plant. It is known as a masquerade poison because ricin-caused symptoms are easy to confuse with those from a viral or bacterial infection. Victims experience abdominal pain, nausea, cramps, seizures, and dehydration. Death usually ensues from cardiac arrest due to an electrolyte (key minerals such as sodium and potassium) imbalance.

Riverboats pass beneath a span of Waterloo Bridge in London, where the Bulgarian dissident Georgi Markov was murdered with a ricin-filled dart fired from an umbrella in 1978. © PATRICK WARD/CORBIS

Scotland Yard announced the medical examiner's findings and reported that a similar attack had failed in France. In Paris, another Bulgarian defector, Vladimir Kostov, was attacked with an umbrella in late August. Kostov was ill for a few days with stiffness and fever, but he recovered. By chance, the poison pellet that struck Kostov had lodged in muscle in his upper back, away from major blood vessels.

Markov's assassin has never been captured. In June 1992, General Vladimir Todorov, the former Bulgarian intelligence chief, was sentenced to sixteen months in jail for destroying ten volumes of material on the case. A second suspect, General Stoyan Savov, the deputy interior minister, committed suicide rather than face trial for destroying the files. Vasil Kotsev, widely believed to have been the commander of the **assassination** plot, died in an unexplained car accident. The Soviet KGB is also suspected of providing technical assistance.

Markov's spectacular death proved to be a public relations disaster for Bulgaria. In 1998, Bulgaria's democratically elected President Peter Stoyanov stated that the Markov assassination was one of the darkest moments in his country's communist era. Stoyanov said authorities would continue to investigate the case. Scotland Yard has also kept the case open.

SEE ALSO Assassination; Assassination weapons, biochemical; Death, cause of; Medical examiner; Ricin.

Marks and scars SEE Body marks

James Marsh

9/2/1794–6/21/1846
ENGLISH
CHEMIST

With a distinguished career as an English chemist in the 1830s and 1840s, James Marsh (1794–1846) is historically well-known for the research and development of a dependable, simple laboratory test for the **identification** of minute traces of arsenic.

The Marsh test (or the Marsh Arsenic test), as it is known today, involved the testing of given samples of food, fluid, or deceased human tissue by forensic toxicologists from the middle part of the nineteenth century to well into the latter half of the twentieth century. In fact, the test was often used by **Mathieu Joseph Bonaventure Orfila** (1787–1853), the person who is often considered as the originator of forensic **toxicology**. The Marsh test gave experts an effective and accurate way to detect small amounts of arsenic—a sometimes-fatal chemical contaminant when placed accidentally or intentionally within the body. In Marsh's day, arsenic poisoning was a very large problem throughout the world, and was often not discovered by ordinary analysis. The development of this testing method and accompanying apparatus by Marsh helped to promote the scientific advancements of poisoning investigations, along with assisting the outcome of several notable **murder** trials.

Little is known about Marsh as he grew up in England and began his professional career at the Royal British Arsenal (also called the Woolwich Arsenal), which was located east of London in the town of Woolwich. His scientific abilities were probably first noticed in 1836 when leaders of the neighboring town of Plumstead asked advice of him as to the possible reason of arsenic poisoning within the deceased body of a local leader. As a qualified chemist who was familiar with the accepted German methods of testing autopsies, Marsh applied yellow precipitates, ammonia solvents, and various other laboratory materials to the tissues of the dead body and to the coffee that was alleged to have contained the poison. Marsh presented his **evidence** at the inquest, which clearly identified arsenic in the victim's body. However, at the trial the jury did not understand his technical testimony and acquitted the accused grandson of the decedent. (The grandson later confessed to the crime after being convicted of later wrongdoings.) Because of this work, Marsh is considered today as the first person to present the results of toxicology analysis in court.

Because of his inability to convince the jury, Marsh became determined to develop new laboratory tests that could prove the presence of even small traces of arsenic and make the results understandable to even uninformed people. Basing his investigations on the previous work (of transforming arsenic to a related gas called arsine) by Swedish scientist Karl Wilhelm Scheele (1742–1786), Marsh produced hydrogen from a reaction of adding solid zinc metal to a glass receptacle containing either hydrochloric acid or sulfuric acid. When Marsh added tissue or body fluid to the hydrogen-generating container, its reaction with the zinc and acid would create hydrogen gas. If any type of arsenic was present, the hydrogen gas when heated by Marsh would react with it to produce arsine gas, which fumed off to deposit a silvery-black film—that is, metallic arsenic—on a porcelain bowl.

Marsh was able to produce visible stains on the bowl when only very small amounts of arsenic were present. In fact, as little as 0.1 milligrams (0.0000035 ounces) of arsenic were detected by using the test designed by Marsh. Later, Marsh designed a U-shaped glass tube with a narrowed nozzle at one end to provide a controlled reaction and to help ignite the exiting gas. Marsh wrote a report based on his pioneering research and resulting test that was published in the *Edinburgh Philosophical Journal* in October 1836, and followed with two other Marsh test articles in 1837 and 1840.

Upon publication of the article, toxicologists and other scientists around the world experimented with the information that Marsh provided. French toxicologist Orfila, already famous in his own right, made important improvements to the Marsh test such as recommending that all reacting chemicals be shown free of arsenic before being used in an investigation. In 1840, the Marsh test was instrumental in making a conviction in a major murder case, one that was decided by a report by Orfila. Specifically, Orfila applied the Marsh test to decide the controversial trial of Marie Lafarge, who was charged with murder in the arsenic poisoning of her husband. Based on his results, Lafarge was found guilty and sentenced to death (which was later reduced to life in prison). Due to the scientific work of Orfila and his expert application of the Marsh test, procedures were first formalized for proving poisoning in court cases with the use of **toxicological analysis**.

Throughout his career, Marsh worked at the Woolwich arsenal where he was employed in the fields of electromagnetism and artillery technology. While still employed at the arsenal, March died in London at the age of 51. After his death, the Marsh test was extensively applied by forensic toxicologists until more technically-advanced methods of instrumental analysis such as atomic absorption **spectroscopy** and x-ray fluorescence spectroscopy replaced it in the latter half of the twentieth century.

SEE ALSO Autopsy; Toxicological analysis.

Nancy E. Masters

AMERICAN
FORENSIC LATENT PRINT ANALYST

For more than thirty years, Nancy E. Masters has made significant contributions to the field of **fingerprint identification**. As a latent print analyst, she has participated in crime scene investigations and testified as an expert in court trials in accordance with her extensive **training** in examining fingerprints found at crime scenes. Masters also has developed curriculum, written books, and lectured nationally and internationally on the subject of latent print techniques.

Masters attended Sacramento State University, Sacramento, California, earning a bachelor's degree in political science in 1969 and a secondary teaching credential in 1972. She launched her career in **forensic science** immediately, working for the California Department of Justice (CDJ) in its Fingerprint Program from 1967 to 1981. Masters then moved into the CDJ's Latent Print Program, as a latent print analyst, for the next seven years. During this time, and throughout her career, Masters continued her training and education in the field by attending seminars and programs run by the Federal Bureau of Investigation, the **International Association for Identification**, and the CDJ. She was awarded the California Governor's Safety Award in 1987.

In 1988, Masters began working with the CDJ's Criminalistics Institute. As an instructor there, she developed curriculum for courses on latent print techniques, latent print comparisons, and specialized latent print techniques, including physical, chemical, photographic, and **laser** techniques. Using her experience and knowledge, she has instructed law enforcement personnel throughout the world.

Masters has also significantly contributed to literature on the subject of fingerprint identification. In 1995, she wrote the textbook *Safety for the Forensic Identification Specialist*, with a second edition released in 2002. In the book, Masters instructs technicians on safety issues while dealing with fingerprint **evidence**, **physical evidence**, and crime scene hazards. She was also a contributing author to the *Clandestine Laboratory Manual of Instruction and Procedure*, used by law enforcement agencies in the United States.

Since 1996, Masters has continued her work in fingerprint identification as a consultant for the CDJ and other entities. She has also worked as a speaker and article author, contributing to trade journals such as the *Journal of Forensic Identification* and the *FBI Law Enforcement Bulletin*. In 2004, she won the John A. Dondero Award from the International Association for Identification.

SEE ALSO Careers in forensic science; Evidence.

Fuseo Matsumur

JAPANESE
TRACE EVIDENCE EXAMINER

Louis Pasteur, the nineteenth century medical researcher, once noted, "Where observation is concerned, chance favors only the prepared mind." And so it occurred, almost a century after Pasteur's death, that an ordinary **trace evidence** examiner in Japan made a rather profound observation. In 1977, Fuseo Matsumur was preparing microscope slides for an investigation being conducted by the Japanese National Police Agency. The crime involved the **murder** of a taxi driver, and Fuseo's task was to glue hair samples from the crime scene to glass slides for later microscopic examination. While carrying out this routine task, Matsumur made a seemingly simple observation: the fumes from the Superglue® (cyanoacrylate adhesive) he was using caused his fingerprints to become visible on the glass slides.

Fingerprint "dusting," the print retrieval technique commonly seen on television, is somewhat limited in its use, because the perspiration which forms a fingerprint evaporates rather quickly, leaving nothing to attract and hold the dusting powder. Long after the moisture in a fingerprint has evaporated, however, the amino acids found in human sweat remain behind, sometimes for months. These amino acids attract the fumes from Superglue® and other brands of cyanoacrylate adhesive, forming a sticky image of the latent print, which is then dusted and lifted with a wide piece of transparent tape.

While Matsumur knew none of the science behind what he had observed, he recognized its potential importance in the field of **criminology**. Matsumur quickly relayed his observation to Masato Soba, a print examiner at the agency, who began exploring the technique further. Soba's subsequent work, along with that of researchers in other organizations, has led to numerous advances in this technique, though the basic concept remains unchanged. A typical analysis today involves placing the evidentiary objects inside a sealed box with an open container of cyanoacrylate. The glue is heated to release its fumes, and after about 15 minutes, when the prints have become clear, the box is pumped clear and the objects are removed and dusted. Prints discovered using this method can be removed with tape and placed on a transparent plastic card.

"Fuming" has become a routine procedure in criminal investigations today, allowing investigators to collect otherwise unusable latent prints.

SEE ALSO Crime scene investigation; Fingerprint; Latent fingerprint.

Luke Sylvester May

12/2/1892–7/11/1965
AMERICAN
DETECTIVE

Considered one of the first American criminalists, Luke S. May had a long career as a detective dedicated to the advancement of scientific method in relation to crime investigation. He pioneered striation analysis in tool mark comparison, and invented the Revelarescope. In addition, May was a regular contributor to the popular magazine *True Detective Mysteries*, and wrote many books on **forensic science** topics.

May cultivated an interest in **criminology** as a young man, reading works by authors as diverse as **Arthur Conan Doyle** and **Hans Gross**. At the age of seventeen, he began working as a private detective in Salt Lake City, Utah. A few years later, he opened Revelare International Secret Service, an independent detective agency, with noted forensic experts J. Clark Sellers and John L. Harris. With an emphasis on scientific method and forensic specialties like **fingerprint identification**, May and his colleagues were able to provide lab services to law enforcement officials before the officials had these capabilities on their own.

In 1919, May moved to Seattle, Washington, and opened Scientific Detective Laboratories, parting way with Sellers and Harris. It is here that May invented his best-known forensic tool, the Revelarescope, in 1922. The instrument, a comparison magnascope, featured two lenses that projected a split image on a ground glass screen. May's invention was used in a high-profile child abduction case in Washington, one that produced a ground-breaking decision in the use of tool mark identification. At this time, May also intensified his role as an educator, allowing criminology students to study with him at his laboratory. He later served as an instructor in the law programs at the University of Washington, University of Oregon, and Willamette University.

May was well-known as an ongoing contributor to the popular true crime magazine, *True Detective Mysteries*. He collaborated with writers to create a number of case articles for the magazine, and also wrote a question-and-answer column regarding investigation techniques. In 1936, May wrote *Crime's Nemesis*, a book in which he outlines the details of some of his most unusual cases. May also wrote two crime investigation handbooks, *Scientific Murder Investigation* and *Field Manual of Detective Science*, in 1933.

SEE ALSO Literature, forensic science in; Microscopes.

Walter C. McCrone

6/9/1916–7/10/2002
AMERICAN
CHEMICAL MICROSCOPIST

For more than sixty years, Walter C. McCrone worked as a chemical microscopist, consultant, and educator. He is best known for his work on analyzing The Shroud of Turin and the Vinland Map, but McCrone also made significant contributions to his field by establishing the McCrone Research Institute, a not-for-profit center for teaching microscopy. He is also the author of more than 600 articles and sixteen books and chapters, including the well-known text *The Particle Atlas.*

McCrone pursued his interest in chemistry early on. He attended Cornell University, earning an undergraduate degree in chemistry in 1938 and a doctorate in organic chemistry in 1942. Continuing his work in the academic field, McCrone worked for Cornell for two years before becoming a chemist and professor at Armour Research Foundation (now Illinois Institute of Technology).

After twelve years at the Armour Research Foundation, McCrone left to start his own consulting firm. He founded McCrone Associates, a company that grew from a one-man shop to a renowned facility serving more than 2,000 clients each year. And while he enjoyed his work as an independent consultant, McCrone was also interested in promoting the education of microscopy. So in 1960, McCrone founded the McCrone Research Institute in Chicago, Illinois. The not-for-profit organization has taught more than 22,000 students in every facet of applied microscopy, as well as conducted research in that field. Later, McCrone opened its sister organization, McCrone

Scientific, in London, England. In addition, McCrone continued to write about his research and findings in the field of microscopy, publishing 600 technical papers and sixteen books and chapters. His best-known publication is *The Particle Atlas*, a handbook for solving materials analysis problems.

McCrone is also known for his analytical work on a number of famous antiquities. In the 1970s, he analyzed the Vinland Map, a map possibly depicting parts of North America some sixty years before the arrival of Christopher Columbus. McCrone found the ink on the map to contain a mineral commonly found in inks after 1920. In 1978, McCrone was asked to analyze the Shroud of Turin, a strip of cloth thought to be the shroud Jesus Christ was buried in. After studying the shroud, McCrone concluded that the material was instead a medieval painting. While many contested McCrone's findings, carbon dating tests conducted ten years later upheld McCrone's assessment. In 2000, he received the American Chemical Society National Award in Analytical Chemistry for his work on the Turin Shroud.

SEE ALSO Anthropology; Art forgery; Microscopes.

Measurements of anatomical features SEE Biometrics

Medical examiner

The medical examiner (ME) is the person in charge of the forensic investigation of a death that has occurred in his or her area of jurisdiction, whether it is a homicide, suicide, accident, or other suspicious death. He or she has a number of tasks to carry out, chief of which is the determination of the cause and manner of the death through performing an **autopsy**. The medical examiner also takes charge of the analysis of **evidence**, works with the police investigating the scene of the crime, and presents evidence in court. In short, the ME is involved in both the medical and legal sides of a forensic investigation.

The role of the medical examiner is one that has been evolving since the nineteenth century. There has always been a tradition in investigating unexplained deaths. Initially, the people appointed to take charge of these investigations were known as coroners and they were elected or appointed but did not necessarily have any special legal or medical **training**. During the

nineteenth century, the practice of **medicine** became more professional in many countries, with an increasing requirement for proper academic training. At the same time, **forensic science** and **pathology** were being established as disciplines in their own right. The old office of **coroner** was out of step with these new trends. Increasingly, regions began to demand that the coroner have medical knowledge so that scientific principles could be brought to bear on the investigation of a death. In 1877 Massachusetts became the first state to pass a law replacing the office of coroner with that of medical examiner and requiring that the ME have a license to practice medicine.

Increasing urbanization in the United States during the early years of the twentieth century led to several cities introducing the ME system. This change was accelerated by various scandals where deaths had allegedly been improperly or inadequately investigated by ill-qualified coroners. Today, there is a mixture of the coroner and the ME system in many counties, with the former still tending to predominate in rural areas.

Many modern medical examiners have training not just in pathology, but in forensic pathology and so are well qualified to carry out all the medical and legal tasks involved in investigating a suspicious death. However, the ME is not actually required to be a forensic pathologist, as there are not enough specialized forensic pathologists to meet the needs of every community. When a death requires investigation and the relevant region does not have an ME who is a forensic specialist, the area will contract out the work to the nearest center which does offer such services.

The medical examiner has many varied duties when investigating a suspicious death. First and foremost is the task of establishing the cause and manner of the death. For instance, the person may have died of asphyxia and this would be the **cause of death**. However, there are many different manners in which asphyxia can occur—drowning, strangulation, or hanging, for example. The **time of death** also needs to be determined as accurately as possible so it can be put into context with the events unfolding at the crime scene. It is also important for the ME to establish the identity of the victim, if this is not already known. Where the body has wounds, they should be thoroughly investigated and correlated with any weapons that may have been used to inflict them. The presence of **body marks** and signs of disease may also be significant and must be recorded and interpreted.

The autopsy findings are clearly highly relevant in establishing the cause and manner of death. However,

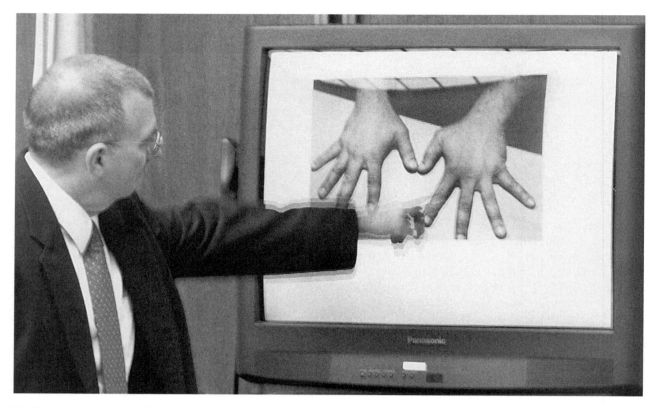

Medical examiner presents video evidence during a manslaughter trial in Massachusetts in 2002. © REUTERS/CORBIS

autopsy findings must be supported by other available sources of evidence, including witness reports, evidence collected at the scene of the crime such as bloodstains or weapons, and the results of crime lab testing. All of this involves working closely with the police and forensic scientists, assisting them with tasks such as the collection of evidence directly from the body. Sometimes there are surviving victims, who will be important witnesses, at the scene of a crime. The medical examiner is usually charged with examining their wounds and determining their cause and timing, because this is also a valuable source of evidence.

When a sudden and unexplained death is reported to the medical examiner, he or she takes the usual systematic approach to investigating it, as any good doctor would with a living patient presenting with a medical complaint. The only difference, of course, is that the ME cannot take a direct history from the deceased. Instead, the ME must gather as much information as possible from witnesses, family members, the police, and anyone else who might be able to shed light on the death. The ME may require people to give evidence, such as **blood** samples or fingerprints, that may help in the investigation.

When it comes to examining the body, there may be no obvious signs of physical trauma. Often this suggests a death from natural causes. Consultation of the medical records of the deceased and discussion with their physician can establish whether this is likely. An autopsy might then be carried out to confirm any tentative conclusions the ME comes to. Tests for drugs, alcohol, and poisons may also be carried out to see if they played a role in the death. When the investigation is complete, the ME prepares a report which covers the essentials of the case and lays out a conclusion of the cause and manner of death.

While the cause of death can often be established by the ME, deciding on the manner is an opinion based upon their reading of the evidence and circumstances. They will record a verdict such as homicide, suicide, accident, or an open verdict. This opinion will not necessarily be accepted in court and may be challenged by the police, lawyers, or the victim's family. Thus, even if a verdict of homicide is returned by the medical examiner, the police will not necessarily bring a prosecution. Families often object to a verdict of suicide, in cases of drug overdose for instance, and will appeal for it to be changed to accidental death. The ME's verdict on the manner of death may also change if new evidence emerges. A death previously thought to be natural may turn out to be a homicide or suicide, for instance. Finally, it is the ME's job to prepare and sign the death certificate.

The medical examiner often works with a forensic investigator, who is the person who deals with the body at the crime scene. It is usually the forensic investigator who makes the first examination of the body and takes its temperature, which is needed to estimate the time of death. The investigator also directs the taking of photographs of the body and the removal of trace or insect evidence from it. Then the forensic investigator wraps and transports the body to the ME's office. Throughout, the body is in the custody of the medical examiner, while the crime scene is under the control of the police. The forensic investigator provides a useful interface between the two entities.

The forensic investigator often assists the medical examiner in the morgue, with the performance of the autopsy and the preparation of the autopsy report. The task of communication with family members, the media, and the police in matters relating to the ME's office might also fall to the forensic investigator. Finally, the forensic investigator may represent the ME by testifying in court.

The range of cases referred to the medical examiner can be very wide. He or she will be called in to look at any traumatic death that is due to injuries that could be homicidal, self-inflicted, or suicidal. The death need not, however, be violent to be referred. Any death that is unusual, unexpected, or in some way suspicious would have to be investigated. For instance, if a fit, healthy teenage girl was found dead in bed, this would be a clear case for the medical examiner. Sudden deaths occurring within hours of the onset of symptoms need to be examined also; this could indicate a poisoning, although such crimes are relatively rare these days. It is also usual for deaths in police custody, in prison, or during medical or surgical procedures to be investigated. Discovered bodies, such as those washed up on a seashore or found in a shallow grave, also clearly require a full investigation.

The medical examiner need not always perform an autopsy. The frequency with which this is done varies from place to place, but usually up to a quarter of reported deaths are followed up with an autopsy. Often, the deceased person's physician will be involved in the autopsy if it is felt that the death occurred from natural causes. Sometimes all that is needed to clarify a death is a cursory external examination. An experienced forensic pathologist will be able to assess the extent of the investigation needed. Some cases are challenging and it is always important for the medical examiner to come to the right conclusion. Often the medical examiner is the only expert witness that a judge and jury can rely on to explain complex medical matters.

SEE ALSO Autopsy; Death, cause of; Death, mechanism of; Pathology; Toxicology.

Medicine

Medicine is one of the branches of the health sciences. It deals with restoring and maintaining health, but is also used in determining the causes of death. It is a practical science that applies knowledge from biology, chemistry, and physics to treat diseases. Biological knowledge is derived from anatomy, biochemistry, **physiology**, histology, **epidemiology**, microbiology, genetics, **toxicology**, **pathology**, and many other disciplines. Biology forms the basis for understanding how the human body works and interacts with its environment. An understanding of chemistry is required to determine the interactions between different drugs, to detect chemicals in the body, and design drugs for treatment. Physics has an impact on understanding how the body works and on understanding how the various instruments and equipment are used in diagnosis and treatment. The need to understand interactions between all of these areas makes medicine one of the most complex scientific disciplines.

In its early days medicine was not based on science. Many aspects of it were considered forms of magic, encompassing everything from disease causes to treatments. This was because the disease process was not understood. There was no knowledge of infectious agents (such as bacteria and viruses). Therefore, unless the cause of a disease was obvious and visible, sickness was considered a punishment from gods or an interference of an evil spirit. As a result, some treatments were logical, while others were irrational and often involved magic incantations and spells.

The practice of medicine goes back to at least 3000 B.C., when the first written medical records appeared in Mesopotamia. Babylonian medical texts provided the first anatomical descriptions and an early code of conduct for doctors. Their understanding of diseases was very basic; they recognized trauma and **food poisoning**, but a lot of the illnesses were still a mystery. Despite advances in anatomy and surgery, ancient Egyptians, as the Babylonians before them, still believed in supernatural causes for many illnesses.

The scientific basis of medicine was laid down by Hippocrates, who rejected magical causes of diseases. He believed in medical examination and keeping detailed records of a disease history. His influence on medicine is present even today, in form of the "Hippocratic Oath," which all new doctors have to take. It sets out ethical guidelines for doctors.

The importance of clinical examination of the patient was made even more important by Claudius Galen, another Greek physician. He worked extensively on anatomy and experimented with live animals.

Great advances in all areas of medicine, especially in epidemiology and hygiene, took place in the middle ages. Avicenna, a Persian physician, was the first to recognize the contagious nature of tuberculosis. In his many works, he gave important advice to surgeons, especially on cancer treatment and advanced use of oral anesthetics (painkillers). Another great advancement of the times was the use of silk thread for stitching wounds, developed by Abul Qasim al-Zahrawi.

A number of scientific discoveries, starting from the late 1800s with the work of E. Jenner, L. Pasteur, R. Koch, A. Flemming and others, established that microbes are the cause of infectious disease; these diseases can be prevented by vaccinations; and there are drugs that can kill the infectious agents (microbes). These findings shaped modern western medicine.

Furthermore, discoveries in physics, such as x rays, ultrasounds, magnetic resonance, and lasers, led to the development of equipment that allows quicker and better diagnosis, as well as easier and safer surgical procedures.

As a result of these scientific and technological changes, the knowledge that medical students have to acquire is immense. Therefore, all doctors learn the same basics but later they have to specialize in narrower areas in order to be highly skilled and able to effectively treat all of the diseases of a particular organ or tissue.

There are doctors specializing in various areas of medicine, such as emergency medicine, intensive care medicine, internal medicine, pediatrics, surgery, neurology, obstetrics, and others. While obstetrics is a relatively narrow area, dealing with childbirth and female health, surgery or internal medicine is further subdivided into sub specializations. Some of those subspecialties are hematology (**blood** and its diseases), cardiology (heart and cardiovascular system), oncology (cancer), ophthalmology (eyes), orthopedic surgery (mostly skeletal system), or neurosurgery (brain). On the other hand, pediatrics deals with childhood diseases and most of the specialties and subspecialties have their pediatric equivalent. Some doctors specialize in narrow medical fields, while others specialize in areas requiring wide medical knowledge such as sport, aerospace, or forensic medicine.

The most important doctor for the majority of the population is the family doctor (or general practitioner, GP). It is the GP who makes the first examination and keeps a record of the medical history of the patient. He or she also makes an assessment if more tests are required before a diagnosis can be made or if a referral to a specialist is required.

The process of determining the cause of a disease and prescribing treatment is quite complex. It consists of clinical examination, diagnosis, and treatment.

Clinical examination can consist of a number of different aspects, including visual, pathological, toxicological, and genetic analysis. Visual examination addresses the general symptoms: a patient's appearance, heart rate etc. Pathological analysis is often required to identify any non-obvious cause of disease. The tests can include blood or urine analysis, electrocardiogram (ECG), ultrasound, computed tomography (CT) scan, biopsy, histology of removed tissues, or bacteriological analysis of body **fluids**. Most people have blood and urine tests during their lives. **Toxicological analysis** is usually carried out on blood, but can be done on tissue samples (bones or hair) and can detect alcohol, certain drugs, toxic metals, and other compounds (for example dioxins). Genetic testing is not usually required for the majority of patients, but in cases of inherited diseases, or genetic predisposition, they can be carried out. Often it is not just the adults that undergo this procedure. Amniotic fluid surrounding the embryo can be tested to determine if a child will develop a life-threatening disease.

Diagnosis is based on the combination of all of the examinations that have been performed and the accumulated knowledge of the doctor. Depending on the illness, it can be quick and simple or time consuming and difficult.

Treatment is the ultimate result of a visit to the doctor. It can include prescription of drugs, surgery,

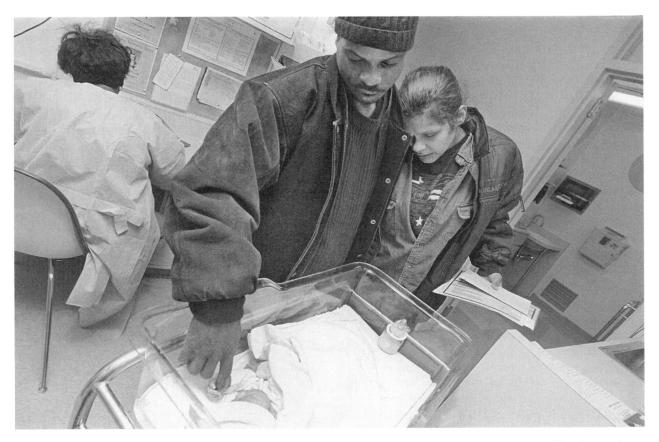

Couple visits with their newborn who will be placed in foster care. Toxicology tests revealed that the baby was born addicted to cocaine.
© BRENDA ANN KENNEALLY/CORBIS

or special diet. Any treatment can be simple or complex depending on the illness.

Not all doctors treat patients. Pathologists study disease processes. They analyze clinical tests and base their diagnosis on the results. They can work with isolated tissues and samples, or, in the case of forensic pathologists, the deceased. Pathological analysis is very important in the diagnosis of an illness in the case of regular pathology and in determining a **cause of death** in forensic pathology. Forensic pathology is a part of a forensic medicine, a branch of medicine answering questions important to the law.

Forensic medicine is important in determining the cause of death, **time of death**, and **identification** of the remains. This allows doctors to determine the cause of death as accident, suicide, or **murder**. A forensic pathologist describes the state of the body (**decomposition** if any), and subsequently examines the body for a cause of death, but also notes any abnormalities found on the surface or in the tissues. The surface of the body is initially checked for the presence of trauma injuries (bruises, broken bones),

cuts or stab wounds, thermal injuries (burns), firearm injuries (gunshot wounds), or **defensive wounds**. An internal examination of the body is carried out on organs or isolated tissues (histology). It might reveal presence of water in lungs (drowning), or asphyxia (lack of oxygen).

The analysis of a corpse is often carried out in the same way as for normal patients using x rays, toxicology, and genetics. Forensic medicine requires great attention to detail and a wide medical knowledge, especially in the areas of anatomy and physiology.

Modern western medicine is not the only existing medical system. There is also traditional medicine and complementary or alternative medicine. Traditional medicine includes folk and indigenous practices. The best known and most widely accepted areas are Chinese medicine and western herbal medicine. Complementary medicine uses non-invasive and non-pharmaceutical methods. Examples of alternative treatments include yoga, chiropractic or osteopathic manipulation, or various massage methods, as well as many others.

The first written evidence of Chinese medicine comes from 1766 B.C. The philosophy of medicine and methods used by Chinese doctors differed widely from those of the ancient Mediterranean and current modern medicine. The Chinese have based their medicine on a philosophy of yin and yang, and on The Five Elements (metal, wood, water, fire, and earth). A healthy person would have a harmonious mix of these elements. Among the practices developed in Chinese medicine are acupuncture, moxibustion (a technique that involves the use of heat, through burning specific herbs, to facilitate healing), and traditional herbal medicines. A physical examination with a doctor can include detailed interview, pulse taking, breath analysis, and tongue inspection. Some of the traditional Chinese treatments are quite widely accepted by modern western medicine, for example acupuncture.

A new approach to practicing medicine is the development of integrative medicine. It combines the modern western practices with alternative treatments. It only accepts methods for which there is scientific evidence for safety and effectiveness. Acupuncture, herbal treatment, music, and massage therapy are just some of the accepted treatments. The aim of this approach is not to just treat the illness, but to provide support to patients and induce their general well-being.

SEE ALSO Autopsy; Epidemiology; Pathology.

Medicolegal death

Medicolegal death is the term used to describe any unclear or vaguely suspicious death that must be investigated such as unexpected, sudden, or violent deaths. Besides all cases of homicides such as those involving criminal violence, medicolegal death investigations usually include persons who were in detention centers and jails, in apparently good health, poisoned, apparent suicides, with diseases that could threaten the health of the public, undergoing medical treatment (or when death occurred less than 24 hours after admission to a hospital) or a surgical procedure, infants and children, prominent or famous involved with accidents, or unclaimed after death.

Generally, members of the medical examiner's office or coroner's office are authorized to investigate all medicolegal deaths. The basic tool used in any death investigation is the **autopsy**, either a medical examination performed by a pathologist in order to determine the **cause of death** or a medicolegal exam-

ination performed by a **medical examiner** (and ordered by legal authorities) in order to ensure that justice is carried out and to determine the cause of death under the auspices of medicolegal death. During a medicolegal autopsy, a law enforcement representative, such as the investigating police detective at the crime scene, will be present during the examination in order to contribute any information that might be important to the investigation. In addition, relatives or friends of the deceased may be asked to make a positive **identification** either at the scene of the crime or later during the medicolegal autopsy.

The series of steps that is usually required for a medicolegal autopsy include: (1) an examination of the scene of the death (such as taking photographs of the body and the surrounding area), (2) an identification of the body (with the help of photographic identification cards and acquaintances of the victim), along with appropriate tagging of the body, (3) an external examination of the corpse (including a detailed description of all injuries and wounds), (4) a dissection and internal examination (including skeletal and dental characteristics), along with a recorded verbal account of the autopsy, and (5) a toxicological examination of all body **fluids**, organs, and tissues (for **evidence** of alcohol, drugs, poisons, and other relevant forensic substances).

SEE ALSO Autopsy; Coroner; Death, cause of; Identification; Medical examiner; Pathology; Toxicology.

Mens rea

To hold a person criminally responsible before law, *mens rea* must be established. *Mens rea*, from the Latin *mens*, meaning mind and *rea*, meaning guilty or guilty mind, is presently established according to several criteria.

Consideration for criminal responsibility can involve intent, knowledge or recognition of one's own acts, recklessness (irresponsible acts that put at risk or cause harm to a third part's well being or property), and negligence (willful omission in exercising the proper care of a person or property under the individual's responsibility, or the failure in providing a service as required by law under the circumstances). *Mens rea* is therefore the basis of legal accountability both in civil and criminal courts. In its absence, or if the offender's *mens rea* is diminished or impaired due to a mental disorder or another circumstance, the offender cannot be blamed or punished by his act or omission. In other words, the prosecution has to prove that the accused not only committed the offense, but also that the individual had the required state of mind to be legally responsible for the act.

Criminal responsibility is often questioned by defense lawyers on the grounds of temporary or chronic insanity. These grounds require the assessment of the defendant by forensic psychiatrists and the testimony of the psychiatrist in court. As a general rule, criminal offenders diagnosed as not responsible for their acts by reason of mental retardation or a psychiatric disorder, will be, at the court's discretion, subjected to compulsory confinement or hospitalization in a psychiatric institution for treatment. Legislation of each country regulates the extension, duration, termination, and supervision of treatment and reclusion of mentally ill offenders.

Because criminal responsibility implicates liability for punishment, the establishment of *mens rea* has been required in some countries for centuries. This legal principle has been known and required since the thirteenth century in some European countries such as Italy and Scotland. However, the admission of **expert witnesses** to assess mental capacity in criminal courts is a relatively recent practice that encountered much resistance during the last decades of the nineteenth century, when psychiatry was still in its infancy. In the United Kingdom, the Report of the Royal Commission on Capital Punishment stated that criminal responsibility should not be founded solely on legal principles, but also on the establishment of moral responsibility. The report defined moral responsibility as the ability of a person to know that their action was legally and morally wrong, according to the criminal law and the moral standards of the community. Much controversy existed about whether or not it was possible to establish such moral responsibility. The English physician and philosopher John Locke (1632–1704), for instance, argued that a person's actions are completely separated from his thoughts. Later the English Lady Wootton stated that not even science could provide any answers to the questions concerning the moral responsibility of an individual. In 1863, an English judge recommended jurors to "not be deprived of the exercise of your common sense because a gentlemen comes from London and tells you scientific sense."

The common law test to establish criminal responsibility, known as M'Naghten rule, originated in Great Britain in the nineteenth century and was later applied in the United States. Daniel M'Naghten was what is now defined as a paranoid schizophrenic who murdered the secretary to British Prime Minister Robert Peel in 1843. M'Naghten was acquitted under the grounds of delusion and lack of control over his actions, and sent to a mental institution instead of receiving the capital penalty. His case, in addition to other previous similar judicial decisions, established by common law the M'Naghten rule, which assumed that if an individual could distinguish right from wrong, he or she was not insane and therefore, was criminally responsible. Conversely, if the offender was not able to make such distinction, insanity was established and acquittal was required.

Some English jurists have criticized the ambiguities of the standards for insanity under the M'Naghten rules and have proposed three parameters for acquittal of criminal responsibility: the illegality standard, the subjective moral standard, and the objective moral standard. The illegality assumed that if the offender lacked the capacity to understand that his acts were against the law, he could not be held accountable for those actions. The second standard stated that those offenders suffering from a disease of the mind that caused a delusional belief of being morally justified in their actions or that God dictated their acts, should be considered mentally insane and not criminally responsible. The third standard assessed the capacity for understanding the social moral standards and the capacity to abide by them. The United States, Tasmania, and Queensland have added another parameter to these rules, that of partial insanity and irresistible impulse, which characterize diminished responsibility, implying that if a person was under a temporary delusion, even if not insane, mitigation of responsibility (and penalty) could be considered by the defense. In Great Britain, however, due to the many cases of acquittal and even release of offenders who made attempts against the lives of members of the royal family and other political personalities, such revisions of the test by the Atkin Committee on Insanity and Crime in 1923, and by the Royal Commission on Capital Punishment in 1953 were rejected by the Judiciary. Queen Victoria even tried to change the Trial of Lunatics Act of 1883 to an "insane but guilty" connotation. However, the common law was maintained, with the special verdict of insanity implying a qualified acquittal, although not an absolute acquittal. More recently, the American model penal code required the establishment of a lack of substantial capacity by the offender to conform his behavior to the law and admit insanity defense pleas.

Diminished responsibility due to partial insanity existed in Scottish penal law since the seventeenth century. It did not imply acquittal, but only penalty mitigation, by changing the charge from **murder** to **manslaughter**. Partial insanity was defined as an abnormality of the mind arising from a condition of arrested or retarded mental development, or a disease or injury that significantly impaired mental responsibility for acts or omissions in relation to a killing. Therefore, manslaughter opened a wide range of possibilities for courts, which ranged from conviction for life, or compulsory commitment to a mental institution, to absolute acquittal.

It is important to emphasize that all the above descriptions and definitions of insanity were non-scientific in nature and the tests were merely cognitive, as medical psychiatry was still in its infancy. The first attempts to assess criminal responsibility in courts used non-specialist physicians and even apothecaries as expert witnesses, during the late nineteenth and early twentieth centuries, both in England and the U.S., with convictions or acquittals due much more to lawyers' rhetorical skills than to sound scientific data. When psychiatrists began to serve as expert witnesses, a standardized psychiatric evaluation procedure was not still in use, often giving rise to allegations of inferential, inconclusive diagnoses from both the prosecution and the defense.

Forensic psychiatry is a relatively recent specialty that differs from clinical psychiatry in its objectives. While clinical psychiatry aims at diagnosing and treating neuropsychiatric disorders, forensic experts must establish to courts whether an offender was, at the time the offense was committed, mentally impaired or sane. In the first case, a precise diagnosis and the explanation of how the mental condition interferes with the cognitive, emotional, and behavioral capacities of the offender is necessary. Forensic psychiatry is a sub-field of psychiatry that requires special **training** in order to perform specific types of clinical assessments and diagnoses, such as retrospective, transversal, or prospective assessments to prosecutors, defense lawyers, probation boards, judges, and police investigators. The adoption of psychiatric diagnostic guidelines by several countries in the last 20 years gave the forensic experts a new level of credibility in courts, thanks to the advances in neurosciences and diagnostic resources and technologies.

A more clear description in the last 30 years of biological factors associated with each psychiatric disorder and the detailed description of related symptoms, led to the publication of the *Clinical Descriptions and Diagnostic Guidelines* and the *Diagnostic Criteria for Research* of psychiatric disorders by the World Health Organization (WHO), which is used by several countries around the world to establish forensic criminal responsibility. In the United States, the American Psychiatric Association (APA) is responsible for the guidelines used by forensic psychiatrists, published under the title *Diagnostic and Statistical Manual of Mental Disorders*. WHO and APA guidelines are regularly updated to incorporate new scientific information and diagnostic techniques. Such advances and improvements in science and law released the task of establishing *mens rea* from the realm of conjecture and philosophical arguments, and gave it the status of an objective evidence-based scientific field. In many countries, forensic psychiatry has become a field of expertise apart from clinical psychiatry, and a qualified psychiatrist is the only expert witness recognized in court to establish criminal responsibility.

SEE ALSO Criminal profiling; Expert witnesses; Federal Rules of Evidence; Psychiatry; Psychology; Psychopathic personality.

Metal detectors

Metal detectors use electromagnetic fields to detect the presence of metallic objects. They exist in a variety of walk-through, hand-held, and vehicle-mounted models and are used to search personnel for hidden metallic objects at entrances to airports, public schools, courthouses, and other guarded spaces; to hunt for landmines, archaeological artifacts, and miscellaneous valuables; and for the detection of hidden or unwanted metallic objects in industry and construction. Metal detectors detect metallic objects, but do not image them. An x-ray baggage scanner, for example, is not classed as a metal detector because it images metallic objects rather than merely detecting their presence.

Metal detectors use electromagnetism in two fundamentally different ways, active and passive. Active detection methods illuminate some detection space—the opening of a walk-through portal, for example, or the space directly in front of a hand-held unit—with a time-varying electromagnetic field. Energy reflected from or passing through the detection space is affected by the presence of conductive material in that space; the detector detects metal by measuring these effects.

Passive detection methods do not illuminate the detection space, but take advantage of the fact that every unshielded detection space is already permeated by the Earth's natural magnetic field. Ferromagnetic objects moving through the detection space cause temporary, but detectable, changes in this natural field. (Ferromagnetic objects are made of metals, such as iron, that are capable of being magnetized; many metals, such as aluminum, are conducting but not ferromagnetic and cannot be detected by passive means.)

Walk-through or portal detectors are common in airports, public buildings, and military installations. They bracket their portal with two large coils or loop-type antennae, one a source and the other a detector. Electromagnetic waves (in this case, low-frequency radio waves) are emitted by the source coil into the detection space and interact with objects there. When the electromagnetic field of the transmitted wave impinges on a conducting object, it induces transient currents on the surface of the object; these currents, in turn, radiate electromagnetic waves. These secondary waves are sensed by the detector coil.

Metal detectors small enough to be hand-held are often used at security checkpoints to localize metal objects whose presence has been detected by a walk-through system. Forensic investigations can also utilize hand-held metal detectors. Some units are designed to be carried by a pedestrian scanning for metal objects in the ground (e.g., nails, loose change, landmines). All such devices operate on variations of the same physical principle as the walk-through metal detector, that is, they emit time-varying electromagnetic fields and listen for waves coming back from conducting objects. Some ground-search models further analyze the returned fields to distinguish various common metals from each other.

Gradiometer metal detectors are passive systems that exploit the effect of moving ferromagnetic objects on the Earth's magnetic field. A gradiometer is an instrument that measures a gradient—the difference in magnitude between two points—in a magnetic field. When a ferromagnetic object moves through a gradiometer metal detector's detection space, it causes a temporary disturbance in the Earth's magnetic field, and this disturbance (if large enough) is detected. Gradiometer metal detectors are usually walk-through devices, but can also be mounted on a vehicle such as police car, with the intent of detecting ferromagnetic weapons (e.g., guns) carried by persons approaching the vehicle. Gradiometer metal detectors are limited to the detection of ferromagnetic objects and so are not suitable for security situations where a would-be evader of the system is likely to have access to nonferromagnetic weapons.

Irish police officer examines the entrance to an underground bunker said to be a firing range for the Irish Republican Army in 1999. Police searched nearby fields with metal detectors after discovering a weapons cache in the bunker. AP/WIDE WORLD PHOTOS. REPRODUCED BY PERMISSION.

The magnetic imaging portal is a relatively new technology. Like traditional walk-through metal detectors, it illuminates its detection space with radio-frequency electromagnetic waves; however, it does so using a number of small antennas arranged in a ring-like formation around its portal, pointing inward. Each of these antennas transmits in turn to the antennas on the far side of the array; each antenna acts as a receiver whenever it is not transmitting. A complete scan of the detection space can take place in the time it takes a person to walk through the portal. Using computational techniques adapted from computed axial tomography (CAT) scanning, a crude image of the person (or other object) inside the portal is calculated and displayed. The magnetic imaging portal may for some purposes be classed as a metal detector rather than as an imaging system because it does not produce a detailed image of the metal object detected, but only reveals its location and approximate size.

SEE ALSO Crime scene investigation.

Meteorology

Meteorology, the study of the atmosphere, is a related field of **geology** used by forensic investigators, lawyers, and prosecutors to look for specific information to be used in court when climate conditions are of relevance in explaining an event. The term meteorology originates from the Greek, *meteoros*, for airborne, and *logos*, for discourse or study.

Meteorologists may be requested by courts or by companies to give information necessary for reconstructing ship or airplane accidents, or on wind chills affecting outdoor workers, or to present a detailed weather reconstruction for a given area on a particular day. Meteorologists are sometimes requested to explain events associated with air pollution and airborne spread of dangerous substances, or to clarify whether a given meteorological event is abnormal or expected in a certain region and period of the year.

Forensic meteorologists may also help in crime investigations. For instance, they can calculate the wind and ocean currents in a particular body of water and thus indicate the most probable area where a disabled boat or even a corpse could be washed onshore.

Mankind has been intrigued since antiquity by meteorological phenomena such as sudden climate changes, the cycle of seasons, and the origins of winds, lightning bolts, storms, and tides. However, meteorology is a relatively young science whose importance and impact on the economic activities and military strategic planning became increasingly evident in the industrial era. Agricultural communities have regulated their activities for thousands of years through the empirical observation of local climatologic cycles. But weather prediction was a very imprecise and challenging task until the end of World War II (1939–1945). The date for the invasion of Normandy by the Allied forces, the famous D day, had to be changed several times because of such limitations. The field was able to remarkably advance after satellites, Doppler radar, and computer technologies allowed the development of more efficient research methods for the understanding and prediction of meteorological phenomena.

Climate variations are determined by the interchange between the atmosphere and terrestrial topography, with noticeable differences in temperature, moisture, and pressure between two localities of a given area due to such features. A large body of water, or the presence or absence of forests and mountains are topographic factors responsible for climate variations, known as local effects. For instance, a mountain chain running parallel to a coastal seashore functions as a dividing barrier, with different local effects on opposite sides of the mountains. Big cities also function as topographic factors, with their industrial and automotive emissions of carbon dioxide increasing the local temperature and changing the patterns of rain and snow precipitation compared with the surrounding countryside. Differences in air temperatures over the sea and coastal lands give rise to breezes and winds that circulate between the two surfaces. Breezes usually start blowing from the sea to the land in the morning, increasing speed until mid afternoon, and then reversing direction in late afternoon and during the night. The main reason for this event is that the air over land heats faster than over the ocean. Water absorbs a great amount of solar radiation and slows down the heating process of the air, whereas land surfaces reflect most of the radiation to the atmosphere. As air temperature rises, atmospheric pressure lowers over the land, allowing the air to move from the sea to land. At night, however, land surfaces loose heat faster than water, causing the wind direction to reverse.

The presence of a maritime current of cold or warm water flowing along a coastline also will interfere with wind patterns as well as the presence of a mountain chain nearby the coastline. Mountains create their own thermal circulations, even when atmospheric pressures are weak, because of the heating variations among different altitude gradients. Air over the valleys heats faster than over the mountain slopes, creating the anabatic air currents that move toward the mountaintop. At evening, the current reverses, and the katabatic winds move down from the mountaintops to the valleys. Anabatic winds are more frequent and stronger in summer and in tropical regions, whereas katabatic winds are more frequent in wintertime and in temperate latitudes. Mountain chains along the coastal line have anabatic, or upwardly moving, winds increased by the breeze blowing from the ocean. They also act as a partial barrier against sea wind propagation toward inland, and promote the formation of cumulus clouds on mountaintops because air is gradually cooled and water vapor condenses as it ascends. Late afternoon or evening precipitation is common in tropical coastlines with these topographic features.

Winds blowing perpendicular to mountain slopes create phenomena known as convergence, by forcing the air around the slopes to move upward, being

Method of operation (M.O.)

A researcher poses by blocks of ice, some as big as basketballs, in a lab in Spain. Chemical analysis helped determine meteorological condiitons that enabled the ice chunks to fall from Spanish skies over a 10-day period in 2000. AP/WIDE WORLD PHOTOS. REPRODUCED BY PERMISSION.

continuously deflected by the wind as they rise. When the air reaches the top, a strong current is released and sinks on the other side, except when a temperature inversion is present near the mountain summits. Temperature inversion refers to a descending air mass that is warmer than the ascending air. When the ascending air encounters the warmer, less-dense air, it loses pressure and a wavelike turbulence pattern is formed, known as lee waves or orographic waves, which are felt as a "bumpy road" when airplanes fly through them. When a large front of cool high-pressure air descends from higher altitudes and encounters a large warm low-pressure front, complex interactions take place. These may lead to the onset of tropical storms, gusty winds, thunderstorms, or tornadoes, depending on the particular conditions of the resulting super cell.

SEE ALSO Accident investigations at sea; Accident reconstruction; Aircraft accident investigations; Careers in forensic science; Crime scene reconstruction; Geology; Satellites, non-governmental high resolution.

The concept of method of operation (M.O.) or *modus operandi*, as it has been historically termed, is a means of identifying a single perpetrator in a series of criminal events. Forensic **evidence** such as crime scene photographs, **physical evidence**, **autopsy** photographs and report, and an extremely detailed study of the characteristics of the criminal's behavior is compiled. Methodology, weapons, means of victim acquisition, location of crime, victim demographics, methods and types of ligatures or bindings, and crime-scene characteristics are also compiled and analyzed in order to create a picture of the unique perpetrator, as well as to link geographically or temporally remote crimes that were previously believed to be unrelated, but that actually encompass a serial pattern.

The offender's method of operation undergoes an evolutionary process, one that changes as he or she becomes more skilled at committing a particular act (or a series thereof). That is, the perpetrator learns to be more successful at achieving his or her particular aim in the commission of the crime over time (with practice, skills improve). Another aspect of the M.O. is referred to as the signature, consisting of those behaviors emitted but not actually required in the commission of the crime. Signature behaviors are suggestive of the personality of the offender and help to distinguish similar or copycat offenses. Some examples of signature behaviors are use of specific ligature or binding materials, type and order of knots used, repeated unusual injuries such as laceration pattern, bites, disfiguration, mutilation, amputation of specific regions, evidence of torture or sadistic injuries, location and type of crime scene, victim posture, body arrangement, and actual messages left at the crime scene or divulged to the media.

The study of criminal method of operation offers the forensic investigator a window into the psyche of the perpetrator; it is a means of identifying or characterizing a criminal by his or her behavior, motivation for commission of particular acts, victim choice, and crime scene characteristics. By diligent development of the specific perpetrator's M.O., it is possible to link crimes committed in different parts of the country (or the world), across time and across venues. Because people have become progressively more able to move rapidly from place to place, it is possible for a single perpetrator to commit crimes in multiple areas within short periods of time. Successful analysis and identification of an individual's M.O. can facilitate rapid identification of an offender, and markedly increase ease or rapidity of apprehension.

SEE ALSO Antemortem injuries; Autopsy; Bite analysis; Body marks; Cold case; Criminal profiling; Physical evidence; Psychological profile.

Micro-fourier transform infrared spectrometry

Spectrometry of various kinds is used in the laboratory analysis of **trace evidence**, because it can produce a chemical "fingerprint," which helps in **identification** and comparison. Fourier transform infrared spectrometry (**FTIR**) is a particularly useful tool for the forensic scientist because it allows the analysis of such a wide variety of trace **evidence** including paint, drugs, lubricants, cosmetics, and adhesives. Micro-fourier transform infrared spectrometry combines a microscope with an FTIR instrument, providing even more information because microscopic examination is always the first step in the examination of trace evidence.

The basic technique of micro-FTIR is infrared spectrometry. Fourier transformation is a mathematical process that improves the quality of the signal at the detector. Infrared spectrometry can provide chemical fingerprints for both organic and **inorganic compounds** that are components in trace evidence. It works on the principle of chemical bonds absorbing energy in the infrared region of the **electromagnetic spectrum**. The frequency at which a bond absorbs energy depends upon its polarity, that is, the nature of the constituent atoms making up a bond. A carbon-hydrogen bond absorbs energy at a different frequency from a carbon-carbon bond, for instance.

The sample is inserted into the FTIR machine and then exposed to a scan of different infrared frequencies over the whole of the infrared range. As each bond absorbs energy, a peak appears on the detector. The scan produces a fingerprint, or spectrum, that is characteristic of that compound. Mixtures of compounds also give characteristic fingerprints. Research has produced huge libraries of reference infrared fingerprints for known compounds and products. Therefore, the spectrum of the trace evidence can be compared, by rapid computer analysis, with reference samples that should provide an identification match. Micro-FTIR can also be used in comparison work—comparing a flake of

paint from the scene of a crime to a **reference sample** taken from a suspect's car, for instance, which could be helpful in investigating a hit and run accident. The technique has also been found particularly useful in the analysis and comparison of hairs and **fibers**.

SEE ALSO Infrared detection devices; Microspectrophotometry.

Microphones SEE Bugs (microphones) and bug detectors

Microscope, comparison

A comparison microscope is a device used to observe side-by-side specimens. It consists of two **microscopes** connected to an optical bridge, which results in a split view window. The comparison microscope is used in forensic sciences to compare microscopic patterns and identify or deny their common origin. Without this device, the **identification** of **toolmarks** and **firearms** would be such a cumbersome process that it would be carried out on a very limited basis.

The idea behind the comparison microscope is simple. Two microscopes are placed next to each other and the optical paths of each microscope are connected together by the optical bridge. The optical bridge consists of a series of lenses and a mirror that brings the two images back together at the single eyepiece. The user looks through the eyepiece as with a regular microscope, except that a line in the middle separates the circular view field into two parts. The left side of the view field is the image produced by the left microscope, and the right side of the view field is the image produced by the right microscope. In some more modern or sophisticated comparison microscopes, it is also possible to superimpose the view fields generated by the two microscopes. This is particularly convenient when the forensic scientist compares impressed patterns rather than striated patterns. It is important that the two microscopes are identical. In order for a comparison to be valid, the two images produced in the circular view field needs to be at the same magnification and present the same lens distortion (if any). Comparison microscopes are mostly used in a reflected light setting, but a transmitted light setting is also available in some instances, and fluorescent light settings are found on higher-end models. This

An Oregon State Police forensic scientist uses a comparison microscope on two bullets for firearms identification at the crime lab in Portland, Oregon, 2003. AP/WIDE WORLD PHOTOS. REPRODUCED BY PERMISSION.

allows for comparison of more than just bullets and toolmarks.

Use of a comparison microscope is straightforward. The incriminated impression, typically a bullet or casing found at a crime scene or a toolmark's cast from a crime scene, is placed under the left microscope and thus, appears in the left part of the circular view field. A comparison impression, such as a bullet fired from a revolver found on a suspect, is placed under the right microscope and thus, appears in the right part of the view field. When comparing striations, the forensic scientist moves the comparison object until the striations match the ones present on the incriminated object. If the striations do not present similarities, then the two objects cannot be associated with a common origin. If the striations match, then a common source between the two objects is established. When comparing impression marks, the forensic scientist can use the superimposition option and, again, by moving the comparison object on the right, try to find common characteristics between the two objects.

The comparison microscope is used to compare **impression evidence** that requires a magnification ranging from 5× to approximately 100×. Items that are commonly observed under the comparison microscope are fired bullets, fired casings, and toolmarks. These items are observed under a reflected light setting. Other **evidence**, including impressions of serial numbers or characters from a typewriter, can also be compared using the comparison microscope. These are compared using a reflected light setting. This comparison might allow for the link between a stamped serial number and a die or between a sheet of paper bearing characters and the typewriter that was used to write it. The comparison microscope is also used to compare layers of a paint chip. This might allow for the identification of the vehicle from which the paint originated. Finally, when used in a transmitted light setting, hair, **fibers**, or the extruding striations of plastic bags can be compared. This allows the comparison of fibers found on a seat with the clothing of a suspect, for example. Plastic bag striations might establish links between different plastic bags and to demonstrate that they originate from the same batch. This is particularly useful with the small bags used to sell drugs. When dealing with fibers and plastic bags, the comparison microscope can also be used in an ultraviolet light setting or a polarized light setting.

The comparison microscope was invented in the 1920s by American Army Colonel Calvin Goddard (1891–1955) who was working for the Bureau of Forensic **Ballistics** of the City of New York. Goddard also benefited from the help of Colonel Charles Waite, Philip Gravelle, and John Fisher. At that time, the comparison microscope was used to compare fired bullets and casings. In the late 1920s, Swedish criminalist **Harry Söderman** (1902–1956) drastically improved the comparison microscope by inventing a system for rotating the bullets under the objectives. This allowed for a much faster comparison of lands of grooves of bullets by simultaneous rotation of both the suspect and comparison bullets. Söderman gave the name Hastoscope to his invention.

SEE ALSO Criminalistics; Drugfire; Integrated Ballistics Identification System (IBIS).

Microscopes

A microscope is the instrument that produces the high magnification image of an object that is otherwise difficult or impossible to see with the unaided eye. A microscope's resolving power allows the user to differentiate two objects from one another that could not be distinguished with the naked eye.

Microscopes assume a central role in **forensic science**. Forensic **evidence**, particularly **trace evidence**, is often so tiny as to escape detection with the naked eye. But the magnified examination of samples can reveal a great deal of detail. For example, examination of **gunshot residue** using a scanning electron microscope can allow an investigator to determine the shape of the spent residue and even its elemental composition, both of which are critical to the **identification** of the gunpowder used. The microscope can aid in matching the residue on a victim to residue present on a suspect. As another example, examination and identification of **fibers** would be impossible without the use of light microscopy.

Microscopic examination of documents can reveal information that cannot otherwise be seen. The high magnification and analysis possible using specialized techniques of scanning and transmission electron microscopy can reveal the presence of mate-

rial that is otherwise undetectable in the elements that make up a sample.

Today's sophisticated use of microscopes in forensic analysis had its beginnings hundreds of years ago. In ancient and classical civilizations, people recognized the magnifying power of curved pieces of glass. By the year 1300, these early crude lenses were being used as corrective eyeglasses.

In the seventeenth century Robert Hooke published his observations of the microscopic examination of plant and animal tissues. Using a simple two-lens compound microscope, he was able to discern the cells in a thin section of cork. The most famous microbiologist of this century was Antony van Leeuwenhoek (1632–1723). Using a single lens microscope that he designed, Leeuwenhoek described microorganisms in environments such as pond water. His were the first descriptions of bacteria and red **blood** cells.

By the mid-nineteenth century, refinements in lens grinding techniques had improved the design of light microscopes. Still, advancement was mostly by trial and error, rather than by a deliberate crafting of a specific design of lens. It was Ernst Abbe who first applied physical principles to lens design. Abbe combined glasses that bent light beams to different extents into a single lens, reducing the distortion of the image.

The resolution of the light microscope is limited by the wavelength of visible light. To resolve objects that are closer together, the illuminating wavelength needs to be smaller. The adaptation of electrons for use in microscopes provided the increased resolution.

In the mid-1920s, Louis de Broglie suggested that electrons, as well as other particles, should exhibit wavelike properties similar to light. Experiments on electron beams a few years later confirmed this hypothesis. This was utilized in the 1930s in the development of the electron microscope.

There are two types of electron microscope: the transmission electron microscope (TEM) and the scanning electron microscope (SEM). The TEM transmits electrons through a sample that has been cut so that it is only a few molecules thin. Indeed, the sample is so thin that the electrons have enough energy to pass right through some regions of the sample. In other regions, where metals that were added to the sample have bound to sample molecules, the electrons either do not pass through as easily, or are restricted from passing through altogether. The different behaviors of the electrons are detected on

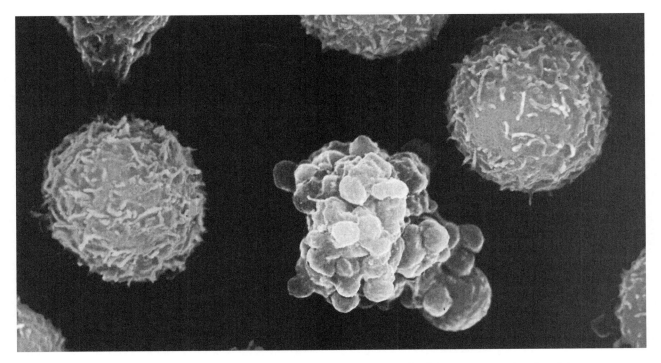

Scanning electromicrograph of apoptosis (center) showing cell death due to normal cellular processes rather than injury.
© GOPAL MURTI/PHOTOTAKE

special film that is positioned on the opposite side of the sample from the electron source.

The combination of the resolving power of the electrons, and the image magnification that can be subsequently obtained in the darkroom during the development of the film, produces a total magnification that can be in the millions.

Because TEM uses slices of a sample, it reveals internal details of a sample. In SEM, the electrons do not penetrate the sample. Rather, the sample is coated with gold, which causes the electrons to bounce off of the surface of the sample. The electron beam is scanned in a back and forth motion parallel to the sample surface. A detector captures the electrons that have bounced off the surface, and the pattern of deflection is used to assemble a three dimensional image of the sample surface.

In the early 1980s, the technique called scanning tunneling microscopy (STM) was invented. STM does not use visible light or electrons to produce a magnified image. Instead, a small metal tip is scanned very close to the surface of a sample and a tiny electric current is measured as the tip passes over the atoms on the surface. When a metal tip is brought close to the sample surface, the electrons that surround the atoms on the surface can actually "tunnel through"

the air gap and produce a current through the tip. The current of electrons that tunnel through the air gap is dependent on the width of the gap. Thus, the current will rise and fall as the tip encounters different atoms on the surface. This current is then amplified and fed into a computer to produce a three dimensional image of the atoms on the surface.

Without the need for complicated magnetic lenses and electron beams, the STM is far less complex than the electron microscope. The tiny tunneling current can be simply amplified through electronic circuitry similar to circuitry that is used in other electronic equipment, such as a stereo. In addition, the sample preparation is usually less tedious. Many samples can be imaged in air with essentially no preparation. For more sensitive samples that react with air, imaging is done in vacuum. A requirement for the STM is that the samples be electrically conducting, such as a metal.

Scanning tunneling microscopes can be used as tools to physically manipulate atoms on a surface. This holds out the possibility that specific areas of a sample surface can be changed.

Other forces have been adapted for use as magnifying sources. These include acoustic microscopy, which involves the reflection of sound waves off a specimen; x-ray microscopy, which involves the transmission of x rays through the specimen; near field optical microscopy, which involves shining light through a small opening smaller than the wavelength of light; and atomic force microscopy, which is similar to scanning tunneling microscopy but can be applied to materials that are not electrically conducting, such as quartz.

SEE ALSO Fibers; Fluorescence; Microscope, comparison; Polarized light microscopy; Scanning electron microscopy; Scanning electron microscopy; Trace evidence.

Microscopy, confocal SEE Confocal microscopy

Micro-spectrophotometry

Micro-spectrophotometry (MSP) is an essential tool in the forensic analysis of many kinds of **trace evidence**. It uses either visible or infrared light to determine the light transmission, absorption, or reflectance properties of a material. MSP is particularly valuable in the investigation of hair, textile **fibers**, and paint.

The chemical bonds within the molecular components of trace **evidence** interact with light in a characteristic way. They will absorb, transmit, or reflect specific frequencies of visible and infrared light. When we see a piece of cloth as red, for example, this means that although white light falls upon the material, all the color frequencies making it up except red are absorbed by the dye molecules in the material. It is therefore the red frequencies of light that are reflected back. A blue cloth contains different dye molecules, which reflect back only blue frequencies. MSP is a more sophisticated and highly accurate way of recording exactly what color an object is.

When an opaque or translucent specimen is inserted into an MSP instrument, it is exposed to a range of visible or infrared frequencies. The frequencies where it reflects, absorbs, or transmits, depending on the mode of the instrument, are recorded at a detector as a spectrum or fingerprint of that material. Comparisons can be made with materials whose spectra are held in databases. It is also possible to compare a piece of trace evidence with a control sample. A fiber found at the scene of the crime can be compared with one found on a suspect's clothing,

for instance. If the two fibers' MSP spectra are identical, then they come from the same source. The same is true of hairs and paint flakes. Indeed, MSP can reveal whether someone's hair has been dyed, bleached, or treated in some way, as well as when the person last visited the hairdresser. This could be useful, for example, in linking hair found on a suspect to that taken from the victim and so place the suspect at the scene of the crime, or eliminate them as a suspect.

SEE ALSO Micro-fourier transform infrared spectrometry; Spectroscopy.

Military police, United States

Forensic science is not the exclusive domain of civilian law enforcement agencies. Various branches of the military also undertake investigations into accidents and deaths and must utilize the same forensic techniques and skills as those used by local, state, and federal police. Military police are also concerned with crimes and accidents that call for forensic analyses, albeit of a more specialized nature than their civilian counterparts.

The United States military police, whose establishment dates back to the early twentieth century, are the law enforcement corps within each of the major services. The Army has the Military Police Corps (the largest of the armed forces police services), the Navy has the Shore Patrol, the Air Force has the Air Force Security Police, and the Marine Corps has the Military Police. These forces are staffed almost entirely by military personnel, and are responsible for all the ordinary civilian-analogous functions of a police force, as well as additional military duties.

Military police personnel are involved in law enforcement operations ranging from protecting school crossings and writing parking tickets to **murder** investigations and undercover drug stings. Personnel at U.S. bases around the country and the world provide temporary confinement of service members charged under the uniform code of military justice (UCMJ). Assuming the individual is found guilty after trial in a military court, where he or she is represented by a member of the judge advocate general (JAG) corps, if the sentence warrants, the convicted will serve time at a federal facility such as Fort Leavenworth in Kansas.

In addition to the regular military police activities, several branches have special undercover contingents—for example, the forensically-relevant Army Central Investigation Division (CID)—as well as corrections officers.

SEE ALSO Careers in forensic science; Navy Criminal Investigative Service (NCIS); United States Army Medical Research Institute of Infectious Diseases (USAMRIID).

Minerals

Minerals have played many important roles in the world of **forensic science**, from forensic **geology** used in criminal **identification** and crime scene investigations, to forensic **toxicology** and the study of poisons.

Historically, metal-based mineral poisons were commonly used as murder weapons, with arsenic a favorite. In fact, arsenic was often referred to as "inheritance powder" for its efficacy in hastening the demise of wealthy relatives. In the eighteenth century, the Dutch physician Hermann Boerhaave (1668–1738) was the first expert witness to use basic forensic toxicological methods as the basis for testimony at a **murder** trial. In this case, Mary Blandy was encouraged by her fiancé to use a powdered preparation in order to get the money from her father's estate (he was very much alive at the time). She dutifully put the white substance into her father's food; he became ill. The servants became suspicious. One of the servants found the white powder and took it to a local apothecary for examination, where the hypothesis was arsenic. The servant relayed her concerns to her employer, who dismissed them, and not long after, was dead. Mary was tried for murder, and four medical toxicologists served as **expert witnesses**. They noted that the appearance of Mr. Blandy's organs at **autopsy** was suggestive of arsenic poisoning. Boerhaave reported that he had taken some of the white powder saved by the servant, treated it with a hot iron and smelled it (not a safe test for poisons, by any means). The smell was that of arsenic. Equally important was the testimony of the servant, who was able to describe the white powder that she had observed Mary putting into her father's food. Mary Blandy was found guilty of murder, sentenced to death, and hanged shortly thereafter. This trial set the stage for development of forensic toxicological methods for detection of metal-based (and other) poisons.

In 1911, a forensic method for determining the quantity of metal-based poisons in internal organs

was developed by the English physician William Willcox, who was particularly interested in arsenic poisoning. He ran several tests for arsenic, and then used this method to determine how much arsenic was in each of the internal organs of Elizabeth Barrow, a victim of murder by poisoning. His method was used as the basis for far more sophisticated toxicological testing, which can now determine the amount of arsenic down to the microgram (one one-millionth of a gram) in both the human body and in soil.

After the middle of the twentieth century, thallium, a new metal-based poison, was popular for use in rat poison. Although it was banned from commercial use in 1984, it remained readily available in rat poison for at least another decade. In August 1991, Robert Curley developed a barrage of confusing symptoms and was repeatedly hospitalized. The cluster of symptoms included uncontrollable vomiting, abrupt hair loss, numbness of the extremities, general weakness, and burning skin. Shortly before his death in September 1991, he became combative, agitated, and aggressive; at that point, heavy metal exposure was hypothesized. A battery of tests revealed markedly increased thallium levels in his system.

Curley worked in a chemistry laboratory at Wilkes University in Wilkes-Barre, Pennsylvania. Five bottles of thallium salts were found in a stockroom there, although none of his coworkers became ill or evidenced any signs of accidental thallium exposure. Upon Curley's death, an autopsy was performed; it revealed extremely high thallium levels, confirming intentional poisoning, and leading to a ruling of homicide. During the investigation, the Curley home was examined, and several thermoses tested positive for thallium. Curley's widow reported that her husband brought iced tea to work in the thermoses daily. Curley's widow and her daughter by a previous marriage were found to have slightly elevated thallium levels, but they were well below the toxic range. Curley's widow sued the university for wrongful death. Upon further investigation, it was found that she had collected more than one million dollars from a car accident involving her first husband, and had also gained nearly three hundred thousand dollars in life insurance proceeds after Curley's death. At that point, she became a suspect, and the local criminal authorities requested **exhumation** of the body in order to perform more sophisticated testing.

Frederic Reiders, of National Medical Services, agreed to run forensic toxicology tests on Curley's hair shafts, toenails, fingernails, and skin. From the length of the victim's hair, Reiders was able to create a timeline extending 329 days before Curley's death. He used atomic absorption spectrophotometry to record thallium levels at different times. The surprising conclusion was that Robert Curley had been systematically exposed to thallium, through ingestion, for a period of nine months before his death. There was a sharp spike several days before his death, indicating intentional poisoning. Hair from other parts of his body, as well as the skin, fingernail, and toenail samples, all supported the conclusions reached by Reiders after testing the head hair. It was further determined that the valleys, corresponding to drops in thallium level, occurred whenever Curley was away from home (or in the hospital). When confronted with conclusive **evidence**, Curley's widow plea-bargained and confessed to poisoning her husband in an effort to gain his life insurance proceeds.

As testing for metal-based poisons has become progressively more conclusively detectable, the criminal use of these substances as a "murder weapon" has dramatically decreased in favor of plant-based **toxins**.

SEE ALSO Chemical and biological detection technologies; Energy dispersive spectroscopy; Food poisoning; Gas chromatograph-mass spectrometer.

Misdemeanor

A misdemeanor, when applied to criminal law, is defined as any offense other than a **felony** or treason. Being the least serious of these three classifications of crimes, a misdemeanor usually covers all minor offenses. In the United States, criminal codes vary among the fifty states but generally include such offenses as libel, slander, assault in the third or fourth degrees, conspiracy in the third and fourth degrees, and criminal tampering; along with more minor infractions such as violations of driving, fishing, hunting, and boating laws.

A misdemeanor is generally prosecuted by means of information (or prosecutor's information) rather than by indictment, which is how a felony is prosecuted. Both are accusatory documents that must supply information about the alleged illegal act such as time, place, and nature of the crime. However, when a misdemeanor is involved, the prosecutor's information is used to formally file a charge with the court based on the information gathered during the investigation. When a felony is involved, an indictment must be given to the court

and presented to a grand jury because of the more serious nature of the crime. Persons found guilty of a misdemeanor are usually punished by probation, fine, or imprisonment in a jail (such as a county jail) or prison (excluding a federal or state penitentiary). The maximum penalty for a misdemeanor could likely be imprisonment in a county jail for less than one year, while a more minor penalty could be a fine of $100 for violating, for example, a municipal code.

Through the use of high-tech devices and modern laboratory techniques, **forensic science** is often used to prove that misdemeanors have occurred by detecting the presence of various substances in a victim or suspected criminal at a crime scene. For example, most DUI (driving under the influence) and driving while intoxicated/impaired (DWI) cases are misdemeanor offenses. Police officers who have stopped drivers suspected of driving under the influence of such intoxicates as alcohol and illegal drugs will often use a breath test (such as a **Breathalyzer®**) to ascertain whether the reasonable cause of the suspect's erratic behavior is due to such a substance.

A breath test—originating within the field of forensic science—which is given to an alleged intoxicated driver by a police officer involves collecting an exhaled sample of a suspect's breath at the scene of the incident. The police officer then analyzes the sample at the scene in order to measure the concentration of alcohol consumption; that is, to measure the amount of alcohol as a percentage of blood (0.08, for example, indicates that alcohol makes up 0.08 percent of the total amount of blood in a person's blood stream). Using such forensic analysis, the police officer can make a determination, based on specific state law, as to whether or not a person should be arrested. Today, alcohol breath-testing instruments are so accurate that their results are regularly used as **evidence** to prosecute misdemeanor cases involving drunk driving.

SEE ALSO Breathalyzer®; Felony.

Missing children

Children can disappear inadvertently or as a result of deliberate abduction, or **murder**. Typically, an investigation will assume that the child is still alive, and so will be geared to locating the child. While much of this effort involves police work that is not forensically-oriented, **forensic science** plays an important role.

The nature of the forensic activities can change with the length of time a child is missing. For example, as will be dealt with in more detail subsequently, computerized techniques can alter the photographic image of a child to approximate the child's appearance through adolescence and into adulthood. Such a visual cue can prove valuable in recognizing a children years after they have been reported missing.

Forensic science plays a grimmer role when a child is discovered dead, or when an unidentified body or skeleton that may potentially be the missing child is discovered. In this case the focus naturally shifts from a happy reunion of the child with loved ones, to the **identification** of the body.

As sad as the latter task may be, this aspect of forensic science can help grieving family members to begin to deal with the reality of what has transpired. Finally, forensic science is invaluable in establishing the **cause of death** of a missing child, especially when foul play is suspected.

In age progression, a forensic artist uses a facial photograph of the missing child to render an image of how the child might look as a pre-adolescent, adolescent or even an adult.

An image can be created the old-fashioned way, using a pencil and sketchpad. This type of image recreation actually has become quite sophisticated. In the 1950s a facial identification kit was developed that consisted of a series of clear stackable sheets ("foils") that allowed a myriad of different hand-drawn facial features to be laid on top of one another on different-shaped faces. The thousands of possible combinations made it possible to produce a final image that proved to be very similar to a person's true appearance.

Today, computer programs enable the forensic artist to digitally scan the child's image into a program and then digitally manipulate the image to approximate the effects of aging. Forensic age progression is a combination of science and art. It relies on the rendering skill of the artist and knowledge of the development of facial muscles, features such as the eyes and nose, and the change in shape of the **skull** with age.

Predictably, faces broaden and lengthen during the transition from the childhood years to adolescence. Primary teeth are lost and secondary teeth appear. The bridge of the nose will tend to rise. As the skull expands, the eyes tend to narrow, the mouth becomes wider and the nose lengthens. Hair that is lighter colored tends to darken.

By about the age of 12, the facial features that are present will persist throughout life, unless surgically altered. Some subtle changes can occur; eyebrows can become more extensive and the cheekbones more prominent. However, other changes may occur that may need to be factored into an image. As examples, hairstyles will change, a hairline can recede, and changing optics of the eyes may necessitate the use of glasses.

In an age progressed image that is within a few years of the child at the time she/he went missing, these age-related changes will be kept to a minimum. However, if the child has been missing for an extended number of years, then a series of images can be made, to give a better overall portrayal of the person's possible appearance.

If the missing child has older biological siblings, then their appearance will be scrutinized, as will parental features, since some of their facial features acquired by the siblings from their biological parents will likely have been acquired by the missing child.

Medical records of the missing child can provide useful information in image reconstruction. For example, the presence of a facial scar from a childhood accident, moles, and even tattoos can remain with the child for life, and will be a feature of the age progressed image.

In a related area, image rendering is also done if the missing child is suspected of being abducted and the identity of the kidnapper is unknown. In this case, since the abductor may well try to disguise their appearance, different images may be produced, based on information gleaned from witnesses, surveillance **cameras** or other means. For example, a man can be shown clean shaven, with various styles of facial hair, and with a face that reflects a weight gain or loss.

Particularly in the case of an abduction of a child by an unknown person, the need for eyewitness information is pressing. Such information can be valuable in producing an image of the suspect, and for trying to piece together the events of the abduction.

Obtaining information from eyewitnesses calls for tact and special skills on the part of the forensic investigator. Eyewitnesses, who themselves may be traumatized by what they have witnessed and whose memory can be subject to manipulation, need to be given the time and emotional encouragement that unlocks accurate recollections of the event.

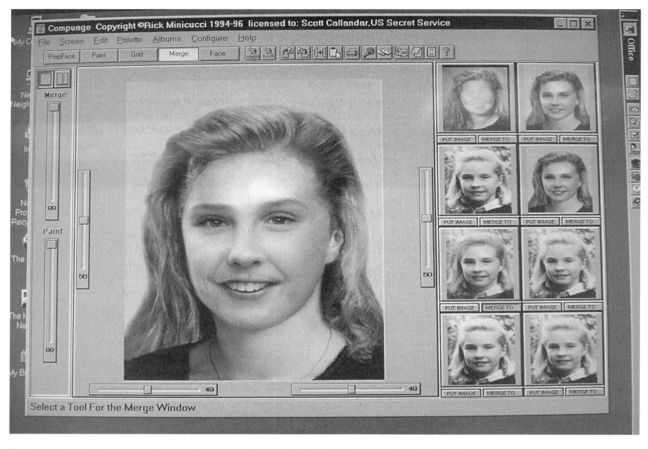

Software available at the National Center for Missing Children in Arlington, Virginia, provides a digital image "aged" to the current chronological age of the missing child. © RICHARD ELLIS/CORBIS SYGMA

A forensic investigator will assess the information provided by a witness while considering the person's involvement with the event. For example, the information provided by someone who had only a brief glimpse of the missing child and/or suspect may not be as reliable as the information from someone who had a more prolonged view. As another example, if the eyewitness normally wears glasses but was not at the time, then the quality of the information, while not necessarily suspect, needs to be considered cautiously.

Other forms of eyewitness information are available. Surveillance cameras that are an ever-present facet of daily life can provide a picture of the child and an abductor, for example.

Fingerprints are unique identifiers that are invaluable in the identification of a missing child and, in the case of an abduction, the suspect. For fingerprints to be useful, a child's fingerprints need to be already recorded and on file. Programs such as ID Me Now, sponsored by the Child Protection Education Foundation of America, incorporate on a card high quality images of **fingerprint** patterns with a digital facial photograph, dental records, contact numbers and personal information, and even information on how to collect a cell sample for deoxyribonucleic acid (**DNA**) extraction.

Fingerprint patterns can also be submitted to a databank that is administered by the Federal Bureau of Investigation. The fingerprint patterns obtained from a missing child (or recovered corpse) can be compared to the hundreds of thousands of digitized patterns resident in the database to determine an identity match.

Such child fingerprint collection is, however, more the exception than the norm. In this case, a forensic investigator may instead be able to obtain a fingerprint of a missing child from an object known to be handled by the child.

The conclusion of a missing child case can be tragic with the discovery of a corpse or skeleton. Identification of the body or remains as that of the missing child becomes the priority. If an intact skull is found, it can be used to create a three-dimensional reconstruction of the facial appearance of the person. The shape of the skull, combined with knowledge of the typical thickness and arrangement of facial and head muscles and tissue can be used to physically create a face.

For this task, modeling clay is applied to the skull. The clay mimics the muscles and tissues that underlie the skin. The shape of the nose can be deduced from measurements of the nasal aperture; the hole in the skull where the nose once was. Typically, the width of the nasal aperture is increased by five millimeters on either side. Other measurements of the nasal aperture are used to calculate the approximate length of the nose. Appropriate facial hair and prosthetic eyes are inserted, and the reconstruction is photographed. The final image can be very similar to the actual image of the deceased.

Skin, tissue, muscle and even bone that can be recovered can be used as a source of DNA or a related genetic material known as ribonucleic acid (RNA). Through various sophisticated means, the genetic material can be amplified in number, and the sequence of nucleotide building blocks that comprise the DNA or RNA can be determined. These genetic sequences can be as unique to an individual as is a fingerprint pattern. People inherit genetic material from their parents; indeed, this is the basis of paternity testing that is used to establish if a man is the biological father of a child.

The genetic identification utilizes specialized DNA that is known as mitochondrial DNA. The pattern of mitochondrial DNA between mother and child can be identical. This generational similarity of genetic material has been used in El Salvador to identify the remains of children who were abducted and murdered by the Salvadoran military in the 1980s and, more happily, to reunite children who were abducted but not killed, with their biological parents.

SEE ALSO Anthropometry; Autopsy; DNA profiling; Integrated automated fingerprint identification system; International Association for Identification; Mitochondrial DNA typing; Paternity evidence; STR (short tandem repeat) analysis.

Mitochondrial DNA analysis

In human cells, **DNA** is found in both the nucleus and the mitochondria. The mitochondrion is an organelle responsible for the molecular products that provide the energy to the cell. There is a single nucleus in human cells and it contains two copies of DNA, one originating from the father and one from the mother. In contrast, there may be hundreds or thousands of mitochondria in human cells and the DNA in a single mitochondrion may be copied numerous times. Nuclear DNA is much longer than mitochondrial DNA, also written mtDNA, however the fact that there are so many more copies of mtDNA makes it extremely useful in cases in which there is only a small sample or the sample has been degraded. In addition, some biological materials such as hair shafts, teeth, and bones do not contain any cell nuclei, but mitochondria may be present and mitochondrial DNA analyses can be performed.

When a **sperm** fertilizes an egg, the DNA-containing head of the sperm fuses with the egg, but the tail and midsection are left on the outside of the egg. The mitochondria of a sperm are found in the tail and midsection as these parts require energy in order to propel the sperm. Because the mitochondria of the sperm never reach the inside of the egg, all the mitochondria in the embryo come from the egg. As a result the mitochondrial DNA in a child is identical to that of the mother. Mitochondrial DNA is therefore useful for proving maternal relationships in forensic investigations.

The DNA molecule is made up of a sequence of four different smaller molecules called nucleotides: adenine (A), guanine (G), cytosine (C) and thymine (T). DNA is a double stranded molecule and its nucleotides always associate themselves with a complementary nucleotide; if adenine is on one of the strands, thymine is across from it on the other strand. Similarly, if cytosine is on one strand, guanine will be found across from it on the other strand. Because the nucleotides of DNA are found in pairs on the two strands, the nucleotide sequence is also called a sequence of base pairs (bp).

Mitochondrial DNA is approximately 16,569 base pairs long and the genome is usually found in a ring-like conformation. There are two major parts of the molecule. A coding region accounts for the majority of the molecule and the DNA from this section codes for biochemical products related to providing energy to the cell. The other section of the mtDNA is called the control region and it is responsible for regulating the production of the **gene** products from the coding region. Within the control region there are two regions that have been found to contain a disproportionate number of variations in humans. These regions are called Hypervariable Region 1 and Hypervariable Region 2, or HV1 and HV2. HV1 is approximately 342 bp and HV2 is approximately 268 bp.

There are five major steps to mtDNA analysis. First, the sample is visually examined, cleaned, and prepared. Cleaning is extremely important because extraneous cells from handling can easily contaminate a sample. Usually the sample is immersed in detergent and an ultrasonic bath. Teeth and bones are sanded and cross-sectioned. In teeth, the dentin and pulp are used in the analysis. In all cases, the sample is ground to a powder and then placed in an extraction solution to release the cellular material, including the mtDNA, from the cells.

The second step involves extracting the mtDNA from the cellular material. This is accomplished by adding to the solution a mixture of chemicals that separate DNA from other organic molecules and then spinning the mixture in an ultracentrifuge. The mtDNA is concentrated in the top layer and then purified. The third step involves a technique called **PCR, polymerase chain reaction**, which uses carefully regulated cycles of heating and cooling to produce many copies of the mtDNA. This process is called amplification. After amplification, the mtDNA product is purified and quantified to ensure that the PCR yielded the expected quantity of mtDNA. The final step in mtDNA analysis is **sequencing** the amplified mtDNA. This is done using a technique similar to PCR, but special fluorescently labeled nucleotides that terminate the growth of a strand are added to the solution. This technique is referred to as Sanger's method and the result is many strands of DNA that vary in length by one nucleotide. This collection of DNA is then sorted by length, using a technique called gel **electrophoresis**. A **fluorescence** detector then reads the labels at the end of each strand of DNA and computer software reconstructs the mtDNA sequence. Finally, a DNA examiner edits and verifies the sequence.

When performing mitochondrial DNA analysis, about 610 bp are sequenced and compared to a standard. Any nucleotides in the sample sequence that differ from this standard are listed by location and nucleotide. For example, if a sample contained cytosine at position 263 while the standard contained adenine in this location, then the results would be presented 263 C.

The **FBI** has been using mtDNA to solve crimes since 1996. By 2002, they had processed more than 500 cases using mtDNA analysis and had established the National Missing Persons DNA Database to gather information on missing persons for the law enforcement community. A database of mitochondrial DNA can also be accessed through the FBI's **CODIS** (Combined DNA Index System) software.

Mitochondrial DNA has been used successfully in a broad range of instances such as solving missing persons cases and identifying human remains and disaster victims. In 2005, the FBI decided to expand its mitochondrial DNA work and planned to open four new facilities focusing directly on mitochondrial DNA analysis.

SEE ALSO Human migration patterns; Identification of the son of Louis XVI and Marie Antoinette; Mitochondrial DNA typing.

Mitochondrial DNA typing

The field of **forensic science** has benefited significantly from the identification, characterization, and basic understanding of the mitochondria. The mitochondrion is a subcellular organelle that is located within the cell and functions to produce energy for various tissues of the body. It contains its own genome distinct from the genome found in the nucleus (nuclear **DNA**) due to many features, including: how it is inherited; how it is replicated; its copy number; and its size. Mitochondrial DNA is circular, double stranded, and inherited maternally.

Mitochondrial DNA typing is a method used by forensics scientists to match DNA from an unknown sample to a sample collected at a crime scene. It is ideally used in special cases where the DNA is degraded or the source of the sample doesn't contain enough genomic nuclear DNA for analysis. As it is maternally inherited, the DNA from siblings and all maternal relatives should be identical (in the absence of spontaneous mutations). For this reason, the remains of missing persons can be rapidly identified by using **mitochondrial DNA analysis** of relatives. Additionally, there is generally a lack of recombination, an event that takes place during nuclear DNA cell division in which two stands of DNA cross over and exchange information, thereby creating greater sequence diversity. Therefore, even matriarchal relatives separated by several generations can serve as reference samples. Nuclear DNA samples cannot provide this function, due to multiple recombination events that take place throughout the nuclear DNA genome.

The two genomes are not mutually exclusive, instead they rely on each other for survival. The nuclear DNA can encode roughly 1,000 proteins that are targeted for the mitochondria and play a role in oxidative phosphorylation, or energy production, while the mitochondrial DNA produces energy by producing

ATP as well as several other functions. All other **DNA typing systems** use nuclear DNA analysis.

There are several advantages to studying the mitochondrial DNA of a sample. The application of mitochondrial DNA analysis in forensic sciences stems from characteristics of the mitochondrial DNA genome, including its copy number within the cell, its hypervariable region, its size, and its sequence variations. The mitochondrial genome is roughly 16,569 base pairs in size (compared to the 3 billion base pairs in the nuclear DNA). Whereas nuclear DNA has only two copies of each **gene**, tightly woven into chromosomes, mitochondrial DNA can be copied 2–10 times per mitochondrion and there can be hundreds to even thousands of mitochondria per cell. With the mitochondria's role as an energy provider, different tissues contain different amounts of mitochondrial DNA, depending on the energy requirements of the cell. A higher copy number equates to greater sensitivity. This is particularly important if the DNA sample is significantly degraded, or the DNA is present only in a very small quantity. The likelihood of recovering mitochondrial DNA from a small or degraded sample is, therefore, greater in mitochondrial DNA samples compared to nuclear DNA samples since the mitochondrial DNA has a larger copy number.

The low fidelity of DNA repair mechanisms to correct specific mitochondrial DNA mutations has lead to a 5–10 fold higher mutation rate, and, in turn, a higher rate of evolution. Human identity testing employs these regions where there is hypervariability as a consequence of a higher mutation rate. Two hypervariable (HV1 and HV2) regions are part of a control region. On average, there are roughly 8 nucleotide differences between Caucasians and 15 differences between individuals with African decent in these two hypervariable regions. Mitochondrial DNA typing using HV1 and HV2 can be readily performed by using a mitochondrial DNA-specific **polymerase chain reaction** and amplification of genomic mitochondrial DNA. This is followed by direct DNA **sequencing** and identification of sequence variations.

The sample source can often determine which DNA typing system represents the ideal approach. For example, if a hair is left at the scene of the crime, nuclear DNA can only be analyzed if the root is intact. However, mitochondrial DNA can be analyzed from anywhere along the hair follicle, including the shaft. Bones and teeth also contain mitochondrial DNA and can be used in mitochondrial DNA analysis.

There are several disadvantages of using mitochondrial DNA typing in forensics in lieu of nuclear DNA markers. As all individuals of the same maternal lineage are virtually indistinguishable by mitochondrial DNA analysis, identification of the remains of an individual would not be possible without comparing it to maternally-related relatives. Additionally, using mitochondrial DNA analysis to match a suspect to a sample by comparing different genomic locations might reveal a similar profile. Mitochondrial DNA should not be viewed as a unique identifier, since seemingly unrelated individuals might have an unknown shared maternal relative in their distant past. If this is the case, a mistaken match might be suggested. Finally, using a more sophisticated (multi-locus) nuclear DNA analysis will provide far greater discriminatory power.

SEE ALSO DNA fingerprint; DNA profiling; DNA sequences, unique; DNA typing systems.

Andre A. Moenssens J.D., LL.M.

BELGIAN
FORENSIC CONSULTANT

Andre Moenssens did both his pre-legal studies and his early forensic studies in his native Belgium. In 1950, he began a formal study of fingerprints and **fingerprint** analysis under the mentorship of Major Georges E. Defawe. In 1953, Moenssens joined the **International Association for Identification** (IAI); in 1956 he immigrated to the United States. He studied law at the Illinois Institute of Technology-Kent College of Law, where he received his J.D. cum laude in 1966. He completed his Master of Laws degree (LL.M.) at Northwestern University in 1967.

Moenssens continued to pursue his **forensic science** interests as head instructor in fingerprint **identification** at the Institute of Applied Science in Chicago (1960–1967). He was also the associate editor of the *Fingerprint and Identification* magazine from 1960 to 1968.

After completing his academic legal studies, Moenssens began his professional tenure as a law professor at Chicago-Kent College of Law (1967–1973), the University of Richmond in Virginia (1973–1995), and the University of Missouri at Kansas City (1996–2002), where he was on the doctoral faculty and held the Douglas Stripp Professorship in Law. From 1993 to 1995, and again in 2004, Moenssens was Visiting Professor of Law, holding the William J. Mayer Chair, at West Virginia University. After retirement from teaching, he again turned his attention to the world of forensic science.

Moenssens has been the editor of the *Illinois Law Enforcement Officers Law Bulletin* since 1972; he was elected to membership in the prestigious Scientific Working Group on Friction Ridge Analysis, Study, and Technology (SWGFAST). He has been a fellow of the **American Academy of Forensic Sciences** since 1966, where he has served two terms as secretary-treasurer (among other leadership positions). Moenssens is also a member of the Canadian Identification Society, The United Kingdom's Forensic Science Society, and the Indiana Division of the IAI (formerly a member of the Virginia Division of the IAI as well).

Andre Moenssens authored *Fingerprints and the Law* (1969) and *Fingerprint Techniques* (1971), was the senior co-author of *Scientific Evidence in Civil and Criminal Cases* (5th edition, 2005), and *Cases and Comments on Criminal Law* (7th edition, 2003). He has also written dozens of articles, presentation and position papers, books and book chapters, and commentaries on criminal justice and the forensic **evidence**. He remains a sought-after forensic consultant and public speaker, and has also made consistent contributions to the field of forensic science via both the Computer Forensics International Web site and his evolving Forensic Evidence Web site and database.

SEE ALSO Criminal responsibility, historical concepts; Criminology; Fingerprint; Friction ridge skin and personal identification: a history of latent fingerprint analysis.

Monochromatic light

Technologies using monochromatic light have a wide range of application, from astrophysics and astronomy to **forensic science**. The term monochromatic derives from the Greek words *monos*, meaning one or sole, and *chromos*, meaning color. Monochromatic light, or one-color light, is essentially electromagnetic radiation derived from photon emissions from atoms. Photons propagate, or travel, as energy wave fronts of different lengths and levels of energy. Energy levels determine the frequency of light, and the length of a wave determines its color. The bands of light wavelengths that humans can see are called visible light.

Visible light includes red light (in the lower energy level of the **electromagnetic spectrum**)

and violet light in the higher visible energy level of the electromagnetic spectrum. As light propagates through different media, it interacts with atoms present in molecules, such as atmospheric gases, water, and organic matter. These interactions are known as atomic transitions, and consist of emission or absorption of specific wavelengths (or energy packages). The particular structure of isotopes (atoms or molecules of one element of the periodic table) as well as the structure of complex molecules (containing more than one element) defines their physical-chemical properties. Such properties will determine which wavelengths are absorbed and which ones are emitted. Absorption and emission of light by atoms occur in energy packages known as quanta. Absorption occurs when light excites atoms, making electrons suddenly jump to specific outer orbits. This is not a progressive movement between orbits, but a sudden change of energy state by which a given energy quanta is absorbed.

Emissions occur in the inverse manner, resulting in the release of the absorbed quanta. Monochromatic light and **laser** technologies take advantage of these atomic transitions as well as another atomic property known as ground state energy. Ground state energy refers to the tendency of electrons to return to the lowest energy level, therefore undergoing spontaneous emission of the energy quanta.

A monochromatic light beam is characterized by its brightness or light intensity, direction of propagation, and color (all visible characteristics) and by its state of polarization (an invisible characteristic). Light waves oscillate, or swing back and forth, perpendicularly to the direction of propagation. For example, if a light wave is propagating horizontally, it is oscillating vertically. The best example of monochromatic light is a laser beam. A laser light results from one atomic transition with a specific single wavelength, which results in a monochromatic light beam.

When a monochromatic light is directed to a substance or material, it induces transitions which are characteristic to the chemical properties of the constituent elements of such material. Optical **spectroscopy** instruments record the peaks and troughs of the resulting wave lights in a spectrometer that measures the changes in frequency and intensity of these transitions. The resulting wave patterns indicate the chemical composition of the sample. Scanning monochromators are optical instruments that disperse light, permitting the scanning of forensic samples or **evidence**, using one wavelength (or light color) at a time, and scan for the entire spectral range. Battery powered ultraviolet monochromatic devices are used to scan for evidence not easily detected by the naked eye at crime scenes. They allow hidden bloodstains, **fibers**, fingerprints, and lesions that are just beneath the skin on corpses to be visualized by the examiner.

Credit cards, currency, and important documentation are often marked with imprinted holograms on security stamping foils, which are created by monochromatic laser beams. Security standard holography represents the first generation of a security technology known as optically variable devices (OVDs). Other non-holographic OVDs technologies exist, and are detectable in marked materials with ultraviolet light devices.

SEE ALSO Alternate light source analysis; Isotopic analysis; Laser.

Arthur Ernest Mourant

4/11/1904–8/29/1994
ENGLISH
SEROLOGIST, GEOLOGIST

A. E. Mourant was born in the city of Jersey in the United Kingdom. He graduated from Exeter College Oxford, where he studied chemistry, with a specialization in crystallography. He obtained a doctorate (PhD) in **geology** from Leeds University in 1931. In 1933, Mourant founded the Jersey Chemical Pathology Laboratory, which he ran until 1938. At that point, he decided to become a psychoanalyst and moved to London to undergo his own preparatory psychoanalysis training; he began medical studies at St. Bartholomew's Hospital Medical College in London in 1939. During the course of his medical studies, he developed a strong interest in hematology and changed the direction of his career. Mourant completed his coursework in 1943 and was appointed to the position of Medical Officer in the National Blood Transfusion Service in 1944.

Mourant began researching blood **serum**; this led to his discovery of the **antibody** anti-e and his work on the Rhesus system, the Lewis factor in blood grouping, his co-discovery of the Kell factor, and his work on the creation of the antiglobulin test with Race and Coombs. Mourant's discovery of the antibody anti-e was of forensic importance in establishing the three-factor system of Rh blood typing. As a result of his finding of an antibody that reacted with the Lewis system, he was credited with the first publication documenting the Lewis blood grouping system in

1946. There are two genes associated with the Lewis Blood Grouping system: the Lewis **gene** and the **secretor** gene. Mourant also shared in the discovery of the Kell system, which has been found to be comprised of twenty-two different blood group antigens, some of which are associated with allelic genes. An important forensic aspect of the Kell system is its relationship to certain specific racial groups: the more specifically biological **evidence** is able to point to (or exclude) a suspect, the more likely it will be to successfully identify an individual perpetrator, to link crimes, and to achieve successful (and accurate) criminal prosecution.

Mourant authored numerous forensically important hematology texts, the most well-known of which are: *The Distribution of Human Blood Groups and Other Biochemical Polymorphisms* (1953), *The ABO Blood Groups and Maps of World Distribution* (1958), *Blood Group and Disease* (1978) and *Blood Relations, Blood Groups and Anthropology* (1985).

In 1945, Mourant became the Medical Officer at the Galton Laboratory Serum Unit; in 1946 he accepted the Directorship of the Medical Research Council's Blood Group Reference Laboratory at the Lister Institute of Preventive Medicine in London, where he remained until 1965. In 1952, the World Health Organization named the Laboratory as their International Blood Group Reference Laboratory.

Over time, Mourant's interests turned progressively more to **anthropology**. He published two forensically important books about human blood group distribution worldwide: in 1953 he published *The Distribution of Human Blood Groups and Other Biochemical Polymorphisms*, and in 1958 he published *The ABO Blood Groups and Maps of World Distribution*. Of particular forensic significance is the suggestion by Mourant that specific geographic areas and their populations could be associated with particular blood groups and blood types. By so stating, he was indicating that it might be possible to pinpoint the race or geographic origin of an unknown suspect by means of blood typing and blood group analysis. This is of scientific significance because the more specifically it is possible to define an unknown suspect, the more likely it will be to identify (or rule out) an individual.

SEE ALSO Antibody; Anthropology; Blood; Serology; Serum.

M.P. SEE Military Police, United States

Robert S. Mueller III

8/7/1944–
AMERICAN
DIRECTOR, FEDERAL BUREAU OF INVESTIGATION

Robert S. Mueller, III assumed his current position as sixth Director of the Federal Bureau of Investigation on September 4, 2001, exactly one week before the September 11, 2001, terrorist attacks against the United States.

Mueller was born in New York City and raised near Philadelphia, Pennsylvania. He graduated from Princeton University in 1966 and completed a master's degree in International Relations at New York University in 1967. After completing his education, Mueller spent three years as an officer in the Marine Corps. He served in Vietnam, earning the Vietnamese Cross of Gallantry, a Bronze Star, two Navy Commendation Medals, and a Purple Heart. After returning to the United States, Mueller attended Virginia Law School, graduating with a J.D. in 1973. He worked as a litigator with a San Francisco law firm until 1976, and then spent 12 years working in the United States Attorney's Offices. While at the Northern District of California in San Francisco, he achieved the position of criminal division chief. In 1982, he assumed the Boston-based position of Assistant United States' Attorney. His primary areas of investigation and prosecution were terrorist and public corruption cases, major financial fraud, international money laundering, and narcotics conspiracies. He spent a brief period as a partner in a Boston law firm before accepting the position of Assistant to Attorney General Richard L. Thornburgh at the United States Department of Justice (USDOJ) in 1989.

In 1990, Mueller took over responsibility for the criminal division. There, he oversaw the John Gotti crime boss prosecution, the case surrounding the bombing of Pan Am Lockerbie Flight 103, and the conviction of Panamanian leader Manuel Noriega. He was elected a fellow of the American College of Trial Lawyers in 1991. In 1993, he joined the Boston Law Firm of Hale and Dorr as a partner, specializing in white-collar crime. In 1995, he resumed public service as a senior litigator in the homicide division of the District of Columbia United States Attorney's Office. From 1998 until 2001, Mueller was posted in San Francisco as the United States Attorney. Before becoming the sixth Director of the Federal Bureau of Investigation on September 4, 2001, Mueller spent several months as the Acting Deputy Attorney General of the U.S. Department of Justice.

Mueller has stated his conviction that the **FBI** must be responsive to the changing face of American security in the post-9/11 era. Since 9/11, there has been increasing emphasis on field work, due to efforts at improving homeland security as well as an increased need for mobile response to criminal activity and suspected or threatened acts of terrorism. Mueller maintains that in order to remain effective, the FBI must improve core competencies, increase workforce skills specificity, significantly improve ability to gather and protect the security of confidential information, become better able to collaborate with partner agencies, develop and expand its proficiency with emerging technologies, and use that technological acumen to buttress investigations, analyses, and operations.

Historically, the FBI's method of operations has been reactive; it responded to potential or actual events. It is Mueller's plan to fully shift the Bureau to a proactive stance, reshaping the philosophy of the FBI for increased compatibility with current world events. His proactive emphasis involves broadening the working relationship between American and international intelligence and law enforcement communities, particularly in three areas: counterterrorism, cybercrime and infrastructure protection, and counterintelligence.

As of March 2005, Mueller has outlined three major tenets underlying the FBI management shifts: the mission and the priorities of the FBI must be refocused in accordance with the changing face of terrorism and threats to national security; the FBI workforce must be realigned in order to address its new priorities; and the operational culture and philosophical stance of FBI management must support enhanced agility, flexibility, effectiveness, and accountability.

SEE ALSO FBI (United States Federal Bureau of Investigation); FBI crime laboratory; September 11, 2001, terrorist attacks (forensic investigations of).

Kary Banks Mullis

12/28/1944–
AMERICAN
BIOCHEMIST

American biochemist Kary Banks Mullis is famous in **forensic science** circles as the designer of the **polymerase chain reaction** (**PCR**). PCR is a fast and effective technique for reproducing specific genes or deoxyribonucleic acid (**DNA**) fragments that is able to create billions of copies in a few hours. Widely available because it is now relatively inexpensive, PCR has revolutionized not only the biotechnology industry, but also many other scientific fields and it has important applications in forensic science and law enforcement.

Mullis was born in Lenoir, North Carolina, on December 28, 1944. He entered Georgia Institute of Technology in 1962 and studied chemistry. As an undergraduate, he created a laboratory for manufacturing poisons and **explosives**. He also invented an electronic device stimulated by brain waves that could control a light switch.

Upon graduation from Georgia Tech in 1966 with a B.S. degree in chemistry, Mullis entered the doctoral program in biochemistry at the University of California, Berkeley. At the age of 24, he wrote a paper on the structure of the universe that was published by *Nature* magazine. He was awarded his Ph.D. in 1973 and he accepted a teaching position at the University of Kansas Medical School in Kansas City. In 1977, he assumed a postdoctoral fellowship at the University of California, San Francisco. In 1979, he accepted a position as a research scientist with a growing biotech firm, Cetus Corporation, that was in the business of synthesizing chemicals used by other scientists in genetic cloning.

In the late 1970s, the most effective way to reproduce DNA was by cloning. The cloning process is not only time-consuming, but it replicates the whole DNA strand, increasing the complexity. The revolutionary advantage of PCR is its selectivity; it is a process that reproduces specific genes on the DNA strand millions or billions of times, effectively amplifying or enlarging parts of the DNA molecule for further study.

A commercial version of PCR and a machine called the Thermal Cycler have been developed. With the addition of the chemical building blocks of DNA, called nucleotides, and a biochemical catalyst called polymerase, the machine would perform the process automatically on a target piece of DNA. The machine is so economical that even a small laboratory can afford it.

In the field of genetics, the PCR process has been particularly important to the Human Genome Project, a huge undertaking to map human DNA. The ability of this process to reproduce specific genes has made it possible for virologists to develop extremely sensitive tests for acquired immunodeficiency syndrome (AIDS), capable of detecting the virus at early stages of infection. PCR has been particularly useful for diagnosing genetic predispositions to diseases such as sickle cell anemia and cystic fibrosis.

PCR has also revolutionized evolutionary biology, making it possible to examine the DNA of woolly mammoths and the remains of ancient humans. PCR has been used to identify the bones of Czar Nicholas II of Russia. Scientists are preparing to use PCR to amplify DNA from the hair of Abraham Lincoln, as well as bloodstains and bone fragments, in an effort to determine whether he suffered from Marfan's syndrome.

In law enforcement, PCR has made genetic fingerprinting more accurate and effective. It has been used to identify murder victims, and to overturn the sentences of men wrongly convicted of rape.

In 1988, Mullis became a private biochemical research consultant. In 1993, he won the Nobel Prize in chemistry.

SEE ALSO DNA; Fingerprint; PCR (polymerase chain reaction).

Multisystem method

Serologists (scientists who study **blood serum**, and immune factors in blood serum) **Brian Wraxall** and **Mark Stolorow** pioneered the "multisystem method" for the simultaneous separation of three isoenzymes (glyoxalase I, esterase D, and phosphoglucomutase) from bloodstains in 1978. They also created and developed a multisystem method involving the use of **electrophoresis** analysis and an immunoelectrophoretic technique for use in forensic **identification** of bloodstains. The goal of the multisystem method is to carry out several different procedures simultaneously, thereby vastly reducing the amount of bloodstain needed for the analysis (cutting it by two-thirds), multiplying accuracy, markedly reducing the time previously involved in the sequential analysis of all three isoenzyme components, and accomplishing all of this without any loss in sensitivity or resolution.

Blood remains the single most important type of **evidence** in the world of **forensic science** and of criminal investigation. It can link perpetrator to act of violence, to victim, to crime scene, and to other evidence. A bloodstain is first typed for blood group. While quite useful, this is considered only class evidence (evidence that links to a specific group), as it can exclude suspects, but cannot conclusively identify a specific individual. At a slightly higher level of sophistication, the sample can then be typed for Rh factor, and sub-grouped beyond this.

In order to type the stain to the greatest possible level of specificity, with the goal of accurately linking a sample or bloodstain to a single individual, the typing of proteins and enzymes is utilized. Blood proteins and enzymes share the characteristics of isoenzymes, or polymorphisms; that is, they exist in multiple molecular forms that have the same or very nearly identical enzyme activities and therefore, they have subtypes. Among the more common isoenzymes found in blood (and in bloodstains) are: transferrin, glucose-6-phosphate dehydrogenase, 6-phosphogluconate dehydrogenase, esterase D, adenyl kinase, glutamic pyruvate transaminase, glyoxalase I, erythrocyte acid phosphatase, adenosine deaminase, and phosphoglucomutase. Each isoenzyme, as well as every blood group subtype, has a known population distribution. By breaking the blood sample down to the level of maximum specificity, it is possible to progressively exclude the population of suspects until only one individual is left who could possibly match the set of specific blood group, type, and polymorphism markers. For example: the sample and the suspected perpetrator both have blood type A (42% of the population), and basic subtype A2 (25%), protein adenyl kinase (15%), and enzyme phosphoglucomutase (6%). The probability that there could be two individuals with this exact blood type is: (0.42 x 0.25 x 0.15 x 0.06), or less than 0.000945 percent.

By creating multisystem methods for bloodstain typing, Wraxall and Stolorow revolutionized the field of individualized blood typing, and made lasting contributions to the accuracy, validity, and reliability of forensic science, by dramatically decreasing required sample size, increasing efficiency and saving considerable cost by allowing for the simultaneous testing of three isoenzymes, and doing so without sacrificing either resolution or accuracy.

SEE ALSO Antibody; Antigen; Bloodstain evidence.

Mummies

For legal **medicine** purposes, the state of conservation of a corpse is crucial to determining the cause and **time of death**. Conservative-transformative phenomena, also called spontaneous mummification, can occur when a body is exposed to favorable conditions, such as dehydration combined with heat, or dehydration combined with freezing temperatures.

Mummification may occur naturally or may be achieved through artificial methods. Ancient Egyptians, Incas, and the natives of the Canary Islands used different methods to embalm and conserve the bodies of their dead. In modern societies, embalming is also practiced when requested by the family of the deceased or to preserve corpses for academic teaching and research.

Forensic scientists, forensic anthropologists, and forensic archeologists work together to unwrap the mysteries surrounding both preserved and naturally occurring mummies. **DNA** fingerprinting and **skull** reconstruction, techniques originally developed to solve crimes, are useful in investigating mummified human remains. Investigators may also use CT scans to help determine the **cause of death**, radiocarbon dating to help determine the time of death, and knowledge of forensic **entomology** (insect **evidence**) to determine what happened to the mummy at different stages after death.

The natural mummification process usually happens in extremely dry environments that allow the fast dehydration of tissues, simultaneously slowing down or inhibiting the **decomposition** by bacteria and other microorganisms. Bodies buried in the sands of the Takla Makan Desert in Asia and the Atacama Desert in the north of Chile have been found mummified even thousands of years after death. Mummification also happens to the bodies of people who die on the desert surface, where direct exposure to sunlight and the highly dry atmosphere favor rapid dehydration. Stone crypts sometimes house conditions favorable for natural mummification, such as occurred in the catacombs of the Franciscan Brotherhood in Tolosa, Spain, and in the crypt of Saint Boumet-le-Chatêau, where more than 30 mummies exist in a perfect state of conservation. These two locations share in common a dry climate, crypts that have a natural constant temperature of about 59°F (15°C), and enough air movement to prevent vapor from the bodies to build up in the crypts.

Natural mummification is also favored by some other factors, such as age (it is more common in newborns), gender (occurs more often in female corpses), and cause of death (large hemorrhages, ante-mortem prolonged administration of **antibiotics**, and poisoning by arsenic and potassium cyanide). The external aspect of both natural and man-made mummies includes drastic body-weight reduction, dried leather-like shrunken and darkened skin, reduced volume of the head, and well-conserved teeth and nails. Facial features are in a measure preserved, but tendons and muscles are very fragile and

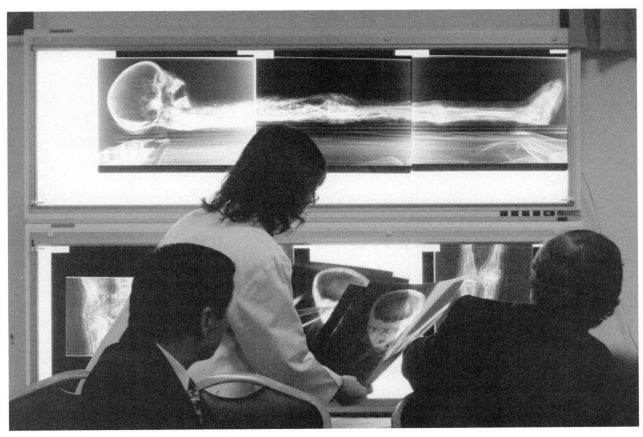

Scientists discuss the x ray of a 3,000-year-old Egyptian mummy at the National Taiwan University Hospital in Taipei, 2003.
© RICHARD CHUNG/REUTERS/CORBIS

disintegrate at touch. Another environment that favors mummification is freezing temperatures associated with dry climates such as those found in upper altitudes in the Himalayas, Alps, as well as in the Artic and Antarctic caps. The famous Otzi mummy, also known as "Iceman," was found in the Tyrolean Alps in 1991, after approximately 5,000 years, in highly conserved conditions and still bearing the wounds of the weapon that killed him. From the position of his fallen body and his wounds, it was possible to make a **crime scene reconstruction**, 5,300 years after the **murder**.

Peat bogs, the soft moist soil formed by the partial decay of vegetation, are very acidic due to high kevels of tannin, one of the compounds used in leather conservation. Marshes and other peat bogs in Scandinavia, Ireland, and Scotland have yielded from time to time well-preserved mummies from the Bronze and Iron Ages. Perhaps the first peat bog mummy to draw the attention of anthropologists was the one known as Tollund Man, found in a peat bog on Denmark in 1950. An **autopsy** revealed even

his last meal and estimated the time of death as having occurred 12 hours after that meal, through the analysis of the well-conserved partially digested grains in his stomach. The mummy was dated as having died around 350 B.C., at the approximate age of 40. Among the seeds present in his stomach were found barley, knotweed, bristle grass, chamomile, and some other wild seeds, suggesting that such a meal was a soup. Since those seeds were only cropped in the spring in those latitudes, researchers could conclude that he died during a spring season. As he had a rope with a knot and noose around the neck and clear marks of the knot in the skin of his neck, they concluded that he had been hung (cause of death), although his bones were very deteriorated to allow the verification of a neck fracture. These and other lines of analysis are what a forensic anthropologist considers when investigating a "cold case."

Calcification is a conservative-transformative phenomenon by which a corpse is "petrified" due to the rapid absorption of calcium salts by the skeleton in the presence of bacterial decomposition of internal organs. Fetuses that die in the womb are more likely to undergo calcification than other bodies. However, most fetuses undergo maceration (softening of the tissues) and not calcification when death occurs in the womb, due to the presence of the amniotic fluid in the mother's uterus. Colorification is a very rare mummification phenomenon, described in 1985 by Della Volta, occurring in cadavers kept in perfectly sealed zinc urns. The mummies' skin has the appearance of rawhide, with a flattened and depressed abdomen, muscles, and subcutaneous tissues well preserved, and internal organs softened and generally conserved. A small quantity of a viscous liquid of a brown-yellowish tonality is usually found at the bottom of such urns. The exact process underlying this type of mummification is not yet understood.

SEE ALSO Anthropology; Autopsy; Body marks; Coroner; Crime scene reconstruction; Death, cause of; Entomology; Hanging (signs of); Medical examiner.

Murder vs. manslaughter

Killing another person is commonly referred to as murder. However, the precise term for the killing of one person by another is homicide. Murder is a form of criminal homicide that has a precise legal meaning. Murder is usually defined as the "unlawful killing of another with malice aforethought (or "an abandoned and malignant heart"). Malice aforethought refers to the perpetrator's intention of doing harm.

There are different legal variations of murder, known as degrees. Degrees of murder vary by the gravity (seriousness) of the offense (usually measured by the intent of the perpetrator) and the sentence assigned to that offense. For example, murder in the first degree, or first-degree murder, carries the sternest sentences and is usually reserved for murders committed with premeditation or extreme cruelty.

Manslaughter is also a form of criminal homicide. The difference between murder and manslaughter is in the element of intent. In order to commit voluntary manslaughter, a person must have committed a homicide, but have acted in the "heat of passion." This mental state must have been caused by legally sufficient provocation that would cause a reasonable person of ordinary temperament to lose self-control. To convict a person of manslaughter, it must be proved that the person who committed the homicide had adequate provocation (this cannot involve words alone), acted in the heat of passion, and lacked the

opportunity to cool that passion. There must also be a connection between the incident of provocation, the heat of passion, and the act that caused the homicide.

Involuntary manslaughter is manslaughter resulting from a failure to perform a legal duty expressly required to safeguard human life, from the commission of an unlawful act not amounting to a **felony**, or from the commission of an act involving a risk of injury or death that is done in an unlawful, reckless, or grossly negligent manner. Involuntary manslaughter is a relatively new legal concept. Its exact definition varies greatly by jurisdiction, and is sometimes known as second- or third-degree manslaughter.

In order to convict someone of either murder or manslaughter, the distinct elements of each crime must be proved beyond a reasonable doubt, and the actions of the perpetrator cannot be explained or excused by any legal defense, excuse, or justification. Murder and manslaughter also differ in the sentences imposed for each crime. As the perpetrator of manslaughter is assumed to have evidenced less mental culpability, the sentence for manslaughter is usually less than that for murder.

SEE ALSO Assassination; Criminal responsibility, historical concepts; Death, cause of; Death, mechanism of; Serial killers.

Murders, serial SEE Serial killers

Raymond C. Murray
**7/2/1929–
AMERICAN
FORENSIC GEOLOGIST**

Over the course of his career, Raymond C. Murray turned his knowledge of **geology** into a critical tool for crime investigators. He worked for several years as a geology professor before also becoming a forensic geologist, aiding law enforcement officers and testifying in criminal cases. Murray has written numerous books on the subject, including *Forensic Geology*, the first textbook of its kind.

Murray had an early interest in geology. He attended the University of Wisconsin, Madison, earning a master's degree in geology in 1952 and a doctorate in geology in 1955. After graduation, he was hired by Shell Development Company in Houston, Texas, to work as a manager of geology research, a position he held for the next eleven years. But ultimately, Murray decided to move into academia, taking an associate professor position at the University of New Mexico in 1966.

In 1967, Murray was offered a job at Rutgers University, and became the chairman of the geology department there. It was at Rutgers where Murray first became involved in forensic geology. A Bureau of Alcohol, Tobacco, and Firearms agent had come to Murray with soil involved in a crime investigation, and asked Murray for help. From that point forward, Murray continued his work as a professor, but also expanded his knowledge and expertise into the world of forensic geology. In 1975, along with fellow Rutgers professor John Tedrow, Murray published *Forensic Geology: Earth Sciences and Criminal Investigation*. It was the first textbook written on the science. A revised edition was published in 1991.

Murray left Rutgers in 1977 to take a position at the University of Montana. There he continued his work in forensic geology, often testifying as an expert witness and lecturing at crime laboratories around the world. He retired from the University of Montana in 1996, devoting more time and attention to his private forensic geology practice. In 2004, Murray wrote and published his latest book on the subject, *Evidence from the Earth: Forensic Geology and Criminal Investigation*. In this text he details the many ways geologists have been able to analyze forensic data and reveal soil and rock **evidence**.

SEE ALSO Careers in forensic science; Soils.

Mustard gas

Among the toxic agents that can injure or kill people are noxious gases. One example is mustard gas. Its use as an offensive chemical weapon makes mustard gas of particular relevance for military forensic scientists. Mustard gas is the popular name for the compound with the chemical designation 1,1-thiobis(2-chloroethane) (chemical formula: Cl-CH2-CH2-S-CH2-CH2-Cl). Mustard gas has also been called H, yprite, sulfur mustard and Kampstoff Lost.

The name mustard gas arose because the odor of the impure substance is similar to mustard, garlic, or horseradish. However, in the pure form, mustard gas is odorless and colorless.

The gas was used for the first time as an agent of **chemical warfare** during World War I, when it was distributed with devastating effect near Ypres in Flanders on July 12, 1917.

In 1860, Frederick Guthrie observed that when ethylene reacted with chlorine a substance was produced which, in small quantities, could produce toxic effects on the skin. Exposure to low concentrations of mustard gas classically causes the reddening and blistering of skin and epithelial tissue. On inhalation, the gas causes the lining of the lungs to blister and leads to chronic respiratory impairment. Higher concentrations of mustard gas will attack the corneas of the eyes and can cause blindness.

Exposure to mustard gas can lead to a slow and painful death and any moist area of the body is especially susceptible to its effects. The compound is only slightly soluble in water, but it undergoes a hydrolysis reaction, liberating highly corrosive hydrochloric acid and several other vesicant intermediates, which are able to blister epithelial surfaces.

Despite the ease of hydrolysis, mustard gas may be preserved underground in a solid form for up to ten years. The reason for this is that in an environment where the concentration of water is relatively low, the reaction pathway proceeds to form an intermediate known as thiodiglycol. In a low moisture environment, most of the water available at the solid surface is used in this reaction. Subsequently, another intermediate in the reaction pathway, a sulfonium ion, reacts with the thiodiglycol in the place of water. This reaction then creates stable, non-reactive sulfonium salts, which can act as a protective layer around the bulk of the solid mustard and prevent further degradation.

Mustard gas as a chemical weapon is a particularly deadly and debilitating poison and when it was first used in 1917, it could penetrate all the masks and protective materials that were available at that time. In more recent years, urethane was found to be resistant to mustard gas, and also has several other advantages for use in combat; urethane is tough, resistant to cuts, and is stable at a wide range of temperatures.

Detoxification procedures from mustard gas are difficult because of its insolubility and also because of the drastic effects it can have on lung epithelial tissue following inhalation. During World War I, physicians had no curative means of treating the victims of mustard gas exposure. The only method of detoxification that was known involved a rather extreme oxidation procedure using superchlorinated bleaches, such as 5% sodium hypochlorite. Today, several novel methods of detoxification have been developed to counter the effects of mustard gas and these include the use of sulfur-amine solutions and magnesium monoperox-yphthalate. The most effective method to date employs peroxy acids, because they are able to react quickly with the mustard gas. Furthermore, the addition of a catalyst can speed up the detoxification reaction even more effectively.

Although mustard gas has been shown to have long-term carcinogenic properties, it can also be used as an agent in the treatment of cancer. In 1919, it was observed that victims of mustard gas attack had a low white blood cell count and bone marrow aplasia (tissue growth failure). More detailed research in the years following 1946 showed that nitrogen mustards, which differ from traditional mustard gas by the substitution of a sulfur atom by a nitrogen, could reduce tumor growth in experimental mice by cross linking **DNA** strands. It had been shown previously that the sensitivity of mouse bone marrow to mustard gas was similar to that of humans and more detailed research eventually led to successful clinical trials. Today, nitrogen mustards are also part of the spectrum of substances used in modern anti-cancer chemotherapy. They are primarily used in the treatment of conditions such as Hodgkin's disease and cancers of the lymph glands.

SEE ALSO Chemical warfare; Chemical Biological Incident Response Force, United States; Nerve gas; Sarin gas; Tabun.

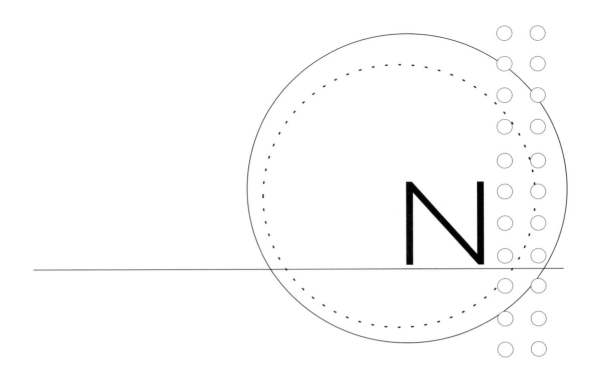

Narcotic

The detection of narcotics and other drugs of abuse in the **blood**, body **fluids**, and tissues of drug abusers and corpses where the suspected **cause of death** is related to drug overdose is routine procedure in forensic laboratories. The National Institute on Drug Abuse (NIDA), the Federal Bureau of Investigation (**FBI**), the Drug Enforcement Administration (**DEA**), and the Department of Justice are the agencies responsible for drug research and preventive programs, regulatory control, classification of drugs of abuse, and law enforcement.

Narcotics are opium (a substance naturally occurring in poppy seeds) and semi-synthetic opioid substances used to relieve intense pain. These drugs block specific receptors that processes pain information in the central nervous system (CNS), such as the brainstem, medial thalamus, spinal cord, hypothalamus, and limbic system, along with peripheral nerve fibers. Narcotics are addictive substances due to the euphoric effect they have on mood and general disposition. Morphine, codeine, and heroin are the main drugs of abuse in the narcotic category.

Morphine is a controlled medication prescribed for the treatment of intense chronic pain and for post-surgery pain due to its strong analgesic (pain-relieving) properties. However, morphine is highly addictive and can present dangerous side effects. Ordinary doses of morphine may lead to respiratory depression, or the slowing or cessation of breathing, through the reduction of sensitivity of the brain cells

that regulate breathing. A study funded by the National Institute on Drug Abuse has shown that the chronic administration of morphine to rats reduced the size of nerve cells that produce dopamine by 25%. Dopamine is a natural brain chemical messenger (neurotransmitter) that causes sensations of pleasure, joy, and reward. The euphoric effects of morphine and other opiates indicate that they act upon the dopamine receptors. It is also known that cells decrease sensitivity to a given medication when frequently exposed to it. Therefore, such observed cell size reductions may be the result of cell desensitization to the drug. This explains the tolerance effect that morphine and other drugs of abuse cause in the CNS, leading addicts to intake increased doses to obtain the same initial effects of euphoria. It also explains the deep depressive episodes that take place when the effect of the drug ceases, or when abusers are under detoxification treatment. Besides addiction, the other side effects of morphine chronic intake are sedation, constipation, nausea and vomiting, urinary retention, and respiratory depression. Withdrawal causes acute depression, tremors, emotional instability, and irritability.

Heroin is an illegal and highly addictive narcotic with the fastest action on brain receptors. Heroin is a semi-synthetic derivate of morphine, sold on the black market either as a black gluey substance known as "black tar" or in a more "purified" form, mixed with sugar, starch, powdered milk, or quinine. The purification process is done by reacting heroin with other drugs or poisons, such as strychnine, which increases the risk of death or irreversible brain

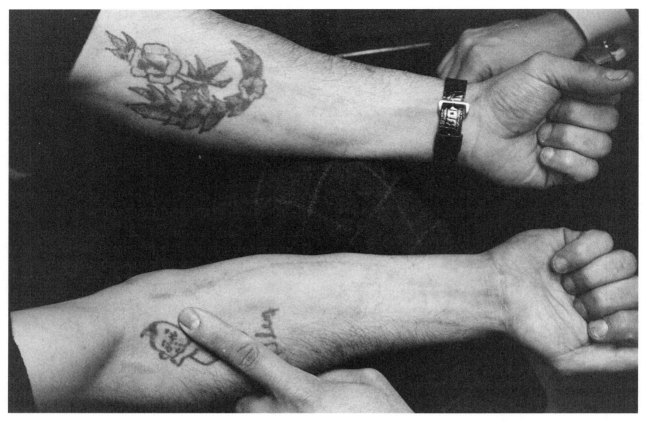

Tattoos on a heroin addict's arm, done for the purpose of covering up needle marks. © TED STRESHINSKY/CORBIS

damage. Since abusers usually inject heroin in an intravenous or intramuscular solution, often while sharing needles, the risk for abusers contracting hepatitis C and HIV is a large concern among public health authorities. Other forms of heroin consumption involve inhaling it through the nose (snorting) or smoking the drug. As tolerance develops, abusers may inject heroin three or four times per day. After the initial rush of euphoria, users become drowsy, respiratory depression sets in, and higher mental functions are clouded. Heroin is converted into morphine in the brain, so the withdrawal symptoms are the same as with morphine, although more severe with heroin. Another risk imposed by heroin is that its illegal manufacture is accomplished by criminals who use toxic compounds and poisons in the process. The product can also be mixed with other dangerous drugs. In addition, the user does not know exactly how much heroin is in the purchased drug; it may have enough to induce an accidental overdose. It can also be contaminated with fungus and other **pathogens**, leading to infections. Lung complications, such as tuberculosis and pneumonia, are common among drug abusers. Inflamed veins or arteries are also common, due to the poor solubility (dissolvability) of substances mixed with the abused drugs.

Law enforcement against international drug traffickers who illegally bring narcotics and other **illicit drugs** of abuse into the United States requires a continuous effort and strategic planning from the FBI and DEA. It also involves collaboration with other international agencies, such as **Interpol** and the police of other countries where these drugs are originally produced, as well as those that are used as routes for drug dealers.

Forensic **identification** of addicts involves the examination of physical indicators such as needle marks in the veins of arms and legs, bluish bruises due to collapsed veins in these areas, and pinpoint pupils. Frequent snorting of cocaine or heroin leads to the destruction of nasal cartilages and nosebleeds. To determine what drugs a suspect is using, laboratory tests are performed on blood or urine samples that allow for the detection of both classes of drugs and specific drugs of abuse. **Interrogation** of arrested addicts helps local investigators to identify and arrest street drug dealers. The use of trained dogs in ports and airports is also a useful resource for the rapid identification of packages and luggage containing drugs. In the past, "mules," or people hired to carry drugs between countries, hid drugs wrapped in plastic inside their own body cavities. After the installation of x-ray scanners in airports, mules were more easily detected and arrested.

SEE ALSO DEA (Drug Enforcement Administration); FBI (United States Federal Bureau of Investigation); Homogeneous enzyme immunoassay (EMIT); Illicit drugs; Immune system; Interpol; Nervous system overview; Neurotransmitters; Psychotropic drugs.

National Institute of Justice

Various branches of the federal government in the United States are concerned with the forensic investigations of accidents, deaths, and crimes, and in determining both the cause of a particular incident and in taking steps to lessen the likelihood of a recurrence.

The National Institute of Justice (NIJ) serves the United States Department of Justice in the areas of research, development, and evaluation. Established under the authority of the Omnibus Crime Control and Safe Streets Act of 1968, its purpose is to provide independent, evidence-based tools to assist state and local law enforcement. Its programs address a variety of law-enforcement issues, including use of **DNA evidence**, drug abuse, and domestic violence.

Appointed by the President and confirmed by the Senate, the director of the NIJ is responsible for establishing objectives in alignment with Justice Department priorities, as well as the current needs of the field. It works to take account of views from professionals in all areas of criminal justice and related fields in its search for knowledge and tools to guide the policy and practice of law enforcement nationwide. On January 12, 2003, it reorganized, streamlining its structure from three offices to two, the Office of Development and Communications and the Office of Research and Evaluation.

NIJ has set research priorities in a number of fields, including law enforcement/policing; justice systems (sentencing, courts, prosecution, defense); corrections; investigative and forensic sciences (including DNA); counterterrorism/critical incidents; crime prevention/causes of crime; violence and victimization (including violent crimes); drugs, alcohol, and crime; interoperability, spatial information, and automated systems; and program evaluation. Among its programs are the Arrestee Drug Abuse Monitoring Program (ADAM); Community Mapping, Planning, and Analysis for Safety Strategies (COMPASS); National Commission on the Future of DNA Evidence; and the Violence Against Women and Family Violence Research and Evaluation Program.

SEE ALSO FBI (United States Federal Bureau of Investigation); Law Enforcement Training Center (FLETC), United States Federal.

Navy Criminal Investigative Service (NCIS)

In addition to civilian law enforcement agencies, various branches of the military conduct forensic investigations into accidents and deaths. One of these branches is the Navy Criminal Investigative Service (NCIS). NCIS is responsible for providing law enforcement on behalf of United States Navy and Marine Corps personnel and their families. Originally part of the Office of Naval Intelligence (ONI), the organization was staffed primarily by military personnel, whereas today it is largely staffed with civilians. NCIS has been involved in **murder** investigations and drug sweeps, and since September 11, 2001, it has also taken on a homeland security role. All these activities can involve forensic analyses.

NCIS began as part of ONI, which was deployed during World War II to detect potential spies and saboteurs on the domestic front. Through the end of World War II, the investigative branch of ONI was composed mainly of military personnel. In the postwar era, however, the Secretary of the Navy developed a coterie of civilian agents responsible for conducting criminal investigations, counterintelligence, and security background investigations on naval and marine personnel and civilians associated with the U.S. Navy and Marine Corps.

Only on February 4, 1966, did the Naval Investigative Service (NIS), as NCIS's predecessor was called, gain an identity separate from that of ONI. Nonetheless, it remained a part of the naval intelligence office. In 1972, the newly formed Defense Investigative Service took over responsibility for background checks, leaving NIS free to concentrate on counterintelligence and criminal investigations. During the 1980s, the organization went through a number of name changes until, in December 1992, it gained its present identity.

NCIS has received numerous accolades for its efficiency, not least for the work of its "cold-case squad," which attempts to solve old, previously unsolved crimes. The latter has reopened scores of previously unsolved homicide cases, and successfully solved dozens. This work is not possible without the application of modern **forensic science** techniques.

Working with the cold-case squad of the Fairfax County, Virginia, law-enforcement authorities, for instance, NCIS helped solve a homicide case that was extremely "cold"—so much so that the accused had finished high school, had a full career in the Navy, and retired—all in the quarter-century between the murder and his arrest.

The case involved Paul S. Sorensen, who was 16 years old in 1975, when he allegedly stabbed to death a convenience store clerk while robbing a 7-Eleven. Sorensen entered the Navy after graduating high school in 1976, and in 1999, having attained the rank of chief petty officer, retired to Corpus Christi, Texas. Three years later, and five years after NCIS and Fairfax County reopened the **cold case**, Sorensen—knowing that he would soon be arrested anyway—turned himself in to authorities.

Another example of NCIS at work was the drug sweep that in July 2002 netted 84 marines and sailors at Camp Lejeune, North Carolina. Code-named Operation Xterminator, the sweep took two years and yielded $1.4 million in narcotics.

SEE ALSO Careers in forensic science; Cold case; Military police, United States; United States Army Medical Research Institute of Infectious Diseases (USAMRIID).

NCIC (National Crime Information Center)

As part of the Federal Bureau of Investigation (**FBI**), the National Crime Information Center (NCIC) is a national computerized repository system of criminal justice data used by local, state, and federal law enforcement agencies throughout the United States, Canada, Puerto Rico, and the U.S. Virgin Islands. Now under the direction of the FBI's Criminal Justice Information Services (CJIS) division, located in the city of Clarksburg, West Virginia, the NCIC provides North American **forensic science** departments with search information for such data involving convicted

sex offenders, **fingerprint** impressions, and missing persons.

The NCIC was created by the FBI in January 1967 in response to an alarming increase in crime within the United States. Recognizing that law enforcement agencies throughout the country needed instantaneous access to standardized criminal data, the FBI established a computer system and a telecommunications network to initially assist fifteen metropolitan and state regions with about 95,000 records in five databases (Wanted Persons, Stolen License Plates, Stolen or Missing Guns, Stolen Autos, and Other Identifiable Stolen Articles). By 1971, all of the U.S. states and the District of Columbia were part of the NCIC system. Then, in February 1992, the CJIS was created by the FBI in order to serve as the primary information repository for criminal justice data. The NCIC was consolidated under the jurisdiction of the CJIS, along with other relevant federal programs such as Fingerprint Identification and Uniform Crime Reporting.

Open around the clock, the NCIC is well equipped to search for a wide range of forensic data due to the use of its expanding number of databases that contain a growing amount of historical and current data. For example, by using the New York State Identification and Intelligence System, NCIC personnel are able to search for phonetically similar names (such as Clark and Clarke) or derivatives (such as William, Willy, and Billy). In addition, fingerprint searches of wanted and missing persons are made using stored images of the right index fingerprint. NCIC personnel can also search records within the Convicted Persons or Supervised Release File for suspects under probation and parole.

Photographs, commonly called mugshots, can be searched through a signature, fingerprint, or other identifying images (such as scars and tattoos). NCIC personnel can also search for digital images of physical possessions (such as automobiles and boats) associated with a suspect. Records of convicted sexual offenders and violent sexual predators can also be searched through a Convicted Sex Offender Registry. Convicts currently held in the U.S. federal prison system can be identified through the NCIC's Sentry file.

As of March 2005, the NCIC possesses more than ten million records in around seventeen database files (some recently added ones include Foreign Fugitive, Missing Persons, Violent Gang/Terrorist, Unidentified Persons, and U.S. Secret Service Protective) and about 24 million criminal history records contained in the Interstate Identification Index. In the business of law enforcement, the NCIC deals with more than 80 thousand law enforcement and criminal justice agencies.

SEE ALSO DNA databanks; DNA profiling; FBI (United States Federal Bureau of Investigation); Tattoo identification.

NDIS, FBI database

The National DNA Index System, or NDIS, is a United States Federal Bureau of Investigation (**FBI**) DNA database that facilities the electronic comparison and exchange of DNA profiles between participating local, county, state, and federal law enforcement agencies and forensic laboratories. First made operational in 1998, the NDIS is a highly valued instrument that is used by law enforcement professionals in order to better coordinate and communicate information related to serial violent crimes committed across the United States. Authorization to establish the NDIS came about from the DNA Identification Act of 1994.

The NDIS is a critical component of the Combined DNA Index System (**CODIS**), an FBI software support program developed in 1990, which uses DNA (deoxyribonucleic acid) technology to generate leads in crimes where forensic **evidence** is recovered from crime scenes. In its role, the NDIS enables participating organizations to compare DNA profiles on a national level in order to more efficiently investigate crimes. Managed by the FBI as the nation's DNA database, DNA profiles typically are generated at the local level, transferred to state and national levels, and uploaded electronically through the Internet at the state level to the NDIS. At this point, the data is compared to determine if a convicted offender can be associated with a previous or current crime, or if two or more crimes can be joined together.

An actual example that shows how the NDIS works involves the unsolved (and previously unconnected) rape and **murder** cases of a college professor in Flint, Michigan, in 1986; and of a flight attendant in Romulus, Michigan, in 1991. With access to CODIS in 2001, Michigan State Police submitted DNA from the 1986 case to the NDIS. When the sample was matched with DNA from the 1991 case, latent fingerprints from the 1986 case were sent to the FBI's Latent Fingerprint Unit. While searching through the FBI's **Integrated Automated Fingerprint Identification System** (IAFIS), one of the prints

was identified. Based on this information, the Flint Police Department followed the suspect, recovered a restaurant napkin used by the suspect, and after the material found on the napkin was forensically matched with evidence left at both homicide scenes, the suspect was arrested and charged with murder.

From its beginnings on October 13, 1998, to today, the NDIS has gained participants and now includes over 130 federal, state, and local laboratories representing all fifty states, the District of Columbia (the FBI Laboratory), Puerto Rico, and the U.S. Army. On June 12, 2002, the NDIS achieved a major milestone when the Florida Department of Law Enforcement contributed the one millionth DNA profile to the program. As of December 2004, the total number of DNA profiles within the NDIS is 2,132,470; the total number of convicted offender profiles is 2,038,470; and the total number of forensic profiles is 93,956.

SEE ALSO CODIS: Combined DNA Index System; DNA; DNA databanks; DNA profiling; FBI (United States Federal Bureau of Investigation); FBI crime laboratory; Integrated automated fingerprint identification system; Serial killers.

Nerve gas

Noxious gases can injure or kill people, and so can be of significance in a forensic investigation. One example is nerve gas. Its offensive military use makes nerve gas of particular relevance for military forensic scientists. As well, the specter of the use of agents like **sarin gas** by rogue organizations and extremists has made the forensic detection of nerve gas a national security issue.

Nerve gases, or nerve agents, are mostly odorless compounds belonging to the organophosphate family of chemicals. Nerve gasses are either colorless or yellow-brown liquids under standard conditions. Two examples of nerve gases that have gained some notoriety through their powerful physiological effects are sarin and VX.

Even in small quantities, nerve gases inhibit the enzyme acetylcholinesterase and disrupt the transmission of nerve impulses in the body. Acetylcholinesterase is a serine hydrolase belonging to the esterase enzyme family, which acts on different types of carboxylic esters in higher eukaryotes. Its role in biology is to terminate nerve impulse transmissions at cholinergic synapses. It does this by rapidly hydrolyzing the neurotransmitter, acetylcholine, which is released at the nerve synapses. Inhibition of the acetylcholinesterase results in the excessive build up of acetylcholine in, for example, the parasympathetic nerves leading to a number of important locations in the body, such as the smooth muscle of the iris, ciliary body, the bronchial tree, gastrointestinal tract, bladder and blood vessels; also the salivary glands and secretory glands of the gastrointestinal tract and respiratory tract; and the cardiac muscle and endings of sympathetic nerves to the sweat glands. An accumulation of acetylcholine at parasympathetic sites gives rise to characteristic muscarinic signs, such as emptying of bowels and bladder, blurring of vision, excessive sweating, profuse salivation, and stimulation of smooth muscles. The accumulation of acetylcholine at the endings of motor nerves leading to voluntary muscles ultimately results in paralysis.

Nerve gases are highly toxic, stable, and easily dispersed. They produce rapid physiological effects both when absorbed through the skin or through the respiratory tract. They are also fairly easy to synthesize and the raw materials required for their manufacture are inexpensive and readily available. This means that anyone with a basic laboratory can produce them. Nerve gases are, therefore, a significant concern for authorities as they are an easily available weapon for terrorist groups.

In 1936 the German chemist Gerhard Schrader of the I. G. Farbenindustrie Laboratory in Leverkusen first prepared the agent **tabun** (ethyl-dimethylphosphoramidocyanidate). At the time, Schrader was leading a program to develop new types of insecticides, working first with fluorine-containing compounds such as acyl fluorides, sulfonyl fluorides, fluoroethanol derivatives, and fluoroacetic acid derivatives. Schrader's research eventually led to the synthesis of tabun as an extremely powerful agent against insects. Schrader found that as little as 5 parts per million (ppm) of tabun killed all the leaf lice used in his experiments. Soon after Schrader's experiments, the potential use of this substance as an agent of war was realized.

In 1939, a pilot plant for tabun production was set up at Munster-Lager, on Luneberg heath near the German Army training grounds at Raubkammer. In January 1940, Germany began the construction of a full-scale plant, code named Hochwerk, at Dyernfurth-am-Oder (now Brzeg Dolny in Poland). A total of 12,000 tons of tabun was produced during the ensuing three years (1942–1945) and at the end of WWII, large quantities were seized by the Allied Forces. In addition to tabun, Schrader and his collea-

gues produced some 2,000 new organophosphates, including sarin in 1938 and the third of the "classic" nerve agents, soman, in 1944. These three nerve agents, tabun, sarin, and soban, are known as G agents. The manufacture of sarin was never fully developed in Germany and only about 0.5 tons were produced in a pilot plant before the end of WWII in 1945.

After 1945, a great deal of research began to focus on understanding the physiological mechanisms of nerve gas action, so that more effective means of protection could be devised against them. However, these efforts also allowed for the development of new and more powerful agents, closely related to the earlier ones. The first official publications on these compounds appeared in 1955. The authors, British chemists Ranajit Ghosh and J. F. Newman, described amiton, one of the newly developed nerve agents, as being particularly effective against mites. At this time, researchers were devoting a great deal of energy to studying organophosphate insecticides both in Europe and in the United States. At least three chemical firms independently studied and quantified the intense toxic properties of these compounds during the years 1952–53 and some of them became available on the market as pesticides. By the mid-1950's, following in the wake of the intensive research activity, a new group of highly stable nerve agents had been developed. These were known as the V-agents and were approximately ten-fold more poisonous than sarin. The V-agents can be numbered among the most toxic substances ever synthesized. VX, a persistent nerve gas, was discovered by Ghosh and was touted as being more toxic than any previously synthesized compound. Since the discovery of VX, there have been only minor advancements in the development of new nerve agents.

A contemporary use of nerve gas occurred during the Iran-Iraq war of 1984–1988. In this conflict, the United Nations confirmed that Iraq used tabun and other nerve gases against Iran. This incident is a prime example of how the technology of chemical weapons was shared during the Cold War. The Soviets armed their allies while the U.S. did the same for its allies. Iraq was a benefactor and implemented its chemical stockpiles during this period.

Another contemporary incident of nerve gas use occurred in Japan in 1995. Members of the Aum Shinrikyo cult introduced sarin gas into Tokyo's subway system. This incident gives an example of the possible new roles that nerve gases may play in the future, as tools of insurrection rather than the weapons of powerful nations.

SEE ALSO Chemical warfare; Chemical Biological Incident Response Force, United States; Mustard gas; Sarin gas; Tabun.

Nervous system overview

The knowledge of the structure and functioning of the nervous system can be very relevant to a forensic examination that seeks to determine the cause of an illness or death. For example, in cases where suspected drugs or **toxins** may have been used, a forensic scientist may be able to determine what compounds were used by the symptoms produced. Drugs including **barbiturates** can slow or cripple the transmission of nerve impulses, while **amphetamines** stimulate the nervous system by causing the excessive release of norepinephrine, which is involved in the transmission of the nerve impulses. The toxin produced by the bacterium *Clostridium botulinum* inhibits nerve transmission by binding to sites at the junction between adjacent nerves.

The nervous system is responsible for short-term immediate control of the human body and for communication between various body systems. Although the endocrine system achieves long-term communication and control via chemical (hormonal) mechanisms, the nervous system relies on a faster method of alternating chemical and electrical transmission of signals and commands through a network of specialized neural cells (neurons).

There are three differing types of neurons, including sensory neurons, neurons associated with transmission of impulses, and effecter neurons such as motor neurons that transmit nerve impulses to specialized tissues (e.g., motor neurons to muscle tissue) and glands. In addition to neurons, there are a number of cell types that play a supportive role in the nervous system. Principal among these neuron-supporting cells are Schwann cells, which are associated with an insulating myelin sheath that wraps around specific types of neural fibers or tracts.

Neurons contain key common components. At one end, the dendrite end, specialized cell processes and molecular receptor sites bind **neurotransmitters** released by other neurons and sensory organs across a gap known as the neural synapse. At the dendrite, the nerve impulse within a particular neuron is generated by a series of chemical and electrical events associated with the binding of specific neurotransmitters. The nerve impulse then travels down the neuron cell body, the axon, via an electrical action potential that results from rapid ion movements across the neuron's outer cell membrane. Ultimately, the action potential reaches the presynaptic terminus region where the electrical action potential causes the release of cell specific neurotransmitters that diffuse across the synapse (the gap between neurons) to start the impulse generation and conduction sequence in the next neuron in the neural pathway. The major chemical neurotransmitters include acetylcholine, norepinephrine, dopamine, and serotonin.

Neural transmission and the diffusion of neurotransmitters across the synapse do not always produce a subsequent action potential without the combined input of other neurons in a process termed summation. Depending on the specific neurotransmitters, receptor binding can produce either excitation or inhibition of action potential production. Subject to a refractory period, during which a neuron returns to its normal state following the production of an earlier action potential, once the neuron reaches a properly timed threshold stimulus, it will produce an action potential. The production of action potentials is an "all or none" process and once produced the axon potential (nerve impulse) sweeps down the axon.

The nervous system is organized along morphological (structural) and functional lines. Structurally, the nervous system can be divided into the central nervous system (CNS) that includes the brain and spinal cord, and the peripheral nervous system (PNS) that contains all other nerves (e.g., sensory and motor neurons), ganglia, and associated cells.

The CNS is protected by a tri-fold layer of specialized membranes, termed the meninges. The brain and spine are organizationally reversed. The spinal cord contains gray matter tracts surrounded by white matter. In contrast, the brain contains centralized white matter.

Functionally, the nervous system can be divided into the somatic or voluntary nervous system (VNS), which coordinates voluntary muscles and reflexes, and the autonomic nervous system (ANS), which is associated with the regulation of viscera, smooth muscle, and cardiac muscle. The autonomic nervous system is further subdivided into sympathetic and parasympathetic systems.

The sympathetic nervous system (SNS), when related to the classic "fight or flight" response,

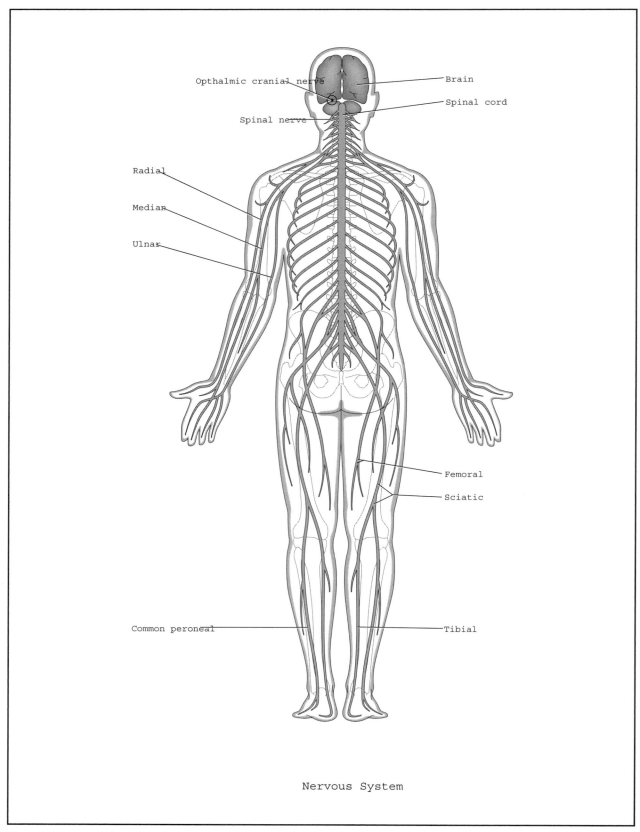

Opthalmic cranial nerve

Brain

Spinal cord

Spinal nerve

Radial

Median

Ulnar

Femoral

Sciatic

Common peroneal

Tibial

Nervous System

Nervous system overview. ILLUSTRATION CREATED BY ARGOSY

heightens activity in bodily organs or systems (e.g., the respiratory system) and the metabolic rate (the rate at which energy is consumed by bodily processes such as respiration). In contrast, the parasympathetic nervous system (PNS) lowers response and decreases the metabolic rate. The sympathetic and parasympathetic systems work in opposition to control bodily systems.

The brain is divided into various areas or lobes. The large left and right anterior lobes represent the convoluted (wrinkled) cerebral cortex or cerebrum. Posterior lobes represent the cerebellum. At the top of the spinal cord lie the pons and medulla. The cerebellum, pons, and medulla together are referred to as the hindbrain and are associated with many basic process involved in body maintenance, metabolism (e.g., breathing and heart rate), and homeostasis. In general, the forebrain (the cerebrum and some related areas) is the area responsible for higher intellectual functions involved in sensory interpretations, memory, language, and learning. The midbrain tract acts as a switching system that directs, coordinates, and integrates impulses among various regions of the brain.

Within the peripheral nervous system, mechanoreceptors, most of which are located in the skin (integumentary system), respond to physical stimuli such as pressure and motion. Thermoreceptors are specialized to respond to changes in temperature. Chemoreceptors associated with taste and smell senses respond to specific molecules. Highly developed complex sensory structure such as the eyes and ears respond to light (electromagnetic radiation) and sound.

In addition to a complex network of nerves throughout the body that act as a transmission system, the PNS contains specialized nerve cells to interface and transmit signals to muscles and glands.

Nerves usually contain neuron cell bodies that lie in tracts or fibers. Unmyelinated axons form gray matter. When Schwann cells wrap around the axon they create a myelin sheath around neurons (in the peripheral nervous system) that in tracts or fibers are termed white matter. Because the myelin sheath disrupts the normal transmission of the electrical action potential down the neuron, a specialized form of conduction of the nerve impulse or action potential occurs between spaces in the myelin sheath termed the nodes of Ranvier. Accordingly, diseases that disrupt or destroy the myelin sheath (demyelinating diseases) can impair or destroy normal nerve function.

Schwann cells are only one form of neuroglia or glial cells that are required to support normal neural function. Other glial cells include astrocytes, microglia, ependymal cells, oligodendrocytes, and satellite cells. Astrocytes are necessary for the proper vascularization of nerve cells and for the transport of nutrients and the removal of cellular waste products across the blood brain barrier. Microglia cells engage in phagcytosis and are capable of helping defend neural cells from attacks by a range of pathogenic agents. Ependymal cells line brain and spinal ventricles (fluid filled cavities in the brain and spine) and produce and maintain cerebrospinal fluid. Oligodendrocytes are responsible for the production of the myelin sheath in the CNS. Satellite cells protect neurons in ganglia.

SEE ALSO Amphetamines; Barbiturates; Botulinum toxin; Epilepsy; Neurotransmitters; Psychotropic drugs; Toxicology.

Neurotransmitters

The forensic investigation of an accident or death is not always aided by the presence of physically obvious signs, such as a stab wound or gunshot wound. Injury or death inflicted by toxic agents may have less subtle physical effects. **Toxins** can interfere with the normal physiological functions of the body. Then, their presence is forensically evident by a physiological change in the norm. One example is agents that disrupt the action of neurotransmitters.

Neurotransmitters are chemicals released in minute amounts from the terminals of nerve cells in response to the arrival of an action potential. There are now more than 300 known neurotransmitters and they act either locally in point-to-point signal transmission (e.g., the motor nerve of a neuromuscular junction) or at a distal site (e.g., the hypothalamic releasing hormones acting on the anterior pituitary). Locally acting neurotransmitters relay the electrical signal traveling along a neuron as chemical information across the neuronal junction, or synapse, that separates one neuron from another neuron or a muscle. Neurons communicate with peripheral tissues, such as muscles, glands etc., or with each other, largely by this chemical means rather than by direct electrical transmission.

Neurotransmitters are stored in the bulbous end of the nerve cell's axon. When an electrical impulse traveling along an axon reaches the junction, the neurotransmitter is released and diffuses across the synaptic gap, a distance of as little as 25 nanometers (nm) or as great as 100 micrometers (μm). The interaction of the neurotransmitter with the postsynaptic receptor of the target cell generates either an excitatory postsynaptic potential (EPSP) or an inhibitory postsynaptic potential (IPSP). Transmitters that lead to EPSPs appear to open large, non-specific membrane channels, permitting the simultaneous movement of Na^+, K^+ and Cl^-. IPSPs are caused by Cl^- flux only.

Neurotransmitters include such diverse molecules as acetylcholine, noradrenalin, serotonin, dopamine, γ-aminobutyric acid, glutamate, glycine and numerous other small monoamines and amino acids. There are also small peptides, which appear to act as chemical messengers in the nervous system. They include substance P, vasopressin, oxytocin, endorphins, angiotensin, and many others. A rather unusual but interesting neurotransmitter is the gas nitric oxide. This diverse range of chemical neurotransmitters may suggest that chemical coding could play as important a part in communication between neurons as do the strict point-to-point connections of neural circuitry.

Acetylcholine is one of the neurotransmitters functioning in the peripheral nervous system. It is released by all motor nerves to control skeletal muscles and also by autonomic nerves controlling the activity of smooth muscle and glandular functions in many parts of the body. Norepinephrine is released by sympathetic nerves controlling smooth muscle, cardiac muscle, and glandular tissues. In these tissues acetylcholine and norepinephrine often exert diametrically opposed actions.

The neurotransmitters used by the majority of fast, point-to-point neural circuits in the central nervous system (CNS) are amino acids. Of these, the inhibitory substance γ-aminobutyric acid (GABA) is well characterized and it is present in all regions of the brain and spinal cord. GABA rapidly inhibits virtually all CNS neurons when applied locally by increasing cell permeability to chloride ions, thus stabilizing resting membrane potential near the chloride equilibrium level. Although GABAergic (GABA-producing) neurons also exist in the spinal cord, another inhibitory amino acid, glycine, predominates in this region of the CNS. Glycine is present in small inhibitory interneurons in the spinal cord gray matter and mediates the inhibition of most spinal neurons. The amino acids L-glutamate and L-asparagine depolarize neurons by activating membrane sodium channels and are ubiquitously distributed, appearing as the most common excitatory transmitters for interneurons in the CNS.

In contrast to the point-to-point signaling in which amino acids are involved, the monoamines are mainly associated with the more diffuse neural pathways in the CNS. The monoamines are present in small groups of neurons, primarily located in the brain stem, with elongated and highly branched axons. These diffuse ascending and descending monoaminergic innervations impinge on very large terminal fields and there is evidence that the monoamines may be released from many points along the varicose terminal networks of monoaminergic neurons. Most monoamines released in this way occur at nonsynaptic sites and a very large number of target cells may be affected by the diffuse release of these substances, which are therefore thought to perform modulatory functions of various types.

One of the most remarkable developments was the realization that most peptide hormones of the endocrine and neuroendocrine systems also exist in neurons. These are by far the largest group of potential chemical messengers. For example, the opioid peptides (endorphins) have attracted enormous interest because of their morphine-like properties. They are consequently of considerable interest in the understanding of pain. Endorphins represent a family of chemical messengers found in all regions of the CNS including the pituitary (e.g., beta-endorphin and dynorphin) and the peripheral enteric nervous system. Their presence in regions such as the basal ganglia and the eye's retina, where it is unlikely that they have any connection with pain pathways, suggests that they may also have other diverse functions. There is still much to be learned about the possible functions of neuropeptides in the CNS. In all cases so far examined the peptides seem to be capable of being released by a specialized secretory mechanism from stimulated CNS neurons. They can exert powerful effects on the CNS. For example, the direct administration of small amounts of peptide to the brain can elicit a variety of behavioral responses, including locomotor activity (substance P), analgesia (endorphins), drinking behavior (angiotensisn II), female sexual behavior (LHRH), and improved retention of learned tasks (vasopressin).

An interesting and novel neurotransmitter identified in the 1980s is nitric oxide (NO). This is a highly reactive naturally occurring gas generated in the body from arginine and has the alternative name "epithelium-derived-relaxing factor." Synthesis of NO in blood vessel epithelia occurs in response to the distortion of blood vessels by blood flow. The gas then rapidly diffuses into the surrounding muscle layers, causing them to relax. It, therefore, has vasodilatory (dilation of blood vessels) properties and as a neurotransmitter occurs in a number of nerve networks. For example, it is known to be active in the dilation of arteries supporting the penis and in the relaxation of muscles of the corpora cavernosa (the two chambers filled with spongy tissue which run the length of the penis). NO released from stomach nerves causes the stomach to relax in order to accommodate food. Intestinal nerves also induce the relaxation of the intestinal muscle by releasing NO. In addition, nervous activity in the cerebellum is increased by NO and it appears that NO is an important neurotransmitter associated with memory. Despite its usefulness, nitric oxide can have a toxic effect on body cells and has been implicated in Huntington's disease and Alzheimer's disease.

SEE ALSO Death, cause of; Nervous system overview; Toxicology.

William Nicol

1768–1851
SCOTTISH
MINEROLOGIST, PHYSICIST

William Nicol (aka William Nichol) was born, lived his entire life, and died in Edinburgh, Scotland. He was considered a quiet and unassuming professor at the University at Edinburgh who had a profound effect on the forensic sciences by pioneering the production of polarized light and the creation of the Nicol prism.

Nicol used the double refraction properties of Iceland spar to produce polarized light in 1825 and in 1829 created an optical device called the Nicol prism, a precursor to the polarizing light microscope. Essentially, the Nicol prism consists of a crystal of calcite or Iceland spar that is cut into two equal pieces at an angle; the pieces are then rejoined with Canada balsam. When a beam of light enters the crystal, it undergoes double refraction (birefraction). That is, the beam is split into two parts, each of which is differentially affected. The first part, called the ordinary ray, undergoes total reflection at the Canada balsam joint and is shifted off course to pass out of one side of the Iceland spar crystal. The other part, called the extraordinary ray, continues on through the crystal. By means of the Nicol prism, a beam of light could be polarized or a beam of already polarized light can be subjected to analysis. William Nicol utilized his prism to investigate the optical properties of **minerals** and other substances. He created lenses by grinding semiprecious stones, and used those to investigate fossilized wood and fluid-filled cavities in crystals.

Nicol prisms were first used to measure the polarization angle of birefringent compounds, which led to new developments in the scientific understanding of interactions between polarized light and crystalline substances. (Optical birefringence is when light enters a nonequivalent axis in an anisotropic crystal and is refracted into two rays, each of which are polarized with the vibration directions oriented at right angles to one another, and traveling at different velocities. Anisotropic crystals have crystallographically different axes that interact with light differently, depending on the angle in which the incident light reaches the surface of the crystal.)

Nicol's work set the stage for development of the polarizing light microscope, an important forensic tool. The purpose of the polarizing light microscope is to view and photograph specimens visible due to their anisotropic characteristics. Polarized light is scientifically and forensically useful because it enhances contrast and improves the image quality of birefringent materials when compared to other techniques such as darkfield and brightfield illumination, phase contrast, and **fluorescence**. As a forensic investigative tool, **polarized light microscopy** permits access to a great deal of information not obtainable with any other optical microscopy technique: because it exploits optical properties of anisotropy, it can reveal minutely detailed information about the structure and composition of materials. This is of critical importance for crime scene/criminal **identification**, as well as for forensic diagnostic purposes.

SEE ALSO Alternate light source analysis; Identification; Microscopes; Minerals.

Night vision devices

Forensic investigations are not always conducted in well-lit settings or during daylight. When lighting conditions are diminished, assistance in maximizing the available light using night vision technology can be important in inspecting the scene of an accident or death. Night vision devices have also proved useful in conjunction with lasers to identify altered, obliterated, or over-written documents.

Night vision technology can also be part of surveillance systems. Analyzing the recordings from surveillance **cameras** can reveal aspects of a crime or accident scene before and during the incident that would otherwise not be available.

Night vision scopes are devices that enable machines or people to "see in the dark," that is, to form images when illumination in the visible band of the **electromagnetic spectrum** is inadequate. Although it is not possible to form images in absolute darkness (in the absence of any electromagnetic radiation), it is possible to form images from radiation wavelengths to which the human eye is insensitive, or to amplify visible-light levels so low that they appear dark to the human eye.

There are two basic approaches to imaging scenes in which visible light is inadequate for human vision:

In the first approach, low-level visible light that is naturally present may be amplified and presented directly to the viewer's eye. (Light in the near-infrared part of the electromagnetic spectrum [$\cong$.77–1.0 microns], either naturally present or supplied as illumination, may also be amplified and its pattern translated into a visible-light pattern for the viewer's benefit.) This technique is termed image intensification.

In the second approach, light in the infrared part of the spectrum (>.8 microns) that is emitted by all warm objects may be sensed by electronic devices. A visible-light image can then produced on a video screen. This technique is termed thermal imaging.

Image intensification is the method used for the devices termed night-vision scopes, which exist in a variety of forms that can be mounted on weapons or vehicles or worn as goggles by an individual. Image-intensification devices have been used by technologically advanced military organizations since the 1950s. In a modern, high-performance light amplifier, light from the scene is collimated—forced to become a mass of parallel rays—by being passed through a thin disk comprised of thousands of short, narrow glass cylinders (optical fibers) packed side by side. The parallel rays of light emerging from these optical fibers are directed at a second disk of equal size, the microchannel plate. The microchannel plate is also comprised of thousands of short, narrow cylinders (.0125–mm diameter, about one fourth the diameter of a human hair), but these microchannels are composed of semiconducting crystal rather than optical fiber. A voltage difference is applied between the ends of each microchannel. When a photon (the minimal unit of light, considered as a particle) strikes the end of a microchannel, it knocks electrons free from the atoms in the semiconducting crystal. These

are pulled toward the voltage at the far end of the microchannel, knocking more electrons loose as they move through the crystal matrix. Thousands of electrons can be produced in a microchannel by the arrival of a single photon. At the far end of the microchannel, these electrons strike a phosphor screen that is of the same size and shape as the microchannel disk.

The phosphor screen contains phosphor compounds that emit photons in the green part of the visible spectrum when struck by electrons; thus, that part of the phosphor disk affected by a single microchannel glows visibly, the brightness of its glow being in proportion to the intensity of the electron output of the microchannel. (Green is chosen because the human eye can distinguish brightness variations in green more efficiently than in any other color.) The phosphor-disk image is comprised of millions of closely packed dots of light, each corresponding to the electron output of a single microchannel. The light from the phosphor disk is collimated (made parallel) by a second fiber-optic disk and presented to the viewer's eye through a lens. The function of the lens is to allow the user's eye to relax (i.e., focus at infinity), rather than straining to focus on an image only an inch or so away. Alternatively, the phosphor-disk image can be filmed by a camera.

Either a pair of night-vision goggles may contain two such systems, one for each eye, or, as in the case of the U.S. Army's AN/PVS-7B night vision goggles, a single image may be split into identical copies and presented to both the user's eyes simultaneously.

A "third generation" image intensifier has been described above; several other image-intensification technologies remain in the field. All, however, operate by using photons to liberating electrons, amplifying the resulting electron current, and using the amplified electron current to liberate visible photons.

Infrared imaging systems are bulkier and more expensive than image intensification systems. However, they work even in a complete absence of illumination (since all scenes "glow" in infrared) and can detect otherwise invisible phenomena, such as hot, nonsmoky exhaust plumes, that may be of forensic interest. Infrared imagers are also used for a wide variety of forensic and industrial purposes, as they can reveal chemical compositional differences not evident in visible light.

SEE ALSO Alternate light source analysis; Crime scene investigation.

NIST Computer Security Division, United States

A phenomenal amount of information is computerized. Whether isolated or connected to the global computerized community via the Internet, computers house countless pages of text, graphics, and other forms of information. Without safeguards, this information is vulnerable to misuse or theft.

Forensic computing is concerned with **computer security**, particularly when a breach has occurred. This aspect of **forensic science** is a national priority. The Computer Security Division (CSD) is one of eight divisions within the Information Technology Laboratory of the National Institute of Standards and Technology (NIST), itself a bureau of the Chamber of Commerce. CSD is concerned with raising awareness of information technology (IT) risks, vulnerabilities, and protection requirements, especially for new and emerging forms of technology.

In addition to its support and security role with regard to new technologies, CSD is involved in researching IT vulnerabilities, advising federal and state agencies of these, and developing means to provide cost-effective protection. Also, in line with its mission as a part of NIST, it helps develop standards, tests, validation programs, and metrics in computer systems and services with an eye toward security.

NIST involvement in "digital sleuthing," or the use of computers in detective work, often allows the division to team up with a consortium of law-enforcement agencies to develop **computer forensics** technology. NIST and CSD scientists worked with agents from the Federal Bureau of Investigation, United States Customs Service, and other agencies, along with software vendors, to create the National Software Reference Library (NSRL), which allows easier review of the contents of a computer, especially with regard to material potentially relevant to a criminal investigation. By examining file tag attachments, NIST CSD programs can easily identify certain types of files (e.g., picture files that may be hidden in other programs).

Presidential Decision Directive 63, signed by President William J. Clinton in 1998, earmarked $5 million to NIST and CSD (far less than the $50 million Clinton had requested from Congress) to encourage the development of secure information systems for support of the telecommunications, transportation, and government service infrastructures. In the heightened security environment of the post-September 2001

United States, the work of CSD has become—like that of most agencies either within or at the periphery of the security and intelligence apparatus of the federal government—critical to national defense. Among the forensically-relevant areas of focus for CSD are development of cryptographic standards and applications, security testing, and research in the interests of emerging technologies.

SEE ALSO Computer forensics; Computer hackers; Computer hardware security; Computer software security; Computer virus.

NTSB (National Transportation Safety Board)

The investigation in the aftermath of a transportation accident is a federal responsibility in most countries, including the United States and Canada. The investigations are entirely forensic in scope, from the physical piecing together of the shattered train or aircraft to the **identification** of victims based on genetic material, dental samples, or bone and tissue samples.

The United States National Transportation Safety Board (NTSB) is an independent national agency responsible for investigating transportation accidents within the United States. The agency has custody of all debris and wreckage from accidents that it investigates, and thorough investigations sometimes take years to complete. The primary focus of NTSB operations is the investigation of civil aviation accidents, however the agency is also required to report on railroad, pipeline, and significant marine and highway accidents. For the NTSB to be involved in an accident investigation, the accident must involve a national transportation infrastructure, a public vessel, or hazardous materials.

The NTSB was established on April 1, 1967. In its early days, the agency worked closely with the Department of Transportation. Concerned with the NTSB's ties to the nation's transportation regulatory agency and the transportation industry, Congress sought to make the NTSB an independent, and impartial, entity. In 1975, the agency became independent, receiving funding in its own right through the Independent Safety Board Act.

In addition to accident investigation, the NTSB maintains the government database of civil aviation accidents. The database permits NTSB researchers to search for patterns in accident occurrence, as well

Aerial view of the wreckage of the Amtrak Sunset Limited that plunged into a bayou north of Mobile, Alabama, in 1993, killing 47 people when a barge rammed the bridge and caused the derailment. Coast Guard rules on towing vessels changed because of the accident. **AP/WIDE WORLD PHOTOS. REPRODUCED BY PERMISSION.**

as publish safety statistics for carriers and airports. The NTSB conducts regular studies of transportation safety procedures, making improvement suggestions to transportation officials and Congress when necessary. Since its inception in 1967, the NTSB has issued nearly 12,000 recommendations. Though the NTSB does not have the power to act as a regulatory authority, most of its recommendations have been adopted by the national transportation industry.

Although the investigative jurisdiction of the NTSB does not extend beyond national borders, the agency provides investigators to international accidents involving United States registered aircraft or maritime vessels. United States NTSB investigators, or foreign NTSB Accredited Representatives, have occasionally been welcomed by foreign governments that do not have their own investigative services to report on accidents.

While in the wake of September 11, 2001, the NTSB's mandate shifted to reflect increased concern

with airline safety and screening procedures, forensic investigations remain the heart of the board's work.

SEE ALSO Accident investigations at sea; Aircraft accident investigations.

Nuclear detection devices

In the Gulf Wars of 1991 and 2003, much effort was spent on the detection of nuclear and biological weapons that were suspected to be stockpiled by the government of Iraq. One aspect of this forensic sleuthing was the use of devices to detect nuclear weapons and their radioactive payloads. Nuclear detection devices, also termed radiation detectors, are systems designed to detect the presence of radioactive materials. These materials may take the form of gases, particles suspended in air, or solid metals (often alloys of uranium or plutonium).

Although radioactive materials can be (and, in the laboratory, often are) detected by direct chemical assay, or analysis, it is far easier in practice to detect them at second hand by measuring the radiation they emit. Nuclear materials emit two kinds of radiation as the nuclei of their atoms spontaneously break apart: fast particles (i.e., neutrons, electrons, and ions) and electromagnetic radiation (i.e., x rays and gamma rays). Different nuclear materials emit different blends of these radiation types. This radiation, unless blocked by layers of matter (shielding), reveals the presence of the nuclear material. The use of nuclear detection devices or radiation detectors is thus, key to monitoring for the presence of radioactive substances. The arms-control monitoring programs of the International Atomic Energy Agency, for example, depend heavily on both automated and hand-carried detection devices that seek to measure the telltale radiations emitted by nuclear materials.

Radiation can cause illness, injury, or death. A single fast particle, x ray, or gamma ray can damage a **DNA** molecule so that a healthy cell is converted to a cancer cell, and sufficiently large numbers of particles or rays can disturb enough of a cell's molecules to kill it. Therefore, nuclear detection devices are also used to alert to releases of radioactive material, whether deliberate (e.g., caused by a "dirty bomb") or accidental (e.g., material escaping from a nuclear power plant, waste-storage facility, or fuel-reprocessing plant).

To be detectable, radiation must be partly or wholly absorbed by ordinary matter. Radiation is said to have been absorbed by a mass of material when it has given up most or all of its energy to that material; radiation that is difficult to absorb (e.g., neutrino flow) is correspondingly difficult to detect. There are several different radiation-absorption phenomena, each of which is exploited in the design of a different class of detection devices. The most important form of absorption is ionization, that is, the separation of neutral atoms in the absorbing medium into free electrons (negatively charged) and free ions (positively charged atoms lacking one or more electrons). All forms of radiation mentioned above can cause ionization. Ionization, in turn, can be detected in numerous ways. One way is chemical; because ions lack electrons they readily combine with other atoms to form new molecules. In a photographic film, this recombination appears as the chemical change known as exposure. Film-badge dosimeters measure radiation by accumulating chemical changes in response to ionizing radiation.

Researcher holding uranium at the Oak Ridge, Tennessee Y-12 plant, where uranium-235 powder is converted to metal discs or "buttons," which then are manufactured into nuclear weapon components. © CORBIS

A more precise and continuous measure of ionizing radiation is obtained by electronic amplification of individual ionization events. The best known of the tools that measures radiation in this way is the Geiger counter. In a Geiger counter, a voltage is placed across a chamber filled with gas (usually argon or xenon); this causes an electric field to exist between one end of the chamber and the other. When a fast particle or high-energy ray passes through the chamber, it ionizes neutral atoms, that is, splits them up into free electrons and positively charged ions. Under the influence of the electric field, the electrons accelerate toward one end of the chamber and the ions toward the other. If the electrical field is strong enough, it accelerates them enough so that when they strike other atoms in the gas they ionize them as well. The electrons and ions thus produced may also be accelerated enough to cause ionization, and so on. The resulting brief avalanche of charged particles constitutes a pulse of electrical current that can be detected, amplified, and counted by appropriate circuitry. In the audio output circuit of a Geiger counter, a single ionization event is amplified to produce the device's trademark "click." Although the arrival of any one ray or particle is a randomly timed event, the average rate of such arrivals, smoothed over time, gives an accurate idea of how much radiation is present.

Another type of radiation-detection device is the scintillation detector. Certain crystals, when struck by a single high-energy photon or particle, produce a scintillation, that is, a flash of light consisting of thousands or tens of thousands of visible photons.

U.N. weapons inspectors search inside a storage tank at Tikrit University in Iraq for evidence of alleged nuclear weapons programs, 2003. © REUTERS/CORBIS

In the early twentieth century, one method of measuring radiation was to count scintillation rates under a microscope; modern detectors use electronic circuits for the same purpose.

The interactions of radiation with semiconducting crystals such as silicon can also be measured. Semiconducting radiation detectors have the advantages of small size, high sensitivity, and high accuracy.

SEE ALSO War forensics.

Nuclear spectroscopy

Nuclear **spectroscopy** is a powerful tool in the arsenal of scientists and forensic investigators because it allows detailed study of the structure of matter based upon the reactions that take place in excited atomic nuclei.

Nuclear spectroscopy is a widely used technique to determine the composition of substances because it is more sensitive than other spectroscopic methods and can detect the trace presence of elements in an unknown substance that may only be present on the order of parts per billion.

Nuclear spectroscopy analysis techniques provided forensic investigators with **evidence** that linked several of what were eventually to be known as the Washington, D.C.-area "sniper shootings" in late 2002.

A number of methods can be used to excite atomic nuclei and then measure their decaying gamma ray emissions as the atoms return to normal energy levels (i.e., their ground state). The emissions are then analyzed and separated into an emission spectrum that is characteristic for each element. Excitation can be accomplished by colliding nuclei, heavy ion beams, and a number of other methods, but the fundamental purpose remains to measure the spectral properties of a sample as a tool to learn something about the quantum structure of the atoms in the sample.

Like other forms of spectroscopy, the fundamental measurements of nuclear spectroscopy involve recording the emissions or absorption of photons by atoms. The specific emissions or absorptions reflect the energy levels, spin states, parity, and other properties of an atom's structure (e.g., quantized energy levels).

A qualitative analysis identifies the components of a substance or mixture. Quantitative analysis measures the amounts or proportions of the components in a reaction or substance.

Because each element—and each nuclide (i.e., an atomic nucleus with a unique combination of protons and neutrons)—emits or absorbs only specific frequencies and wavelengths of electromagnetic radiation, nuclear spectroscopy is a qualitative test (i.e., a test designed to identify the components of a substance or mixture) to determine the presence of an element or isotope in an unknown sample.

In addition, the strength of emissions and absorption for each element and nuclide can allow for a quantitative measurement of the amount or proportion of the element in an unknown. To perform quantitative tests, that is, to measure amounts of an element present, the measured spectrum needs to be narrowed down to analysis of photons with specific energies (i.e., electromagnetic radiation of specific wavelength or frequency). Quantitative computation using Beer's Law is then applied to the measured intensities of photon emission or absorption. Many other spectroscopic methods use this technique (e.g., atomic absorption spectroscopy and UV-visible light spectroscopy) to determine the amount of a element present.

One of most widely used methods of nuclear spectroscopy used to determine the elemental composition of substances is nuclear activation analysis (NAA).

In neutron activation analysis the goal is to determine the composition of an unknown substance by measuring the energies and intensities of the gamma rays emitted after excitation and the subsequent matching of those measurements to the emissions of gamma rays from standardized (known) samples. In this regard, neutron activation analysis is similar to other spectroscopic measurements that utilize other portions of the **electromagnetic spectrum**. Infrared photons, x-ray florescence, and spectral analysis of visible light are all used to identify elements and compounds. In each of these spectroscopic methods, a measurement of electromagnetic radiation is compared with some known quantum characteristic of an atomic nucleus, atom, or molecule. With NAA, of course, high energy gamma ray photons are measured.

Neutron activation analysis involves a comparison of measurements from an unknown sample with values obtained from tests with known samples. Depending on which elements are being tested for, the samples are irradiated with energetic neutrons. The process of radioactivity results in the emission of products of nuclear reactions (in this case, gamma rays) that are measurable by instruments designed for that purpose. After a time (dependent of the length of radiation) the gamma rays are counted by gamma ray sensitive spectrometers. Because the products of the nuclear reactions are characteristic of the elements present in the sample and a measure of amounts of the amounts present, neutron activation analysis is both a qualitative and quantitative tool.

Although NAA usually involves the measurement of gamma rays emitted from the radioactive sample, more complex techniques also measure beta and positron emissions.

Nuclear magnetic resonance (NMR) is another form of nuclear spectroscopy that is widely used in **medicine** and in forensic analysis.

NMR is based on the fact that a proton in a magnetic field had two quantized spin states. The actual magnetic field experienced by most protons is, however, slightly different from the external applied field because neighboring atoms alter the field. As a result, however, a picture of complex structures of molecules and compounds can be obtained by measuring differences between the expected and measured photons absorbed. NMR spectroscopy as an important tool used to determine the structure of organic molecules.

When a group of nuclei are brought into resonance—that is, when they are absorbing and emitting photons of similar energy (electromagnetic radiation, e.g., radio waves, of similar wavelengths)—and then small changes are made in the photon energy, the resonance must change. How quickly and to what form the resonance changes allows for the non-destructive (because of the use of low energy photons) determination of complex structures. This form of NMR is used by physicians as the physical and chemical basis of a powerful diagnostic technique termed magnetic resonance **imaging** (MRI). MRI can also be used for non-invasive examination for concealed substances or implanted objects.

SEE ALSO Nucleic acid analyzer (HANAA).

Nucleic acid analyzer (HANAA)

Forensic analysis often involves the analysis of samples for the presence of disease-causing microorganisms (**pathogens**). In the past, this analysis required the specialized media, incubators and other equipment housed in a laboratory. However, miniaturization of equipment has enabled some of the pathogen technology to be taken into the field in a portable form.

In the months preceding the 2003 war in Iraq, United Nations inspectors conducted forensic analyses throughout the country, searching for **evidence** of chemical, nuclear, and biological weapons. One of the portable devices utilized enabled detection of some bacterial pathogens based on the detection of target regions of nucleic acid.

The device used is a hand-held advanced nucleic acid analyzer (HANAA). It was developed by the Lawrence Livermore National Laboratory in 1999 based on a previous model of the nucleic acid analyzer ANAA produced in 1997.

HANAA is a real-time **polymerase chain reaction** (PCR)-based system for detecting pathogens. It is highly sensitive as it can detect 200 organisms per milliliter. Typical lab-based tests that require the growth of bacteria require the presence of millions of living bacteria.

The instrument takes advantage of real-time **PCR** technology that was developed in recent years. PCR amplification of **DNA** (deoxyribonucleic acid) requires repetitive sample heating (to approximately 203°F [95°C]) and cooling to a lower temperature specific for the sample (usually 122–161°F, or 50–72°C). Traditional instruments require two to three hours to complete a PCR run and additional time to run the products on a gel to detect positive samples. New real-time PCR instruments have heating and cooling systems allowing a reduction of the running time to less than 30 minutes. The same instruments also allow observation of product formation during the run. This is achieved by incorporation of fluorescent detection methods to visualize product formation.

The main part of the instrument is a sample module containing a miniaturized silicon thermal cycle of high heating and cooling efficiency. These small thermal units are a major breakthrough in technology, as batteries can efficiently support them. In comparison, most of the existing real-time systems are comparatively larger and heavier and cannot be operated in a field with ease, despite the similarly good technology for detection or time of analysis. HANAA also has an advantage over its predecessor ANAA, which was as big as a small suitcase. HANAA fits into the palm of a hand and weighs around two pounds (1 kg). It can operate 1.4–5.5 hours depending on the battery used. A run on the instrument is approximately 7–20 minutes depending on the program used for detection.

The PCR process used by HANAA is based on using TaqMan-type probes, which rely on a short DNA oligonucleotide being labeled by two fluorescent molecules, a quencher and a reporter. When a probe anneals to DNA, there is no signal as the short distance between the quencher and the reporter results in the reporter's **fluorescence** being quenched. However, during amplification, the reporter molecule is released and an increase in fluorescence is observed.

HANAA has four chambers for analysis and can perform two independent identifications in each chamber, therefore is able to test for up to eight pathogens at one time. Each of the sample units can be run independently, which makes the instrument highly flexible in use. The unit is operated by a keypad, with all the menu options and results displayed on a LCD (liquid crystal display) screen as text or bar charts. A positive sample is announced by an audible alarm.

The instrument and technology are still dependent on the quality of the sample and lack of any possible PCR inhibitors in the sample. However, sample preparation is relatively simple. A template for PCR is prepared by placing sample in a liquid buffer in a small (0.020 ml) test tube and reagents are added directly to the same tube.

SEE ALSO Biological weapons, genetic identification; DNA fingerprinting; DNA recognition instruments; DNA sequences, unique; PCR (polymerase chain reaction).

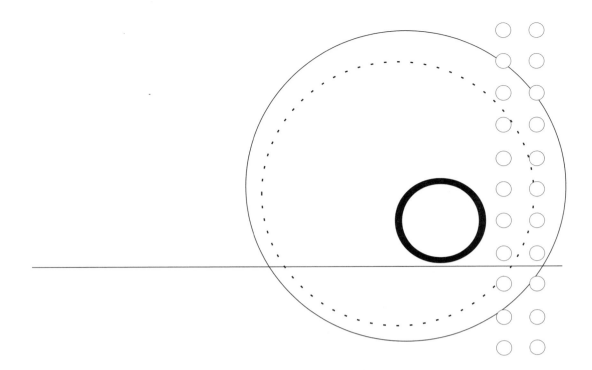

Odontology

Forensic odontology is the application of dentistry to the investigation of crime. It has its main applications in **identification** of corpses and human remains and in **bite analysis**. Although each person is born with the same number and type of teeth, the dental pattern of each individual is unique. Most people have dental records, or these can be created through making a dental impression from a suspect. These can then be compared to either teeth found on a corpse or bite marks found at the scene of a crime. However, the interpretation of dental **evidence** is a specialist task, undertaken by a forensic odontologist who may be called as an expert witness in a case.

One day, **DNA** analysis may become the "gold standard" for identifying an individual. However, if skeletal remains or fragmented corpses from mass disasters are involved, recovery of DNA is by no means certain. Identification by dental records remains the most reliable source of identification under such circumstances. Dental enamel is the hardest substance in the human body, so it does not decay alongside other tissue and will be found alongside skeletal remains.

Although everyone starts out with the same number of teeth, these differ naturally in length, width, and shape. During life, people sustain damage to their teeth; there may be missing teeth, chips, dental work, or misalignments. Taken together, these individual features create a unique pattern. If the person visited a dentist, then there will be a dental record that can be used to establish identity. Even if only a few teeth are available with a set of human remains, the forensic odontologist can still offer an opinion as to the age and habits of that person. This opinion can be set into context with other identifying information.

Bite marks are a valuable type of **impression evidence** that can be used to identify or eliminate a suspect. They sometimes appear as characteristic curved bruises on the flesh of victims of sexual assault or child abuse. The odontologist will study a dental cast of such bite marks and compare them with dental impressions made from suspects. Bite marks may also be found in soft materials at the scene of crime such as cheese, chocolate, pencils, or apples. They can be an important form of individualizing evidence in the hands of the forensic odontologist. Bitemark evidence has been used to in the trials of many criminals, including the serial killer Ted Bundy.

SEE ALSO Casting; Odontology, historical cases.

Odontology, historical cases

Odontology is the study of teeth for the investigation of identity and crime. One of its main applications is in the **identification** of corpses and human remains, especially in mass disasters where other forms of identification may not be available because

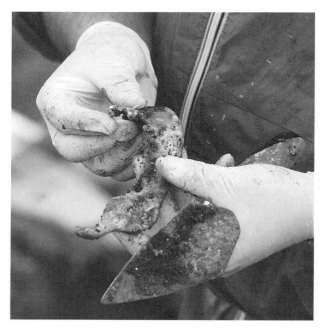

A forensic expert examines a human jaw with gold teeth found in a mass grave near the Bosnian town of Miljevina in 2004.
© DANILO KRSTANOVIC/REUTERS/CORBIS

the bodies have been burned or otherwise destroyed. Teeth are the most enduring part of the human body, apart from bone. Odontology is also used in the analysis of bite marks left at the scene of a crime. Although we are all born with the same number and type of teeth, the dental pattern of each individual is unique. Most people have dental records, or these can be created through making a dental impression from a suspect. These can then be compared to either teeth found on a corpse or to bite marks. Odontology has been used in many historical cases of identification and crime.

The use of teeth for identification goes back to Roman times. In the first century A.D., the Roman Emperor Claudius had his mistress, Lollia Paulina, beheaded and then demanded to examine the teeth on the body to ensure the right woman had been put to death. He knew she had a discolored front tooth. In another early example of dental identification, William the Conqueror, King of England in the eleventh century, would bite into wax used to seal official documents. His teeth were misaligned, so his bite mark guaranteed the documents' authenticity. In 1775, Paul Revere, famous for alerting American colonists to the approach of British forces, made a set of dentures for a friend, Dr. Joseph Warren, who was killed at the Battle of Bunker Hill that year. Warren was buried in a mass grave, but his family wanted the body for a private burial. Revere was able to identify Warren's body through the dentures he had made. In a similar case in 1914, a dentist in Scotland helped to identify a corpse in a grave-robbing case. Such crimes were not uncommon at the time as the bodies were furnished to medical schools. The victim had recently been fitted with a denture and this was presented in court as **evidence** of her identity.

In United States courts, dental evidence was first presented in court in 1849 when the incinerated remains of a George Parkman were identified by Nathan Cooley Keep through a partial denture he had made for this patient. He proved identity by fitting the prosthesis onto the cast that had been used in its manufacture. The evidence led to the conviction and execution of a J.W. Webster for the **murder**.

The first use of dental records in the identification of victims of mass disaster was probably the fire at the Vienna Opera House in 1878. Dental remains were also used to identify some of the 126 dead in a fire in Paris in 1897, which prompted the writing of the first textbook on forensic dentistry by the pioneering figure Oscar Amoedo. Since then, forensic odontology has been used to identify the victims of many other major incidents such as plane crashes, fires, and terrorist attacks. For instance, in the year 2000, Alaska Airlines Flight 261 crashed in California, killing 88 passengers and crew. A team of forensic dentists summoned to the scene found few intact jawbones and worked with partial post-mortem records, comparing these with the full ante-mortem dental charts which were sent to them from the victims' dentists. Over 100 dental remains were studied and compared with 68 complete dental records. In total, 22 of the victims were identified through their dental records. In the attacks on the World Trade Canter on September 11, 2001, only around half of the estimated 2,749 victims were ever identified, through a mixture of **DNA**, jewelry, and dental records.

Forensic dentistry has also been used to identify some notorious figures from the Nazi era, including Adolf Hitler, Martin Bormann, Eva Braun, and Joseph Mengele. The identity of John F. Kennedy's assassin, Lee Harvey Oswald, was confirmed through dental records. The remains of Czar Nicholas II and his family, who were shot during the 1917 Russian Revolution, were also initially identified from their teeth.

The first time bite marks were ever used as evidence in a criminal trial was in the 1954 case *Doyle v. State of Texas*. This involved an assailant who left his bite mark in a lump of cheese at the scene. A more

Arrest of notorious serial killer Nikolai Dzhurmongaliev in Russia in 1992 (shown handcuffed, center). Dental evidence helped link Dzhurmongaliev to over 100 murders, in part due to his false metal teeth. © PATRICK ROBERT/SYGMA/CORBIS

famous case is that of serial killer Ted Bundy who left a bite mark on the buttock of a victim, which helped secure his conviction in 1978.

SEE ALSO Bite analysis; Bundy (serial murderer) case; Casting.

O. J. Simpson trial SEE Simpson (O. J.) murder trial

Oklahoma bombing (1995 bombing of Alfred P. Murrah building)

At 9:02 a.m. on April 19, 1995, a powerful truck bomb exploded on the street in front of the Alfred P. Murrah Federal Building, a U.S. government complex in Oklahoma City, Oklahoma. The explosion caused enormous damage, completely destroying a third of the seven-story building, including a day care center on the first floor near the front, and damaging more than three hundred buildings in the vicinity. The bomb killed 168 people, including 19 children and one rescue worker. It injured over 800 others, some of them blocks away, as the explosion turned street signs, shards of **glass**, and other debris into missiles and blew pedestrians off their feet. It was the largest domestic terror attack in U.S. history and the largest terrorist attack on U.S. soil until the attacks of September 11, 2001.

Less than an hour later, an Oklahoma highway patrolman stopped and arrested Gulf War veteran Timothy McVeigh for driving without a license plate and carrying a concealed weapon, a 9 mm Glock handgun. While McVeigh was being taken to the jail in Perry, Oklahoma, he left behind in the police cruiser a business card for Paulson's Military Supply. On the back McVeigh had written "TNT $5/stick need more" and "Call after 01 May, see if I can get some more." This would be the first piece of **physical**

evidence that would implicate McVeigh in the bombing.

While McVeigh awaited his bail hearing for the traffic and concealed weapon charges, the investigation of the bombing in Oklahoma proceeded. Many experts and members of the public initially assumed that the bombing was the work of foreign terrorists, but at the FBI's behavioral sciences unit in Virginia, psychological profiler Clinton R. Van Zandt arrived at a different conclusion. Noting that the bombing occurred on the two-year anniversary of the Branch Davidian siege in Waco, Texas—a day of infamy among right-wing militia and antigovernment groups—he concluded that the bomber was probably a white male in his twenties, a military veteran, and a member of a militia group.

As events turned out, this profile closely fit Timothy McVeigh. From an early age he had been fascinated with weapons. In 1988, he joined the U.S. Army, and he served with distinction as a gunner in the Gulf War in Iraq, earning a Bronze Star. When he failed in his effort to become a Green Beret, he left the army and became increasingly paranoid about what he saw as the oppressiveness of the U.S. government, particularly its efforts to curb the spread of guns, which McVeigh saw as a violation of the "right to bear arms" guaranteed by the Second Amendment of the Constitution. His antigovernment rage reached a boiling point in 1993 with the events in Waco. That siege, based on the government's belief that the cult's leader, David Koresh, had a cache of illegal weapons, had begun on February 28, 1993. It ended on April 19 when federal agents stormed Koresh's compound, a fire erupted, and seventy-five people inside were killed.

Enlisting the aid of army companions Terry Nichols and Michael Fortier, McVeigh decided to take action against the government. He had long admired the book *The Turner Diaries*, written by American Nazi leader and white supremacist William L. Pierce under the name Andrew Macdonald. In this book, the protagonist Earl Turner blows up an **FBI** building in Washington, D.C., with a truck bomb. McVeigh's goal was to wreak vengeance in similar fashion against the Bureau of Alcohol, Tobacco, and Firearms (**ATF**) for its role in the events in Waco. As it turned out, McVeigh's choice of target was a mistake, for the ATF did not maintain an office in the Murrah building.

Evidence that McVeigh was behind the bombing quickly accumulated. The bomb was contained in a yellow Ryder rental truck. The truck's 250-pound rear axle, which had landed on a car near the scene of the bombing, had an identifying number, and the rear bumper, license plate intact and legible, was found nearby. The truck was traced to a Ryder rental agency in Junction City, where the rental agreement had been signed by a "Robert Kling." Employees at the agency helped an FBI artist create a sketch of Kling, referred to as John Doe #1; they also created a sketch of another man who was in the agency at the same time, John Doe #2, although this person was never found or identified. Investigators showed the pictures throughout the area. That evening, the manager of a local motel told investigators that she recognized John Doe #1 and that he had registered at the motel under the name Timothy McVeigh. Additionally, McVeigh had parked a yellow Ryder truck in the motel's parking lot two nights before the bombing.

Later investigation would piece together the actions of McVeigh and Nichols in the weeks and months before the bombing. Following the advice of various bomb-building manuals, they gathered and stored their materials. Forensic examination of the bombsite showed the bomb consisted primarily of ammonium nitrate, an agricultural fertilizer, and nitromethane, a volatile motor-racing fuel. Experts estimate that the size of the bomb ranged from 4,000–5,000 pounds and detonated with an initial explosive force of 500,000 pounds per square inch. Traces of these chemicals were found on McVeigh's clothing, as well as on the victims. Shortly before 9:00 on the morning of April 19, McVeigh drove the truck to the street outside the Murrah building and walked away. Minutes later, the bomb detonated. Some experts argued that the pattern of the bomb blast and the amount of damage suggest more than one bomb, but these views were not widely accepted.

McVeigh was arrested for the bombing while still in jail on the traffic and gun charges. His trial began in Denver, Colorado, on April 24, 1997. Damaging testimony was offered by Fortier, as well as by Fortier's wife, Lori, and McVeigh's sister Jennifer, all of whom knew details of the plot. Physical evidence included not only the Ryder truck parts and the bomb residue on McVeigh's clothing but also his fingerprints on receipts from his purchase of the bomb's materials and calling-card records that tracked his movements. McVeigh was found guilty and executed on June 11, 2001. Nichols was later sentenced to life in prison, and Michael Fortier was sentenced to twelve years in prison for failing to warn authorities of the attack.

Although **forensic science** played a role in the investigation of the bombing, its chief role was in

Rescue workers and investigators sift through the rubble after a planted fuel and fertilizer truck bomb exploded in 1995 in front of the Alfred P. Murrah Federal Building in Oklahoma City, killing 168 people. © RALF-FINN HESTOFT/CORBIS

victim **identification**. Some of the bodies were complete enough to allow for **fingerprint** identification, but many were fragmented, making the work of identification painstaking and arduous. The forensic investigators' first step was to gather antemortem information, including lists of people who were believed to be at or near the bombsite. Families and funeral directors provided demographic information, and potential victims' dentists were contacted to provide records. As each body was brought to a temporary morgue across the street from the Murrah building, the task of postmortem information gathering began. A prominent role was played by forensic odontologists, who faced the grim task of identifying the remains of the victims from teeth. They estimated the age of children based on patterns of primary and permanent teeth. Many of these children had pieces of wallboard embedded in their teeth, suggesting that the explosion had blown them through the wall of the day care center.

Radiologists also played a key role. After a body was discovered, an average of fifteen x rays of it were taken. Pathologists, anthropologists, and FBI bomb specialists examined these x rays to identify the victims as well as to uncover crime scene evidence. In many cases, the x rays revealed either healed fractures or degenerative conditions. One victim, for example, was identified from degenerative changes in the spine; another was identified from healed fractures in the tibia and fibula. X rays of missing persons who were thought to be victims of the bombing were compared with these postmortem x rays for possible matches. X rays also revealed the presence of foreign objects in the bodies, including evidence of the bomb itself, and they were used to distinguish bomb evidence from leaded-glass shards from the building's windows.

Finally, forensic anthropologists also played a key role in victim identification. In many instances, only a single disembodied body part was found, and body parts were often commingled. Forensic anthropologists could, for example, measure a limb, then use a computer program that determines age and race from bone measurements to pin down the demographics of the victim, which could then be compared with antemortem information to provide a possible match. This procedure sometimes had to be used in tandem with other methods. In one instance, a forensic anthropologist identified a lower leg as belonging to a white male about 30 years of age. Because the leg had two pairs of socks, a military boot, and blousing straps, the question arose as to whether a second bomber may have been present and killed in the explosion. The leg, however, underwent **DNA** testing, which contradicted the earlier results, showing that it came from a twenty-one-year-old African American woman. This instance showed that forensic anthropologists often cannot rely on a single method of identification, but may have to use two or more methods to achieve a positive identification.

By the time all of the victims had been identified three weeks after the explosion, forty-four had been identified through teeth alone; twenty-five through fingerprints alone; seventy-seven through a combination of teeth and fingerprints; one through teeth and palm prints; one through teeth, fingerprints, and DNA; six through x rays alone; four through palm prints; three through DNA alone; one through footprints; one through a toe print; one through marks and scars; and four through visual identification.

SEE ALSO Anthropology; Bomb (explosion) investigations; Explosives; Odontology; Osteology and skeletal radiology; Profiling; Psychological profile.

Mathieu Joseph Bonaventure Orfila

4/24/1787–3/12/1853
SPANISH, NATURALIZED FRENCH
CHEMIST, PHYSIOLOGIST

Mathieu Orfila helped initiate the study of **toxicology**. His massive treatise on poisons appeared in three languages in the second decade of the nineteenth century and immediately propelled the medical, biological, chemical, physiological, and legal sciences in new directions.

Born as Mateu José Bonaventura Orfila i Rotger in Maó, Minorca, Spain, he eschewed his family's traditional career of merchant seafaring when he was fifteen in order to study **medicine**. From 1804 to 1807, he attended courses in medicine at the University of Valencia and chemistry at the University of Barcelona. He won a scholarship to the University of Madrid to study chemistry and mineralogy, but went instead to Paris in June 1807 to study medicine and pharmacy. There Orfila

became the protégé of pharmacist and chemist Louis-Nicolas Vauquelin and chemist Louis-Jacques Thénard. As hostilities brewed that led to the 1808–1814 Peninsular War, Napoleonic France threatened Orfila with expulsion, but Vauquelin interceded on his behalf and Orfila was allowed to remain in Paris.

Orfila continued working with Vauquelin and Thénard after receiving his medical degree from the Faculté de Médecine de Paris in 1811. He married Anne Gabrielle Lesueur in 1815, succeeded Thénard as professor of chemistry at L'Athénée in 1817, became a naturalized French citizen in 1818, was named professor of legal medicine at the Faculté de Médecine in 1819, and succeeded Vauquelin there as professor of medical chemistry in 1823. He became dean of the Faculté de Médecine in 1831 and in 1834, was created Knight of the Legion of Honor.

All this success was due to Orfila's first book, his masterpiece, *Traité des poisons, tirés des règnes minéral végétal et animal; ou toxicologie générale, considérée sous les rapports de la physiologie, de la pathologie et de la médecine légale*, which was published in two volumes in Paris in 1814–1815. Three translations soon appeared: *A General System of Toxicology, or, a Treatise on Poisons, Drawn from the Mineral, Vegetable, and Animal Kingdoms, Considered as to their Relations with Physiology, Pathology and Medical Jurisprudence*, translated by John Augustine Waller in London in 1816–1817; Joseph Nancrede's abridged translation, *A General System of Toxicology, or, a Treatise on Poisons Found in the Mineral, Vegetable and Animal Kingdoms, Considered in their Relations with Physiology, Pathology and Medical Jurisprudence*, in Philadelphia in 1817; and Sigismund Friedrich Hermbstädt's German translation in Berlin in 1818–1819. All were received with enthusiasm in the scientific community.

One of Orfila's other major works includes *Elémens de chimie medicale*, published in two volumes in 1817 and translated as *Elements of Medical Chemistry* in 1818. Another is *Secours a donner aux personnes empoisonées ou asphyxiées, suivis des moyens propres a reconnaître les poisons et les vins frelatés, et a distinguer la mort réelle de la mort apparente*, published in 1818 and translated twice the same year, once by William Price as *A Popular Treatise on the Remedies to be Employed in Cases of Poisoning and Apparent Death, Including the Means of Detecting Poisons, of Distinguishing Real from Apparent Death, and of Ascertaining the Adulteration of Wines*, and once by R. Harrison Black as *Directions for the Treatment of Persons who have Taken Poison, and Those in a State of Apparent Death, Together with the Means of Detecting Poisons and Adulterations in Wine, also of Distinguishing Real from Apparent Death.* He also wrote *Leçons de médécine legale [Lessons in Legal Medicine]*, which appeared in three volumes from 1821 to 1823, and *Traité des exhumations juridiques [Treatise on Juridical Exhumations]*, published in 1831, as well as several later works specifically about arsenic, the poison most commonly preferred by murderers of that era.

Orfila was the founding editor of two important medical journals, *Journal de chimie médicale, de pharmacie et de toxicology* in 1824 and *Annales d'hygène publique et de médecine ĺgale* in 1829. He also founded the Society of Medical Chemistry in 1824, the Museum of Pathological Anatomy, known as the Musée Dupuytren, in 1835, and the Museum of Comparative Anatomy, now called the Musée Orfila, in 1845.

Serving as an expert witness in several famous legal proceedings further enhanced his reputation. Using his own improvements on the arsenic detection methods of **James Marsh**, Orfila helped to uncover the truth about the murders of Nicolas Mercier in 1838 and Charles LaFarge in 1840. However, because he wished to avoid controversy, he refused to participate as an expert witness after 1843.

Like many European scientists of the early nineteenth century, Orfila fell victim to political intrigue. He was honored during both the Bourbon Restoration and the reign of Louis Philippe, but quickly fell out of favor in the 1848 revolutions. Although his medical deanship was abruptly terminated on February 28, 1848, he was still able to serve as president of the Académie de Médecine from 1850 to 1852. It is said that the stress he suffered during the Second Republic hastened his physical decline and led to his death.

SEE ALSO Physiology; Poison and antidote actions; Toxicology.

Organic compounds

Organic compounds are based on carbon and are found in living things. They are thus distinguished from **inorganic compounds**, which are those containing the other elements such as nitrogen, phosphorus, and metals (such as iron and zinc). In fact,

this distinction between organic and inorganic is perhaps a little simplistic. Carbon-based compounds need not always come from living things, synthetic **fibers** like polyester and nylon are carbon-based, but are not found in plants or animals. As far as **forensic science** is concerned, both organic and inorganic compounds are found in items of **evidence**. The techniques used for determination of the chemical composition of such evidence will depend upon whether its component compounds are organic or inorganic.

An important feature of compounds based on carbon is that their chemical bonds—with other carbon atoms or with hydrogen, oxygen, or nitrogen atoms—absorb energy in the infrared, visible, and ultraviolet region of the **electromagnetic spectrum**. This is the basis of **spectroscopy**, which involves scanning samples containing organic compounds (such as textile fibers or paint fragments) with light, producing a "fingerprint" that is characteristic of the compound. The fingerprint shows the intensity of absorption in the infrared, visible, and ultraviolet region at each wavelength. This sample fingerprint can be compared to those from a reference database, which can reveal the origin of the paint or textile sample. If samples from a suspect—such as fibers found on their clothing—give the same fingerprint as the evidence, then it can be argued they came from the same source.

Another important technique for analyzing organic compounds in evidence is **thin layer chromatography**. A colored sample, such as a minute sample of ink from a questioned document, is placed on an absorbent paper that is dipped into a solvent mixture. When the mixture is drawn up the paper, it sweeps the sample with it and separates it into its components as a pattern of spots on the paper. As with spectroscopy, this pattern is characteristic of the compound and can be compared with reference or suspect samples for **identification**.

SEE ALSO Micro-spectrophotometry.

Organs and organ systems

Many forensic examinations include an **autopsy**. The surgical inspection of the exterior and interior of a body can reveal details about the death, including signs of trauma, wounds, and the presence of poisons, drugs or **toxins**.

Examination of various organs (two or more different types of tissue that work together to carry out a complex function) and organ systems (a group of organs that perform intricate functions necessary for the survival of an organism) is of paramount importance in an autopsy, since they can be the targets of the physical and chemical damage.

Sometimes an organism can survive with an impaired or nonfunctioning organ. However, when a whole system of organs shuts down, the life of the organism becomes compromised. Thus, the organ systems work together to maintain a constant internal environment, called homeostasis, within the body to ensure survival of the organism. The physical and chemical insults that are of forensic relevance (e.g., disease, use of **firearms** or poisons, drowning, asphyxiation) can disastrously disrupt the homeostatic balance.

There are 11 organ systems within the human body: integumentary, skeletal, muscular, nervous, endocrine, circulatory, lymphatic, respiratory, digestive, urinary, and reproductive.

The integumentary system acts as a protective barrier for the human body against microorganisms, dehydration, and injuries caused by the outside environment. Additionally, the integumentary system regulates body temperature. Organs of the integumentary system include hair, nails, sebaceous glands, sudoriferous glands, and the largest organ of the body, the skin.

The skeletal system is a structural framework providing support, shape, and protection to the human body. Additionally, the skeletal system provides attachment sites for organs. The skeletal system also stores minerals and lipids and forms **blood** cells. Bones, cartilage, tendons, and ligaments are all organs of the skeletal system.

The muscular system provides movement to the human body as a whole, as well as movement of materials through organs and organ systems. This system also functions to maintain posture and produce heat. The muscular system consists of skeletal muscle, smooth muscle, and cardiac muscle.

The nervous system conducts electrical impulses throughout the body to regulate and control physiological processes of the other organ systems. Organs of the nervous system include the brain, spinal cord, and nerves.

The endocrine system also functions to regulate and control physiological processes of the body. However, these functions are accomplished by sending out chemical signals called hormones into the blood. Glands, the organs of the endocrine system, secrete hormones and include: the pituitary gland, pineal gland, hypothalamus, thyroid gland, parathyroid glands, thymus, adrenal glands, pancreas, ovaries, and the testes.

The circulatory system circulates blood throughout the body and in doing so transports gases, nutrients, and wastes to and from tissues. Organs of the circulatory system include the heart, blood vessels, and blood.

The lymphatic system, also known as the **immune system**, defends the body against microorganisms and other foreign bodies. Additionally, fluids are transported from the body's tissues to the blood, thus helping to control fluid balance in the body. This system also absorbs substances from the digestive system. The organs of the lymphatic system include the lymph, lymph nodes, lymph vessels, thymus, spleen, and tonsils.

The respiratory system exchanges gases between the body's tissues and the external environment. Oxygen is inhaled from the external environment and passes from the lungs into the blood, where it is exchanged for carbon dioxide that passes from the blood to the lungs and is expelled. The respiratory system consists of the nose, pharynx, larynx, trachea, bronchi, and lungs.

The digestive system functions to digest and absorb nutrients from the food ingested into the body. Additionally, the digestive system transports foodstuff through the gastrointestinal tract. The primary organs of the digestive system include the mouth, pharynx, esophagus, stomach, small intestine, large intestine, rectum, and anal canal. Accessory organs that aid the primary organs include the teeth, salivary glands, tongue, liver, gallbladder, pancreas, and appendix.

The urinary system removes excess water and nutrients and filters wastes from the circulatory system. Additionally, the urinary system aids in red blood cell formation and metabolizes vitamin D. The urinary system's organs include the kidneys, ureters, urinary bladder, and urethra.

The reproductive system of the human body can be either male or female. The male reproductive system synthesizes gametes called spermatozoa that are responsible for fertilizing the female gametes, or oocytes, during reproduction. The female reproductive system is designed to undergo conception, gestation, and birth once a spermatozoon fertilizes an oocyte. The male reproductive system is composed of the testes, vas deferens, urethra, penis, scrotum, and prostate. The female reproductive system consists of the ovaries, uterus, fallopian tubes, vagina, vulva, and mammary glands.

SEE ALSO Autopsy; Decomposition; Poison and antidote actions; Toxicology.

Orthotolidine solution

Testing of **fluids** such as urine and **blood** is a part of routine diagnostic forensic testing. As well, such testing can yield useful forensic **evidence** of disease, presence of **toxins** and other chemicals, and even genetic material.

While fluid testing can involve sophisticated instruments, simple and reliable tests that can be done at the scene of an accident or death are still in popular use. Several urine-based tests utilize a chemical known as orthotolidine.

In the past, orthotolidine was a popular chemical used to monitor swimming pool water for the presence of excess chlorine. While that use has been supplanted by other chlorine monitoring methods, orthotolidine has remained popular in routine diagnostic testing and in forensic investigations.

The presence of glucose in the urine can be detected using a paper strip impregnated with orthotolidine and two enzymes—glucose oxidase and peroxidase. A yellow dye is also infused into the strip. When the paper strip is immersed in the glucose-containing urine, the glucose is catalytically converted by glucose oxidase in the presence of air to gluconic acid and hydrogen peroxide. Subsequently, peroxidase converts the hydrogen peroxide into a compound that reacts with orthotolidine. The result is a blue color.

The blue reacts with the yellow dye in the strip to form a potential spectrum of color ranging from light green to a dark blue color. The intensity of the color depends on the amount of glucose present in the urine.

This simple test, which can be done within a minute, allows a forensic examiner to gauge if the victim or deceased was diabetic.

Orthotolidine can be combined with another chemical, toluidine, to assess the presence of myoglobin in urine. Presence of the latter is characteristic of a malady called myoglobinuria. If myoglobin (or **hemoglobin**, as the test cannot distinguish between the two) is present in urine, the orthotolidine-toluidine chemical pair forms a blue color.

Both orthotolidine-based examinations can help identify a victim or corpse.

Albert Sherman Osborn

1858–1946
AMERICAN
QUESTIONED DOCUMENT EXAMINER

Albert Sherman Osborn was the first American to achieve prominence in the world of questioned document examination and forged document analysis. He authored *Questioned Documents* in 1910; it remains in print, and still stands as a seminal text in questioned document analysis. In 1937, near the end of his career (and not long from the end of his life), he published *The Mind of the Juror as Judge of the Facts*, or, *The Laymen's View of the Law*, another well-known forensics tome. Osborn was at the forefront of questioned document examination for more than 50 years, and was renowned for his success within the legal system as an expert witness and scholar. By the thoroughness and professionalism of his work, he was able to make significant headway with the court system's acceptance of expert testimony about forged documents as legal **evidence** in **criminal trials**. He founded the American Society of Questioned Document Examiners in 1942; this organization has continued to grow and expand in its research, knowledge base, and cadre of subject matter experts to the present day.

Albert Osborn was the first American to utilize the scientific method in the examination of **questioned documents**. His legendary texts, *Questioned Documents*, and *The Problem of Proof*, published in 1910 and 1922, respectively, were met with wide acclaim by public and private criminal justice and law enforcement agencies, the legal professions, and the public. Although the American Society of Questioned Document Examiners was chartered in 1942, Albert Osborn began holding annual informal meetings designed to share ideas and research information among experts in the fields of forged documents and questioned document analysis in 1913.

The premise inherent in questioned document analysis is to examine and compare data appearing on written or electronic evidence. It has grown from **handwriting analysis** and signature comparisons to include: handwriting; typewriting; hand printing; electronic and other printing methods; alterations; erasures; obliterations; studies of impressions on paper or other printing media; physical features of printing media (watermarks, seals, fiber contents, etc.); studies of the materials used to make the documents such as inks, ribbons, cartridges, and papers; and even shoeprint and vehicle tread impression analysis. Questioned document examiners also study and compare edges, perforations, and tears in documents, stamps, seals, and other pieces of **physical evidence**.

Albert Osborn was an acknowledged expert in the fields of **document forgery** (it was his contention that no two individuals could produce exactly the same handwriting characteristics) and questioned document analysis. His forensic methods and scientific conclusions are still studied, and his expertise is still quoted in contemporary courts of law.

SEE ALSO Document forgery; Fibers; Handwriting analysis; Impression evidence; Tire tracks.

Osteology and skeletal radiology

Within approximately two years of death, and sometimes considerably sooner, all that remains of a body is a skeleton. **Identification** of skeletal remains can sometimes be an important task in the investigation of a suspicious death. A forensic pathologist or anthropologist will use osteology, the study of bones, to find out as much as possible about the identity of a skeleton or collection of bones. Sometimes they rely on skeletal radiology, the study of bones through x rays or **fluorescence** (light-emission) to help make the identification.

When confronted by skeletal remains, the investigator works from general concepts to the more specific when trying to identify them. First, they will ensure that the items are in fact bones. It is not uncommon for the public, who often discover such remains, to mistake stones or bits of wood for bones. A physician will recognize the shape and texture of bone. It can, however, be a little more difficult to determine whether the bones are human. When it comes to intact skulls, it is relatively easy to distinguish humans from other animals. With smaller bones, especially those from children, identifying them as human is more challenging. Bear paws, for instance, can be remarkably similar to human hands and feet once stripped of their flesh. Sheep and deer ribs can be hard to distinguish from those of humans.

The investigator is fortunate if he or she gets a whole skeleton to work with. Over time, natural forces and predators tend to scatter bones, so it is more likely that a collection of bones, a single bone, or even just a fragment will be all there is to examine. If necessary, the investigator will have to extract **DNA** from the bone marrow for analysis to confirm the identification.

Bones discovered in the ground may be anything from around two to hundreds of years old. Establishing their probable age is clearly important as very old bones will not be relevant to a current forensic investigation, although they may well be of great interest in a historical or archaeological context. There are various methods for aging bones. The level of nitrogen in bones decreases over time, although this depends upon temperature and moisture. High levels of nitrogen can distinguish between bones that are a few years old and those that are decades old. Fresh bones glow when exposed to ultraviolet light. This fluorescence decreases from the outside of the bone to the inside over time. A bone that is hundreds of years old may not show any fluorescence.

Nuclear weapon use in World War II and weapons testing in the 1950s and 1960s led to the accumulation of certain radioactive materials in bones of that era. Finding substantial levels of carbon-14, strontium-90, cesium-137 or tritium, a radioactive isotope of hydrogen, suggests the bones date back from around 1950.

Having established the relevance of the bones, the investigator then sets out to discover some general characteristics which will narrow down the search for the identity of the deceased. Information on sex, age, height and race can all be deduced from careful study of skeletal remains. Of course, much depends on how many bones are available for study; far less can be deduced from single bones than from a whole skeleton.

Gender-specific changes in the skeleton do not start to appear until puberty, so distinguishing the sex of a child can be difficult. In general, males have bigger and thicker bones than females. But much depends on nutrition and level of physical activity. A woman who ate well and carried out manual labor will have bigger, stronger bones than a malnourished and inactive male. The long bones, that is, the bones of the arms and legs, are often indicative of sex. The diameter of the heads of the humerus (upper arm bone) the radius, (lower arm bone) on the thumb side, and the femur (thigh bone), are usually bigger in males. The pelvis of a male and female are quite different. A female pelvis is wider and has a wider outlet to allow

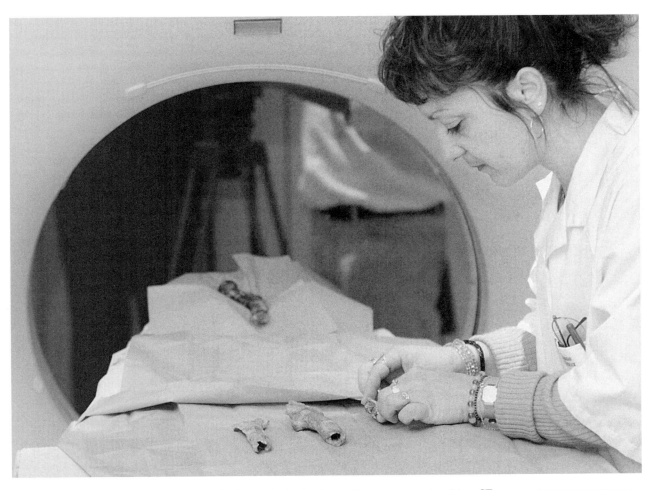

Skeletal remains of the "Millennium Ancestor," a hominid who lived six million years ago, placed in a CT scanner. © LIO/CORBIS SYGMA

for childbirth. A pathologist will look at the sciatic notch, which is the point where the sciatic and other nerves pass from the pelvic cavity to the leg. Typically, this is wider in females than in males. The back side of the pubic bone may be pitted or scarred in a woman who has borne a child. The **skull** may also be indicative of gender, for male skulls are larger and thicker, particularly in the jaw area.

Determining the age at death from skeletal remains is easier for children and adolescents than for adults. The way the skeleton grows and develops from birth to adulthood is well defined. For instance, the skull can be quite useful in determining the age of an infant. The bones of the skull knit together gradually in early childhood along lines called suture lines. The pattern of closure of these lines does, however, vary widely between individual infants so age estimation from this observation is not highly accurate. The symphysis, a thin band of cartilage attaching the pelvis to the spine, has a zigzag shape

at birth, which straightens as someone ages up to the age of 50. Bone density decreases with age, as calcium is lost. Radiological examination of skeletal remains can determine bone density and this may help indicate the person's age; however, malnutrition and osteoporosis can also decrease bone density independent of age.

The long bones continue to grow till someone has reached the age of about 25. Therefore, their length may be indicative of age. The areas where the ribs join the breastbone also change with age. They start off smooth and rounded, but become more pitted and sharp over time. In general, the age at death of a skeleton can be determined to around five to ten years, inaccuracy increasing with age.

The height of a person can be estimated from a full skeleton. It will not, however, be the same as the head to heel length of the skeleton itself, because of factors like muscle relaxation and shrinkage of the

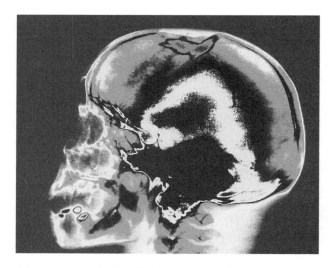

Enhanced x ray of a skull showing evidence of trauma. © FIREFLY PRODUCTIONS/CORBIS

discs between the spinal bones. If only long bones are available, the investigator can use standard tables that associate the length of these bones with height. The thickness of the bones can also indicate whether the person was of slight or muscular build. Right-handed people tend to have thicker bones on the right side of the body and vice-versa.

Using skeletal remains to determine a person's race is a difficult task, as no single trait is racially distinct. It may, however, be possible to assign a skeleton to one of three racial groups: Caucasoid, Negroid, or Mongoloid. Caucasians tend to have high, rounded, or square skulls with a straight face and a narrow nose. Negroid skulls are lower and narrower with wider, flatter noses. Monogoloids have broad, round skulls with an arched profile. Eye sockets can be distinctive as well; Caucasians' are triangular, Negroids' more squared, and those of Mongoloids tend to be rounded. If someone is of mixed racial origin, they will have a blend of these features making determination of race extremely difficult.

Once the investigator has narrowed down the search for the identity of the skeleton as above, they will look for individualizing characteristics. Should there be ante-mortem x-ray images of the deceased, they can be very useful in establishing identity. A skull x-ray can be distinctive for each person has a unique shape to the frontal sinus area which is evident on comparing the x-ray images with the skull. Ribs, the humerus, and the femur can also be usefully compared between x-rays taken in life and skeletal remains.

Clothing or jewelry found with skeletal remains can be a useful aid to identification, as can injuries found on the body. Of course, many injuries do not affect the skeleton at all. If someone is strangled, it will not be apparent by examining his or her skeleton. However, blunt and sharp force injuries do sometimes impact on bone and these marks may be informative. Similarly, bullet entry and exit wounds may sometimes be apparent. It is important for the investigator to distinguish when the wounds may have been made. During life, wounds heal and create scar tissue, which is apparent on examination of the bone. Wounds without scar tissue may have been inflicted close to the **time of death** and may, indeed, have been the cause of it. Bones may be damaged after death, but a post-mortem injury looks very different from an ante-mortem injury. Dead bones are brittle and they crumble and break cleanly. The fracture would usually occur parallel or perpendicular to the long axis of the bone. Living bone fractures in a twisted or splintering manner.

X-ray examination of skeletal remains may also indicate disease such as bone cancer or osteoporosis that may be correlated with medical records. Some people have medical appliances like hip replacements or cardiac pacemakers. It is possible that they will even bear a reference number that will reveal the identity of the deceased. DNA analysis provides the ultimate identification. It is possible to extract DNA from the bone marrow or the bone itself. There is increasing interest in looking at mitochondrial DNA, genetic material that occurs in the mitochondria of the cell rather than its nucleus. Mitochondrial DNA is passed down the maternal line and is very resistant to destruction, so is likely to be present in even very old skeletal remains. Mitochondrial DNA from the bones can be compared to that of a living family member to try to establish identity.

SEE ALSO Anthropology; Sinus print; Skeletal analysis.

Ouchterlony test

Örjan Thomas Gunnarson Ouchterlony, a Swedish bacteriologist who was born 1914 in Göteborg (Gothenburg), developed a double immunodiffusion technique in 1948 that, when used in forensics, determines whether a bloodstain is human or animal. This technique is commonly called Ouchterlony double gel diffusion test, which refers to Ouchterlony's critical analysis in 1968 in his *Handbook of Immunodiffusion and Immunoelectrophoresis*. Another synonym employed is the agar gel immunodiffusion test, AGID.

The binding of an **antibody** to an **antigen** is a fundamental reaction of immunology. Antibodies and antigens form complexes that result in the formation of a visible white aggregate, which is called precipitation, making it possible to assay antibody-antigen systems. The antigen in precipitation reactions is soluble and so small that it must combine with many antibodies to form visible clumps. Soluble antigens can be attached to particulate material serving as carriers that can be detected using the more sensitive agglutination technique. Antigen-antibody reactions are widely used in research, laboratory diagnosis of diseases, pregnancy tests, and forensic **identification** of blood.

The technique involves cutting cylindrical wells into a purified preparation of semi-solidified agar gel in a Petri dish. The wells are filled with antibody or antigen and the dish is allowed to incubate. Homologous antigen and antibody diffuse toward each other from the individual wells to a point in the agar where optimum concentration of each is reached. Subsequently, a precipitin line will form within 18–24 hours somewhere between the two wells. If challenges are mixed together in a single well and allowed to diffuse out into the agar towards the **serum** test well, multiple precipitin bands are seen routinely. Non-specific reactants diffuse past each other, forming no precipitate. The precipitation reaction is subject to inhibition if either antigen or antibody is present in excess. The qualitative Ouchterlony test can simultaneously monitor multiple antibody-antigen systems and can be used to identify particular antigens.

The Ouchterlony method is wearisome due to the time and interpretative expertise required, and the need for reagent sensitivity and selectivity validation. Today, immunoassay tests are used that rely on immunological principles similar to the Ouchterlony test. Results are accurate, more sensitive, and visible within ten minutes, however, the test apparatus is portable and simple to use, requiring no prior experience to conduct and interpret the results. They can give the crime scene examiner a rapid indication as to whether a sample should be taken for **DNA** analysis from a bloodstain. Similarly, the laboratory analyst can utilize these tests to confirm whether a bloodstain is of human origin, which may be important where DNA results have failed. If animal blood is suspected, then the Ouchterlony test is utilized.

SEE ALSO Antibody; Antigen; Blood; Bloodstain evidence; Crime scene investigation; DNA; Homogeneous enzyme immunoassay (EMIT).

Paint analysis

Painted surfaces are everywhere, so it is not surprising that paint is an important source of **trace evidence**. Typically, paint chips are transferred in car accidents, either from one car to another or, in the case of a hit-and-run, from the car to the victim. If there is wet paint at the scene of a crime, the perpetrator may also get it on their clothing. When tools like a crowbar are used in a breaking and entry crime, they may end up with microscopic flakes of paint on them. Analysis of paint **evidence** can therefore make an important contribution to an investigation.

Paint is a complex mixture consisting of pigments, modifiers, extenders, and binders. The pigments give the paint its color. Blue and green pigments tend to be **organic compounds**, while reds, yellows, and whites are often **inorganic compounds**. The modifiers control the properties of the paint such as gloss, flexibility, toughness, and durability. An extender adds bulk and covering capacity and is usually inorganic in nature. Some substances, such as titanium oxide, which is white, may act as both a pigment and an extender. A binder is a natural or synthetic resin that helps stabilize the mixture and form a film when it is spread. Topcoat, primer, and undercoat all have different types of chemical composition. The sample may also have been exposed to dirt, rain, and other contaminants, which can complicate the analysis.

Paint samples can be difficult to collect from the scene of a crime. They can be found on a variety of objects, including clothing, vehicles, and tools. Often the paint is mingled with other materials such as dirt or grease, and its removal may well be a specialist task. In the case of paint chips on cars, it is often the undermost layer of the surrounding paint that is most informative; great care has to be taken to preserve it. Matching chips with flakes of paint that have been knocked off a vehicle can be important individualizing evidence, so great care must be taken not to disturb any features of the surface during evidence collection to allow an accurate match.

Because paint has both organic and inorganic components, a variety of different chemical analysis techniques may be used to find out its actual composition. **Micro-spectrophotometry** in its reflectance mode will help determine the nature of the pigments, while infra red spectrometry will determine its organic components. X-ray powder diffraction is useful for determining the identity of any microcrystalline components. Because paint in the form of a chip is solid, a specialized technique called pyrolysis gas **chromatography** might be used to determine its composition. Pyrolysis involves heating the sample until it turns into a vapor. This is then injected into a gas chromatograph that separates the components. These can be identified by molecular weight using mass spectrometry, which creates a chemical fingerprint that can be compared to reference samples.

If the paint is in the form of a flake, then information on the number of layers can be obtained by various microscopic techniques. The forensic investigator compares the sample to known paints or

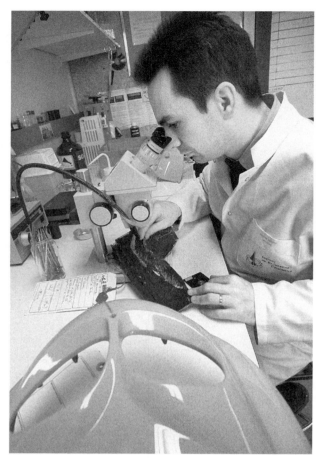

French researcher takes a sample of paint with a scalpel to help identify a car driven by suspects while committing a crime.
© ALAIN NOGUES/CORBIS SYGMA

control samples, by whatever techniques are most appropriate, to see if they came from the same source. The most individualizing type of paint evidence consists of flakes whose fractured edge can be matched to an area of paint loss. Thus, if a paint flake is found on the clothing of the victim of a hit and run accident, then the perpetrator's car should show a chip whose edge exactly matches that of the flake. The investigator uses a light microscope, a stereomicroscope, and perhaps even a scanning electron microscope to look for a jigsaw-like fit of the edge of the chip and the flake. Analysis of a paint can narrow down a sample to this kind to the make, model, and maybe even the year of a car, making it easier to catch the driver.

Paint analysis was used to help convict British serial rapist Malcolm Fairley, also known as "The Fox," in 1985. After one attack, investigators found minute specks of yellow paint on a tree branch around 45 inches (114.3 cm) from the ground. The paint was analyzed and identified as a type of car paint used on a single model, the Austin Allegro, between 1973 and 1975. Other evidence accumulated and the police went to an address in North London to interview a suspect. A young man was cleaning a yellow Austin Allegro outside. Examination revealed scratches on the paintwork about 45 inches from the ground that matched the paint flakes found at the scene of the crime. On this, and other evidence, Fairley was convicted on several accounts of indecent assault, rape, and burglary and given six life sentences.

SEE ALSO Gas chromatograph-mass spectrometer.

Skip Palenik

1948–
AMERICAN
RESEARCH MICROSCOPIST

For more than thirty years, Skip Palenik has worked as a research microscopist, identifying the origins of tiny pieces of materials. His work has helped provide crucial **evidence** in many criminal investigations, and Palenik has testified in and worked on many high-profile cases. As a lecturer and writer, he has also contributed to the education and literature regarding microscopy and chemistry.

Palenik was eight years old when he obtained his first microscope. This childhood hobby would later turn into a career path. From 1966 to 1969, he worked as an intelligence analyst in Germany for United States Army Intelligence. Returning to college, Palenik earned a B.S. degree in chemistry from the University of Illinois at Chicago. He also studied microscopy with two of his mentors, the Swiss microscopist **Max Frei-Sulzer** and Chicago microscopist **Walter C. McCrone**. In 1974, Palenik joined McCrone's lab, McCrone Associates, as a research microscopist. He worked for the company for eighteen years, in various positions.

As an independent researcher, Palenik developed a reputation for skill and unbiased analysis. He has worked on hundreds of criminal investigations across the United States, including such high-profile cases as the 1995 Oklahoma City bombing, the Tylenol tampering murders, the Narita Airport bombing, and the JonBenet Ramsey case. Palenik has also worked on identifying potentially fake artwork, the remains of a body thought to be that of the Sundance Kid, and the identity of Nazi war criminal Ivan the Terrible. In 1992, Palenik started his own laboratory, the Elgin, Illinois-based Microtrace. He is often consulted by the **FBI**, New Scotland Yard, and the Royal Canadian Mounted Police.

In addition to his work as a microscopist, Palenik has taught at the Illinois Institute of Technology, the University of Illinois at Chicago, and the McCrone Research Institute, as well as at individual laboratories and conferences across the United States. He has been a contributor to many books, including the *Encyclopedia of Forensic Science* and *Forensic Examination of Fibers*. He has also written articles for many trade publications, and serves on the board of directors for the McCrone Research Institute. Palenik was named the 2003 Distinguished Scientist by the Midwestern Academy of Forensic Scientists.

SEE ALSO Art identification; Careers in forensic science; Locard's exchange principle; Scanning electron microscopy.

Timothy Palmbach

8/16/1960–
AMERICAN
FORENSIC INVESTIGATOR AND EDUCATOR

From the 1980s to the present, Timothy Palmbach has been a qualified expert witness in the **processing** of crime scenes, interpretation of **blood spatter** patterns, and digital enhancement of forensic photographs, due to his expertise, experiences, and education in the investigation of hundreds of crime scenes. Some of the more famous investigations performed by Palmbach include: helping to identify in 1999 the burial site of Native American princess Pocahontas in the town of Gravesend, England; researching in 2000 into the July 1985 death of Douglas Bruce Scott, an Australian aboriginal prisoner; participating in research during 2000 with regard to the murder of Mary A. Sullivan by "The Boston Strangler," and the activities leading up to the 2001 **exhumation** of the body of Richard DeSalvo. After a distinguished career with the Connecticut State Police, Palmbach is currently the chairperson for the **forensic science** department at the University of New Haven, in West Haven, Connecticut.

In 1982, Timothy Palmbach received a bachelor's of science degree in forensic science and chemistry from the University of New Haven. Three years later, Palmbach completed a master's of science degree from the University of New Haven in forensic science with a concentration in **criminalistics**. Later, in May 1998, Palmbach received a juris doctor degree in law

from the University of Connecticut School of Law in Hartford.

From 1982 to 1986, Palmbach worked as a resident trooper/trooper with the Connecticut State Police. Then, from 1986–1992, Palmbach worked as a detective in the Major Crime unit with the Connecticut State Police and, from 1992–1993, as a patrol supervisor. In these two capacities, he processed about 300 crime scene investigations, during which time he was assigned as the coordinator/liaison for the Crime Scene Processing unit with the Forensic Laboratory. In 1993, Palmbach was promoted to a supervisor in the Major Crime unit, a role he maintained until 1997. During these four years, he managed a wide variety of criminal investigations into cases including murders, kidnappings, **serial killers**, and robberies.

In January 1997, Palmbach transferred to the Connecticut Forensic Science Laboratory where, at the rank of lieutenant, he became the organization's assistant director. For the next year and one half, Palmbach managed the Support and Administrative Services area; designed and implemented a pre-accreditation program from the American Society of Crime Laboratory Directors; implemented the Laboratory Management Information Systems program; and assisted the well-known Chinese-American forensic scientist **Henry C. Lee** with case reports of crime scene reconstructions. Then, in July 1998, Palmbach transferred to the Department of Public Safety. There he was promoted to the rank of major and managed the operations of the Commissioner's Office including Legal Affairs, Legislative Liaison, and Public Information, and the operations of the Division of Scientific Services including the Forensic Laboratory, Computer Crime Unit, and Toxicology Laboratory. He also continued his assistance with Lee.

In June 2000, Palmbach became the commanding officer and director of the Division of Scientific Services, and served in this position until 2004. As division head, Palmbach had general jurisdiction over such areas as the Forensic Science Laboratory, Computer Crime and Electronic Evidence Unit, and Controlled Substance and Toxicology Laboratory. Palmbach is a certified law enforcement instructor, a classification he has held since 1992. In this capacity, Palmbach is certified to instruct such courses as Crime Scene Procedures, Principles of Investigation, Photography, Fingerprinting, and Sexual Assault/Rape crisis.

Since August 2000, Palmbach has held the positions of practitioner-in-residence and distinguished lecturer at the University of New Haven. At this institution, Palmbach teaches undergraduate and graduate courses in forensic science including Physical Analysis in Forensic Science, Pattern Analysis and Crime Scene Procedures, and Advanced Criminalistics. Some of the many workshops and seminars that he has taught include Cold Case Investigations, Effective Presentation of Expert Testimony, and Advances in DNA Profiling and Technologies for Attorneys.

Palmbach has been an adjunct lecturer at Central Connecticut State University in New Britain; where he has lectured on special topics within **criminology**. In addition, Palmbach has been a guest lecturer at such universities as the University of Connecticut School of Law, Western Connecticut University, Saint Joseph College, and Northwestern Connecticut Community College. Besides his college lectures, Palmbach also gives many professional forensic science presentations at conferences and seminars around the world, including in 2002: "Blood Stain Pattern Analysis" at the 9th Annual New Jersey State Police Advanced Homicide Investigation Conference at Princeton University, New Jersey, and "Reconstruction of Shooting Incidents" at the Southeast Law Enforcement Training Seminar in Lawrenceburg, Tennessee.

Palmbach has collaborated with other authors on such publications as: "Henry Lee's Crime Scene Handbook," (with Henry Lee and Marilyn Miller, 2001), "Digital Enhancement of Sub-Quality Bitemark Photographs," (with Henry Lee and Constantine Karazulus, 2001, *Journal of Forensic Science*), and "The Green Revolution: Botanical Contributions to Forensics and Drug Enforcement," (with H. M. Coyle, Carll Ladd, and Henry Lee, *Croatian Medical Journal* [2001]). Palmbach holds a professional affiliation with the American Academy of Forensic Scientists and is on the board of directors of the Henry C. Lee Institute of Forensic Science, which is affiliated with the University of New Haven.

SEE ALSO American Academy of Forensic Sciences; Blood spatter; Crime scene investigation; Expert witnesses.

Palynology

Palynology is the science of fossil and modern pollen, **spores**, algal cysts, and other microscopic plant bodies. It is a multi-disciplinary field with applications in **forensic science**, **geology**, geography, **botany**, **entomology**, zoology, **archaeology**, immunology, and environmental sciences. The term palynology is derived from the Greek terms *paluno*, meaning to strew, or to sprinkle, and suggestive of

palé, meaning fine meal, or the Latin *pollen*, meaning also fine flour or dust.

The study of palynology has, by necessity, been closely associated with the development and later improvements of **microscopes**. Because pollen grains are microscopic, mankind had to wait until the invention of the compound microscope in the mid 1600s before pollen grains could be seen in any detail. During the next two centuries following the invention of the microscope, botanists studied the morphological features of pollen grains, their form and structure, and began to develop taxonomic keys for their **identification**.

Pollen carries the male gametes of flowering and cone-bearing plants, and spores are the asexual reproductive bodies of ferns, mosses, and fungi. Plants produce vast quantities of microscopic pollen and spores, which they disperse with the help of animals, wind, or water. Although individual pollen grains are invisible to the naked eye, they occur on almost every surface in nature. They are also highly resistant to decay, being found in rocks many millions of years old, and also persisting on or in soil, dirt, and other materials for many years. Pollen and spores come in an infinite variety of shapes and have complex surface ornamentation. Each plant type has distinctive pollen that can be distinguished from the pollen of other plants. For this reason pollen and spores are often called nature's fingerprints for plants.

The major commercial application of palynology is in geology, where it is used to date sediments to assist in petroleum, mining, and underground water exploration. Aeroallergy is the branch of **medicine** concerned with the seasonal occurrence, abundance, and allerogenic effect of spores and pollen. The study of extant palynomorphs, which are either living, still retain their cell contents, or whose cell contents have been removed by maceration, is called actuopalynology. It includes the disciplines mellisopalynology (study of pollen in honey or other bee products), pollination ecology (distribution of pollen by wind or animals and its efficacy in fertilization and seed set), aeroallergy, and **criminology** (i.e., forensic palynology). In the discipline of archaeological palynology pollen, spores, and other palynomorphs from archeological sites are employed to reconstruct prehistoric diet, funeral practices, artifact function and source, archaeological feature use, cultivation and domestication of plants, and human impact on vegetation.

The term forensic palynology refers to the use of pollen and spore **evidence** in legal cases. It is often possible to be very specific about where a person or thing has been from the pollen types that occur together in a sample. Pollen and spore production and dispersion are important considerations. The expected production and dispersal patterns of spores and pollen (called pollen rain) for the plants in a given region will yield the type of "pollen fingerprint" to expect in samples that come from that area. Therefore, the first task of the forensic palynologist is to try to find a match between the pollen in a known geographical region with the pollen in a forensic sample. Knowledge of pollen dispersal and productivity often plays a major role in solving such problems.

Pollen can help destroy or prove alibis, link a suspect to the scene of a crime, or link something left at the crime scene to a suspect. It can also help to determine what country or state drugs, food, merchandise, and antiques among other things, have come from. In its broader application, the field of forensic palynology also includes legal information derived from the analysis of a broad range of microscopic organisms such as dinoflagellates, acritarchs, and chitinozoans that can be found in both fresh and marine environments. One of the earliest successful cases where forensic palynology was used pertained to a criminal case in Austria in 1959.

Soil, dirt, and dust are common elements at almost every crime scene. Woven cloth, woolen blankets, ropes, clothing, and fur all make excellent traps for pollen and spores. Woven materials and fur are made of tiny interwoven **fibers**. When air comes in contact with woven materials, the fibers become filters that retain solid particles, such as pollen and spores. Woolen garments, including blankets, skirts, suits, ties, and sweaters, make the best pollen and spore traps.

If working on a case, pollen is extracted from exhibits (washed or scraped from items, or taken off with tape lifts); **control samples** are collected; and if possible, the crime scene attended. The samples are then taken through various preparation procedures so that the detail of the pollen can be examined with microscopes. Some cases are quite easy and require only the comparison of assemblages in the control and forensic sample; others require much research in the laboratory with other scientists, the public, and police.

SEE ALSO Botany; Crime scene investigation; Entomology; Fingerprint; Forensic science; Geology; Identification; Microscopes; Pollen and pollen rain; Reference sample; Soils; Spores.

Parasitology

Parasitology is the study of parasites, organisms that live, grow, and feed on or in other organisms. The prevention of parasite-infested consumption of raw (or undercooked) meat, fish, seafood, vegetables, and dairy products, as well as contaminated water, is a matter of public health. The **United States Food and Drug Administration** (**FDA**), the Centers for Disease Control (**CDC**), and several other local and state sanitary agencies are responsible for regulatory food safety measures and regular inspections of food and water quality to prevent the outbreak of epidemics caused by parasites and other **pathogens**.

When an epidemic outbreak occurs in a city or when several cases of food-related poisoning suddenly happen in an area, forensic pathologists or forensic parasitologists help epidemiologists to identify the source of the problem. For example, in 1980, 32 patients, including four physicians, reported to hospitals in Los Angeles within a short period of time complaining of abdominal distention, diarrhea, intermittent abdominal cramps, and flatulence. They were diagnosed as having been infested by a flatworm, *Diphyllobothrium spp.*, a common parasite in freshwater and sea fish. All patients recalled that they had eaten sushi, a raw fish dish, ten days prior to the onset of symptoms. Alerted by hospitals, the CDC tracked the illness back to sushi made of salmon contaminated with the flatworm.

Another field where parasitology is also important is legal **medicine**, as some parasitic pathogens (disease-causing organisms) are transmitted through sexual contact and may constitute **evidence** of crime, especially in cases of child molestation.

Although some pathogenic (disease-causing) bacteria such as Chlamydia and Ricketsia can be thought of as obligate intracellular parasites (i.e., they can only be replicated inside living cells using the host cell's metabolic machinery) the strict definition of parasites refers to protozoa and helminthes or worms, also known as Metazoa. Pathogenic protozoa are unicellular (e.g., single-celled) organisms divided into four groups: Sarcodina (amoebas), Sporozoa (sporozoans), Mastigophora (flagellates), and Ciliata (ciliates). Metazoa or worms classified are divided in two groups, Platyhelminthes or flat worms, such as Trematoda (flukes) and Cestoda (tapeworms), and Nemathelminthes or roundworms. The most commonly occurring parasites in humans can be also grouped according to the areas of the body they infest, such as: 1) the intestinal tract (*Giardia* lamblia, *Entamoeba histolytica*, and Cryptosporidium); 2) urogenital tract (flagellate *Trichomonas vaginalis*); 3) blood and tissues (flagellates Leishmania and Trypanosoma, protozoans Toxoplasma and Plasmodium).

Giardiasis, or infestation by *Giardia lamblia*, occurs in two forms: Giardia trophozoites (active Giardia) and cysts (latent, non-mobile Giardia). Water and food contaminated with fecal residues are the main means of transmission, with the cysts developing into Giardia trophozoites in the duodenum (upper part of the stomach). Giardia attaches to the duodenal mucosa where it competes for protein and fat nutrients, causing inflammation, flatulence, foul-smelly diarrhea, intestinal cramps, nausea, anorexia, and associated protein and fatty acid deficiency. Although 50% of the hosts do not present with symptoms, giardiasis is very common among children in daycare centers, and people who camp, hike, or drink unfiltered water directly from streams, with symptoms appearing especially in those with certain immune deficiencies. Giardiasis is an endemic infestation in the United States, affecting about 5% of the population.

Entamoeba histolytica have two life-cycle phases: trophozoites or mobile amoeba and cyst (non mobile) phases. They cause intestinal cramps, dysentery, and liver lesions, being transmitted by ingestion of cysts present in water or uncooked food, as well as through fecal-oral contact in sexual intercourse. Once inside the body, the cysts mature to the trophozoites phase, the active ameba. By causing necrosis (cell and tissue death and decay) of the intestinal epithelium, amebas invade the submucosa layers of the colonic tract and reach circulation, being transported to the liver where they cause systemic hepatic disease and liver abscesses. Approximately 2% of the American population suffers from amebiasis. Other types of amebiasis are rare, such as those caused by *Acanthamoeba ssp.* and *Naegleria fowleri*, which are pathogenic free-living amebas transmitted by water inhalation (while swimming) and by air. They can multiply in the tissues of the brain and spinal fluid, causing nerve damage and death if untreated. Naegleria causes primary amoebic meningoencephalitis (PAM) and Acanthamoeba leads to granulomatous amoebic encephalitis (GAE). If untreated, PAM can kill within a week of the onset of symptoms. GAE occurs in patients with immunodeficiencies and leads to death within several weeks to a year after the onset of disease. Both diseases cause eye infections that can lead to blindness. Between 1985 and 1986, 22 cases of amoeba-related ocular lesions were reported

to the Centers for Disease Control. Investigators found out that the majority of the cases were associated with poor disinfection of contact lenses and homemade saline solutions.

Cryptosporidium is another pathogen that induces diarrhea, which is more severe in small children, senior patients, and those with immunodeficiencies such as HIV. Transmission is generally under the form of oocysts present in water and may cause collective outbreaks of watery diarrhea with risk of severe dehydration, particularly to those belonging to the more vulnerable groups. Water filtration is the most effective way of preventing both giardiasis and Cryptosporidium-related diarrhea because these two parasites are resistant to water chlorination.

Almost two billion people live in parts of the world where malaria is an endemic (naturally occurring in the environment) disease. Malaria is a parasitic disease caused by four different species of the Plasmodium parasite, and is transmitted by the bite of infected mosquitoes. The worldwide use of pesticides containing DDT greatly reduced the incidence of malaria, but since DDT was found to contain possibly carcinogenic (cancer-causing) chemicals in the late 1960s, its use has declined greatly, and in turn, the incidence of malaria has increased sharply around the world. As of 2005, malaria is estimated to have killed more than 300–500 million people over the centuries and still kills an estimated 2.5 million people per year (including 1 million children) in Africa and the world's tropical areas. Many countries in these regions are returning to the use of DDT to control the mosquitoes carrying the parasite that causes malaria.

Trichomonas vaginalis is a sexually transmitted parasite that exists only as trophozoites, causing genital itching and smelly-greenish vaginal secretions as well as urethritis (a burning sensation when urinating). In men, the only symptom is urethritis, although the parasite is transmitted in the prostatic secretions (secretions of the prostate gland). The use of condoms prevents infection. When found in a child, this and other sexually transmitted diseases may suggest a case of child molestation. Some rare cases of trichomoniasis appear to be associated with contact with wet toilet seats.

Toxoplasma gondii, a blood parasite, may be transmitted through the contact with infected feces of cats and other mammals, or by consumption of raw or undercooked meat or contaminated water, causing toxoplasmosis. It can be also transmitted from mother to the fetus, in what is known as congenital toxoplasmosis. Congenital infection favors miscarriage, neonatal mental retardation, or chorioretinitis (inflammation of the choroids portion of the eye), which leads to blindness during childhood. In immunodepressed adults, toxoplasmosis may cause encephalitis, although most of the infected population remains asymptomatic, due to the action of the **immune system**. However, *T. gondii* passes from the intestinal tract to other tissues of the body, such as brain, liver, lungs, and eyes, where it remains as cysts for years. As long as the infected individual's immune system is healthy, antibodies and the immune cells will keep the infection at bay, preventing disease progression.

Diarrheal parasites and other pathogens account for 4% of deaths worldwide each year. Periodical tests for these and other parasitic infestations are a valuable preventive measure that can avert serious and unnecessary diseases and even death.

SEE ALSO Air and water purity; Antibiotics; Antibody; FDA (United States Food and Drug Administration); Hemoglobin; Immune system; Medical examiner.

Paternity evidence

The general concept of testing for paternity is centered on the establishment of information about hereditary factors that either exclude an individual from consideration of being the biological father of a child, or reveal a convincing pattern of consistency that supports a claim of biological paternity. Exclusion can be absolute—it is indeed possible to disprove a person's role as biological father. It is not possible, however, to make a positive proof of paternity. This side is always a probability calculation. Thus, the development of paternity evidence involves both physical testing, through **DNA** or other biochemical markers, and probability calculations using the laws of probability.

One important aspect of paternity testing is the development of a list of potential candidates for paternity. Since the timing of conception is fairly tightly clustered around the middle of the menstrual cycle, the mother of a baby generally knows with a fair amount of certainty who the father is, or knows the list of possible candidates with whom she has had sexual intercourse near enough to the time of conception for determining paternity to be a realistic possibility. In some cases, and for various reasons, the mother may not have a conscious awareness of all of the events surrounding the pregnancy. This may

be the situation in cases of rape by an unknown assailant, intercourse which has taken place under the influence of drugs or alcohol, or when the mother is mentally retarded or has certain forms of mental illness. The first step in the process of paternity testing is to determine the candidates for whom testing makes sense. This type of testing is centered on elimination or retention of individuals who have been placed on the list of reasonable candidates.

In previous years, testing was focused on the testing of **blood** group types and the evaluation of biochemical markers for which there were significant differences among individuals in the population. This testing seems crude compared with the more precise and informationally rich DNA marker systems for testing that are currently in use. In principle, any marker that is inherited from the parents can be used as a part of the testing process, however.

In the laboratory testing phase of the analysis, the laboratory chooses a number of markers, which have different forms in the general population, for analysis. These markers are called polymorphic markers, meaning each marker has many forms. Simple markers may have just two forms, and each individual has two copies of each marker. Thus, with these simple two-marker systems, a person would fall into one of three categories: he could have two copies of the first form, one copy of each of the two forms, or two copies of the second form. There are just three possibilities for anyone in the population, and it is common to match with a genotype consistent with paternity just by chance. The greater the number of possible forms, however, the greater the number of different combinations in the population, and the lower the likelihood of matching purely by chance. For example, if there are three different forms of a marker, there are 6 combinations possible; four forms yields 10 different combinations; five forms yields 15 combinations. For many of the genetic markers available for testing, such as short tandem repeats, there may be 10 to 20 different forms and therefore many, many combinations possible.

The testing strategy would then be to select several markers for testing, and to test the mother, the child, and the suspected father for each of the markers selected. Starting with the child, for each marker studied, one would ask which of the two copies that the child has came from the mother. For highly polymorphic systems it is often true that one and only one of the child's markers could have come from the mother. The remaining marker that the child carries must have come from the father. Sometimes, the child and mother match exactly for both forms of the marker, and it is not clear which one came from the mother and which came from the father. In this case, if either form matches one of the forms of the marker that the father carries, it is consistent with paternity.

As an example, let us say that there is a marker we will call X that has twelve forms that can be found in different people. We will let X be a trinucleotide repeat that is found to have anywhere from six to seventeen copies in normal individuals in the population. Each person will have two alleles of X, one that was inherited from his mother and one that was inherited from his father at conception. Upon testing, let us say that the child has one allele that has 7 copies of the repeat, and the second allele has 11 copies of the repeat. In the mother, we find one allele that has 7 copies of the repeat, and the other has 8 copies of the repeat. We know that the mother must have passed along the allele with 7 copies of the repeat. The other allele that the child has must come from his father. We can now exclude any suspected father who does not carry at least one allele of X that has 11 copies of the repeat. But what if the father does have an allele that has 11 copies of the repeat? Does this prove paternity? No, this could be a match purely by chance. While it is consistent with paternity, it is not conclusive by itself.

In real practice, one would not use just a single marker, even if it were highly polymorphic. One would generally include several informative markers to increase the chance that the suspect will be eliminated by failing to match. By choosing markers with a lot of variability in the population, the chance of matching can be minimized. For a person to be retained as a candidate for paternity, matching has to occur for all of the markers. Even a single inconsistency can eliminate a person from consideration.

If a person matches on all of the markers included in testing, and if those markers are reasonably informative markers for testing, the individual being tested is the presumptive father. In this case, it will be necessary to compute the likelihood of a person matching purely by chance using the simple laws of probability.

The probability of an individual carrying a marker of some given size can be found by studying a large number of people and computing the number who carry the marker divided by the total number of people studied. Suppose 500 people are studied, and 50 of those people have are found to have at least one copy of marker X with 11 repeats; the chance is 50/500 or 0.10 of carrying a marker of that size.

Peruvian President Alejandro Toledo recognized 14-year-old Zarai Toledo as his daughter for the first time in 2002 after a court ordered him to take a DNA paternity test. © REUTERS/CORBIS

One rule of probability is that the probability for both of two different events happening is found by multiplying their individual probabilities together. Likewise, to compute the chance of three or more separate events each happening one would multiply each of their individual probabilities together. When the probabilities are each small, the product of the combined probabilities becomes very small. It is possible to end up with likelihood of paternity that says that the chance of matching purely by chance is one in a million or less.

A reasonable question that many people ask is what is the chance that the testing is wrong. The simple answer is that the chance of being wrong when the father has been excluded by DNA testing is very near to zero. This assumes, however, that the specimen that was studied actually came from person that you think is being testing. Great care must be given to ensuring that the blood sample or other specimen that is taken for paternity testing actually comes from the person that is suspected as being the father. It is standard practice for laboratories that perform paternity testing to document a **chain of custody** for the specimen from the time it is drawn, until the time it reaches the laboratory for testing.

What about the chance of being wrong when the testing is consistent with paternity? As the result is expressed as a probability statement, it always remains true that there is a possibility of a match by chance. When there is reason to suspect that this is the case, the study of additional markers can further reduce the likelihood of a match by chance. While it is not possible to get this probability to zero, the probability can always be further reduced by adding additional markers. This adds expense, however, and most people will quickly realize that such expense is not warranted unless there is some compelling reason to doubt the findings. It is rarely the case that a person enters paternity testing without some fairly high likelihood that he is in fact the father.

The last twenty years of the twentieth century saw dramatic developments in the understanding of genetics and the development of markers that can be used in paternity and forensic testing. Compared with the testing available in previous generations, determination of paternity is now extremely reliable and relatively inexpensive.

SEE ALSO DNA; DNA evidence, social issues; DNA typing systems; Evidence, chain of custody; Gene; Genetic code; RFLP (restriction fragment length polymorphism); Statistical interpretation of evidence; STR (short tandem repeat) analysis.

Pathogen genomic sequencing

The forensic detection of disease-causing (pathogenic) bacteria is facilitated by knowledge of target sequences of the genome of the particular organism. **Sequencing** of some **pathogens** has been undertaken by organizations such as the Institute for Genomic Research. In the national interest, the United States has embarked on a genomic sequencing program of pathogens that will have forensic applications.

The Pathogen Genomic Sequencing program initiated by the Defense Advanced Research Project Agency (DARPA) in 2002 focuses on characterizing the genetic components of pathogens in order to develop novel diagnostics, treatments, and therapies for the diseases they cause. In particular, the program will collect an inventory of genes and proteins that

are specific to pathogens and then to look for patterns among these molecules.

This information will facilitate the development of tools for identifying pathogens in a variety of vectors. It will also provide a foundation for engineering antibodies to identify pathogens. Initially, one representative strain of the bacteria that cause a variety of diseases (or their close relatives) are being studied for this program: *Brucella suis* (brucellosis), *Burkholderia mallei* (melioidosis), *Clostridium perfringens* (botulism), *Coxiella burnetti* (Q fever), *Franciscella tularensis* (tulareremia), and *Rickettsia typhi* (Rocky Mountain spotted fever).

As part of the Pathogen Genomic Sequencing project, a website focusing on orthopox viruses has been created. Known as the Poxvirus Bioinformatics Resource, this website serves as a repository for genetic sequence data for orthopox viruses. It currently contains sequence data for 35 viral pathogens including the virus that causes **smallpox**. In addition, the website contains data-mining and sequence analysis software and a poxvirus literature resource. The goals of the Poxvirus Bioinformatics Resource are the development of novel therapies for human diseases caused by orthopox viruses, the ability to detect orthopox viruses in the environment and the development of quick diagnostic tools for detecting pox diseases.

SEE ALSO Biological weapons, genetic identification; DNA; *Escherichia coli*; PCR (polymerase chain reaction).

Pathogen transmission

Forensic investigation of an illness, outbreak, or a death can be concerned with disease causing (pathogenic) microorganisms and, more specifically, with their route of transmission. Unearthing how an organism infected the victim(s) can be crucial when the organism is capable of spreading through a population quickly, or is a threat to public health.

Pathogens are microorganisms such as viruses, bacteria, protozoa, and fungi that cause disease in humans and other species. Pathogen transmission involves three steps: escape from the host, travel, and infection of the new host. Pathogen transmission occurs in several ways, usually dependent on the ecology of the organism. For example, respiratory pathogens are usually airborne, while pathogens of the digestive tract tend to be food- or waterborne. Epidemiologists group pathogen transmission into two general types—direct and indirect contact—within which there are several mechanisms.

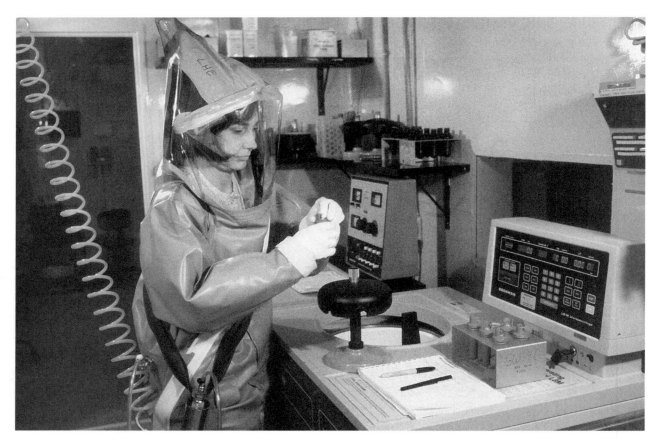

A Centers for Disease Control scientist wearing a protective suit with helmet and face mask is protected from pathogens as she conducts studies in the CDC BSL-4 laboratory. © CDC/PHIL/CORBIS

Pathogen transmission by direct contact takes place when an infected host transmits a disease directly to another host. The pathogens that travel this way are extremely sensitive to the environment and cannot be outside of the host for any length of time. For example, pathogens that cause sexually transmitted diseases (STDs) are transmitted via **blood**, **semen**, or **saliva**. Some pathogens responsible for STDs include *Tremonema palidum* (syphilis), *Neisseria gohorrhoeae* (gonorrhea) and human immunodeficiency virus (HIV) (acquired immunodeficiency syndrome or AIDS). The viruses responsible for hemorrhagic fever, such as Ebola, are also transmitted by direct contact via the blood.

Indirect transmission occurs when an agent is required to transfer the pathogen from an infected host to a susceptible host. The agent may be either animate or inanimate. Inanimate forms of transmission include air, water, and food, which are referred to as disease vehicles. Inanimate agents also include fomites, which are objects on which the pathogen has been deposited. Examples of fomites are toys, clothes, bedding, or surgical instruments. Animate,

or living, agents of disease transmission are most often insects, mites, fleas, and rodents. Living agents of transmission are referred to as vectors. Diseases that are spread via indirect contact in hospitals are specifically referred to as nosocomial infections.

Many respiratory viruses and bacterial **spores** are light enough to be lifted by the wind. These agents can subsequently be inhaled, where they cause lung infections. A particularly important example of an airborne bacterial pathogen is the spore form of the anthrax-causing bacterium *Bacillus anthracis*. This bacterium forms spores that can spread through the air and causes a severe respiratory disease when inhaled.

A common route of indirect pathogen transmission is via water. The ingestion of contaminated water introduces the microbes into the digestive system, where they can attack the gastrointestinal tract. Some pathogenic organisms use the cells that line the digestive tract in order to gain entry to the bloodstream. From there, an infection can become systemic. A common waterborne pathogen is *Vibrio cholerae*, the bacterium that causes cholera. The contamination of drinking water by this bacterium still causes cholera epidemics in some areas of the world.

Foodborne pathogens are grouped in two categories. Those that produce **toxins** that poison the host and those that infect the host and then grow there. **Food poisoning** is most often caused by the bacterium *Staphylococcus aureus*, which produces enterotoxins that result in vomiting and diarrhea. The bacterium *Clostridium botulinum* is responsible for the disease botulism, which is an extremely severe and sometimes fatal food poisoning.

Vectors harbor the microorganisms that cause disease and transfer them to humans via a bite or by other contact. *Coxiella burnetti*, the bacterium that causes Q fever, is transmitted to humans from the handling of animals such as sheep. Insects are common vectors of disease. Mosquitoes spread the protozoan *Plasmodium vivax* that causes malaria. Deer ticks are responsible for infection by the spirochete *Borrelia burgdorferi* that causes Lyme disease. The bacterium that causes plague, *Yersina pestis*, is transmitted by the rat flea.

SEE ALSO Anthrax; Bacterial biology; Biosensor technologies; Bioterrorism; *Escherichia coli*; Spores; Toxins.

Pathogens

Forensic analysis often involves the determination of the circumstances surrounding an illness outbreak or death. Medical examiners search for pathogens in body tissues and **fluids** to determine if the cause of a death was due to an infectious process.

Pathogens are organisms, frequently microorganisms or components of these organisms, that cause disease. Microbial pathogens include various species of bacteria, viruses, and protozoa. Many diseases caused by microbial pathogens, and the frequency of these diseases, are a national security issue.

A disease is any condition caused by the presence of an invading organism, or a toxic component, that damages the host. In humans, diseases can be caused by the growth of microorganisms such as bacteria, viruses, and protozoa. Bacterial growth, however, is not mandatory to cause disease. For example, some bacterial pathogens cause disease by virtue of a toxic component of the bacterial cell such as lipopolysaccharide. Finally, the damaging symptoms of a disease can be the result of the attempts

by the host's **immune system** to rid the body of the invader. One example is the immune-related damage caused to the lungs of those afflicted with cystic fibrosis, as the body unsuccessfully attempts to eradicate the chronic infections caused by *Pseudomonas aeruginosa* (a cause of pneumonia).

Not all pathogens cause diseases that have the same severity of symptoms. For example, an infection with the influenza virus can cause the short term aches and fever that are hallmarks of the flu, or can cause more dire symptoms, depending on the type of virus that causes the infection. Bacteria also vary in the damage caused. For example, the ingestion of food contaminated with *Salmonella enteritica* causes intestinal upset. But, consumption of ***Escherichia coli*** O157:H7 causes a severe disease, which can permanently damage the kidneys and which can even be fatal.

There are three categories of bacterial pathogens. Obligate pathogens are those bacteria that must cause disease in order to be transmitted from one host to another. These bacteria must also infect a host in order to survive, in contrast to other bacteria that are capable of survival outside of a host. Examples of obligate bacterial pathogens include *Mycobacterium tuberculosis* (tuberculosis) and *Treponema pallidum* (syphilis).

Opportunistic pathogens can be transmitted from one host to another without having to cause disease. However, in a host whose immune system is not functioning properly, the bacteria can cause an infection that leads to a disease. In those cases, the disease can help the bacteria spread to another host. Examples of opportunistic bacterial pathogens include *Vibrio cholerae* (cholera) and *Pseudomonas aeruginosa* (bacterial pneumonia).

Finally, some bacterial pathogens cause disease only accidentally. Indeed, the disease actually limits the spread of the bacteria to another host. Examples of these "accidental" pathogens include *Neisseria meningitides* (bacterial meningitis) and *Bacteroides fragilis* (normal intestinal flora that can cause serious infection if it gets into the bloodstream, usually through intestinal ulceration or trauma).

Pathogens can be spread from person to person in a number of ways. Not all pathogens use all the available routes. For example, the influenza virus is transmitted from person to person through the air, typically via sneezing or coughing. But the virus is not transmitted via water. In contrast, *Escherichia coli* is readily transmitted via water, food, and blood, but is not readily transmitted via air or the bite of an insect.

While routes of transmission vary for different pathogens, a given pathogen will use a given route of transmission. This has been used in the weaponization of pathogens. The best-known example is **anthrax**. The bacterium that causes anthrax—*Bacillus anthracis*—can form an environmentally hardy form called a spore. The spore is very small and light. It can float on currents of air and can be breathed into the lungs, where the bacteria resume growth and swiftly cause a serious and often fatal form of anthrax. As demonstrated in the United States in the last few months of 2001, anthrax **spores** are easily sent through the mail to targets. As well, the powdery spores can be released from an aircraft. Over a major urban center, modeling studies have indicated that the resulting casualties could number in the hundreds of thousands.

Contamination of water by pathogens is another insidious route of disease spread. Water remains crystal clear until there are millions of bacteria present in each milliliter. Viruses, which are much smaller, can be present in even higher numbers without affecting the appearance of the liquid. Thus, water can be easily laced with enough pathogens to cause illness.

Food-borne pathogens cause millions of cases of disease and hundreds of deaths each year in the United States alone. Frequently the responsible microbes are bacteria, viruses, or protozoa that usually reside in the intestinal tract of humans or other creatures. Examples of microorganisms include *Escherichia coli* O157:H7, *Campylobacter jejuni*, and rotavirus.

Pathogens can be transmitted to humans through contact with animals, birds, and other living creatures that naturally harbor the microorganism. The agent of anthrax—*Bacillus anthracis*—naturally dwells in sheep. Other examples include *Brucella abortic* (Brucellosis), *Coxiella burnetti* (Q fever), and viruses that cause hemorrhagic fevers such as Ebola and Marburg.

Microorganisms have various strategies to establish an infection in a host. Some microorganisms recognize molecules on the surface of the host cell, and use these as receptors. The binding of bacteria or viruses to receptors brings the microorganism in close contact with the host surface.

The nature of the interaction between the host receptor molecule and the attachment molecule on the surface of the bacteria, virus, or protozoan has in some cases been defined, even to the genetic level. The use of recombinant **DNA** technology—where a target section of genetic material is removed from

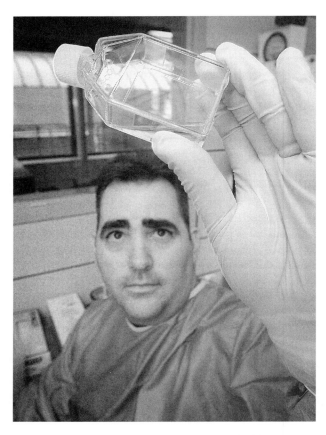

A scientist at the Centers for Disease Control (CDC) examines a T-25 flask used in the SARS virus isolation, as part of a global collaboration to address the emergence of the SARS virus. © CDC/PHIL/CORBIS

one organism and inserted into a certain region of the genetic material of another organism, in a way that does not affect the expression of the gene—allows the genetic manipulation of a microorganism so as to enhance its ability to cause an infection. Alternatively, the addition of a **gene** that codes for a toxin into a bacterium that is a normal inhabitant of an environment like the intestinal tract could produce a formidable pathogen. This altered bacteria would readily associate with host cells, but would also carry the toxin.

Viruses almost always damage the host cells. Because viruses cannot reproduce on their own, they rely on the replication mechanism of the host cell to make more copies of themselves (i.e., they are obligate pathogens). Then, the new viral particles will exit the cell and search for another cell in which to infect. This exit is often very physically damaging to the host cell. Thus, viral infections can be detrimental because of the loss of function of host cells.

Some viral pathogens are capable of causing a disease long after they have infected a host. This delayed response occurs because the viral genetic material becomes incorporated into the genetic material of the host. Thereafter, the viral genetic material is replicated along with that of the host, using the replication enzymes and other machinery of the host. But, in response to a number of signals, the viral material can be excised from the host material and form the template for the manufacture and assembly of new virus particles. A prominent example of such a virus is the human immunodeficiency virus (HIV), which is acknowledged to be the cause of acquired immunodeficiency syndrome, or AIDS.

SEE ALSO Bacterial biology; Biosensor technologies; Bioterrorism; Prions; Toxins.

Pathology

Pathology is the scientific study of disease processes that affect normal anatomy and **physiology**. Anatomical and physiological changes are pathological changes when they result from an underlying disease process or abnormality. **Forensic science** is geared towards deducing the nature of the physical and chemical insults that have been inflicted on one or more persons. Sometimes these insults can cause changes in the body. When that occurs, the forensic examination overlaps with pathology. Forensic pathology is the study of the anatomical or physiological changes that are suspicious in their origin.

Pathologists play an increasingly important role in diagnosis, research, and in the development of clinical treatments for disease. A specialized branch

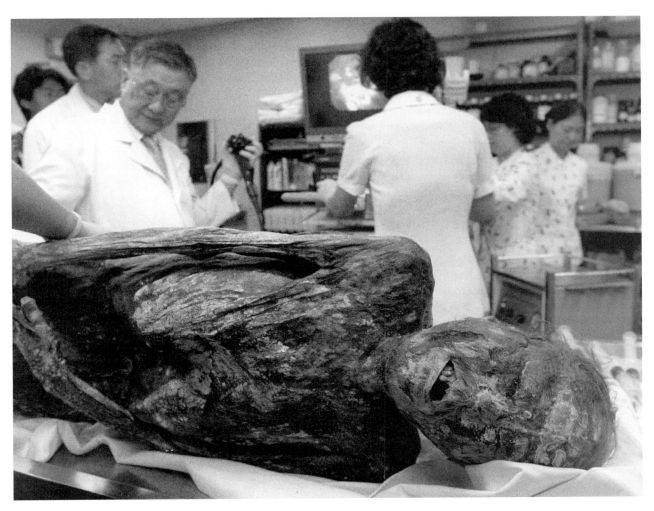

South Korean pathologists inspect a 600-year-old mummy through an endoscope at a laboratory in Seoul, July 2004.
© YOU SUNG-HO/REUTERS/CORBIS

of pathology, forensic pathology, offers a vast array of molecular diagnostic techniques (including **DNA fingerprint** analysis) toward **identification** of remains, gathering of **evidence**, and identification of suspects.

Modern pathology labs rely heavily on molecular biology techniques and advances in biotechnology. During the last two decades, there have been tremendous advances in linking changes in cellular or tissue morphology (i.e., gross appearance) with genetic and/or intracellular changes. In many cases, specific molecular tests can definitively identify disease processes and help make a correct diagnosis at an earlier stage in the disease process.

Pathologists attempt to relate observable changes to disease process. Whether the changes are evident morphologically (structurally) or are distinguishable only via sophisticated molecular tests, the goal is to determine the existence and/or etiology of disease (the cause of disease). Once the etiologic agents are identified, the general goal of research is to document and gather evidence of the pathogenesis of disease (i.e., the mechanisms by which etiologic agents cause disease).

On a daily basis, pathologists perform a broad spectrum of tests on clinical samples to determine anatomical and physiological changes associated with a number of disease processes, including the detection of cancerous cells and tumors.

Major branches of pathology include the study of anatomic, cellular, and molecular pathology. Specific clinical studies often focus on transplantation pathology, neuropathology, immunopathology, virology, **parasitology**, and a number of clinical subspecialties (e.g., pediatric pathology).

Forensic pathology has several specific aims in addition to the aforementioned. The pathological examinations seek to establish what weapon was used, if that is relevant. Also, whether a death was self-inflicted or was a **murder** is another goal. Finally, the contribution to the death of a pre-existing disease or condition is a goal. For example, a person who is infected with the Human Immunodeficiency Virus often has a compromised **immune system** that lays them open to the development of other maladies that might otherwise not be fatal (i.e., fungal infections).

SEE ALSO Amphetamines; Barbiturates; Botulinum toxin; Death, mechanism of; Electrical injury and death; Food poisoning; Hemorrhagic fevers and diseases; Pathogens; Toxicological analysis.

Pathology careers

Pathology is the investigation of death and disease. It emerged as a discipline from the mid-nineteenth century with the development of the microscope. Physicians began to see that the microscopic examination of tissue was relevant to the study of disease and had practical application in diagnosis and research. Two branches of pathology emerged; anatomic pathology involved the study of cells, tissues, and organs, while clinical pathology covered the study of body **fluids** such as **blood** and urine. The discipline of forensic pathology developed during the twentieth century, and is the application of pathology to the investigation of crime, particularly when injury or death have occurred.

The **medical examiner** (ME) is a key person in a forensic investigation. He or she is charged with looking into any suspicious death reported to them, be it a homicide, suicide, accident, or in any other way suspicious. To this end, their work involves specific tasks, chief of which is the determination of the cause and manner of the death through performing an **autopsy**. The ME also takes control of the analysis of **evidence**, works with the police investigating the scene of the crime, and presents evidence in court. Ideally and increasingly, the ME is a forensic pathologist. In practice, they must merely be medically qualified and may not even be a pathologist. In such cases, they may well contract out some of their duties, such as carrying out the autopsy, to a forensic pathologist elsewhere.

Becoming qualified as a forensic pathologist involves a lengthy course of study. After completing an undergraduate degree, the individual completes four years of medical school (in the United States; course lengths elsewhere may differ). Then, postgraduate **training** in pathology, which is done in a teaching hospital, takes at least four years more. After that, a further year's training is needed to become a forensic pathologist, and this is usually done in an ME's office, to get the necessary experience. The forensic pathologist can then take an exam to become board certified, which means he or she is finally qualified to assume the job of a medical examiner. Given the strong legal content of the ME's work, some forensic pathologists may also have some training in the law, or even a law degree.

The work of the forensic pathologist is quite varied. They will, like any other physician, often be involved in reviewing a patient's medical history. Many of the apparently suspicious deaths reported to the ME are actually from natural causes and the pathologist must be as aware of common diseases as of the methods used for homicide and suicide. If it appears as if a crime has been committed, then witness statements will be reviewed and, ideally, the scene of crime visited. Evidence of many types must be considered, from bloodstains and **DNA**, to **toxicological analysis** of blood and urine. All of this will help the medical examiner to determine the cause and manner of death.

Perhaps the most important part of the forensic pathologist's job is to carry out the autopsy, if one is required. This is done according to a standard procedure with notes and photographs taken at every stage. The forensic pathologist is also responsible for writing up a report on the investigation, which includes autopsy results and other findings, and presenting this to the court.

The forensic pathologist does not operate alone; he or she is part of an investigating team. In a large jurisdiction, the ME may have one or more assistants who may also be medically qualified. There are also posts for those who have degrees in science rather than **medicine**. A degree in biology, chemistry, or physics may secure a job as a technician, scientist, or laboratory manager in a facility where forensic pathology is done, particularly for candidates who have the appropriate post-graduate training in a branch of **forensic science** or experience in an appropriate laboratory.

Forensic pathology itself includes a number of specialties, including **toxicology**, **serology**, **odontology**, **anthropology**, and **taphonomy**. Laboratories, both governmental and private, devoted to each discipline will have openings for those qualified in medicine or science. A forensic pathologist needs to undertake further training to specialize in any of these disciplines. Toxicology involves the analysis of body fluids and tissues for poisons or drugs of abuse. There are two kinds of tests, a screen, which determines whether the drug is present, and a confirmatory test, which determines the amount of drug present. The two main applications of toxicology testing are in autopsy and in workplace drug testing, including **sports testing**. Work in the toxicology laboratory involves chemical analyses using techniques such as **thin layer chromatography**, gas **chromatography**, and ultraviolet **spectroscopy**. Technicians may be qualified in chemistry and chemical analysis. The pathology side involves determining the contribution that an individual drug may have made to a death. Drug overdose is involved in many deaths, but it can be challenging to work out whether such a death has been a suicide or an accident.

Homicide by poisoning is rare nowadays, thanks, at least in part, to developments in toxicological analysis that make it easy to detect the most common poisons in human tissues.

Forensic serology is the study of blood and other body fluids. The work requires clinical pathology technicians to type blood that can incriminate or eliminate a suspect. Analysis of other body fluids, like **semen**, can help in the investigation of serious crimes such as rape. Body fluids, including **saliva**, can also be used to extract DNA, the ultimate form of individualizing evidence. The analysis of DNA and the interpretation of results is a specialized task, even though much of the instrumentation is automated these days. DNA technicians are expected to have training in molecular biology techniques.

DNA analysis is rapidly becoming the "gold standard" for identifying an individual. Dental records can be very useful in the **identification** of skeletal remains, one of the main uses of forensic odontology, or the application of dentistry to the investigation of crime. The other major application of forensic odontology is the analysis of bite marks left behind at the scene of a crime. Dental technicians may create casts of impressions of bite evidence; the interpretation of dental evidence is a specialist task involving comparison between dental records or impressions and the evidence. Even if only a few teeth are available with a set of human remains or if a bite mark is incomplete, the forensic odontologist can still offer an opinion as to the age and habits of that person, which can be set into context with other identifying information.

Like teeth, bones are enduring and their forensic analysis can often be used to make an identification. Forensic anthropology is the study of human skeletal remains to estimate, first of all, the age, sex, and race of the deceased. The anthropologist may also use toxicological and DNA analysis if these can be obtained from the remains. If a **skull** is available, identification can sometimes be made by comparing it with x rays obtained antemortem (before death). The forensic anthropologist needs a depth of knowledge to be able to estimate the age of bones (they may be so old as to be of little forensic significance), and whether they are indeed human.

The forensic pathologist deals with a "fresh" body, the anthropologist with bones. The study of the in-between stage, the decomposing body, is the realm of the forensic taphonomist. A human body undergoes specific changes after death. The rate of these changes, however, depends very much on the individual and the environment. Evaluation of these changes may help establish the all-important **time of death**.

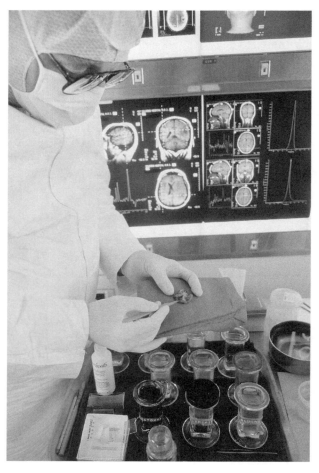

A pathologist prepares a microscope slide from a tumor that was removed in a brain biopsy. © ROGER RESSMEYER/CORBIS

Any pathologist working in the above disciplines may be called in as an expert witness to help resolve cases where the facts are unclear or in need of some explanation. A pathologist can help with the difficult question of **cause of death** when a body is recovered from water or how long it may have been in a shallow grave.

Being an expert witness is not a profession in its own right and a pathologist who carries out this work does not need to have special legal qualification. The expert witness is created and recognized as such by the judge and the court; he or she will usually have undergone training in court procedures so they can present their evidence to the best of their ability to help the judge and jury come to their decision.

Either the prosecution or the defense may call in a forensic pathologist as an expert witness. He or she is expected to look at the evidence relevant to their discipline, whether it is skeletal remains or analyses of body fluids, and put it in the context of the whole

case. They will produce a report that can be taken up to the witness stand. First of all, the party who engaged the expert witness will ask questions that prove their identity, qualifications, experience, and background to the court. Then they will ask questions that generally take the court through the expert witness's report.

The expert witness can expect to be cross-examined by the opposing counsel who will ask questions as to the reliability of the evidence and the expert's conclusions. Many pathologists are experts in their subject, but it takes special skill and training to defend one's findings in public while still remaining objective and impartial.

The expert witness is the only one in court who is allowed to give opinion as well as facts. This is because the court has confidence in the facts and knowledge on which the opinion is based. Thus, the forensic anthropologist is allowed to say, for example, "I believe these bones are only about two years old and the cause of death was probably a blow to the head."

SEE ALSO Expert witnesses; Forensic science.

Pattern evidence

Pattern **evidence** is defined as any forensic evidence that can be read and analyzed from a specific type of pattern left by the physical contact between different people (such as victim and assailant), persons and objects (such as victim and automobile), and different objects (such as automobile and tree). These types of pattern evidence can result in various designs such as depositions, imprints, recesses, residues, and striped markings. When injuries result on the victim's body, so-called patterned injuries can oftentimes identify the features of the assailant or object and describe the specific characteristics of injuries. For example, burns result when an assailant shoves a victim into a container of hot water. Burns that are characterized as symmetrical (balanced) and bilateral (appearing on both sides) provide a reasonable initial indication that they were intentional.

Specific examples of sources that often result in pattern evidence include **blood** splatters (such as from a bullet's exit wound), fire burns (such as from **accelerant** residue), footwear, furniture positions (such as what results after a fight between victim and assailant), projectile trajectories (such as a bullet's path from an assailant's gun, through a victim, and into an object), shattered **glass** fractures (such as from vehicle windshields), and tire and skid marks.

Forensic experts examine all forms of pattern evidence in order to eliminate any possible accidental and natural causes for the pattern. For example, fires from flammable liquids often leave behind certain residue patterns. Such fires will normally burn downward unless specifically forced to burn upward. Specifically, accelerants poured from a container will often flow to the lowest spot and accumulate in a pool. After being ignited, the liquid will generally scorch the floor in a puddle configuration. Well-defined boundary lines between the burned and unburned areas will often be obvious to the investigator. In addition, flammable liquids will frequently penetrate cracks and other similar holes, and flow beneath surfaces. The ignited liquid may burn beneath the surface where it was first poured. Areas around such holes will often burn more rapidly when liquid concentrates in those places. All such actions must be considered by the forensic expert.

Pattern evidence, which is for the most part permanent in nature, is often compared to transient evidence, which is evidence that is temporary in nature. Examples of transient evidence that can easily change or disappear include odors, temperatures, and vapors. Forensic scientists, when specializing in pattern evidence, use many different types of instruments and methods to determine the chemical and physical characteristics of pattern evidence. Such professionals also perform investigations of crime scenes to collect and preserve pattern evidence in order to reconstruct relevant events through the analysis of such patterns.

SEE ALSO Ballistics; Blood spatter; Flame analysis; Gunshot residue; Shoeprints; Tire tracks.

PCR (polymerase chain reaction)

PCR, or polymerase chain reaction, is a biochemical technique that can generate millions of copies of a template strand of **DNA**. The technique relies on the same enzymes that cells use to replicate DNA, however it is performed in a simple test tube using controlled cycles of heating and cooling. PCR has revolutionized the field of biotechnology, making it quick and inexpensive to replicate, or amplify, specific segments of DNA.

PCR was conceptualized by molecular biologist **Kary Mullis** in 1983. While driving the highway between San Francisco and Mendocino, California, Mullis realized that very simple molecules could be used to replicate DNA in vitro, given the proper conditions. Prior to PCR, molecular biologists relied on bacteria to make copies of DNA. This process was both slow and subject to inaccuracies. After developing a conceptual model for PCR, Mullis refined the technique over the next seven years while working for Cetus Corporation in Emoryville, California. In 1993, Mullis was awarded half of the Nobel Prize in Chemistry for his work.

The DNA molecule is a double helix, which means that it consists of two long strands of smaller molecules. These long strands twist around each other. Each strand is made up of a sequence of four different smaller molecules called nucleotides. The four nucleotides are adenine (A), guanine (G), cytosine (C), and thymine (T). Each nucleotide always associates itself with a complementary nucleotide so that if adenine is on one of the strands, thymine is found across from it on the other strand. Similarly, if cytosine is on one strand, guanine is found across from it on the other strand.

Each strand of DNA has an orientation. One end of the molecule is known as the $5'$ (or 5 prime) end and the other is called the $3'$ (or 3 prime) end. This is because each nucleotide contains a $5'$-phosphate on one side and $3'$hydroxyl on the other side. The nucleotides are linked together by a reaction between the phosphate and the hydroxyl. The nucleotide on one end of the strand has an unconnected phosphate, the $5'$ end, and the nucleotide on the other end has an unconnected hydroxyl, the $3'$ end. The two strands of DNA are oriented in opposite directions so that the $5'$ end of one strand matches the $3'$ end of the other.

In order to make copies of DNA, the two strands are first separated from each other. Then a short molecule called a primer attaches itself to a location toward the $5'$ end of the part of the DNA to be replicated on one of the strands. A primer is usually about 20 nucleotides long. Next, a special enzyme called DNA polymerase attaches itself to primer. This enzyme has the unique ability to add nucleotides to a growing DNA molecule. DNA polymerase uses the original strand of DNA as a template as it, in effect, slides along the original strand of DNA and pieces together a strand of complementary nucleotides. If, for example, the original strand contains the sequence CGGTA, then the DNA polymerase builds a strand with a sequence GCCAT. Because of the complementary nature of the nucleotides that make up DNA, after the original strands are separated and copied by DNA polymerase, the result is two copies identical to the double-stranded original. DNA polymerase moves along the DNA in the 5′ to the 3′ direction only.

The primer is extremely important to DNA replication because DNA polymerase can only add nucleotides to a growing chain, it cannot begin a new molecule. In cells, the primer is often a piece of RNA that binds to the DNA on the 5′ end of a **gene**. In biotechnological applications, primers are synthesized so that specific portions of DNA are reproduced. In order to copy both strands of DNA for a specific gene, two primers are needed, one for each strand. These two primers are not simple complements of each other because, due to the orientation of the two strands, the two primers will attach to DNA on opposite sides of the gene.

The biochemicals required for PCR are: at least one strand of the target DNA; two primers, one for each strand of the DNA; the enzyme DNA polymerase; and the four nucleotides found in DNA, adenine, guanine, cytosine, and thymine. These molecules are all combined in an instrument that carefully controls the heat of the mixture.

The steps required for PCR are fundamentally simple. First the strands of DNA are separated from each other by heating them to about 90°C (194°F) for roughly 30 seconds. At this high temperature, DNA is denatured and does not form a double strand. As a result, the primers are unable to bind to the target DNA. In the second step, the mixture is cooled to about 55°C (131°F), a temperature at which the DNA molecule takes on its double-stranded conformation. During this step, the primers bind to each of the target DNA strands on the 5′ side of the region to be copied. An excess of primer is added to the mixture to ensure that the primers anneal to the target DNA strands rather than the target DNA strands reattaching to each other. This second step takes about 20 seconds. Finally, the temperature is raised to about 75°C (167°F), which is the temperature that the DNA polymerase most commonly used in PCR is most effective. The DNA polymerase then extends the complementary strand of DNA, which takes about a minute. The result, after the first cycle, is two complete copies of the target DNA.

The cycle is then repeated multiple times. The second time it is repeated, both the original target DNA and the newly synthesized strands are copied; the result is four complete copies of the target DNA. The third time the cycle is repeated, eight copies result and so on. Usually between 20 and 30 cycles

are completed, taking just a few hours, and the result is between one million and one billion copies of the original target piece of DNA.

The DNA polymerase usually used in PCR is known as *Taq* polymerase, because it is derived from the bacterium *Thermus aquaticus*. This bacterium is thermophyllic, meaning that it lives in locations with very high ambient temperatures, such as hot springs. In particular, the DNA polymerase of *T. aquaticus* is thermally stable at temperatures as high as 95°C (203°F), and so the high heating required to separate the double strands of DNA has no effect on the molecule. In addition, at higher temperatures, the chance of a primer binding to non-target DNA decreases. Because the *Taq* polymerase operates optimally at 72°C (161°F), the specificity of the PCR reaction is high and the DNA copied by the process is homogeneous.

Because PCR can be used to generate a large number of copies of very small amounts of DNA in very little time, it has quickly become an extremely useful and popular technology. Only ten years after it was developed, PCR had been referenced in more than 7,000 scientific publications. The applications of PCR are so great that it has become a standard research tool.

In forensics, the field of DNA fingerprinting relies on PCR. A very small sample of **blood**, **semen**, hair root, or tissue can be used to identify a person using PCR on the DNA from the nucleus of cells. The Federal Bureau of Investigation houses a genetic database called **CODIS** (Combined DNA Index System) that holds genetic information on convicted criminals and missing persons. A sensitive technique that can be used to establish maternal relationships between people is called **mitochondrial DNA analysis**, which relies on PCR. Biological material that is degraded or very old or tissues that do not contain nuclei, such as hair shafts and bones, are often more likely to yield information using this technique instead of DNA fingerprinting.

PCR is also important in answering basic scientific questions. In the field of evolutionary biology, PCR has been used to establish relationships among species. In anthropology, it has used to understand ancient **human migration patterns**. In **archaeology**, it has been used to help identify ancient human remains. Paleontologists have used PCR to amplify DNA from extinct insects preserved in amber for 20 million years. The Human Genome Project, which had a goal of determining the sequence of the 3 billion base pairs in the human genome, relied heavily on PCR. The genes responsible for a variety of human diseases have been identified using PCR. For example, a PCR technique called multiplex PCR identifies a mutation in a gene in boys suffering from Duchenne muscular dystrophy. PCR can also be used to search for DNA from foreign organisms such as viruses or bacteria. For instance, the presence of the HIV virus that causes AIDS can be determined using PCR on blood cells.

SEE ALSO DNA banks for endangered animals; DNA databanks; DNA fingerprint; DNA sequences, unique; Electrophoresis; Hair analysis; Mitochondrial DNA typing; RFLP (restriction fragment length polymorphism); STR (short tandem repeat) analysis; Y chromosome analysis.

Pentagon, 2001 attack upon SEE
September 11, 2001, terrorist attacks (forensic investigations of)

Performance-enhancing drugs

The use of performance-enhancing drugs in athletics began to accelerate in the 1960s. Then, athletes from East Germany received drugs as part of a state-sanctioned program designed to ensure Olympic dominance. In 1988, such drug use became infamous when Canadian sprinter Ben Johnson was stripped of his Olympic 100-meter gold medal (and then world record time) following the detection of a metabolic remnant of an anabolic steroid in his urine.

Aside from any moral or ethical considerations of this behavior, the use of performance-enhancing drugs can pose health dangers. Recognizing these dangers, many professional and amateur sporting organizations are increasingly imposing their own standards for performance enhancement and monitoring participants to try to ensure athletic performance is determined by natural talent and training excellence.

In the realm of Olympic sports, the World Anti-Doping Agency, which is headquartered in Montreal, Canada, is responsible for actively discouraging the use of illegal performance-enhancing drugs. A list of prohibited drugs is maintained and updated annually.

Part of the agency's efforts also involves the accreditation of analysis laboratories for the examination of samples. The obtaining and analysis of urine and other samples is essentially a forensic process. The investigators delve back in time to determine what chemical methods might have been used to enhance performance.

Performance-enhancing drugs may exert their effects in different ways. Some, like anabolic steroids, increase the mass and the strength of muscles. Bones can also be strengthened. Other drugs cause more oxygen to be delivered to muscles, which allows the muscles to perform at an intensity that could not otherwise be possible. Still other drugs can blunt pain, stimulate the production of chemicals that spur the body to greater levels of athletic activity, or reduce weight. Some drugs are even taken just to mask the presence of a performance-enhancing drug.

A number of drugs can be used to enhance the amount and strength of muscles. This list includes anabolic steroids, beta-2-agonists, human chorionic gonadotrophin, luteinizing hormone, human growth hormone, insulin-like growth factor, and insulin.

A steroid is derived from cholesterol. Anabolic steroids, which build muscle and bone by stimulating protein production from muscle and bone cells, derive their name from the constructive process of anabolism (the opposite breakdown process is called catabolism).

Anabolic steroids include testosterone, a hormone that predominates in men, and other steroids structurally similar to testosterone. As a result, these steroids, in addition to increasing the intensity and length of athletic training that muscles and bones can tolerate, enhance male reproductive and secondary sexual characteristics including development of testicles, body hair growth, and thickening of the vocal cords (females taking anabolic steroids can thus experience a deepening of their voices).

Besides testosterone, other examples of anabolic steroids include dihydrotestosterone, androstenedione (commonly known as Andro, which reputedly was taken by baseball star Mark McGuire), dehydroepiandrosterone, clostebol, and nandrolone.

The gains in athletic performance bestowed by anabolic steroids come with a price. Mood swings and feelings of depression and aggression (commonly known as "roid rage") can occur, as can liver damage and jaundice. Males can become infertile and experience breast growth, while females can develop facial and body hair and an altered or completely suppressed menstrual cycle.

Beta-2 adrenergic agonists can be life saving to an asthmatic. When inhaled, they mimic the action of epinephrine and norepinephrine, which are secreted by sympathetic nerves, and cause airway muscles to relax, making breathing easier. However, when injected into the bloodstream, the agonists can help build muscle mass and stimulate the utilization of fat. The result is a leaner and stronger athlete, but an athlete who can be prone to nausea, muscle cramps, and even an irregular heartbeat. Examples of beta-2 adrenergic agonists include clenbuterol, tertbutaline, salbutamol, fenoterol, and bambuterol.

Human chorionic gonadotrophin (HCG) is produced naturally by a developing fetus. Indeed, its detection is the basis of home pregnancy tests. HCG functions to stimulate the development of male and female sex steroids. This is exploited as a muscle-boosting performance enhancer in male athletes via the increased production of testosterone.

Luteinizing hormone (LH) is produced by the pituitary gland, which is located at the base of the brain. Normally, the peptide hormone regulates the level of testosterone in males and the ovulation-signaling estrogen in females. In men, excess LH or synthetic forms of LH, such as tamoxifen, boosts levels of testosterone and so produces the increased muscle mass.

Human growth hormone (HGH) is another natural hormone that is produced by the pituitary gland. Normally, the hormone functions to promote growth in childhood and adolescence. But, when exploited as an athletic performance enhancer, the hormone builds muscle, strengthens bone, and stimulates the destruction of fat. Side effects of deliberate misuse include: abnormal enlargement of the hands, feet, and face (acromegaly); enlarged heart, kidneys, tongue, and liver; and heart malfunction.

Both LH and HGH function to promote increased muscle mass. The enhanced athletic performance that can result comes at a potentially lethal price of low blood sugar (hypoglycemia).

Muscles need a supply of oxygen to function. Supplying more oxygen increases the capacity of the muscles to perform. Protein hormones, artificial oxygen carriers, and blood doping (the addition of whole blood into an athlete) are all illicit means of increasing the oxygen content in tissues.

A protein hormone called erythropoietin (EPO) is naturally produced and secreted by the kidneys when oxygen levels are low. The hormone stimulates bone marrow cells to manufacture red blood cells, which function to bind oxygen and ferry the molecule to tissues throughout the body.

By boosting the oxygen levels in the body's tissues, EPO can be a performance enhancer for athletes engaged in sports that require endurance, as opposed to the raw power of an activity like power lifting. Thus, marathon runners, cyclists, and cross-country skiers have all been accused of injecting EPO. Indeed, American cyclist Lance Armstrong, who has won the Tour de France six times in succession through 2004, has long been under a cloud of suspicion regarding EPO use, despite his repeated and vehement denials and lack of evidence of impropriety.

While EPO does boost oxygen levels by up to 10%, the increased number of red blood cells can thicken the blood. The blood, honey-like in consistency, does not flow as well through blood vessels, which causes the heart to work harder. The risk of a stroke or heart attack is increased.

Artificial oxygen carriers are synthetic compounds that mimic the oxygen-binding behavior of **hemoglobin** (the active component of the oxygen-binding red blood cell). They were initially conceived and made to help assist in conditions of clinical distress, such as breathing difficulties experienced by premature infants or those whose lungs have been damaged. However, the compounds have been exploited in the quest for greater athletic excellence.

The athletic benefits of artificial oxygen carriers are not clear. Moreover, this dubious benefit increases the risk of kidney damage, cardiovascular difficulties, and problems with the **immune system**.

Blood doping, by transfusing whole blood to an athlete, increases the amount of blood in the body (or more precisely the number of oxygen-binding red blood cells) and the overall oxygen carrying capacity is increased. This process occurs naturally when athletes train at higher altitudes, where the oxygen content in the air is less than at sea-level.

While altitude training is an ethically acceptable training practice, deliberate infusion of blood is not. Furthermore, injection of blood can cause infections and the increased amount of blood can cause similar problems as EPO. As well, if the infused blood is from someone else, there is a risk of acquiring a blood related infection such as acquired immunodeficiency syndrome or hepatitis.

Injury is a natural part of training and competition. A natural part of injury is pain; the signal to cease whatever is causing the damage. Many injuries heal with time and therapy. But, pressure to continue the athletic activity can drive an athlete to dull the pain rather than to stop training.

Narcotics including morphine, methadone, and heroin are effective at masking pain. They are, however, very addictive and can disrupt the mental focus that can be vital to peak athletic performance.

Adrenocorticotrophic hormone (ACTH) is produced by the pituitary gland. Normally, ACTH stimulates the production of other hormones by an organ called the adrenal cortex. The hormones reduce inflammation and so can be used illicitly to ease the trauma of injured muscles. However, immediate side effects include stomach irritation and ulcers. In the longer term, bones and muscles can become weaker.

Stimulants such as caffeine (the wake-up ingredient of coffee), cocaine, and **amphetamines** increase the beating of the heart, lung activity, and even brain activity. For an athlete, these physiological responses are manifest as increased alertness, decreased fatigue, and promotion of an aggressive, competitive attitude. Side effects include an irregular heartbeat and high blood pressure.

Relaxants such as alcohol and marijuana decrease brain and nervous system activity. They can ease competition jitters. However, impaired focus and coordination can undermine athletic performance.

Beta-blockers are another illicitly used relaxant. They slow down the heartbeat, which can help lessen the movement of the hands and arms that occurs in concert with pumping of blood by the heart. Thus, they can be used by athletes competing in archery or shooting competitions, where steady hands can be a key to the first-place podium.

Paradoxically, athletes may need to take drugs to hide the use of other **illicit drugs**. One example is epitestosterone. The compound is a natural form of testosterone. Testing for elevated levels of testosterone rely on the comparison of the levels of testosterone and epitestosterone. By artificially increasing the levels of the latter, the presence of increased testosterone can be masked.

The tendency of blood to thicken because of the administration of agent like EPO can be masked by diluting the blood with additional fluid. This process is called plasma expansion.

Organizations such as the World Anti-Doping Agency are actively engaged in testing samples obtained from athletes during training and following competition.

Urine is most often tested. Illicit chemicals can be detected using the technique of gas chromatograph/mass spectrometry, where individual components can be separated from one another based on their different rates of movement through a medium.

Compounds including HCG, LH, and ACTH stimulate the production of antibodies by the body's immune system. These antibodies are used to detect the presence of the compounds in urine samples.

Testing procedures are constantly being refined. Some drugs such as EPO remain difficult to detect. A San Francisco a company called BALCO was exposed in 2004 as the source of a variety of performance-enhancing drugs for athletes, including New York Yankees star Jason Giambi, who has admitted his steroid use. A forensic investigation of BALCO uncovered evidence that existing drugs were being chemically modified to be undetectable.

SEE ALSO Illicit drugs; Saliva; Souvenirs from athletic events; Sports testing.

PERK (physical evidence recovery kit)

The physical evidence recovery kit (PERK) is an assembled set of necessary materials, instructions, and forms for the purpose of collecting and protecting the physical **evidence** of a sexual assault investigation whenever the victim decides to initiate criminal charges against the alleged assailant. Under most circumstances, the only requirements with regard to using the PERK is that the assault must have taken place within 72 hours of the medical examination and the assailant's **semen** must be collected from the victim within 24 hours of the sexual assault.

The PERK, also called a sexual assault determination kit, assists the attending doctor and nurse in collecting specimens for evidential analysis by forensic experts. In many cases, a Sexual Assault Nurse Examiner (SANE nurse) or Forensic Nurse Examiner (FNE nurse) will perform the collection of evidence through the use of the PERK, along with documenting any physical damage on the victim. The kit may be used at the hospital or at the crime scene by a qualified criminal investigation team.

In addition to the medical examination, the victim will be asked about details of the assault to be included within the PERK. To document all aspects of the sexual attack, a variety of information will be recorded, such as the type of assault, type of sexual penetration, location of the attack, and past medical history of the victim, along with her past and present health conditions, date of last menstrual period, history of contraceptive use, date of most recent consensual sexual activity, and other such personal information.

In order to obtain all relevant materials and information in the most accurate, consistent, and methodical way possible, the PERK is a very convenient way to collect and document the forensic evidence. Usually within a container made of cardboard or other similar material, the PERK generally contains (but is not limited to) the following items: instructions for the medical examination; one procedural checklist; one report form; one patient consent form; one patient information form; tape for sealing evidence; one label for the outside container; one roll of wrapping material such as cellophane tape; numerous paper envelopes for hair samples (from the pubic area, head, chest, face, and other body areas), **saliva**, **blood**, foreign materials, and other necessary specimens; one orange stick for fingernail undersurface scrapings; one blood vacuum tube; two standard-sized combs; one pre-sharpened pencil; three sets of prepackaged swabs and smear (usually for collecting vaginal, rectal, and oral smear samples); three frosted-end microscope slides; and three rectangular cardboard tubes.

SEE ALSO Privacy, legal and ethical issues; Rape kit; Semen and sperm.

Perspective analysis

As used in crime scene analysis, **photography**, and **photogrammetry**, perspective analysis involves the use of measurement techniques to determine the relative (and exact) sizes of objects within a photograph, digital image, or video image. Essentially, the process involves measurement of the distance between the camera and target item in the image of a known size, and utilizing those two measurements to calculate the size of other objects in the image.

At a crime scene, there are several important perspective aspects or views for photographic documentation. First, the entire scene is captured from a distance (a known or marked distance) in order to gain an overview of the entire scene before it is disrupted. Next, images are taken from midrange in order to estimate the size, or to document the relationships, of items. Finally, close range photographs are taken of individual items of **evidence**. For evidence items, one-to-one photography is used when possible. This technique involves taking actual size photographs of specific evidentiary items, and using them to make direct comparisons with the suspect.

This technique is most often employed with fingerprints, bare footprints, and shoe prints.

In its most rudimentary form, perspective analysis can be used when examining a photograph containing an object of known size by measuring the image of the known object and developing a ratio of the image size to the sizes of other objects in the photograph. This is a cruder and less accurate form of perspective analysis than that involving the direct use of a scale, or the use of camera distance measurement techniques.

Several pieces of equipment are essential for accurate perspective analysis and object measurement: a ruler or scale, a tripod, and a level, in addition to a multilensed camera (35 mm, digital, instant, video, and other **cameras** are often utilized at crime scenes). When a ruler or scale is used for actual item measurement, the object should first be photographed alone, and then photographed again with the ruler lying in exactly the same plane as the object, and the camera situated in a plane parallel to both. It is also essential to measure the distance from the focal area of the camera to the object being photographed, in order to calculate the size of the objects being photographed.

The ruler or scale used for perspective measurement must be at least as precise as the camera doing the scene recording. The same scale used at the scene should be used to measure with when printing the photographs to a particular magnification. All rulers and scales should be individually marked so as to be readily identified both in the photographs and later during legal proceedings (court testimony or evidentiary presentation).

SEE ALSO Architecture and structural analysis; Automobile accidents; Bullet track; Computer modeling; Crime scene reconstruction; Photogrammetry.

Peruvian Ice Maiden

The Peruvian Ice Maiden is a 500-year-old mummy that was discovered in the Peruvian Andes in 1995. She is the first mummy found frozen, rather than dried, and as a result her **DNA** is very well preserved. **Mitochondrial DNA analysis** demonstrated that the mummy shares ancestry with Native Americans and with the Ngobe people of Panama.

In 1990, Nevado Sabancaya, a volcano in the Peruvian Andes, began erupting. The heat of its

The frozen mummy known as the "Ice Princess," the first frozen Incan mummy ever found, is displayed in Arequipa, Peru, in this Oct. 26, 1997, photo. **AP/WIDE WORLD PHOTOS. REPRODUCED BY PERMISSION.**

eruption, as well as the hot ash that spewed from it cleared a layer of snow pack from the mountains in the area, including Mount Ampato. Five years later, in September 1995, anthropologist Johan Reinhard and his climbing partner Miguel Zarate climbed Mount Ampato to get a look at the active volcano nearby.

As they neared the summit, they spotted some bright feathers in the snow. Reinhard recognized the feathers as part of an Inca headdress of a ceremonial statue. It was made from a spondylous shell, the shell of an oyster that was sacred to the Incas, and it was preserved perfectly, with its textile clothing in excellent condition. The find had likely been uncovered by the melting of snow during the volcanic eruptions. Nearby, the two explorers noticed stones that appeared to be from an Inca ceremonial platform. As they looked down a ravine near the platform, they spotted a cloth bundle, which was frozen in place.

When Zarate hiked down the ravine to recover the bundle, he found a frozen mummy. The mummy was in the fetal position wrapped in colorful textiles made of alpaca (llama) wool. Pottery shards, bones from llamas and corn kernels surrounded her. The mummy was from a teenage girl, probably between 12 and 14 years old. Reinhard believed that Inca priests had sacrificed her, probably as part of a ritual to the gods they believed were part of the mountain. Reinhard recognized that mummy was a major archaeological find because she was the first frozen female mummy discovered in the Andes. She was later determined to be about 500 years old.

Reinhard and Zarate documented the site with photographs and collected the artifacts associated with the mummy. They knew that either exposure to sun and ash would damage the mummy or looters would destroy her remains and therefore they decided to take her from the mountain so she could be preserved. They carried the body down from the mountain and brought her to Universidad Catolica de Santa Maria in Arequipa, where refrigeration was arranged.

In 1996, the mummy was brought to the United States and several types of forensic techniques were performed to learn more about the girl's life, her last hours and about the people who may have descended from the Incas. Because a traditional **autopsy** would destroy the mummy, less invasive techniques were used. At Johns Hopkins Hospital in Baltimore, Maryland, computerized tomography (CT)—which is similar to a 3-dimensional x ray—was performed in order to determine the girl's bone structure and condition. Researchers at Johns Hopkins also removed small samples from the girl's heart and stomach using thin needles.

Radiologists determined that the mummy's bones were in good condition. She also had plenty of muscle mass and healthy teeth. She showed no evidence of disease or nutritional deficiency. This indicates that the girl was in excellent health at the time of her death. The girl's **skull** shows evidence of a violent blow. There was a fracture above the right eye and damage to the eye socket. The girl's brain was displaced to one side. These findings suggest that the girl was killed by being hit on the side of the head with a club, fracturing her skull. Subsequent bleeding filled the skull and pushed the brain to one side.

A sample of the contents of the girl's stomach contained only vegetable material. No meat was present. Because it probably took the girl several weeks to freeze, the fact that any material was found in her stomach suggests she had a full stomach when she died.

The tissue samples were sent to the Institute for Genomic Research in Rockville, Maryland. The mitochondrial DNA in the sample was copied using **PCR (polymerase chain reaction)**. In old tissues or tissues that might be degraded, mitochondrial DNA is often easier to study than nuclear DNA because cells contain many more copies of mitochondrial DNA than nuclear DNA. The mitochondrial DNA extracted from the Ice Maiden was of excellent quality, probably because she had been frozen rather than "dried" as is common in most **mummies**.

Mitochondrial DNA can be divided into two major regions. The first is a region that codes for the genes that make the molecular products used by mitochondria, which are sub-cellular organelles. The other region is a non-coding region and it does not contain any genes. Within the non-coding region, two regions on mitochondrial DNA have very high rates of mutation and are therefore optimal for studying differences among people. The two regions are called HV1 and HV2 (hypervariable region 1 and hypervariable region 2).

Comparisons of the sequence of the Ice Maiden's mitochondrial DNA from HV1 showed four differ-

ences from a reference sequence. Searching through databases of sequences of HV1, researchers found that these four differences exactly matched those differences found in a group of Native Americans. These people belong to a group called Haplotype A and they are one of the four founding lineages of Native Americans.

The HV2 sequence of mitochondrial DNA from the Ice Maiden varied in eight nucleotides from a reference sequence. These variations did not match any sequences found in databases of HV2 sequences. The closest match agreed in six of the eight nucleotide positions and was from a group of people called the Ngobe who live in Panama. Because of its unusual sequence, the Ice Maiden's mitochondrial DNA from the HV2 region is of great value for learning more about ancient people.

SEE ALSO Mitochondrial DNA typing.

Petechial hemorrhage

A petechial hemorrhage is a tiny pinpoint red mark that is an important sign of asphyxia caused by some external means of obstructing the airways. They are sometimes also called petechiae. Their presence often indicates a death by manual strangulation, hanging, or smothering. The hemorrhages occur when blood leaks from the tiny capillaries in the eyes, which can rupture due to increased pressure on the veins in the head when the airways are obstructed. If petechial hemorrhages and facial congestion are present, it is a strong indication of asphyxia by strangulation as the **cause of death**.

The forensic pathologist usually needs a very good light source and maybe even a magnifying glass to detect petechial hemorrhages. They range in size from the size of a speck of dust to around two millimeters and may occur in distinct groups. Often they are seen in the conjunctiva of the eyes and also on the eyelids, especially after hanging. They may also be found elsewhere on the skin of the head and face, such as in the mucous membrane inside the lips and around or behind the ears. When found in a case of suspect hanging, the presence of petechial hemorrhages strongly suggests the victim was hung when still alive. This helps distinguish hangings staged to make a **murder** look like a suicidal act.

Petechial hemorrhages on the face are also found in other conditions such as cardiac arrest. Internal examination may reveal petechiae on the surfaces of the lungs and heart in cases of death by heat stroke and sudden infant death syndrome (SIDS, or crib death). In the latter circumstances, they are not considered a cause of the child having been smothered or otherwise asphyxiated. The forensic pathologist will also look out for petechiae in cases of sexual assault. Petechial hemorrhage may also occur postmortem as the capillaries start to break down, but these lesions tend to be rather bigger than pinpoint size and may blur into one another rather than occurring as distinct groups. As ever, the pathologist must be aware of all the circumstances surrounding the death when interpreting these findings.

SEE ALSO Asphyxiation (signs of); Hanging (signs of).

Photo alteration

A common sight at the scene of a forensic investigation is one or more photographers. Recording the details of the scene prior to the removal of **evidence** is an essential step to the subsequent reconstruction of the course of events. Whether using traditional photographic film or the recently developed digital photographic capability, photographs can be manipulated or altered to enhance the information.

However, as a caveat, the ability to add or remove details digitally from photographs requires the authentication of the photographic file to ensure that the photographs produced of a crime or accident scene, in fact, represent reality.

The camera was invented in 1839. By the next decade, photographers had already begun to manipulate photographic images. Initially, the manipulation was part of the exploration of the artistic potential of the new medium. Soon, the informational power of the photograph became recognized.

The ability to produce photographs that reveal more detail than do traditional photographs, especially at longer distances or using small **cameras**, has increased the information that can be gathered.

With new technology, the ability to alter a photographic image is easier than ever before. For example, in a traditional photograph, the difference in skin tone between a face and the neck or shadows that point in different directions can be clues that an image has been manipulated. However, these visual discrepancies can be eliminated in the digital image. Thus, the ability to generate false or misleading information has become routine.

In the days before digital technology, photo alteration was accomplished in the darkroom during the development and printing of the photograph. In a technique called dodging, the light shining through the photographic negative onto light-sensitive paper was obscured. Because less light strikes the paper, that region appears lighter in the developed image. In contrast, the technique of burning allows an increased amount of light to strike the photographic paper. The result of burning is to make the region appear darker in the print.

The traditional techniques of dodging and burning are used to enhance or disguise aspects of the photo. As well, details can be excluded from an image by the use of cropping, where only the selected portion of the image is printed. Photographs can also be enlarged to selectively print portions of the image. Enlarging cannot be done indefinitely, however, since the eventual inability to separate the informational components of the image from one another produces a blurry picture.

The coming of digital **photography** revolutionized the ability to alter photographs. The laborious darkroom manipulations of preceding times could be accomplished by a few commands in specialized photographic software.

In traditional photography, the reflected light from the subject enters the camera through the lens and is focused onto the surface of a light-sensitive emulsion. The emulsion records the image, which can be beamed onto light-sensitive photographic paper. The paper is subsequently treated with chemicals to make the image appear. It is during this latter printing process that the alteration of the photograph can be accomplished.

In digital photography, the reflected light that enters the camera is focused onto a chip that is known as a charged coupling device (CCD). The surface of the CCD contains an array of light-sensitive photo diodes. Each diode represents a pixel (the basic unit of programmable color in a computer image). Each photo diode is hooked up to a transistor, which sends an electrical signal (whose voltage corresponds to the light intensity that registered on the photo diode) to another chip. The second chip converts the electrical signal to digital information—1s and 0s—that can be interpreted by computerized photo manipulation software programs.

Colors are assigned a code sequence between 0 and 255, 0 is black and 255 reveals the most intense shade of red possible by the software. These coded assignments are in turn converted to sequences of 0s and 1s. Black, for example, is 00000000, while the most intense red is 11111111. Shades in between are mixtures of the eight-digit sequence of 0s and 1s.

Digital photo manipulation involves the alteration or elimination of the digital 1s and 0s. Changing an eight-digit sequence is trivial. When the digital information is reconstructed into an electronic image, the result can be an altered color.

In addition to color change, a myriad of effects are possible, including color enhancement, elimination of regions of the image, increased contrast, correction of a blurred image, and the merging of other images with the original image (a photographic version of the "cut and paste" operations in word processing). Images of **missing children** or crime victims also can be digitally manipulated to create an aged appearance, and have proved useful in identifying victims years later.

As digital photo manipulation software has increased in technical sophistication, and people have become more adept at using the software, the task of detecting manipulated images has become very challenging. Digital photographic manipulation is now so sophisticated that it can sometimes be impossible to discern whether people or objects in a photographic were actually there when the photo was taken. This has spurred efforts, especially in the military and intelligence communities, to establish a system of image verification. In this regard, the United States Air Force Research laboratory in Rome, New York, has developed a technique called digital watermarking. Akin to the watermarking of paper currency to establish authenticity, digital watermarking embeds an encrypted image over the actual photo image. The encrypted image is invisible to the naked eye, but can be detected by specially designed image scanners. The lack of the digital watermark is evidence of a altered image.

SEE ALSO Crime scene investigation; Digital imaging.

Photogrammetry

The American Society for Photogrammetry and Remote Sensing (ASPRS) defines photogrammetry as "the art, science, and technology of obtaining reliable information about physical objects and the environment through the processes of recording, measuring and interpreting photographic images and patterns of electromagnetic radiant energy and other phenomena." In this context, "art" refers to an advanced level of skill that can only be achieved through significant practical experience.

Photogrammetrists are skilled at using photographs to obtain reliable measurements. As used in **forensic science**, photogrammetry involves applying scientific and mathematical techniques to two-dimensional images in order to accurately measure two- or three-dimensional objects or to create three-dimensional models or reconstructions from the two-dimensional images. Photogrammetry is sometimes referred to as remote sensing, because it is used to measure objects without coming into physical contact with them.

Although photogrammetry can encompass far range and aerial image creation, it is most often used in crime scene documentation at close range for either object **identification** or measurement. At crime scenes, it can be used to derive the locations of the perpetrator and victim during the event. It can be scientifically applied, long after the crime, to photographs and other images taken on-scene by forensic investigators in order to extract additional detail such as **blood spatter**, wound patterns, bite marks, and other minute **evidence** from photographs and other images. The extracted information can be used to develop evidence measurements or to create detailed crime scene maps.

During fire and **explosion investigations**, there may be minimal **physical evidence** and poor visibility, but much photographic (or other image) evidence gathered. Photogrammetric digital image processing techniques can produce enhanced images that may be readily viewed and interpreted, often providing important forensic information.

Photogrammetric techniques can be used to make corrections in oddly angled images in order to place objects in the correct planes and at the proper angles for **crime scene reconstruction**, as well as to make virtually unlimited three-dimensional measurements from available crime-scene photographs. This can be done at any time, which is useful for providing answers to new questions, or for allowing more detailed analysis of existing data.

Forensic photogrammetrists utilize specialized **cameras** and/or other **imaging** equipment, targets, measurement devices, and **computer modeling** software for the purposes of crime scene measurement and reconstruction. By so doing, they make it possible to create scaled images, diagrams or three-dimensional models in which there is accurate placement of evidence without necessitating physical contact with any aspect of the original scene.

SEE ALSO Architecture and structural analysis; Biosensor technologies; Bomb (explosion) investigations; Crime scene reconstruction; Fire investigation; Imaging; Photography.

Photographic resolution

Photographic recording of an accident or crime scene, or other venues where a forensic investigation is held, is vitally important. After the scene has been cleaned, photographs preserve the scene in time and allow visual analyses to be done long after the fact. The quality of the photographs is therefore extremely important. This is the reason why forensic **photography** is the domain of a professional photographer, rather than, for example, the investigating officers.

A critical aspect of photographic quality is resolution. The term resolution in the context of photography refers to the degree to which adjacent objects can be distinguished from one another in a photographic image. Obviously, the higher the degree of resolution—which is a function of the acuity of the photographic equipment used, as well as the abilities of the operator—the better the quality of the photograph.

The lower the figure given for the resolution, in metric or English units, the higher the degree of resolution. For example, the first four satellites of the CORONA project, which remained aloft throughout most of the period from June 1959 to December 1963, had a relatively high resolution of 25 feet (7.6 m), meaning that objects smaller than that size were likely to be indistinguishable from one another. Higher still was the resolution of the fifth satellite in the series, KH-4B (September 1967 to May 1972), at 6 feet (1.8 m). Photographs taken by KH-5, a satellite deployed for mapping purposes between February 1961 and August 1964, had a much lower degree of photographic resolution: 460 feet (140 m).

Modern satellite **cameras** such as Landsat, SPOT, and Quickbird **digital imaging** systems send photographic images that show resolutions of 2 feet (0.62 m) for panchromatic images and 7.9 feet (2.4 m) for color images. Quickbird images were used to help identify debris from the space shuttle *Columbia*, when it exploded over Texas in 2003.

SEE ALSO Crime scene investigation; Digital imaging; Geospatial Imagery; GIS; Photo alteration; Photography; Satellites, non-governmental high resolution.

Photography

Photography has many applications in **forensic science**. It is used in the first instance to photograph the crime scene. Then, photographs are taken of individual items of **evidence**, from fingerprints and bloodstains, to wounds on a victim's body both at the scene and during an **autopsy**. Specialized techniques such as microphotography and infrared photography can be extremely useful in particular settings. Forensic photography is a skilled job, for all photographs must be of high enough quality to be admissible as evidence in court.

A crime scene is always photographed as soon as possible, so there is a permanent record of the location in its original condition. This will probably occur after the preliminary survey of the scene when, ideally, nothing will have been touched or moved. Sometimes, however, the priority is to get emergency help for a victim and this may lead to some movement of objects. The photographer will take shots of these items in the place they have been moved to. Returning them to their original position would amount to disturbing the scene, which is bad practice. It is not possible to specify how many photographs will be taken for so much depends on the type and nature of scene. As a general guide, the forensic photographer will err on the side of caution and take too many pictures instead of too few.

Three types of photographs are taken, overall, mid-range, and close-up photographs. Overall photographs will be taken of the exterior and interior of the crime scene. Exterior photographs will show buildings and other major structures, roads, or paths to and from the scene, streets signs, and address numbers. If possible, aerial photographs will be taken because these give the broadest possible view of a crime scene in relation to its surroundings. Interior photographs are taken using the corners of the room as a guide. Overlapping views are taken, to ensure everything is covered. It is also important to take photographs of the common approach path, that is, the agreed route through which investigators enter and leave the scene of the crime. This comprises an access point and a focal point and is chosen so that there will be minimal disturbance of evidence. For instance, investigators would not choose a common approach path involving the perpetrator's possible entry point for fear of contaminating evidence at this location. A body, if there is one, is often the focal point of a common approach path. The photographer will also take shots of any possible routes taken by perpetrators or victims including entry or exit points.

Mid-range photographs will show items of evidence and any bodies in their immediate surroundings. Close-ups will focus on evidence like weapons, victims, footprints, and other evidence. A scale, such as a ruler, will give a guide to the size of the item of evidence. This is important because the photographs will later be enlarged to the appropriate size for comparison work, with **shoeprints**, for instance. Photos with and without this scale are generally taken. An L-shaped ruler that shows the length and breadth of the item is particularly useful. All photos taken must be recorded in a special photo log with the date, time, photographer, film, camera settings, and a brief description of what the photo shows. The settings of the camera must be such as to allow good illumination, filling in shadows with flash where needed. Flash can also be used to enhance detail or patterns. No extraneous objects such as investigators or their equipment should be seen in any of the photographs. The forensic photographer's scene of crime kit typically will include a 35-millimeter camera, normal, wide-angle, and close up lenses, an electronic flash with a cord, color and black-and-white film, scales or rulers, and a tripod. Photography is often supplemented by taking a video of the scene. But the still photographs are essential, because they are of higher resolution than a video film. The aim is to take examination quality photographs which can be studied back in the forensic laboratory in comparison with samples taken from suspects or from reference databases.

When it comes to photographing evidence that could easily be damaged or lost, such as fingerprints, shoeprints, **tire tracks**, and toolmarks, it is important to take the photographs as soon as possible. Fingerprints may need to be made visible, by exposing to **laser** or ultraviolet light, or by applying special powders before they can be photographed at the scene. Similarly, shoeprints may need treatment before they can be visualized, although those in mud or **blood** can usually be captured on film without special preparation. It is important to take photographs of shoeprints at a 90-degree angle to its surface and centered in the camera lens. This avoids distortion in the image and makes comparison with control shoeprints more reliable. Tire track photographs need to be taken both as part of a general scene photograph, so that their location can be precisely determined, and also close up, to determine the pattern detail on the tire so it can be identified. Photographs of toolmarks should at least show the location of this important source of evidence. However, even macrophotography may not reveal enough detail to allow the photographs to be used for laboratory comparison with suspect tools. Each item of evidence is photographed individually before being touched if at all possible, and several shots of each item are taken.

Bloodstains are found in many different locations and patterns at crime scenes. The overall photographs

will show their location and distribution, which may be significant in revealing the relative positions of the victim and perpetrator. Then the photographer takes more shots close up of the individual stains that reveal the detail needed to back up pathological analysis of the injuries inflicted. Bloodstains and **blood spatter** patterns on the victim's body are also photographed.

It is also important to photograph any injuries on living or dead victim. A corpse is always photographed before being moved from the scene of a crime. Full body and close-ups are taken. The place where the victim lay will also be photographed again once the body has been moved and then searched for evidence. If the victim is living, the photographer will take pictures of only the minor injuries at the scene. Serious **knife wounds** or gunshot injuries will generally be photographed at the hospital in the interests of getting the victim medical help as soon as possible. Photography plays an important role in an autopsy, too. The body is photographed both clothed and unclothed. Frontal and profile photographs of the face and body are important, especially if there is a question of **identification**. Each birthmark, tattoo, scar, and any other body mark is also photographed. Photographs are taken at each stage during the autopsy process.

Photography may be an important aid to identification of a body. Photos of the face of a corpse may be simply compared with images or descriptions of missing persons. A forensic anthropologist, who is an expert in human remains, may be able to determine whether two pictures are of the same person by analyzing their bone structure. Even though two pictures may be very different in quality and in their age, similarities or differences in certain elements of bone structure may be apparent. The investigator will superimpose the two pictures, at the same image size, and compare the eyebrow area, nasal openings, and the contours of the chin.

Special illumination techniques are often used to take photographs in particular situations. Photographs taken in infrared light can sometimes help distinguish two types of ink, which look very similar in ordinary light. This may help determine whether writing has been added to an original document. Ultraviolet illumination enhances images of injuries while laser light illumination is valuable in recording fingerprints. There is also a trend towards using digital rather than conventional photography in forensics as well as in other applications. Digital images can be readily enhanced. For instance, if a **fingerprint** appears on an interfering background, such as a bank note, then the background can readily be removed to make the actual evidence clearer. However, it is this very ability to manipulate which makes some courts wary of digital photographic evidence.

Good quality photographs have many uses in the investigation of a crime. They can help investigators carry out a **crime scene reconstruction**, where the sequence of events leading up to and occurring after the actual crime is deduced. Sometimes photographs are used to help witnesses recall more about what they saw. Photographs can be faxed and widely distributed in the media or throughout a neighborhood in the search for missing persons or suspects. Judge and jury may be presented with photographs during a trial to help them understand the nature of a crime. Sometimes a photograph of an item of evidence will even be allowed to stand in for the real thing if the actual item could not be removed from the scene of crime for some reason. Photographic techniques are advancing all the time and it is the task of the forensic photographer to make best use of these to create strong, detailed images of all the evidence pertaining to a particular crime.

SEE ALSO Imaging; Photo alteration; Ultraviolet light analysis.

Physical evidence

A successful crime investigation depends upon the collection and analysis of various kinds of **evidence**. Forensic scientists classify evidence in different ways and have specific ways of dealing with it. One major distinction is between physical and biological evidence. Physical evidence refers to any item that comes from a nonliving origin, while biological evidence always originates from a living being. The most important kinds of physical evidence are fingerprints, tire marks, footprints, **fibers**, paint, and **building materials**. Biological evidence includes bloodstains and **DNA**.

Locard's Exchange Principle dictates that evidence, both physical and biological, is to be found at the scene of a crime because the perpetrator always leaves something behind by having contact with victims and objects there. Similarly, he or she will often take something away with them, which can be found on a search of their person, their garment, a vehicle, or their premises. Such evidence is often found in minute quantities and known as **trace evidence**. One important source of physical trace evidence is textile fibers, which usually comes from clothing or furniture involved in the crime. It may either be left

behind by the perpetrator or picked up from the victim. Typically, trace evidence is invisible to the naked eye and is collected by brushing or vacuuming a suspect surface. Once collected and back in the laboratory, microscopic techniques will often be used in its examination and analysis as, for example, in the case of paint fragments or textile fibers.

Impression marks are another important kind of physical evidence. When an item like a shoe or a tire comes into contact with a soft surface, it leaves behind a pattern showing some or all of its surface characteristics, known as an impression. The collection and analysis of **impression evidence** found at the scene of a crime can often be very important to an investigation.

The collection of objects, marks and impressions that make up the physical evidence of a crime is a specialized task. The general principles of preserving physical evidence and assuring a secure **chain of custody** apply whatever the crime. However, the time and effort put into collecting evidence will be more if a serious crime, like **murder** or rape, is involved compared to a so-called volume crime such as burglary or car theft. In the latter case, the investigators will concentrate on the entry and exit points taken by the perpetrator where they will hope to find, above all, fingerprints and possibly tool marks.

Fingerprints are perhaps the most significant type of physical evidence in most crimes. The technology of collecting and analyzing fingerprints has been well known for over a century and has been refined over the years. A **fingerprint** is important as individualizing evidence. It can tie a specific person to a crime, because no two individuals have ever been found to have the same fingerprint. If a fingerprint from the scene of a crime can be linked to one in a database or from a suspect, then an **identification** can be made. The courts will readily accept fingerprint evidence, so long as it is properly collected and analyzed. DNA evidence, however, is rapidly becoming the gold standard of identification evidence, and when it is made less costly, will likely take over from fingerprints as the foremost manner of identification. At present, the technology is too expensive for routine use. DNA is, of course, biological rather than physical evidence.

Other kinds of physical evidence such as **tire tracks** and **shoeprints** are class evidence, rather than individualizing, evidence. This means that on its own such evidence may not be enough to convict. A shoe print taken from a relatively new shoe merely suggests the make, style, and maybe the size of a shoe. However, no shoe wears down in the same way. People walk with their own individual gait. They also take a unique path when they walk; no two people walk the same streets over time, and encounter different types of damage to the soles as they encounter the ground. Thus, over time, shoe prints may change from being class evidence to being individualizing evidence.

Class evidence such as prints from relatively new shoes or textile fibers can be valuable in identifying a suspect if taken together. A victim may have been wearing a sweater or jacket from a chain store and fibers could be found on the clothing of a suspect. If this is taken with shoe prints found at the scene from a type of trainer owned and worn by the suspect, then both items of physical evidence are strengthened and link that suspect to the crime scene.

Physical evidence can, therefore, be a highly significant part of a crime investigation. However, to play its role, the evidence must be collected and analyzed properly. In the case of a serious crime, every possible item of physical evidence must be collected. As some evidence is trace evidence, this means an extremely thorough search, or "fingertip" search, of the scene is conducted. The way this search is accomplished depends largely on the nature of the scene, but will often focus on a point such as a body, and then work outwards or inwards in a spiral. Sometimes, investigators will work in a grid formation to ensure nothing is missed. The body itself is an important source of physical evidence and a search for fibers or fingerprints will always be made before it is moved to the mortuary.

Some items of physical evidence, such as weapons, can be easy to locate and collect. However, the investigator must take care not to contaminate these items by, for instance, leaving their own fingerprints. Investigators generally cover themselves with protective clothing in order to avoid contaminating evidence at the scene. When it comes to trace evidence, other methods must be used to collect it. Hairs and fibers may stick onto a piece of sticky tape laid down on a surface. Dusting with special chemicals may reveal fingerprints or shoe prints that are otherwise invisible. Sometimes a cast is made of impression evidence like shoe prints. All the physical evidence will be photographed before anyone touches it because it is so important to keep a record of the crime scene.

It is crucial that physical evidence, whatever its nature, is not contaminated by handling. Packaging methods vary according to the nature of the evidence. Tape lifts of hair and fibers may be adhered to a piece of film and then sealed into a clean polythene bag. Fibers lifted with tweezers will be placed inside clean slips of paper called druggists' folds or **bindle paper**, and then sometimes sealed in plastic bags. Collection of an impression is a specialized forensic task for, unlike a hair or bullet, an impression cannot just be packaged and taken back to the lab. Impression evidence is often fragile; a tire track may deteriorate or even be destroyed by rainfall, for example.

If physical evidence is to be admissible in court, then the chain of custody must be proved. That is, each person who handled the evidence from its collection to its appearance in court must have signed for it. Therefore, the court knows who had custody of it at each stage of this journey. Precautions will have been taken to prevent any **cross contamination**. If someone attended the crime scene and then examined a suspect, it is possible they could transfer evidence such as textile fibers from the scene to the suspect. Ideally, the same officer would not transfer between the scene and a suspect's residence. If they do, owing to limitations on the number of personnel investigating a crime, they must undergo decontamination between locations and be able to prove to the court they have done so.

In the case of a murder, a further search for physical evidence will be made at the mortuary. Once the body is removed, the search for evidence at the scene will continue, particularly around the site where the body was found. While items of evidence are being collected, thought must also be given to collecting **control samples** from the scene. Thus, if chemicals have been spilled on a carpet in an incident, then it is important to have comparison samples from an unaffected piece of carpet.

Once physical evidence has arrived at the forensic laboratory, it must be stored under secure conditions. Care must be taken that items not deteriorate under their storage conditions in case there is a long interval before any criminal trial begins. There are a number of different techniques in the laboratory that can help to analyze and identify the source of physical evidence. For instance, **visible microspectrophotometry** is useful in identifying the chemical nature of fragments of paint or textiles. Typically, these will be compared to reference samples or to those taken from a suspect. It may be that not all the items of physical evidence will turn out to be relevant to solving a crime, but it is better the investigators collect too much physical evidence than too little. As long as they know how to keep it safe and the best way to interpret it in the context of other evidence, physical evidence can be a powerful guide as to the circumstances and perpetrator of a crime.

SEE ALSO Crime scene investigation; Evidence; Paint analysis; Trace evidence.

Physiology

Physiology is the study of how various biological components work independently and together to enable organisms, from animals to microbes, to function. This scientific discipline covers a wide variety of functions from the cellular and sub-cellular level to the interaction of organ systems that keep the complex biological machines of humans running.

Because a forensic examination involving an injury or death is often concerned with establishing cause, a forensic investigator will of necessity be concerned with physiology. By understanding the proper functioning of **organs and organ systems**, a forensic investigator is able to recognize abnormalities. Moreover, the nature of an abnormality can provide clues as to the nature of its cause.

For example, if a person experienced a rapid onset of paralysis prior to their death, the investigator might suspect the involvement of the toxin produced by the bacterium *Clostridium botulinum*. Appropriately, nervous tissue and **blood** would be examined for the presence of the toxin.

More generally, physiological studies are aimed at answering many other questions in addition to forensic questions. Physiologists investigate topics ranging from precise molecular studies of how food is digested to more general studies of how thought processes relate to electrical and biochemical patterns found in the brain (a branch of this discipline known as neurophysiology). It is often physiology-related investigations that uncover the origins of diseases.

While physiological studies are one of the cutting-edge tools in a forensic examination, the roots of the discipline date back to at least 420 B.C. and the time of Hippocrates. More refined physiological approaches first appeared in the seventeenth century when scientific methods of observation and experimentation were used to study blood movement, or circulation, in the body. In 1929, American physiologist W. B. Cannon coined the term homeostasis to describe how the varied components

of living things adjust to maintain a constant internal environment conducive to optimal functioning. Proper physiology relies on homeostasis.

Homoestasis is an important aspect of **forensic science**. A specific disturbance to the body caused by, for example, a poison such as a toxin can have other effects (e.g., loss of muscle control, difficulty breathing, mental confusion) as the body is more generally affected.

Physiological studies have evolved from the first visual-based methods to now encompass a variety of analytical procedures. The use of analytical instruments such as the gas chromatograph, electrophoretic techniques that can detect and identify components such as **toxins**, the elemental analytical power of mass **spectroscopy**, and various other techniques have made forensic physiological determinations highly sensitive and specific.

SEE ALSO Analytical instrumentation; Blood; Death, mechanism of; Epilepsy; Hemorrhagic fevers and diseases; Immune system; Nervous system overview; Organs and organ systems.

Plague, bubonic SEE Bubonic plague

Plant identification SEE Botany

Point-by-point analysis

Point-by-point analysis (also referred to as side-by-side comparison) is a subset of the **forensic science** of image analysis, although it is also widely utilized in many other disciplines. Essentially, it involves the photographic, or other image, comparison between two objects for the purposes of **identification**, or to draw conclusions about the contents of the image. **Photogrammetry** is sometimes used as a means of conducting a point-by-point analysis involving measurement, or measurement comparisons, of the object depicted in the image.

Side-by-side assessment with photographic, digital, or video images is used to make comparisons between aspects in images and known objects in order to proffer an expert opinion on either elimination or identification. Some common subjects of point-by-point analysis are facial comparisons made between identified suspects and images captured on surveillance video film (used at banks, retail and convenience stores, ATMs, etc.). Questioned images are often compared with those of a known camera in order to ascertain if the image was created by that specific camera. Cars, boats, planes, or other motor vehicles captured on surveillance or chase video are often compared with those impounded or recovered during the course of an investigation.

In the process of making the analysis, the image is examined in order to extract as much information from it as will be necessary in order to accurately compare the two objects (image and actual object). It is sometimes necessary to create an enhanced or otherwise improved version of the features within the image in order to optimally assess each point of comparison. An important aspect of point-by-point analysis involves the examination of content of the image. The process of content analysis involves arriving at conclusions based on the comparisons made, such as the exact contents of the image, the means or the process with which the image was created, the physical environment captured in the image (the lighting, composition, etc.), and the attributed origin (also called the provenance) of the image. Some examples of content analysis include patterned injury analysis, correlation of apparent injuries depicted in am image with **autopsy** or emergency medical records, adjudication of the type of camera used to create a particular image, and verification of a specific feature in an image, such as the registration or license plate number on a motor vehicle.

SEE ALSO Art identification; Ear print analysis; Fingerprint; Identification; Photogrammetry.

Poison and antidote actions

A variety of chemical and biological compounds can damage tissues, organs, and organs systems of the body. **Amphetamines**, **barbiturates**, and **botulinum toxin** debilitate the nervous system, for example. Other **toxins** produced by bacteria such as *Escherichia coli* and *Vibrio cholerae* can damage the cells lining the intestinal tract. A particularly vicious strain of *E. coli* designated O157:H7 produces a toxin that can permanently disable the kidneys.

These and other poisons can become an important focus of a forensic examination that seeks to determine the cause of an illness or death.

A poison is a compound that produces a deleterious change on or in the body. Toxicity is a general term used to indicate adverse effects produced by poisons. As touched on above, these adverse effects can range from slight symptoms such as headaches or nausea to severe symptoms such as coma, convulsions, and death.

The hallmark of a poison is the change elicited in a body function. This change can involve the speed of a function. Examples of this can include increased heart rate, excessive sweating, and decreased (or completely stopped) breath.

The target of poisons vary widely. With some poisons only a particular region or organ may be damaged, while other poisons, such as a bacterial toxin that can circulate in the bloodstream, may have more general effects. Another example of the latter is an insecticide called Parathion. It inactivates a particular enzyme that functions in communication between nerves. The enzyme is very widespread in the body, and thus many varied effects are seen.

These differing manifestations of poisoning mean that a forensic investigator must be familiar with the spectrum of possible poison hazards and their toxic effects.

Toxicity is based on the number of exposures to a poison and the time it takes for toxic symptoms to develop. Acute toxicity is due to short-term exposure and happens within a relatively short period of time. Chronic toxicity is due to long-term exposure and happens over a longer period.

Some poisons produce a mild reaction. Poison ivy, poison oak, and poison sumac all contain a sticky sap comprising a compound called toxicodendrol. For individuals who are allergic to the compound—more than half the population—a red, blistering rash called rhus dermatitis results upon contact with the plant. There are no antidotes per se, as the rash cannot be reversed. Antihistamines or drying agents such as calamine provide comfort and lessen the rash.

The toxins produced by bacteria are can be far more potent poisons than toxicodendrol. The effects of bacterial toxins are varied, ranging from the vomiting and diarrhea associated with toxins of *E. coli* and Shigella, to the paralysis and death caused by the toxin produced by *Clostidium botulinum*. If detected early enough, relief is brought by the injection of an antitoxin, which neutralizes the toxin that has not yet bound to its target. This antidote is ineffective on toxin that has already bound to host tissue.

Plants are another source of poisons. Very many plants, if ingested, can cause vomiting, depression, tremors or convulsions, stomach pain, kidney or liver failure, coma, or death. The antidote depends on the type of plant. Treatment with ipecac to induce vomiting is a common antidote, but in some cases, an antidote does not exist.

Compounds that are effective in one setting, or drugs that are therapeutic at certain concentrations, can be poisonous if used in an inappropriate way or at too high a concentration. As examples, bleach and other household detergents and cleaning agents are poisonous if ingested. Barbiturates taken in a prescribed quantity can help calm a person, but an accidental or deliberate overdose of the drugs can kill. And, while two aspirin are effective for treatment of a headache, 30 aspirin at one time are poisonous.

SEE ALSO Amphetamines; Barbiturates; Bioterrorism; Botulinum toxin; Chemical and biological detection technologies; Food poisoning; Nervous system overview; Toxins.

Polarized light microscopy

One of the microscopy techniques that can be beneficial in a forensic examination involves the use of polarized light (light in which the electromagnetic waves all vibrate in the same plane). The use of polarized light microscopy can not only detect the presence of small pieces of **evidence** including **fibers**, crystals, and soil, but can help identify this **trace evidence** based on the distinctive appearances of different materials under the polarized illumination.

The basis of polarized light microscopy is the wave nature of light. From its source, a beam of light moves outward. Similar to the waves in a pond that move outward from the point of entry of a rock, light waves consist of a series of alternating crests and troughs. These crests and troughs can be oriented vertically, horizontally, or in any other plane in between. In general, this form of light, which is known as unpolarized light, can be thought of as vibrations in the horizontal and vertical planes.

Unpolarized light can be transformed into polarized light. The most common means, which is used in microscopy and even in polarizing sunglasses, is to pass the unpolarized light through a special filter. This Polaroid filter, or polarizer, blocks the vibrations in either the horizontal or vertical plane while permitting the passage of the remaining plane of light. The light emerging from the filter represents the polarized light.

The construction of the filter allows for this selectivity. Within the filter, molecules comprising long carbon chains are arranged in the same direction. The effect is visually akin to the pattern of a picket fence. If the alignment is horizontal, then the "polarization axis" will be vertical. The filter will block all light waves that are vibrating in the horizontal plane, while permitting waves vibrating in the vertical plane to pass through. Alignment of the filter molecules in the vertical direction produces a horizontal polarization axis, so that only waves vibrating in the horizontal plane will pass through the filter.

Some polarization light **microscopes** are equipped with two filters that can be rotated to permit the sensitive tailoring of the light wavelengths that emerge (since, in reality, waves vibrate in other than the horizontal and vertical planes). If these filters are in exact opposition (i.e., vertical polarization axis superimposed on horizontal polarization axis) then the passage of all the light is blocked and no image is seen. At other filter configurations, different vibrational forms of the light will pass through.

Polarized light has a number of uses other than for microscopy. One of the most appreciated is three-dimensional (3-D) movies. The use of two slightly offset projectors casts two movie images on the screen. One is aligned horizontally and the other is aligned vertically. By wearing the distinctive 3-D glasses, which contain polarization filters, the viewer experiences a sense of depth in the viewed image.

Polarized light microscopy can be used with different types of materials. Materials such as cubic crystals and **glass** that is not under stress are symmetrical in their optical properties. Light impinging from any direction on these so-called isotrophic materials will behave the same. In contrast, anisotrophic materials have optical properties that vary depending on the orientation of the object in the light beam and on the vibrational property of the light (unpolarized, polarized, horizontally- or vertically-polarized). In the latter, which includes almost all solid materials, the appearance of the object can vary depending on the above parameters.

These different appearances can be exploited to determine the compositional nature of the object being examined. For example, as an object is reoriented, areas of brightness can appear or the color can change. These changes can be directly related to the height differences of the surface and on the presence of differently composed regions. An experienced forensic microscopist can learn a great deal about a sample from these patterns.

As one example, chrysotile, crocidolite, and amosite forms of asbestos can be differentiated from one another based on their microscopic appearance under polarized light. This can be important in a forensic examination, since the chrysotile form of asbestos does not pose the health threat that the latter two forms do. Without the rapid discrimination power of polarized light microscopy, such an assessment could not be made.

Polarized light microscopy can also be done using light that passes through thin and transparent objects (transmitted light) and light that has reflected back off from the surface of an opaque object (reflected light). Thus, the technique can be used to examine the surface of objects like rocks, computer chips, and fibers.

Other potential forensic uses of polarized light microscopy include the determination of the mineral content of a rock chip, the **identification** of natural and synthetic polymers, and the identification of nylon fibers.

SEE ALSO Alternate light source analysis; Fluorescence; Monochromatic light; Scanning electron microscopy; Trace evidence.

Pollen and pollen rain

Pollen is an important form of **trace evidence**, which can help link a suspect to a crime scene. This branch of **forensic science** has developed alongside advances in microscopy. Experts in forensic pollen analysis are called palynologists. They can determine whether the pollen species and patterns found on a suspect are characteristic of a particular area. It is not just the identity of the pollen that is important, but also the way in which it is dispersed, known as pollen rain. Each area has its own type of pollen rain that depends upon its native flora.

Pollen is the male sex cells of flowering or cone-bearing plants. It is microscopic and found on nearly every surface and object, so suspects will be carrying it, unknowingly, on their clothes, hair, and body. Pollen is also found on victims and on significant items such as ransom letters and money involved in crimes like bank robberies or drug dealing. The investigator has to know where to look to collect pollen samples; good places include any samples of soil, dust, mud or dirt, on clothing or perhaps in the suspect's vehicle.

Each plant spreads its pollen in a different way and a different plant ecology is found in each region. Wind-pollinated plants produce a lot of pollen, while self-pollinated and insect-pollinated plants produce much less. These properties lead to the characteristic pollen rain patterns of different regions.

Pollen rains down continually and can contaminate the sample containing the pollen of interest. It has been found useful to brush the desired sample with a clean, dry, cosmetic brush to get rid of this contaminating pollen that has nothing to do with the crime event. Then a sample of the pollen-containing material is scraped or brushed into a clean container. If the sample is dust, then a lift onto adhesive tape might be made. Hair is a very good source of pollen. Every time wind blows through someone's hair, pollen clings to it. The pollen sample can be washed off a hair sample with detergent. Pollen can also be found on many other surfaces which may be relevant, such as blankets, carpets, and packaging, including envelopes, and can be brushed or scraped off. The usual precautions in handling trace **evidence** apply—the **chain of custody** of the evidence—must remain intact if the evidence is to be admissible in court. Great care must be taken to prevent contamination; this is particularly important with pollen because the investigators will also have pollen on their own clothes and hair.

Examination of pollen from a victim sometimes provides evidence not otherwise readily available. Since pollen settles on food, analysis of pollen found in stomach content can give a clue as to where the individual was just prior to their death. Since pollen takes a long time to decay, samples taken from decomposed and even skeletal remains can still be informative.

It is important that the investigator collects plenty of control pollen samples from the scene. This will provide a baseline of the pollen type and pollen rain expected for that area. The forensic samples are compared to these and so help determine their relevance. If a body has been moved, for instance, the pollen will differ from that which is characteristic of the place where it is found.

Once back in the lab, the pollen has to be extracted from the evidence for microscopic examination. There are standard ways for doing this, but they are usually destructive of the evidence. If that particular piece of evidence, such as hair, has to be subjected to other analysis, then the pollen analysis must be done last. Microscopic evidence can identify a pollen grain by comparison with standard samples held in a database. The pollen rain pattern can also be identified by looking at the different pollens present and their density. Low density of grains suggests self-pollinating species; high density suggests wind-pollinated species.

In one early case, which was solved with the help of forensic **palynology**, a man had disappeared near the Danube River in Vienna in 1959. There was a suspect with a motive, but no body had been found and the suspect denied any crime. However, the investigators found mud on the suspect's shoes, revealing spruce, willow, and alder pollen, as well as a fossil hickory pollen grain that had survived for millions of years. Only one small area in the Danube valley had this particular pollen mix. When confronted with this fact, the suspect broke down, confessed, and led police to the body that was, indeed, buried in this area.

SEE ALSO Botany.

Polygraph, case histories

Since antiquity, civilizations have assumed that there were means to make individuals tell the truth against their own will and interests. Torture was (and still is) one of the most common tools used by interrogators around the world. Along with its inhumane aspects, torture is highly imprecise in revealing the truth, as under torture, a person may confess to exactly what the torturers want to hear in order to end his or her discomfort.

Among ancient Romans, alcoholic intoxication was another way of obtaining information from politicians or foreign diplomats who could not be simply arrested and tortured. This gave rise to the expression, *"In vino veritas,"* meaning the truth is in the wine. The Italian physician Cesare Lombroso was a pioneer in the late 1880s in the search for devices that could measure physiological changes associated with lies during **interrogation** of criminal suspects, such as the pletymosograph. The device was a modest ancestor of modern **polygraphs** that recorded blood circulation variations during interrogation. Lombroso asserted that through the observation of how physiological signs changed during interrogation, a reliable and humane means of detecting when individuals were telling the truth or lying could be developed. In 1915, William M. Marston at Harvard University developed an instrument to measure blood pressure that he named the "lie detector." In the early 1920s, American criminologist and psychiatrist John Larson started to develop the first modern polygraph machine that recorded blood pressure levels, pulse rates, breathing rates, and perspiration.

By the 1980s, polygraphing had a one-billion-dollar industry in the United States, with different models and testing methods of application not only for criminal investigation, but also as a tool for testing employees in the workplace. However, its efficacy and accuracy became increasingly disputed by scientists who labeled the polygraph a tool of "junk science" because of the many variables involved physiological changes, the subjective nature of data interpretation by polygraph examiners, the misuse and abuse found in many cases, and the many documented cases of false positive and false negative results. Increased privacy law protection and a string of notable failures in polygraph examinations by those who successfully defeated counterintelligence polygraph examinations brought polygraph practice into increasing disrepute. The failures were well publicized, especially in the wake of the 1985 arrest of Navy spies in the Walker family spy ring and the 1994 arrest of CIA officer Aldrich Ames for selling secret information to the Soviets for years despite being "cleared" by repeated polygraph examinations.

In contrast, many individuals who were convicted for crimes based on polygraph tests in the first half of the twentieth century were later found to be innocent (false positive results), which led courts in general to deny the acceptability of polygraph tests as valid **evidence**. For that matter, even **J. Edgar Hoover**, during his many years as director of the Federal Bureau of Investigation (**FBI**), banned polygraph testing of FBI employees, deeming it a waste of time and money. Nevertheless, polygraphs were again introduced in the FBI and gained increasing prestige in other agencies as well as a tool of interrogation rather than as an accurate scientific test. Today they are largely used in both criminal and security investigations by the police, governmental agencies, and private enterprises.

More controversy on the validity of polygraph tests was sparked in 1999, when Chinese American nuclear physicist Wen Ho Lee was accused of mishandling highly classified data on nuclear weapons. Lee was tested by two different polygraph examiners from the U.S. Department of Energy (DOE). Lee passed one polygraph test, failed a second one, and then passed a third test. Department of Energy (DOE) polygraph examiners still disagree about the tests' contradictory results. Former Energy Secretary Bill Richardson, elected in the wake of the Lee controversy, recommended a wide polygraph-screening program for DOE employees instead of using guards and x-ray scanning at the entrances of DOE laboratories, which had been cancelled by his predecessor.

When Congress approved Richardson's petition, another great controversy ensued as scientists and engineers working in some facilities unanimously refused to be tested. The scientists claimed that polygraphs did not increase security, but rather undermined it, since spies are trained to pass the tests; polygraphs create a false sense of security; polygraphs drain valuable resources from other effective and sound security measures; and polygraph tests demoralize the staff, possibly jeopardizing the safety of information in such vital issues as nuclear technology.

A leading voice in this issue was Alan P. Zelicoff, the senior scientist at the Center for National Security and Arms Control at Sandia National Laboratories. Zelicoff decided to take the case against polygraphs to the public after both the DOE and the Congress had ignored scientists' concerns. Among his arguments, Zelicoff (who is a physicist and physician) alerted the public that polygraphs are deceptive devices subject to the manipulation and incompetence of polygraph examiners. Such examiners, he noted, routinely induce nervousness and anxiety in the subjects being tested by telling them that the machine is indicating "deception" (which it is actually not) and by continuously pressing the individual to "clarify" his or her answers by providing more personal, intimate information.

Zelicoff also reinforced his case by citing how innocent people had their lives and careers ruined by erroneous interrogation of polygraph tests. Such was the case of David King, a Navy veteran held in prison for 500 days under the suspicion of selling classified information. King was arrested after failing a polygraph test and was subjected to repeated polygraph scrutiny, with some of these sessions lasting up to 19 hours, all with contradictory results. After a military court dismissed all charges against King, he was released, but his further military career prospects were tainted. As a physician, Zelicoff argued that the four parameters measured by polygraphs—blood pressure, pulse, perspiration, and breathing rates—can be affected by a myriad of emotions. He asserted that there is no medical literature that associates variations in these parameters with the intention of hiding the truth by individuals.

Charles R. Honts, a psychologist at Boise State University in Idaho, is considered one of the most qualified U.S. experts on the use and misuse of polygraphs, and is frequently requested to serve as an expert witness in court. Honts has spoken against the use of polygraphs in the workplace by government and private companies. Since the appearance of polygraphs, the main advocates of polygraphs have been psychologists and law enforcement agents. However, a growing number of studies by psychologists are concluding that polygraphs constitute incomplete science and are more likely a tool for suspect intimidation, where suspects are led by examiners to believe that polygraphs are high-precision devices that detect lies without human inference. The ethical aspects of how tests are conducted by inexperienced or poorly prepared examiners, plus the alleged use of unethical intimidation techniques by some examiners, have been the object of questioning in scientific literature, as well.

FBI forensic scientists, in turn, are testing methods of improving polygraph accuracy by using the test in association with a variety of known psychological methods utilized for detecting deception. One such psychological method is known as the guilty knowledge test/technique (GKT). GKT was adopted in 1959 as a valid psychological test for interrogating suspects in association with polygraphs. GKT is based on the premise that guilty subjects will show higher levels of physiological reactions when exposed to details of a crime that were not publicized when such facts are presented among incorrect information. It also assumes that innocent people will not show the same levels of physiological reactions. GKT is a popular test in association with polygraph tests among the Israeli law enforcement and security agencies. A paper published in *Forensic Science Communications* in 2003 showed the results of a study with 758 examinations made by polygraph examiners of 25 FBI field offices from November 1, 1993, to August 31, 1994, indicating that GKT should be used as a supplement in order to improve prevention of false positive results in polygraph tests.

Despite the controversies, the use of the polygraph is still advocated by some. Besides the strong power for lobbying that a billion-dollar industry has, polygraphs remain die-hard devices because they were also ingrained in the popular imagination as an infallible tool, partially due to the way they are portrayed in movies, **television shows**, and in thriller novels. Electroencephalograms (EEGs), however, are much more useful in detecting facts, because the brain stores true experiences and the fabricated facts in different areas. When individuals wired to an EEG machine are shown a sequence of images, including a crime scene and pictures of other persons, the brain areas responsible for true memories are activated by the recognition of images associated with the individual's real experiences.

In 2005, experiments on lie-detector technologies were being assessed by forensic experts at the Human Brain Research Laboratory in Fairfield, Iowa. Scientific methodologies and specific criteria for tests must first be adequately developed and validated, in order to prevent the birth of another popular myth.

SEE ALSO Brain wave scanners; Circumstantial evidence; Ethical issues; Evidence; Expert witnesses; FBI (United States Federal Bureau of Investigation); Federal Rules of Evidence; Interrogation; Malicious data; Psychology; Statistical interpretation of evidence.

Polygraphs

A forensic investigation may implicate an individual or group of people as suspects in a crime. Once identified as a suspect, an individual can typically expect to be questioned about the incident and their potential role. Questioning can involve the use of a polygraph test. As well, an individual may choose to participate in a polygraph test to exonerate themselves.

A polygraph test is administered to determine whether or not statements made by the subject taking the test are deceptive. During the test, the subject is monitored by a polygraph machine and interrogated by an administrator trained in forensic psychophysiology. The machine measures changes in the subject's blood pressure, heart rate, respiration rate, and sweat production. The theory underlying the polygraph test is that a person who is lying exhibits involuntary physiological responses that can be detected by the polygraph instrument. These changes include rapid breathing and heartbeat and increased blood pressure and perspiration.

The polygraph test usually measures four to six physiological reactions made by three different medical instruments that are combined in one machine. Older polygraph machines were equipped with long strips of paper that moved slowly beneath pens that recorded the various physiological responses. Newer equipment uses transducers to convert the information to digital signals that can be stored on computers and analyzed using sophisticated mathematical algorithms.

The three components of the polygraph instrument include the cardio-sphygmograph, the pneumograph, and the galvanograph. Blood pressure and heart rate are measured by the cardio-sphygmograph component of the polygraph, which consists of a blood pressure cuff that is wrapped around the subject's arm. During the questioning the cuff remains inflated. The movement of blood through the subject's veins generates a sound that is transmitted through the air in the cuff to a bellows that amplifies the sound. The magnitude of the sound relates to the blood pressure and the frequency of the changes in the sound relates to the heart rate. The pneumograph component of the polygraph records the subject's respiratory rate. One tube is placed around the subject's chest and a second is placed around his or her abdomen. These tubes are filled with air. When the subject breaths, changes in the air pressure in the tubes are recorded on the polygraph. The galvanograph section records the amount of perspiration produced. It consists of electrical sensors called galvanometers that are attached to the subject's fingertips. The skin of the fingertips contains a high density of sweat glands, making them a good location to measure perspiration. As the amount of sweat touching the galvanometers increases, the resistance of the electrical current measured decreases and these changes are recorded by the polygraph. Most forensic psychophysiologists consider the cardio-sphygomgraph and the pneumograph components more informative than the galvanograph.

During the polygraph test, the examiner and the subject are alone in the questioning room. Before the test begins, the examiner spends about an hour talking with the subject. This permits the examiner to obtain a baseline reading on the subject's emotional state. Before the test begins, the examiner goes over each question with the subject so that he or she knows exactly what to expect. When they are ready start, the person administering the polygraph attaches the various components of the polygraph instrument to the examinee.

The polygraph test itself usually consists of about 10–12 questions that require yes or no responses. Several methods of composing questions for polygraph tests exist, but all include asking the subject both relevant questions and control questions. Relevant questions relate directly to the focus of the polygraph test. Examples of relevant questions are "Did you commit crime X?" or "Did you ever use drug Y?" Control questions vary depending on the type of test administered. The most common type of polygraph test is the Control Question Test (CQT), in which control questions are composed so that the subject can answer them honestly, however, the examiner may make them slightly provocative to evoke an emotional response. Examples of control questions are "Did you ever think of doing crime Y?" or "Were you ever drunk in the last year?" This allows the examiner to understand the subject's physiological responses to challenging questions. In the CQT, greater physiological responses to the relevant questions than to the control questions indicate deceptive behavior.

There are variations to the CQT. In Directed Lie Tests (DLT), the examiner substitutes very broad questions for the control questions and the subject is directed to answer them with lies. An example is "Have you ever told a lie?" to which the subject is directed to respond "No." This response gives an examiner an understanding of the subject's physiological response associated with lying. In Positive Control Tests (PCT), a relevant question itself is used as a control. The subject is instructed to answer truthfully the first time the question is asked and falsely the second time it is asked. The only factor that influences the response is whether or not the subject is lying. In the Truth Control Test (TCT), the control questions are composed to make the subject think that he or she is being accused of a fictitious crime. This gives the examiner information on how the subject responds to a truthful denial.

During the post-test, the forensic pschophysiologist analyzes the subject's responses to the questions and scores them. Each channel of the polygraph is scored individually. For any channel, if the control response is larger than the relevant response, the score is from +1 to +3, dependent on the magnitude of the difference. If the relevant response is larger the score is from −1 to −3. The scores are summed over all channels and all repetitions of the questions to get to the total score. If the final score is sufficiently large and positive, then the subject is considered to have made truthful statements. If the final score is sufficiently large and negative, then the statements are considered deceptive. If the result is close to zero, then the test is inconclusive.

There is much debate as to the accuracy of polygraph tests. Forensic psychophysiologists generally concur that the rate of detecting deceptive behavior is greater than the rate of detecting truthful behavior. The American Polygraph Association claims that the accuracy rate for polygraph tests is between 85 and 95%. However, reports of false positives have reached as high as 75% in research done by the Congressional Office of Technology Assessment.

In the 1980s, the scientific validity of polygraphs was brought into question by psychologists. In 1988, the federal Polygraph Protection Act was passed, prohibiting employers from using polygraphs for employment screening. As a result of this legislation, businesses can ask an employee to take a polygraph, but the employee's refusal will not result in any disciplinary treatment. This law does not protect government employees including people who work in schools, prisons, public agencies, and businesses under contract with the federal government.

The use of polygraphs in court was brought to trial in 1989. In the case of *United States v. Piccinonna*, a polygraph was deemed admissible as **evidence**, only if both sides agree to its use or the judge allows it based on criteria set forth in the case. A Supreme Court ruling in 1998 expanded the judge's authority in the use of polygraphs in federal cases. Some states accept this ruling, but not all. On the state level, polygraph use is dependent upon the judge and the case.

SEE ALSO Interrogation; Polygraph, case histories; Truth serum.

Polymerase chain reaction analysis SEE PCR (polymerase chain reaction) analysis

Georg Popp

GERMAN
FORENSIC GEOLOGIST

Georg Popp is credited as the first forensic scientist to utilize geological **evidence** to solve a crime. In October 1904, while working as a forensic scientist in Frankfurt, Germany, Georg Popp was asked to assist in solving the **murder** of a young woman named Eva Disch, who had been strangled in a field. The murder weapon was Ms. Disch's scarf, and the perpetrator had apparently left his own well-used handkerchief near the body. Upon microscopic examination of the contents of the handkerchief, Georg Popp noted that the enclosed mucous contained particles of snuff and bits of coal. The most forensically interesting aspect of the mucosal contents were a variety of **minerals**, particularly that of hornblende.

The principal suspect in the case was a man named Karl Laubach, who was known to use snuff, who worked part-time in a gasworks fired by burning coal, and who was also employed part-time at a local gravel pit. Popp examined the body of the murder victim and extracted bits of coal and grains of several minerals, including hornblende, from under her fingernails. Georg Popp was able to obtain the clothing worn by the suspect on the day of the murder; he made a close examination of the legs of Mr. Laubach's trousers and removed a variety of soil samples from them. When he performed a microscopic examination of the soil samples, he discovered a lower layer consistent in makeup to a soil sample previously obtained from the murder scene. When he examined an upper layer of soil from the trousers, he found a mineral blend consistent with soil samples removed from the path between the murder site and the suspect's home.

Popp's forensic scientific conclusion was that the suspect's clothing picked up the lower layer of soil at the scene of the murder; this layer was then covered by mineral-laden mud splashed upon the trousers during the suspect's return home. When interrogated and presented with the analysis of evidence found in his handkerchief and clothing, Karl Laubach confessed to the murder. The publicity surrounding the solution of this case established Georg Popp as a forensic geological expert.

The use of geologic information in forensic settings was established internationally in 1908, when Georg Popp was again called upon to assist in the solution of a murder. In this case, he focused his examination on the shoes of the principal suspect; he examined the layers of dirt encrusted between the sole and the front of the heel. The shoes were known to have been cleaned by the suspect's wife on the night before the murder occurred, so it was Popp's hypothesis that the soil had been sequentially accumulated on the day of the murder with the layer closest to the shoe leather deposited first, and so on. By carefully removing each individual layer of soil and examining it microscopically, Popp was able to retrace the steps, literally, taken by the suspect on the day of the murder. He was able to match the soil from the shoes to the soil surrounding the suspect's home, to the scene of the crime, and to the location where the shoes had been hidden by the suspect. His solution of this case firmly established Georg Popp at the forefront of forensic **geology**. Georg Popp's microscopic examination of minerals and soil samples set a precedent for the continuing use of soil samples as an integral part of forensic investigation.

SEE ALSO Crime scene investigation; Geology; Inorganic compounds; Microscopes; Minerals.

Post death injuries SEE Antemortem injuries

Posterior SEE Anatomical nomenclature

Presumptive test, blood SEE Blood, presumptive test

Prions

Forensic investigations can often be focused on an illness outbreak or death that is suspected of being of infectious origin. Then, a critical task of forensic scientists is to identify the source of the illness and, if it is determined to be contagious, to track the pattern of the infection in order to help quell the present and future outbreaks.

Bacteria, viruses, fungi, and protozoa are the usual causes of infections. However, within the past several decades, a protein found in the brain has been determined to be the cause of one or more similar diseases of humans and animals (variant Creutzfeld-Jacob disease in humans; Bovine Spongiform Encephalopathy [BSE] or "mad cow" in cattle) that produce a progressive destruction of brain tissue.

The determination of the involvement of the protein, dubbed prion, is an example of **forensic science**. Post-mortem examinations of tissue samples are geared toward unearthing the indications of prion activity and in detecting the presence of the abnormal form of the protein. As in other infectious disease investigations, establishing the origin of the infection becomes a priority.

Prions are proteins that are infectious. Indeed, the name prion is derived from "proteinaceous infectious particles." The forensically relevant investigations that have implicated prions in degenerative brain diseases have been revolutionary. The discovery of prions and confirmation of their infectious nature overturned a central dogma that infections were caused by intact organisms, particularly microorganisms such as bacteria, fungi, parasites, or viruses. Since prions lack genetic material, the prevailing attitude was that a protein could not cause disease.

Prions were discovered and their role in brain degeneration was proposed by Stanley Pruisner. This work earned him the Nobel Prize in medicine or physiology in 1997.

In contrast to infectious agents that are not normal residents of a host, prion proteins are a normal constituent of brain tissue in humans and in all mammals studied thus far. The prion normally is a constituent of the membrane that surrounds the cells. The protein is also designated PrP (for the aforementioned proteinaceous infectious particle). PrP is a small protein, being only some 250 amino acids in length. The protein is arranged with regions that have a helical conformation and other regions that adopt a flatter, zigzag arrangement of the amino acids. The normal function of the prion is still not clear. Studies from mutant mice that are deficient in prion manufacture indicate that the protein may help protect the brain tissue from destruction that occurs with increasing frequency as someone ages. The normal prions may aid in the survival of brain cells known as Purkinje cells, which predominate in the cerebellum, a region of the brain responsible for movement and coordination.

The so-called prion theory states that PrP is the only cause of the prion-related diseases, and that disease results when a normally stable PrP is "flipped" into a different shape that causes disease. Regions that are helical and zigzag are still present, but their locations in the protein are altered. This confers a different three-dimensional shape to the protein.

As of 2005, the mechanism by which a normally functioning protein is first triggered to become infectious is not known. One hypothesis, known as the virino hypothesis, proposes that the infectious form of a prion is formed when the PrP associates with nucleic acid from some infectious organism. Efforts to find prions associated with nucleic acid have, as of 2005, been unsuccessful.

If the origin of the infectious prion is unclear, the nature of the infectious process following the creation of an infectious form of PrP is becoming clearer. The altered protein is able to stimulate a similar structural change in surrounding prions. The change in shape may result from the direct contact and binding of the altered and infectious prion with the unaltered and still-normally functioning prions. The altered proteins also become infective and encourage other proteins to undergo the conformational change. The cascade produces proteins that adversely effect neural cells, and the cells lose their ability to function and ultimately die.

The death of regions of the brain cells produces holes in the tissue. This appearance led to the designation of the disease as spongiform encephalopathy. This appearance is a hallmark of forensic examinations.

The weight of evidence now supports the contention that prion diseases of animals, such as scrapie in sheep and BSE in cattle, can cross the species barrier to humans. In humans, the progressive loss of brain function is clinically apparent as Creutzfeld-Jacob disease, kuru, and Gerstmann-Ströussler-Scheinker disease. Other human diseases that are candidates (but as yet not definitively proven) for a prion origin are Alzheimers disease and Parkinsons disease.

In the past several years, a phenomenon that bears much similarity to prion infection has been discovered in yeast. The prion-like protein is not involved in a neurological degeneration. Rather, the microorganism is able to transfer genetic information to the daughter cell by means of a shape-changing protein, rather than by the classical means of genetic transfer. The protein is able to stimulate the change of shape of other proteins in the interior of the daughter cell, which produces proteins having a new function.

The recent finding of a prion-related mechanism in yeast indicates that prions may be ubiquitous features of many organisms and that the protein may have other functions than promoting disease.

SEE ALSO Animal evidence; Mad cow disease investigation.

Privacy, legal and ethical issues

Evidence collection, searching of private premises, obtaining samples for genetic and various biochemical examinations, and questioning suspects are all parts of a forensic investigation. Although the need to acquire evidence is pressing, the need to preserve and protect the privacy and liberty of individuals is also paramount.

Among the foundational principles of the Western liberal tradition that binds the American political system is the belief that the rights of the individual, wherever possible, must be preserved against the authority of the state. Emanating from that principle is the implication that individuals have a right to privacy, a right implied—as noted by several distinguished Supreme Court justices over time—in the United States Constitution. Balancing, and sometimes contradicting, this right to privacy is the need for security on a national and local level, which can include the collection of forensic evidence and the use of forensic testing.

An array of U.S. tort and constitutional laws support the individual's right to privacy. In tort law, persons have a right to seek legal redress for invasions of privacy undertaken for the purposes of material gain, mere curiosity, or intention to defame. These protections extend to all persons under U.S. law, though public figures—a term strictly defined in legal statutes—have somewhat less broad rights of privacy.

Some national constitutions spell out the rights of the individual, with the assumption that all other privileges belong to the government. The U.S. Constitution, by contrast, outlines government authority, with the provision that all other rights belong to the states and individuals. To James Madison and other founders of the republic, these guarantees did not go far enough, and therefore, Congress passed the Bill of Rights, or the first ten amendments to the Constitution. Among these are several that would later figure heavily in debates over privacy: the First Amendment, with its protection of free speech; the Fourth Amendment, which stands against unlawful search and seizure; and the Fifth Amendment, which provides for due process under law. The Fourteenth Amendment, passed after the Civil War to protect the rights of freed slaves, extended Fifth Amendment provisions to states as well, because citizenship of both the nation and the resident state was extended to persons born or naturalized in the United States (i.e., rights of citizenship could not be denied at the state level because of race).

Contrary to popular belief, neither the Constitution nor its amendments contains any reference to privacy as a right *per se*. The concept of "The Right to Privacy" comes from an influential 1890 *Harvard Law Review* article by that title, under which Supreme Court Justice Louis Brandeis, writing with Samuel Warren, put forward the proposition that privacy rights extend beyond mere protection against clear-cut intrusions on privacy. Thereafter, a number of landmark decisions in the Supreme Court broadened the concept of privacy as defined in constitutional law. Among these was *Griswold v. Connecticut* (1965), involving a state law that prohibited the use of contraceptives. Writing for the Court, which struck down the law, Justice William O. Douglas held that the "penumbra" of the First, Fourth, and Fifth collectively provides a "zone of privacy."

The 1970s saw a revolution in privacy rights, not only through the Court—whose *Griswold* decision

set the stage for the protection of abortion rights in *Roe v. Wade* (1973)—but also in the legislative branch of government. In 1974, Congress passed the Privacy Act, which restricts the authority of government agencies to collect information on individuals or to disclose that information to persons other than the individual. The Privacy Act also requires agencies to furnish the individual with any information on him or her that the agency had in its files.

In 1967, Congress had passed the Freedom of Information Act (FOIA), which limits the ability of U.S. federal government agencies to withhold information from the public by classifying that information as secret, but it greatly expanded FOIA provisions in 1975. Together with the Privacy Act— the two are often referred to collectively as the Freedom of Information-Privacy Acts (FOIPA)—these served to further extend the rights of individuals against government intrusion. Like FOIA, the Federal Wiretapping Act of 1968 had been passed earlier, but it, too, was extended in the 1970s. Today, all U.S. states have laws against wiretapping and telephone recording.

Many of these changes occurred as a response, either directly or indirectly, to the Watergate scandal and the subsequent revelations of illegal wiretapping, recording, and surveillance activity conducted by the Nixon White House and other compartments of the federal government. In 1976, Congress passed the Foreign Intelligence Surveillance Act (FISA). FISA, which became law in 1978, placed checks and balances on the authority of government agencies to conduct surveillance on persons accused of conducting espionage—authority that had been misused by Federal Bureau of Investigation director **J. Edgar Hoover** in some domestic intelligence campaigns during the 1950s and 1960s.

In September, 1997, Congress passed the Fair Credit Reporting Act (FCRA), which requires potential employers to obtain written authorization from a job candidate or employee before accessing records from a consumer reporting agency. The employer is also required to notify the employee or applicant if any adverse action is taken pursuant to a negative report. Thus federal law extended privacy rights to protect the individual from intrusion by businesses as well as the government.

Many privacy issues at the dawn of the twenty-first century involved new technologies and new developments in science. In the area of technology, the broadening of access to the Internet brought with it a number of concerns regarding government monitoring of e-mail and other electronic communications traffic.

With specific regard to forensic evidence, debate still exists about the extent of privacy protections. In particular, the collection and matching of **DNA** sequence information in **DNA databanks**, especially if the information is used for other than **identification** of remains.

SEE ALSO Criminal responsibility, historical concepts.

Processing

It is of critical importance to properly identify, collect, preserve, and transport forensic scientific **evidence** for processing. During the investigation of a crime, the initial objectives regarding evidence are to thoroughly document and photograph the scene and to annotate the description and location of evidence to be gathered. A systematic process is then used to collect and package evidence for transport to the laboratory. Photographing may continue throughout the sample collection process, particularly if there are multiple layers of evidence that can only be seen as those above them are removed.

Paper packets, envelopes, and bags are most commonly used for specimen collection, because they do not gather evidence-destroying moisture or condensation. Nonporous, leakproof, and unbreakable containers are used for collecting and moving liquids, and clean, airtight metal canisters are used to transport **arson** evidence. Plastic bags are sometimes used to collect dry or powdered evidence. **Blood** and other moist evidence can be moved from the crime scene to the lab in plastic containers only if the transport time is less than two hours, in order to avoid the introduction and proliferation of contamination-causing bacteria. Upon receipt at the processing area, all items of evidence must be cataloged, then removed and allowed to completely air dry. After drying, evidence can be repackaged in paper or other suitable containers as necessary.

When packaging evidence, it is imperative to avoid cross-contamination by separately and securely packaging and sealing different items. At the start of the custody chain, the evidence container must be clearly marked with the initials of the collector, the date and time of acquisition, a detailed description of both the evidence specimen and the location from which it was collected, and the investigating agency's name and case file number.

The **chain of custody** typically refers to the paper trail, evidence log, or other forms of documentation pertaining to the collection (whether by sampling or legal seizure), custody, control, transfer, analysis, presentation, and final disposition of material and/or electronic evidence.

In order for evidence to be admissible and credible in court, it is essential that the chain of custody remain intact. Every contact with, or movement of, a piece of evidence must be documented in detail in order to verify that it was never unaccounted for or potentially tampered with. A specific, and appropriately credentialed, individual must be assigned physical custody of individual items of evidence. In law enforcement proceedings, this generally means that a detective will have overall responsibility for the integrity of the evidence; he or she will document its receipt and sign it over to an evidence clerk who is responsible for storing the evidence in a locked and secured area. Every single transaction involving any piece of evidence must be chronologically documented in minute detail from the moment of collection through presentation in court, in order to establish authenticity, and to defend against allegations of tampering. The documentation must include a detailed description of the location and conditions under which the evidence was collected, the identity (and possibly the credentials) of every handler of the evidence, the duration of each movement of the evidence, the level of security for each movement, as well as the overall storage of the item, and a specific description of the manner and conditions under which each transfer of the evidence occurred. If the chain of custody is broken at any time, the evidence is likely to be inadmissible or of minimal, if any, legal value.

SEE ALSO Bloodstain evidence; Cameras; Crime scene investigation; Disturbed evidence; Physical evidence; Quality control of forensic evidence.

Product tampering

Product tampering is the deliberate contamination of goods after they have been manufactured. It is often done to alarm consumers or to blackmail a company. The individual involved may have mental health problems or be politically motivated. Investigation of product tampering often involves forensic **toxicology** to discover the nature and timing of the contamination. Psychological **profiling** of the perpetrator may also prove useful. Both tampering itself and threatening to tamper are criminal offences, as is claiming tampering has occurred when it has not. Although there have been few deaths from tampering, compared to the number of complaints about it, the potential for spreading fear and doing actual physical harm to large numbers of people is great.

As consumers, trust is put in companies to provide safe foods, beverages, and medicines. Occasionally errors are made during manufacture and a harmful substance is added to a product, such as Sudan 1, the illegal dye that turned up in over 160 food products in the United Kingdom in 2005. When this happens, retailers generally remove the product from their shelves and issue prompt warnings to customers. Even so, consumer confidence is impacted and the manufacturer and retailer may suffer financially. With product tampering, contamination is done deliberately and generally to goods that are already in circulation. It is then up to a forensic investigation team to trace the source and nature of the contamination before people are harmed.

A wide variety of contaminants have been found in products that have been tampered with. Mice, syringes, cyanide, needles, liquid mercury, and **glass** have all turned up in a wide range of goods. The forensic laboratory must take a look at the physical and chemical nature of the contaminant using a range of techniques. If the contaminant is an organic compound, then infrared **spectroscopy** and either gas or liquid **chromatography** in conjunction with mass spectrometry can rapidly provide an identity. Chromatography experiments against an uncontaminated sample, in the case of a soft drink, for example, will reveal the proper composition of the product. Extra components could be contaminants and these will be analyzed more closely. Inorganic contaminants, such as acids or sodium hydroxide (lye), can be examined with techniques such as atomic absorption, which can show the elements involved.

The lab will then carry out more tests to find out when the tampering occurred, as this will help the search for the perpetrator. A contaminant may change chemically once inside the product, and analysis may show how long it has been there. Rarely, a disenchanted employee will contaminate a product during manufacture. More often, however, the perpetrator interferes with the product when it is on the shelf of the retailer's, or once it is in circulation. Most big supermarkets have video **cameras**, so if the store where the tampering took place can be found out through investigation of the packaging and its contents, it may be possible to identify a perpetrator in the act on camera.

Probably the most famous case of product tampering occurred in 1982 when seven people died in Chicago after ingesting capsules of the pain reliever Tylenol® laced with cyanide. Autopsies showed cyanide poisoning but, at first, no one could see the connection between the victims. Then it turned out they had all purchased a pack of Extra-Strength Tylenol®. These had been contaminated with cyanide. Psychological profilers were fascinated by the case, because this was a new kind of crime, with no apparent motive. As the victims were random and probably unknown to the attacker, it was a crime involving great psychological distance probably motivated by rage at society and seeking power through the fear generated by the tamperings. Naturally, the crimes aroused great public anxiety, for anyone could become a victim at any time. Yet the incidents stopped as suddenly as they began and no one was ever arrested or convicted. However, one man was imprisoned after trying to blackmail the manufacturers of Tylenol®.

There must, however, be a large psychological element to product tampering, because the publicity surrounding the 1982 Tylenol poisonings triggered a wave of other attacks. Many of these turned out to be fake or staged tamperings, often carried out by attention-seeking individuals. Sometimes criminals have sought to defraud companies by blackmail with threats of tampering. There have been 20 arrests in connection with such threats in the U.S., but no one was injured as no tampering took place. Some suicides have tried to cover up the true nature of their death by staging a tampering.

Publicity about tampering in the media also leads to an increase in reports of suspect tampering. That is, a consumer reports packaging that appears to have been interfered with, or links a symptom they experience with possible contamination of a product. Most of these complaints prove unfounded although they must, of course, be investigated.

In 1984, the Food and Drug Administration (**FDA**) began to compile figures on tampering. Unlike other crimes, where rates either increase, decrease, or stay steady, the rate of tampering is linked to the publicity about a specific case. In early 1984, pins and needles were found in cookies meant for a group of young girl scouts and reports of tampering went up from 20 to 200 in the following month. Once press coverage died down, the rate fell to 10 incidents reported a month. There was another fatal Tylenol poisoning in Westchester in February 1986 and, again, the reports of other tamperings went up to 326 a month. Later that month, there was huge publicity when glass was found in baby food. The next

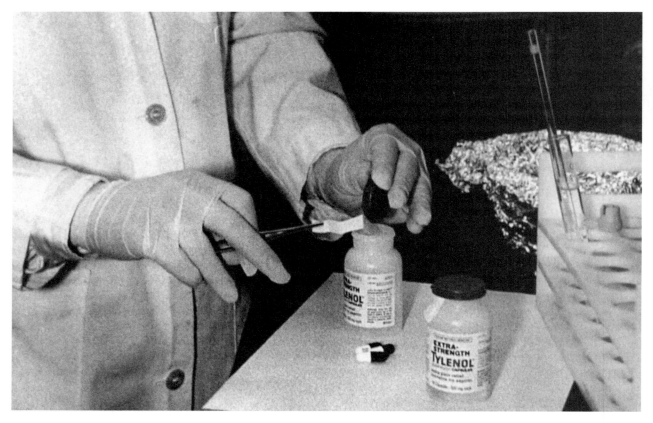

Bottles of Extra-Strength Tylenol® are tested after tampered, cyanide-laced Tylenol killed seven people in 1982. The incident lead to tamper-resistant packaging on most foods and drugs sold today. AP/WIDE WORLD PHOTOS. REPRODUCED BY PERMISSION.

month, reports of tampering reached an all time high of 456. It was in 1987 and 1988 when there were no publicized incidents that reports fell to an all time low. Some experts suggest that publicity should be minimized in cases of tampering but, of course, the public has to be warned and, indeed, may have valuable information that could lead to the perpetrator.

In another famous case, **murder** was staged to look like tampering. Sue Snow collapsed suddenly and died in 1986 at her home in Seattle. It looked like a drug overdose, but the only medication she had been taking was Excedrin, a normally safe painkiller. During **autopsy**, however, the pathologist noted the telltale odor of almonds around the corpse, suggesting cyanide poisoning. Toxicology tests revealed its presence. As with the 1982 Tylenol case, all packs of Excedrin had to be removed from the shelves of drugstores across the country. The police found two other contaminated bottles, one in Auburn, WA and one in nearby Kent, WA.

This proved to be no random case of product tampering, however. A few days later, Stella Nickell told police her husband had also died suddenly after taking Excedrin. His death certificate gave **cause of death** as emphysema. The police would have exhumed Bruce Nickell's body, save that a **blood** sample had been retained because he was a registered organ donor. Toxicological investigation showed that he had died of cyanide poisoning. Nearly 250,000 Excedrin capsules were examined by the Food and Drug Administration in an attempt to find a link between the two victims. Five contained cyanide and two of them were in the possession of Stella Nickell. The finding of another chemical contaminant in the capsules, an algicide used to clean fish tanks, suggested her guilt when a fish tank was discovered on her premises. Other **evidence** helped to convict Nickell, who is now serving a 99 year prison term for murder.

Product tampering could, of course, be a potent tool for terrorists. There have been various incidents and hoaxes involving a number of groups such as animal rights activists, extreme religious groups, and others. In 1978, for instance, a Palestinian group told the Dutch government it was responsible for injecting mercury into citrus fruits from Israel. These turned up in The Netherlands, the United Kingdom, Belgium, Germany, and Sweden. Investigation suggested the poisoning had occurred at point of retail because the pattern of discoloration in the fruit was not consistent with it having occurred in Israel. No one died, but a dozen were affected by mercury poisoning and Israeli orange exports fell 40% as fruit sales plummeted all throughout Europe.

Following the Tylenol incidents, over-the-counter drugs have been sold in tamper-proof packaging. This may deter the impulsive criminal, but those bent on spreading harm and anxiety could find a way around the packaging. The Food and Drug Administration (FDA) recently expressed some concern that Al Qaeda might tamper with the domestic food and drug supply and may find a way of specifically targeting illegally imported prescription drugs. The FDA has a special unit dedicated to the forensic investigation of product tampering. Recent incidents included the contamination of baby food with ground castor beans, which contain the deadly poison **ricin**. In what may have been a hoax, a shipment of lemons from Argentina was said to be impregnated with an unspecified biological toxin. Nothing harmful, however, was found in the fruit on examination at border control.

SEE ALSO Food supply; Toxins.

Professional publications

Forensic science is a fast moving field, with new techniques, theories, and information being introduced all the time. The forensic professional, whether he or she is a **medical examiner**, a specialist, or a laboratory technician, needs to keep up-to-date. There are several professional publications that the scientist can consult to learn about the latest research. If they so wish, they can use the journals to correspond and debate with colleagues all over the world on the latest forensic science issues. They can also build their scientific reputation, and that of their laboratory, by publishing original research. The Internet has made using professional publications much easier. Often, a paper will be published online before it appears in the print edition so that everyone can have access to it earlier. A searchable online index for a journal means that a subject can be researched easily by those who do not have ready access to an academic library. Subscriptions to journals are expensive, but most now provide a "pay for view" facility so that one can purchase a copy of an article

of interest without having to visit a library or take our a subscription to a journal.

Like other academic journals, forensic science publications are usually overseen by a panel of experts whose opinions ensure that all the work published there is accurate, timely, and relevant. It is usual for all research papers to be peer-reviewed, that is, scrutinized by professionals to check the originality and quality of the research. The peer review system can lead to delays in publication, although these are now reduced as communications are handled electronically. Although peer review is open to abuse, and accusations of bias or favoritism are not unknown, it is the best guarantee that research published in a professional journal is of a high standard.

There will always be a role for the academic library for those consulting professional publications. Universities and hospitals providing postgraduate **training** in forensic science are likely to subscribe to at least the main journals. These will usually be shelved in the **pathology** section in a medical library. Forensic science publications may often be found near the chemistry section of a science library. The range of journals available is wide. There are academic journals containing important and groundbreaking research papers on the one hand and, on the other, newsletters containing items about the business of a society or association and articles of more general interest.

One of the most comprehensive and popular academic publications for the forensic scientist is the *Journal of Forensic Sciences*. This is the official publication of the **American Academy of Forensic Sciences**. The editors accept original investigations, observations, scholarly inquiries, and reviews. The following areas are covered by the Journal: **anthropology**, **criminalistics**, engineering, law, **odontology**, pathology, **psychiatry**, **questioned documents**, and **toxicology**. The *Journal of Forensic Science* began publication in 1956 and appears once every two months.

Forensic Science International is a more commercial journal and has been published since 1978. It is produced by Elsevier, an academic publisher, every two weeks. The journal's scope is broad, covering forensic pathology and histochemistry, chemistry, biochemistry and toxicology, biology (including hair and fiber analysis), **serology**, odontology, psychiatry, anthropology, physical sciences, **firearms**, and document examination. The editors accept research papers, review articles, preliminary communications, letters, book reviews, and case reports. There are also articles on specialist topics such as accident investigation and mass disaster, **fingerprint evidence**, **toolmarks**, and bite mark evidence.

The *American Journal of Forensic Medicine and Pathology* is essential reading for forensic pathologists and medical examiners, because it is published by the National Association of Medical Examiners. First published in 1980, it appears four times a year and features articles on new examination and documentation procedures. This journal is a useful discussion forum for the expansion of the role of the forensic pathologist in new areas including human rights protection, suicide and drug abuse prevention, and occupational and environmental health. It also includes case reports, technical notes, and reports of medico-legal practice worldwide.

Legal Medicine is a relatively new journal, first appearing in 1999 and comprising five issues a year. It is the official journal of the Japanese Society of Legal Medicine and it is intended for forensic scientists, forensic pathologists, anthropologists, serologists, odontologists, toxicologists, and lawyers specializing in the medico-legal area. *Legal Medicine* is an international forum for the publication of a wide range of original articles, reviews, and correspondence. Besides covering all the main areas of forensic science, it also accepts submissions on malpractice, insurance, child abuse, and medical ethics.

The Australian Academy of Forensic Sciences launched its official publication, the *Australian Journal of Forensic Sciences*, in 1968. It covers a wide range of topics: **arson**, aircraft accidents, money laundering, sex offenders, voiceprints, and even the philosophy of evil. There are also topics that are of special interest to Australian forensic scientists, such as the treatment of aboriginal people within the justice system.

Science and Justice is the official journal of the Forensic Science Society, founded in 1959 and one of the world's oldest and largest associations for forensic scientists. The journal has a comprehensive range of articles and appears four times a year.

The American College of Forensic Psychiatry publishes the *American Journal of Forensic Psychiatry*, which first appeared in 1979. It publishes papers written by psychiatrists who act as **expert witnesses** and by attorneys who deal with civil and criminal mental health cases. The Journal appears quarterly and has published over 800 papers at the interface between psychiatry and the law. It covers historical and cultural aspects of mental health. Topics that have been written about include anti-social behavior, suicide, air rage, stalkers, malingering, and violent behavior.

Laboratory-based forensic scientists have their own specialist professional publications. For instance, The American Society of Crime Laboratory Directors publishes an online newsletter. This is intended as a forum for the discussion of issues concerning the management of the crime laboratory as well as a channel for informing members about the business and activities of the Society.

There are several journals which deal in detail with specialized branches of forensic science. One example is *Environmental Forensics*, the journal of the International Society of Environmental Forensics. The publication deals with legal and technical aspects of environmental pollution, a subject that is of importance for those working to protect the air, water, soil, and biological ecosystems. In a completely different area, the American Society of Questioned Document Examiners publishes an academic journal for its members, and other interested parties, twice a year.

Busy forensic scientists often do not have the time to read all the journals they would like to. That is why abstracting journals, such as *Forensic Science Abstracts*, are so useful. They provide what is known as a current awareness service, scanning all the relevant journals. A short summary, known as an abstract, of the articles in each journal is produced and all the scientist needs to do is to browse through the abstracts on a regular basis and then track down the articles of major significance to his or her work. *Forensic Science Abstracts* is part of a larger publication called *Excerpta Medica*, which surveys over 4,000 biomedical journals.

Another important type of publication for the busy professional is the communications journal. This contains short papers or letters which are meant to give the reader a rapid update on developments in their field. One good example is *Forensic Science Communications*, which is published by Federal Bureau of Investigation scientists and appears four times a year.

A recent development is the appearance of the electronic journal with no paper equivalent. Anyone can set up an electronic journal; it may be free to access to all, or it may be restricted by password. Papers may or may not be peer-reviewed. One example is *Scientific Testimony*, which is produced by the faculty and students at the Department of Criminology, Law and Society at the University of California, Irvine. Its declared aim is to improve the quality of scientific testimony in the courts. The editors invite research papers, tutorials, where a specific scientific or technical topic is reviewed, and have set up a debating forum where people can advance their views. Areas that will be covered regularly include the work of the expert witness, forensic science in general, and science and the jury.

However, probably the first online forensic journal of this kind was Anil Aggrawal's *Internet Journal of Forensic Medicine and Toxicology*, which was set up in 2000 and goes on-line twice a year. Anil Aggrawal is a professor of medicine in New Delhi, India, and chose a forum where those working in forensic medicine and toxicology could share their experiences. Often, a professional will make an observation or try something out which they may not have time to write up for an academic journal. It is easier, however, to email the idea to an Internet journal where the work is more likely to appear and interesting feedback from others can be generated. Professor Aggrawal's journal has now developed so it can accept full-length research papers with color photographs. No doubt, there will be other online developments of this kind. If professionals can communicate with one another easily in a journal format and have the chance for exposure to new ideas, it can only help develop their knowledge and accelerate the progression of their science.

SEE ALSO Careers in forensic science; Training.

Profiling

Profiling is the process of developing descriptions of the traits and characteristics of unknown offenders in specific criminal cases. It is often used in situations for which authorities have no likely suspect. There are two basic varieties of profiling: inductive, which involves the development of a profile based on known psychological typology; and deductive, which reasons exclusively from the details of the victim and crime scene to develop a unique profile. Profiling as a law enforcement tool emerged in the late 1960s, and today, the leading entity engaged in profiling is the National Center for the Analysis of Violent Crime (NCAVC) of the Federal Bureau of Investigation (**FBI**).

Profiling should not be confused with racial profiling. Racial profiling, a topic surrounded with considerable controversy, came to the forefront in the late 1980s and 1990s, when a number of activists and social scientists maintained that law enforcement officials tended to single out African Americans, particularly young males, for arrest and abuse. After the September 2001, terrorist attacks, random searches and other forms of attention directed against Middle Eastern males were also dubbed in some quarters as racial profiling.

Criminal profiling is still controversial among law enforcement authorities and forensic scientists, not all of whom agree on its merits or on the proper approach to obtaining a profile. However, profiling is acceptable by the general public. In fact, television programs concerning crime, as well as dramatic portrayals in popular films have raised considerable public interest in profiling. Thanks to this interest, leading profilers are well-known outside the law-enforcement community.

Indicative of this popularity was the attention given to profiling opportunities on a frequently asked questions (FAQ) page in the employment section of the FBI's Web site in 2003. Alone among FBI specialties, profiling was featured with the question "I just want to be a FBI 'profiler.' Where do I begin the application process?" As the bureau noted in its response, "You first need to realize the FBI does not have a job called 'Profiler.'" The answer went on to discuss the NCAVC, located at FBI headquarters in Quantico, Virginia. The FBI also noted on the site that "These FBI Special Agents [involved in profiling] don't get vibes or experience psychic flashes while walking around fresh crime scenes. [Instead, profiling] is an exciting world of investigation and research. . . ."

Criminal profiling originated from the work of FBI special agents Howard Teten and Pat Mullany in the late 1960s. It is especially used in cases involving **serial killers**, who usually are not personally acquainted with their victims. Most murders involve people who know one another, and in most **murder** investigations, likely suspects can be readily identified. For example, if a married woman is murdered, her husband often quickly becomes the focus of police investigation. If, however, there is nothing to suggest that a victim has been murdered by someone he or she knows, or if the victim's identity is unknown, profiling may be necessary in order to develop a set of leads for investigators.

Criminal profilers make use of two types of reasoning, which, in the view of some profiling experts, constitute two schools of thought. Inductive criminal profiling, like the larger concept of induction in the philosophical discipline of epistemology (which is concerned with the nature of knowledge) develops its portrait of a suspect based on the results gathered from other crime scenes. Inductive criminal profiles draw on formal and informal studies of known criminals, on the experience of the profiler, and on publicly available data sources, to provide guidance.

By contrast, deductive criminal profiling relies purely on information relating to the crime scene, the victim, and the **evidence**. Instead of drawing on the facts of other crimes, the deductive profile draws only on the information relating to the crime in question. For instance, if a search of the crime scene reveals that the killer had smoked an expensive variety of cigar, this would lead the deductive profiler to presume that the killer was wealthy and probably well educated. The profiler working through pure deduction would not, however, seek to compare this fact with information on other killers in the past who had smoked expensive cigars.

FBI profilers are supervisory special agents with NCAVC. In order to be considered for the program, an individual must have served as an FBI special agent for three years. However, due to high competition for placement in the program, individuals selected usually have eight to ten years of experience with the bureau. Newly assigned personnel typically undergo a structured **training** program of more than five hundred hours. Alongside these special agents work other, civilian, personnel in positions that include intelligence research specialists, violent crime resource specialists, and crime analysts. It is their job to research violent crime from a law enforcement perspective, and to provide support to NCAVC special agents.

In addition to developing criminal profiles, NCAVC provides major case management advice and threat assessment services to law-enforcement officials around the nation and the world. Special agents may also provide law enforcement officials with strategies for investigation, interviewing, and prosecution. Among the services provided by NCAVC to the law enforcement community at large is VICAP, the Violent Criminal Apprehension Program. VICAP is a nationwide data information center tasked with collecting, collating, and analyzing information on violent crimes, particularly murder. Cases eligible for VICAP include solved or unsolved homicides or attempts, especially ones involving an abduction; apparently random, motiveless, or sexually oriented homicides; murders that are known or suspected to be part of a series (i.e., serial murder); unresolved missing persons cases, particularly those in which foul play is suspected; and unidentified dead bodies for whom the manner of death is known or suspected to be homicide.

Local law enforcement agencies participating in VICAP are able to draw on its information database in solving crimes. For example, if a murder was committed with a rare variety of handmade pistol, VICAP could be consulted for information on other cases involving such a weapon. Once a case has been entered into the VICAP database, it is compared continually against all other entries on the basis of certain aspects of the crime. VICAP has been used to solve a number of homicides nationwide.

SEE ALSO FBI (United States Federal Bureau of Investigation); Interrogation; Psychological profile; Psychopathic personality.

Profiling, criminal SEE Criminal profiling

Profiling, ethical issues

Profiling is known by a variety of terms, including criminal investigation analysis, crime scene analysis, behavioral **evidence** analysis, psychological profiling, biopsychosocial profiling, psychosocial profiling, investigative process management, **criminal profiling**, psychological criminal profiling, criminal behavioral profiling, offender profiling, and criminal personality profiling. As part of the criminal investigative process, profiling can add depth to crime scene investigations; the behavior of an offender is reflective of his or her underlying psychological process. The appearance of a crime scene can also reveal important information regarding the perpetrator's underlying psychopathy, sociopathy, psychopathology, or enduring character traits. Profiling is also useful when attempting to find subtle commonalities in serial crimes.

Profiling has not been developed as a means of identifying a specific offender in a particular case; rather, it has evolved as a means of adding depth to an investigation. Profiling aids in conducting psychological examination in cases of equivocal death, where a profile can assist investigators in establishing the likelihood that the death was a result of natural, accidental, suicidal, or homicidal origin. Profiling can suggest new avenues of investigation, support the working hypotheses of investigating officers, create a framework for **interrogation** after suspect apprehension, and assist the defense or prosecution in formulating a strategy for case presentation in the courtroom, or paving the way for plea construction.

There are many typologies and definitions of profiling, most likely at least as many as there are names for the cluster of activities that fall under the profiling heading. In the Unites States, the wide-spread use of profiling largely resulted from the Federal Bureau of Investigation's (**FBI**) work with serial murders and the perpetrators thereof. Its formal use was popularized by the FBI's Behavioral Science Unit (BSU), starting in the 1970s, as part of an effort to incorporate the principles of behavioral science into the law enforcement community. Profiling has received a great deal of attention in the media. It has been the subject of novels and nonfiction crime books (including a large number written by former FBI BSU staff members), featured in movies, and the central topic in numerous **television shows** and series. Because there are so many labels and definitions, the field of profiling has suffered a lack of credibility in the legal, and often the public, arenas. Additionally, the lack of uniformity has led to a significant number of **ethical issues** with the entire concept of profiling.

There are two predominant methodologies currently utilized for profiling: inductive, which is typically used by the FBI and moves from specific case findings to general theories, and deductive, which builds from general theories to specific case findings.

Profiling is currently practiced by a large number of professionals (and paraprofessionals), in a variety of occupations and, as such, currently lacks standardization or uniformity of practice. The concept of profiling is, by its very nature, one that involves interplay among numerous disciplines. In order to achieve some degree of homogeneity, the practice of profiling must attain several developmental milestones; it must have an infrastructure, or set of rules, procedures, guidelines, standards of practice, and requires a universally, or at least consensually, agreed upon vocabulary and set of ethical guidelines. There has been considerable resistance in the field to the concepts of standardization and "professionalization" of profiling, to which a number of reasons have been attributed. Profilers in different disciplines have displayed an inability to find common ground in which to discuss the principles of practice (a police detective has different mandates than a forensic psychiatrist or an FBI Special Agent, forensic nurse, forensic anthropologist, and so on). Profilers often decline (or are prohibited from so doing) to publicly discuss the details of cases due to issues of confidentiality (this can be circumvented by de-identifying case materials). There is also a vocal group of diverse profilers who oppose standardization because it may limit their creativity. In many ways, the art of profiling may be likened to a niche market, in which individuals have honed their expertise (often local) to the

point that they have achieved some degree of indispensability in their law enforcement arena. To standardize the profession would be to suggest that any trained profiler (by whatever means trained were to become defined) could be contracted by any jurisdiction to be brought in, create the necessary profiling process, and then leave. This possibility could conceivably threaten to create a loss of livelihood for private, small, and local agencies.

There are a significant number of ethical issues raised by the lack of professionalization of profiling. There are no specific educational or **training** requirements in order to label oneself a profiler. The lack of educational or training requirements also means that there are no minimum standards for the measurement of competency; the lack of competency standards leads to an inability to either discipline or sanction practitioners who are irresponsible or incompetent. There is no juried or peer-reviewed system of practice measurement, there is no agreement as to what the process of creating a profile entails, nor what one should contain, and there is no agreed upon methodology for the conduction of the profiling process. That means, there is no scientific basis upon which profiling rests, as it cannot be subject to analysis and its process cannot, therefore, be replicable. In terms of the actual outcome of the practice of profiling, there are ethical difficulties associated with the use of personality and psychological theories as a means of directing the outcome of a criminal investigation. Profiling has been portrayed by the media as a romantic or heroic profession, possibly resulting in an inaccurate perception of the life and role of a profiler. As a result, the field may attract individuals who are poorly suited to competent practice. When not credibly accomplished, profiling can cause serious harm or impose delays in the actual solution of a case by suggesting inappropriate directions of investigation. The pursuit of suspects who fit a typology suggested by the profiler that is very different than that of the actual perpetrator could also result in the implication or arrest of innocent parties. Finally, there are no official ethical standards for the practice of profiling.

The Academy of Behavioral Profiling (ABP), an internationally recognized, not-for-profit corporation, was initiated in 1999 and incorporated in 2004. The ABP was created, in part, to address some of the ethical concerns raised by the lack of standardization in the field of profiling. Its mission statement describes a commitment to raising the professional bar for profilers by promoting the concepts of peer review, multidisciplinary education and training, and common professional standards for practitioners of evidence based criminal profiling. Among its initial goals were: the creation of written multidisciplinary practice and ethical code of conduct guidelines; development of readily accessible, uniform educational and continuing professional education opportunities; creation and promulgation of a profiling general knowledge exam in order to create some common competency standards; promotion of research opportunities for the advancement of the field of knowledge in evidence-based profiling as well as replicability of results; creation of an informational profiling database; to evolve the peer review process in the professionalization of the practice of profiling; and to increase positive public awareness of behavioral profiling.

The ethical guidelines and code of professional conduct created by the ABP suggest the need for increased professionalism on the part of profilers. They call for a universal attitude embodying integrity and support the need for an unbiased approach to the profiling and reporting process by mandating impartiality, independence, and objectivity. As such, they set standards for maintenance of confidentiality of case information to ensure the dignity of crime victims and their families. They also require that the interpretations and conclusions developed as a result of the profiling process be strictly limited to the information and evidentiary materials reviewed and discovered to avoid the introduction of bias. The ABP ethical code of conduct requires limiting expert witness testimony to the facts of the case, and mandates against the use of conjecture and the offering of opinions regarding guilt or innocence of a suspect in a particular crime. Finally, the ethical guidelines set the standards for reporting unethical conduct, or ethical code violations, to the appropriate authorities associated with the governing bodies of the profession in which the violator was credentialed.

Within the ABP, there are three levels of possible sanction for members who violate the ethical guidelines for professional conduct: (1) advisement—an individual who is responsible for the violation receives a written notice that they are to cease and desist the unethical activity. A member who receives two such advisements is automatically issued a warning; (2) warning—the individual who is responsible for the ethical violation is given a written warning that failure to immediately end the unethical conduct may result in expulsion form the ABP. Notification of a warning is made publicly available to all ABP members, and receipt of two warnings will result in automatic expulsion form the ABP; (3) expulsion—an individual responsible for the ethical transgression will be given written notice of expulsion from the ABP. Such notices of expulsion are made available to the general public. The underlying premise of the sanction process is to educate membership about the importance of maintaining the highest standards of ethical professional behavior.

The ABP has achieved all of its initial goals and continues to grow internationally, suggesting that it may be possible to unite the professionals involved in the practice of profiling, and to someday achieve standardization and adherence to the highest standards of ethical conduct, while maintaining the art of the multidisciplinary process.

SEE ALSO Careers in forensic science; Crime scene investigation; Criminal profiling; Criminalistics; Forensic Science Service (U.K.).

Profiling, screening

Screening of all kinds plays an increasing role in everyday life. Luggage is screened by x rays at the airport to ensure it does not contain any dangerous items. People are screened for cancer to enable cases to be caught and treated early. Employees may be screened at random for the presence of alcohol or drugs. Psychological screening is carried out to ensure someone's suitability for a particular job. Screening is a useful way of a forensic psychologist gaining some basic knowledge of a suspect's mental and psychological characteristics before proceeding to more specialized testing and a full **psychological profile**. The tests used in screening are quick and simple. Sometimes they can even be done and assessed by computer. These tools differ from the psychology quizzes sometimes found in magazines in that they usually have been validated by years of research and experience so the results are meaningful. There are two basic types of psychological screening used in forensic investigation, personality and cognitive screening. Each type gives the psychologist a mini-profile of the suspect which can form a useful basis for more detailed and individual examination.

Personality screening often involves standardized tests such as the Minnesota Multiphasic Personality Inventory or the California Psychological Inventory. These are designed to measure key personality characteristics such as introversion or extroversion, intuition, honesty, neuroticism, optimism, and so on. The results may give the psychologist a feel for whether the person was likely to have committed the crime in question. In the forensic context, more specific screening tools, such as the Psychopathy Check List may also be used. Psychopathy, or anti-social personality disorder, is very common among criminals and a high score may be a useful pointer although not, in itself, proof of guilt. Another specialized screening tool is the Structured Interview of Reported Symptoms, which detects malingering (pretending to be still ill or injured).

Most people are used to taking personality tests in everyday life—after all, they are often used in recruitment so they have become a standard part of a job interview. In many kinds of work, such as teaching and law enforcement, there will be an emphasis on trying to discover the person's integrity and this is often a focus in a criminal investigation. People may think they can cheat a personality test but, in reality, the list of questions is designed to minimize this possibility because certain items are designed to spot untruthfulness and the test as a whole looks for consistency in the replies. Outright lying on the part of the suspect is also common during an investigation. That is why the forensic psychologist will always take the mini-profile alongside other **evidence** to form his or her conclusions. Thus, if the person does not want to seem like a loner in the belief that makes them look guilty of the crime, they may try to skew the answers on the personality test to make themselves look sociable. However, in an interview their true tendencies will emerge.

The other kind of basic screen which is done by the forensic psychologist is the cognitive test which profiles a person's mental ability. He or she may use a standard instrument such as the Wechsler Adult Intelligence Scale, which measures the intelligence quotient or IQ. On its own this is limited, as people have different kinds of intelligence. Someone who is good with numbers, for example, may have little verbal ability. Nevertheless, it is useful, because a person of very low intelligence is unlikely to have committed a sophisticated computer crime, for instance. They may, however, have carried out a violent attack. Other tests of cognitive ability such as memory, verbal reasoning, and comprehension can also help reveal whether the suspect was capable of the crime. Sometimes the crime scene will yield evidence of detailed planning. This may or may not match the mini mental profile the psychologist builds of the suspect. Again, most people encounter such tests on an everyday basis. In most jobs, the employer wants to know if the person has at least minimal mathematical ability and the ability to follow instructions.

The advantage of psychological screening tools is that they are standardized, validated, and therefore, accepted by the courts as part of the evidence. However, on their own they are limited. Just as recruitment for a top job cannot be done on testing alone, it must be followed up with one or more interviews, a criminal cannot be convicted by the use of a screening tool. Nevertheless, preliminary psychological screens play a very useful role in the assessment of suspects.

SEE ALSO Psychological profile; Psychology.

Proximal SEE Anatomical nomenclature

Pseudoscience and forensics

For over a century, science has held out the hope that the administration of criminal justice can be placed on a firmer and more rational footing, one that does not have to rely on ambiguous **circumstantial evidence** or potentially unreliable eyewitness testimony to put criminals behind bars. Defendants may lie, and witnesses are often mistaken about what they know or have seen, but science relies on observable and testable facts. A criminal usually leaves behind **physical evidence** that can be found, examined, and identified through scientific techniques, and linked to the criminal in a way that gives new meaning to the phrase "beyond a reasonable doubt."

In the twentieth century, science began to take on an almost mystical aura of infallibility as some of the tools of the forensic trade began to emerge. The first case that relied on **fingerprint** analysis, for example, was heard in 1911 in Illinois (*People v. Jennings*), and soon the claim that no two persons have identical fingerprints became axiomatic (taken for granted). In 1936, Bruno Richard Hauptmann was convicted for kidnapping and murdering the infant son of Charles Lindbergh, Jr., the first criminal of note to be executed largely on the basis of **handwriting analysis**. In 1979, the profile of forensic odontologists was boosted when bite mark testimony was allowed in the trial of serial killer Ted Bundy. In 1990, testimony about **DNA**, with its seemingly incontrovertible statistical claims about DNA matches, was admitted into **evidence** for the first time. Judges, juries, and members of the public accepted the testimony of forensic scientists with little question.

Skeptics, however, have demanded proof—in the form of clinical trials, publication, peer review, and measurement of error rates—that what forensic experts practiced was science and not pseudoscience. In the early years of the twentieth century, these skeptics performed a valuable service. They exposed the pseudoscientific claims of phrenologists, who asserted that the shape of the **skull** was indicative of mental faculties and character, so that criminal tendencies could be measured with a pair of calipers. Similarly, early handwriting analysts had little in the way of science to back their claims, and their analysis often shaded off into graphology, a pseudoscience that attempts to assess personality through unique handwriting characteristics. In the 1920s, toolmark examination was all the rage; in a rape trial, one examiner testified with apparent breathtaking scientific accuracy that to find an exact match of the knife blade used in the crime, "every one of the hundred million people in the United States" would have to have "six hundred and fifty quadrillion knives each." In the 1930s, efforts were made to link criminal tendencies with particular **blood** types, but the claims were abandoned when they were rejected by the scientific community as pseudoscience.

The skepticism that scuttled these pseudosciences was given renewed life in the aftermath of *Daubert v. Merrell Dow Pharmaceuticals*, a 1993 U.S. Supreme Court case that interpreted the 1975 **Federal Rules of Evidence** as they pertained to the admissibility of expert testimony, including that of forensic scientists. Under the so-called Daubert standard, judges were required to act as gatekeepers for scientific testimony and to demand that the testimony of forensic scientists (and other experts) has a valid, reliable, and relevant foundation.

Arson investigators, for example, have long searched for signs of chipped concrete at fire scenes. Their assumption is that an **accelerant** such as gasoline causes concrete to "fragment," but laboratory tests have called this assumption into question, casting doubt on the validity of this mainstay of arson investigation science. Similarly, many defendants have been convicted of crimes based on visual comparisons of hair **fibers**. However, 26 of the first 74 prisoners to be exonerated by DNA evidence in the 1990s had been convicted largely on the basis of a supposed match between their hair and hair follicles found at the crime scenes. In 1997, a Vancouver, Washington, man was convicted of **murder** largely on the strength of a Dutch expert's claim that he was 100% confident that an ear print found at the crime scene was made by the defendant, even though no peer-reviewed studies confirm the validity of ear

print comparison. As of 2005, **ear print analysis** is still used in Europe, and the European Commission is conducting research in hopes of supporting or denying its validity. The **FBI** asked the National Academy of Sciences (NAS) to conduct an examination of voice-print technology, which is premised on the theory that a spectrograph can produce a unique pattern for an individual's speech, but the NAS concluded that the theory had not been validated. Firearm **identification** has come under similar scrutiny because while some of the marks found on a crime scene bullet are unique to the individual gun, other marks are shared by bullets fired from the same model of gun. Further, different brands of bullets can take on identifying marks differently, even though they have been fired from the same gun. In the early 2000s, research was under way to give firearm identification testimony more precision, especially in measuring error rates.

The judiciary began to show similar skepticism in 1999. Massachusetts Federal District Court judge Nancy Gertner assumed the role of gatekeeper that year when she refused to allow a forensic handwriting expert to testify as to the authorship of a stick-up note and restricted the expert to noting points of similarity between the note and the accused robber's handwriting. Said Gertner, "one's handwriting is not at all unique in the sense that it remains the same over time, or uniquely separates one individual from another." In 2001, a federal court in *United States v. Saelee* said that the testing that has been done on handwriting analysis "raises serious questions about the reliability of methods currently in use." In 2002, a federal judge in Philadelphia refused to admit a fingerprint comparison based on his belief that its techniques had not been scientifically validated (he later reversed this decision). The controversy this aroused followed on the heels of a February 1999 report issued by the **National Institute of Justice**, the research arm of the U.S. Justice Department, saying that the "theoretical basis" for fingerprint comparison "has had limited study and needs a great deal more work." A new study of the science behind fingerprint comparison was scheduled to begin in early 2005.

Although judges and others are demanding more scientific evidence from forensic scientists, few are willing to dismiss these branches of forensics as pseudoscience altogether. Many judges are, however, less shy about branding as pseudoscience some other branches of forensics, including forensic **animation** and forensic **odontology**.

A new branch of forensics, forensic animation, creates computerized illustrations of the events of a crime. The technology was first used in a 1984 New York car accident case. In 1992 it was used to convict a San Francisco man of murdering his brother. It has also been used in product liability and baby-shaking cases. By the early 2000s, over a hundred firms were specializing in the creation of forensic animations. Typical of these was a 72-second animation used to convict a Scranton, Pennsylvania, man accused of shooting his wife. The video broke down the crime second by second, illustrating the angle from which the shots were fired, where they entered the body, and the like. Judges like forensic animation because of its efficiency; a video can show in minutes what might take a day or more to establish with traditional witness-stand testimony. Prosecutors like it because it brings a crime to life in a way that such phrases as "posterior exit wound" uttered by dour scientists do not. Others dismiss the technology as a form of pseudoscience for at least three reasons. First, the animation creates an aura of accuracy and precision, similar to the 650 quadrillion knife blades mentioned above, about the reconstruction of events that is often based, at best, on human analysis and interpretation of physical evidence. Second, the animation fills in blanks in the sequence of events that cannot really be known. And finally, noting that in functioning as executive producers of such videos, many attorneys admit it is possible to manipulate camera angles or lighting to achieve a desired effect that may mislead a judge or jury.

Also coming under severe fire is bite mark evidence offered by forensic odontologists. These experts originally limited their efforts to identifying crime or disaster victims through dental records, but after gaining recognition as a division of the **American Academy of Forensic Sciences** in 1970, they began to branch out into criminal investigations. Relying on low-tech tools like putty to make impressions of bite marks and plaster casts of a suspect's teeth, as well as such high-tech tools as image-enhancing software to make bite mark features more visible, they have testified at hundreds of trials, often involving such crimes as rape, murder, and child abuse, where bite marks are often found on the victims. Some have gone so far as to say that bite marks are as good as fingerprints for identifying a criminal. However, says David Faigman of the University of California Hastings College of Law, "Bite marks probably ought to be the poster child for bad forensic science." He and others point to numerous cases in which convictions have been won after forensic odontologists testified with high certainty that bite marks identified defendants who were later exonerated by DNA evidence. Noting that the field lacks a firm research base, they point to studies in which forensic odontologists in controlled settings arrived at false conclusions anywhere from a quarter to two-thirds of the time and sometimes even failed to identify marks caused by something other than a human bite.

The American Academy of Forensic Sciences, founded in 1948, serves to promote accurate scientific practices within the **forensic science** community through education, professional association, and with its peer-reviewed publication, the *Journal of Forensic Sciences*.

SEE ALSO Animation; Expert witnesses; Federal Rules of Evidence; *Frye* standard; Handwriting analysis; Odontology; U.S. Supreme Court (rulings on forensic evidence).

Psychiatry

Forensic psychiatric evaluations are crucial to many civil and criminal court decisions. Psychiatrists are requested to assess the level of criminal and legal responsibility of defenders in cases of fraud, embezzlement, **murder**, physical aggression, disputes for child custody, and other crimes and court proceedings. In some countries, when a person decides to write a will, his or her mental sanity has to be established in order to prevent disputes among heirs about the legal validity of the will based on allegations of the author's mental health at the time the document was written. Other roles of forensic psychiatry involve studying the psychiatric risk factors for criminal behavior among the population, to evaluate inmates for probationary release, and to research the neurobiological aspects of psychopathic personalities and the risk they may pose to society.

Psychiatry is the field of medical sciences that studies mental diseases and behavioral disorders associated with biological causes. Congenital (present at birth), hereditary, or acquired psychosis, mania, and schizophrenia can often lead to violent or self-destructive behavior and deviant patterns of social interactions. In contrast to psychiatry, **psychology** investigates behavioral, emotional, and cognitive disorders. Psychology also studies the unconscious mechanisms underlying life experiences and mental illness. Both psychiatry and psychology study the development of personality from birth to adulthood, and the psychological (emotional and cognitive) and social or interpersonal developmental needs of each phase of life. However, the medical diagnosis and treatment of psychosis and other psychiatric disorders is the exclusive domain of the psychiatrist, whereas the counseling and cognitive re-education of patients suffering from nonpsychotic disorders, such as neurosis, behavioral problems, and emotional traumas, is usually the role of the psychologist.

Neuropsychiatry or the clinical application of the findings of neuroscience to the diagnosis and treatment of psychiatric disorders has yielded a better understanding of the biological bases of violent and criminal behavior associated with some psychopathologies, as well as a number of new effective diagnostic techniques. Since the 1970s, many neuroscience studies have shown that the brain structures and neurochemistry can be modified during infancy and childhood by the repetitive exposure to traumatic experiences or to neglect. Whereas less than 1% of any given population may present hereditary psychosis, these studies have shown that children born with a healthy brain can be neurologically damaged by chronic exposure to maternal neglect, child abuse, or a violent environment, even if the child is not the direct target of the violence. The brain adapts to such situations by undergoing detrimental and often permanent changes in its structures and neurochemical functions that often lead to psychosis and violent behavior, or to self-destructive patterns and other psychiatric pathologies. Such knowledge is leading many psychiatrists to work in the early detection of children at risk in order to prevent further damage through early diagnosis and treatment of abused children. Forensic psychiatry is therefore, crucial to the evaluation of children victimized by domestic or social violence and/or neglect, and for informing courts and social agencies on the therapeutic needs and available treatments in this vulnerable age group.

Forensic psychiatry differs in nature from clinical psychiatric practice because it aims to prove a fact in court, and is subjected to scrutiny and cross-examination by opposing parts. It requires a wide range of specific studies and adequate techniques as well as a special **training** in order to enable the psychiatrist to act as an expert examiner and witness in court. The psychiatric examiner supplies prosecutors, judges, probation boards, and police investigators with expert diagnosis on the mental state of defenders, convicts, and suspects. Such forensic diagnosis will constitute **evidence** to be considered by judges and/or by the court.

Expert psychiatric evaluation may be divided in three categories: transversal (or horizontal) evalua-

tion, retrospective evaluation, and prospective evaluation. Transversal evaluations aim to establish whether the defendant is suffering in the present from a psychiatric disorder that would acquit him of civil or criminal responsibility. However, an insanity diagnosis implies in many cases the compulsory reclusion to a psychiatric hospital and treatment. If the psychiatric offender poses serious threat to himself and to other people's lives, he can be committed to a mental institution for life. Transversal evaluations are usually requested by the defense or by the prosecution before the trial or in the initial phases of the trial, and are obligatory by law in many countries. Retrospective evaluations require great expertise and technical preparation from forensic psychiatrists in order to infer the mental condition and legal responsibility of the defender at the time he committed the crime. Prospective evaluations, or risk assessment, consist of evaluations based on the present and past history of a convict, or a defendant to determine future risk of recidivism (repeated criminal behavior). It is usually carried out by a multidisciplinary team when prisoners are being assessed for probation, or by the forensic psychiatrist alone to enable the judge to determine the length of a new sentence in cases of repeated offenses.

Another field of forensic psychiatry involves researching the incidence of crime in the population, and is known as crime epidemiology. One such study sponsored by the National Institute of Mental Health (NIMH) was completed in 2002. An entire generation of boys in the city of Dunedin, New Zealand, was periodically evaluated from birth through physical, psychiatric, neurological, and psychomotor tests. In 2002, the group donated **blood** for genetic tests, including those who had a record as juvenile offenders in recent years or were serving sentences for violent crimes. It was found that in addition to having been victims of serious abuse or neglect during childhood, a subpopulation among the delinquent group had a genetic mutation that affected the regulation of a chemical messenger in the brain. Although this subgroup represented only 12% of the delinquents, they accounted for 44% of convictions for violent crimes.

The adoption of psychiatric diagnostic guidelines by some countries in the past 20 years, which are regularly updated to include new scientific advances, are essential for modern forensic psychiatry. The process of forensic psychiatric evaluation can be generally described as requiring interviews with the examinee, clinical physical examination, neurological and endocrine tests, neurological and functional diagnostic tests, neuropsychological assessments, and interviews with third parties. Based on the results of these various tests, forensic psychiatrists issue expert reports and prepare evidence for presentation in court. In the United States, a forensic psychiatric diagnosis is based on the *Diagnostic and Statistical Manual of Mental Disorders*, developed by the American Psychiatric Association. In many other countries the World Health Organization (WHO) guidelines are used, such as the *Clinical Descriptions and Diagnostic Guidelines* and the *Diagnostic Criteria for Research.*

Advancements in neuroscience and the establishment of objective criteria for psychiatric diagnostics as well as the clear and detailed description of the etiology (causes) and ethology (progression) of psychopathologies (serious mental disorders) were important to forensic psychiatry, as these advancements rid the profession of the controversial character often attributed to forensic psychiatry in the past. The APA system adopts objective formulations, similar to those used in other medical specialties. Diagnostic techniques introduced or improved in the last two decades, such as functional brain magnetic resonance **imaging** (fMRI), PET scans, and computer tomography, allow the identification of structural asymmetries and functional abnormalities of the brain associated with some mental illnesses. The same is true for new laboratorial neuroendocrine tests, which give insight into brain chemistry. The advances of neurosciences and the better understanding of brain chemistry gave forensic psychiatry a new scientific status as an objective science, using clear diagnostic parameters and criteria. Therefore, allegations of insanity by defenders can now be proved or disproved on the basis of solid scientific evidence.

SEE ALSO Brain wave scanners; Criminal profiling; DNA typing systems; Epidemiology; Expert witnesses; Forensic science; Genetic code; Nervous system overview; Psychology; Psychopathic personality.

Psychological profile

A psychological profile is a tool that can help crime investigators by telling them the kind of perpetrator they are seeking. The development of psychological **profiling** began in the Federal Bureau of Investigation (**FBI**) Behavioral Science Unit during the 1960s in an attempt to understand violent criminal behavior. Although psychological profiling has been used in the pursuit of **serial killers**, it is also applied to the investigation of **product tampering**, poison pen letter writing, serial bombing, serial rape, kidnapping, **arson**, and single murders.

A psychological profile is built through **evidence** from the scene of the crime, which is integrated into psychological theory. Forensic researchers have built a body of knowledge based upon interviews with criminals and data from a wide range and number of crimes. It is important that the profiler has access to all the information about a crime, from witness statements and analysis of **physical evidence** to **photography** and **autopsy** findings. A perpetrator does not leave behind just physical evidence like fingerprints at the scene when he or she commits a crime. Also left behind clues are clues about behavior and personality which are revealed by a study of the scene and all the evidence connected to it.

Victimology, the study of the victim, is an important part of psychological profiling. The investigator wants to know what attracted this perpetrator to this victim and what the relationship was between them. This may shed light on the motivation for the crime which can reveal much about the personality of the perpetrator and maybe the fantasies driving them.

The perpetrator's *modus operandi* (**method of operation** or M.O.), which describes the tools and strategies used to carry out the crime, can be very revealing. It demonstrates some of the suspect's behavior that, in turn, is linked to their personality. Forensic **psychology** has revealed three main types of offenders. The organized offender plans the crime, sometimes in great detail, bringing tools and taking them away again. The type of offender will take care not to leave evidence behind and will also hide or dispose of the body. The organized offender is usually of average to high intelligence with a stable lifestyle. They normally tend to be married and employed. The disorganized offender often leaves a mess. They don't plan or bring tools; instead they use whatever is to hand to carry out their attack. This type of offender lives alone or with a relative, may be unemployed, of lower intelligence, and have a history of mental illness. Their attacks are often accompanied by considerable violence. The third category is the mixed offender, who shows mixed characteristics of the first two types. While their approach may be carefully planned, the assault itself may be frenzied, showing a person losing control over deep-seated urges and fantasies.

The psychological profile of a criminal can be very revealing of their habits, employment, marital status, mental state, and personality traits. A profile works best if the offender displays some form of mental disturbance such as employing torture or mutilation. Some take a trophy away from the victim, possibly an item of no obvious value but of deep symbolic significance to the perpetrator. They may also use a signature, which is a behavioral sign such as positioning the corpse in a certain way or tying a ligature with a complicated knot. This, again, can reflect a specific personality quirk which may be very revealing to the profiler.

Psychological profiling first proved its worth in the capture of Richard Trenton Chase, the so-called "Vampire of Sacramento," who murdered a woman and drank her blood in 1978. Concerned at the brutality of the crime, the FBI called in the profilers. They noted the disorder at the scene and, from a study of body type and mental temperament, concluded the murderer was white, thin, undernourished, and in his mid-twenties. As a disorganized type, he'd be unemployed and live alone. They also guessed he would kill again and, unfortunately, three days later he did. He murdered three people in their own home, stole the family car and then abandoned it. The second **murder** provided more information to refine the profile. Chase was soon found, living locally. His appearance was just as the profile had suggested. He had a history of mental illness, admitted the crimes, but did not see he had done wrong. He told his interrogators that his own blood was turning to sand, so he had to become a vampire. The profile saved many lives, for Chase had more murders planned and marked down on a calendar found in his room.

SEE ALSO Criminal profiling.

Psychology

Psychology is the science of the mind. An appreciation of what is happening of the mind of a criminal and why he or she acts as she does can be an important part of any investigation. A forensic psychologist (or psychiatrist, if they are medically qualified) can carry out a number of functions, such as assessing the mental stability of a suspect, building a **psychological profile** of the perpetrator and victim, and trying to understand the motivation for a crime.

Psychological tests can be useful in learning more about a suspect and their behavior. Standardized personality screening tests, of the kind that are sometimes also used in recruitment, can reveal the suspect's basic personality type. The tests are lists of questions to be checked which elicit

responses about behavior, emotion, social skills, and beliefs. One common personality test includes the Minnesota Multiphasic Personality Inventory (MMPI), which can reveal if someone is suffering from a mental disorder such as anti-social personality disorder.

The psychologist may also use more subjective tests known as projective tests, which reveal more about inner conflict, fantasies, and thought processes. In the widely used Rorschach inkblot test, the suspect is shown a series of abstract inkblots and asked to describe what he sees. Another approach is to ask the subject to draw something like a house or a frightening scene. This can be very revealing of the suspect's fantasies and may be in complete contradiction to what they actually say to the psychologist.

The third kind of psychological test that may be administered is a cognitive test that measures the suspect's intelligence, mental competency, thought processes, and ability to understand his or her behavior. A common example is the Wechsler Adult Intelligence Scale. Less structured interviews will also be carried out, where the suspect may be encouraged to talk about their family, childhood, relationships, and problems. The psychologist will lead up to a discussion of the events that brought the suspect in for **interrogation** and try to find out how they feel about what happened. Of course, many suspects lie, but a skilled psychologist will be able to sort out the truth from the fiction by analysis of the subject's body language.

SEE ALSO Profiling, screening; Psychiatry.

Psychopathic personality

For both forensic **psychiatry** and legal purposes, the correct diagnosis of psychiatric disorders in criminal offenders is crucial to establish legal and criminal responsibility. Psychopathic personality disorder (PPD) is a psychiatric disorder. The majority of patients with a psychiatric disorder do not commit crimes. For that matter, although psychopathic personality disorder shows a high prevalence among criminals, it does not imply that all carriers of the disorder will necessarily become involved with criminal activity. Conversely, all criminals do not have a psychiatric disorder. An estimated 1–4% of individuals among the general population present some degree of the symptoms described for psychopathic personality disorder.

Psychopathic personality disorder is a chronic psychiatric condition with specific manipulative and exploitive behaviors that persist for many years. The cause of PPD is unknown, although genetic factors and a history of child abuse are thought to play a role. The condition affects more men than women, and often, persons with psychopathic personality do not seek treatment unless ordered to do so by a court. The diagnosis of psychopathic personality is most often made by a forensic psychiatrist.

Perhaps the main characteristic of PPD is the inability to feel remorse. The American psychiatrist and neuroscientist Bruce Perry defines remorse as a painful emotional reaction that results from the realization of how much suffering the individual has caused to another person. Remorse, therefore, implies the capacity to empathize with the pain one has caused another person. People with psychopathic personality disorder have no such capacity. They can repent or intellectually recognize they were wrong, when they are caught, especially if such recognition brings some advantage to his or her situation. However, repenting is a rational exercise, and not an emotional event, according to Perry. People with PPD are often highly intelligent and have able manipulative skills, but often have poor emotional intelligence and are unable to understand or consider other people's feelings. In essence, they are predators, often presenting a cunning intuitive perception of other's psychological fears and weaknesses, which they exploit for self-benefit. Persons with PPD are not solely found among criminal ranks; often they are present at the workplace, in social circles, and in the political scenery. Swiss psychiatrist Karl Jung (1875–1961) made an interesting psychological assessment of Hitler in the late 1930s, describing characteristics belonging to Hitler which resemble the main criteria for PPD: superficial charm, grandiose sense of self worth, keen manipulative skills, lack of realistic long-term goals, irresponsibility, lack of remorse or guilt, callous lack of empathy, poor behavioral control, self-centered and self-important feelings, blaming others for his failures, predatory attitudes, easily-frustrated, impatient, and ambitious.

People with psychopathic personality disorder who do not commit crimes are likely to have troubled relationships at home and in the workplace, due to their destructive personality characteristics and need to manipulate and control others. They have the ability to undermine self-esteem and self-confidence in others. They feel superior to others and consider themselves above the rules that regulate society. Their main aim is self-gratification,

even when they pretend to be caring and concerned with the well being of others. Self-image and self-interest are a high priority for people with these characteristics. They often lie, abuse, steal, cheat, and are unscrupulous in business partnerships and commercial transactions. Appearing fearless, they may put at their lives and the lives of others at risk during thrill-seeking activities. Many white-collar criminals share characteristics with this personality group, and often elude authorities.

Violent psychopaths who end up in prisons are usually less intelligent or have little education, and began criminal activities as juveniles. Violent psychopaths may have a childhood history of torturing small animals and/or of repeated acts of vandalism, systematic lying, thefts, violent behavior towards smaller children, and defiant attitude with parents, teachers, and other authority figures.

In contrast with other psychiatric offenders, criminals with psychopathic personality disorders have a clear understanding that they are breaking the rules. They are convinced, however, that rules exist only for those who are inferior to themselves. Breaking the rules without being caught is a means of proving their superiority. Rehabilitation programs usually provide little benefit to criminals with psychopathic personality disorder, as they do not view incarceration as deserved punishment, and they have no remorse for their actions or wish to alter their behavior.

SEE ALSO Criminal profiling; Criminology; Hitler Diaries; Psychiatry; Psychology.

Psychotropic drugs

Determining the presence of various drugs in samples, including **blood** and urine, is an important facet of **forensic science**. A variety of analytical techniques can be used, depending upon the drug being tested. Eyewitness information concerning the behavior of the victim or suspect, and physical aspects of the investigation scene (i.e., presence of syringes, open liquor bottles, or the smell of marijuana), can guide the law enforcement officer or forensic investigator in recommending particular drug tests.

Psychotropic drugs are forensically relevant. The drugs are a loosely defined grouping of agents that have effects on psychological function and include antidepressants, hallucinogens, and tranquilizers.

They are all compounds that affect the functioning of the mind through pharmacological action on the central nervous system. Psychotropic drugs are widespread in today's society and encompass both prescription psychiatric medications and illegal narcotics, as well as many over the counter remedies. Because these compounds affect human behavior, there is much suspicion, misunderstanding, and controversy surrounding their use. Sedative drugs first appeared in the late 1800s. They were followed by **barbiturates** and **amphetamines** in the early 1900s. But it was drugs such as chlorpromazine hydrochloride (Thorazine) and lithium, introduced in the 1950s, that dramatically affected psychiatric medicine. Medicine essentially recognizes four main psychotropic drug categories: antipsychotics, mood stabilizers, antianxiety agents, and antidepressants.

Antipsychotics include chlorpromazine, which was released in 1954 for the treatment of schizophrenia. Originally designated as a major tranquilizer, it was also found to be effective in subduing the hallucinations and delusions of psychotic patients. Since then, other antipsychotics, including haloperidol (Haldol) and clozapine (Clozaril) were developed for the treatment of various kinds of psychosis.

Mood stabilizers were first recognized following Australian psychiatrist John F. J. Cade's 1949 discovery of the beneficial effects of lithium on manic-depressive disorder. Patients with schizophrenia, however, did not respond to lithium, leading psychiatrists to a degree of diagnostic precision that was previously not possible. Recently, some antiepileptic medicines—valproic acid (Depakene) and carbamazepine (Epitol, Tegretol) have also been used to treat manic-depressive disorder.

Barbiturates were widely prescribed before the 1960s to relieve anxiety, but were found to be highly sedating and addictive and did not always work successfully. Chlordiazepoxide (Librium) and the other benzodiazepine agents developed from the 1960s to the 1980s rapidly replaced barbiturates.

Antidepressants are possibly the most widely used psychotropic drugs in the United States. In any given six-month period, about 3% of adult Americans experience severe depression. For the millions whose depressed mood becomes a clinical syndrome, though, psychotropic therapy is one way to relieve the symptoms. The tricyclic imipramine hydrochloride (Tofranil), developed during the late 1950s and introduced during the early 1960s, was the first of the now-available antidepressants and still is often prescribed. Research has progressed considerably since then and current theories attribute depression to psychological causes (low self-esteem, important losses in early life, history of abuse) and biological causes (imbalance of **neurotransmitters**, including serotonin and dopamine; disruptions in the sleep-wake cycle) as well as social factors. The various classes of antidepressants—tricyclics, MAOIs, serotonin-specific agents—and individual drugs—including nefazodone (Serzone), mirtazapine (Remeron), venlafaxine (Effexor), and bupropion hydrochloride (BuSpar)—target the biological causes. At present, the selective serotonin reuptake inhibitors (SSRIs) hold center stage, and fluoxetine hydrochloride (Prozac) is in the spotlight. The result of years of focused research and design, fluoxetine was rapidly accepted and prescribed to millions within a few months after its introduction in December 1987. As of 2005, long-term effects of SSRIs and potential elevated risks of suicide in young people taking SSRIs are under study.

Though much of the research and understanding of psychopharmacology comes from the field of medicine and **psychiatry**, there are, of course, other areas where psychotropic drugs have been used, ranging from illegal recreational use to the possibility of applying them as agents of "mind control." The Central Intelligence Agency (CIA) Crime and Narcotics Center monitors, reviews, and delivers information about international trafficking in illegal drugs and international organized crime to the nation's leaders and law enforcement agencies. Former Director of Central Intelligence William Webster created what became today's DCI Crime and Narcotics Center in April 1989. The center is staffed by people from the 13 agencies making up the US Intelligence Community, including the CIA, as well as from law enforcement agencies. The Crime and Narcotics Center's staff are responsible for estimating the amount of illegal drugs, mainly coca, opium poppy, and marijuana, produced around the world. They also assist law enforcement agencies to break up drug and organized crime groups and help law enforcement agencies detect and capture illegal drug shipments.

Psychotrophic drugs are potentially useful in the **interrogation** of suspects. One such drug is sodium pentothal, more commonly known as **truth serum**, which is used as a sedative and anesthetic during surgery. It depresses the central nervous system, slows the heart rate, and lowers blood pressure. Patients on whom the drug is used as an anesthetic are usually unconscious less than a minute after it enters the veins. Because of its effectiveness as a sedative, it was also one of the first of three drugs to be used by the U.S. prison system during executions. In milder doses, the drug affects people such that they often become more communicative and share their thoughts without hesitation. Despite its name, however, sodium pentothal will not make a person tell the truth against their will, but a recipient is only more likely to lose inhibitions and therefore, may be more likely to volunteer the truth.

SEE ALSO Interrogation; Truth serum.

Puncture wound

A puncture wound is the piercing of the body by a sharp-tipped object. It can be as trivial as pricking a finger with a needle or drawing pin, or as serious as the fatal penetration of the heart or lungs with a knife. Puncture wounds tend to have more depth than width, which distinguishes them from cuts, where the reverse is true. In a forensic context, the most significant kinds of puncture wounds are stab wounds, which are often fatal.

A stab wound can be homicidal, suicidal, or accidental and **autopsy** can often shed light on the manner of death in such cases. Many different weapons can be used to inflict stab wounds. Typically, a knife is used but screwdrivers, fragments of **glass**, hat pins, or hypodermic needles may also cause stab wounds. The weapon need not even be held by an assailant. In some accidents, people sustain broken ribs which puncture the lungs, or fall on broken glass or spiked railings.

During an autopsy, the pathologist will look at the location, depth, and track of puncture wounds.

He or she will try to work out from what direction the weapon entered the body, the track it took, and the damage caused. X rays can be useful in establishing the track of the wound and may also be indicative of the dimensions of the weapon. It is also important to examine any damage to clothing; the direction of any tears and **blood** patterns may reveal something of the victim's position relative to the assailant.

Relatively little force need be applied to the weapon to build up a penetrating pressure on its pointed end. Once the weapon has penetrated the victim's clothes, then the body itself offers relatively little resistance to its penetration, unless it impacts on bone. Weapons that break into bone will have been applied with considerable force. Often, the tip of the weapon is left behind in the victim's body and, if the pathologist retrieves it, they will have a valuable piece of **evidence**.

Wounds that enter an organ are known as penetrating and if they also pass out the other side they are known as perforating. Much of the bleeding in a stab wound is internal. Indeed, a trivial looking puncture of the skin may conceal a very deep and possibly fatal wound. Cause of death is usually massive hemorrhage. Most deaths by stabbing are homicidal in nature and common sites for the wounding are the heart, abdomen, back, and throat. The pathologist will want to deduce as much as possible about the circumstances of the event by the analysis of the nature of the stab wounds.

SEE ALSO Knife wounds; Wound assessment.

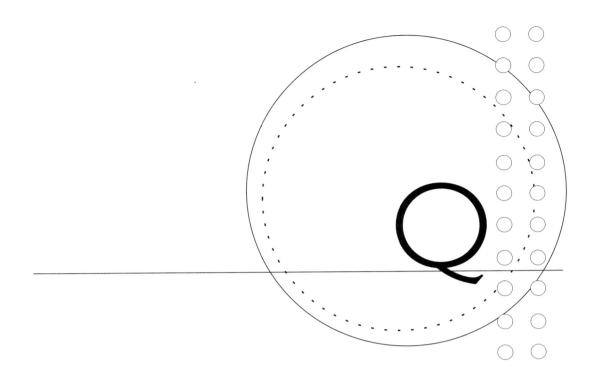

Quality control of forensic evidence

When an item of **evidence** that could be crucial to securing a conviction appears in court, judge and jury want to be sure that it really is relevant to the crime. The only way of fulfilling this requirement is to make the concept of quality central to everything the forensic investigator does with the evidence, from collecting it to presenting it in court. This striving for quality is not confined to **forensic science**; it is found in most other industries, from pharmaceuticals to aerospace. The underlying goal is to offer products and services to the public that are safe and effective. In forensic science, quality of evidence is important because if first-rate evidence is not submitted in court, the guilty may go unpunished or, equally, an innocent person may lose their liberty.

The terms quality control (QC), and quality assurance (QA) are often used interchangeably. What is more, their meanings may differ from place to place and between different kinds of activity. Put simply, QC covers all the different activities done to fulfill quality requirements for a product or service. In forensic science, this might cover the need to run **control samples** when doing a **DNA** analysis or to keep records of exactly what was done in the microscopic examination of a hair sample. The term QA is a broader one, covering the overall system of dealing with evidence and includes issues such as staff training and qualifications and the laboratory environment. A disorganized laboratory, with no

clear chain of command, cannot reasonably be said to be providing good QA. In this article, the term QA/QC will be used to cover all aspects of quality in forensic investigation.

The idea of quality began with medieval craftsman who organized themselves into guilds dedicated to making products of a high standard. Products that reached the quality standards of an inspecting committee would receive a special quality mark. Master craftsmen began to add their own quality marks to their products to guard their reputation and standards. Customers who bought products bearing inspection and master craftsman marks were assured of the quality of their purchase. It was in the twentieth century that the concept of quality was broadened to include many more products and services, including forensic science. The medieval quality marks have evolved into a more general idea of standards, which are procedures, metrics (measurements), behaviors, or whatever is needed in a particular activity to guarantee a quality output.

Standards vary from place to place, so there is a need for some kind of international reference. After all, the result of DNA **identification** should not vary depending on the country or laboratory where it was done. If the defense orders a second opinion, then it merely confuses matters if the second lab follows a different procedure from the first one. The ISO (International Organization for Standardization) 9000 series is a set of international standards on quality management and QA/QC, which was established in 1987 and is constantly being updated and revised. A lab dedicated to forensic investigation can be registered to ISO 9000 standard, which gives proof of the quality of its work. Another important idea in the improvement of quality is benchmarking. This involves a search for a benchmark, an example of best practice or the best way of doing something, and comparing current practice with the benchmark. Quality is an evolving concept, with organizations and individuals continually being challenged to reach ever-higher standards. In science, methods and equipment are changing all the time, and laboratories and their personnel must keep up and adapt. For crime investigation, this can only be a good thing, for it means enhancing the court's confidence in the evidence being presented.

In the context of forensic investigation, QC/QA covers scientific, legal, and ethical aspects of the work of both laboratory scientists and the police scene-of-crime officers. Forensic science involves many different disciplines, from **pathology** and chemistry to engineering and **entomology**. Whatever the nature of the evidence, however, its preservation from deterioration or contamination is paramount. **Trace evidence**, in particular, is vulnerable in this respect. Protective clothing at the scene and restricted access can help preserve the evidence that is present. After that, proper and securing packaging is essential. Once in the laboratory, the evidence must be correctly stored, which may involve refrigeration or protection from moisture, and it must never be left unattended or unsecured in case of tampering or theft.

When it comes to laboratory investigation of the evidence, there will be Standard Operating Procedures (SOPs) and Standard Methods (SMs) that must be followed. These are written instructions as to how to carry out a given task using properly tried and tested methods. These SOPs and SMs will change over time, as new methods, equipment. and evidence emerge. A court would, rightly, not be impressed to discover that a forensic laboratory was still carrying out, for example, **fingerprint** analyses according to a method from the 1950s.

A wide range of equipment, including spectrometers, **microscopes**, **cameras**, and gas chromatographs is used in the forensic laboratory. An important part of QA/QC is ensuring all this equipment is properly used by staff that have received correct training. The equipment must also be properly and regularly calibrated, that is, run with reference samples to ensure its correct operation. It must also be regularly maintained and replaced or upgraded if faults occur.

Quality standards apply as much, if not more, to the people working in the forensic laboratory as to the equipment and methods they use. First, the person must have the appropriate scientific qualifications for the job. Requirements may vary, but each person should have a written job description including their responsibilities, duties, and skills required. The manager of the laboratory will have had several years of experience of forensic work. Technicians will have qualifications appropriate to the type of work they are carrying out. Everyone's work needs to be supervised and audited, both internally and externally. Because forensic science is such a rapidly evolving discipline, it is essential that there be provision for continuing education for everyone employed in the laboratory. This might include the opportunity to take a higher degree and will certainly involve taking courses to learn new techniques from time to time and keeping up with the professional literature to increase awareness of developments. In addition, an important part of being a forensic science professional is to be prepared to testify in court. This may involve fierce cross-examination and the individual must be objective and confident enough to defend their work as well as making the principles and detail involved accessible to the judge and jury.

Everyone working in a forensic laboratory must do all they can to take a scientific, objective, approach to their work, just as one would in any other laboratory setting. This means being unbiased, prepared to repeat experiments, using control and reference samples, and keeping accurate records of procedures carried out and results obtained. Over and above this, there are special requirements for forensic investigators relating to ethical and legal aspects of the work. Perhaps the most important requirement here is an awareness of the importance of the **chain of custody** of evidence. This means that it must be clear to the court exactly what has happened to the evidence from the moment of its collection to its presentation in the courtroom. Everyone who handled the evidence in any way must sign for it and record what they did with it. Only with an unbroken chain of evidence can the judge and jury be sure of the relevance of the evidence to the crime under investigation.

Not only must the evidence itself be properly handled and accounted for at all times, careful records must also be kept of all operations carried out on it. At one time, these would have been hand written. Now, however, there are many computerized laboratory information handling systems. The forensic laboratory should be using a recognized and

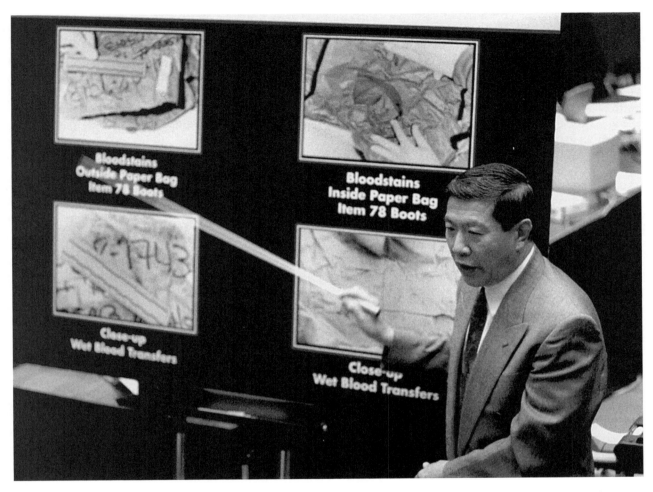

A defense witness forensic scientist uses a pointer as he describes how blood stains were transferred from evidence items to the paper bags they were carried in during the O.J. Simpson double-murder trial in 1995. **AP/WIDE WORLD PHOTOS. REPRODUCED BY PERMISSION.**

acceptable system and all personnel should be trained in its correct use.

People who choose to work in forensic science generally do so because they have a keen interest in the subject and are motivated to help solve crimes and see justice done. However, it is not unknown for a forensic investigator, maybe under the stress of his or her workload or maybe for more sinister reasons, to lose or destroy evidence, make mistakes, or even to falsify results. The QA/QC system should allow for the rapid detection and correction of this kind of incident.

Laboratories doing forensic work can apply for accreditation by an independent third party, which is also seen as an important part of QA/QC. In the United States, this accreditation is carried out by the American Society of Crime Laboratory Directors through their Laboratory Accreditation Board. A satisfactory evaluation and on-site inspection of the organization, staffing, and facilities of a laboratory can lead to accreditation. After this, a full re-inspection will be carried out every five years. Many laboratories in the United States have been accredited in this way and similar schemes apply in other parts of the world, such as the United Kingdom. Forensic science cannot stand still when it comes to quality; the discipline must always be striving to improve.

SEE ALSO Disturbed evidence; Evidence.

Questioned documents

In 1795 an Englishman named William Henry Ireland made an astonishing claim: that he had in his possession a manuscript of the play *Kynge Leare*, written in the hand of William Shakespeare himself. Such a discovery would have been invaluable, for no manuscript version of any of Shakespeare's plays is known to exist. A year later, however, Edward Malone was able to refute Ireland's improbable claim. In examining the manuscript he discovered twenty distinct paper watermarks among its leaves. Surely, Malone concluded, by the time he had written *King Lear*, Shakespeare would have been financially secure enough to be able to purchase a single batch of paper on which to write. The hodge-podge of different papers in the Ireland manuscript could be explained only as the work of a forger, who would likely raid a variety of old manuscripts for paper that would appear authentic, which is exactly what happened. In 1805, Ireland confessed that the manuscript was a forgery and that indeed he had obtained the paper by paying a bookseller to tear pages out of old manuscripts.

Malone was not the first questioned document examiner. In 1681, a French monk named Jean Mabillon (1632–1707) published *De Re Diplomatica*, which outlined a science he founded called diplomatics, or the analysis and verification of documents. Neither Mabillon nor Malone could have known that their efforts would eventually evolve into a branch of **forensic science** called questioned document examination (QDE). In Malone's day and later, a document examiner relied primarily on a good set of eyes, a microscope, and perhaps rudimentary chemical tests, but as new scientific tools emerged in the twentieth century, the field evolved into a complex specialty, demanding from its practitioners a high level of **training** and scientific knowledge.

To that end, in 1913, prominent questioned document examiner Albert S. Osborne invited a select number of colleagues from around the United States and Canada to join him to discuss problems and share research in QDE. For three decades Osborne, whose *Questioned Documents* (1910) and *The Problem of Proof* (1922) are regarded as classic books in the field, continued to meet informally with his colleagues until they formally founded the American Society of Questioned Documents Examiners, the field's leading professional organization, in 1942.

The term "questioned document" refers to any handwriting, typewriting, signature, or mark whose authenticity is in dispute. The types of documents that come under the examiner's purview include wills, contracts, letters, threatening letters, suicide notes, ransom notes, photos, lottery tickets, passports, voter registrations, drivers licenses, checks, tax returns, sales receipts, torn pieces of paper (such

as matches torn from a matchbook), photocopies, carbon paper, charred paper, faxes, and the like. Although typically such documents are paper, examiners can be called on to examine any surface on which marks or writing appears, including, for example, walls, blackboards, or rubber stamps. In one noteworthy 1989 case, an apparent kidnapping and **murder** of a young girl, document examiners were called on to examine the plastic garbage bag in which the victim was found. Minute markings created by the heat-seal process used in manufacturing such bags enabled investigators to determine that the bag was manufactured on the same machine within seconds of other bags found in the parents' house, key **evidence** that resulted in the conviction of the girl's mother for murder.

Questioned document examination is a catch-all term for a field that encompasses a number of subspecialties, some of which overlap and any of which could play a role in the investigation of a crime. These include: (1) **handwriting analysis**, which attempts to show whether a questioned document came from the same hand as a document known to have been written by a particular person; (2) historical dating, which uses such techniques as carbon-14 dating to determine the age of a document; (3) typewriting analysis, which can trace the origin of a document to a make and model of typewriter and to an individual typewriter, a technique used in the investigation surrounding Unabomber Ted Kaczynski; (4) fraud investigation, which follows money trails and often relies on questioned document examination to demonstrate criminal intent; (5) paper and ink specialists, who use chemical and other methods to identify and date different types of paper, ink, watermarks, copy machines, printer cartridges, and the like; (6) forgery specialists, who use lighting, spectography equipment, and the like to determine whether a document or parts of a document have been erased, changed, or otherwise doctored; and (7) forensic stylistics, in which examiners look at linguistic style, grammar, and word choice, to determine whether a person was the likely author of a document. A new and evolving subspecialty is (8) **computer crime investigation**. This subspecialty uses some of the same techniques as typewriting analysis, examining ink cartridges, paper alignment, the alignment of images produced by printers, and fiber analysis of paper, as well as discovery of hidden, protected, temporary, or encrypted computer files, recovery of deleted files, analysis of unallocated space on a computer disk. Any of these subspecialties can merge under the general heading of questioned document examination.

While many state crime labs have questioned document units, the Federal Bureau of Investigation (FBI) often serves as the lead investigative agency or provides technical expertise because of its enormous resources. The FBI's reference files include information drawn from previous casework; thus, evidence such as a threatening note can be compared with other threatening notes that were part of earlier investigations. Examples include the Anonymous Letter File, the Bank Robbery Note File, and the National Fraudulent Check File. The agency's standard files are banks of legitimate documents used for comparison with questioned documents. Examples of these include the Checkwriter File, the National Motor Vehicle Certificate of Title File, the Office Equipment File, and the Watermark File. Watermarks have proven invaluable in many cases to show that a document could not have been written when it was alleged to have been written because the watermark did not exist at the time.

QDE has played a major role in the investigation of cases involving murder, forgery, counterfeiting, art crimes, gambling, kidnapping, organized crime, fraud, con games, theft, **arson**, burglary, serial murders, and sex crimes. The majority of cases in which the FBI Questioned Documents Unit (QDU) becomes involved require handwriting analysis. A typical FBI case arose in 1956, when a one-month-old child was kidnapped from his Long Island home. In the baby's carriage, investigators found a ransom note torn from a notebook purporting to be from the child's babysitter. FBI investigators called in to examine the note discovered distinguishing characteristics in the way the writer formed 16 letters of the alphabet. Of particular interest was the writer's lowercase *m*, which looked much like a sideways *z*. Investigators searched through nearly two million documents looking for similar writing until a Brooklyn, New York, probation officer found in his files documents written by a 31-year-old auto mechanic with the same peculiar *m*. After the FBI determined that the suspect was indeed the writer of the ransom note, he was arrested, tried, convicted, and executed in 1958.

Other questioned document cases have gained national and even international notoriety. In 1976, document examiners examined the infamous "Mormon Will," a holographic will allegedly written by reclusive billionaire Howard Hughes. According to the terms of the will, which had been mysteriously delivered to the offices of the Mormon Church, the bulk of the estate would pass to the church, but $156 million would go to one Melvin Dummar of Gabbs, Nevada. For months, Dummar claimed that he was a beneficiary under the will because a bum he had picked up in the desert and driven to Las Vegas was in fact Hughes, who was rewarding him for his kindness. Eventually, document examiners determined that the will was a hoax. In a similar case, in 1983, after *Stern* magazine in Germany began publishing portions of a set of diaries purportedly written by Nazi dictator Adolf Hitler, document examiners at Germany's Federal Archives, using ink and paper analysis, determined that the diaries were forgeries created by an artist and petty criminal named Konrad Kujau.

Questioned document examiners bring to bear a number of high-tech tools, many of which are manufactured by the UK firm Foster and Freeman. The firm's ESDA[2] is named after the process it uses, called electrostatic detection, to render visible indented writing, such as writing that appears only as indentations on the next sheet of paper in a pad. The Video Spectral Comparator 5000 is used to examine questioned documents in the visible and near infrared regions of the light spectrum and can determine the presence of indented writing, make obscured writing visible, and differentiate inks and papers by their optical properties.

An invaluable tool has been the company's FORAM 685–2, which uses surface enhanced resonance Raman **spectroscopy**, or SERRS, to compare ink samples as small as 5 microns. Raman spectroscopy, developed in 1928 by Indian scientist Chandrasekhara Raman, has a wide variety of applications in law enforcement. It is used, for example, to identify explosive materials and to detect the presence of **illicit drugs**. Librarians and archeologists also use it to determine the chemical makeup of ink or paint found on ancient documents. Armed with this technology, a document examiner can measure the vibrational structure of molecules by exciting them with photons and examining the light the substance emits when its molecules "de-excite." More specifically, the technique directs light from a monochromatic **laser** down an optical microscope to a sample. The sample absorbs the light, but when it re-emits the light, the light is at a different wavelength. This re-emitted light is fed to a diffraction spectrometer, which records the spectrum and displays it on a computer. The light spectrum is a kind of fingerprint that identifies the substance from which it was emitted, for example, a specific kind of ink on a questioned document.

SEE ALSO Art forgery; Computer forensics; Document forgery; Handwriting analysis; Hitler Diaries; Howard Hughes' will; Spectroscopy; Typewriter and printer analysis.

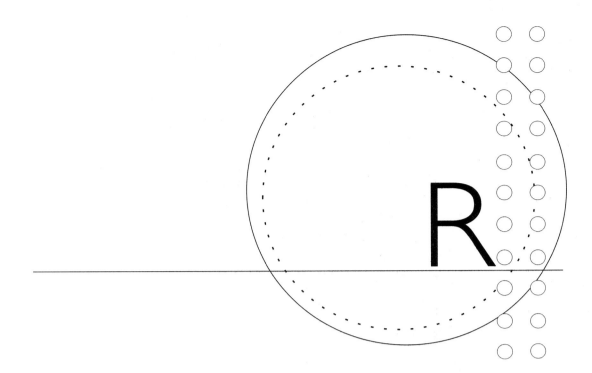

Radiation damage to tissues

Some forensic **evidence** is easy to detect. Gunshot and **knife wounds** and the burns inflicted by chemicals or fire are obvious examples. However, other causes of injury or death are not as easily detected, at least in their early stages. An example of the latter is exposure to radiation. While exposure to a high level of radiation can cause rapid death and massive burning of the skin, the exposure to less immediately harmful levels of radiation cause subtle internal changes in the body. Knowledge of these changes can be useful to a forensic investigator.

Certain types of radiation exposure may cause mutations (**DNA** damage and genetic alterations) or accelerate the types of mutations that occur spontaneously at a very low rate. Ionizing radiation was the first mutagen that efficiently and reproducibly induced mutations in a multicellular organism. Direct damage to the cell nucleus is believed to be responsible for both mutations and other radiation-mediated genotoxic effects like chromosomal aberrations and lethality. Free radicals generated by irradiation of the cytoplasm are also believed to induce **gene** mutations even in the non-irradiated nucleus.

There are many kinds of radiations that can increase mutations. Radiation is classified as ionizing or non-ionizing depending on whether ions are emitted in the penetrated tissues or not. X rays, gamma rays, beta particle radiation, and alpha particle radiation (also known as alpha rays) are ionizing forms of radiation. An example of non-ionizing radiation is sunlight, more specifically the ultraviolet component of the visible light spectrum of wavelengths.

Critical lesions leading to mutations or killing of a cell include breaks in the DNA strands, damaged bases (the building blocks of DNA: adenosine, thymine, cytosine, guanine) and sites where a base is deleted. Large chromosomes can also be deleted when cells damaged by radiation are replicating. Except for large deletions, most of these lesions can be repaired to a certain extent, and the lethal and mutagenic effect of radiation is assumed to result principally from incompletely or incorrectly repaired DNA. This view is supported by experimental studies, which showed that mice given a single radiation dose, called an acute dose, develop significantly higher levels of mutations than mice given the same dose of radiation spread over a period of weeks or months, allowing time for DNA repair.

Biologically, the different effects produced by the different types of radiation involve the way energy is distributed in irradiated cell populations and tissues. For example, alpha radiation ionizations occur every 0.2–0.5 nanometers (nm), which leads to an intense localized deposition of energy. Accordingly, alpha radiation particles will travel only about 50 nm before expending of their energy. Primary ionization in x rays or gamma radiation occurs at intervals of 100 nm or more and traverses centimeters into tissues. This penetration leads to a more even distribution of energy as opposed to the more concentrated or localized alpha rays.

Thus, in a forensic examination, the pattern of radiation damage can be a clue to the type of radiation that was involved.

SEE ALSO Chromosome; DNA; Dosimetry; Radiological threat analysis.

Radiation, electromagnetic radiation injury

An important facet of a forensic investigation is the determination of the cause of the injury or death. This may not always be self-evident, since some causes of trauma do not leave readily apparent external clues. This is especially so when the harmful agent originates at some distance from the scene. One example is electromagnetic radiation.

Any nuclear explosion 25 miles (40 km) or higher above the ground produces a high-altitude electromagnetic pulse (HEMP), a short-lived, overlapping series of intense radio waves that blanket a large swath of ground. Electromagnetic bombs have also been developed and tested.

These radio waves can induce electrical currents in metallic objects and so cause damage to electrical and electronic equipment, including electrical power grids, telephone networks, radios, and computers. Since the basis of human **physiology** is the transmission of electrical impulses, disruption of the passage of currents in the body can have debilitating or even dire consequences to cardiac and neurological functions.

The electromagnetic pulse from a nuclear explosion consists of a series of overlapping radio pulses. When a nuclear weapon detonates, large numbers of gamma rays (high-energy photons with wavelengths less than .1 nm) radiate outward from the burst point. Many of these collide with atoms in the Earth's atmosphere, knocking electrons free. These free electrons are created almost simultaneously in a large volume of the atmosphere surrounding the explosion, and travel rapidly away from the burst point in all directions. Because any charged particle crossing magnetic field lines experiences a force at right angles to its direction of motion, the Earth's magnetic field forces these electrons to follow curved paths. Because charged particles following curved paths emit electromagnetic waves (synchrotron radiation), the explosion-liberated electrons spiraling through the Earth's magnetic field emit a strong radio pulse. Additional pulses, of longer duration but lower magnitude, are subsequently caused by scattered neutrons and gamma rays (radiation that has made one or more bounces, rather than following a straight radial path from the burst point) and by the expansion and ascent of the ionized nuclear fireball through the Earth's magnetic field. The electromagnetic pulse caused by the latter effect, termed the magnetohydrodynamic EMP or HD-EMP, is of low intensity but long duration, and is thought to be a particular threat to power transmission lines.

Two other forms of electromagnetic pulse may be caused by nuclear explosions. The first is generated inside electronic devices by the passage of ionizing radiation (e.g., neutrons and gamma rays) directly into metallic cases, circuit boards, semiconductor chips, and other components, where it can cause brief electrical currents to flow by knocking electrons loose from atoms. This effect is termed systems-generated electromagnetic pulse (SGEMP). The other form of EMP—source-region EMP or SREMP—occurs when a nuclear weapon explodes at low altitude. In this situation, a highly asymmetric electric field is produced in the vicinity of the burst (e.g., within a radius of 3–8 km) having intensities that are much greater than those produced by the high-altitude electromagnetic emission.

SEE ALSO Electrical injury and death; Electromagnetic weapons, biochemical effects.

Radiological threat analysis

Many countries have stocks of radioactive materials arising from nuclear weapon and nuclear power programs. Therefore, there is an ongoing threat of release of significant amounts of radiation into the atmosphere either by accident or by sabotage. Since the World Trade Center attacks of September 11, 2001, fears that terrorists might steal material from a nuclear facility to build a bomb have grown. Experts are now trying to analyze and take precautions to deal with such threats.

Radiological threat analysis starts with assessing and managing the potential dangers of nuclear sites and activities and reducing their vulnerability to accident or attack as far as is possible. Sites where large amounts of material are stored, a nuclear power station, for instance, need to be protected by the police or the military. Security should be tight, but must not interfere with the activities of the site, which may be making a significant contribution to the country's energy supply.

Potential radiological threats are of three kinds. A group may actually steal a nuclear weapon, they may steal radioactive materials or they may attack or sabotage a nuclear installation. There have been no known instances of the first scenario, but plutonium and highly enriched uranium have been known to go missing and may have fallen into the hands of terrorists. There have also been several cases where people have tried to break into nuclear installations but none of them have led to serious harm. Indeed, the perpetrators of the World Trade Center bombing of 1993 threatened to target nuclear installations in a letter to the *New York Times*. Experts have tried to analyze various scenarios such as the sabotage of vulnerable areas, like the control room or electricity supply, inside nuclear installations. These exercises have led to new approaches to tightening up security.

One important finding that has emerged from forensic radiological threat analysis is that no nuclear installation in the world could currently withstand an air strike. Since September 11, officials consider this fact a significant vulnerability. The special hazards presented by nuclear reprocessing plants have also been highlighted by scientific analysts. Nuclear transport trains, which carry plutonium for hundreds of miles in countries like France, are also potential targets for a radiological threat. Such transportation should be minimized, if not eliminated, wherever possible. The analysts must always keep one step ahead of the terrorists, trying to imagine the worst-case scenario of what they might do and then taking steps to prevent it.

SEE ALSO Chemical and biological detection technologies; Chemical Biological Incident Response Force, United States; Chemical warfare; Radiation damage to tissues.

Rape kit

A rape kit, also known as a sexual assault **evidence** kit (SAEK), is a collection of biological evidence taken from a rape or sexual abuse victim after an assault. The kit, which varies by state and situation, aids in arresting and convicting a suspect. It should be collected within 72 hours of the attack, with complete retrieval often requiring up to four hours. The victim's informed consent is necessary for a rape kit to be used.

Once the rape kit is opened, the "chain of evidence" must be maintained. Evidence cannot be left unattended. The recommended contents of a rape kit typically include: instructions and check-off sheet; large paper sheet; filter paper; small paper bags; cotton-tipped swabs; small cardboard boxes; comb; wooden splints; envelopes; red-topped and purple-topped tubes for **blood** sample collection; history and physical documentation forms; patient discharge information form; patient's clothing; fingernail scrapings, broken fingernail pieces; hair strands; oral swabbing; pubic hair; vaginal swabbing; vaginal washings; cervical smear; rectal swabbing; blood samples; and microscope slides.

To begin the process of collection, a nurse individually bags each article of the victim's clothing to be submitted to the investigating police officer or directly to the crime laboratory. Items of clothing are placed in paper bags, not plastic bags, as plastic may promote bacterial growth on blood or **semen** stains. Clothing can be collected up to one month after the assault, provided the items have not been laundered.

The pubic hair region is combed to recover any foreign hair that may have been deposited by the assailant. The comb is then placed in an envelope that is sealed and initialed. The patient is examined for visible blood or seminal stains. If the nurse observes such stains, a gauze pad is moistened, the stain is collected on the pad, the pad is allowed to air dry, and then it is placed in one of the plastic bags. The area swabbed is documented. Ten to fifteen pubic hair **control samples** are taken from the victim. A representative hair sample is also obtained, preferably pulled and not cut from the victim.

A set of swabs is used to prepare two vaginal and cervical smears on the microscopic slides. The speculum used to examine the cervix should be lubricated only with saline, since K-Y jelly may be spermicidal and may interfere with wet mount procedures and forensic evaluation. The slides are sprayed with a cytological fixative and allowed to air dry for three to five minutes before being labeled.

The condition of the hymen and any perineal trauma are noted. If a Wood's lamp (an ultraviolet light lamp) is available, the patient's thighs are examined for fluorescing semen stains (urine and pus may also fluoresce) and any positive areas swabbed. If genital anal contact is indicated, anal smears for **sperm** are collected. Lastly, a blood sample needs to be obtained from the victim for later typing.

Head of the Connecticut State Police Forensic Laboratory hands out new kits for the collection of evidence in sexual assault investigations at the end of a training class in the use of the kits in October 2004. AP/WIDE WORLD PHOTOS. REPRODUCED BY PERMISSION.

If any blood, hair, or foreign tissue is observed on the fingernails, the nurse will scrape under the nails with the wooden splints over a clean white paper. If blood is present, the nurse will clip the nails. Oral samples are obtained by swabbing the mouth twice. Sperm have been recovered from the oral cavity up to six hours after an assault, even if the teeth were brushed or mouthwash was used. A second **saliva** sample is collected on the filter paper disk to determine characteristics (such as **secretor** status) of the victim.

Throughout the examination, the person is observed for signs of trauma outside of the genital region. The most commonly injured extragenital areas are the mouth, throat, wrist, arms, breasts, and thighs. The presence, size, and location of bruises, lacerations, bite marks, and scratches are documented. If the patient consents, the areas of trauma are photographed. If consent is refused, diagrams are used to accurately portray the physical condition of the victim.

Those responsible for collecting a rape kit are trained to recognize the psychological impact of the examination. Although the examination experience itself is generally not physically painful, it can be experienced by victims as psychologically humiliating. For many rape victims, the collection of a rape kit can be experienced as a second source of victimization.

The collection of a rape kit does not mean that the kit will be processed. Historically, many states have not possessed the financing to process every rape kit that was turned into evidence. In response, some states have changed their statute of limitations for rape prosecution, allowing for longer statutes when **DNA** evidence is uncovered.

SEE ALSO Blood; Bloodstain evidence; Body marks; DNA databanks; DNA typing systems; Fibers; Fluorescence; Hair analysis; Physical evidence; Saliva.

Reconstruction, accident SEE
Accident reconstruction

Reconstruction, crime scene SEE
Crime scene reconstruction

Reference sample

Analysis of forensic samples can often involve the use of sophisticated instruments. While the presence of even minute quantities of a compound can be detected, the data can be suspect and legally inadmissible unless it can be demonstrated that the instrument was functioning properly. In a proper sample analysis, various quality control procedures need to be included along with the samples. One critical aspect is the inclusion of a reference sample.

A reference sample is a sample that is comprised of a similar matrix as the forensic sample. For example, if a forensic sample is a water-based solution, the reference sample must be a water-based solution. In addition, a reference sample contains a precisely defined amount of a target compound or microorganism.

Analysis of a reference sample should yield, within defined limits, the quantity of the target agent. If the analysis precision is faulty, then the reliability of the equipment and/or the operator is questioned.

For example, a microbiological reference sample will contain a defined number of living bacteria (such as *Escherichia coli*). The sample is rapidly shipped to the laboratory and must be analyzed within a defined time (typically 48 hours). The results are sent back for evaluation and determination of the laboratory's performance.

Reference samples are commonly used in accreditation procedures, which are designed to verify that a laboratory is competent to perform the analyses. Achieving and maintaining accreditation adds credibility to a laboratory's performance and makes it less likely that the legal admissibility of sample analyses will be questioned.

In the United States, the American Board of Forensic Technology maintains a laboratory accreditation program in forensic **toxicology**. Proficiency testing involves the analysis of reference samples for the detection, **identification** and quantitative analysis of alcohol, various drugs, and **toxins** in biological matrices including urine and **blood**.

Other reference samples are available, depending on the analytical capability of the lab. Examples include **DNA** and metal ions.

Other countries have their own reference sample programs. For example, the Standards Council of Canada oversees the reference sample-mediated accreditation program that includes the six Royal Canadian Mounted Police forensic laboratories located across the country.

Laboratories that participate in reference sample-mediated accreditation programs are required to analyze a determined number of samples each year. This schedule ensures that the lab's equipment and personnel are continually proficient.

SEE ALSO Analytical instrumentation; Control samples; Quality control of forensic evidence.

Kathleen J. Reichs
AMERICAN
FORENSIC ANTHROPOLOGIST, WRITER

Kathleen J. Reichs is a professor of **anthropology** at the University of North Carolina, Charlotte. In addition, she investigates up to 80 cases a year as forensic anthropologist for both the State of North Carolina and the Province of Quebec, Canada, the latter a position offered to her because she is one of the few certified forensic anthropologists fluent in French. Forensic anthropology is the application of the science of physical anthropology to the legal process. In her professional capacity, Reichs identifies bones and analyzes fracture patterns, bullet wounds, and stab marks in cases where she is called in by a pathologist. Reichs is also the author of a series of bestselling novels featuring protagonist Temperance Brennan, a female forensic anthropologist.

Reichs was born in Chicago, Illinois. She received her Ph.D. from Northwestern University. An internationally recognized forensic anthropologist, in the capacity of her work she has testified at the United Nations Tribunal on Genocide in Rwanda, helped identify remains from mass graves in Guatemala, and performed forensic investigations at Ground Zero in New York. She has also examined the remains from the Tomb of the Unknown Soldier. Additionally, she has taught **FBI** agents at the Federal Bureau of Investigation laboratories in Quantico, Virginia how to detect and recover human remains.

Writing under the name Kathy Reichs, she draws on her experience as a forensic scientist to create her forensic thrillers, which began with *Deja Dead* in 1997. Protagonist Temperance "Tempe" Brennan's work parallels that of her creator. The fictional stories spend a great deal of time explaining the processes used in forensics.

"The hard part was interweaving the science, making it brief enough so that it isn't boring, and doing it totally without jargon," Reich related in an interview. "I tried to make it accurate," the author also explained, "not just grisly or sensational. I wrote it to give people the feel of what it's like to do this kind of work." Reichs described the difference between her own work and the investigation undertaken by Tempe, saying, "While I do go out to exhumations if we get a tip, I would never pursue the investigation in the way that she does. I stay in the lab."

Reichs has published seven forensic novels and three technical books.

SEE ALSO Anthropology; Literature, forensic science in.

Rudolph Archibald Reiss

7/8/1875–8/8/1929
SWISS
CRIMINALIST

Rudolph Reiss is considered one of the pioneers of **criminalistics**, or the analysis and interpretation of **physical evidence** gathered from crime scenes. His groundbreaking work at the beginning of the twentieth century created advances in forensic sciences. Reiss also contributed to the development of the forensic institute of the University of Lausanne, which is among the world's prominent forensic education facilities.

Rudolph Archibald Reiss was born in Hechtsberg, Germany, about 400 miles southwest of Berlin. He was the youngest of ten children. He attended different schools in Germany until he graduated from high school. As a child, he was frequently in poor health, and moved with his family to Lausanne, Switzerland in August of 1893 in order to improve his physical condition. Reiss began his studies in chemistry at the University of Lausanne and in June 1898, obtained his doctoral degree in chemistry.

Reiss was also interested in photography from a young age. While studying in Lausanne, he actively participated in photography clubs and contests. He also co-founded the *Revue Suisse de Photographie* (Swiss Photography Review). This attraction to photography was crucial to the development of his forensic career. In 1899, the University of Lausanne appointed him to lead the photography laboratory of the university.

In 1909, the *Insitut de Police Scientifique* (Institute of Scientific Police) at the University of Lausanne was founded. This first university level forensic school provided the highest quality of teaching in forensic sciences. While other subsequently founded schools did not survive World War I and World War II, this school endured the wars because it was located in neutral Switzerland. It is now called *Ecole des Sciences Criminelles* (School of Criminal Sciences) and is still one of the world-leading university forensic **institutes**.

In 1911, Reiss published the *Manuel de Police Scientifique. Vol. I Cambriolages et Homicides* (Manual of Scientific Police. I. Burglaries and Homicides), which presents techniques used by the scientific police at the time to investigate, collect, and analyze **evidence** related to burglaries and homicides. Reiss held as his goal to publish *Volume II. Faux* (Volume II. Counterfeits), *Volume III. Identification* (Volume III. Identification), and *Volume IV. Organisation de la Police Criminelle Moderne* (Volume IV. Organization of Modern Criminal Police). Unfortunately, his engagement in the ongoing Serbian war throughout the following years prevented him from accomplishing his goal.

Countries such as France, Germany, Russia, and Brazil invited Reiss to present at conferences and to help with the development of forensic sciences. Reiss spent three months of 1913 in Sao Paulo, Brazil, teaching forensic sciences to police investigation personnel. Then, in 1914, the Serbian government requested Reiss' help in order to investigate the war crimes committed by the armies of Austria-Hungary against the Serbian people. Reiss responded in such haste that he forgot to advise the University of Lausanne about his departure. In 1915, the Serbian government requested his services again and, with the support of the university, Reiss returned to Serbia. During Reiss' absence, funding for the Institute of Scientific Police was threatened, as the university wanted to downgrade it. Reiss immediately responded from Serbia and wrote several letters to support the status of the teaching facility. In 1919, Professor Reiss resigned from the University of Lausanne. First, he explained that he had been absent for so long from the university that it would not be fair for his substitutes to be subordinated again. Second, Reiss' affinity with the Serbian cause conflicted with the neutrality policy of Switzerland. Swiss Criminalist Marc Bischoff replaced him as the director of the Institute of Scientific Police. Reiss died suddenly in 1929 while in Serbia.

Reiss contributed to the development of police organizations in Switzerland and in many other countries. Reiss was also one of the participants of the International Congress of Police, which eventually evolved into **Interpol**.

Reiss developed many techniques used by the forensic community to investigate crimes of all kinds. He advanced the use of photography to document crime scenes and forensic evidence. Finally, his teaching allowed several police agencies around the world to develop their own criminal investigation divisions and to solve crimes using science.

SEE ALSO Fingerprint.

Remote sensing

Remote sensing is broadly defined as the act of obtaining images or data from a distance, typically using a manned spacecraft, a satellite, or a high-altitude spy aircraft. The term was invented in the 1950s to distinguish early satellite images from aerial photographs traditionally obtained from fixed wing aircraft. As such, remotely sensed images can be considered to be one kind of **geospatial imagery**. Although the application of unclassified remote sensing images to civil and criminal investigations has been limited, they have proven to be useful for documenting international atrocities in areas that are otherwise inaccessible to outside observers.

Sufficiently detailed satellite imagery has been used to document international crimes such as possible genocide in the Darfur region of Sudan and the existence of concealed mass graves in Iraq. In Iraq, potential gravesites were identified with the help of satellite image and aerial photograph interpretation and then investigated in more detail using ground-penetrating radar and other methods. A total of 270 mass graves were reported, of which 53 had been confirmed by early 2004, with some 400,000 bodies discovered. Features such as mass graves are generally not directly visible. Instead, analysis reveals features such as otherwise inexplicable areas of freshly moved earth or signs of heavy construction equipment used to excavate the graves. Comparison of publicly available Landsat satellite images obtained in 2003 and 2004 was also used to document the burning of 44 % of the villages in the Darfur region of Sudan during a period of civil strife, which some observers believe amounted to genocide. Burning was inferred in areas where the albedo, or amount of radiation reflected by the ground surface, had changed significantly during the times at which the two images were obtained. This was accomplished by using a computer algorithm to calculate albedo from the satellite data, then subtracting one albedo map from the other to calculate the change. This kind of mathematical operation on entire maps or digital images, as opposed to single numbers, is known as map algebra.

Modern remote sensing satellites provide panchromatic grayscale images (popularly known as black and white) and multispectral images in which channels representing discrete bands of the **electromagnetic spectrum** are combined. The most common multispectral images consist of some combination of red, green, blue, and near infrared bands. Hyperspectral sensors can produce images composed of dozens or hundreds of bands. Using information about the spectral reflectance characteristics of different kinds of **soils**, rocks, and plants, image analysts can fine tune the ratios of bands in multispectral and hyperspectral images to identify specific targets.

Image resolution has historically limited the use of satellite images, particularly those that are unclassified and easily available, in criminal and civil forensic work. The *Landsat 1* satellite launched by the United States in the early 1970s, which provided the first publicly available satellite images, had a maximum resolution of 80 m. Therefore, objects smaller in size than several hundreds of meters could not be analyzed because objects must be many times larger than the maximum resolution in order to be clearly shown. *Landsat 7*, launched in 1999, had maximum resolution of 15 m for its panchromatic band, 30 m for its multispectral bands, and 60 m for its thermal infrared band. Although imagery with maximum resolution of 10 m or more can be useful for regional investigations, it is generally not useful for detailed forensic investigations of activities that have occurred through time on individual parcels of land. A new generation of commercial satellites such as the *Quickbird* satellite launched in 2001, however, has 0.61 m panchromatic resolution and 2.44 m multispectral resolution. The commercial IKONOS satellite, which was launched in 1999, has a maximum resolution of 1 m for color imagery. Although no images have been released as of early 2005, many intelligence experts believe that the most recent KeyHole surveillance satellites operated by the United States have a resolution of about 2 cm (0.02 m).

The resolution of panchromatic images is higher than that of multispectral or hyperspectral images because panchromatic information requirements are lower. In a panchromatic digital sensor, each light-sensitive photosite responds to all colors of light. In a multispectral sensor, however, the same number of photosites must be divided among each of the spectral bands. A multispectral sensor with infrared, red, green, and blue bands but the same number of photosites as a panchromatic sensor would have a resolution only 1/4 as high as the panchromatic sensor. This explains, for example, the ratio of 4 between the panchromatic 0.61 m resolution and multispectral 2.44 m resolution of the *Quickbird* satellite. In some cases, multispectral images can be combined with brightness information from more detailed panchromatic images. The apparent effect is a sharper image, although the resolution of the multispectral layer is not actually changed.

SEE ALSO Digital imaging; Geospatial imagery; Satellites, non-governmental high resolution.

Robert K. Ressler

AMERICAN
CRIMINOLOGIST

Former Supervisory Special Agent and Federal Bureau of Investigation (**FBI**) criminologist Robert K. Ressler was with the FBI's elite Behavioral Sciences Unit (BSU) for sixteen of his twenty years with the Bureau. Ressler served on active duty in the United States Army for ten years, and then remained in the Reserves until his retirement at the Rank of Colonel, with thirty-five years of service. While in the Army, he served in the Military Police Corps and was a criminal investigation officer with the Criminal Investigation Division (CID) in Washington, D.C. Ressler attended graduate school at Michigan State University and earned a master's degree. A Special Agent in the FBI's Lansing, Michigan, office who eventually became the Assistant Director of the FBI's Training Academy in Quantico recruited him. When the Academy opened in 1972, the BSU was established. Special Agents Howard Teten and Pat Mullany were the pioneers in developing the BSU's metatheory and psychological approach to criminal behavioral **profiling** that was to strongly influence both the FBI and the worldwide **forensic science**

community for the remainder of the century. Mullany and Teten formed the original FBI profiling and crime scene assessment team. As the profiling program began to gather momentum, more agents were recruited for training. When the FBI's Training Academy opened in 1972, the Unit was officially established. Ressler was recruited into the BSU in 1974, and was initially involved as a training instructor for new Academy students.

Ressler remained with the BSU for the next sixteen years, until his retirement from the Bureau in August of 1990. During that time, he was responsible for creating many programs leading to the development of the National Center for the Analysis of Violent Crime. He was the catalyst and director of the FBI's first research program concerning violent criminal offenders, and, as such, interviewed and collected data on thirty-six serial and sexual murderers. The program resulted in the publication of two textbooks: *Sexual Homicide: Patterns and Motives* (1988) and the *Crime Classification Manual* (1992). Ressler is credited with having originated the term "serial killer."

In 1985, he became the first Program Manager for the Violent Criminal Apprehension Program (VICAP). The goal of VICAP was to gather all possible information about both solved and unsolved homicides, concentrating on those that were random, involved abduction and/or were serial in pattern. Added to the database was information about unidentified corpses for whom the manner of death appeared to be homicide, and missing persons for whom foul play was strongly suspected. The database was could be accessed and added to as a crime-solving tool, by law enforcement agencies, both within the United States and internationally.

Since his retirement from the FBI, Ressler has continued to play an active role in the world of forensic science. He is a criminologist in private practice as well as a popular international lecturer and public speaker. He continues to consult with law enforcement agencies, and to testify as an expert witness on both civil and criminal cases. Robert Ressler is the Director of the Virginia-based Forensic Behavioral Services, a training, lecturing, expert witness, and consulting agency. His particular areas of interest remain **criminology**, criminal personality profiling, sexual assaults, workplace violence, crime scene analysis, hostage negotiation, homicide (especially serial and sexual murders), and threat assessment.

SEE ALSO Civil court (forensic evidence); Criminalistics; Criminal profiling; Serial killers.

RFLP (restriction fragment length polymorphism)

RFLP, or restriction fragment length polymorphism, is a molecular biological technique used to compare **DNA** from two samples. Special enzymes that cleave the DNA in specific locations are used to digest strands of DNA. Mutations within the DNA result in strands of different lengths. **Electrophoresis** is then used to separate the strands according to their length. RFLP is used as part of DNA fingerprinting, to detect genetic diseases and to determine genetic relationships between species.

The DNA molecule is made up of a sequence of four smaller molecules called nucleotides. The four nucleotides are adenine (A), guanine (G), cytosine (C), and thymine (T). The sequence of these nucleotides is extremely important, as it determines the structure of all of the molecules in an individual. Differences in individuals result from small variations, called mutations, in the sequence of DNA. There are a variety of types of mutations in DNA. Insertions are regions of DNA where nucleotides have been added to a sequence. Deletions are regions where nucleotides have been removed. In vertebrates (animals with a backbone), there are regions of DNA that contain many repetitions of the same sequence. Two families of these repeats are found quite often in DNA: variable number of tandem repeats (VNTRs) and short tandem repeats (STR). Point mutations may also occur in DNA. This is simply the replacement of a single nucleotide by a different one.

A special type of protein called a restriction enzyme, or a restriction endonuclease, can recognize specific sequences of nucleotides on DNA and then cleave the DNA at these locations. For example, the restriction enzyme HaeIII recognizes the sequence GCGC and it cleaves the bond between middle cytosine and guanine. Bacteria naturally produce restriction enzymes and they use them to cleave the DNA from foreign organisms. Over 90 different restriction enzymes have been isolated from different species of bacteria. Each of these enzymes cleaves DNA between different, and specific, sequences of nucleotides.

When performing RFLP, the target DNA is usually subjected to polymerase chain reaction, which produces millions of copies of strands of DNA identical to the original. This amplified DNA is then combined with a set of restriction enzymes, which cleave the DNA in specific locations. For example, consider the strand of DNA from one individual with the sequence GCGCAAGGC-GAATTCGCGC. The restriction enzymes HaeIII and EcoRI are both added to the mixture. As discussed, HaeIII cleaves between C and G on the sequence GCGC. EcoRI recognizes the sequence GAATTC and it cleaves the bond between the adenine and the thymine. The resulting strands from this RFLP would be GC, GCAAGGCGAA, TTCGC, and CG. Next, consider a sample of the same region of DNA from a second individual. This individual has a point mutation so that their DNA sequence is GCGCAAGGC-GAATTCGCCC. After exposure to the same restriction enzymes, the resulting strands of DNA would be GC, GCAAGGCGAA and TTCGCCC.

After exposure to the restriction enzymes, the two mixtures are transferred to a gel and electrophoresis is performed. In gel electrophoresis an electrical current is transmitted through the gel causing the fragments of DNA to migrate through the gel according to their electrophoretic mobility. This distance is roughly proportional to the inverse of the fragment's length. As a result, shorter fragments migrate farther from the origin as they move through the gel.

After the gel is run, the DNA is labeled using a radioactive probe and the gel is exposed to x-ray film, which changes color in the presence of radioactivity. The locations of the fragments of DNA show up on the film as bands. Different samples can be loaded onto the gel in different lanes so that the banding patterns can be compared side-by-side. In the example above, if the digested DNA is loaded into two lanes on the same gel, three bands will appear in both lanes but the pattern will be different. Both lanes will have a band very far from the origin containing the small sequence GC and a band close to the origin containing the sequence GCAAGGCGAA. Both lanes will also have a third band between these two. However, the band from the first individual will be farther from the origin than the band from the second individual, because it is shorter.

In cases where the DNA under consideration contains VNTRs or STRs, restriction enzymes that do not cut within the VNTR or STR sequence are used. The resulting gel has bands closer to the origin that represent fragments with more repeats and bands farther from the origin for fragments that contain few repeats.

The applications for RFLP are many. DNA fingerprinting uses the presence of STRs at thirteen different locations on the chromosomes. The lengths of these STRs are detected using RFLP analysis. Several genetic diseases are detected using RFLP analysis including cystic fibrosis, Huntington's chorea and sickle-cell anemia. In particular, sickle-cell anemia is caused by a single mutation of a single nucleotide: thymine is replaced by adenine. This mutation occurs at a point in the DNA sequence that is recognized by the restriction enzyme MstII in a person without the disease. The RFLP from a person suffering from sickle-cell anemia will have a long band instead of two shorter ones because the cleavage by MstII will not occur. Finally, mutations in DNA between species are often investigated using RFLP analysis. Species with more different banding patterns are suspected of being less closely related than species with more similar banding patterns.

SEE ALSO DNA banks for endangered animals; DNA fingerprint; DNA sequences, unique; Mitochondrial DNA analysis; Y chromosome analysis.

Dieter Max Richter

AUSTRIAN
FORENSIC SCIENTIST

In 1900, Dieter Max Richter made two important contributions to the world of **forensic science**. First, he adapted the Austrian Nobel Prize winning immunologist Karl Landsteiner's (1868–1943) technique for **blood** group typing for use on bloodstains. His second major contribution to the world of forensic science was his application of the scientific method; it was the first time that performance validation experiments were used to adapt a technique specifically for use within the field of forensic science.

With Landsteiner, Richter studied the agglutination of blood that occurs when one person's blood is brought into contact with that of another. They found that the blood of a person with type A would be agglutinated by anti-A **serum**; the blood of a person with type B would be agglutinated by anti-B serum; and the blood of an individual with type O blood would not be agglutinated by either anti-A serum or anti-B serum. Eventually, it was learned that blood types follow predictable distribution patterns: O is most common among indigenous peoples and Latin Americans; type A is most prevalent among Europeans and Caucasians; and B is most common among African Americans and some Asians.

When the pair had firmly established their methodology for typing and grouping human blood, they began to work with blood serum and other bodily **fluids** such as **saliva**, **semen**, and vaginal secretions, and were able to replicate their earlier work. They found the blood serum of some people could agglutinate the blood of others. From his earlier work, Landsteiner had devised the idea of three mutually incompatible blood groups, and labeled them A, B, and C (later referred to as O). Eventually, a fourth group, AB, was added. Landsteiner and Richter used the same methodology employed in the blood group typing of human blood, blood serum, and other bloodstains, with equally reliable results. By so doing, they opened up the world of forensic science to the use of old **evidence** to make new **identification**, or to gain new knowledge about a crime, a crime scene, a victim, or a perpetrator.

SEE ALSO Blood spatter; Blood, presumptive test; Bloodstain evidence.

Ricin

Ricin is a highly toxic protein that is derived from the bean of the castor plant (*Ricinus communis*). The toxin causes cell death by inactivating ribosomes, which are responsible for protein synthesis. Ricin can be produced in a liquid, crystal or powdered forms and it can be inhaled, ingested, or injected. It causes fever, cough, weakness, abdominal pain, vomiting, diarrhea, dehydration, and death. There is no cure for ricin poisoning, and medical treatment is simply supportive.

Ricin comes from castor beans, which produce castor oil, a component of brake fluid and hydraulic fluid. One million tons of castor beans are processed each year and the resulting waste mash contains 5–10% ricin. The 66,000 Dalton protein can be purified from the mash using **chromatography**. Once purified, ricin is a very stable molecule, able to withstand changes in environmental conditions.

The protein composed of two hemaglutinins and two **toxins** (RCL III and RCL IV). The toxins are made up of an A polypeptide chain and a B polypeptide chain, which are joined by a disulfide bond. The general molecular structure of ricin is similar to other biologically produced toxins, such as botulinum, cholera, diptheria and tetanus.

The B portion of ricin binds to glycoproteins and glycolipids that terminate with galactose on the exterior of cell membranes. The toxin is then transported inside the cell by endocytosis. Once inside the cytosol of the cell, the A portion of the molecule binds to the 60S ribosome, stopping protein synthesis. A single molecule of ricin can kill a cell.

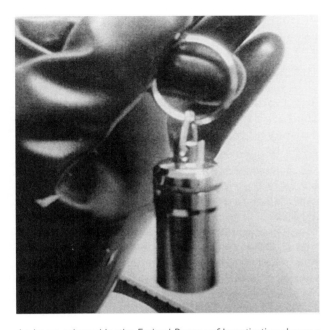

An image released by the Federal Bureau of Investigation shows a small metal vial of ricin found in a threatening letter addressed to the Transportation Department discovered at a U.S. Postal facility in Greenville, S.C., in October 2003. AP/WIDE WORLD PHOTOS. REPRODUCED BY PERMISSION.

Ricin poisoning can occur by dermal (skin) exposure, aerosol inhalation, ingestion, or injections and the symptoms vary depending on the route of exposure. If ricin comes in contact with the skin, it is unlikely to be fatal, unless combined with a solvent such as dimethyl sulfoxide (DMSO). Aerosol inhalation can cause fever, chest tightness, cough, nausea, and joint pain within four to eight hours. Respiratory cell death can prelude respiratory failure. If ricin is ingested, it can cause severe lesions in the digestive system within two hours of exposure. It may cause abdominal pain, nausea, vomiting, and bloody diarrhea. Eventual complications include cell death in the liver, kidney, adrenal glands, and central nervous system. Injection of ricin causes local cell death in muscles, tissue, and lymph nodes. Ricin poisoning causes death generally within three to five days, although a victim may survive after the fifth day.

There is no cure for ricin poisoning, although a vaccine is currently under development. Treatment for dermal exposure includes decontamination using soap and water or a hypochlorite (bleach) solution, which deactivates Ricin. In case of aerosol inhalation, treatment is the administration of oxygen, intubation, and ventilation. Ingestion of ricin is treated with activated charcoal.

The most famous case involving ricin is the **assassination** of the Bulgarian dissident, Georgi Markov. In 1978, Markov was working in London as a British Broadcasting Company (BBC) correspondent. As he was walking across Waterloo Bridge, a man jabbed the tip of an umbrella into Markov's right thigh, murmured an apology and slipped away into the crowd. Markov died four days later. After the collapse of the Soviet Union, the new Bulgarian government admitted that their Secret Service had been responsible for the murder. The KGB produced the murder weapon: an umbrella modified to inject a 1.7 mm platinum pellet filled with ricin into Markov's leg.

SEE ALSO Pathogens; Toxicological analysis; Toxins.

Ridge characteristics

Humans have characteristically ridged skin on their fingertips, palms, and soles. This roughened skin makes it easier to grip things and, up close, it appears as patterns of tiny ridges and furrows. The fingertips, palms, and soles can sometimes create a transfer of these patterns when they come into contact with surfaces and objects. The most important of these transfers are fingerprints, made when the tips of the fingers and thumbs make impressions. Fingerprints have long been used for forensic **identification** purposes thanks to features within their patterns called ridge characteristics or minutiae.

All fingerprints fall into one of three basic overall patterns, the arch, the loop, and the whorl. However, the ridges themselves form a wide variety of patterns within these basic three types. **Fingerprint** experts describe various ridge characteristics. For example, ridge endings refer to an abrupt cessation of ridge. A bifurcation occurs when a ridge splits into two. A dot is a very small segment of ridge. There are also combinations of ridge characteristics, such as the island that is two bifurcations together. When a control fingerprint, either taken from a suspect or obtained from a database, is compared with one from the scene of a crime, the investigator will look at the ridge characteristics.

The control and the sample fingerprint are placed in the same orientation and a search is made for ridge characteristics that match. Each person has a unique pattern of ridge characteristics and it is this mark of identity for which the investigator must search. The number of ridge characteristics that must match to allow identification remains debatable. For many

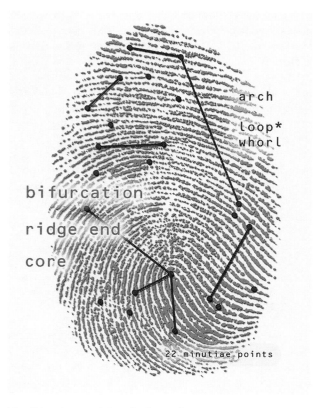

arch
loop*
whorl

bifurcation

ridge end

core

22 minutiae points

Identifying characteristics of a fingerprint. © DIGITAL ART/CORBIS

decades, investigators had to match a minimum of 12 ridge characteristics in a control and sample fingerprint to be able to say they came from the same finger. Now, however, it is accepted that having a fixed minimum is not appropriate in all cases and it is best left to the experience of the investigator to make the decision on identification. Of course, he or she should be prepared to defend this decision in court.

SEE ALSO Fingerprint; Fingerprint analysis (famous cases); Latent fingerprint.

Rigor mortis

Rigor mortis, from the Latin for "stiffness of death" is the rigidity that develops in a body after death. This rigidity may begin shortly after death—within 10–15 minutes—or may not begin until several hours later, depending on the condition of the body at the **time of death** and on environmental factors, such as moisture content of the air and particularly temperature. A colder temperature promotes a slower onset of rigor mortis.

Knowledge of the progression of rigor mortis can be very useful for a forensic investigator in a determination of the time that has lapsed since death.

Typically, rigor mortis affects facial muscles first. Spreading to other parts of the body follows. The body will remain fixed in the rigid position until **decomposition** of tissue begins, about 24–48 hours after death.

Rigor mortis occurs because metabolism continues in muscles for a short while after death. As part of the metabolic activity, adenosine triphosphate (ATP) is produced from the metabolism of a sugar compound called glycogen. ATP is a principal energy source for muscular activity. As long as ATP is present, muscles continue to maintain their tone. As the store of glycogen is exhausted, ATP can no longer be made and its concentration decreases.

One of the consequences of ATP depletion is the formation of abnormal links between two components of muscle tissue, actin and myosin. The leakage of calcium into the muscle cells also contributes to the formation of abnormal actin-myosin links. The abnormality produces the stiffening of the muscle, which persists until the links are decomposed.

SEE ALSO Autopsy; Coroner; Fluids; Death, mechanism of.

Ritual killings

Ritual killings are relatively unusual, but sometimes bear some of the hallmarks of a serial killing, such as mutilation of the corpse or some kind of special positioning. Many ritual murders involve the idea of human sacrifice, usually for religious reasons. The term religion is, however, used quite loosely in this context, as it can include belief systems such as satanism and vampirism. There may also be cultural, psychological, and psychosexual elements to a ritual **murder**. The hallmark of a ritual killing is **evidence** of acts not necessary to bring about death. For example, bite marks, excessive violence, and sexual assault may be found in connection with a ritual killing.

Human sacrifice is a feature of some, but not all, occult belief systems. The word occult means hidden and by its very nature, this kind of ritual killing can be hard to investigate. Violence motivated by religion may not be a crime in the eyes of the perpetrator, but it is treated no differently from any other murder in

Rigor mortis sets in to the body of a victim of a fuel tanker explosion in 1978. The tanker was delivering propane to a Los Alfaques campsite in the Tarragona Province of Spain. More than 150 people, mainly tourists, died and 500 people were injured.
© RICHARD MELLOUL/SYGMA/CORBIS

the eyes of the law. Research into motivation for ritual killings has shown that the practice is thought to lead to transformation, self-deification, and healing. Many people also believe that satanic human sacrifice is done as a way of drawing down dark forces. Investigators may assume that those involved in human sacrifice are simply mentally disturbed and hiding behind a belief system that seems to justify their actions. Yet understanding the beliefs that led to the crime, however distorted they appear, may actually be helpful in solving it and aid in the prevention of future occurrences.

Many ritual killings have involved teenage perpetrators drawn into satanic cults. In 1997, 16-year-old Luke Woodham of Pearl, Mississippi, killed his mother and then went to school with a rifle, killing two classmates and wounding seven more. Woodham had been instructed by his peers in a satanic group that murder was a way of achieving their purposes. The jury rejected an insanity defense and he was sentenced to a life term for each murder. In another case, three teenage girls in Italy murdered a nun,

having formed their own satanic group. There have been other murders, in both Europe and the United States, involving young people who have been in satanist groups.

In vampirism, there is a belief that drinking blood and practicing cannibalism can help the individual to achieve power and immortality. There have been a number of ritual homicides committed in the vampire tradition, some of them involving teenagers. For instance, 17-year-old Michael Hardman broke into the home of 90-year-old Mabel Leyshon in Anglesey, Wales. After killing her by stabbing, he arranged her body with the legs propped on a stool and placed two candlesticks on her body and a candle on the mantelpiece. He then removed her heart and drained blood from her leg to drink in a vampire ritual, thinking these actions would render him immortal. When police searched his bedroom, they discovered a large amount of vampire-related books and Internet material. Hardman, known as the "Vampire Boy Killer," was sentenced to a minimum of 12 years in jail in 2002.

The above cases of ritual killing involve young people who appeared to be dabbling in the occult rather than being committed to it. Often they acted alone or in a small group. There are others who are committed to a belief system, or pretend to be for the purposes of committing the crime. It can be difficult to distinguish between the two motives. For example, Richard Trenton Chase, the so-called "Vampire of Sacramento," murdered a woman and drank her blood in 1978. Psychological profilers noted the disorder at the scene and concluded the murderer was white, thin, undernourished, and in his mid-twenties. As a disorganized type, he'd be unemployed and live alone. They also guessed he would kill again, which he did. Trenton had a history of mental illness and admitted the crimes, but did not see he had done wrong. He told his interrogators that his own blood was turning to sand, so he had to become a vampire.

Another case of a killer incorporating some ritual elements into his crime was the Night Stalker, Richard Ramirez, who terrorized Los Angeles between 1984 and 1985 with a rampage of rape and murder. He would try to make victims declare a love of Satan. At his conviction for 13 murders in 1989, he raised a hand with a pentagram design on it and shouted, "Hail Satan." It is widely believed that killers like Ramirez use belief systems like satanism as a cover or justification for their crimes. Whether or not they are also mentally deranged is debatable.

Even more difficult for forensic psychiatrists are those cases where a murder has been committed by a true believer who considers murder to be a sacred act of sacrifice. Such deaths tend to occur outdoors in a designated sacred area on a significant date. Generally such acts are blood rituals involving a knife. Depending on the belief system involved, the killing may involve a rapid slitting of the throat or be slower and more tortuous. The blood may be drained from the corpse, which will be an unusual finding at **autopsy**. Mutilation post-mortem, along with sexual abuse, carving symbols into flesh, and dismemberment, are not uncommon in such killings.

A recent case of murder, committed by apparent true believers, involved the discovery of the mutilated torso of a young boy found floating in London's River Thames in 2002. The body was found close to seven half-burned candles. An autopsy showed hallmarks of a ritual killing and the body had been dismembered in a manner consistent with a human sacrifice. There was a name on the sheet in which the candles had been wrapped and African experts suggested the signs were consistent with a ritual homicide of the kind sometimes carried out in Nigeria to bring good luck to the perpetrators. It may be that the boy was sacrificed to an ancestor god of the Yoruba people, Nigeria's second largest ethnic group. Orange shorts, orange being the color associated with the god, were placed on the corpse.

Genetic testing, including **mitochondrial DNA analysis**, suggested the boy came from West Africa, probably Nigeria or a nearby country such as Togo or Benin. The boy was circumcised, which commonly occurs after birth in West Africa, but later on as a passage to adulthood in Southern Africa. Analysis of stomach contents and bone chemistry further revealed that the boy could not have been brought up in London. Forensic examination of the cuts where the head and limbs had been severed from the body suggested the expert use of very sharp knives. The flesh had first been cut down to the bones, which were then slashed with a single blow from a weapon like a butcher's meat cleaver. The body was then held while the blood was drained from it.

Investigators believe that those involved in this case included a magician or priest who would have carried out the ritual. The limbs may have been kept as magical trophies. The orange shorts have been traced to Germany, suggesting the boy was brought into Britain by a common route used in human trafficking. It is a complex case and, so far, a so-called *muti* (the African Zulu word for medicine) killing (in which body parts are taken for use in traditional medicines) has been ruled out. The reason is that the boy's genitals were left intact. In a *muti* killing, the genitals are removed, because they are believed to be a powerful medicine. Forensic investigators assume that the killers were more interested in the boy's blood. A number of Nigerians were arrested in 2003 in connection with the murder. It appears the boy may have been kidnapped and brought to Britain purely for the purpose of carrying out this ritual murder.

In terms of conventional psychological **profiling**, the ritualistic aspects of a killing are sometimes rather similar to the signature of a serial killer. So far, the theory of psychological profiling has not been developed to distinguish the serial killer from the ritual killer. To do this, various cultural and religious aspects would have to be added to current psychological theory. Those who indulge in religious violence know it to be illegal but do not believe it to be wrong. Many killers who are mentally ill do not understand they have done wrong and may or may not believe their acts are illegal. Understanding the difference between these two groups is clearly challenging for

Skulls discovered by Nigerian police from religious shrines in forests are displayed at a Nigerian police station in 2004. Officials said that a secretive sect was believed to have carried out traditional ritual killings. AP/WIDE WORLD PHOTOS/SUN NEWSPAPER NIGERIA. REPRODUCED BY PERMISSION.

the forensic psychiatrist but is worthwhile in terms of appreciating the context of certain brutal murders.

SEE ALSO Autopsy; Serial killers; Trace evidence.

RNA expression patterns and time of death SEE Time of death, contemporary determination

Nicholas Romanov

Nicholas Romanov, also known as Czar Nicholas II, was the last in a line of the Romanov dynasty that ruled Russia for more than 300 years. Nicholas was forced to abdicate his throne at the beginning of the Russian Revolution of 1917. After a brief period of confinement, Nicholas, his entire family, and four servants were executed. The fate of their remains was questioned for nearly 80 years and involved both political and religious debate. A variety of forensic techniques, including **mitochondrial DNA analysis**, identified the human remains from a pit near Yekaterinburg in the Ural region of Russia as those of the murdered family.

Nicholas Romanov married a German Princess, Alexandra, with whom he had four daughters, Olga, Tatiana, Marie, and Anastasia, and one son, Alexis. His rule of Russia was fraught with domestic and international turmoil. Russia was poorly prepared for World War I and suffered heavy losses. In addition, Alexandra became closely allied with a mystic, Rasputin, who was seen as dangerous by many in the royal court. A series of riots intensified to the level of civil war and Nicholas was forced to abdicate in March of 1917.

After Nicholas was removed from the throne, he and his family were confined. In November of 1917 they were moved from Siberia to the town of Yekaterinburg. On the evening of July 16, 1918, the Romanov family, Alexis' doctor, and three servants were told to dress, as they were to be photographed for a family picture. A Bolshevik execution squad led by Yakov Yurovsky burst into the room, firing shots at the family and their servants. Bullets ricocheted off of jewels that were sewn into the bodices of several of the women. Those who did not die quickly were bayoneted.

The bodies were taken to a spot called Four Brothers, north of Yekaterinburg. They were undressed and the valuables were removed, including about 40 kg of jewels. The bodies were dropped into a deep mine shaft. After word of the killings spread throughout the town, Yurovsky decided to move the bodies to try to better conceal them. Two of the bodies were allegedly set on fire, but this was found to be too time consuming, so the rest were doused with sulfuric acid and buried in a shallow pit about 20 km north of Yekaterinburg.

In 1978 Geli Ryabov, a filmmaker, and Alexander Advonin, a local expert on the executions, decided to try to find the bodies of the Romanov family. They contacted Yurovsky's son, who had a report that his father had written about the murders. It described the location to where the bodies had been moved. Ryabov and Advonin located the burial site on May 30, 1979, and secretly removed two of the skulls. Because of the political situation in the Soviet Union at the time, the two men were unable to provide any further insight into the assassinations, so they reburied the skulls one year later. When the Soviet Union changed its policies to allow for more open exchange of information, Ryabov told the story of the find in 1989. In 1991 Prime Minister Boris Yeltsin called for an official investigation into the origin of the remains.

Approximately 1,000 bones were collected from the burial site. They were reconstructed to form nine bodies, five of which were female and four male. The male skeletons were those of adult men, which suggested that the body of Alexis, who was 13 at the time of his death, was missing. Also missing was the skeleton of one of Nicholas' daughters, though there remained some discrepancy as to which daughter. A Russian team of scientists used a forensic technique called superimposition to identify the skeletons. This technique involves comparing photographic images with skeletal remains to try to link physical features with bone structure. The Russian team concluded that Marie was absent. Using dental comparisons and by study of various bone fragments, a team of scientists from the United States concluded that Anastasia was missing.

In 1992 Pavel Ivanov, a Russian molecular biologist, and Peter Gill of the British Forensic Science Service performed both nuclear and mitochondrial **DNA** (mtDNA) analyses on the skeletal remains. **STR (short tandem repeat) analysis** showed that the skeletons belonged to two parents and three female children and four other unrelated people. Prince Philip of England was maternally related to Alexandra and his mtDNA exactly matched the DNA from the skeleton believed to belong to Alexandra.

Results of the mtDNA analysis from the skeleton believed to belong to Nicholas were more difficult to interpret. Nicholas' younger brother Grand Duke Georgij was not alive and the suggestion of exhuming his remains was not an option in 1992. One of Nicholas nephews, Tikhon Kulikovsky, refused to cooperate with the investigation. Eventually, two of Nicholas' distant maternal relatives, Xenia Sfiri and the Duke of Fife, offered to contribute samples of their DNA to the study.

Like nuclear DNA, mitochondrial DNA is made up of a long sequence of four different nucleotides. Mitochondrial DNA analysis compares the sequence of nucleotides in two regions of mtDNA that are highly variable between different people. The mtDNA sequence of Xenia Sfiri and the Duke of Fife matched that of Nicholas except for one single nucleotide. The sequence of mtDNA from bone analyzed from the skeleton believed to belong to Nicholas had a thymine at position 16169, and the mtDNA sequence

from Nicholas' relatives had a cytosine at that location.

Additional samples of bone from the skeleton believed to belong to Nicholas were then analyzed to try to reconcile the difference. About 70% of the bone samples contained cytosine at position 16169 and about 30% contained thymine at that location. This variation in mtDNA sequence is known as heteroplasmy and it is exceedingly rare. Some critics claimed that the bone samples must have been contaminated.

In order to convincingly establish whether or not the skeleton actually belonged to Nicholas, the Russian Orthodox Church ordered the body of Nicholas' brother Grand Duke Georgij exhumed in 1994. Analysis of mtDNA from the remains of Georgij resulted in the exact same heteroplasmy as was found in the skeleton believed to belong to Nicholas. Given the rarity of agreement of mtDNA sequence between two people, combined with the unusual occurrence of a heteroplasmy, the probability that the skeletal remains belonged to Nicholas were greater than 100 million to one.

After the source of the remains was established, Nicholas was given a funeral according to the traditions of the Greek Orthodox Church. On July 17, 1998, the remains of Nicholas were laid to rest in the St. Peter and St. Paul Cathedral in St. Petersburg. Two years later, the Church canonized Nicholas, along with his wife Alexandra, stating that their "meekness during imprisonment and poise and acceptance of their martyr's death" deserved great honor.

SEE ALSO DNA fingerprint; Exhumation; PCR (polymerase chain reaction); Skeletal analysis.

Rule of Sixes

The rule of sixes describes a method of determining the distance from which a shotgun was fired. In 1963, shotgun wounds were classified into three types based upon distance and penetration. The distances of six feet, less than six yards, and beyond six yards originally identified by firearm experts brought up the name "rule of sixes." At close range (less than six feet) a shotgun wound appears as a central hole. A blast fired from a distance of up to six yards leaves a central hole with satellite entry wounds. Beyond six yards, the wound appears as only a pattern of scattered shot, with no central hole.

In terms of forensic investigation, the determination of the gun's position is the specialty of both the **firearms** expert and the pathologist. If the gun is pressed close against the skin, all the little shots are concentrated in one place, leading to large wounds. At fairly close range, the shot begins to expand. At about two feet away, the wound begins to look like a large central hole with a few little holes surrounding the edge. Beyond four or five feet, the shot disperses and is more likely to make many smaller wounds and less likely to be fatal.

The wound itself can give important indications on the position of the gun. If the gun is pressed close against the skin, there is a small ring of soot, which is burned into the flesh and cannot be removed. The gun that was fired a few inches away leaves a large ring of soot, since it had the space to disperse and was not embedded. If the gun was held at an angle, the ring of soot will be distorted in one direction.

The distance at which the gun was still close enough to leave residue is called the intermediate range. Tattooing is a pattern of tiny orange-brown lesions on the skin made by a reaction to the gunpowder. It occurs before death, so is an indication that the person was alive at the time they were shot. If the

victim was dead at the time of the shooting, there will still be powder marks, but they will be grey-yellow in color. Size and position of the soot can be used to determine the direction and distance of the gun. However, this is affected by the type and make of gun, so it is helpful to have that information first. As the gun gets further away, the area covered by soot becomes wider but the concentration becomes less dense. At long-range distance, no powder marks are generated. The only mark is the bullet hole.

Because distances are often unknown, the groups defined by the "rule of sixes" were reclassified in 1993 by pathologists according to the patterns of pellet scatter. Type I patients had >25 cm (10 inches) of scatter, Type II had <25 cm (10 inches) but >10 cm (4 inches), and Type III had <10 cm (4 inches). In terms of forensic **pathology**, pellet scatter proved to be a more accurate system, as well as more useful to physicians in determining patient treatment and recovery prognosis for persons with shotgun wounds. The term "rule of sixes," however, was kept.

SEE ALSO Firearms; Gunshot residue; Pathology; Wound assessment.

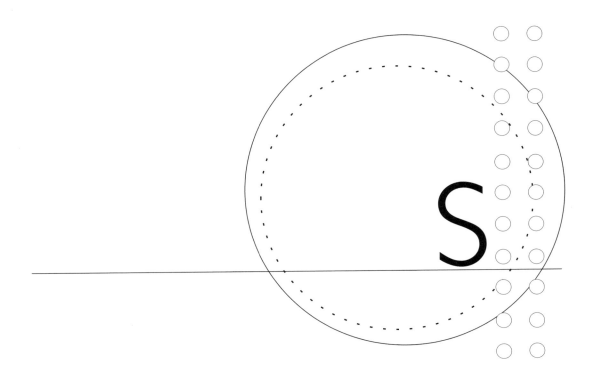

Sacco and Vanzetti case

The Sacco and Vanzetti case is widely regarded as a miscarriage of justice in American legal history. Nicola Sacco and Bartolomeo Vanzetti, Italian immigrants and anarchists, were executed for **murder** by the state of Massachusetts in 1927 on the basis of doubtful ballistics **evidence**. For countless observers throughout the world, Sacco and Vanzetti were convicted because of their political beliefs and ethnic background.

The Sacco and Vanzetti case began in South Braintree, Massachusetts, on April 15, 1920. Workers at the Slater & Morrill shoe factory were paid in cash. The money to be paid out that day, $15,773.51, was placed in two steel boxes, each secured by a Yale lock, and picked up by payroll guard Alessandro Berardelli and paymaster Frederick A. Parmenter for escort to the factory. The two guards began walking toward the shoe factory at 3 o'clock in the afternoon. Just as they passed two men leaning against a pipe-rail fence, the men attacked the guards. In the struggle that followed, Berardelli was shot four times, with the last shot coming as he had fallen to his knees. Parmenter was shot once in the chest and once in the back as he staggered and fell in the street.

The two attackers fired several other shots, apparently to signal accomplices. A dark-colored touring car, with three men inside, picked up the robbers and the payroll boxes. The car headed west, out of town. Berardelli was dead when the **medical examiner** arrived on the scene at 4 p.m. Parmenter regained consciousness long enough to make a statement that he did not recognize the gunmen. He then died at 5 a.m. the next day.

Eyewitness reports differed on almost every crucial part of the evidence. The description of the gunmen's builds, appearances, and clothes varied widely among the many people on the street that day. There was also disagreement about when the bullets were fired and who fired them. Some witnesses reported that a third robber had fired shots. Even the exact sequence of the crime varied among observers.

The police suspected anarchists, in part because anarchists at the time were engaged in a number of bombings and robberies. Michael Stewart, the police chief of Bridgewater, Massachusetts, had been assisting the Justice Department in rounding up Italian anarchists for deportation. One of the anarchists, Ferrucio Coacci, failed to report for deportation at the east Boston immigration station on the same day as the payroll robbery. Stewart concluded that the robbery and murders must have been committed by Coacci and his comrades, among whom were Sacco, Vanzetti, Riccardo Orciani, and Mario Buda. Stewart also considered them responsible for a botched holdup of a shoe factory in Bridgewater in December 1919.

Nicola Sacco (1891–1927) and Bartolomeo Vanzetti (1888–1927) both immigrated to the United States from Italy in 1908. Sacco found work as an edge-trimmer in shoe factories, while Vanzetti labored as a fish peddler. Both men were followers of Luigi Galleani, an anarchist who advocated revolutionary violence, including bombings and assassinations. On May 3, 1920, they learned that an Italian anarchist had died of a purported suicide while in federal custody. The dead man had been involved in a bomb plot with other anarchists, including Sacco and Vanzetti.

On May 5, 1920, Sacco and Vanzetti were either hiding Italian anarchist literature, including a bomb manual, or moving dynamite. Both men were carrying pistols and ammunition when arrested, and during their interrogation—initially about their radical activities, not the payroll robbery and murders—they told lies and gave contradictory statements to the police. The authorities concluded that the behavior of Sacco and Vanzetti meant that the men were guilty of something—presumably the payroll murders.

The trial of Sacco and Vanzetti for the South Braintree murders was held in Dedham, Massachusetts, from May 31 to July 14, 1921. Police believed that Sacco was one of the gunmen and that Vanzetti had been one of the three men seen in the getaway car. During the trial, 169 witnesses testified about 226 items of evidence. Sacco claimed to be in Boston on April 15 to arrange for passports so that he could return to Italy with his family. An Italian consul officer supported Sacco's statement. More than twenty witnesses, all of Italian background, testified that Vanzetti had sold them fish on the day of the crime.

The prosecution's chief expert, Captain William Proctor of the state police, did not hold that Sacco's Colt .32-caliber automatic fired the bullet that killed Berardelli (The remaining five bullets taken from the two bodies could not have been fired from the guns found on Sacco and Vanzetti.) Nevertheless, by prearrangement with District Attorney Frederic G. Katzmann, Proctor testified that the bullet in question was consistent with having been fired from the gun, meaning any Colt .32-caliber automatic, not necessarily Sacco's weapon. Katzmann also knew that the .38-caliber revolver found on Vanzetti at the time of his arrest could not have been taken from the slain guard, as the prosecution claimed. The guard's weapon was a .32-caliber revolver with a different serial number—evidence withheld from the defense.

The jury returned a guilty verdict on July 14, 1921. Each of the defendants was found guilty of first-degree murder. The weight of evidence—the weapons, ballistic tests, and eyewitness testimony—and the issue of consciousness of guilt were crucial in convicting Sacco and Vanzetti, but emotional factors were also heavily present. The presiding judge, a

man who had requested to work on the trial because he hated anarchists, influenced the jury against the suspects with his instructions about the guilty behavior of the men. The prosecutor emphasized the Italian background of Sacco and Vanzetti.

A six-year struggle to save Sacco and Vanzetti followed the trial. Countless observers worldwide were convinced that political intolerance and racial bigotry had condemned two men whose only offense was that of being foreigners, atheists, and anarchists. Sacco and Vanzetti defenders eventually included radicals, trade unionists, intellectuals, liberals, and even some conservatives. Others were steadfast in their belief that the American system of justice could do no wrong and that the two subversives were guilty as charged, had been fairly tried, and deserved the maximum penalty.

The fate of Sacco and Vanzetti, however, was not decided in the arena of public opinion. Eight motions for a new trial in accordance with Massachusetts law were submitted to the trial judge. Several pertained to perjured testimony by prosecution witnesses and to collusion between local police and Justice Department agents. Another addressed a jailhouse confession by a convicted bank robber, Celestino Madieros, who claimed he and other members of the Morelli gang of professional criminals had committed the South Braintree holdup and murders. Each motion was denied. After the Massachusetts Supreme Court ruled that no errors of law or abuses of discretion had been committed, the judge sentenced Sacco and Vanzetti to death on April, 9, 1927.

In the face of mounting criticism of the legal proceedings and the impending death sentence, Massachusetts Governor Alvan T. Fuller appointed a committee on June 1, 1927 to review the case and advise him on the issue of clemency. The Lowell committee, named after its chair, Harvard University President A. Lawrence Lowell, ignored exculpatory evidence the defense had discovered since the trial while validating the prosecution's every step. Reporting its findings to Governor Fuller on July 27, the Lowell Committee declared that the trial and appeals process had been fair and advised against clemency. Governor Fuller followed the committee's recommendation. Despite continuing worldwide protests and demonstrations, Sacco and Vanzetti were electrocuted at Charlestown State Prison on August 23, 1927.

By this point, the case had become too controversial to quietly fade away. Scholars and scientists have spent the subsequent decades reexamining the evidence and the trial testimony. In the most current thinking about the case, Vanzetti is regarded as

Italian immigrants Nicola Sacco and Bartolomeo Vanzetti (middle, foreground) were accused of killing a paymaster and stealing about $16,000 in 1920. Many believed they were convicted and executed in 1927 because of their anarchistic beliefs. AP/WIDE WORLD PHOTOS. REPRODUCED BY PERMISSION.

innocent of any involvement in the murders. The weight of opinion is that Vanzetti, although innocent, was willing to die to become a martyr for the cause of anarchy.

Less certainty exists about the innocence of Sacco. **Ballistics** tests in 1983 showed that the bullet that allegedly killed Berardelli came from the Colt revolver taken from Sacco at the time of his arrest. A panel of **firearms** experts concluded that Sacco was probably guilty either as a conspirator or a perpetrator of the crime. Another group of experts insists that there exists an overwhelming probability that a substitution of bullets took place and that Sacco was completely innocent. They contend that both Sacco and Vanzetti were innocent victims of a frame-up.

Forensic evidence in the Sacco and Vanzetti case has badly deteriorated in the passage of time. It is unlikely that anyone will ever be able to conclusively prove the guilt or innocence of the two anarchists at this late date.

SEE ALSO Ballistic fingerprints; Ballistics; Circumstantial evidence; Firearms.

Sagittal plane SEE Anatomical nomenclature

Saliva

A forensic investigation can involve the analysis of body **fluids**, including saliva, for **evidence** of **toxins** and both prescription and **illicit drugs**. Obtaining a saliva sample is far less obtrusive and

A staff research associate at the University of California-Davis veterinary genetics lab takes a swab of a spot of saliva off a sweatshirt worn by a victim in a dog attack case in 2002. AP/WIDE WORLD PHOTOS. REPRODUCED BY PERMISSION.

cumbersome than obtaining a **blood** or urine sample, especially at the scene of an accident or crime.

Saliva is a clear liquid that is made and is present in the mouth, where it has a number of functions. It wets food and makes the food easier to swallow. As well, specialized proteins that are present in saliva trigger chemical reactions that begin to break apart chemical bonds in the food (the proteins are generically termed enzymes). This begins the process of digestion, whereby the food is converted to a form that can be utilized by the body to provide energy. For example, the salivary enzyme alpha-amylase initiates the breakdown of starch into its constituent maltose sub-units.

In addition to wetting the food, saliva also wets the tongue, which aids the various receptors on the surface of the tongue in differentiating the different tastes of foods. Washing of saliva over the surface of teeth, and the presence of antibacterial enzymes, helps keep teeth clean and helps lessen the chance of infections.

Saliva production lessens during sleep. The resulting build-up of bacteria on the teeth and in the mouth produces the characteristic objectionable morning breath. Even though production lessens during sleep, the production of saliva is a round-the-clock affair. Every day, 2–4 pints (approximately 1–2 liters) of saliva are produced. This large volume is secreted by three pairs of salivary glands located in the mouth.

Within each gland a cluster of cells called the acinus secrete the salivary fluid. The fluid contains water, electrolytes (minerals such as sodium, potassium, and calcium that are present in body fluids and cells, and whose concentrations are important in maintaining proper body function), mucus (a slippery, jelly-like substance that helps coat and protect cells) and the aforementioned enzymes.

From the acinus, the fluid collects in ducts within each salivary gland. Here, the composition of the fluid is changed. Most of the sodium is reabsorbed and potassium and bicarbonate ions are added. The latter is particularly important in ruminant animals like cows, since, when swallowed, it helps counteract the corrosive action of the large quantity of acid that is produced in the forestomachs.

From the collecting ducts, the saliva passes to larger ducts, which ultimately merge to form a single large duct, from which the saliva empties into the mouth.

Most animals, including humans, have three pairs of salivary glands that are located on either side of the mouth in three different locations. They differ in the nature of the saliva that is produced.

The parotid glands are located near the upper teeth, in a broad area underneath the earlobe. The secreted saliva is watery and reminiscent of the serum portion of blood; indeed, it is described as being serous. Submaxillary (or submandibular) glands are located on the floor of the mouth, underneath the back portion of the tongue. The saliva produced by these glands is a mixture of serous and mucus portions. Finally, the sublingual glands are located on the floor of the mouth in the region of the chin. Sublingual saliva is predominantly mucous in composition.

In addition to the three pairs of glands, hundreds of small glands called minor salivary glands are located in the lips, inside of the cheeks, and throughout the remainder of the mouth and throat.

Saliva can be of forensic significance because traces of drugs that are circulating in the body can be present in saliva. The composition of the saliva accurately mirrors the proteins that are present in both the blood and the urine. Thus, testing of saliva, which is easier and less obtrusive than obtaining a blood or urine sample, can be used to reveal the presence of prescription and illicit drugs.

Similar tests are being refined that will enable the detection of viral and bacterial infections as well as diseases such as cancer. These tests are based on the presence of signature proteins that are unique to the maladies, such as antibodies, from the microorganism or cancerous cells.

For example, an antibody-based saliva test for the human immunodeficiency virus (HIV; the accepted cause of acquired immunodeficiency syndrome) is available for clinical use. No home-use tests are officially approved as of yet, although a number of non-sanctioned and independently evaluated tests are available through Internet-based companies.

Promising preliminary research results published in February 2005 have shown that aberrant genetic material (deoxyribonucleic acid; **DNA**) and the messenger ribonucleic acid (mRNA) that helps process the genetic information into a protein from cancerous cells can also be detected in saliva. In the future,

forensic analysis of saliva may help determine if the subject has (or did have) cancer.

SEE ALSO Barbiturates; Illicit drugs.

Sample control SEE Control samples

William C. Sampson
AMERICAN
CRIME SCENE INVESTIGATOR

Retired crime scene investigator William C. Sampson worked for the Miami-Dade Police Department for almost forty years, and is recognized as an expert in recovering latent fingerprints from skin. Using his experience and expertise, Sampson has consulted with and taught hundreds of law enforcement personnel on his innovative techniques. He has also written and lectured widely on the subject.

Sampson's career was spent serving the Miami-Dade Police Department, where he held posts as a training advisor, liaison to the department's crime laboratory, administrative supervisor, and crime scene investigator. He is a certified instructor by the Florida State General Police Standards Commission, and has worked as an adjunct professor at Miami-Dade Community College.

During the course of his career, Sampson made the discovery that the environment can affect the ability to obtain latent fingerprints from materials like skin and cloth. Previous to this, it was widely accepted that this type of **fingerprint** was unlikely, if not impossible, to obtain. Sampson experimented with manipulating the environmental ambient temperature and humidity and keeping the skin at a certain temperature, thus creating readable prints. He consulted with doctors, medical examiners, funeral directors, and even air conditioning companies. Working on his technique, he was able to yield a very high success rate, and as a result Sampson's work led to the **identification** and conviction of numerous perpetrators. Sampson has been teaching his techniques to law enforcement personnel across the country, and lecturing at many industry events and conferences. He has also written about developing latent fingerprints for trade publications such as the *Journal of Forensic Identification*, *The Print*, and *Evidence Technology*.

In 1995, Sampson, along with his wife and fellow forensic scientist Karen Sampson, formed

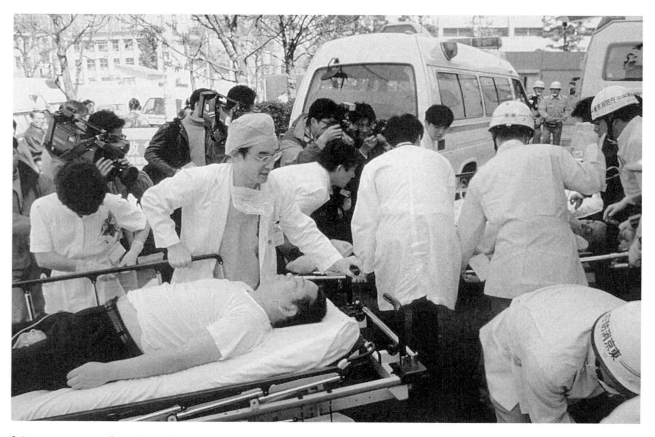

Subway passengers affected by sarin gas planted in central Tokyo subways by the Aum Shinri Kyo cult's are carried into St. Luke's International Hospital in Tokyo in 1995. **AP/WIDE WORLD PHOTOS. REPRODUCED BY PERMISSION.**

KLS Forensics Inc. The company assists law enforcement agencies and provides training in many crime scene related topics.

Sampson was awarded the 1997 John A. Dondero Award from the **International Association for Identification**. He previously was the recipient of the Ford Foundation Award and the Miami-Dade Police Department's Distinguished Service Award. He is also a retired fellow of the British Fingerprint Society, and a member of the Florida division of the International Association for Identification.

SEE ALSO Careers in forensic science; Latent fingerprint.

Sarin gas

Sarin gas (O-Isopropyl methylphosphonofluoridate), also called GB, is one of the most dangerous and toxic chemicals known. It belongs to a class of chemical weapons known as nerve agents, all of which are organophosphates. The G nerve agents, including **tabun**, sarin, and soman, are all extremely toxic, but not very persistent in the environment. Pure sarin is a colorless and odorless gas, and since it is extremely volatile, can spread quickly through the air. A lethal dose of sarin is about 0.5 milligrams; it is approximately 500 times more deadly than cyanide.

Sarin, which has become infamous in contemporary times from its use in Iraq, and by the Aum Shinrikyo doomsday cult, was first synthesized in 1938 by a group of German scientists researching new pesticides. Its name is derived from the names of the chemists involved in its creation: Schrader, Ambros, Rudriger, and van der Linde. A pilot plant to study the use of sarin was built in Dyernfurth. Although they produced between 500 kg and 10 tons of sarin, the German government decided not to use chemical weapons in artillery during World War II. The Soviet army captured the plant at Dyernfurth at the end of the war and resumed production of sarin in 1946. The Russian government currently has about 11,700 tons of sarin.

Between about 1950 and 1956, the United States produced sarin. It is estimated to have stockpiles totaling 5,000 tons of the nerve agent stored in different parts of the country. Several other countries including Syria, Egypt, Iran, Libya, and North Korea have confirmed or suspected stocks of sarin.

Like other organophosphate nerve agents, sarin inhibits the break down of the enzyme acetyl-cholinesterase. Under normal conditions, this enzyme hydrolyzes the neurotransmitter acetylcholine. When sarin is present, the build up of acetyl-cholinesterase results in the accumulation of excessive concentrations of acetylcholine in nerve synapses. This overstimulates parasympathetic nerves in the smooth muscle of the eyes, respiratory tract, gastrointestinal tract, sweat glands, cardiac muscles, and blood vessels.

After exposure to sarin, symptoms begin within minutes. If a person survives for a few hours after exposure, he or she will likely recover from the poisoning. The first symptoms of sarin poisoning include a runny nose, blurred vision, sweating, and muscle twitches. Longer exposures result in tightness of the chest, headache, cramps, nausea, vomiting, involuntary defecation and urination, convulsions, coma, and respiratory arrest.

Atropine acts an antidote for nerve agent, including sarin. Atropine binds to one type of acetylcholine receptor on the post-synaptic nerve. A second antidote is pralidoxime iodide (PAM), which blocks sarin from binding to any free acetyl-cholinesterase. Both should be administered as soon as possible following exposure to the toxin. Diazapam can also be used to prevent seizures and convulsions.

SEE ALSO Toxicological analysis; Toxicology.

Satellites, non-governmental high resolution

High-resolution satellites, generally understood to be those with a spatial resolution of 2 meters (6.6 feet) or less, have the capability to provide forensic information from areas that are otherwise inaccessible to law enforcement officials.

Resolution is a measure of the ability of an image to depict detail. When used in reference to digital images such as those produced by **remote sensing** satellites, resolution generally refers to size of the pixels, or fundamental elements, comprising the image. A 2-meter resolution image consists of elements representing the average color or intensity of a 2x2 meter area of Earth's surface. Nothing smaller than 2x2 meters will be depicted as a distinct object.

The smallest objects that can be clearly identified on an image, however, will be much larger than the resolution because many pixels are required to represent the characteristic shape or outline of an object. A 2-meter resolution satellite image might, therefore, show distinct images of buildings covering tens or hundreds of square meters, but not a small shed or automobile covering an area the size of a 2x2-meter pixel.

The best commercial satellites operating in 2005 had resolutions of 1 meter (3.3 feet) or less. However, intelligence satellites operated by the U.S. government were believed to have a resolution of about 2 centimeters (0.8 inches). Images with that resolution, however, have never been released for public use.

The first remote sensing satellites were built, launched, and operated by government agencies in the 1960s. In the interest of national security, images from these satellites were tightly controlled and generally inaccessible to civilian officials and forensic scientists. Imagery from the first Landsat satellites, launched by the United States in the 1970s, was publicly available but its low resolution (tens of meters) made it useful only for regional studies. After an attempt to privatize and eliminate government subsidies for the Landsat program in the 1980s, the United States passed the Land Remote Sensing Policy Act of 1992. This act emphasized the importance of satellite imagery, returned the Landsat program to government operation, mandated that its data be made available at cost, and included a provision for the licensing of commercially operated remote sensing satellites. At about the same time, the French government developed the SPOT (Satellite Pour l'Observation de la Terre) program and marketed its imagery through a subsidized corporation. Like Landsat imagery, however, SPOT imagery generally did not provide the resolution necessary for detailed forensic work.

The Landsat and SPOT satellites paved the way for a new generation of high-resolution commercial satellites that provide images detailed enough for forensic work. The commercial IKONOS satellite, launched by the multi-national Space Imaging consortium in 1999, orbits Earth at an altitude of 680 kilometers (422.5 miles) and provides panchromatic (black and white) images with 1-meter resolution. The *EROS A1* satellite, built by the ImageSat International consortium in Israel and launched from Russia in 2000, provides 1.8-meter (6-foot) resolution. Its successor, the *EROS B1*, will have 0.70-meter (2.3-foot) resolution when operable in 2006. The highest resolution commercial satellite imagery available in 2005 came from the *QuickBird* satellite operated by the Colorado company DigitalGlobe. QuickBird produces 0.62-meter (2-foot) resolution panchromatic images and 2.4-meter (7.9-foot) resolution color images. The panchromatic images, in particular, are detailed enough to depict individual automobiles, pieces of machinery, or ground disturbance associated with illegal activities.

Panchromatic images have higher resolutions (smaller pixel size) than color, or multi-spectral, images. This is because **digital imaging** sensors have a fixed number of photosites that respond to light. When a panchromatic image is made, each photosite senses the total intensity of light. When a multi-spectral image is made, in contrast, the photosites must be divided among the spectral bands being depicted. Thus, a color image consisting of infrared, red, green, and blue bands would have one-fourth the resolution of a panchromatic image from a sensor with the same number of photosites.

One particularly high profile application of commercial high-resolution satellite imagery was the search for debris from the space shuttle *Columbia*, which exploded over Texas in 2003. The *QuickBird* satellite was immediately redirected to cover the accident area, and the resulting images showed areas of broken trees and highly reflected debris. The detailed satellite images allowed accident investigators to better document the extent of the debris field and recover pieces of the shuttle.

High-resolution commercial satellite imagery is also invaluable in the aftermath of natural disasters such as the 2004 Indian Ocean tsunami. There, it was used to help guide relief efforts and provided important information for researchers studying the effects of tsunamis.

Other applications of commercial satellite imagery in **forensic science** are less exotic. Government officials in Arizona, Georgia, and Minnesota have used satellite imagery to detect illegal cotton cultivation, logging, and pollution. Because satellites pass over any given location no more frequently than every few days, they are best suited for the characterization of slow processes such as growing crops or persistent problems such as air or water pollution. For the same reason, it is unlikely that satellite imagery will provide images that catch thieves, kidnappers, rapists, or murderers committing crimes.

Like photographs and videotapes, satellite images can be manipulated and must therefore be authenticated for use in court. Prosecutors or plaintiff's attorneys must establish that any processing or enhancement techniques used on the imagery were properly documented and followed accepted professional standards, whereas defendant's attorneys may question the authenticity of imagery used against their clients. Although some manipulation must be done in order to transform digital information into a visible image, it is critical to establish that the manipulation did not distort or otherwise misrepresent the area being depicted in the imagery.

SEE ALSO Digital imaging; Geospatial Imagery; GIS.

Scanning electron microscopy

The scanning electron microscope (SEM) is an important tool in modern **forensic science** due to its wide range of applications. SEM allows the rapid analysis of elements that compose very small specimens and the conclusive determination of the origin of many materials that are crucial to the chain of **evidence**. Paint particles, **fibers** (both natural and artificial), bullet fingerprints, **gunshot residue**, counterfeit bank notes, forged documents, and **trace evidence** are all examples of specimens that can be analyzed using the scanning electron microscope. Scanning electron microscopy also renders detailed three-dimensional (3-D) images of extremely small microorganisms, 3-D anatomical pictures of insect, worm, spore, or other organic structures, and the analysis of gems and gem fragments.

Conventional **microscopes** use light and several lenses to magnify images, whereas SEM uses electron beams to sweep the surface of specimens, producing magnified images in black and white. In most SEMs, samples are placed in a vacuum chamber after being adequately prepared to conduct electricity. Once the sample is in the chamber, the air is extracted and an electron gun at the top of the chamber emits a beam of electrons, which passes through a series of magnetic lenses that condense the beam into an extremely fine focus, capable of sweeping nano spots on the sample surface. A scanning device near the bottom of the vacuum chamber controls the movement of the electron beam across the specimen, row by row. As the electron beam sweeps the surface, it excites electrons present in the atomic structure of molecules, causing some of them to escape from the surface. These escaping electrons, known as deflected secondary electrons, have specific energies that can be measured. As they are released from each area of the sample, they are collected and counted by a detector that sends their amplified signals. The various electronic energies produced are analyzed by computer software, and the resulting image is displayed on a computer monitor.

Some modern SEMs offer an additional advantage for forensic purposes because of new methods of biological sample analysis that do not corrupt the specimen, a major drawback with conventional SEMs. In conventional electron microscopy, biological samples have to be dehydrated and then coated with a material that conducts electricity, such as a thin layer of gold or carbon. Modern SEMs allow the adjustment of the internal pressure in the chamber to dissipate the electric charge that would otherwise charge the sample, thus dispensing with coating and dehydration. Examples of non-conductive materials that require special preparation in conventional SEMs are paper, paint, textiles, bone, hair, and **glass**.

Each chemical element consists of an atomic structure composed by a given number of particles in the nucleus and of electrons vibrating in different levels or shells around the nucleus, each at a specific distance from the nucleus. Electrons in different shells ("orbits") have different energies and the atomic weight of the nucleus determines the quantity of electrons of an atom. Atoms are usually neutral because all their positive and negative particles are in a state of dynamic electrical balance. However, when free atoms collide or when they are bound through molecular chemical reactions, some atoms gain or lose an extra electron, thus becoming positive or negatively charged (cations or anions). When the electron beam of a SEM hits the sample, it deflects two types of electrons from the sample: inelastic electrons and elastic electrons. Inelastic electrons are low-energy particles that give information about the topographic variations on the sample surface and are responsible for 3-D black and white images. They are also known as secondary electrons and most of them have charges inferior to ten electron Volts (<10 eV). Elastic electrons are those that collide with the electrons generated by the SEM (that are present in the beam). The collision of electrons produces specific energy quanta that are retained by the elastic electrons. By calibrating the microscope to different beam intensities, analysts can study several types of data provided by elastic electrons, such as the sample composition and crystallographic structure of the surface, the internal structure of semi-conductor materials, the distribution and energy levels of phosphorous compounds, and information about the elements and chemicals present in the several layers of the surface.

Forensic analytical tests such as scanning electron microscopy, spectrometers, **chromatography**,

and x-ray dispersion aim at producing individualized evidence that allows the **identification** and origin of samples and the accurate interpretation of data in relation to a crime or a suspect investigation or to help explain an explosion, **arson**, or airplane crash. Modern scanning electron microscopy provides nondestructive analysis of both organic and inorganic samples. Another application of this method in forensics is the analysis and identification of dust particles in the air of indoor environments to either assess the air quality or to detect possible **pathogens** (disease-causing organisms) or hazardous substances. Mineral grains (such as carbonates, glass, quartz, or mica), biological materials (such as mold **spores**, pathogen spores, insect particles, skin cells, and rodent fecal dust), fibers (such as hair, textile fibers, carpet fibers, cellulose, and asbestos), and miscellaneous particles (such as metallic particles, paint, soot, rubber, and plastic) are all materials that have been used in forensic analysis done with scanning electron microscopy.

SEE ALSO Accelerant; Aircraft accident investigations; Analytical instrumentation; Arson; Artificial fibers; Ballistic fingerprints; Bomb (explosion) investigations; Document forgery; Fibers; Filaments; Hair analysis; Handwriting analysis; Ink analysis; Isotopic analysis; Minerals; Organic compounds; Paint analysis; Point-by-point analysis.

Scanning technologies

The forensic examination of an accident or crime scene can involve the direct visual observation of the surroundings. As well, **evidence** may be present or even hidden within objects. For detection of the latter, more specialized scanning technologies are necessary.

X rays are electromagnetic waves in the 10^{-8} to 10^{-11} meter (3×10^{16} to 3×10^{19} Hz) range of the spectrum. (Alternatively, x rays can, like all electromagnetic waves, be conceived of as particles termed "photons.") Because x rays have more energy than visible light, they can pass through solid objects that are otherwise opaque. However, they do not, in general, pass through them as if they were almost transparent, as air is to visible light; rather, when x rays encounter materials of different densities and compositions, they are absorbed and deflected from their original straight-line paths (scattered) to different degrees. This allows x rays to be used for **imaging** the interiors of many objects. The two commonest commercial applications of x-ray scanning technology are medical imaging of the interior of the body and security scanning of baggage and cargo. X rays also have a place in **forensic science**.

Projection radiography (also termed transmission imaging or fluoroscopy), discovered in 1895, is the oldest and simplest form of x-ray scanning. In projection radiography, a beam of x rays is directed at an object behind which a detector or x-ray sensitive surface (i.e., electronic-device array or photographic film) is placed. Volumes of different absorptive properties in the object absorb and scatter the incident x rays to different degrees, causing an x-ray shadow to be cast on the detecting surface. This shadow pattern is the x-ray image.

There are two essential limitations on projection radiography. Firstly, it can readily resolve only structures that contain strong x-ray absorption contrasts. In human beings, this means that the soft tissues are difficult, or impossible, to image. Secondly, all three-dimensional structure in the x-rayed object is collapsed or flattened onto the image plane, destroying information. Nevertheless, because of their speed, simplicity, and economy, projection-type x-ray systems are still commonplace in hospitals, and standard in security systems that examine cargo, baggage, and other inanimate objects.

Computed tomography (CT, also known as computerized axial tomography, CAT) was first made commercially available in the mid-1970s. CT combines projection radiography with computer processing to recover the three-dimensional information that is lost in a traditional two-dimensional x-ray. In a CT scanner, the object to be scanned (e.g., person or baggage item) is placed in a cylindrical or doughnut-shaped device. Inside the cylinder or doughnut is an x-ray source that is mechanically rotated entirely around the object. Also, the cylinder or doughnut is lined with detectors that measure the x rays that pass through the scanned object at all angles. By collating all the information that is gathered during a full revolution of the x-ray source, a computer can form a three-dimensional model of the irradiated volume of the object. This information can then be presented to the user on a video screen in any desired form; most commonly, a thin slice of the object is modeled, with the details of its structure imaged as a black-and-white cross section. To examine more of the object, the user looks at multiple slices.

"Backscatter" consists of waves that are reflected back from an obstacle. In backscatter imaging, x rays are beamed at a target object and a sensor co-located with the beam source records reflected (backscattered) waves. Since denser objects tend to create more backscatter, backscatter x-ray systems create a density-contrast image that reveals different information about objects' interiors than does transmission imaging.

Using specially constructed sensors it is possible to acquire transmission-type x-ray information that can be formed into stereoscopic images (that is, a left-eye, right-eye image pair that the user's brain combines into a three-dimensional impression). Because such an image has apparent depth but cannot be rotated, it is sometimes referred to as "2 1/2 dimensional."

While still in its infancy as an examination technique, stereoscopic x-ray scanning is quicker and cheaper than CT scanning, as it requires less computation and does not need to rotate the x-ray source around the object being scanned. Its limitations are that it provides neither fully rotatable three-dimensional knowledge of an object nor density data, both of which are provided by CT scanning.

The atomic orderliness of a substance affects the way in which x rays are diffracted (i.e., forced to mutually interfere) when passed through it. By recording the scattering patterns characteristic of specific compounds (e.g., drugs), and comparing these templates to patterns observed when scanning objects, a substance-specific detection system can be devised. This technique is now in the early development stage, and is not ready for deployment.

Several other techniques for imaging object interiors exist, including ultrasound, positron emission tomography (PET), nuclear magnetic resonance (NMR) imaging, nuclear quadrupole resonance (NQR) scanning, and neutron emission analysis. All, like x-ray scanning, have security, medical, or scientific applications; the question of which technique is best for any given application is decided based on physics (i.e., which imaging modalities can do a particular job) and, if more than one technique is usable for a given task, on economics (i.e., which imaging modality yields the minimum acceptable image quality for the least cost). For enhanced efficacy, airport security systems are now being planned that will combine complementary techniques to increase the probability of weapon or contraband detection. Such a system might combine x-ray scanning for suspicious-object detection with neutron emission analysis for chemical **identification**.

SEE ALSO Bomb detection devices.

Scene examination SEE Crime scene examination

Sculpting

Sculpting is a way of creating a three-dimensional reconstruction of the head from skeletal remains. It is useful for **identification** when traditional methods have failed to yield a result. Sculpting is carried out by a forensic artist. The forensic artist first makes a plaster cast of the **skull**. This is placed on a stand, facing horizontally, so that it can be tilted and turned in all directions as the artist works with it.

The head is built up by placing successive layers of clay on the plaster cast. The artist is guided during the reconstruction by tissue depth data tables. These are compiled from information of how deep a layer of flesh is over various parts of the human skull and how this varies with age, gender, and ethnic origin. Artificial eyes are placed in the eye sockets and hair can be added, either in the form of a wig or as clay layers. The artist may also add various items of clothing as appropriate as aids to identification. Full notes are taken throughout the process and the end product is photographed.

Manual sculpting of a head may take several weeks and is a skilled task. The end result is limited in that the face tends to be devoid of expression. Often, however, it is the expression, or range of expression, on someone's face that is the key to identification. There are now computer programs that can build not just the three-dimensional representation of the face, but also add expression. The program first makes a scan of the skull and then sculpts the face using the same tissue depth tables as the forensic artist. The end result is available much more quickly than it would be by manual processes.

The head can be animated by the computer program by using a virtual head that has simulations of the 24 muscles that control our facial expressions. The head can thus be given various expressions, which may provide additional information that will lead to a positive identification of a skull. If the forensic artist had to do this manually, several trips back to the workbench might be needed to create the different expressions. The program can also show the face with different hairstyles and hair colors. In the future, a computer program may also be developed to add a range of varying skin textures, to make the head come to life to an even greater degree.

SEE ALSO Composite drawing.

Secret writing

Forensic analysis often involves the examination of hand-written material, computer files, bank account and other account information, and other sources of data. Sometimes, the information needs merely to be retrieved for analysis, having been recorded in a straightforward and readily understandable way. However, information can be encrypted or even physically hidden so as to make its detection and deciphering challenging, even virtually impossible.

One such forensically relevant means of communication is known as secret writing. Secret writing is any means of written communication whereby written text can be concealed, whether it is enciphered/encoded or not. **Codes and ciphers** are sometimes mistakenly placed under the heading of secret writing, but this is accurate only if that expression is taken in its most general sense, as writings that are concealed in any way. Whereas codes and ciphers conceal the meaning of a message, secret writing conceals the actual message.

Techniques of secret writing include the use of invisible ink and carbon copies. Widely applied from ancient times until the early twentieth century, secret writing has been almost entirely eclipsed by more modern methods of concealing messages, such as microdots.

There has long been a desire to keep messages hidden from prying eyes. Indeed, secret writing dates from antiquity. Herodotus described a method of secret writing employed in the Persian Wars. As the Persian emperor Xerxes was preparing to march on the Greek city-states in 480 B.C., a Spartan expatriate name Demaratus learned of the plans and contrived to warn his compatriots. The problem was how to do so in such a way that the Persians themselves would not intercept the message, a challenge for which Demaratus contrived a clever solution.

As Herodotus recorded, Demaratus scraped the wax from a pair of wooden tablets, wrote his message on the wood beneath, then poured hot wax onto the tablets again. Of course the Spartans lacked the advantage of knowing that they were receiving a secret message, but according to Herodotus—who qualified his claim with the caveat "as I understand [it]"—Gorgo, the daughter of a citizen named Cleomenes, received a divine revelation. Thanks to the intervention of the gods, the Spartans realized that they had simply to scrape off the wax and read the message written on the wood beneath it. The Greeks thus began to prepare for the coming invasion, and routed Xerxes' navies at Salamis.

One form of secret writing known to many children from school projects involves invisible ink. This technique uses an acidic citrus juice; lemon juice is most often the preferred choice because it dries without leaving any evidence it has been applied. The juice takes the place of ink, and is applied using a fine stylus, or even an ordinary toothpick. After the juice dries, the acid remains on the paper, which it weakens. When the paper is gently heated, or examined under alternate illumination, the message becomes visible.

Other liquids for invisible ink include milk, which is mildly acidic, as well as white wine, vinegar, or apple juice. In the past, prisoners of war have used their own sweat, **saliva**, or even urine, all of which contain acidic secretions that adhere to the paper, weakening it, even after the water in those bodily fluids has evaporated. A slight variation on this technique is the use of a baking soda and water mixture as the invisible ink, and, after drying, applying grape juice concentrate with a paintbrush. The acid in the grape juice reacts with the baking soda (a base or alkali in chemical terms), exposing the message.

During the late nineteenth and early twentieth centuries, carbon copies provided a means of secret writing. This method involved a means not unlike the one still used today when signing a credit-card receipt. The back of the receipt is impregnated with graphite, a carbon allotrope (a version of a chemical element distinguished by molecular structure) also used in pencil lead. Therefore, when one signs the front of the receipt, the pressure transfers the graphite to the second page, leaving an impression as though one had written on it in pencil.

In a version utilized in the intelligence community, one piece of paper contains a special chemical that will be invisible when transferred to a second sheet. This makes it possible to inscribe secret writing on the back of an envelope, which can be mailed. Upon receipt, the message can be developed by exposure to water or heat.

The use of secret writing has declined since the middle of the twentieth century. Among the techniques that have become prominent is the microdot, or photographic image miniaturized to the size of a dot, which was actually developed in the mid-1800s.

Much more sophisticated is the technique of **steganography**, the concealment of information within other, apparently innocuous, data in a computer file.

SEE ALSO Codes and ciphers; Computer forensics; Decryption; Handwriting analysis; Linguistics, forensic stylistics; Questioned documents; Steganography.

Secretor

Secretor is the name given to the condition that a person secretes their blood-type antigens into **saliva** and other bodily **fluids**. It is also the name of the **gene** that causes this to happen.

Blood type (ABO) is determined by the presence of complex carbohydrates on the surface of blood cells that elicit an immune response in laboratory testing or in the case of bodily exposure by means of a blood transfusion. Blood type is a fundamental biological characteristic of an individual that does not change during their lifetime.

In forensic work, a person's blood type can be ascertained from very small traces of blood found at a crime scene. It is often possible, therefore, to know a person's blood type early on in an investigation based on this testing. The ABO blood system is not a complex information system; there are only three basic blood types, each of which can be further designated as Rh positive or Rh negative, yielding a total of six major blood types.

In some cases, no blood is found by the investigators, but there may be saliva or other mucus-containing bodily fluid that can be identified. If the person from whom the bodily fluid originates carries the dominant secretor gene, that individual will secrete the ABO antigens in mucus, and it is possible to infer the blood type from these fluids. Secretion of soluble blood type antigens is now know to be a function of the alpha(1,2)fucosyltransferase gene. Careful study of this gene reveals that the secretor gene is present in the vast majority of people tested, but non-secretors carry a nonsense mutation in both copies of their secretor gene, rendering them silent. Approximately 75%–80% of Caucasians carry at least one copy of the secretor gene, and they therefore, secrete soluble antigens into bodily fluids. The secretor phenotype also is a fundamental biological characteristic of a person that remains constant throughout life. This is another piece of biological **evidence** that can be collected in trying to match a sample found at a crime scene with potential suspects.

Blood typing and secretor analysis are not highly informative systems of information compared with existing **DNA** technologies such as **STR analysis** because of the limited numbers of different categories into which all people can be placed. Nevertheless, they played a significant role in the collection and analysis of forensic specimens prior to the advent of more informative DNA systems, and they continue to play a small role today. These kinds of evidence are far more persuasive as negative evidence (to rule out a suspect) than as positive evidence (to confirm a suspect) because many people can match by random chance.

SEE ALSO Blood spatter; Crime scene investigation; Serology.

Semen and sperm

The presence of sperm and semen can be important to a crime investigation. The visual detection of semen can provide **evidence** in the case of a suspected rape. As well, the genetic material present in the sperm can be analyzed and used as a genetic fingerprint to identify a suspect.

In the male, semen is the fluid expelled during ejaculation. In addition to plasma, the semen ejaculate contains secretions from the seminal vesicles and other glands to support and nourish the living sperm cells (spermatozoa) contained within the semen. Sperm cells are haploid sex cells of the male. Unlike eggs (oocytes and the mature ovum) that are large, non-motile, and generally ovulated one at a time, sperm are tiny, motile, and produced in the millions. While a human sperm contains a relatively long tail (flagella), the volume of an entire sperm, tail and all, is only 1/85,000 of the mature ovum.

Motility of the sperm is due to the long tail, which is a modified flagellum. Cilia and flagella, from protozoa through humans, all have a similar structure that has been intensively investigated since first described in early electron microscope studies. Microtubules that run the length of the sperm tail are arranged in a ring of nine pairs surrounding a pair in the center. Ciliary dynein is associated with each of the nine microtubule pairs. It is the interaction of the dynein with the microtubules which causes flagellar bending and thus propulsion.

It is estimated that a quarter of a billion sperm are released in a single ejaculate of semen in a healthy male human. In addition to a nutrient function, the semen plays an important role in thermal and hydration regulation that promotes viable sperm cells. The semen also provides initial protection against the acidic gradient of the vagina and cervical region.

In a forensic examination, semen can be detected by the presence of the enzyme acid phosphatase. Because this enzyme is present elsewhere in the body, however, the test is not absolute proof of the presence of semen on clothing or in material recovered in a case of suspected sexual assault. But, detection of acid phosphatase is powerful **circumstantial evidence**, and indicates that further efforts should be made to investigate the possibility that semen is present.

The microscopic detection of sperm is much more conclusive. The chance of recovering intact sperm is less when a sample is older, due to **decomposition** of the biological material. However, samples that are analyzed soon after collection can be positive for sperm.

Semen can be visualized on clothing and other surfaces using an ultraviolet light. The semen fluoresces under ultraviolet illumination. This test has the advantage of being non-destructive to the scene of the investigation.

SEE ALSO Crime scene investigation; DNA; DNA profiling; Luminol; Rape kit.

September 11, 2001, terrorist attacks (forensic investigations of)

Forensic investigations can occur in relative obscurity or can be front-page news. A horrific example of the latter occurred in the aftermath of the terrorist attacks on September 11, 2001.

At 8:46 A.M. on September 11, 2001, American Airlines Flight 11, hijacked from Boston's Logan Airport with 92 people on board, crashed into the upper floors of the World Trade Center's North Tower in lower Manhattan, New York. Seventeen minutes later, United Airlines Flight 175, also hijacked from Logan and with 65 people on board, crashed into the South Tower. By this time, virtually the entire nation had tuned in to witness the after-effects on television of what at first seemed a terrible accident, but was quickly revealed as a terrorist attack. Over the course of the next 85 minutes, the South Tower collapsed, followed by the collapse of the North Tower. The incident, in which nearly 3,000 people died, ranks as the worst case of mass murder in U.S. history, the worst building disaster in human history, and the largest terrorist incident in the history of the western world.

Watches recovered from the debris of the World Trade Center are assembled in an evidence decontamination room on Staten Island in New York City. Debris from site was examined for evidence, property and remains of victims. © REUTERS/CORBIS

Terrorist hijacked United Airlines flight 175 flies into the South Tower of the World Trade Center in New York City during terrorist attacks on September 11, 2001. © ROB HOWARD/CORBIS

The forensic determinations that occurred in the aftermath of the tragedy were multi-pronged. Forensic inspectors sought to identify the dead and to determine the nature of the events that led to the collapse of the two buildings. Amid the carnage, investigators needed to observe the wreckage in an effort to find clues to the collapse of the buildings, while at the same time try to locate survivors.

On the same day, American Airlines Flight 77, departing from Washington, D.C.'s Dulles International Airport bound for Los Angeles, was hijacked and crashed into the Pentagon building in Washington, D.C. Another hijacked aircraft, United Airlines Flight 93, en route from Newark, New Jersey, to San Francisco, California, was also commandeered. The ultimate target of that hijacked plane remains unknown as its passengers fought back against the terrorists, crashing the plane in a field near Pittsburgh, Pennsylvania.

In the Washington and Pennsylvania crashes, the forensic investigations initially focused on **identification** of victims from clothing, dental **evidence**, **fingerprint** patterns, and analysis of genetic material. The goal was to ascertain the sequences of deoxyribonucleic acid (**DNA**) that can be as unique as a fingerprint.

A group of firefighters stand in the street near the destroyed World Trade Center in New York on September 11, 2001. © REUTERS/CORBIS

Later, forensic efforts were also geared toward determining the cause of the crashes, including searches to locate the **flight data recorders** that are a feature on aircraft, and analysis of the communications between the pilots and air traffic control personnel.

In New York, the forensic engineering work needed to proceed at the same time as wreckage was being cleared away. Because the priority was to uncover any survivors trapped beneath the rubble, steel beams and other rubble were removed from the site before investigators had an opportunity to inspect the structural remains on site in great detail. In retrospect, this hampered efforts to establish a cause of the towers' collapse. Ironically, one the forensic inspectors was able to assess the damage to some of the trade center's structure when a truck transporting the wreckage parked in front of his hotel.

Pieces of the structure that were recovered were instructive. For example, gouge marks on steel beams that were made by a wing and nose section of one of the planes indicated that the plane was traveling at a high rate of speed. In another example,

beams were recovered with rivets still intact, which indicated that the buildings withstood the impact of the aircraft.

When the true scope of the loss of life became apparent, forensic efforts shifted to the identification of the dead. Indeed, DNA analysis was instrumental in identifying more than 1,600 victims. More than 800 of the victims were identified by their DNA alone.

As the identification of the victims came to a close, the longer term forensic engineering work continued. This work has continued until 2005, when reports on the cause of the buildings' collapse were issued.

A necessary part of the forensic engineering investigations involved the design and construction of the World Trade Center towers. Designed by architect Minoru Yamasaki—who, ironically, had a fear of heights—and engineered by Leslie Robertson and John Skilling, the 110-story towers soared 1,360 feet (415 m) above an open plaza, which made them the world's tallest buildings at the time of their completion in 1973. Whereas the Empire State

Building and other older skyscrapers drew support from an interior grid of steel girders, support for the trade towers came from the exterior and the inner core. Horizontal floor trusses joined the perimeter support structure to the central area, which the engineers envisioned as a great "tube" running through the building and containing not only its support structure, but also its utilities such as elevators. This design had two advantages. First, it made the buildings extremely stable—not prone to swaying in high winds as the Empire State did. And, it left much of the interior available as rentable space.

By the 1980s, New Yorkers had become accustomed to the trade towers, which punctuated the skyline as the ultimate symbol of American and international commerce. Then, in February 1993, just months before the towers turned 20, the towers became the target of a bombing by Islamic terrorists operating a van filled with **explosives**. In this, the first terrorist attack, six people were killed, but the structural integrity of the towers themselves was not threatened.

When Flight 11 crashed into the North Tower of the World Trade Center at 8:46 A.M., smoke and flames began to gush from the upper stories, and workers began to evacuate the lower floors. Some, however, chose to remain at their desks. For workers on the floors above the impact area, there was no choice but to remain in place.

For 17 minutes, it was possible to assume that what had happened to the North Tower was an accident; then, Flight 175 smashed into the South Tower. Once again, smoke and flames erupted from the heights of the building, and tenants down below began a slow, but steady evacuation while others—many with no choice—stayed where they were.

Seventeen minutes after the impact, with little warning, the South Tower, succumbed to the stress caused by the fire and began to crash from the top down. As it fell, it created a vast cloud of dust and ash above and filled the streets below with noise, heat, and terror.

Shortly thereafter, the North Tower began to implode, once again crashing downward from the top. The area around what had once been the World Trade Center became smoke, ash, and dust.

In late 2001, a team of investigators that included representatives of the American Society of Civil Engineers and the Federal Emergency Management Agency (FEMA) commenced a study on the structural collapse of the towers, the details of

which they made public in April 2002. In August 2002, the National Institute of Standards and Technology (NIST) began its own study, scheduled to last two years. The actual timing was a bit longer, and findings of the study were released in April 2005.

The forensic analyses revealed that the aircraft impacts severed columns in each building, which distributed the weight of the upper floors onto the remaining columns. As the fires subsequently raged, these columns weakened to the point of buckling inward and eventually collapsed.

Thus, it was not the impact, but the heat from the burning jet fuel, that heated the temperature of the buildings' steel support structures up to 1,472°F (800°C), causing them to buckle and the floors to collapse downward. (Both jets were bound for Los Angeles and had almost a full tank of fuel on board.) The initial crash neutralized sprinkler systems, allowing the spread of the fire, which was fed by caches of paper and other flammable materials in the buildings' offices.

In another forensic aspect following the incident, forensic accountants began the task of tracing the perpetrators using financial records and other materials. These investigations led to the al Qaeda terror network as the perpetrators of the attack.

SEE ALSO Aircraft accident investigations; Architecture and structural analysis; DNA profiling; World Trade Center, 1993 terrorist attack.

Sequencing

Molecular techniques of analysis are a vital part of **forensic science**. Analysis of genetic material is instrumental in detecting pathogenic (disease-causing) microorganisms and in identifying a victim or implicating a suspect.

These molecular examinations rely on the determining of the arrangement of the building blocks of the genetic material. This determination is called sequencing.

Sequencing refers to the techniques used to determine the order of the constituent bases (i.e., adenine, thymine, guanine, and cytosine) of deoxyribonucleic acid (**DNA**), ribonucleic acid (RNA) or the constituent amino acid building blocks of protein.

DNA is typically sequenced for several reasons: to determine the sequence of the protein encoded by the DNA, the location of sites at which restriction enzymes can cut the DNA, the location of DNA sequence elements that regulate the production of messenger RNA, or to detect alterations in the DNA.

The sequencing of DNA is accomplished by stopping the lengthening of a DNA chain at a known base and at a known location in the DNA. Practically, this can be done in two ways. In the first method, called the Sanger-Coulson procedure, a small amount of a specific so-called dideoxynucleoside base is incorporated in a mixture with the other four normal bases. This base is slightly different from the normal base and is radioactively labeled. The radioactive base becomes incorporated into the growing DNA chain instead of the normal base, and growth of the DNA stops. This stoppage is done four times, each time using one of the four different dideoxynucleosides. This generates four collections of DNA molecules. Also, because replication of the DNA always begins at the same point, and because the amount of altered base added is low, for each reaction many DNA pieces of different lengths will be generated. When the sample is used for gel **electrophoresis**, the different-sized pieces can be resolved as radioactive bands in the gel. Then, knowing the location of the bases, the sequence of the DNA can be deduced.

The second DNA sequencing technique is known as the Maxam-Gilbert technique, after its co-discoverers. In this technique, both strands of double-stranded DNA are radioactively labeled using radioactive phosphorus. Upon heating, the DNA strands separate and can be physically distinguished from each other, as one strand is heavier than the other. Both strands are then cut up using specific enzymes and the different sized fragments of DNA are separated by gel electrophoresis. Based on the pattern of fragments, the DNA sequence is determined.

Several decades ago, sequencing involved scrutinizing the gels by eye. However, the marriage of powerful computational hardware and software to the sequencing process has automated the procedure.

The Sanger-Coulsom approach is the more popular method. Various modifications have been developed, and it has been automated for very large-scale sequencing. During the sequencing of the human genome, a sequencing method called shotgun sequencing was very successfully employed. Shotgun sequencing refers to a method that uses enzymes to cut DNA into hundreds or thousands of random bits. So many fragments are necessary since automated sequencing machines can only decipher relatively short fragments of DNA about 500 bases long. The many

sequences are then pieced back together using computers to generate the entire DNA genome sequence.

Protein sequencing involves determining the arrangement of the amino acid building blocks of the protein. It is common to sequence a protein by determining the DNA sequence encoding the protein . This, however, is only possible if a cloned **gene** is available. It is still often the case that chemical protein sequencing, as described subsequently, must be performed in order to manufacture an oligonucleotide probe that can then be used to locate the target gene. The most popular direct protein chemical sequencing technique in use today is the Edman degradation procedure. This is a series of chemical reactions, which remove one amino acid at a time from a certain end of the protein (the amino terminus). Each amino acid that is released has been chemically modified in the release reaction, allowing the released product to be detected using a technique called reverse phase **chromatography**. The identity of the released amino acids is sequentially determined, producing the amino acid sequence of the protein.

Another protein sequencing technique is called fast atom bombardment mass spectrometry, or FAB-MS. This is a powerful technique in which the sample is bombarded with a stream of fast atoms, such as argon. The protein becomes charged and fragmented in a sequence-specific manner. The fragments can be detected and their identity determined. The expense and relative scarcity of the necessary equipment can be a limitation to the technique, though.

Still another protein sequencing strategy is the digestion of the protein with specialized protein-degrading enzymes called proteases. The shorter fragments that are generated, called peptides, can then be sequenced. The problem then is to order the peptides. This is done by the use of two proteases that cut the protein at different points, generating overlapping peptides. The peptides are separated and sequenced, and the patterns of overlap and the resulting protein sequence can be deduced.

SEE ALSO Analytical instrumentation; DNA sequences, unique; PCR (polymerase chain reaction).

Serial killers

Serial killers, those who kill more than once, pose a special problem for crime investigators because the their motives are often far less obvious than those of the person who commits a single homicide. Investigators describe three types of killer who commit multiple murders. The mass murderer kills several people at one time. Often these killers turn out to be disgruntled employees who show up at their places of work with shotgun in hand, bent on revenge. Spree killers often go on rampages with knives or guns, killing one person after another. Such people often have serious mental health problems. The serial killer, however, dispatches one victim at a time, with a time interval that may be as long as several years between each **murder**.

The "Washington Sniper" (aka, "Beltway Sniper" or "D.C. Sniper") killed ten people within a three-week period in the Washington, D.C., area in 2002. Originally thought to be a lone gunman, the killers turned out to be Gulf War veteran John Allen Muhammad and 18-year-old Lee Boyd Malvo, who were both convicted of capital murder. The media quickly labeled them "spree killers." Forensically speaking, however, they are probably more accurately described as a serial killers.

The serial killer tends to prey upon people at random. Usually, the attacker does not know the victims personally. The Federal Bureau of Investigation (**FBI**) Behavioral Science Unit developed the concept of psychological **profiling** in the 1960s to aid in the pursuit of serial killers and to let police know what kind of man (serial killers are nearly always men) is instigating the crimes.

Despite attempts by authorities to profile and find serial killers, some killers can continue killing and elude authorities for years. The so-called Green River Killer murdered at least 48 victims over a span of 16 years, from 1982 to 1998. The confessed murderer, Gary Leon Ridgway (now serving a life sentence), claimed that strangling young women was his "career."

Despite all the work that has been done on the **psychology** of the serial killer, forensic psychologists and psychiatrists are still far from understanding such people. Although it may be easier to comprehend someone who kills out of greed or revenge, the work of a serial killer is so far removed from normal behavior that most people have little understanding of his motives.

Many serial killers are psychopaths. Psychopathy, or anti-social personality disorder, is not considered completely curable. There is even debate by some scientists as to whether it is a mental illness at all. The hallmark of the psychopath is an extreme lack of guilt or empathy for others, which means the serial killer can carry out terrible crimes without emotional distress. Studies of serial killers in prison and evidence gathered from those who know them

suggest that many of these murderers were the targets of physical, psychological, or sexual abuse in early childhood. This may lead them to build a world based on fantasy as a protective measure. These fantasies are then acted out in the course of a violent crime, often with a sexual context. The killer feels satisfied after the crime and then relaxes for a while. However, it is only a matter of time before the fantasies push them toward the next killing.

As the homicides mount, it becomes increasingly urgent for police to track down the killer. Also, as the killings mount, so too does the evidence, no matter how clever the killer may consider himself to be. As he continues, he may become careless or complacent, and the chances of his capture increase.

The forensic psychiatrist uses evidence from the crime scene to build a **psychological profile** of the serial killer. One categorization that has been found useful is to decide whether the investigators are dealing with an organized or a disorganized killer. If the crime scene suggests the murder was carefully planned and executed, then the killer may be a man of average to high intelligence who has a stable social network. He may be married with a family. He may also be employed. Living a "normal" life on the surface requires a degree of self-control, which manifests itself in the way the crime is carried out. Sometimes, though, the organized offender does lose control in the actual attack when the fantasy motivation takes over. In such cases, a violent or frenzied attack may occur, yet there may also be careful attempts to conceal or destroy evidence.

The disorganized offender leaves a mess at the crime scene. He may use any weapon that is available to strike out and makes little effort to cover his tracks. This lack of planning and control often suggests low intelligence. He is likely to be unemployed and may be a bit of a loner with few friends. The attack may be marked by excessive violence and could also include sexual contact with the victim after death. The disorganized serial killer often turns out to have a history of mental illness.

A number of other factors can be added to the profile. Many serial killers are young adults in their twenties or thirties. They tend not to cross racial lines. White killers tend to kill white victims; black killers tend to kill blacks. Many kill close to home the first few times, but then start to move farther away. Serial killers are eventually often highly mobile, which can make the logistics of catching them difficult.

Of particular interest to those investigating serial killers is what is taken from the scene or from the victim. In most crimes, the perpetrator will take items of monetary value, like cash or jewelry. They may also take evidence, such as a weapon. The serial killer often takes something known as a trophy or souvenir, of no obvious value except to him in his fantasy world. The item is known as a trophy if it is seen as a symbol of achievement and a souvenir if it is to remind the killer of the crime.

Trophies and souvenirs are an important part of the killer's *modus operandi* (**"method of operation,"** or M.O.), the name given to the particular tools and strategies that distinguish the killer's work. The M.O. includes factors such as the location of the crimes, the tools used, the time of day, the alibi, and any accomplices involved. The M.O. may, of course, evolve over time as the killer becomes more experienced. The investigators will be particularly interested in any details that are unique to that killer, such as leaving a note behind. They will also look for the signature of the crime. Trophies and souvenirs can be part of the signature, as can mutilating or having sex with the corpse, or placing the body in a certain position.

Victimology, the study of the victim, can be crucial in tracking down a serial killer. The investigators need to know what it was about that particular person that attracted the killer. Was the victim truly chosen at random or had the person been stalked previously? The killer may have been searching for the one person who fit his fantasy and, if a common link can be found between the victims, this may be very revealing. For instance, nearly all of the victims of serial killer Ted Bundy had dark hair parted in the center.

The location of the serial killer's crimes is also of significance. Geographical profiling is based on the premise that the killer will operate in a zone where he feels comfortable. This may be near home or, alternatively, far away from it, depending on his psychological make-up. Location is not just where the crime was committed, but is also where the victim was abducted and where the body was taken and left after the crime. Establishing a geographical profile can be challenging if the victim was a prostitute, for instance, or someone who might not be missed by relatives or co-workers for a while. The Yorkshire Ripper killed several prostitutes in the United Kingdom from 1977 to 1981, and the difficulty of tracking the victims' movements sometimes hindered the investigation. Sometimes bodies are dumped in remote places and may not be found for some time. In such cases, a forensic anthropologist may be called in to judge the times of death so the order in which victims were killed can be determined.

The world's most prolific serial killer was Dr. Harold Shipman, a British physician who took his own life in prison in 2004. He may have been responsible for up to 300 deaths, but the true figure will never be known as he always denied the killings. Prior to this, the so-called "Monster of the Andes," Pedro Lopez, held this dubious distinction, having been convicted of 57 murders in 1980. He may have killed many more; his victims were young girls in Colombia.

Despite his notoriety, Shipman was, in many ways, an unusual type of serial killer. His victims, many of whom were elderly women, met their end through morphine injections, one of the main methods of assisted suicide, which some believe to be a compassionate act. He was well known and liked in his community, and there was no obvious motive for the crimes. Some psychiatrists have suggested Shipman disliked older women, or that he was trying to re-enact the death of his mother. Others believed he gained pleasure from the power of life and death that he could exercise as a doctor. Shipman may have begun to kill patients very early on in his medical career, before he had even finished **training** to be a doctor. Initially, it was thought he began his career as a serial killer in 1974 when he first became a family doctor. This would put the number of deaths between 216 and 260. If, however, he began to kill almost as soon as he had the opportunity, then at least 24 more deaths, and maybe more, could have been at the hands of Shipman.

SEE ALSO Bundy (serial murderer) case; Psychological profile; Psychopathic personality.

Serology

Serology testing (assay) is largely used by forensic laboratories to analyze **blood** samples from suspects and bloodstains collected at the crime scene, in order to identify blood types of victims and assailants. The main objective of forensic tests, whether serological or other types, is to individualize samples through the **identification** of their sources.

Blood is the most common **physical evidence** in accidents, murder cases, and violent crime investigations. Besides blood, crime scene technicians may also find other stains and residues similar to blood in appearance at the scene, such as tomato sauce, red paint, or animal blood. To identify human blood, forensic scientists test samples at the crime scene with the chemical phenolphthalein, in an assay known as the Kastle-Meyer color test. Phenolphthalein releases hydrogen peroxide that reacts with an enzyme known as catalase in the blood. Catalase breaks down the hydrogen peroxide into water and oxygen, therefore releasing bubbles. However, as vegetables, animals, and some bacteria also produce catalase, this test only rules out the inorganic samples. Organic (plant or animal derived) samples are then collected for further serological analysis at the crime laboratory.

Body **fluids** such as blood, **semen**, **saliva**, and sweat, all contain **serum**. Serum is a liquid component of blood composed of water, trace minerals, several proteins including albumin, and immunoglobulins or antibodies. Albumin is the sticky protein that gives blood enough density for the water within it to remain inside the walls of arteries and veins. (Egg white contains high levels of albumin, which gives it the characteristic consistency.) When red and white blood cells are removed from blood, the resulting clear golden yellowish liquid is serum. Serology is therefore the study of the properties of serum. Serological tests have a wide range of applications in **medicine**, such as immunology and allergy assays, infection diagnosis, and blood typing. Serology can determine whether an individual was exposed in the past or if he is presently infected with a variety of **pathogens** (disease-causing organisms), such as hepatitis, measles, **anthrax**, syphilis, or HIV. Serology tests can also determine the presence of alcohol, illegal drugs, and poisons in the serum. Serological tests are also used in forensics to identify blood ABO groups, whose results, although not conclusive, may help to exclude or include suspects in the investigation process. If for instance, a suspect is blood type B and the samples from the crime scene are all types A and O, the suspect with type B blood can be excluded from the investigation.

Serology is such a convenient diagnostic tool because the **immune system** produces specific molecular tags in the blood for practically each foreign substance or invading microorganism. Each one specializes in binding to a specific molecule such as a viral, parasite, or bacterial protein, as well as to foreign substances such as poisons and drugs. For minutely small drug molecules against which the immune system is not very sensitive, special immune reagents were developed for the detection of drug abuse. An example is the Homogeneous Enzyme Immunoassays (EMIT), which is commercialized in kits ready for use.

To determine whether a blood sample is from a human or animal source, samples are tested with anti-human serum. This method was discovered by the German biologist Paul Uhlenhunth in the late 1870s. He injected protein from a chicken egg into a sample of rabbit's blood. After a few days, he extracted the rabbit's serum and mixed it with egg white, causing the separation of egg proteins from the solution to form a whitish clotting substance, precipitin. Precipitin is now a generic name for the resulting agglutinated complex formed when antibodies present in the serum of a species agglutinate the proteins in the blood of a different species. The forensic test consists of collecting the blood sample in a test tube containing serum from a rabbit containing antibodies against human blood, known as anti-human antibodies. If an insoluble complex of precipitin (clumping) occurs, the test is positive for human blood. This test can also be conducted using gel-electrophoresis, when a blood sample is put on a glass slide and covered by a layer of agar gel. The slide is positioned side by side with another containing the rabbit anti-human serum, inside a box filled with a solution that conducts electric current. As the current passes through, protein molecules are filtered into the gel and toward each glass slide. If precipitin is formed, the test is positive, and the blood sample is identified as human blood.

Electrophoresis is also used in typing the different groups of human blood, known as the ABO grouping system. After the discovery of antibodies and antigens (molecules to which antibodies bind), scientists identified four blood types among humans between 1875 and 1901. All human blood contains antigens in red cells that vary in type among individuals in accordance with inheritance (e.g., maternal and paternal inherited genes). Genes A and B (**chromosome** 9) encode enzymes that add specific sugars to an **antigen** at the ends of a complex sugar molecule (polysaccharide) that is present on the surface of erythrocytes (red blood cells). Individuals who inherit neither A or B genes have type O blood. As genes A and B are codominant (they do not dominate each other), individuals who inherit both genes (one from each parent) are type AB. The following other inherited combinations may occur: AA, BB, AO, BO, OO. Individuals AO or BO are respectively heterozygous type A and type B. AA or BB are homozygous types A or B.

Blood typing tests consist of mixing blood samples with anti-serum A on one side of the slide, and with anti-serum B at the other side. If the agglutination (clumping) occurs on both sides of the glass slide, the blood is AB. If it occurs only with anti-serum A, the blood is type A, or if it occurs only with anti-serum B, the blood is type B. If no agglutination occurs, the blood is type O. Because a person with type O blood does not present antigens to either A or

B antibodies, they can donate blood to most blood groups. Carriers of **gene** A that have antibodies against B antigens in their blood plasma, and vice versa, can only receive transfusions of the same blood type or from type O blood. Individuals with AB blood type can receive transfusions from all donors. Type O carriers however cannot receive blood from the other types because their plasma contains antibodies against A and B antigens.

Population prevalence of blood types is approximately as follows: type A is more common in Caucasians and Europeans; type B among Africans, African descendents, and South Asia populations; AB type is predominant in China, Japan, and Korea; and Type O is predominant in Native Americans, Aborigines, and Latin American populations, and is common in Middle-Eastern populations as well. A small portion of the world population carries a rare variation of AB type subgroups that present weak reactions or no reaction at all to antibodies.

Another breakthrough of significance for both medical and forensic sciences was the discovery by **Karl Landsteiner** in 1940 that 85% of the human population carries erythrocytes that express the Rh(D) antigen, or Rhesus disease antigen (a protein also present in Rhesus monkeys). Blood is designated as being either Rh positive ($^+$) or Rh negative ($^-$). If an Rh$^-$ person receives blood from a donor who is Rh$^+$, his immune system will develop antibodies against the antigen, causing disease or death, depending on the quantity of blood transfused. There are thirty possible combinations between ABO groups and Rh factors. Approximately two thirds of all people have an O$^+$ or A$^+$ blood type, with all other types comprising the remaining third. These variations allow the number of suspects in a crime investigation to be narrowed.

Another singular characteristic of proteins and enzymes is the presence of discrete variations in a single base pair of the genes that encode them, known as polymorphisms (or multiple forms of the same gene). More than 1% of any given population has polymorphisms in specific genes. Specific polymorphisms are also more prevalent in certain populations. For instance, the CYP enzymes of the gene Cytochrome P 450 show a specific polymorphed version in 40% of the Asian population, whereas another polymorph is more prevalent among Caucasians and Europeans. Several other enzymes also present a known prevalence among races, and are therefore, useful in forensic testing.

Genetic screening for polymorphisms in forensic samples is very helpful when combined with blood type and Rh factors, because it sharply reduces the probability the existence of two persons with the same blood characteristics being involved with the same crime to very insignificant odds. In addition, other serological tests can also be used to estimate age, sex, and race of suspects, such as hormonal levels in blood and other fluids, as well as genetic analysis such as chromosomal typing (or karyotyping), and **DNA profiling**.

SEE ALSO Animal evidence; Antibody; Antigen; Blood; Chromosome; Circumstantial evidence; Crime scene investigation; Cross contamination; DNA; Epidemiology; Fluids; Hemoglobin; Homogeneous enzyme immunoassay (EMIT); Illicit drugs; Immune system; Luminol; Parasitology; Paternity evidence; Saliva; Serum; Toxicological analysis.

Serum

Serum, or **blood** serum, is a useful medium for a range of forensic analyses, as well as for laboratorial diagnostic assays, due to its biological contents. Pure serum, however, does not contain blood cells, platelets, or fibrinogen (coagulation factors). The sticky consistency of serum is due to albumin, a protein that provides the proper density for blood, and prevents it from leaking through cell vessel walls. The main function of serum is to moisten the surfaces of cell membranes and to transport to organs and tissues diluted water-soluble nutrients such as blood red cells (erythrocytes), hormones, fat-soluble nutrients (chyle), white blood cells, and antibodies present in the lymphatic fluid as it enters the blood circulation. Serum is also present in seminal fluid and lymphatic **fluids**, and exudates from wounds and blisters as a clear watery substance. The presence of these and other contents in serum allowed the development of several types of analytical assays (tests) useful for both clinical and forensic purposes, such as for detecting tumor markers, detecting antibodies for specific infectious agents, anti-doping tests, blood typing, and **DNA** tests. Serological tests are also used in postmortem **identification** of poisons or illegal drugs in the body fluids of corpses.

Blood plasma is formed by serum and lymphatic fluid, and contains suspended leukocytes (white blood cells), erythrocytes, coagulation factors, electrolytes (e.g., mineral ions), gases, proteins, glucose, water, and micronutrients essential for cells. Plasma may contain poisonous metabolites resulting from enzymatic transformation of drugs, poisons, allergenic substances, or environmental pollutants, known as exogenous metabolites. Additionally, serum transports endogenous toxic metabolites resulting from cellular and enzymatic processing of gases and nutrients, which are released in blood plasma to be excreted through urine, sweat, and feces. Serum and plasma contents can therefore be analyzed for various purposes: the forensic determination of environmental **toxins** in outbreaks of illness due to either water or food contamination, DNA screening for the identification of suspects and/or victims, paternity tests, and drug screening.

The most common serological immunoassays used by forensic technicians are: enzyme-multiplied immunoassay technique (EMIT), radio-immunoassay (RIA), fluorescence polarization immunoassay (FPIA), cloned enzyme donor immunoassay (CEDIA), enzyme linked immunosorbent assay (ELISA), gel diffusion analysis (immunodifusion), serum protein **electrophoresis** (immunoelectrophoresis), and Western immunoblotting. EMIT, RIA, FPIA, and CEDIA allow the screening of very small amounts of antibodies against all classes of drugs and the identification of specific drugs as well. As some small drug metabolites do not trigger natural **antibody** formation, specific **commercial kits** are used to recognize these potential antigens in suspects of drug abuse. Antigens are proteins and substances recognized either by the **immune system** as foreign to the host (such as viral and bacterial particles or allergens) or by an assay antiserum reagent. The following specific drugs can be detected in serum through the above immunoassay tests: benzoylecgonine, a cocaine metabolite, phentanyl, methadone, phenylciclidine, and propoxyphene. Additionally, the following classes of drugs can be identified: **amphetamines**, **barbiturates**, benzodiazepines, cannabinoides, and opiates. ELISA is more commonly used for HIV and hepatitis C diagnosis, although this method can also detect drugs in the serum or in urine. ABO blood grouping and Rh factor typing is usually performed through gel diffusion analysis (immunodiffusion) or serum protein electrophoresis, known as immunoelectrophoresis. These assays can also determine whether a blood sample has a human or animal origin. Serum proteins can also be sorted by immunoelectrophoresis, and the resulting protein complexes can be further screened for specific antibodies against HIV antigens or very small drug metabolites through the Western immunoblotting technique.

Another immunoassay technique, the antibody profile assay (APA), was developed in the late 1990s, and has proved to be useful in forensics. The test design is based on the fact that the serum of each individual contains a variety of antibodies, each one specific to a given foreign protein to which a host was exposed in different periods of life. Therefore, each individual has a unique antibody serological profile, consisting of all the different antibodies that he or she carries. At birth, babies have in their blood plasma only the antibodies received from the mother; gradually, each will develop his or her own particular antibody profile through exposure to infectious agents and other antigens during life. APA determines the unique set of individual specific antibodies (ISA) by embedding a paper strip containing antigenic proteins into blood samples, which causes specific immune reactions by the antibodies present in the sample. The strip is then stained to reveal a unique ISA pattern of bands that identifies the donor of the sample. Several hospitals use APA to identify newborns and their respective mothers.

The Wyoming State Crime Laboratory has collaborated with APA researchers in testing APA specificity for forensic application in identifying contaminated and tainted samples. The laboratory received ten blood samples and proceeded to subject them to all possible conditions found in crime scenes: tainting, contaminating, mixing the samples with other human or animal blood samples, urine, or gasoline, and putting them in upholstery, car hoods, and side walks. Researchers also exposed some samples to a variety of temperatures, ranging from $-68°F$ ($-56°C$) to $140°F$ ($60°C$). The resulting 422 tainted samples were then returned to researchers for APA testing, and resulted in 91% correct identifications.

SEE ALSO Amphetamines; Antibody; Antigen; Autopsy; Barbiturates; Blood; Bloodstain evidence; Commercial kits; DEA (Drug Enforcement Administration); Death, cause of; FBI crime laboratory; Fluids; Homogeneous enzyme immunoassay (EMIT); Illicit drugs; Immune system; Narcotic; Paternity evidence; Pathogens; PCR (polymerase chain reaction); Poison and antidote actions; Rape kit; RFLP (restriction fragment length polymorphism); Saliva; Semen and sperm; Serology; Toxicological analysis; Toxins; Vaccines.

Sex determination

Sex determination is the process by which organisms develop as males or females. Some organisms reproduce only by asexual methods, and thus they may possess no system for sexual differentiation. For most species of plants and animals, however, sexual development is a basic element of the normal life cycle. In humans, sex is a fundamental characteristic that influences the development of many of the features of the body. This includes some obvious traits such as genital and breast development, but it also includes structures in the brain and other internal organs, the shape and mineral composition of bones, and a wide array of features observable at the cellular level.

The many clues, overt or subtle, that can be collected from careful examination of the bodies, organs, tissues, and even cells of the deceased remove much of the mystery of the sex of a victim whose remains are recovered from the scene of a crime, or the site of a fire, explosion or other disaster.

In humans, where there are two distinct sex chromosomes, the X and the Y chromosomes, it is the presence of the Y **chromosome** that specifies male development. More specifically, there is a **gene** on the Y chromosome called the sex-determining region of the Y chromosome (SRY) that causes male development. In fact, female development seems to be the default pathway, and in the absence of SRY, the urogenital tract develops as a female. The elementary structures for both male and female development are present in the early embryo, however, development of the female ductal system, called the Mullerian system, is inhibited by a substance produced by the early male embryo. Likewise, in females, the primordial male ductal system, called the Wolffian duct, degenerates as the Mullerian ductal system advances. The Mullerian ducts give rise to the fallopian tubes, uterus, and upper portion of the vagina. The Wolffian ducts give rise to the spermatic ducts and seminal vesicles which carry **sperm** from the mature testes during ejaculation. Although SRY, the primary sex-determining gene, is found on the Y chromosome, many of the genes responsible for development of both male and female reproductive structures and other sexual characteristics are found on the autosomes.

One of the earliest events in male development is the production of testis-determining factor within the sex cord cells. The sex cords begin to differentiate into Sertoli cells when SRY is present. The Sertoli cells secrete male-specific factors such as Mullerian inhibitory substance (MIS), which causes the female ductal system to degenerate. MIS also promotes the development of another male-specific cell population called Leydig cells, which produce testosterone. For female embryos, because of the absence of SRY, the sex cords develop along a different pathway to develop structures associated with the ovaries. As the embryo develops, hormones produced by the testes in males and the ovaries in females create a biochemical environment in which the more subtle elements of sexual development occur.

Sexual development is not always so straightforward in humans. Although people are usually considered either male or female, various disruptions can occur during sexual development and differentiation that give rise to atypical or mixed sexual development. These include sex chromosome abnormalities, where there are extra or missing copies of the sex chromosomes. This would include Turner syndrome, where females receive only a single X chromosome; Klinefelter syndrome, wherein males receive not only an X and Y chromosome but also an extra copy of the X chromosome; and a wide variety of other more rare numerical sex chromosome abnormalities where extra copies of the X and/or Y chromosomes are present. In addition, the SRY gene that is normally transmitted on the Y chromosome can become translocated to an X chromosome or an autosome, resulting in a reversal of sex. Also, when multiple cell lines are present, with different sex-chromosome allocations, individuals may develop both male and female characteristics. True hermaphrodites have both testes and ovaries, and may have both intact male and female external genital structures. Pseudohermaphrodites have external genital structures that are opposite of what would be expected on the basis of having either testes or ovaries internally. In addition, the development of the external genital structures can be incomplete, and it may initially be difficult to determine sex at birth. Occasionally, some of the male or female structures fail to form altogether for reasons that are not usually clear. In cases where external genitalia are ambiguous, it was common practice for many years to assign a female gender, and to perform surgical alterations to make the external genitals look more completely feminine. In recent years, it has been recognized that the sexual identity of genetic males after puberty is typically male regardless of whether the child was reared as a male or female, and thus more consideration is given to sex assignment now than in previous years.

Sexual determination is not always as straightforward in other species as it is in humans, and there are many different basic mechanisms by which sex is determined. In fruit flies (*Drosophila melanogaster*), for example, sex is determined by the ratio of X chromosomes to the number of sets of autosomes. Normal females have a ratio of 1:1, usually having two X chromosomes and two complete sets of autosomes. Males typically have one X chromosome and two sets of autosomes for a ratio of 1:2. Any ratio greater than 1.0 will result in female sex development, and any ratio below 0.5 results in male development. In between 0.5 and 1.0, the pattern of development is intermediate, bearing some aspects of both femaleness and maleness.

WORLD of FORENSIC SCIENCE

In most species, female development is associated with the presence of two X chromosomes, and male development with the presence of an X and a Y chromosome. Females are therefore typically the homogametic sex, meaning that their sex chromosomes are identical to one another. Males are said to be the heterogametic sex, have two different sex chromosomes. In some species, most notably in certain birds and butterflies, the male is homogametic, and the female is the heterogametic sex. In these species, the male sex chromosomes are referred to as Z chromosomes, and the females are said to have a W chromosome and a Z chromosome.

Sex determination in plants is also variable. The male-associated structures in flowering plants are the stamen and pollen. Female associated structures are the pistil and ovaries. Most plants exist as hermaphrodites, producing both male and female structures, often in the same flower. Other plants may exist as male or female individuals, producing only male or female flowers. The common sexual differentiation schemes among plants that produce seeds encased in ovaries are dioecy and gynodioecy. In dioecy, plants can be either male or female. In gynodioecy, plants are either female or hermaphroditic. Sex determination in plants is often less genetically deterministic than in humans. That is, genetic factors may not sufficiently specify the sex of the plant. This results in male, female, or hermaphroditic development being somewhat dependent on environmental conditions.

Sex determination in animals can also be heavily influenced by the environment in some species. For example, sex-determination in some species appears to be primarily dependent upon temperature at the time of development rather than on the presence or absence of specific genes or chromosomes. In certain species of fish, sexual development can change over time with individuals functioning as females for part of the life cycle and as males for other parts of the life cycle. This can be influenced by the relative abundance of individuals of the same or opposite sex in the environment, even when the other individuals are separated by an insuperable barrier such as a glass partition in an aquarium. Environmental pollutants can also influence sexual development in many species.

Bacteria are generally considered to be asexual reproducers, however, *Escherichia coli* sometimes contain a plasmid called the F-factor that contains 30 or so genes in a small plasmid. The presence of the F-factor permits a bacterium to conjugate with another bacterium lacking the F-factor. During conjugation, copies of the F-factor are transmitted to recipient cells, converting them from F^- to F^+. This system is reminiscent of sexual systems in higher organisms.

There are many other unusual systems for sexual development and differentiation, and there seem to be as many exceptions as there are rules. For example, the parasitic wasp, *Habrobracon juglandis* can reproduce without a partner. This process is called parthenogenesis. Female wasps produce eggs at maturity and begin laying eggs regardless of whether there are males in the environment with which to mate. Both fertilized and unfertilized eggs hatch out and produce viable offspring. Eggs that are not fertilized contain only a single copy of each chromosome, a state that is called haploidy. Haploid offspring are male, and will produce sperm at maturity, and will mate with females to fertilize their eggs. The fertilized eggs receive two copies of each chromosome, one from each parent. This is called diploidy. Diploid offspring develop as females. Thus in this species, sex determination is dependent on the number of copies of each chromosome that are present at the time embryogenesis begins. When few males are present in the environment, most eggs will go unfertilized and the offspring will be haploid and thus male. When many males are present in the environment, most eggs are fertilized, giving rise to diploid offspring, which develop as females. While this system for sexual development is not common in nature, it illustrates one of the many innovative ways that sex can be determined in nature.

The benefits of sexual systems for reproduction are not very well understood in nature, but the presence of such elaborate and complex systems for development suggests that there must be benefits to sexual reproduction compared with asexual methods.

SEE ALSO Anthropometry; Chromosome; Gene.

Sexual dimorphism

The natural occurrence of physical differences between males and females is referred to as sexual dimorphism. Often, these physical differences are quite striking and obvious, such as the differences seen in humans where external genitalia at birth can usually be used to tell boys from girls unambiguously. As children develop and mature into adulthood, a whole host of other physical traits emerge such as body hair patterns, breast development, and a wide array of other growth characteristics. While it might seem self-evident that physical differences exist between males and females, some species, such as Quaker parrots, do not exhibit any outward differences, and cannot be sexed externally. Even avian experts must rely on genetic testing to sex these birds. Quaker parrots could, therefore, be described as sexually monomorphic.

The sex of an animal can oftentimes be determined by external physical traits such as overt differences in the appearance of the external genitalia. Dogs, for example, are sexually dimorphic at this level as one can easily determine gender from observation of external genitalia, even at a distance. Other species, such as hamsters, exhibit differences in external genitalia that are more subtle and require careful examination. Many birds may be sexed by the scientist, despite a lack of observable differences in external genitalia, because of striking differences in coloration patterns in the feathers.

In fruit flies (*Drosophila melanogaster*), it has long been recognized that the ratio of X-chromosomes to Y-chromosomes is the primary determinant of whether the embryo will develop as a male or as a female. Males can easily be discriminated from females based on external differences such as length and coloration patterns of the abdomen, and the presence of sex combs being limited to the foreleg of males. There are indeed differences in external genitalia of fruit flies, but these differences are far more subtle, making discrimination of gender on the basis of external genitalia impractical. There has recently been a revolution in scientific understanding of how sex-determination in fruit flies (*Drosophila*) generates sexual dimorphism in somatic tissues at the molecular level. The mechanisms for **sex determination** alter the activities of various signaling molecules and transcription factors within cells to direct various sex-specific elements of growth and differentiation.

In flowering plants, there are two dimorphic breeding systems that are fairly widespread among species that develop seeds within an ovary. The first system, called dioecy, involves males and females. Male expression in plants involves stamen and pollen production. Female expression involves production of the pistil and ovaries. The second and more common system, called gynodioecy, involves females and hermaphrodites (plants which express both male and female components). Hermaphrodites are individuals that produce both male and female sexual parts. Hermaphrodites are very common among plants.

Conditions within the environment such as the availability of water or soil nutrients can alter the sexual expression in hermaphroditic plants, resulting in differences in the balance of male to female flowers over time.

The concept of sexual dimorphism can be applied at many different levels. Thus, while one might ask at the most basic level whether males and females are physically different and therefore distinguishable from one another, the question of sexual dimorphism can be applied toward specific traits, both internal and external. Differences in hormone levels between males and females constitute a kind of sexual dimorphism of their own at the biochemical level. Genetic differences between males and females, even prior to the rise of hormonal differences, can give rise to differences in both structure and function in the brains of vertebrate animals when comparing males and females. Even in cell **culture**, response to hormonal supplementation can be different in male and female neurons even when the neurons in culture are taken from the embryo prior to time that the testosterone surge masculinizes the male embryonic brain. This leads to differences in structural development as well as differences in the biochemical environment. One can even consider behavioral traits to be sexual dimorphisms if the patterns of behavior are consistently different between males and females.

Evidence of sexual dimorphism may be seen even in the circadian rhythms (daily physical patterns) of males compared with females in many species. Careful study of the development and the differences in circadian rhythms in male and female rodents shows that differences arise after the onset of puberty and require the presence of hormones produced by the testes or ovaries. Removal of the testes or ovaries in animals prior to the onset of puberty prevents the development of distinctive changes in circadian rhythms normally seen shortly after puberty, even when sex-specific hormones are applied.

In the most general sense, any aspect of physical structure, coloration, **gene** expression, **physiology**, biochemistry, or behavior that shows evidence of differences between males and females can be described as a sexual dimorphism. The existence of sexually dimorphic traits at so many different levels of function and development provides researchers with insights into the meaning of sex within nature.

SEE ALSO Anthropology; Biometrics; Gene; Physiology.

Sexual predation characteristics

By legal definition, a sexual predator is a person who has been convicted of or pled guilty to committing a sexually oriented offense, and who is likely in the future to commit additional sexually oriented offenses. Sexual predators present unique challenges to the forensic psychiatrist because their condition is often resistant to current treatments; they may or may not have a concurrent mental illness; and it is often difficult to properly place convicted sexual predators, whether within the prison population or in mental health facilities. Offenders can be classified as sexual predators in one of the following ways: (1) The offender is convicted of a sexually violent offense with a sexually violent predator specification, or (2) the sentencing court, after holding a sexual predator hearing (based on legal statutes) determines that the offender is a sexual predator. Offenders who are classified as sexual predators are bound by life-long registration and verification requirements unless an additional hearing is held and a judge makes a decision to modify or to terminate classification of the individual as a sexual predator. Sexual predators are subject to local jurisdictional rules and requirements for neighbor and community notification, and they may be required to report their whereabouts to an officer of the court, or to a law enforcement agency, every 90 days.

According to the Federal Bureau of Investigation's (**FBI**) National Center for the Assessment of Violent Crime (NCAVC), while sexual predators do not always commit homicides, they do typically escalate their criminal sexual behaviors over time. Fantasy plays a key role in the lives of sexual predators, and they are reported (on the basis of extensive research and interviews with incarcerated and convicted sexual predators) to experience violent sexual fantasies well before they begin to act them out. Over time, they progress to the point of carrying out their imagined or fantasized scenarios with both willing and unwilling sexual partners. When sexual predators become lethal (that is, when they kill), they typically refine their means or methods of choosing, pursuing, abducting, and controlling their victims throughout a scenario that leads to the eventual sexual homicide.

It is quite common for sexual predators to report experiencing sexual pleasure, or achievement of sexual gratification, resulting from behaviors that would not generally be considered sexual, such as intentionally causing their victims to experience pain; mutilating or disfiguring their victims; collecting trophies such as articles of clothing or personal items belonging to the victim; taking tokens from the environment in which the crime was committed (in sexual homicides, the latter may be a piece of flesh or other body part); the manner in which the victim is left (bound or tied with the use of symbolic ligatures); or, in the case of **murder**, the manner in which the corpse is arranged or designed to be discovered.

Sexual psychopaths are a subcategory of sexual predators who are characterized as being far more likely to rape (and/or commit homicide) than simply to molest their victims. They are more likely to victimize both children and adults, rather than one or the other. Their criminal sexual predatory behavior, if they are motivated by thrill-seeking rather than by specific fantasies, may be directed into indiscriminate victim choice, not targeting one or a small number of victim types.

SEE ALSO Bite analysis; Blunt injuries, signs of; Bundy (serial murderer) case; Crime scene staging; Criminal profiling.

Shaken baby syndrome

Shaken baby syndrome (SBS) is a collection of findings used to describe the aggressive shaking, jolting, and jerking of an infant or young child primarily about the arms, chest, legs, or shoulders, and the strong impact trauma, or blows, on and about the head and **skull** of a baby. (Other names for shaken baby syndrome include shaken/impact syndrome, abusive head trauma, pediatric traumatic brain injury, shaken brain trauma, shaken impact syndrome, and whiplash shaken infant syndrome.) SBS is most often inflicted by biological fathers, stepfathers, male partners of biological mothers, and caregivers, but can also be inflicted by biological mothers.

Shaken baby syndrome is diagnosed by physicians (in cases of live children) and forensic scientists (those of dead children) when finding such problem areas as retinal hemorrhages (bleeding within the retina of eyes), intracranial hemorrhage (bleeding in and around the brain), increased head size (as a result of too much fluid in brain tissues), spinal cord damage, and broken and fractured ribs and bones. When brain damage is suspected, various diagnostic methods are used including computed tomography (CT) and magnetic resonance **imaging** (MRI) in order to show injuries to the brain. When such problems occur, more subtle symptoms are usually also present such as viral illnesses (such as influenza), infant colic (stomach aches and cramps), swallowing and feeding dysfunction, vomiting, lethargy (sluggishness), and irritability. Enough traumatic force used when shaking a baby can lead to brain damage, hearing loss, blindness, learning disorders, mental retardation, paralysis, seizures, and eventual death of the child.

Shaken baby syndrome, a type of child abuse, is investigated by law enforcement officials as a criminal assault in the United States and in many countries around the world. Such investigations are mostly performed by an expert who can distinguish between common childhood illness and injuries, and symptoms associated with SBS. It could also be investigated by professionals from local or state child welfare, social services, and public health care agencies due to the need to protect the child. Forensic experts must be called in when death has occurred in order to verify that the **cause of death** was shaken baby syndrome.

SEE ALSO Skull.

Shoeprints

Shoes create impressions at the scene of a crime called shoeprints and can be extremely informative to the forensic investigator. The sole of a shoe picks up various kinds of material as a person walks, and this is readily transferred to other surfaces, creating an impression that can reveal the pattern on the sole. Investigators look at soil, particularly around the potential entry and exit points of a crime scene, as well as carpet, linoleum, paper, and dust to try to detect shoeprints. If a shoeprint is found in a pool of **blood**, it can serve as incriminating **evidence**.

There are three kinds of shoeprints: patent, plastic, and latent. Patent shoeprints are clearly visible and come from tracking through a substance like paint or dirt and leaving some behind each time a step is taken. A plastic shoeprint occurs when a shoe sinks into a soft substance like snow or mud. Latent shoeprints are those that are not visible to the naked eye and often occur on a hard surface like **glass** or concrete. The techniques used for collecting shoeprints vary, but include dusting with special powders, electrostatic lifting, and making plaster casts. A photographic record is always taken as well.

Back in the laboratory, the forensic investigator will determine various characteristics of any shoeprints collected. The pattern itself can be linked to specific manufacturers and shoe types. Very few shoe soles are made of plain leather alone, and the patterns on a pair of trainers can be complex. The investigator will probably have access to a shoeprint database to identify the origin of a shoe. It may also be possible to determine the size of the shoe from the size of a sole, and this can help build a physical profile of a perpetrator.

Each individual has their own way of walking, which has an impact on the way their shoes wear down, and this will be evident in the shoeprint. It may be possible to determine if the perpetrator had a foot deformity or a limp from the way their shoes have worn down. As someone walks, the soles of their shoes also acquire a unique pattern of damage consisting of tiny cuts, scratches, and abrasions. Because no two people ever tread exactly the same route over a period of time, this damage pattern is unique to each shoe sole and can be powerful individualizing evidence.

To compare a shoeprint found at the scene of a crime with that from a suspect's shoe, the investigator has to create a print from the latter. One way is to coat the shoe sole with a light oil by pressing it into foam rubber impregnated with oil. The shoe is then pressed onto paper, creating an oily print that can be visualized with magnetic powder. If a plastic print is needed for comparison, the shoe will be pressed into a similar surface to the one in which the shoeprint was found. It is important to try to reproduce the mechanism by which the original shoeprint was made in investigating a suspect's shoeprint. The argument that both came from the same source—the suspect's shoe—then becomes much more convincing.

SEE ALSO Impression evidence.

Silencers

The forensic investigation of a crime that involved the use of a firearm is concerned with establishing the type of weapon used. This knowledge helps piece together the circumstances of the crime and can help apprehend those who committed the crime. These ballistic determinations can include obtaining **evidence** of the use of a silencer.

A silencer, intended to suppress sound, is an attachment to a firearm. Generally, silencers are a six- to twenty-inch steel, titanium, or aluminum alloy barrel addition designed to work with a particular weapon. Silencers have also been constructed from other materials such as plastic soft drink bottles.

Nicknamed "whispering death," these devices give a shooter the ability to strike a target with less risk of being noticed. Contrary to popular image, silencers do not completely muffle the sound of a gun, but instead lessen muzzle flash, reduce muzzle noise, and decrease recoil by delaying the escape of gases from the barrel of the firearm.

To an experienced forensic investigator, then relative lack of **gunshot residue** in a crime involving a firearm can be a clue to the use of a silencer.

Gunsmiths began experimenting with various designs to silence weapons in the nineteenth century. The first person to develop and market a silencer successfully was Hiram P. Maxim, the son of the similarly named inventor of the machine gun. In 1908 Maxim developed a silencer that delayed the release of gases, but he did not market the weapon until making a few improvements. The Maxim Model 1909, released in the year of its name, became the first efficient silencer to be marketed, but the Maxim Model 1910 became the most widely distributed silencer in the United States by capitalizing on an off-center design that allowed it to be used with a weapon's original sights.

Although the military value of silencers quickly became apparent to many observers, Maxim only had the goal of eliminating noise pollution. Many of the first buyers of silencers employed them for target shooting in basements and backyards so that the sound of firing would not disturb others. Silencers also found a market in pest control. Many silencers are still sold for use in eliminating rats, not so much to surprise the rodents, but to avoid the public relations problems associated with shots fired within heavily occupied areas.

The development of a supremely effective silencer has been complicated by many factors. The noise made by the discharge of a firearm has three components: 1) the sounds made by the movement of the parts of the gun; 2) the crack of a bullet passing through the atmosphere at a rate above the speed of sound; and 3) the release of high pressure gases breaking out of the barrel. Silencers only address the last concern, although the use of a heavy subsonic bullet rather than a high velocity bullet greatly adds to sound suppression. High velocity bullets make a noise of their own when traveling through the air outside of the silencer and the substitution of a slower bullet will slow the passage of the projectile through the air, thereby reducing ballistic noise. Silencers that fire regular supersonic ammunition are only a little quieter than those without suppressors. Subsonic ammunition has less power than

regular ammunition making it effective only at shorter ranges of up to 600 feet (200 m). Silencers can be attached to most **firearms**, but they work best as components of purpose built or modified guns.

Silencers are now made for almost every firearm, from fully automatic submachine guns to big bore bolt-action rifles, and the popularity of these weapons is likely to grow.

SEE ALSO Ballistics; Crime scene investigation; Gunshot residue.

Simpson (O. J.) murder trial

The role of forensic scientists is paramount in gathering **evidence** for criminal court cases. In the end, however, the verdict rests with the jury. One of the most publicized and controversial court cases involved the double **murder** of Nicole Brown Simpson, 35, and Ronald Goldman, 25, at approximately 10 P.M. on June 12, 1994. Both were stabbed to death outside Nicole Simpson's Los Angeles condominium. The investigation was complicated by the fact that there were no eyewitnesses and no murder weapon was found. However, crime scene investigators did recover important evidence that linked Nicole's former husband, Orenthal James (O. J.) Simpson, the former football star, to the murders. This evidence was analyzed by forensic scientists and it was used to prosecute Simpson in an internationally watched and discussed court case.

The evidence that was retrieved at the scene of the crime was substantial. It wasn't immediately clear who committed the murders—even though Simpson was an early suspect—until five days after the murders. In front of a televised audience of millions of viewers, police cars, and helicopters, Simpson's white Ford Bronco drove in a 60-mile (97-km) chase across Route 405 in southern California. The car was driven by A. C. Cowlings, a friend and an ex-football player teammate, while Simpson sat in the back seat with a gun. Simpson had failed to show up for his arraignment on the charges of the double murder before the famous car chase. At the end of the car chase, with the Bronco pulling into his Rockingham Avenue estate, Simpson was arrested.

Deputy District Attorney Marcia Clark revealed the evidence to the court. There were hair samples that were found on Goldman's body after his murder. Forensic geneticists matched the **DNA** from the hair samples to DNA retrieved from O. J. Simpson. There was also a trail of bloody **shoeprints** near the murder scene that were estimated by the crime lab to be made by a man's shoe, size 12—the same size that Simpson wears. There was a pair of socks with bloodstains on it that was found in O. J. Simpson's bedroom. Geneticists extracted DNA from the socks and matched it to Nicole's DNA. **Blood** was also found on Simpson's Ford Bronco. After the DNA was extracted and tested, it was found to positively match DNA from both victims. Even blood found at the crime scene was found to have DNA that matched that of O. J. Simpson.

During the police **interrogation** of Simpson, it was discovered that he had a cut on his left hand. A leather glove that was found near both of the victims had blood on it. DNA samples from the blood matched that of both Simpsons as well as Goldman. A matching glove, with bloodstains on it, was also recovered on Simpson's own estate. Cumulatively, this striking evidence led the prosecution to believe that Simpson was guilty. His trial began the following January.

Simpson employed a group of competent, high profile lawyers that became known as "the dream team." They engineered a formidable defense (despite the overwhelming evidence against Simpson) that was focused on discrediting the Los Angeles police department. They claimed that the police failed to conduct a well-constructed, proper investigation. The prosecution launched its attack using O. J. Simpson's prior history of severe domestic violence and a platform for demonstrating both his motive and his capability of violence. There were other women, at one time involved with Simpson, who claimed to have been abused by him. The prosecution asserted that Ronald Goldman was murdered when he went to Nicole's condominium to return her eyeglasses and, in doing so, stumbled upon the murder. He was then allegedly murdered by O. J. Simpson.

For the defense, the strategy was targeted at police detective Mark Fuhrman, who arrived at Simpson's estate and first discovered the matching bloodstained glove on his property. The defense's case was strengthened by a variety of conversations that depicted Fuhrman as a racist based on previous racial remarks he had made. Attorney Johnnie Cochran proved to be a key player on Simpson's defense team. Jurors heard tape recordings of phone calls that Nicole made to 911 in 1989 and 1993 during altercations between her and Simpson. However, Cochran managed to refocus the court proceedings on Fuhrman, who he ultimately accused of planting the matching bloodstained glove on Simpson's property in order to frame the ex-football star for the double murders. It was implied that Fuhrman was motivated to frame Simpson because he was black.

Near the end of the trial, Cochran produced one of the gloves and requested that Simpson put it on his hand. It appeared to the jury that the glove did not fit Simpson appropriately, lending credence to Cochran's defense that the glove might have been planted. On October 2, 1995, a jury of Simpson's peers deliberated for only about three hours before reaching a verdict. On October 3, 1995, the jury acquitted Simpson of the double murder charges. The trial lasted nine months and the state of California rendered him not guilty. Many people throughout the country were shocked by the decision.

This case exemplifies the importance of the police department's handling of evidence and how police officers should conduct a criminal investigation. It also demonstrates that even with the most formidable evidence produced by the forensics scientists, it may not be enough to convince a jury beyond a reasonable doubt that an accused individual is guilty. Following this case, it became clear that top-notch **forensic science**, particularly the DNA analysis and the footwear impression examination determined by the Federal Bureau of Investigation (**FBI**) agents, must be accompanied by top-notch crime scene investigative collection of evidence. Detailed guidelines for the investigations of homicides, crime scene **processing**, and **arson** investigation have since been drafted by the National Institute for Justice. This includes the development of certification programs that specifically train police officers and crime scene technicians in the appropriate approaches to handle the evidence in a **crime scene investigation**.

The O. J. Simpson trial was controversial. The lack of agreement among experts on the reliability of any evidence in a criminal investigation can be crippling for the prosecution. This case also raised controversy regarding DNA evidence and the methods used for linking suspects to biological evidence found at the scene of the crime. An expert witness for the prosecution, Dr. Bruce S. Weir, testified regarding the methods used for the DNA analysis and how the evidence was examined for the case. Unlike a fingerprinting examination, where the methodology has not been demonstrated to be scientifically proven, DNA analysis is scientifically well tested and the methodologies are considered to be solid by most critics. However, how the evidence is obtained and handled can discredit the findings in a forensics DNA laboratory.

Also important in the O. J. Simpson murder case is the length of time that the evidence was collected. Some DNA from blood droplets that were found at the crime scene was determined not to be from the victims. O. J. Simpson's blood was drawn after this was determined (after the blood was collected during the crime scene investigation). The DNA from the blood droplets was compared to O. J. Simpson's DNA and found to match. By the order of events in this case and the fact that the DNA was already being analyzed by the forensics laboratory suggests that this blood could not have been "planted" by police officers after his arrest. In fact, the DNA analysis revealed that O. J. Simpson's blood DNA had matched the blood DNA found at the crime scene with the probability that only approximately one in 57 billion people could have the same type of match. Three different crime labs performed the same analysis and all three found a positive match.

When Dr. Henry Lee, a criminologist, testified that the blood may have been packaged inappropriately, the defense suggested that a sample switching occurred. The defense also claimed that the blood was degraded due to its storage in the lab truck. This was argued by the prosecution's DNA expert, Harlan Levy, who testified that the degraded DNA was not substantial enough to thwart proper DNA analysis and should not mitigate confidence in the results. If the DNA was mishandled due to the storage procedure, then the quality of the controls would also have been abrogated. Regardless of these credible points, the defense managed to convince the jury that the evidence was mishandled. This weakened the credibility of the genetics laboratory results. Moreover, the complicated and confusing testimony from the DNA experts may have confused and worn out the jury, who may not have had an appropriate understanding of the methodologies and scientific merit of these forensic tests.

The O. J. Simpson double murder trial brought forensic sciences and DNA fingerprinting techniques to the media spotlight. In the end, despite the overwhelming evidence in favor of the prosecution, the key to this case was that the jurors were not convinced that the blood samples were handled appropriately. This court case provided a framework for forensics experts to use to develop new ways to properly handle evidence and maintain a high level of quality control.

Civil lawsuits may be filed regardless of the outcome of an associated criminal prosecution or lack of prosecution. A victim can sue in a civil court even if the alleged perpetrator was found "not guilty" in a criminal court. In a civil trial that followed the criminal case, Simpson was found liable for the deaths of Nicole Simpson and Ronald Goldman (in civil court defendants are found liable rather than guilty). Much of the same forensic evidence that was used at the criminal trial was used in the civil trial. In a civil trial, there is a lower threshold for proof of liability. Moreover, Simpson was required to take the witness stand and offer testimony (something he was not required to do at his trial in criminal court). In the O. J. Simpson civil case, the verdict of liability was unanimous, and Simpson was ordered to pay penalties of roughly $8.5 million.

SEE ALSO Bloodstain evidence; Crime scene investigation; DNA databanks; DNA evidence, social issues; DNA fingerprint; DNA sequences, unique; DNA typing systems; Physical evidence; Quality control of forensic evidence.

Sinus print

A sinus print is a bony feature in the **skull** that can be used to make an **identification** of skeletal remains. To use a sinus print in this way, it is necessary that a skull be found among the remains and that ante-mortem skull x rays are available.

The sinuses are four pairs of air-filled cavities, surrounded by bone, at the side and top of the nose. They make the voice resonate and also lighten the bones of the skull. The frontal sinuses are found above the eyebrows and are bounded, at the top, by a scalloped ridge. Research has shown that the detailed shape of this bony ridge is an individualizing characteristic. The pattern is known as a sinus print and, like a fingerprint, it is unique to each individual. Identifications using sinus prints have been carried out since approximately 1921.

When skeletal remains are discovered, the forensic anthropologist, having first confirmed that they are human, will try to date them. Police will usually have a list of persons reported missing around that period of time. Should any of these have had a skull x ray for medical reasons, this will be part of their medical records and can be made available to the investigating team. An x ray is made of the skull and superimposed on the antemortem x ray. Should the sinus prints of antemortem and postmortem x rays match, this is powerful evidence of identity. If they do not match up, the missing person can be eliminated from the enquiry.

Identification from a sinus print may be confirmed by looking for other points of comparison in the antemortem and postmortem skull x rays. For instance, the side profiles of the skulls should also be compared. If there are teeth available with the discovered skull, then dental records can also help confirm identity. If there is no antemortem x ray, the skull may still be useful if there is a photograph of the missing person. In photo superimposition, the forensic anthropologist overlays a photographic transparency of the skull, scaled to match the angle of the head in the portrait. They will look for matches at points such as the chin, teeth, and eyebrow ridge. Lack of fit is usually very obvious. This technique is especially useful for disproving identity. However, it is not as powerful as the sinus print for establishing identity and can only be seen as a guide.

SEE ALSO Anthropology; Osteology and skeletal radiology.

Vittorio Siracusa

ITALIAN
FORENSIC SCIENTIST

In 1923 Vittorio Siracusa was the first to use the absorption-elution technique for the ABO **blood** group typing of bloodstains.

At a crime scene, when there appear to be spatters of dried blood, investigators must follow a logical process in order to identify the unknown substance. The first question to be answered is whether or not the material in question is blood. Once that has been established, it is necessary to determine whether the blood sample originated from an animal. When the unknown sample has been conclusively identified as a sample of animal blood, the next question to be answered is the species of animal from which it came. Assuming that the sample is found to contain blood, that the blood emanated from an animal, and that the animal is human, the next task is to type the blood. After successfully typing the human blood, the investigator will want to try to establish the age, race, and gender of the human blood source. The object of this series of investigative queries is to accurately identify the source of the blood in an effort to tie it to a particular suspect, or to link a perpetrator and a crime, or to link a series of crimes.

The absorption-elution test, promulgated by Vittorio Siracusa, has tremendous forensic utility, because it can be used to identify old and severely dried bloodstains. When a determination has been made that a particular stain contains human blood, but the stain is extremely dry, an absorption-elution test can be conducted. A small sample scraping is taken and compatible antiserum antibodies are added to it. The sample is then heated until it reaches the temperature at which the antibody-antigen bonds are broken. Known red cells from standard blood groups are then added to fragments of the sample, in order to see what causes it to coagulate, in order to determine basic (ABO) blood group type.

By developing the absorption-elution test for use on old or exceedingly dried blood, Siracusa made a lasting contribution to the world of **forensic science**. In fact, his test remains in popular use in contemporary forensic science investigations.

SEE ALSO Blood spatter; Blood, presumptive test; Bloodstain evidence; Microscopes.

Skeletal analysis

The human skeletal system is primarily composed of a supportive structure found inside the body called the endoskeleton. The endoskeleton is made up of either bone or cartilage. Bone is hard, calcified tissue of the skeleton found in vertebrates and consists of collagen, calcium phosphate, calcium carbonate, and is innervated by blood vessels. Analysis of an endoskeleton from the remains of an individual can provide information about the identity of the person that died, as well as information regarding physical characteristics about that person. This is particularly useful to forensics scientists, who are responsible for handling human remains during criminal investigations and determining the identity of a victim, the manner of death, and if a crime was committed.

Ascertaining the **cause of death** can be problematic because the integrity of the remains is often significantly compromised (decomposed) and the cause of death can be due to a myriad of reasons (fires, homicides, explosions, wild animals, poisoning, drowning, among other causes). Forensic anthropologists are often consulted in these difficult cases. They are experts who combine their knowledge and **training** in human evolution, human variability, human development, human genetics, and human osteology (the study of bones) to be used for criminal investigations or following natural disasters. Examinations of skeletal remains are often performed by forensic anthropologists.

There are three primary subspecialties recognized in forensic **anthropology** used for skeletal analysis: forensic osteology, forensic **archaeology**, and forensic **taphonomy**. Forensic osteology involves the study of human bones and includes understanding how bones form, disease states relating to bone, and distinguishing disease from trauma-induced alterations to the skeletal system. Forensic archaeology is the study of human remains at their site, and involves how to excavate human remains found in a potential crime scene. Finally, forensic taphonomy helps forensic scientists determine the skeletal alterations that transpired at the **time of death** and afterwards. These alterations can be analyzed by identifying diffuse or focal traumatic injury to the skeletal system, the rate, extent, and type of **decomposition** that occurs, and any environmental modifications that might be important.

Forensic osteologists usually become involved in the criminal investigation at the beginning of the search (as part of a team) for hidden or buried remains with the assistance of specially trained cadaver search and rescue dogs and law enforcement experts. Once the remains are located, osteologists and archaeologists excavate the remains and help to determine **evidence** relevant to the investigation. Bone collection must follow careful visual analysis of the crime scene to help understand the position of the body or, if buried, what types of tools were used on the body or for burying it.

Once the remains are removed from the site, they are cleaned and analyzed in a laboratory. Forensic osteologists can then apply radiographic techniques to compare skeletal remains to archived x rays, which could help identify the individual. These radiographic techniques are especially helpful if there is suspicion of foul play. If necessary, the skeleton is sectioned or cut and put onto a slide to be analyzed by a bone histologist, who may be able to make assumptions regarding the extent and type of damage inflicted on the bone.

Other techniques such as **scanning electron microscopy** can provide information regarding the extent of decomposition, which helps determine approximate time of death or the nature of the environmental affects on the bones. Scanning electron **microscopes** magnify images using electrons to create three-dimensional images. Bone samples can also be sent to other forensics experts for biochemical or trace element analysis, as well as for **DNA** analysis. Once laboratory tests are complete, the bones are usually casted (molded) and curated (preserved) using commercially available skeletal preservatives.

The race, age (at death), height, size, sex, and type of physique of a person can often be ascertained by examining their skeletal remains. Bone can also be analyzed for traits such as dental hygiene and habits such as smoking and frequent exercise. It is not possible, however, to determine the weight of an individual based on bone structure. Similar bone structures do not indicate similar fat cell size and distribution.

A laboratory that specializes in skeletal biology and forensic archaeology uses equipment such as x-ray machines, microscopes, bone casting supplies, peripheral x-ray bone densitometers (to determine bone density), ultrasonometer, cutting saws, calipers, mandibulometers (specialized calipers for the jaw), and other anthropology equipment. Collections of bones from **autopsy** specimens with known conditions such as arthritis, infections, fractures, cancer, and osteoporosis are also preserved in these laboratories, and aid in distinguishing trauma-induced bone changes from disease-induced bone changes. This distinction could provide critical information to a criminal investigation.

A forensic scientist must be able to analyze the skeletal system given different situations. For example, if a child suffers multiple fractures and dies due to related complications, the parents might be under suspicion for child abuse and homicide. Either the **medical examiner** or the forensic pathologist should identify the rare cases of multiple fractures in deceased children that involve a genetic-based cause of disease, such as osteogenesis imperfecta, where affected individuals are extremely susceptible to multiple fractures with little mechanical force.

Technological advances have paved the way for forensics sciences to gain a plethora of information from scantly detectable evidence in a crime scene. Even in cases where skeletal remains are scattered, contemporary techniques that use three-dimensional digital imagery can help remodel and restore the skeletal remains. Anthropometric (body proportion) measurements from a large enough sample size from a given population can be used for **computer modeling** programs to estimate body measurements. Three-dimensional facial reconstruction techniques can provide a visual representation of the victim. It is possible, based on the size and shape of an individual's **skull**, to estimate race and use computerized programs to help reconstruct what the individual looks like. These computerized models have begun to replace recreating the remains of a person using casts. However, in general, facial reconstructions cannot be used in a court of law as positive **identification**, as they can be subjective, unreliable, and difficult to reproduce.

In examining skeletal remains resulting from natural disasters, knowledge of how the natural surrounding environment participates in the decomposition of the skeletal system is important. For example, certain insects and microorganisms become involved in the decaying remains of an individual in a time-dependent fashion. When the body begins to decay, there are enzymes found in the digestive system that can liquefy the tissues, a process called putrefaction. Maggots are efficient at using rotting flesh for their energy requirements. By examining their life cycles, insect activity can sometimes reveal the time of death.

Additionally, trace amounts of DNA from bone remains can be recovered and analyzed by a molecular geneticist. DNA survival is greatest in dense bone, such as teeth, than in any other type of tissue. In fact, it has been possible to extract small amounts of DNA recovered from bones that are thousands of years old and perform DNA analysis by amplifying the DNA sequences with a technique known as **polymerase chain reaction**, or **PCR**. Bones from murder victims have been successfully identified almost a decade after the person died using comparative DNA typing and DNA markers. DNA markers from the bone sample are compared to DNA markers from samples from the possible parents of the victim. If enough DNA markers are analyzed and these markers match the parents, it is possible to conclude with a high level of certainty the identity of the victim. The degradation rate of DNA extracted from rib bones has also been used to determine the time interval since death of a victim.

In general, although it requires highly trained and specialized experts, skeletal analysis for forensic purposes can be useful and informative, especially in cases where bone is the only recovered evidence.

SEE ALSO Anthropology; Archaeology; Casting; DNA mixtures, forensic interpretation of mass graves; Odontology; Osteology and skeletal radiology; War forensics.

Skeletal system overview (morphology)

When death has occurred weeks or months before a body is discovered, **decomposition** removes much of the body **fluids**, muscle, and tissue from a corpse. What remains is the supporting skeleton. The arrangement of the bones in a skeleton, their condition, and markings that can be present (such as the scrape or gouging left by a knife blade) can tell a forensic investigator much about the deceased.

The bones of the skeletal system can be classified according to their shape and location. The types of bones categorized by shape—long, short, flat, and irregular—also provide evidence of their function. Long bones consist of an elongated shaft called the diaphysis. Each end of the diaphysis is an expanded portion of the shaft and is called an epiphysis. Examples of long bones include the femur in the thigh and the humerus in the arm. These bones function as levers when muscles contract, thus providing support to enable movement. Short bones often have equal dimensions, like those of a cube. Compared to long bones, short bones have a limited range of motion but are able to withstand force. Examples of short bones include the carpals in the wrist and the tarsals in the ankle. Flat bones are thin bones that protect internal organs and provide sites for muscle attachment. The ribs, cranial bones, and scapula are all examples of flat bones. Irregular bones are not shaped like any of the three aforementioned bones and therefore form their own category. The vertebrae and facial bones are categorized as irregular bones.

Location rather than shape classifies other types of bones, such as sesamoid and sutural bones. Sesamoid bones bear pressure as the result of being buried in tendons. The kneecap, or patella, is the best-known example of a sesamoid bone. Sutural bones are tiny bones located between the joints, or sutures, of the cranial bones.

The adult skeleton consists of 206 bones. A baby is born with 270 bones, many of which fuse together during adolescence and adulthood. The bones of males and females differ in that male bones tend to be larger and heavier than female bones.

The skeletal system can be divided into the axial skeleton and the appendicular skeleton. The axial skeleton is composed of the bones that surround the midline or axis of the body, forming the head and trunk. These bones include the **skull** bones, auditory ossicles, hyoid bone, vertebral column, sternum, and ribs.

The skull can be subdivided into eight cranial bones and fourteen facial bones. The cranial bones include the frontal bone, two parietal bones, two temporal bones, occipital bone, sphenoid bone, and ethmoid bone. The facial bones include two lacrimal bones, two nasal bones, two inferior nasal conchae, vomer, two zygomatic bones, two maxillae, two palatine bones, and mandible. Within the middle ear are three auditory ossicles: the maleus, incus, and stapes. These tiny bones transmit vibrations from the eardrum to the inner ear. The hyoid bone is located in the superior part of the neck and attaches the muscles of the tongue.

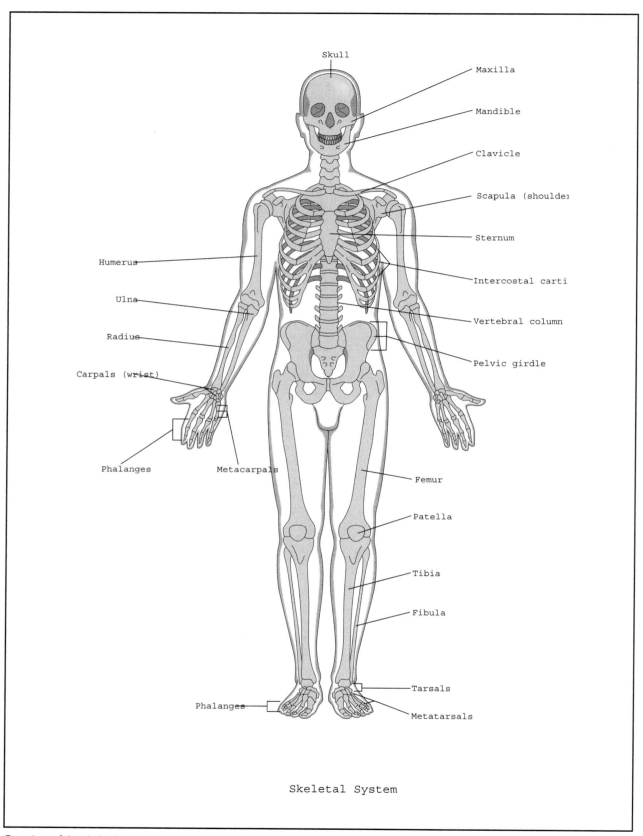

Overview of the skeletal system. ILLUSTRATION CREATED BY ARGOSY

The vertebral column typically consists of twenty-six vertebrae that protect the spinal cord and provide attachment sites for ribs and back muscles. The seven most superior vertebrae are the cervical vertebrae. The first vertebra is called the atlas and enables the head to move forward and backward. The second vertebra, the axis, is unique in that it is the only vertebra that has a process called the dens or odontoid process. The axis enables the head to rotate from side to side. The vertebrae immediately inferior to the cervical vertebrae are the twelve thoracic vertebrae. These vertebrae are larger than the cervical vertebrae and, except for the eleventh and twelfth thoracic vertebrae, have facets that articulate with the ribs. (The point where two bones meet forms a joint and the bones are said to articulate with one another.) Just below the thoracic vertebrae are the five lumbar vertebrae. The lumbar vertebrae are the largest of the vertebrae because they support a tremendous amount of the body's weight. The five sacral vertebrae are actually fused together in adults to form the sacrum. Inferior to the lumbar vertebrae, the sacrum articulates with the pelvic girdle to form the pelvis. The four remaining bones of the vertebral column constitute the coccyx. These individual bones also become fused together in adults.

The sternum, also known as the breastbone, consists of three parts. The manubrium and the body are the superior and middle parts of the sternum that articulate with the ribs. Additionally, the manubrium articulates with the clavicles. The xiphoid process is the inferior part of the sternum that provides attachment for abdominal muscles.

There are twelve pairs of ribs that make up the rib cage. The first seven pairs are true ribs because they are attached directly to the sternum by cartilage. The next three pairs of ribs are false ribs because they are indirectly attached to the sternum by the cartilage of the seventh pair. The two remaining ribs are known as floating ribs because they do not connect to the sternum at all.

The appendicular skeleton is comprised of two pectoral girdles, two pelvic girdles, and the bones of the upper and lower extremities. Each pectoral girdle, or shoulder girdle, includes the clavicle and scapula responsible for attaching the upper extremities to the axial skeleton. The clavicle, or collarbone, is the anterior component of the shoulder that articulates with the scapula and manubrium of the sternum. The scapula, or shoulder blade, is positioned posterior to the clavicle and articulates with the humerus. The humerus constitutes the upper arm and articulates with the two bones of the forearm. The radius is the lateral bone and the ulna is the medial bone of the forearm. The distal end of the radius articulates with the carpals, the first row of bones in the hand. The proximal row of carpals located from lateral to medial includes the scaphoid, lunate, triquetrum, and pisiform. The distal row of carpals that articulates with the metacarpals are the trapezium, trapezoid, capitate, and hamate. The metacarpals are numbered one through five, beginning on the lateral palm of the hand extending medially. The fourteen bones of the fingers, named phalanges, articulate with the metacarpals. Each finger has a proximal, middle, and distal phalanx except for the thumb, which only has two phalanges.

Each pelvic girdle, or hipbone, in an adult is made of three fused bones. Also known as the coxal bones, the hipbones consist of the ilium, ischium, and pubis. The ilium articulates posteriorly with the sacrum. The ischium connects the ilium and pubis. The two pubis bones meet anteriorly to form the pubis symphysis. Together, the hipbones, sacrum, and coccyx constitute the pelvis. One major difference between the male and female skeleton is the bones of the pelvis. In the female, the pelvic bones form a wide, round opening called the pelvic inlet to accommodate for childbirth. The pelvic inlet of males is heart shaped and much narrower than in women. Additionally, the sacrum is wider and shorter in women than in men, allowing the forensic **identification** of the sex of the deceased

The bones of the lower extremities include the femur, patella, tibia, fibula, tarsals, metatarsals, and phalanges. The femur is the leg bone that articulates with the pelvic girdle. The distal end of the femur articulates with the foreleg to form the knee. Anterior to the knee lies the patella, or kneecap. Each foreleg consists of two bones: tibia and fibula. The tibia is the larger of the two bones and forms the shin. The fibula is the lateral bone in the foreleg. At the distal end of the forelegs are the proximal bones of the foot called the tarsals. The tarsals include the calcaneus, talus, navicular, cuboid, and three cuneiforms. The metatarsals form the sole of the foot and are labeled one through five beginning on the medial side of the foot. Each toe consists of three phalanges, the proximal, middle, and distal phalanx. The exception is the big toe, which contains only two phalanges.

SEE ALSO Asphyxiation (signs of); Bite analysis; Exhumation; Skull.

Skull

The skull is the ossified, bony structure that encloses and protects the brain, internal extensions of sensory organs, and some facial structures. The skull is usually considered to consist of a cranial section (the cranium) and a facial region.

When a person has been dead for a long time, much of the body may have decomposed. One body part that will remain intact is the skull. Thus, it can become an important part of a forensic examination designed to determine the **cause of death** and, especially when the teeth are intact, to determine the identity of the deceased.

The cranium is a large, rounded, dome-shaped region of the skull that is composed of paired left and right frontal bones, parietal bones, temporal bones, and an unpaired occipital bone that forms the posterior base of the skull.

The bones of the cranium are fused by sutures—joints that run jaggedly along the interface between the bones. At birth, the sutures are soft, broad, and cartilaginous. This flexibility allows the skull to grow as the child matures. The sutures eventually fuse and become rigid and ossified near the end of puberty or early in adulthood. The coronal suture unites the frontal bone with the parietal bones. In **anatomical nomenclature**, the primary coronal plane is the plane that runs through the length of the coronal suture. At right angles to the coronal suture, the metopic suture separates the frontal bones in the midline region. The area formed by the fusion of the four bones near the top of the skull is termed the anterior fontanel or bregmatic fontanel (also commonly known as the topmost "soft spot" in a baby's skull). As with the sutures, the fontanels are soft at birth to permit growth. The fontanels shrink and close during childhood and are usually fully closed and hardened by young adulthood. The changing suture pattern can be used forensically to help estimate of the age of the deceased.

The sagittal suture unites the two large domed-shaped parietal bones along the midline of the body. The suture is used as an anatomical landmark in anatomical nomenclature to establish what are termed sagittal planes of the body. The primary sagittal plane is the sagittal plane that runs through the length of the sagittal suture. Sagittal planes run anteriorly and posteriorly, are always at right angles to the coronal planes. The lambdoidal suture unites the left and right parietal bones with occipital bone. The area where the two parietals

and the unpaired occipital bone meet is termed the posterior fontanel, lamdoidal fontanel, or lambda point (also commonly called the rear "soft spot" on a baby's skull). Like the anterior fontanel, the posterior fontanel closes and hardens with age, but is an important feature that allows growth of the skull during embryological and childhood development.

Along the sides of the cranium, the squamosal suture unites the temporal bone lying above (superior to) the ear and ear canal with the parietal bone. The anterior region of the temporal bones is united with the great wing of the sphenoid bone by continuation of the squamosal suture. The junction of the temporal, parietal, frontal and great wing of the sphenoid takes place at the sphenoid fontanel. The posterior border of the temporal bone on each side unites with the corresponding mastoid bone.

A mastoid fontanel lies at the posterior region of the side of the skull where the parietal, occipital, and mastoid bones unite. A mastoid process extends anteriorly toward the ear canal. A bony finger-like styloid process protrudes from the interior area to the external auditory opening (external auditory meatus).

The facial area of the skull is composed of the left and right zygomatic arches that extend from the lowest, most anterior margins of the temporal bone where the temporal bones articulate with the mandible (the temporomandibular joint) into the zygomatic bone itself. The zygomatic arches and zygomatic bones thicken to become prominent facial landmarks, forming the lower and side orbits of the eyes. The orbits are separated by a number of smaller bones in the nasal region including the ethmoid, lacrimal, and nasal bones. The maxilla and upper teeth form the most inferior region of the facial portion of the skull and are fused to the zygomatic bones.

The mandible is not considered a formal portion of the skull. In decayed bodies, the mandible becomes detached from the skull as the temporomandibular joint and supporting ligaments deteriorate.

A number of small openings allow nerves and blood vessels to penetrate the skull. These openings are termed foramen and are generally named for the bone they penetrate. For example, openings in the parietal bones are termed parietal foramen. A large foramen magnum at the rear and base of the skull allows the spinal cord to exit the skull into the vertebral column. Rounded, smooth, bony protuberances termed the occipital condyles lie on the anterior sides of the foramen magnum and help articulate the skull with the vertebral column.

The external occipital crest marks the posterior midline of the occipital bone. The crest runs from the foramen magnum upward (superiorly) to a bony knot-like external occipital protuberance.

Forensically, the skull can be used as the basis of a reconstruction, where layers of clay are applied to mimic the muscles and other tissue that formerly overlay the skull bones. When skillfully done, the resulting image offers an approximation of what the person may have looked like.

A less expensive and time-consuming method of reconstructing the facial appearance relies on photographing of the skull from different angles. The photographs can be cut out and mounted side-by-side to give a two-dimensional model that an artist can use to produce a drawing.

SEE ALSO Bite analysis; Exhumation; Skeletal system overview (morphology).

Smallpox

Knowledge of the behavior of disease-causing (pathogenic) bacteria and viruses is especially vital when a forensic investigation is concerned with the possibility of an infection that is a serious threat to health and is easily spread from person to person. A prime example is smallpox.

Smallpox is an infection caused by the **variola virus**, a member of the poxvirus family. The disease is highly infectious. Passage from person to person via contaminated aerosolized droplets (from sneezing, for example) and even by touching objects such as books and blankets that have been previously used by someone who has smallpox occurs easily, and so the spread of smallpox through a population can occur quickly. Like most viruses and other microorganisms, the variola virus can be transported from one location to another without difficulty.

When infected with the virus, there is a twelve to fourteen day symptom-free period, during which the virus is multiplying in the body. There is then a sudden onset of symptoms. The symptoms include fever and chills, muscle aches, and a flat, reddish-purple rash on the chest, abdomen, and back. These symptoms last about three days, after which the rash fades and the fever drops. A day or two later, the fever returns, along with a bumpy rash starting on the feet, hands, and face. This rash progresses from the feet along the legs, from the hands along the arms, and from the face down the neck, ultimately reaching and including the chest, abdomen, and back. The individual bumps, or papules, fill with clear fluid, and, over the course of ten to twelve days, became pus-filled. The pox eventually scabs over, and when the scab falls off it leaves behind a pock-mark or pit, which remains as a permanent scar on the skin of the victim.

Smallpox can be lethal, usually due to bacterial infection of the open skin lesions, pneumonia, or bone infections. A severe and quickly fatal form of smallpox is known as "sledgehammer smallpox." This form of smallpox is characterized by bleeding from the skin lesions, as well as from the mouth, nose, and other areas of the body.

Smallpox has been present for thousands of years. For example, studies of the mummy of Pharaoh Ramses V, who died in 1157 B.C., revealed symptoms of smallpox infection.

Large smallpox epidemics have occurred throughout recorded history. Attempts to protect against smallpox infection began centuries ago, even thought the microbiological nature of the disease was then unknown. In the tenth century, accounts from China and India describe how individuals who had even a mild case of smallpox could not be infected again. Fluid or pus from the skin lesions was scratched into the skin of those who had never had the illness, in an attempt to produce a mild reaction and its accompanying protective effect. Unfortunately, these efforts sometimes resulted in full-fledged smallpox, and helped spread the infection. Such crude vaccinations against smallpox were outlawed in Colonial America.

In 1798, Edward Jenner published his observation that milkmaids who contracted cowpox infection caused by vaccinia virus (a relative of variola) were immune to smallpox. He used infected material from the cowpox lesions to prepare an injection that helped protect the humans. Although Jenner's development of immunization was harshly criticized at first, the work paved the way to the development of **vaccines**.

Until the development of a smallpox vaccine, no treatment for smallpox was known, nor could anything shorten the course of the disease. Until its eradication, smallpox was diagnosed most clearly from the patients' symptoms. Electron microscopic studies could identify the variola virus in fluid isolated from disease papules, from infected urine,

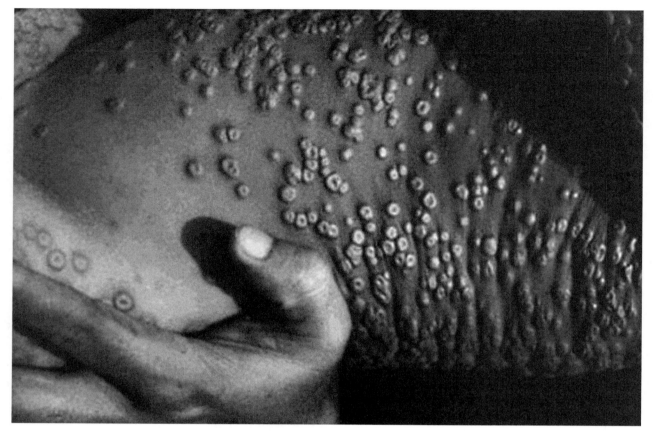

Smallpox lesions on skin are shown in this photograph taken in 1973 in Bangladesh. Smallpox infection was eliminated from the world by 1980, so any further outbreaks would likely be the result of an intentional act. © REUTERS/CORBIS

or from the blood prior to the appearance of the papular rash.

In the 1960s, the World Health Organization (WHO) began a campaign to treat people infected with smallpox and vaccinate those who might be exposed to the infection. The WHO program was extremely successful, and the virus was declared eradicated worldwide in May of 1980. Stored stocks of the virus were maintained in two laboratories. One is housed at the **Centers for Disease Control and Prevention** in Atlanta, Georgia. The other smallpox stock is maintained in Russia.

These stocks were slated to be destroyed in the late 1990s, however, President Bill Clinton halted plans for destruction of the American stocks. Concern that another poxvirus could mutate (undergo genetic changes) and cause human infection has made preservation of the smallpox stock for vaccine development purposes important. As of 2005, the stocks remain undisturbed.

SEE ALSO Bioterrorism; Pathogens; Vaccines; Variola virus.

Ron Smith

AMERICAN
FORENSIC SPECIALIST

Since 1972, Ron Smith has worked in both the government and private sectors as a forensic specialist, consultant, and trainer. He is recognized as an authority on friction ridge **identification** and palm print analysis, and is a certified latent print examiner. Smith also is known for the hundreds of seminars he has conducted on **forensic science** topics throughout the world. In addition, he has served as an expert witness in numerous criminal cases and has lectured extensively on courtroom testimony techniques.

Smith began his career in forensic identification in 1972, when he was hired by the Federal Bureau of Investigation in Washington, D.C. He later held positions with the Alabama Bureau of Investigation and the Mississippi Crime Laboratory, where he worked as assistant director. In these positions Smith did extensive fieldwork and research on the topics of friction ridge identification and palm print analysis.

Because of this experience and knowledge, he has provided testimony in more than 500 criminal cases across the United States. He has also served as the primary courtroom testimony trainer for the Mississippi Law Enforcement Officers Training Academy and the primary expert witness trainer for the Mississippi Crime Laboratory.

For more than fifteen years, Smith has also taught hundreds of forensic workshops for organizations and universities throughout the United States and around the world. He has frequently spoken on the topics of courtroom testimony techniques, latent print examinations, forensic ridgeology, footwear impression comparison, and crime scene examinations. Smith has also been actively involved in the **International Association for Identification** (IAI). He serves on the board of directors and was awarded IAI's 2001 John A. Dondero Award for his contributions to the science of forensic identification.

After his retirement from the Mississippi Crime Laboratory in 2002, Smith opened his own forensic consulting and training company, Ron Smith and Associates, Inc. The company provides technical training and criminal investigation services to government agencies, private corporations, attorneys, and individuals. The company employs professional career forensic specialists located in different cities throughout the United States and Canada, in order to provide forensic services around the world.

SEE ALSO Careers in forensic science; Expert witnesses.

Snowball the cat

In 1994, Royal Canadian Mounted Police (RCMP) found a woman's body in a shallow grave in Prince Edward Island, Canada. She was identified as a 32-year-old woman named Shirley Duguay. The mother of five children, Duguay was separated from her common-law husband Douglas Beamish. Beamish had a criminal record and was on parole during the time of the murder. The primary suspect in the case was Beamish, however RCMP had no **evidence** to associate him with the crime.

Near the scene of the crime, RCMP found a leather jacket that was stained with **blood** that matched that of Duguay. Some of Beamish's friends told RCMP that they thought that Beamish owned such a coat, but they could not be certain. Forensic investigators studying the jacket found 27 white hairs on the inside lining. They initially thought that the hairs might belong to Beamish, but microscopic analysis showed that they were actually cat fur.

One of the investigators on the case remembered seeing a white cat named Snowball at the house of Beamish's parents. At the time of the murder Beamish was living with his parents. Proving that the white fur belonged to Snowball would provide evidence tying Beamish to the crime. While forensics investigators could tell that the hair belonged to a cat, their microscopic **hair analysis** was not accurate enough to assign ownership to a specific cat. Determining the identity of the individual animal that shed the hairs required genetic testing. However, the forensics investigators on the case had no precedent for **DNA** fingerprinting of cats.

An RCMP investigator contacted the Animal Genetics Group at the Laboratory of Genomic Diversity (LGD) in Frederick, Maryland. They agreed to attempt DNA fingerprinting of Snowball. RCMP took a sample of blood from Snowball and one of the hairs found on the jacket contained a root with enough DNA to perform an analysis. The primary geneticist in the case, Marilyn Menotti-Raymond, developed a method that looked for short tandem repeats (STR) in the cat's DNA. Both the DNA from the hair root and the DNA from Snowball's blood sample matched.

Investigators were concerned that because it is an island, Prince Edward Island is relatively geographically isolated. Therefore many of the cats on the island might be close relatives. If this were the case, the match between Snowball's blood sample and the hairs found on the jacket would be insignificant. To test whether this was a problem, RCMP collected cats from all parts of the island, including the area around the crime scene. They took blood samples from these cats and performed the **STR analysis** that Menotti-Raymond developed. The cats on the island showed a high degree of genetic variation, indicating that the STR match between Snowball and the hairs found on the jacket was significant.

Based on the genetic evidence linking Beamish to the jacket, he was convicted of second-degree murder and sentenced to prison for 15 years. The case set a legal precedent allowing DNA fingerprinting of animals to be admitted as evidence in **criminal trials**.

SEE ALSO DNA banks for endangered animals; DNA fingerprint; Hair analysis; PCR (polymerase chain reaction); Wildlife forensics.

Sobriety testing

Sobriety is defined as a physiological and mental state in which a person is unaffected by the presence of a chemical substance. The quintessential example of sobriety is the popular image of a return to an individual's normal behavior after the effects of excessive alcohol consumption have dissipated.

The possibility of alcohol or other intoxicants in a crime, accident, or death is uppermost on the mind of a forensic investigator. In 2002, for example, almost 17,500 motorists were killed in alcohol-related traffic accidents in the United States, according to statistics from the U.S. National Highway Traffic Safety Administration. While the involvement of alcohol in traffic fatalities has been declining in the United States since the 1980s, this fatality toll still represented 41% of all U.S. traffic fatalities.

Alcohol-fueled domestic disturbances can also result in injury and death. Crime Report statistics complied in the late 1980s by the State of New Jersey, and reports examining telephone calls to domestic hotlines indicate that at least 40–50% of domestic disturbances were correlated with abusive behavior linked to the use of alcohol. Sobriety testing is not just a factor in alcohol use. While the term sobriety is commonly linked with the consumption of alcohol, the misuse or overuse of prescription drugs and the use of **illicit drugs** also affect sobriety.

Thus, when responding to a report of a traffic accident (or even stopping a motorist for a suspected traffic infraction) or other incident, police officers can be confronted with need to establish the sobriety of an individual.

Aside from safety issues (operation of a motor vehicle while impaired), sobriety testing is another piece of forensic **evidence** in the investigation of a crime, accident, or death. Sobriety testing involves the recognition of key indicators of impairment, assessment of physical coordination, and the level of ethanol or drugs in the bloodstream.

This assessment begins as soon as the police officer or forensic investigator encounters the person. For example, police officers are trained to inhale when the driver of a vehicle rolls down the window. Use of alcohol, marijuana, and phencyclidine (PCP, also known popularly as angel dust) can be evident on a person's breath. This is also an opportunity for a brief visual inspection of the inside of the vehicle. Open or discarded bottles or cans of alcohol, aside from being illegal in many jurisdictions, can indicate over-consumption, and are grounds for conducting more rigorous sobriety testing.

Another immediate aspect of sobriety testing is the observance of physical appearance and behavior. A red-appearing face, especially the cheeks, can be caused by the overuse of alcohol, which can increase the flow of blood through the capillaries.

Behavioral changes depend on the nature of the intoxicant. Alcohol is a depressant, as are **barbiturates**, sleeping pills, and benzodiazepines. Impairment can be evident as slurred or thick speech, sluggish reactions, features of exhaustion such as yawning and drooping of the eyes, and disorientation with surroundings and events.

Some of the behaviors, such as speech difficulties and disorientation, can also be present when impairment is due to narcotics and inhalants (e.g., vapors produced by solvents like nail polish remover and gasoline or adhesives like airplane glue). Drugs like cocaine stimulate the activity of the central nervous system. The result can be euphoric behavior. This also occurs when narcotics and PCP are taken.

A key early sobriety test is examination of the pupils of the eyes. A police officer will typically make direct eye contact with a driver, even asking the driver to remove sunglasses if necessary. Bloodshot eyes and droopy eyelids can be indicative of alcohol overuse. The use of stimulants, hallucinogens, and inhalants can cause the pupils to be become larger than is normal for the light conditions (dilation). In contrast, narcotics such as codeine, heroin, and opium cause the pupils to become smaller (constriction). A blank or dazed stare can result from the use of PCP, hallucinogens, and inhalants.

If the early assessment of sobriety warrants further action, a police officer or forensic investigator can conduct more rigorous tests.

One standard sobriety test is the indirect measurement of the level of alcohol in the blood by measurement of the alcohol in the expired breath. A portable **Breathalyzer**® displays the level of alcohol as a number that indicates the grams of alcohol per 100 milliliters of blood. In many jurisdictions, this legal limit is 0.08. If the breathalyzer reading exceeds this value, it is evidence that the person may be impaired.

Other sobriety tests typically adhere to a standard field sobriety testing program. Use of established guidelines lessens the chances that the results of the tests will be questioned in court, even in the absence of a Breathalyzer® test, and allows the test results to be the basis of an arrest for driving while intoxicated (DWI) or driving under the influence (DUI).

Standardized Field Sobriety Tests (SFST) were developed in the 1970s by the U.S. National Highway Traffic Safety Administration. The validity of the testing methods and legality of the results was verified by repeated testing under controlled conditions. Without the power of this standardizing procedure, sobriety tests can be merely anecdotal and so less apt to stand legal scrutiny.

SFST involve scoring of the results of a number of requested actions. A determination of intoxication is made if a person fails to successfully perform a sufficient number of these actions: the walk-and-turn, one-leg-stand, and horizontal-gaze nystagmus (eye-movement) tests, which are detailed below. Failing a single test is not grounds for determining that a person is not sober.

The walking and leg-stand tests are assessments of balance, while the eye movement test assesses motor control of the eye muscles. All are tests of coordinated action of muscles and nerve activity. However, the legal admissibility of the first two tests can be challenged more successfully than the eye test. This is because the assessment of walking and standing abilities are more subjective. The eye muscle control that is the basis of the horizontal gaze test is involuntary, and so is able to be assessed more definitively.

Nystagmus is defined as an involuntary rapid and repetitive movement of the eyes. It can occur as a result of brain damage, **epilepsy**, or other pathological disorders. However, for the majority of people, the condition is indicative of impaired motor function. Normally, when concentration and the nervous system are unimpaired, movement is followed by a smooth and controlled change in gaze. However, a sign of impairment can be the loss of this coordinated activity.

Typically, a subject is asked to look straight ahead and, while keeping the head still, to focus on a horizontally moving object (a finger, pen, or pencil, for example). The object must be 12–15 inches from the subject's eyes, at a distance that the subject indicates is comfortable to focus.

People with an eye impairment or an artificial eye are excluded from the test. Evaluating a single eye and then doubling the score with the assumption that the other eye will behave in the same manner is improper technique. Some people do exhibit a difference in the reaction times of their eyes (a condition called lazy eye). In this case, each eye should be tested separately while the other eye is covered.

Police officer giving a sobriety test to a young man suspected of drunk driving; the suspect is walking a line painted on the street.
© HUTCHINGS STOCK PHOTOGRAPHY/CORBIS

A normal eye reaction in this test includes the smooth movement of the pupil from side to side while maintaining focus on the moving object. As well, the pupil should remain still when the object is brought to rest at the end of a leftward or rightward horizontal path. The object can also be moved up or down, to assess if the pupil tracks smoothly.

The side-to-side and up-and-down motions of the object are done a total of at least six times. A score of one is assessed if eye motion in an individual trial is jerky. A score of four or more is indicative of intoxication.

In the walk-and-turn assessment, a reasonably straight line is drawn on a flat surface. The subject is then instructed to place their left foot on the line and then to walk heel-to-toe along the length of the line, by placing the heel of one foot in contact with the toe of the planted foot. In this way the feet remain close together, and balance becomes critical in maintaining progression along the line. When reaching the end of the line, the subject must turn around while keeping one foot planted and repeat the walk in the other direction.

Indications of intoxication include loss of balance (swaying or falling), holding the arms out from the body to maintain balance, stopping and starting rather than walking with a smooth cadence, stepping off of the line, failure to listen to instructions, and starting to walk before being instructed to do so. These aspects of performance are evaluated, scored, and used to assess if coordination is impaired.

For people aged less than 65, who are not judged to be obese, and who do not have a neurological or other disorder that affects balance, another assessment of balance involves standing motionless on one leg. The raised leg must be positioned in front of the body at least six inches off the ground for a time that is determined by the assessor. Swaying, falling, hopping, use of arms for balance, and putting the elevated leg down prematurely are all indications of impairment.

SEE ALSO Automobile accidents; Breathalyzer®; First responders.

Sociopathic personality

In 1941, American physician Harvey Cleckley wrote a groundbreaking book in **forensic science** entitled *The Mask of Sanity.* Before that time, psychopathy had been loosely defined as insanity without delirium (psychotic features such as delusions and hallucinations), psychopathic inferiority, and moral insanity. Cleckley was the first to study this personality syndrome from a more scientific perspective. He generated a list of sixteen traits that clustered together to create an identifiable character sketch (a set of traits, behaviors and attitudes that define a particular way of moving in the world) of the sociopathic personality. The central characteristics in this cluster were: lack of empathy or anxiety, shallowness, self-centeredness, irresponsibility, and manipulativeness. These individuals, Cleckley found, were far more likely to commit crimes, to be more violent, to recidivate (to repeat their criminal behaviors), and less likely to respond to treatment efforts than were other criminal populations. He found the psychiatric community uniformly unwilling to work with this population or to address them in any way, and speculated that this might be due to the fact that they (psychopaths) often afford no outward signs of their **pathology**. In fact, a person with a **psychopathic personality** can be quite charismatic during early interactions. It was Cleckley's contention that it is difficult to fully appreciate the deviancy of the psychopath under treatment or confinement (prison or jail) circumstances; they need to be seen in their social environment, where they often operate as abusers, manipulators, scammers, or con artists.

In 1952, the term psychopath was replaced in the psychiatric literature by sociopathic personality. These terms became synonymous, as the concept of personality disorders evolved. With the advent of *DSM-II (Diagnostic and Statistical Manual of Mental Disorders, Second Edition),* the uniformly accepted manual of psychodiagnosis) in 1968, the term personality disorder, antisocial type replaced sociopathic personality. In contemporary forensic psychiatric, psychological, and sociological literature, the terms psychopath, sociopath, criminal personality and ASPD/APD (antisocial personality disorder) are used commonly to describe the affected criminal population.

Antisocial personality disorder, common among convicted felons, is chiefly characterized by flagrant disregard for the rights of others, a refusal to conform to the rules and norms of society, and an inability to experience feelings of either anxiety or guilt. Other clinical symptoms are predatory behaviors, manipulativeness and deceitfulness, inability to plan for the future or to envision the potential consequences of their behaviors, consistent irresponsibility, irritability and aggressiveness, callous disregard for the safety and well-being of others, and an inability to experience feelings of guilt or remorse after doing material, emotional, or physical harm to others.

The central characteristics of the psychopath are described in somewhat more emotional or affective terms. They are highly self-centered, impulsive, irresponsible, manipulative, and remorseless; they do not experience guilt or regret. They tend to be pathological liars and they persistently violate social norms and rules. Their crimes tend to be described as "cold-blooded," as they are committed without obvious motivation (except to satisfy their own material needs, by robbery, for example). Psychopaths commonly exert power and control over others, and they do so through the use of superficial charm, manipulation, intimidation, and violence. They tend not to outgrow their behavior, do not benefit from treatment, and do not rehabilitate during periods of incarceration.

Sociopaths are typically described as conscience-less. They are extremely shallow, selfish, self-centered, boastful, antagonistic, and unable to bond with others or to form lasting romantic relationships. They also tend to be extreme risk-takers who are unable to refuse temptation of any sort. Sociopaths view other people as vehicles for their own gain, and they fail to recognize their own negative characteristics. Sociopaths are generally adept at rationalizing their behavior and asserting (and believing) that they are victims of the ill will of others, and that they are good people put in bad circumstances. Sociopaths often report difficult childhoods: single parent homes, extreme poverty, neighborhood or family violence, lack of parental supervision, early separation from family, or rearing in foster homes, state-run group homes, or institution-like settings.

There is no effective treatment for these personality disorders: incarceration is merely palliative. That is, an individual with sociopathy, psychopathy or ASPD may either not exhibit the offending behaviors while incarcerated, or may use them adaptively in order to function well in the prison setting, but will immediately (and admittedly) return to utilizing them upon release from prison.

SEE ALSO Bundy (serial murderer) case; Contact crimes; Profiling.

Harry Söderman

8/28/1902–1956
SWEDISH
CRIMINALIST

Harry Söderman was a Swedish criminalist whose career and research is unique in the history of forensic sciences. His name is associated with the greatest contributors to forensic sciences, such as the French criminalist **Edmond Locard** (1877–1966), the French anthropologist **Alphonse Bertillon** (1853–1914), the Austrian criminalist **Hans Gross**, and the Swiss criminalist R.A. Reiss.

At age 22, Söderman began a long journey to the Orient. He persuaded a Swedish bicycle manufacturer to lend him a bicycle to ride to Constantinople (now Istanbul in Turkey). In addition, he obtained extra support from the Swedish police magazine as a correspondent, and while he was visiting different countries, Söderman reported on their police systems and criminal activities. His travel did not stop in Turkey, and he spent many months in Asia, venturing into the interior of China. Söderman returned to Stockholm two years later, in 1924.

The encounter that probably changed his life and made his dreams possible occurred at a small mountain resort in northern Sweden not long after his return from Asia. Because of a bad blizzard that interrupted his hike, Söderman was required to stay for three days and three nights in a hut with three men that he had never met. During their long talks, one of the men revealed that he was an acquaintance

of Edmond Locard, in Lyon, France. Söderman immediately said that he considered Locard the greatest living police scientist and expressed his desire to study under him. Some time later, young Söderman received a letter from Lyon stating that he was accepted as an intern in Locard's laboratory.

In 1926, Söderman left Sweden for Lyon, where he spent the next six years. He was able to absorb a great amount of knowledge and experience from Locard, while also obtaining his doctoral degree from the University of Lyon. His dissertation research was on the scientific study of the individual characteristics present on fired bullets that originate from the barrel of the firearm, as well as those left on cartridges from the firing pin. He was the first researcher to tackle the problem of firearms **identification** from a scientific perspective. Söderman invented the Hastoscope, which is an improved **comparison microscope**. The Hastoscope holds two bullets that can turn on their axles in order to accelerate the identification process by comparison of their striations. The origin of the word Hastoscope is a mystery, but the theory that it is a contraction of Ha(rry) S(öderman) + toscope has been offered. This theory also states that the word contains the word haste, as this microscope accelerated the observation process.

In 1932, Söderman returned to his native Stockholm and started a private forensic laboratory. His work was successful and he obtained a position at the University of Stockholm, where he taught scientific police techniques. In 1933, he left for two years to study American police systems in the United States under a fellowship, spending one full year in New York City. After being back in Sweden for about two years, he left again in 1937 for Dublin, Ireland. He spent one year reorganizing the Irish police force at the request of the Irish government. In 1939, he was asked by the Swedish government to become the head of the National Forensic Science Institute, the equivalent to the **FBI** laboratory in United States. Söderman was at the pinnacle of his career and he remained in this position until his retirement. He continued to be extremely active in international relations, and a few years later, he was one of the founders of **Interpol**.

During World War II (1939–1941), Söderman was asked by the Norwegian minister to train Norwegian police officers in anticipation of the end of the war. Söderman created **training** camps in Sweden, and as a result about 17,000 men were trained between 1943 and 1945. In 1953, Söderman resigned from his position as head of the National Forensic Science Institute to devote himself completely to international activities. The same year, he moved to the

United States, where he worked as a consultant for police organizations from around the world. He died at the age of 54.

Söderman wrote hundreds of articles and books. He was fluent in several languages, including Swedish, English, French, and German. As a columnist for many journals, he was widely read and known in the forensic science community. His most famous books are *Modern Criminal Investigation,* which he co-authored with American Police Deputy Chief John J. O'Connell and *Policeman's Lot.* It is estimated that more than 100,000 copies of *Modern Criminal Investigation* have been sold.

SEE ALSO Firearms; Criminalistics; Microscope, comparison.

Soils

Soil on a suspect's shoe or splattered inside a car fender can provide forensic scientists with information about the travels of suspects and crime victims.

Soil is the product of biological, chemical, and physical alteration of materials at Earth's surface. Soils form in horizons, or layers, that are approximately parallel to the surface, have distinct properties, and are denoted by uppercase letters. The uppermost O horizon consists of decaying organic matter. It is underlain by the A horizon, or topsoil, which consists of a mixture of mineral and organic material. Beneath the A horizon is the B horizon, which consists of slightly altered mineral material, and the C horizon, which consists of the unaltered but loose parent material from which the soil developed (for example, sand). If intact rock is present, it can comprise an R horizon. Desert soils rich in calcium carbonate can also contain Bk or K horizons (the K is used to avoid confusion with the C horizon) that range from light accumulations of calcium carbonate to so-called petrocalcic horizons that are limestone formed in place. The term soil is also used loosely to refer to virtually any unlithified material at Earth's surface regardless of whether it has undergone the soil forming process known as pedogensis. Examples of materials that do not fall under the strict definition of soil include sand in dunes or along beaches and mud deposited by a recent flood. Because soils form by a complicated process that is influenced by factors such as temperature, precipitation, the mineralogical and chemical composition of the parent material, and even the nature of particles that may be washed out of the air during rainstorms, soil

from different locations can have different physical and chemical characteristics that are useful to forensic scientists.

Soil recovered from shoes, clothes, and automobiles can be analyzed in order to determine if a suspect was or was not in a particular location. This is done by carefully comparing the color, particle size and shape, mineralogical composition, and biological components of a soil sample obtained from a suspect to those of soil from a known location. Particle sizes and shapes can be compared using reflected light **microscopes**. The chemical and mineralogical composition of the soil can be compared using techniques such as x-ray diffraction, in which a pulverized soil sample is subjected to x rays that produce patterns indicative of the crystal structure of **minerals** in the soil. Soils that are, or once were, adjacent to water may also contain distinctive shell fragments. The presence of soil unique to a particular area can show that a suspect must have traveled to that area, just as the absence of soil can be used to disprove an alibi. In some situations, layers of soil or mud can be used to establish presence at a sequence of locations.

The fictional British detective Sherlock Holmes is generally credited with the first use of soils as forensic **evidence** in the late nineteenth century, and soils have been employed as real life forensic evidence since the early years of the twentieth century. Holmes possessed the ability to distinguish different soil types and, using that information, make inferences about the travels of suspects. Real-life German chemist **Georg Popp** used goose droppings, sandstone fragments, and three different kinds of dust on a suspect's shoes to link to the same materials found at a murder victim's home, the place where the body was found, and the place where the murder weapon was found. Just as importantly, Popp used the absence of distinctive quartz crystals to disprove the suspected murderer's alibi he was walking in a specific field near his home when the crime occurred.

In more recent times, soil analysis was used in an attempt to track down the killers of Italian prime minister Aldo Moro in 1978. Investigators matched sand found on Moro's body to that found on an 6.8 mile (11-km) long beach north of Rome, which helped to focus their investigation. Another high profile case involved United States drug enforcement agent Enrique Camerena Salazar and his pilot Alfredo Zavala Avelar, who were killed by Mexican federal police in 1985. Their bodies were reported to have been found at the scene of a shootout between police and known drug dealers, implicating the drug dealers as murderers. Close examination of soil samples taken from the bodies, which contained an unusual combination of mineral and volcanic **glass** particles, revealed that the bodies had originally been buried in a remote mountainous area far from the shootout. This, combined with other forensic evidence, eventually showed that the federal police had been involved in the kidnapping, torture, and murder of the two.

Soil analysis is not restricted to cases involving politics and international intrigue. Soil found with a body inside a plastic garbage bag in New Jersey was identified as material that had been dredged from Newark Bay and used as fill to create new land along the shore. This clue led investigators to the victim's wife and daughter, who had killed him and temporarily buried the body beneath their home, which was built on the fill. California authorities were confounded when soil found in a murder suspect's car partially, but not completely, matched the soil around an oil well where the victim's body had been dumped. Further research showed that gravel from a different location had been spread around the well, explaining why the soil from the car was not an exact match with the natural soil in the area.

Small fragments of chert, a sedimentary rock made of silica, in cow manure collected from the back of a truck were used to prove that a herd of cattle had been rustled in Missouri and taken to Montana. Although the cattle rustlers had altered the brands on the cattle in an attempt to cover their tracks, they did not realize that the manure contained evidence that could have come only from Missouri. Another example of agricultural soil forensics is the comparison of soil samples to determine whether valuable plants were removed from protected government land and sold for landscaping.

SEE ALSO Geology; GIS; Minerals.

Souvenirs from athletic events

With the advent of computer technology, counterfeiting of clothing and other goods has proliferated in the world's markets. Basic computer software and hardware can be used to copy, alter, and reproduce almost any item, and sports logos are particularly easy to duplicate. Computers also make it easier to produce and distribute illegally reproduced items. In 2000, the counterfeit market in the United States was estimated to be approximately $1 billion. The **FBI** estimates that between 50–90% of all celebrity and sports collectibles sold in the United States are fakes.

Although many companies producing and selling sports souvenirs have used sophisticated methods, such as holograms and refractive logos, to try to discourage counterfeiting and forgery, pirates have continually been able to circumvent the preventative measures. Beginning around 1996, some companies adopted authentication methods that rely on **DNA** as well as optical taggants (a substance or material added to a product to indicate its source of manufacture).

In 1997 the FBI initiated an undercover operation targeting counterfeiters of sports and celebrity memorabilia. Nicknamed Project Bullpen, the operation culminated in 2000 with the seizure of more than $10 million in illegal goods and the arrests of 25 people. The charges included conspiracy to defraud the United States and tax evasion. Penalties included up to five years of imprisonment and fines up to $250,000 per offense.

Typical memorabilia seized by Project Bullpen operatives included jerseys, shoes, bats and balls, helmets, hockey sticks and pucks, photographs, posters, and trading cards, all of which bear the signature of an athlete or celebrity. The most commonly forged autographs on seized memorabilia included Babe Ruth, Lou Gehrig, Ty Cobb, Sammy Sosa, Mark McGwire, and Tony Gwynn.

The report filed as a result of Project Bullpen claimed that, although there is an extremely large public market for sports memorabilia, almost all of the counterfeit autographs, especially those of deceased athletes, trace back to a small group of forgers. These counterfeiters are able to maintain a low profile by selling much of their merchandise over the internet.

A key player in the marketing chain for forgeries is the authenticator. Sometimes memorabilia are sold with mass produced certificates of authentication, but often people claiming to be experts in verifying autographs assign authenticity to the item. The certificate of authenticity allows sellers to claim that their items are authentic and gives them an excuse if the items are found out to be fraudulent.

In order to evade forgers, some athletes have signed agreements that give certain distributors exclusive rights to their signed memorabilia. For example, all souvenirs autographed by Michael Jordan are sold through the company Upper Deck. Mark McGwire has refused to sign his signature for money since 1990.

Some athletes and professional sports leagues are adopting more technical means to prevent forgeries. DNA markers and optical taggants have proven to be excellent tags for sports memorabilia and they have also been used to authenticate artwork, ID cards, and certificates. Because of their complexity, DNA tags and optical taggants can be used for tracking products during manufacture and shipping. They have also been used to authenticate valuable wines and pieces of artwork.

The DNA molecule is composed of a sequence of four different nucleotides: adenine (A), guanine (G), cytosine (C) and thymine (T). Because DNA is a double stranded molecule, the nucleotides are connected in pairs on opposite strands. Adenine always pairs with thymine and guanine always pairs with cytosine. Because the nucleotides are found in pairs, they are referred to as base pairs. Using biochemical techniques, scientists can engineer short strands of DNA, called oligomers, with any sequence of base pairs. This inherent variability of the sequence can be used as a code to verify the authenticity of objects. For example, there are 10.5 million possibilities for engineering an oligomer that is ten base pairs long. An oligomer that is twenty base pairs long has 1.1 trillion possible variations. If several different oligomers are combined, the possibility of reproducing the DNA code is extremely remote. In addition, masking DNA can be combined with the authenticating DNA to make reverse engineering of the oligomers nearly impossible. Finally, it is sufficiently easy to frequently change the base pair sequence used for authentication.

Once the specific oligomer or several oligomers have been synthesized, they are coated with a protein. This is similar to putting a hard shell around the DNA, protecting it from interacting with other chemicals such as alcohols and dyes. The coated DNA is incorporated into a special matrix, which is then added to ink. The DNA-laced ink can be applied to practically any surface. The ink into which the matrix is added can either be invisible or colored, depending on the intended use.

After DNA has been incorporated into ink and applied to an item, authentication can be performed in a laboratory. A small piece of the item that has ink markings is removed. This piece is digested and the DNA is chemically extracted. **PCR (polymerase chain reaction)** produces many copies of the DNA from the ink. This amplified DNA can then be sequenced to verify that it is the code associated with the item. The ink marks are expected to be permanent and therefore can be used for authentication into the future.

Some chemicals are optically active, which means that they react in the presence of light. These chemicals absorb a photon of light traveling at a particular wavelength and then reemit it at a different wavelength. This process is called excitation and emission. Usually there is a range of wavelengths, or a spectrum of light, that excites a chemical. Similarly, there is a range of wavelengths of light that will be emitted by the chemical. Combining different chemicals with different excitation and emission spectra can result in a mixture with a fairly complex emission spectrum. This emission spectrum is sometimes referred to as a spectral signature.

Companies seeking to authenticate their products have developed a variety of optically active chemicals. Scientists have developed methods to assemble these chemicals in a variety of different combinations so that they emit a unique spectral signature in the presence of the proper excitation wavelengths. These chemicals are referred to as optical taggants and they can be added to a matrix along with engineered oligomers of DNA. Just like the protein-coated DNA, optical taggants are stable molecules that can withstand exposure to alcohols, dyes, plastics, and threads.

Hand-held optical devices have been developed that can be programmed to emit the exact wavelengths of light necessary to excite the optical taggants. They can also be programmed to detect the emission spectra of the chemicals and emit beeps or lights when the correct spectrum is detected. These devices are battery powered and relatively inexpensive. They allow authenticators to scan objects for the presence of the correct spectral signature in the field and to apprehend counterfeiters when the optical taggants are not present.

Counterfeiting of souvenirs and apparel at Olympic games is an enormous market. At the 1996 Olympics in Atlanta, Georgia, it is estimated that as much as 40% of all merchandise sold was unlicensed. Following that enormous loss of revenue, the Australian Government passed the Sydney 2000 Games Indicia and Images Protection Act, which protects the Olympic word and the symbols associated with it from being copied illegally. In order to help uphold the Act, Sydney Organizing Committee for the Olympic Games (SOCOG) contracted with DNA Technologies, a subsidiary of CrossOff Incorporated in Halifax, Nova Scotia, to develop DNA and optical tags for the 2000 Sydney Olympics.

SOCOG decided to incorporate the DNA of an Australian Olympic athlete into the DNA tag as a means to increase public awareness of the counterfeiting detection strategy. DNA was extracted from cells swabbed from the inner cheek of the athlete. A portion of this DNA was then amplified using **PCR** and mixed with other sequences of DNA to mask the original sequence. Both the engineered DNA and a unique optical taggant were used to label nearly everything sold at the Olympics including pins, clothing and hats. More than 34 million labels and tags were produced by DNA Technologies and distributed to 40 official Olympic licensees.

Olympic counterfeit investigators were provided with optical scanners that emit a light in the presence of the optical taggant. They performed more than 3,400 inspections during the course of the Olympics. The inspections uncovered 507 trademark violations and more than three quarters of the violations occurred within the first three months of the inspections. Early seizures of unlicensed items included soccer balls and watches. The Olympic committee estimated that less than 0.5% of the revenue generated by merchandise sales at the Sydney Olympics was lost to counterfeiting.

Beginning in 2000, the National Football League contracted with DNA Technologies to tag football souvenirs. About 100 footballs used at the Super Bowl games were tagged each year. The NFL also used the DNA labeling technology to identify jerseys worn during the Super Bowl and Pro-Bowl games. In 2003, the National Hockey League began a program in which they sold hockey pucks that were used in games. DNA Technologies labeled all these pucks with the DNA and optical taggant-laced ink. The label associates the pucks with the specific game in which they were used and also shows whether or not the puck was used to score a goal.

A variety Major League Baseball souvenirs have been labeled with DNA and optical taggant markers. These include baseballs and bases from the 1999 World Series and the uniforms, baseballs, and bases used by the Detroit Tigers in the final game at Tiger Stadium. A number of historical baseballs have also been labeled with DNA tags. These include the baseballs hit by Mark McGwire for his 70th home run in 1998, Sammy Sosa for his 66th home run in 1998, Mickey Mantle for the 500th home run of his career and Hank Aaron for the 715th home run of his career. DNA Technologies authenticated the bat used by Babe Ruth to hit his first home run at Yankee Stadium in 1923 and a DNA and optical taggant label was applied to that bat. It later sold for almost $1.3 million at a Sotheby's auction. Shoeless Joe Jackson's "Black Betsy" bat was authenticated and labeled with DNA and an optical taggant. In 2001, it sold for $577,000 at auction.

Beginning in 1998, DNA Technologies teamed with Professional Sports Authenticator, a Newport Beach, California company. Called PSA/DNA, the collaboration has developed a method for professional athletes to guarantee the authenticity of their autographs by incorporating DNA and an optical taggant into the ink they use to sign their names. The DNA and optical taggant label is expected to remain detectible in the ink indefinitely. The company guarantees that the chance of duplication of the DNA sequence used in the ink is one in 33 trillion.

SEE ALSO DNA sequences, unique; Handwriting analysis.

Walter Specht
GERMAN
FORENSIC SCIENTIST

In 1937, at the University Institute for Legal Medicine and Scientific Criminalistics in Jena, Germany, Walter Specht introduced the use of **luminol** as a presumptive test for **blood** at crime scenes. This is forensically important, because perpetrators often wash away visible signs of blood at the scene, in an effort to remove all possible **evidence** of the crime.

A presumptive test for blood is used when forensic investigators have strong reason to suspect that blood is present but is not currently visible at the scene. A presumptive test will neither prove nor disprove, in and of itself, the presence of blood at a crime scene—it will merely indicate a likelihood, which should then be further investigated.

Forensic scientists use a spray containing luminol and hydrogen peroxide to detect trace blood at crime scenes. **Hemoglobin** in blood catalyzes the breakdown of hydrogen peroxide into oxygen, which can oxidize the luminol. It works well with both fresh and dry blood, and can be applied several years after the incident. The luminol solution is fine sprayed over the suspected area of a room or object in the room. When sprayed on an area containing blood, luminol produces a chemiluminescent reaction (a glow) instead of color. It is best viewed in total darkness, due to its relatively weak luminescence. The order of use for luminol at a crime scene is: (1) Spray walls first, to illuminate spatter patterns; (2) Spray ceiling next, to highlight cast off patterns; (3) Spray floors, in order to detect **shoeprints**, drag marks, etc., last. Luminol should only be applied once; additional application will only serve to dilute any blood present.

Luminol is considered highly sensitive: it can detect the presence of blood in a ratio of one part per million (1:1,000,000). In contrast to its high sensitivity, it has a relatively low rate of specificity: in addition to reacting to the presence of blood, it can also react to chemical oxidants such as chlorine bleach, certain types of chemical cleaners, and detergents. Crime scene investigators always follow up a positive presumptive indicator with more specific quantifying tests at the luminol-identified sites.

Among the many benefits of presumptive testing with luminol are its heme-specific sensitivity; its relative stability and lack of toxicity (important due to repeated exposures over time at multiple crime scenes); and its reliable yet inexpensive preparation. Of particular forensic significance is the fact that luminol rarely destroys other evidence (if properly prepared and used) and will not interfere with the future **DNA** testing of recovered crime scene blood. In addition, presumptive testing with luminol meets the Frye standard for general scientific and legal acceptance.

Because it works well with both fresh and dry blood, and can be applied several years after the incident, luminol is as useful in cold cases as it is in current **crime scene investigation**. Though originally designed for use in the German copper mining industry as a means of uncovering new sources of ore, Walter Specht's use of luminol in crime scene investigation settings made an enduring contribution to the field of **forensic science**.

SEE ALSO Blood spatter; Cast-off blood; Cast-off trails; Cold case; Crime scene cleaning.

Spectrograph

Forensic analysis of a wide and diversified range of samples seized at crime scenes, accidents, **fire debris**, explosions, and autopsies requires the use of several analytical methods and tools, such as gas chromatography/mass spectrometry (GC/MS), atomic absorption **spectroscopy** (AAS), inductively coupled plasma spectroscopy (ICP), infra-red spectroscopy (IRS), nuclear magnetic resonance (NMR) spectroscopy, and high performance liquid **chromatography** (HPLC). Spectrography and spectroscopy are basically synonyms, referring to "a picture of a spectrum." The terms spectroscopy and spectroscope are more commonly used because they are older and easier to pronounce than the denominations

spectrography and spectrograph. Spectrography is also known as spectral imaging techniques.

Spectrographs or spectroscopes are optical instruments that measure wavelengths and energy levels, radiated from atomic bonds between elements in molecules, or from other light sources such as stars. Spectrographs and spectroscopes disperse light into wave patterns known as a spectral image. The first spectroscope was developed at the beginning of the nineteenth century and consisted of three metallic tubes containing lenses disposed with converging axes and a flint glass prism, which dispersed light originated from a light source or the radiant energy emitted by chemical compounds into a wave spectrum. The spectral image allowed the quantitative analysis of chemical elements, index of refraction, wavelengths, and mass as well as the composition of chemical molecules. Its first application was in astronomy (telescopes) and chemistry (analytical spectroscopy) to determine the composition of chemical elements present in nebulas, stars, and in unknown chemical compounds.

With the advent of photography, spectroscopes were renamed spectrographs because a camera was coupled to the device instead of a telescope, allowing the development of the resulting spectral image into a photographic picture. During the twentieth century, with the advances in physics and electronic technology, the photographic camera was substituted by a photomultiplier that permitted instantaneous spectrographic analyses. A variety of spectral imaging technologies are presently available that are supported by computer software. Examples of forensic applications for these technologies include: isolating trace residues on surfaces; identifying **fibers** and micro particles; detection and quantification of organic and inorganic contaminants in food, water, and air; identifying semivolatile and volatile (explosive) fuel residues; and analyzing paint fragments.

Infrared (IR) spectroscopy uses infrared light to identify substances, due to chemical bonds vibrating in different frequencies, absorbing different amounts of infrared wavelengths, and emitting specific quanta of radiation (e.g., energy at known wavelengths). The device registers the absorbed wavelengths and produces a graph that is compared to those of known substances, which are recorded in a computer database. Each peak in the spectrum represents a different chemical element with unique properties. Each chemical molecule gives a unique spectrum, known as a fingerprint region. Forensic experts may use this method to identify types of drugs in a sample or paint chips from a car. Forensic analysts can gather

physical evidence to support claims of sexual assault by testing samples of **blood** or urine from the victim with infrared spectroscopy. If Rohypnol or other "date-rape" drugs are found, investigators have not only physical **evidence** of the crime, but also information about what investigators should search for in the suspect's house.

Gas chromatography/mass spectroscopy is a combined method used in forensics to identify residual fuels, such as accelerants and chemical residues, in the debris of a fire scene in order to determine whether the fire was accidental or was caused intentionally. These methods are also used to verify the purity of chemical products and the presence of contaminants in cosmetics, hygiene products, and food products. High performance liquid chromatography is another forensic method for **identification** of food and cosmetic contaminants.

Mass spectrometry is used to measure the masses of chemical isotopes (e.g., molecular mass) and to detect impurities in materials. Beams of ionized gas molecules are accelerated in the mass spectrograph, passing through a combined electric and magnetic selector that deflects them, before entering into a vacuum chamber. The amount of deflection is given by the mass/charge ratio, with each molecule being fragmented into smaller particles. In the vacuum chamber, a magnetic field interferes with the beam trajectory creating a spectrum on a photographic plate. Each peak in the spectrum represents a specific mass/charge ratio of a charged fragment and the largest mass/charge ratio indicates the molecular ion used to determine the molecular mass.

Another application of spectrometry is in the forensic analysis of **questioned documents**. Imaging spectrometers equipped with spectral scanners permit the detection of slight differences in inks and paper surfaces, as well as the presence of erased or added lines in numbers or letters. These optical instruments scan the document point by point through absorption, reflection, and **fluorescence** of materials, forming a spectral image where existing adulterations become evident to the naked eye. Spectral imaging is a convenient forensic method because it does not destroy evidence during analysis.

Atomic absorption spectroscopy (AAS) allows the precise quantification of inorganic elements in paints, water, air, or **soils**. AAS can, for instance, determine environmental contamination of water by mercury or other heavy metals. However, when multiple inorganic elements need to be simultaneously analyzed in a sample, inductively coupled plasma

(ICP) spectroscopy is the method utilized. The ICP method can detect multiple metals in a solid matrix, in welding fumes, or in water or paints. Another analytical method used in forensics is Raman spectroscopy, especially when the preservation of samples is important as with court exhibits. This method can identify drugs, chemicals, fibers, and paints through spectral microscopy.

Determining the postmortem interval (PMI) or the time elapsed since death is crucial for investigators of a **murder**, especially when the body was subjected to environmental influences such as water, soil, or insects. In these cases, postmortem metabolic changes can be assessed through high-resolution magnetic resonance spectroscopy (H-MRS). It also provides additional valuable information to other traditional forensic methods used to determine PMI. In one study, decomposing brain tissue was used in H-MRS to identify metabolites and gases that helped to determine the time elapsed since death. The brain metabolites showed expected decreased concentrations that correlated with the estimated PMI of known samples.

In spite of the great utility of analytical instruments in forensic investigations, it is important to keep in mind that nothing substitutes human scientific and technical competence along with the exchange of information when interpreting data, especially when lives are at stake in a criminal court. One example of this was given by a scientist in a 2004 report alerting that bullet matching based on chemical analysis has sometimes been biased by errors in analysts' interpretation of data. In the report, "Forensic Analysis: Weighting Bullet Lead Evidence," the limitations of lead content analysis as a tool for matching evidence and evidence validation were described. Chemical analysis through ICP spectroscopy detects minute amounts of trace elements in bullet fragments such as arsenic, antimony, copper, silver, cadmium, tin, and bismuth, which are present in less than 1% of bullet lead alloys. Although the resulting bullet characteristics are accurate, the way data is interpreted may be misleading. It was long assumed that if two bullets are chemically identical, they originated from the same smelting source or were manufactured at the same day at the same factory. **FBI** examiners even assumed in courts that they came from the same bullet box. The report featured evidence from forensic chemists that even in a single lead smelting pot, sometimes the composition varied from one batch of bullets to the next batch, whereas the composition of different pots matched, implying that bullets made from different pots, by different manufacturers, sometimes matched.

Another forensic analytical chemist at the Committee of the National Academies discovered that bullets made of lead from different sources can get mixed into the supply and manufacturing processes, which can lead to the same ammunition box containing bullets with different elemental compositions. The National Academies Committee concluded in their report that it is impossible to determine with absolute certainty that a bullet from a crime scene came from a specific box of bullets, or that two bullets were manufactured on the same day by the same manufacturer. In the face of these and other gathered data generated from spectrography and shown in the report, the committee has asked the FBI to revise its rules on the interpretation of results from bullet chemical analysis.

SEE ALSO Accelerant; Analytical instrumentation; Ballistic fingerprints; Ballistics; Chemical and biological detection technologies; Chromatography; Circumstantial evidence; Document forgery; Electromagnetic spectrum; Energy dispersive spectroscopy; Fire debris; Gas chromatograph-mass spectrometer; Ink analysis; Isotopic analysis; Micro-spectrophotometry; Paint analysis; Spectroscopy; Trace evidence.

Spectroscopy

Forensic analysis utilizes a variety of physical, chemical, and molecular techniques to detect and, in many cases, determine the quantity and composition of a specific compound. Some of these techniques are extremely sensitive and accurate. One such example is spectroscopy.

Spectroscopy is the measurement of the absorption, scattering, or emission of electromagnetic radiation by atoms or molecules. Absorption is the transfer of electromagnetic energy from a source to an atom or molecule. Scattering is the redirection of light as a result of its interaction with matter. Emission is the transition of electromagnetic energy from a one energy level to another energy level that results in the emission of a photon.

When atoms or molecules absorb electromagnetic energy, the incoming energy transfers the quantized atomic or molecular system to a higher energy level. Electrons are promoted to higher orbitals by ultraviolet or visible light; vibrations are excited by infrared light (thermal energy). Atomic emission spectroscopy (AES) is designed to measure the amount of light emitted by excited atoms. Atomic

absorption spectroscopy (AAS) is more sensitive, because it measures the amount of light absorbed by ground state atoms. Atomic absorption tests are more sensitive because there are more ground state electrons than excited electrons in a sample. UV-VIS absorption spectroscopy is used to obtain qualitative information from the electronic absorption spectrum, or to measure the concentration of an analyte molecule in solution. Molecular **fluorescence** spectroscopy is a technique for obtaining qualitative information from the electronic fluorescence spectrum, or for measuring the concentration of a chemical compound undergoing analysis, also known as an analyte, in solution.

Infrared spectroscopy has been widely used in the study of surfaces. The most frequently used portion of the infrared spectrum is the region where molecular vibrational frequencies occur. This technique was first applied around the turn of the twentieth century in an attempt to distinguish water of crystallization from water of constitution in solids.

Ultraviolet spectroscopy takes advantage of the selective absorbance of ultraviolet radiation by various substances. The technique is especially useful in investigating biologically active substances such as compounds in body **fluids**, and drugs and narcotics either in the living body (*in vivo*) or outside it (*in vitro*). Ultraviolet instruments have also been used to monitor air and water pollution, to analyze dyes, to study carcinogens, to identify food additives, to analyze petroleum fractions, and to analyze pesticide residues. All of these can be forensically relevant. Ultraviolet photoelectron spectroscopy, a technique that is analogous to x-ray photoelectron spectroscopy, has been used to study valence electrons in gases.

Microwave spectroscopy, or molecular rotational resonance spectroscopy, addresses the microwave region of the **electromagnetic spectrum** and the absorption of energy by molecules as they undergo transitions between energy levels. From these spectra, it is possible to obtain information about molecular structure.

In nuclear magnetic resonance (NMR), resonant energy is transferred between a radio-frequency alternating magnetic field and a nucleus placed in a field sufficiently strong to separate the nuclear spin from the influence of atomic electrons. Transitions induced between substrates correspond to different quantized orientations of the nuclear spin relative to the direction of the magnetic field. Nuclear magnetic resonance spectroscopy has two subfields: broadline NMR and high resolution NMR. High resolution NMR has been used in inorganic and organic chemistry to measure subtle electronic effects, to determine structure, to study chemical reactions, and to follow the motion of molecules or groups of atoms within molecules.

Electron paramagnetic resonance is a spectroscopic technique similar to nuclear magnetic resonance except that microwave radiation is employed instead of radio frequencies. Electron paramagnetic resonance has been used extensively to study paramagnetic species present on various solid surfaces. These species may be metal ions, surface defects, or adsorbed molecules or ions with one or more unpaired electrons. This technique also provides a basis for determining the bonding characteristics and orientation of a surface complex. Because the technique can be used with low concentrations of active sites, it has proven valuable in studies of oxidation states.

Atoms or molecules that have been excited to high energy levels can decay to lower levels by emitting radiation. For atoms excited by light energy, the emission is referred to as atomic fluorescence; for atoms excited by higher energies, the emission is called atomic or optical emission. In the case of molecules, the emission is called fluorescence if the transition occurs between states of the same spin, and phosphorescence if the transition takes place between states of different spin.

In x-ray fluorescence, the term refers to the characteristic x rays emitted as a result of absorption of x rays of higher frequency. In electron fluorescence, the emission of electromagnetic radiation occurs as a consequence of the absorption of energy from radiation (either electromagnetic or particulate), provided the emission continues only as long as the stimulus producing it is maintained.

The effects governing x-ray photoelectron spectroscopy were first explained by Albert Einstein in 1905, who showed that the energy of an electron ejected in photoemission was equal to the difference between the photon and the binding energy of the electron in the target. In the 1950s, researchers began measuring binding energies of core electrons by x-ray photoemission. The discovery that these binding energies could vary as much as 6 eV, depending on the chemical state of the atom, led to rapid development of x-ray photoelectron spectroscopy, also known as electron spectroscopy for chemical analysis (ESCA). This technique has provided valuable information about chemical effects at surfaces. Unlike other spectroscopy techniques in which the absorption, emission, or scattering of radiation is interpreted as a function of energy, photoelectron spectroscopy measures the kinetic energy of the electrons(s) ejected by x-ray radiation.

Mössbauer spectroscopy was invented in the late 1950s by Rudolf Mössbauer, who discovered that when solids emit and absorb gamma rays, the nuclear energy levels can be separated to one part in 10^{14}, which is sufficient to reflect the weak interaction of the nucleus with surrounding electrons. The Mössbauer effect probes the binding, charge distribution and symmetry, and magnetic ordering around an atom in a solid matrix. An example of the Mössbauer effect involves the ^{57}Fe nuclei (the absorber) in a sample to be studied. From the ground state, the ^{57}Fe nuclei can be promoted to their first excited state by absorbing a 14.4-keV gamma-ray photon produced by a radioactive parent, in this case ^{57}Co. The excited ^{57}Fe nucleus then decays to the ground state via electron or gamma ray emission. Classically, one would expect the ^{57}Fe nuclei to undergo recoil when emitting or absorbing a gamma-ray photon (somewhat like what a person leaping from a boat to a dock observes when his boat recoils into the lake); but according to quantum mechanics, there is also a reasonable possibility that there will be no recoil (as if the boat were embedded in ice when the leap occurred).

When electromagnetic radiation passes through matter, most of the radiation continues along its original path, but a tiny amount is scattered in other directions. Light that is scattered without a change in energy is called Rayleigh scattering; light that is scattered in transparent solids with a transfer of energy to the solid is called Brillouin scattering. Light scattering accompanied by vibrations in molecules or in the optical region in solids is called Raman scattering.

In vibrational spectroscopy, also known as Raman spectroscopy, the light scattered from a gas, liquid, or solid is accompanied by a shift in wavelength from that of the incident radiation. The effect was discovered by the Indian physicist C. V. Raman in 1928. The Raman effect arises from the inelastic scattering of radiation in the visible region by molecules. Raman spectroscopy is similar to infrared spectroscopy in its ability to provide detailed information about molecular structures. Before the 1940s, Raman spectroscopy was the method of choice in molecular structure determinations, but since that time infrared measurements have largely supplemented it. Infrared absorption requires that a vibration change the dipole moment of a molecule, but Raman spectroscopy is associated with the change in polarizability that accompanies a vibration. As a consequence, Raman spectroscopy provides information about molecular vibrations that is particularly well suited to the structural analysis of covalently bonded molecules, and to a lesser extent, of ionic crystals. Raman spectroscopy is also particularly useful in studying the structure of polyatomic molecules. By comparing spectra of a large number of compounds, chemists have been able to identify characteristic frequencies of molecular groups, e.g., methyl, carbonyl, and hydroxyl groups.

SEE ALSO Analytical instrumentation; Fourier transform infrared spectrophotometer (FTIR).

Spores

Illness and death can occur from pathogenic (disease-causing) microbial infections. Thus knowledge of the ways infections spread and the myriad of symptoms that can develop are a vital part of **forensic science**. This is especially important when the infection is a serious threat to health and is easily spread from person to person. One important contributor to the spread of infection by certain bacteria (including the infamous cause of **anthrax**) is the spore.

A spore is a hard casing that contains the genetic material of those bacteria and other microorganisms that are able to form the structure. This physically and chemically resilient package protects the genetic material during periods when the environmental conditions are so harsh that the growing form of the microbe would be killed.

The effect of temperature on bacterial and spore survival provides a good example of the resilience of bacterial spores. Temperatures of 176–199°F (80°–90°C) typically kill bacteria that are growing and dividing within minutes. These high temperatures cause structural components of the bacteria to dissolve, and strands of genetic material to separate from one another. A group of bacteria known as thermophilic bacteria can survive these temperatures; but, temperatures of (248°F) 120°C kill even thermophiles. In contrast, spores can survive exposure to 248°F for several hours.

Spores of bacteria that subsequently could be revived into the growing form have been recovered from materials that are over a century old. Thus, spores offer an extraordinary form of protection to bacteria. Anthrax spores that could germinate into living bacteria were recovered on Gruinard Island, an island off the coast of Scotland, that was used for biological weapons testing by the British government during World War II.

Bacillus anthracis, the bacterium that causes anthrax, is a spore former. The spores are very light and tiny. As a result, they can be readily dispersed through the air and can be easily inhaled into the lungs. The resulting lung infection, which is called inhalation anthrax, is almost always fatal without prompt medical treatment.

Another prominent example of a bacterial spore former of concern is *Clostridium botulinum*. The bacterium and the spore are widespread in nature. For example, they are a common inhabitant of the soil. This bacterium can also survive in canned foods for extended time periods, even when the food has been heated or is acidic. When the food is eaten, the dormant bacteria begin to grow again and produce a variety of potent **toxins** that disrupt the nervous system, causing serious illness.

Other microorganisms of human concern that form spores include protozoa (e.g., *Microsporidia*) and fungi (e.g., *Actinomycetes*).

The multi-step process of forming a spore is known as sporulation. The process begins when a bacterium senses that the environmental conditions are becoming life threatening. Bacteria are equipped with a whole battery of sensing proteins and other compounds that monitor environmental conditions, such as temperature, pH of the surrounding fluid, water content, and availability of food. After monitoring the environment for a period of time, the deteriorating conditions trigger the microbe to begin the change from a growing and dividing cell to a dormant spore.

The genetic material of the bacterium is duplicated. Then, the membrane coat that surrounds the inside of the bacterium pinches inward until the ends of the inward growing membrane meet. This isolates one of the copies of the genetic material from the remainder of the bacterium. This smaller cell is called a daughter cell. The remainder of the bacterium is called the mother cell.

In the next stage of spore formation, the membrane that surrounds the mother cell surrounds the daughter cell. This creates a daughter cell that is surrounded by two layers of membrane. Between these two membranes a thick layer of a rigid material forms. This layer is called peptidoglycan. Peptidoglycan is normally present in the bacterial cell wall, but not in nearly the same amount as is present in a spore. The thick peptidoglycan makes the double membrane layer very tough and hard to break apart. Finally, this tough membrane is coated on the outer

FBI and Army scientists began the process of opening an anthrax-laden letter sent to Vermont Democratic Senator Patrick Leahy in 2001, containing enough spores to kill thousands of people. © REUTERS/CORBIS

surface by proteins. The proteins are also resistant to breakage.

The remnants of the mother cell dissolve away leaving the spore. The spore is essentially in hibernation. There is very little chemical activity. Nevertheless, the spore is able to monitor the external environment and, when conditions are sensed as being more favorable, the conversion from the spore form to the growing organism begins.

SEE ALSO Anthrax; Bacterial biology; Pathogens.

Sports and drug testing SEE
Performance-enhancing drugs

Sports testing

In 1967, the International Olympic Committee (IOC) and the International Cycling Union became the first sporting organizations in the world to ban the use of performance-enhancing drugs, sometimes also known as doping, in an effort to stop drug misuse during the 1968 Olympics. To be effective, the new measures had to be underpinned by a system of testing athletes and others closely involved in sports for banned substances. Forensic toxicologists carry out sports testing for a range of drugs, from steroids and beta-blockers, to growth hormones and diuretics. It is not clear how widespread the use of drugs in sports really is, but those who do cheat, including trainers, frequently use new substances in an attempt to evade the testers. It is up to the forensic toxicologist to keep a step ahead by developing new, sensitive, and, above all, reliable methods for sports testing.

The technology for sports testing was somewhat primitive prior to the early 1980s. Stimulants, like **amphetamines**, could be detected through reliable tests, but other substances in common use, like anabolic steroids, could not. However, this changed with the introduction of gas chromatography/mass spectrometry (GC/MS) systems, which can accurately analyze most **organic compounds** of the type used in sports doping. Unfortunately, some athletes bent on cheating used GC/MS to their own ends, testing their urine to see how long it took the drugs to leave their system. This enabled athletes to know when to stop taking the drugs before a game or competition where they were likely to be tested. This led to sporting organizations extending testing into the training period, so an athlete could be tested, without warning, at any time. Unfortunately, this too created problems, as some athletes trained in distant locations and could not always be contacted easily to have a test performed.

In the early days of sports testing, organizations did not always appreciate the importance of the **chain of custody** of a sample. Security from tampering and contamination could not necessarily be guaranteed. This led to several successful appeals against "false positives" where an athlete had tested positive for a drug he or she had not in fact taken. Today, many of these logistic problems have been reduced or even eliminated. Athletes competing at high levels are aware of the necessity of testing and are prepared for it, even if they do not all accept it. The **toxicology** laboratories operate more professionally and with a higher degree of scientific accuracy and reliability.

Anabolic steroids are one of the most well known drugs used in sports, both at elite and recreational levels. Related to the male hormone testosterone, anabolic steroids cause muscle growth, increased strength, and sharper reflexes, which is why such drugs have been abused in the context of most Olympic sports as well as team sports. Steroids allow the user to train more often at higher intensity without the risk of injury. However, steroids can damage the user, causing hair loss, impotence, acne, liver damage, heart muscle damage, and aggressive behavior (sometimes known as "steroid rage"). Steroids can readily be detected by GC/MS.

In 2005 the United States Congress tackled the issue of anabolic steroid use in professional baseball when it subpoenaed a panel of former and current all-stars, including former St. Louis Cardinal Mark McGwire—who once held the record for the most home runs hit during a single season—to provide testimony about the frequency of steroid use in the game. The House Committee concluded that officials in charge of baseball have not adequately policed the issue, which resulted in enhanced testing policies, along with increased suspensions and penalties for players who test positive for performance-enhancing drugs. As of April 2005, additional hearings were pending regarding use in other sports, including the National Football League (NFL).

One controversial anabolic steroid is nandralone, which several athletes across the globe have been accused of using. However, some debate exists over testing for the steroid nandrolone. In the body, it is broken down into a substance called 19-norandrosterone (NA) and measurement of levels of this in urine samples is the basis of drug tests. The IOC considers levels of above 2 nanograms/milliliter for men and 5 nanograms/milliliter for women as **evidence** of nandrolone misuse. The number of individuals testing positive for nandrolone appears to have increased in recent years, as the sensitivity of the detection technology has increased. Some athletes claimed false positive results with the new technology. A review found no problem with the testing procedure, but also found a number of reasons why it is at least theoretically possible to test positive for nandrolone without actually taking the banned substance.

The nandrolone test cannot determine the actual source of NA in the urine. Besides coming from knowingly ingested or injected nandrolone, NA can also be produced by the body itself. Self-produced NA levels are not usually above the IOC's limits. There is also some limited evidence that physiological factors, such as vigorous exercise and the stress of injury, might push NA levels into the positive range. Findings against this include a study of 370 male competitors at the 1996 Winter Olympics in Nagano, Japan, which found that none had a concentration of NA above 0.4 nanograms per milliliter.

Some herbal and nutritional supplements also contain anabolic steroids, including nandrolone. The labels on such products may be incomplete or incorrect, or the products themselves might be contaminated. It's possible that some athletes are ingesting nandrolone unknowingly with sports supplements (especially if they take more than one supplement at a time). Current rules state that such ignorance is no defense against a drug charge. Testing methods need to be developed so they can properly distinguish the source of NA in urine, another challenge for the forensic toxicologist.

Most of the other drugs in common use are detected by GC/MS. Stimulants like amphetamines increase reaction time and decrease fatigue. They have been used in American football and cycling, but are perhaps less popular than in previous years because they are so readily detected by GC/MS. Beta-blockers are used to reduce trembling and anxiety in sports such as snooker and archery; however, they also have medical uses such as blood pressure control. Diuretics increase the flow of urine and may be abused in sports where weight control is an issue. They have also been used illicitly to help flush other drugs out of the system.

Human growth hormone seems to be increasing in popularity and has similar effects to anabolic steroids. It increases muscle strength and is thought not to have the same side effects as steroids. Growth hormone was historically in short supply, as it had to be extracted from human pituitary glands. It can now be made in a purer form by genetic engineering and it is this recombinant form that many athletes use, despite its expense. A related substance is insulin-like growth factor (IGF-1). Interest in this substance is sure to increase in the wake of **gene** therapy experiments that show how mice injected with the gene for IGF-1 have up to 30% greater muscle strength and muscle mass than ordinary mice. The animals also have better performance in resistance training.

Genetic engineering has also produced a hormone called recombinant erthyropoietin (EPO), which helps the body to produce more red blood cells and increases endurance in sports like running and cycling. The problem with testing for substances like growth hormone, IGF-1, and EPO is that they so closely resemble the natural versions of these molecules produced by the human body, and the need exists for more sophisticated tests. For instance, a separation technique called isoelectric focusing has shown the differences between natural and recombinant EPO, but more research is needed before it can be generally accepted. Such tests are also quite expensive.

Before the recombinant version became available, it was not unknown for athletes to utilize "blood doping," a process in which the athlete would transfuse himself with his own blood (drawn earlier and then stored for later use) or blood donated by another individual. This process increases the number of red blood cells, allowing the athlete's blood to carry more oxygen to the muscles and theoretically increasing performance levels on the day of the competition. This practice (particularly when the athlete's own blood is used) is difficult to detect in the laboratory. Yet recently forensic tests have been used to expose athletes when the blood is donated from someone else. In April 2005 professional cyclist and Olympic gold medal winner Tyler Hamilton was suspended from racing for two years after blood tests indicated the presence of blood doping via transfusion with donated blood. As of May 2005, Hamilton maintained his innocence and asserted his intent to appeal his suspension.

Canadian sprinter Ben Johnson ponders a question at a news conference where he announced the formation of a foundation to teach youth about the evils of drug abuse in sports. Johnson was stripped of his gold medal and 100-meter record after testing positive for steroids at the 1988 Seoul Olympics.
© REUTERS/CORBIS

Currently, most sports testing is done on urine rather than blood samples. It is easy to perform a random test on a urine sample and such samples are simple to store and process. The way in which drugs are excreted into urine is also well understood, so results from the test can be related to the athlete's drug-taking behavior. More accurate results, however, could perhaps be obtained from taking blood tests. A urine test gives a quick and easy screen, which can indicate the presence of a drug. The urine test, if necessary, can be followed up by confirmatory blood tests. Replacing urine tests with finger-prick blood tests may give more accurate results, especially for newer substances such as EPO, but athletes may see it as unnecessarily invasive. There is also the risk of exposing laboratory staff to infection from blood-borne disease, albeit this risk may be small. More expertise is also needed for the storage and handling of blood samples.

Many of these same issues arise in another emerging field of forensic toxicology—workplace testing. Increasingly, employers will not tolerate their workforce being under the influence of alcohol or drugs and want to carry out random screening to ensure their requirements are being met. Blood testing could be interpreted as an infringement on the employee's liberty as the purpose is non-medical—as it is in sports testing.

A challenge for forensic toxicology is the use of body **fluids** as a medium for accurate drug testing without being unnecessarily invasive. When it comes to sports testing, there may be even bigger questions to address in the future. For example, what if athletes undergo gene therapy to increase their dose of IGF-1 and so increase their strength and endurance? How will it be possible to determine the presence of new genetic material in the genome? The new ethical questions posed by the issue of fairness in sport can only lead to the development of forensic toxicology as a science.

SEE ALSO Gas chromatograph-mass spectrometer; Toxicology.

Standardization of regulations

Forensic work is performed in laboratories worldwide for criminal casework and development of **DNA** databases. Laboratories often have their own particular methods and protocols for performing their analyses, which may present problems when it comes to the final evaluation of the data by a third party, especially when matters of guilt or innocence are at stake. Laboratories must demonstrate that the results they have obtained are reliable and justifiable in court. For this reason, standardized methods and techniques have been generated by governing forensic bodies in order to provide a common means by which forensic laboratories can work. In addition, particular DNA loci (the locations of selected genes on a **chromosome**) have been chosen that represent the basis for the creation of standard DNA databases. Standardized methods and DNA profile databases have revolutionized the manner in which crimes are solved.

Standards and guidelines are extremely beneficial to forensic laboratories as demonstration of conformity establishes a high level of quality assurance and competence within the laboratory. This is especially important when forensic **evidence** is presented in a court of law where it is subjected to the utmost scrutiny and skepticism. Furthermore, because of the nature of the investigations, most forensic DNA work is processed under strict confidentiality. Utilization of a defined standard protocol minimizes both the need to review confidential records and the potential non-inclusion of evidence where methods have been questioned.

Guidelines and standardized methods utilized by forensic labs are created by several different governing bodies in the forensic industry. For example, the Federal Bureau of Investigation (**FBI**) in the United States, the **European Network of Forensic Science Institutes** (ENFSI), and the International Standards Organization (ISO) are a few of the groups that work to ensure validated methods are followed for forensic analyses. The quality assurance guidelines set forth in documentation provided by the aforementioned groups are composed of a variety of specific requirements.

All forensic laboratories must maintain a documented system in which they demonstrate their level of quality of all components of a standard program. These components include much more than guidelines for scientific data evaluation. Specific guidelines are provided on the organization and management of the lab; **training** level and method of training staff; facilities; control of evidence, including complete documentation of the **chain of custody**; the methods, analysis, and validation process; equipment maintenance; review process; proficiency testing; corrective action; and audits.

Standards for DNA testing are constantly being monitored and reviewed. Within each of the organizations and governing bodies, there is a segment of people or expert working group, who meet specifically to ensure that the level of the standards and guidelines are high in all forensic laboratories. These groups include the Scientific Working Group on DNA Analysis Methods (SWGDAM) of the FBI and the DNA Profile Monitoring Expert Group (DNA MEG) of **Interpol**.

Three major DNA databases exist worldwide, each of which hold and catalogue DNA profiles. Each profile consists of the DNA sequence of a particular set of standard loci. The profiles contained in the databases are based on STRs, or short tandem repeats of DNA sequences that are obtained using **PCR (polymerase chain reaction)** to amplify the specific regions of DNA. Although these loci exist in the same place on the chromosome of all humans, the DNA sequence of the region is highly variable, such that when several are combined together, there is an extremely high probability that a particular combination can only be associated with a single person. These databases are maintained by Interpol (ISSOL), the FBI (**CODIS**), and ENFSI and contain several common loci. The FBI's CODIS database contains the most loci, at 13 per profile.

CODIS, ISSOL, and ENFSI databases have greatly increased the ability to solve violent crime on a worldwide level. Because they share loci, it is possible to link offenders to existing samples not only within a single country, but internationally. Two aspects exist to each database, one contains DNA profiles collected from evidence found at crime scenes and the second contains DNA profiles of convicted offenders. Initially, most countries only collected samples from convicted sex offenders or perpetrators of other violent crimes. However, as even small offenders tend toward a pattern of crime, the value of retaining profiles of all convicted offenders has been recognized. Thus, investigators can now compare DNA samples obtained at crime scenes and potentially obtain a match from the offender database.

SEE ALSO CODIS: Combined DNA Index System; DNA; DNA profiling; European Network of Forensic Science Institutes; STR (short tandem repeat) analysis.

James E. Starrs

1930–
AMERICAN
FORENSIC SCIENTIST

James E. Starrs has made significant contributions to the field of **forensic science** as a writer, professor, and investigator. He has taught law and forensic science at George Washington University for more than forty years, and has written many articles and books on his forensic work, including a leading textbook on scientific **evidence**. Starrs is perhaps best known for the numerous scientific investigations he has conducted, on such famous cases as the Boston Strangler, Alfred Packer, Senator Huey Long, CIA agent Frank Olson, Jesse James, and Meriwether Lewis.

Starrs, even as a young man, had a keen interest in criminal law, reading many of the Sherlock Holmes mysteries. He earned an undergraduate degree at St. John's University, and a graduate degree at New York University, where he held a Ford Foundation Fellowship. In 1964, Starrs became a faculty member at George Washington University in Washington, D.C. There he has taught both law and forensic sciences, specializing in criminal law and procedure, forensic **pathology**, fingerprinting, document examination, and polygraph use.

In conjunction with his academic career, Starrs has led a number of scientific investigations of famous historic cases. In the Alfred Packer case, he exhumed the bodies of Packer's five traveling companions to determine if Packer was guilty of cannibalism. In the Boston Strangler case, Starrs exhumed

Forensic scientist James E. Starrs examines a gel x ray of DNA sequences at a George Washington University laboratory.
© RICHARD T. NOWITZ/CORBIS

the body of the Strangler's last victim to determine if her injuries correlated with Albert DeSalvo's confession. Starrs also worked on identifying the remains of Jesse James, determining the **cause of death** of CIA agent Frank Olson and explorer Meriwether Lewis, and determining the true assassin of Senator Huey Long.

Starrs has also contributed to the literature related to forensic sciences. Together with Andre Moenssens and Fred Inbau, he wrote *Scientific Evidence in Criminal Cases*, a leading textbook on scientific evidence. And in 2005, Starrs and co-author Katherine Ramsland published *A Voice for the Dead: A Forensic Pursuit of the Truth in the Grave*. The book details Starrs' work in body **exhumation**. In addition to the many articles Starrs contributed to **professional publications**, he also edited the *Scientific Sleuthing Review* for more than twenty-five years. In 1996, Starrs became a distinguished fellow of the **American Academy of Forensic Sciences**.

SEE ALSO Careers in forensic science; Exhumation.

Jean Servais Stas

8/21/1813–12/13/1891
BELGIAN
ANALYTICAL CHEMIST

Jean Servais Stas was born in Louvain (Leuven), Belgium. There he studied for a medical career and received his medical degree. After a short time as a physician, Stas turned to analytical chemistry.

In 1837, reportedly after much trouble, Stas gained admission to French chemist Jean Baptiste Dumas' laboratory at the Ecole Polytechnique in Paris in order to continue research on phloridzin (a flavonoid compound found naturally in some foods), which he had begun earlier in an attic in his father's house.

In 1840, Stas left Paris when he was appointed the chair of chemistry at the Ecole Royale Militaire in Brussels. He became a professor and worked assiduously on determining atomic weights (i.e., relative atomic masses), including the atomic weights of oxygen and carbon, with more accuracy than had been previously accomplished. Stas produced the first modern table of atomic weights, using oxygen as a standard (set at number 16). Stas' practice of using the number 16 for oxygen on the periodic table as a reference point would continue well into the twentieth century, when chemists returned to basing atomic masses on carbon-12. In 1920, the English chemist Francis Aston (1877–1945) discovered, by means of the mass **spectrograph**, that all atomic masses (isotopes taken into account) are very nearly integral multiples of the same number, a number now taken to be 1/12 the mass of carbon-12, for which Aston received in 1922 the Nobel Prize in chemistry.

Stas also aimed to prove the hypothesis of English physicist William Prout (1785–1850), a hypothesis independently elaborated by the German Johann Ludwig Georg Meinecke, that all atoms were conglomerations of hydrogen atoms. Instead, Stas' results discredited Prout's hypothesis that all atomic weights are whole numbers, but provided the foundation for the work of Dimitri Mendelejew and others on the periodic system. Though Stas started with a predilection in favor of Prout's hypothesis, he was later led by the results he obtained and by his failure to find any evidence of dissociation in the elements to regard it as a pure illusion, and to look upon the unity of matter as merely an attractive speculation unsupported by proof.

Stas also worked in connection with the poisoning of Count Hippolyte de Bocarmé with nicotine in 1850, working out a method for the detection of the vegetable alkaloids, such as caffeine, quinine, morphine, strychnine, atropine, and opium. These poisons affect the central nervous system. Plant alkaloids leave no demonstrable traces in the human body, thus requiring relatively complicated methods of extraction before an analysis can be performed. Stas searched for three months for the agent, and eventually managed to isolate nicotine from the body tissues. Using ether as a solvent, which he then evaporated to isolate the drug, he found the potent drug that was, in fact, the murder weapon. The man's killer had extracted it from tobacco and force-fed it to the victim. With Stas's testimony, the killer was convicted.

Stas thus became the first person to develop a method to extract material containing plant alkaloids from the organic material of the human body, and for many years thereafter, with some modifications, this method was used as the standard. Other toxicologists then developed qualitative tests with the so-called Stas-Otto procedure to determine the presence of various alkaloids in the obtained extract. With his treatise "Forensic investigation on nicotine" Stas became a founder of modern **toxicology** and a pioneer in industrial pollution.

Stas' interests also included the humanities, and in 1851–52, together with Guillaume Claine, he gave a series of lectures at the Cercle artistique et littÕraire de Bruxelles on daguerreotype and its applications in art.

After more than a quarter of a century, but before he had served the thirty years necessary to secure a pension, Stas was obliged to resign in 1869 because of a malady that affected his speech. He then advised the Belgian government on military issues and was also appointed to a post in connection with the Mint. In 1872 he succeeded in preparing pure platinum and iridium, metals necessary to produce the standard measure. Stas was openly critical of the part played by religion in education. He spent the rest of his life in retirement in Brussels, where he died in 1891.

Jean Servais Stas' name is best known for his determination of the atomic weights of a number of the more important elements. His work in this field was marked by extreme care, and he adopted the most minute precautions to avoid error, with such success that the greatest variation of individual determinations for each element are reported to be from 0.005 to 0.01. Stas was one of the most skillful, chemical analysts of the nineteenth century and his measurements remained the standard of accuracy for over 50 years.

SEE ALSO Isotopic analysis; Medicine; Spectrograph; Toxicology.

State courts (rules of evidence)

The state court system in the United States is a complex one, governed by myriad rules and specified procedures. The United States Constitution confers most of the powers in the country to the states, assigning only quite specific and discrete powers to the federal government. The United States has dual judicial systems, those at the federal level, and those operating at the state level. Within each of those judicial systems there are also civil and criminal courts. Violations of federal law are prosecuted through the federal court system; this occurs only in a discrete number of areas. The vast majority of civil and criminal proceedings related to violations of the law occur at the state level.

Using the 1995 **murder** trial in which the former football star O. J. Simpson was the defendant as an example, Simpson was tried in a state criminal proceeding for the murders of his former wife and her friend. Simpson was also tried for the crime of murder at the state civil level. Although at first glance it appears that he was tried twice for the same crime, which would appear to invoke (or violate) the rule of double jeopardy (a person may not be tried twice for the same crime), because the trials occurred at two different jurisdictional levels, a state criminal trial and a state civil trial, this did not constitute double jeopardy. Simpson was not convicted in the state criminal trial, but was found liable and required to pay monetary damages at the state civil trial.

The reason that O. J. Simpson could be tried twice for the murders of Nicole Brown Simpson and Ronald Goldman is this: the criminal and civil court systems in the United States are completely separate. The two courts have different rules of procedure and separate forms and means of imposing penalties. If an individual is convicted as the result of a criminal trial, there is the possibility of being sentenced to prison; this is not the case in a civil trial. A civil conviction typically results in the assessment of financial damages, and may involve being mandated to perform certain actions, like public speaking about the nature of the crime—as in the case of convictions involving the use of alcohol or illegal substances—or being prohibited from behaving in certain ways, such as being prevented from having contact with the individual that the defendant was accused of battering, for example.

In addition to the rules of evidence, there are a considerable number of other rules governing the means and the methods by which trials are to be conducted at the level of the state court system, whether civil or criminal. There are rules about pleading, which create a framework for the manner in which the claim or charge of the plaintiff must be stated. Discovery, the right to assemble information gathered by either the defense or the prosecution, is constrained by specific rules as to how the evidence is obtained, who has the right to custody of the evidence, the manner in which it is delivered or presented, what constitutes acceptable discovery materials, etc. There is a rule regarding burden of proof; in a criminal trial, there must be proof of the defendant's guilt beyond a reasonable doubt. In a state civil trial law, the burden of proof is lowered and the plaintiff's case need only be proven by the preponderance of evidence. That means there must be more weight in favor of guilt than there is in favor of innocence, in order for a conviction of guilt to occur at the state civil level. In a state criminal trial, the defendant is accorded more rights and protections than at the state civil level. For example, a defendant in a state criminal trial cannot be forced to testify. In the case of O. J. Simpson, he invoked his constitutional right against self-incrimination (saying something oneself that could, to a reasonable observer indicate admission of guilt).

The rule of protection states that a defendant has certain specific legal rights and protections in the case of a trial. In a criminal trial, the defendant is entitled to more safeguards and procedural rights than at the state civil level, because the potential penalties for conviction are much more onerous (burdensome, costly, or oppressive).

Whether the trial is at the criminal or civil level, every party has the right to appeal a conviction. In the case of an acquittal at a criminal trial, there is virtually no right of appeal, as a person may not be tried twice for the same crime in the same court of law. In a civil trial, the party for whom the court finds against (the losing party) has the right to appeal.

Although each state views this rule somewhat differently, and exercises the right to set its own parameters and create its own definitions, most states have laws regarding the speed with which cases must be tried. In the case of a criminal trial, there are generally constraints that it must occur within a reasonable time frame after the occurrence of the crime and the indictment of the defendant.

SEE ALSO Evidence; Evidence, chain of custody; Interrogation; Lindbergh kidnapping and murder; Trials, international.

Statistical interpretation of evidence

Because the **identification** of forensic **evidence** is not always obvious, forensic scientists today do not simply identify evidence but must also interpret it statistically. Such evidence—that is, the ways and means by which disputed facts are proven true or false in a legal setting—comes in many forms. Evidence may be spoken or written by expert or ordinary witnesses, law enforcement officials, or other relevant persons; contained in physical objects obtained from crime scenes, victims, and suspects such as **glass** fragments, fingerprints, and firearm marks; and found in physical materials recovered from forensic examinations such as body **fluids**, paint, **DNA** samples, and drugs. There are many other types of evidence, nearly all of which contain variations (or uncertainties) when measured and compared between the observed or calculated value and the actual value. For example, there is little likelihood (actually as low as one chance in 10^{60}) that **fingerprint** characteristics from one person would match the fingerprints of another person, but there is a greater likelihood (about 34 percent) that if one person has **blood** type A+, then another person has the same blood type.

The statistical interpretation of evidence, often performed by forensic statisticians, involves the evaluation and comparison of evidence found during crime scene examinations and in forensic laboratories, and identified from reference samples of suspects. Such matching of characteristics between crime scene and suspect evidence relies on the theory of probability, the branch of mathematics that deals with determining quantitatively the frequency of occurrence of an event. For example, if a coin is flipped 100 times, it is theoretically expected to land as heads 50 times and tails 50 times. Within probability, various statistical models and techniques—such as Bayes' Theorem, deductive and inductive reasoning, graphical modeling, grouping, likelihood ratios, distributions, samplings, and significance tests—are used to help forensic scientists correctly evaluate and accurately interpret evidence that contain elements of uncertainty. For example, a suspect may be identified because a rare blood type (AB−) found at the crime scene matches the suspect's own blood type, which only about one percent of the U.S. population carries.

Although used in both the nineteenth and twentieth centuries, the application of statistics to interpret evidence became especially important during the 1980s when **DNA profiling** first became popular. During those subsequent years, there was doubt within the legal community as to the reliability of such methods and to the appropriateness of the (often) simplistic calculations involved. Eventually, the use of statistics for interpreting evidence brought a positive change in the way quantitative data was viewed from a legal standpoint. Presently, the legal community continues to ask the **forensic science** community for more and better statistics to interpret evidence in order to prove the innocence or guilt of suspected criminals.

Statistics, however, can hinder the solvability of crime when performed improperly. When subjective assessment is introduced—that is, biased evaluations or those based on personal opinion—inaccurate conclusions can be made when comparing evidence characteristics. Subjective qualifiers, such as *high chance* for guilt when used by the prosecution (for example), and as *low chance*, by the defense, can often lead to angry and unproductive legal debates as to whether to implicate or exonerate a suspect. As an example of biased statistical interpretation, if a suspect has a five percent chance of possessing a particular trait in order to be deemed innocent of a crime, then the prosecution could state that the suspect has a 95% chance of being guilty (often called the prosecutor's fallacy), while the defense would simply compute five percent of the population (say one million) to be innocent and declare there is a 1 in 50,000 chance of guilt. Therefore, objective assessment, or the unbiased interpretation of the evidence, is preferred because it requires the rational and sound application of statistics to accurately interpret the uncertainties of evidence.

Although the choice of the statistical method is a subjective one, once it is chosen, different forensic experts with identical data and the same statistical method will produce (theoretically) the same assessment and make the same interpretation of the evidence. Of course, there is still controversy about the assumptions underlying the choice of the method used and the interpretations made thereafter. Debate also exists as to how often statistics are misinterpreted or overvalued as evidence. Although the field of statistics seems to have the potential for uniformity, clarity, and impartiality, it is still in the embryonic stage of development within forensic science. Because of its immature nature there are still risks of misuse by forensic examiners, law enforcement officers, courtroom lawyers, judges, and juries. Incorrect statistical use of evidence still leads to problems such as unnecessary forensic tests, unwarranted appeals against court rulings, and even miscarriages of justice.

In order to make a correct assessment of all the variations within a particular case and to present the information in the most understandable way possible, forensic statisticians need a well-rounded knowledge of both the theory and the application of statistics to forensic evidence. Statisticians must be able to evaluate rationally both subjective opinions and objective analyses in order to check, criticize, and verify all the evidence. For the field of statistics to be successfully applied to the interpretation of evidence, it must be appropriately applied, unbiased in analyses and presentation, and intelligible to the people involved in all phases of the forensic investigation and legal proceedings.

SEE ALSO Forensic science; Quality control of forensic evidence; Uncertainty analysis in forensic science.

Steganography

Forensic **evidence** ranges from the readily evident (i.e., stab or gunshot wound) to the harder to detect (i.e., **trace evidence**) to the invisible or disguised. Whether apparent or not, all evidence is potentially valuable in tracing the course of events of an accident, illness, or crime, and in personal **identification**. Disguised or hidden evidence can be physical or, in the case of **computer forensics**, electronic. An example of the latter is steganography.

Steganography (from the Greek for "covered writing") is the secret transmission of a message. It is distinct from encryption, because the goal of encryption is to make a message difficult to read, while the goal of steganography is to make a message altogether invisible. A steganographic message may also be an encrypted as an extra barrier to interception, but need not be. Steganography has the advantage that even a talented code-cracker cannot decipher a message without knowing it is there.

Steganography has been used since ancient times; Greek historian Herodotus records how one plotter of a revolt communicated secretly with another by shaving a slave's head, writing on his scalp, letting his hair grow back, and sending the slave as an apparently unencumbered messenger. The number of ways a steganographic message might be sent is limited only by human ingenuity. A photograph of a large group of people, for example, might contain a Morse-code message in the expressions of the people in the photograph (e.g., smiling for dot, blank for dash) or in the directions they are looking (e.g., slightly to the left for dot, straight at the camera for dash). Writing in invisible ink or miniaturizing a message, as on microfilm, are also forms of steganography. Probably the commonest form of steganography involves the embedding of messages in apparently innocent texts, with the letters or words of the message indicated either by subtle graphic emphasis (e.g., heavier ink, lighter ink, a small defect) or by special positioning. For instance, reading the first word of every sentence in what appears to be an ordinary letter might yield a steganographic message.

Like most other forms of cryptography and **secret writing**, steganography has thrived in the digital era. Most digital documents contain useless or insignificant areas of data, or involve enough redundancy that some of their information can be altered without obvious effect. For instance, one might conceal a message bitstream inside a digital audio file by replacing the least-significant bit of every waveform sample (or every nth waveform sample) with a message bit; the only effect on the file, if played back as audio, would be a slight, and probably unnoticeable, decrease in the sound quality. Although steganographic messages can be hidden in any kind of digital files, image files, because they contain so much data to begin with, are usually used for digital steganography. Today a number of commercial or shareware programs exist for encoding text into steganographic images, called stego-images), and are used by millions of people worldwide who wish to evade surveillance.

Steganography is also used for *watermarking*, which is the hiding of information indicating ownership or origin inside a digital file. (Physical watermarking, the practice after which digital watermarking is named, is the impression of a subtle pattern on paper using water. A watermark is only visible when the paper is held up to a light.) Watermarking can be used by forensic investigators for digital authentication (i.e., to prove that certain party was indeed the source of a file) or to check whether a digital file was obtained in violation of copyright.

SEE ALSO Codes and ciphers; Computer forensics.

Stimulants SEE Amphetamines

Mark Stolorow

4/28/1946–
AMERICAN
FORENSIC SEROLOGIST

From about the last quarter of the twentieth century to the present, Mark D. Stolorow has provided extensive experience as both a forensic serologist and a forensic laboratory administrator. Because of these qualifications, Stolorow serves as an expert witness in numerous court cases involving **forensic science**. Earlier in his professional career, Stolorow was credited, along with **Brian Wraxall**, with developing the **multisystem method** for simultaneously testing isoenzyme systems in 1978. That same year, Stolorow and Wraxall were also recognized as being the first to develop methods for typing **blood serum** proteins. Today, Stolorow is the executive director of Orchid Cellmark, an internationally recognized leader in providing forensic **DNA** analytical services to law enforcement agencies, lawyers, detectives and investigators, companies, and individuals, and in developing new methods to use DNA testing.

Stolorow gained his bachelor's of science degree from the University of Michigan and his master's of science degree in forensic chemistry from the University of Pittsburgh. He also earned his master's of business administration degree in management from Eastern Michigan University. After graduation, Stolorow was employed as a **training** coordinator for the state forensic **serology** program in Illinois. Later, he was the research program administrator at the Bureau of Forensic Sciences for the Illinois State Police.

After working with the Illinois Police, Stolorow joined Cellmark Diagnostics—a subsidiary of Lifecodes Corporation—as a general manager. When Orchid Biosciences acquired Cellmark Diagnostics in December 2001, Stolorow became the executive director of Orchid Cellmark, located in Germantown, Maryland, the forensic strategic business unit. Stolorow has the responsibility of directing Orchid Cellmark's international network of forensic testing laboratories, which are based in England and the United States. Stolorow and his employees have worked with many of the major U.S. police departments in such cities as New York City, Chicago, and Houston. They have also helped many international law enforcement agencies, including Scotland Yard and the Metropolitan Police Service in London, England. Stolorow has helped to build Orchid Cellmark into the largest independent supplier of DNA analysis services to English police departments, the world's leading country in forensic DNA testing.

Along with fellow Orchid forensic scientists, Stolorow has played important roles in conducting DNA testing for such high-profile cases as the 1995 criminal investigation of O.J. Simpson for the murders of Nicole Brown Simpson and Ronald Goldman; the 1998 **murder** trial of Theodore Kaczynski (the Unabomber); the 1996 murder case of JonBenet

Ramsey in Boulder, Colorado; the 2002 trial of David Westerfield, the murderer/kidnapper of Danielle van Dam of San Diego, California; and the 1982–1984 homicide investigation and serial murder trial of Gary Ridgway (Green River murderer) near Seattle, Washington. In fact, Stolorow presented the DNA **evidence** from the O.J. Simpson case to representatives of the Smithsonian Institute in Washington, D.C., because the case heralded the importance of DNA evidence in crime investigations and courtroom proceedings.

For the **identification** of the 9–11 victims at the World Trade Center in New York City, traditional DNA methods often failed because the crucial genetic materials had been severely degraded by compressed **building materials**, bacterial contamination, high temperatures, and water. Fortunately, Stolorow was able to coordinate the development of innovative technologies that were able to overcome these difficulties. This new forensic technology—called single nucleotide polymorphism (SNP) markers—helped to identify the damaged DNA material found at the disaster site. By using SNP technology, Stolorow and the Orchid scientists were able to identify many more victims that were previously unidentified. Because of their pioneering SNP work with large-scale forensic DNA analysis, Stolorow and his team of scientists are exploring further uses of SNP tests in other difficult medical and scientific cases.

In 2003, Stolorow launched the DNA Express Service, a premium forensic DNA testing service by Orchid Cellmark that is used to help local U.S. law enforcement agencies analyze the estimated 500,000 backlogged cases of DNA evidence from unsolved "no-suspect" and other criminal crimes. Stolorow and his team of forensic scientists deliver DNA results in five business days as compared to the standard four to five weeks for routine casework. In the future, Stolorow intends to make DNA Express Service a key resource for providing quick, but accurate, DNA analysis of criminal cases.

Stolorow is also involved in providing increased DNA testing services that became available when the new law Justice for All Act of 2004 was signed by President George W. Bush. The legislation is providing about $1 billion between 2004 and 2009 in order to eliminate the backlog of unanalyzed DNA evidence in police departments across the country and to expand the FBI's Combined DNA Index System (**CODIS**). Stolorow is guiding Orchid Cellmark as a key partner with law enforcement organizations by reducing the DNA backlog, increasing the use of forensic testing, and adding more criminal information to the federal

CODIS database. Stolorow has already coordinated Orchid Cellmark's work to implement Biotracks, a pilot program with the New York Police Department to solve burglaries by matching DNA crime samples to DNA databases of convicted criminals.

SEE ALSO American Academy of Forensic Sciences; DNA; DNA recognition instruments; DNA sequences, unique; Genetic code; Multisystem method; September 11, 2001, terrorist attacks (forensic investigations of); Simpson (O. J.) murder trial; Unabomber case and trial; September 11, 2001, terrorist attacks (forensic investigations of).

STR (short tandem repeat) analysis

Short tandem repeats (STR) are, as the name suggests, very short stretches of **DNA** that are repeated back to back in various locations throughout the human genome. Typically, the repeating sequence is just two, three, or four base pairs in length, and the number of copies found back to back is variable across a wide range. Unlike the DNA sequences in coding genes, there is no "correct" number of repeats for any specific STR in the genome; they are simply areas within the genome where variation is normal and healthy. For any specific STR, each person will have two copies, one that is inherited from their mother at conception, and the other that is inherited from their father.

STRs are helpful in forensic and paternity testing. Because there is a lot of natural variation for STRs, the chance of two people matching for the exact number of repeats on both inherited copies of the STR is fairly small. By combining analysis of many STRs across the genome, the probability of two people matching by random chance is extremely low.

For example, if the normal variation for certain STR (we will call it STR-A) is from seven to twenty copies, there will be fourteen different lengths that could be passed on from either parent. Since each person has two copies of STR-A, the total number of possible combinations would be 196 (14 x 14). If each of these different STR lengths had an equally probability (1/14), and every possible combination was equally likely, the chance of two people matching on the pattern of STR-A would be 1/196. Now, suppose that there are many other STRs available for study (eg., STR-B, STR-C, STR-D ... STR-Z) each

with the same probabilities we chose for STR-A. The likelihood of matching by random chance alone across these many markers would be found by multiplying the probabilities of each one individually. For two markers, the probability of a random chance match drops to 1/38,416. Adding a third marker drops the probability to 1/7,529,536. The addition of a fourth marker decreases the likelihood to less than one in 14 billion.

The discovery of STRs has greatly advanced **forensic science** by drastically reducing the chances that a suspect will be wrongly identified on the basis of forensic testing.

SEE ALSO DNA fingerprint; DNA profiling; DNA sequences, unique.

Sublimation

Sublimation is the term that describes the change of state of a material from a frozen form to a gas or visa versa. In sublimation, there is no intermediate liquid phase.

A well-known example of sublimation occurs with dry ice, the frozen form of carbon dioxide. When exposed to air, dry ice changes directly to vapor, which is visible as a cloud immediately above the frozen CO_2. In the case of dry ice, the frozen CO_2 is energetically more stable as a gas at room temperature than as the frozen solid.

The gaseous tail that develops behind a comet as it approaches the sun is another example of sublimation. Frost and snowflakes are products of a reverse path of sublimation, where water changes directly from the gaseous state to the solid state.

Sublimation has practical applications in **forensic science**. Forensic analysis of a crime or accident scene often relies on the examination of photographic **evidence** after the scene has been cleaned. A dye-sublimation printer enables digital pictures to be rendered in print form in a very realistic and detailed fashion, which helps investigators in their analysis.

The basis of a dye-sublimation printer is the vaporization of various colored dyes housed in the printer. The vaporized dyes penetrate the glossy surface of the photographic paper before returning to their solid form. The vapor-to-solid dye sublimation creates a gentle gradation at the edge of each pixel of color, rather than a sudden border between the dye and the paper (as is the case with inkjet type printers). The result is a more realistic image that yields more detail.

Dye sublimation is also used to create digital watermarks on documents. This enables a forensic examiner to differentiate an authentic document from a forgery.

Sublimation can be important in the recovery of compounds that are suspended or dissolved in a fluid or a solid like dry ice. The compounds can be recovered, at least in crude form, by allowing the suspending matrix to sublimate away. This method of recovery is usually gentle, which is advantageous in preserving the chemical structure or even activity of the target drug (i.e., cocaine) or enzyme. Many compounds will sublimate when heated. The effective temperature can be characteristic of the compound and can be measured in a forensic laboratory inexpensively, using a common hot plate.

SEE ALSO Analytical instrumentation; Exothermic reactions.

Suicide investigation

When the medical examiner (ME) is faced with an unexplained death, he or she has to determine whether the manner of death is natural, accidental, homicidal, or suicidal. The first involves disease, the other three manners involve some form of physical trauma. In a suicide, trauma is inflicted by the victim on himself. Gunshot wounds, jumping from a great height, hanging, and drug overdose are common causes of suicide. However, such deaths can also be caused by homicide or accident. In the case of a shooting, it can sometimes be obvious from the **autopsy** whether or not the death was likely to be a suicide. With a drug overdose, however, the autopsy findings are the same whatever the victim's intent, and the investigator must look carefully at the circumstances to arrive at the correct verdict. If the investigator comes to the wrong conclusion, a killer may either escape or be unjustly convicted. Suicide is always traumatic for those left behind. If an accident or homicide is wrongly ruled as a suicide, then the family of the deceased is caused unnecessary grief. In other words, suicide investigations must be undertaken with great care, because some cases are complicated.

Poisoning remains the most common method of suicide, especially among women. It is perceived as being less traumatic than other methods and with the widespread availability of alcohol and drugs, the means are easy to obtain. However, poisoning is also often accidental, especially if the victim is confused, which may happen if they have been drinking or ill, for example. Under these circumstances the victim may mistakenly take too many sleeping pills or painkillers. Poisoning could also be a homicidal act. Although **murder** by poisoning today is somewhat less common than in previous centuries, the pathologist should never rule out the possibility.

The suicidal use of corrosive agents such as acid or weed killer has decreased dramatically in recent years, perhaps because such chemicals are now less readily available than they used to be. Cyanide is a deadly poison that often features in books or films about murder and suicide. However, cyanide poisoning is not very common these days, especially as a tool of homicide. Cyanide turns to lethal hydrogen cyanide gas on contact with the acid of the stomach. Hydrogen cyanide prevents the body's cells from using oxygen; this gives the **blood** a characteristic pink color that will be evident to the pathologist on autopsy. The victim's face is often a brick-red hue after cyanide poisoning.

Aspirin and **barbiturates** are also less likely to be used as suicidal agents than previously. Doctors rarely prescribe barbiturates these days, but various other prescription and over-the-counter drugs can be equally lethal. There has been an increase in self-poisoning with antidepressants and acetaminophen. Moves to restrict the amount of some over-the-counter drugs purchased at one time have deterred some impulsive suicides. However, the person who is bent on suicide will merely collect up enough pills to commit the act.

It is not uncommon for a "cocktail" of drugs to be taken in suicide. The pathologist must take samples from blood, urine, and various body tissues and then has the difficult task of trying to work out what contribution each component of the cocktail made to the death. The presence of a suicide note at the scene of a poisoning (or other suicide) may be taken as an indication of suicide rather than an accident. However, the absence of a note does not mean the act was necessarily accidental. Some people simply do not leave a note, perhaps to protect the feelings of loved ones by trying to make the act look accidental. Moreover, forged notes may be used to help stage a homicide as a suicide. As ever, all the **evidence** must be carefully assessed to arrive at the truth.

Carbon monoxide poisoning accounts for many suicides, the classic method being to sit in a car with the engine running in a closed garage. Under such circumstances, it may take only a few minutes for a lethal level of carbon monoxide to build up in

The body of actress Marilyn Monroe is removed to the morgue on a stretcher by a police officer in 1962. Forensic scientists later ruled her death a suicide. © BETTMANN/CORBIS

the atmosphere. Carbon monoxide poisoning is relatively easy to diagnose on autopsy. Carbon monoxide gas interacts with **hemoglobin** in blood to produce a characteristic cherry red color. The skin and internal organs are all pink in color and analysis of the blood will show a high concentration of the gas. However, accidental carbon monoxide poisoning is also a possibility; many cases have occurred in dwellings with faulty gas appliances and heating systems.

Hangings are nearly always suicidal in adults and teenagers, though usually accidental among children. Commonly the **mechanism of death** in hanging is asphyxiation from compression of the carotid arteries and the airways due to the pressure of the ligature. However, if the body drops through a height on hanging, death may be from cardiac arrest from pressure on the vagus nerve in the neck. The **medical examiner** must distinguish between hanging and asphyxiation caused by other means such as manual strangulation and smothering. Neck marks are common, but may not be present if a soft material like a scarf or a sheet has been used. The marks run

diagonally across the neck in a hanging, but are horizontal after manual strangulation. **Toxicology** testing for drugs or alcohol plays an important role in the investigation of a hanging. A suicidal victim may take drugs to get up courage to perform the act; a murder victim may be subdued or made unconscious in the case of a homicide. Homicidal hanging of a fully conscious able-bodied person is virtually impossible. Suicidal strangulation by a ligature is rare, but not impossible, and must be considered when a victim has been strangled. It takes 15 seconds or so to lose consciousness in strangulation, which allows the victim time to loop or knot a ligature around their neck. Another form of suicidal asphyxiation is smothering, where the victim places a plastic bag over the head, securing it in place with tape or a rope. In such cases, the face is often pale and does not exhibit the congestion or protruding tongue seen in strangulation.

When a body is found in water, the pathologist must consider the possibility of suicide, although most drownings, if this is the **cause of death**, are accidental. If the person is weighted down, perhaps by clutching stones or rocks or having them in their pockets, then this may indicate suicide.

Deciding whether a shooting was suicide, homicide, or an accident can be a major issue for the medical examiner. In the case of a suicide, the gunshot wound, or wounds, must be found in a site on the body consistent with the range of the deceased's arm. These wound sites often depend on the type of weapon that is used. Long-barreled weapons such as rifles and short-barreled weapons, like handguns, can both be used to inflict injuries inside the mouth, under the chin, on the front of the neck, and the center of the forehead, all of which will readily inflict a fatal wound to the brain. The classic discharge to the temple is found only with a handgun and the wound will be on the same side of the head as the dominant hand of the victim. A left-handed person cannot readily shoot himself in the right temple.

People rarely shoot themselves in the eye or abdomen. It is also virtually impossible to shoot yourself in the back. Women rarely shoot themselves, either intentionally or by accident. Multiple gunshot wounds are nearly always the result of homicide, although they are not unknown in suicide.

In a suicidal shooting, the weapon must be found at the scene. It may, however, be at some distance from the body because the recoil of the weapon on shooting can fling it away from the victim. If no weapon is found, homicide is the most likely verdict unless someone has been interfering with the scene of the crime and removed the gun. However, investigators must always be alert to the possibility of the staging of a homicide to look like a suicide by placing the gun by the side of the body. In short, deciding the manner of death in a shooting can be difficult, and it is important to consider all the evidence relating to the investigation.

Some railways deaths are suicides. People may lie on the track with their neck across a rail, which results in decapitation. Jumping in front of a moving train is a relatively common form of suicide. The injuries caused depend upon the exact events and are usually extensive. However, some victims do survive jumping in front of a train. It is important to distinguish between homicide and suicide in railway injuries, because it is not unknown for people to be pushed in front of moving trains. Similarly, a homicide may be staged as a suicide by placing a body on a railway track. In such cases, the pathologist may see evidence of injuries that may have been inflicted before the impact of the train on the body.

These are some of the most common methods of suicide, but suicide needs to be considered as a possible manner of death in many cases referred to the medical examiner. Often it is not possible to distinguish between accident and suicide on the evidence given, in which case an open verdict may reasonably be given.

SEE ALSO Death, cause of; Death, mechanism of.

Superglue® fuming

Superglue® fuming, also known as cyanoacrylate fuming, is one of the processes used to chemically enhance fingerprints on smooth or nonporous surfaces. When an object is subjected to superglue fuming, fingerprints that are present on its nonporous parts will appear in white. Further dying is possible, increasing the contrast with the background. This technique is one of the most used **fingerprint** enhancement techniques and has a paramount role in forensic sciences. It allows the observation of fingerprints that would not otherwise be detected. It was first used in 1978 by the Criminal Identification Division of the Japanese National Police Agency.

Superglues are monomeric liquids of cyanoacrylate esters. They are also known as high-strength or rapid glues. When vaporized, the cyanoacrylate ester vapors will selectively polymerize on the secretions left by fingerprints on nonporous surfaces. The resulting hard, white polycyanoacrylate coating covers the fingerprint pattern. This provides the forensic scientist with a first enhancement of the contrast of the fingerprint to the surface. If this enhancement is not enough, it is then possible, after allowing the fingerprint to dry for a moment, to apply different dyes selectively on the polymerized glue. Some of these dyes are also fluorescent (light-emitting) at given wavelengths, which greatly improves the contrast to the background.

In order to process an object for fingerprints with Superglue® fuming, the object is placed in a small chamber. The humidity inside the chamber is important, and a relative humidity of 80% is recommended; air that is too dry provides poor results. The Superglue® is placed on a hot plate and heated to about 212°F (100°C). The surfaces of the object are monitored, and the process is stopped as soon as the fingerprints appear with enough contrast. Many crime laboratories use a homemade unit, comprised of a recycled fish tank, a beaker with water, a small fan to produce humidity, and a modified soldering iron to vaporize the Superglue®. Over time, some companies have developed units specially designed for this process that allow for more accurate control of the humidity, temperature of vaporization, and vapor circulation. Different portable systems have also been developed for field work, and some police agencies have built big chambers to accommodate vehicles.

SEE ALSO Alternate light source analysis; Fingerprint; Fluorescence.

Superior SEE Anatomical nomenclature

Supreme court rulings SEE U.S. Supreme Court (rulings on forensic evidence)

Systematics

In its broadest sense, systematics is where nomenclature and taxonomy intersect. Nomenclature is the assignment of accurate names to taxa. A single group is called a taxon; multiple groups are called taxa; the study of taxa is called taxonomy. Taxonomy refers to the scientific method of classifying and organizing living organisms into specific groups according to their phylogenetic relationships. Phylogeny is the study of the evolutionary relationships occurring among living organisms. Classification is the process of putting organisms together into categories based on their relationships to one another.

Carolus Linnaeus (1701–1778), a Swedish scientist and explorer, is considered the originator of the concept of systematics. He created enormous classifications of plants and animals, and published them as *Species Plantarum* (1753) and *Systema Naturae* (tenth edition published in 1758). In the nineteenth century (1800s), those reference volumes were used as the starting point for the modern systems of botanical and zoological nomenclature. One of the reasons that Linnaeus's work was so widely adopted was his use of simple and logical terminology. Another was his hierarchical framework for grouping organisms. (That is, a system in which organisms, such as plants or animals, are grouped in progressive order, from lowest to highest. This was generally done from least complex to most complex.) And finally his use of binomial nomenclature, in which two-word names, consisting of a generic name and a descriptor, were created in combinations which were unique to a specific species. His naming system was based on observed physical similarities and differences between organisms; he called these "characters."

Systematics has developed into the science both of the diversity of living organisms and of their interrelationships. As conceptualized today, the biological science of phylogenetic systematics seeks to develop novel theories and means for classification that transcend the concepts of taxonomy, and consider not only the similarity of characteristics but also evolutionary processes that result in changes in the original **gene** pool. The English naturalist Charles Darwin (1809–1882) was the first scientist to state that systematic hierarchy should reflect similarities and differences in evolutionary history. In the 1950s, a German scientist named Willi Henning suggested the system that has come to be known as phylogenetic systematics; he reasoned that classification of organisms should closely reflect the evolutionary history of specific genetic lines.

On a molecular level and relative to **forensic science**, every organism has a genome that includes all of the biological materials necessary to replicate itself. The genome's information is encoded in the nucleotide sequence of **DNA** and RNA molecules and is subdivided into units called genes. The Human Genome Project, begun in 1990, was designed to identify each gene in human DNA (estimated to be between 20,000 and 25,000), to classify the sequences of chemical base pairs that make up human DNA (about 3 billion), and to store all of this information in a database. From a forensic science standpoint, the more specifically one can classify living organisms, and the more discretely it is possible to map an individual's DNA, the more accurately it will be possible to match a perpetrator to a crime victim or a crime scene.

SEE ALSO DNA databanks; DNA sequences, unique; Reference sample.

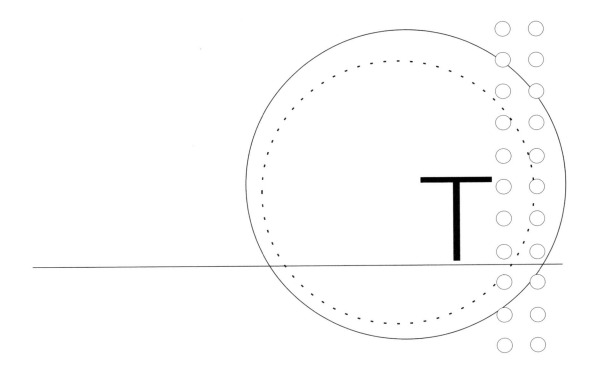

Tabun

Tabun (or "GA") is one of a group of synthetic chemicals that were developed in Germany during the 1930s and 1940s. (Tabun was developed in 1936.) The original intent of these compounds, including tabun, was to control insects. These pesticides were similar to organophosphates (pesticides that contain phosphorus and act as nerve poisons on most animals) in their action on the nervous system. However, tabun and the other human-made nerve agents proved to be much more potent than the organophosphates, and so quickly became attractive as chemical weapons.

Tabun is one of the G-type nerve agents, along with sarin and soman. They are all clear, colorless, and tasteless. As a result, tabun mixes readily with water, and so can be used as a water-poisoning agent. Food can also be contaminated. The fluid form of tabun can also be absorbed through the skin.

When in water, tabun loses its potency relatively quickly, compared to airborne vapors, which can remain potent for a few days. The vapors can even bind to clothing, where they will subsequently be released for 30 minutes or so. People close to the contaminated person can themselves be affected by the vapor. Tabun vapors tend to be denser than air and so settle into low-lying depressions or valleys. People in such regions are especially susceptible.

Like the other members of the G series, tabun is a nerve agent. Specifically, it inhibits an enzyme called cholinesterase. This enzyme breaks apart a compound that acts as a communication bridge between adjacent nerve cells. Normally, the transient formation and destruction of the bridge allows a control over the transmission of nerve impulses. But, the permanent presence of the bridging compound means that nerves "fire" constantly, which causes muscles to tire and eventually stop functioning. In the case of the lungs, this can be fatal.

Symptoms of tabun poisoning, which can begin within minutes of exposure, include runny nose, watery and painful eyes, drooling, excessive sweating, rapid breathing, heart beat abnormalities, and, in severe cases, convulsions, paralysis, and even fatal respiratory failure.

Treatment for the inhalation of tabun consists of three timed injections of a nerve agent antidote such as atropine. Since this may or may not be successful, prevention remains the most prudent strategy. Protective clothing including a gas mask is a wise precaution for forensic investigators who are in an environment where the deployment of tabun is suspected.

SEE ALSO Chemical warfare; Sarin gas.

Tape analysis

One useful tool in the arsenal of a forensic investigator are tapes of telephone conversations and other recordings. These analyses can help determine the identity of the caller and, from background noises, can provide clues as to the location of the call.

Tape analysis of a voice can produce what is known as a voiceprint. Like a fingerprint, a voiceprint can be a unique identifier. A voiceprint relies on anatomical features of the speaker. The dimensions of the vocal cavities including the throat, nose, and mouth, and the length and diameter of the vocal cords are influential acoustic factors in producing a voice whose characteristics are unique to the individual. The chance that more than one person will display the exact voice pattern is very remote.

As well, the interplay of the lips, teeth, tongue, soft palate, and jaw muscles produces intelligible speech, and can also introduce aspects of speech such as a lisp that can help in **identification**. Analysis of the timing and the pitch of the voice can also unearth distinctive intonations.

Tapes can be analyzed to produce a spectrographic pattern of the speech. The aforementioned aspects contribute to this pattern. Attempts to deliberately disguise speech such as whispering, raising or lowering the pitch of the voice, and speaking with an accent, are easily recognized. A suspect may be asked to read a sentence or words in a voice similar to the deliberately altered voice, so as to produce a comparable voice pattern of the two messages. Even the electronic alteration of a voice can be dealt with, since the natural wave form pattern will still be discernable spectrographically, even if the voice is unintelligible to the ear.

Tape analysis is a commonly used facet of law enforcement investigations. Some cases are more famous than others, however. For example, tape analysis of speeches purported to be from the Saudi-born terrorist Osama bin Laden have been carried out to help determine the authenticity of the speaker. Analysis compared the computer-generated wave patterns of the taped voice with other tapes known to be the voice of bin Laden. In particular, common words such as "America" are compared from the different tapes to see if the voice wave patterns are similar or distinct from each other.

While the quality of the recording tape and the acoustics of the room the recording was made in can detract from the analysis, tape analyses of various recordings purported to be from bin Laden as recently as 2004 have concluded that he is the speaker.

SEE ALSO Linguistics, forensic stylistics; Telephone recording system; Voice alteration, electronic; Voice analysis.

Taphonomy

Taphonomy, from the Greek, *taphos*, meaning tomb or grave, and *nomy*, meaning classification, is a field of paleontology, paleo-anthropology, and bioarcheology that studies human and animal remains in relation to the post-mortem (after death) transformations that occur in burial sites. In a broader sense, taphonomy is the study of the processes that leads to fossilization, as well as the stages of transformation of remains through the action of environmental factors. The knowledge gathered by this field is important to **forensic science** as a tool for the analysis of human remains at old crime scenes, mass graves, and mass disaster areas.

Osteology (or the study of bones), geochemistry, and **entomology** (the study of insects) are important aspects of taphonomy, as skeletons and skeletal fragments may yield information on the living conditions, availability of food, presence of infections, wear and tear of specific joints due to repetitive effort, size of muscles, and post-mortem events. Therefore, a scenario of living organism versus environmental characteristics may be inferred from such analysis as well as which forces and agents have acted over the remains after death. When the organism dies and is buried or covered by sedimentary layers of soil, such as clay, sand, volcanic ash, or ice, the taphonomic process of post-mortem transformations begins, which can lead to different types of mummification, **decomposition**, or skeletonization. If the conditions are right, skeletal fossilization will eventually occur. Bones can also be modified by animal scavenging, or be carried by rivers and scattered on riverbanks far from the original site of death before fossilization occurs.

Taphonomy studies three different stages of post-mortem transformation: necrology, biostratinomy, and diagenesis. Necrology refers to the factors present around the **time of death** or directly associated with the **cause of death**. Necrologic studies could include examination of bones or bodies for **skull** fractures, marks of fangs or claws in bones, signs of malnutrition, abscesses, infections, lesions by blunt instruments, bullets, or incineration, among other clues to the cause and events surrounding death. Biostratinomy identifies the changes that occurred after death such as decomposition and changes due to environmental forces acting in burial sites (tombs, graveyards, mass graves), or in places where remains were left or found, such as river or lake bottoms, sedimentary **soils**, or woods. Several events from this stage may leave their marks on the remains, such as animal scavenging, enzymatic and bacterial activity, insect activity, and transportation by water or landslides. Eventually, some bone fragments or entire skeletons may be buried under conditions that favor diagenesis, the process of lithification (compaction) of the sediments that envelop the remains, ultimately resulting in fossilized bones. Fossilization may occur in terrestrial (earth) and maritime (water) environments, and give clues to researchers about the environmental, geological, topographical, and climatic changes that occurred on Earth throughout the process of fossilization. The study of submarine layers of fossilized marine animals and crustaceans, for instance, allows the description of radical climate changes that occurred in different geological eras.

Forensic taphonomy focuses on the perimortem (at the time of death) and intermediate postmortem (days to weeks after death) biological and biochemical transformations in order to determine the cause of death, estimate the approximate time of death, and to identify humans remains including the sex, age, race, and, whenever possible, the individual's identity. The understanding of how different environments interfere with the biological and biochemical changes in human remains, affecting the process of decomposition, is crucial for the forensic interpretation of mass graves, mass disasters, war crimes, and cold cases of **murder**.

SEE ALSO Animal evidence; Anthropology; Body Farm; Death, cause of; Decomposition; Entomology; Exhumation; Geology; Medical examiner; Mummies; Osteology and skeletal radiology; Pathology; Skeletal analysis; War forensics.

Taser

A Taser is a type of gun. It is similar in appearance to a conventional gun, having a handle, squeezable trigger, and a blunt barrel. Instead of firing bullets, however, a Taser incapacitates someone for a short time by the use of electricity. Tasers are most often used by security forces, including police, to quell disturbances without causing injury to the people involved.

The Taser gun is one of three types of weapons that are known collectively as stun guns. The other two devices are known as the hand held stun gun and the liquid stun gun. As their name implies, these weapons are designed to be a non-lethal defense, rather than an offensive weapon capable of causing deadly injury.

Stun guns like the Taser operate by disrupting the electrical flow of signals through nerve cells. This electrical flow drives the ability of the muscles to respond to commands from the brain, and allows information that the body receives from the outside world (i.e., touch, taste, smell) to be communicated to the brain. The disruption of the nerve cells is achieved by the generation of an electrical charge by the Taser that has a high voltage and low amperage. Put another way, the electrical charge has a great deal of pressure, but is not intense. The pressure of the charge allows the charge to penetrate into the body, even through several layers of clothing. In order for it to be effective, the person must be close, even in direct contact, with the electrodes of the Taser. Because the electrical charge is not intense, the brief surge of electricity is not powerful enough to physically damage the person's body.

However, the electricity is powerful enough to temporarily disable the nervous system. This occurs when the added charge mixes with the electrical impulses flowing through the nerve cells. The added electricity overwhelms the meaningful signals, making it impossible for the brain to interpret the signals from the nerve cells. Confusion, difficulty in balance, and muscle paralysis results.

Only about one-quarter of a second is required to incapacitate someone. Once the electrical swamping of the nerve impulses has ceased—within a few seconds to a minute—recovery is complete with no adverse effects. Tests have shown that even heart pacemakers are not affected by Tasers.

The electrical signal from a Taser can be generated as a single burst, or in rapid pulses. If the pulses are similar to the frequency of the natural pulses that occur within the nerve cells, then the muscles are stimulated to contract and relax. However, there is no coordination behind the work, since the connections between the muscles and the brain have been disrupted. The muscles will become depleted of energy and tire. Even when the normal electrical rhythm is restored, the muscles often remain too tired to respond for a short period.

Because a Taser acts on muscles, and as there are muscles all over the body, a Taser applied almost anywhere over the body can cause total immobilization.

Stun guns, including the Taser, consist of a transformer, oscillator, capacitor, and electrodes. The transformer generates the voltage, typically between 20,000 and 150,000 volts. The oscillator introduces the pulsations in the electrical charge. The charge is built up in the capacitor, which releases the charge to the electrodes. It is the electrodes that send the charge into the body, when the electricity bridges the gap between the oppositely charged electrodes.

In a Taser, the electrodes are not fixed in position. Instead, they are positioned on the ends of two long pieces of conducting wire. When a trigger is pulled, a release of compressed gas expels the electrodes out from the gun. In addition, the electrodes have barbs on them, so that they can stick to clothing. This design of the Taser allows a charge to be transferred to someone who is 15 to 20 feet away. Hand-to-hand contact, in this instance, is not necessary. The disadvantage of this design is that only one shot is possible before the electrodes have to rewind, and a new compressed gas cartridge loaded into the gun. Some models of Taser have the attached electrodes, so that if the flying electrodes miss the target, the shooter can move in and try to touch the subject with the stationary electrodes to deliver the stunning dose of electricity.

SEE ALSO Electrical injury and death; Neurotransmitters.

Tattoo identification

A tattoo is a design imprinted onto the skin that can sometimes be a useful mark of **identification** of a non-skeletalized body or a suspect using a false identity. It is believed that tattooing was first practiced in Egypt around 2000 B.C., and its use has spread around the world. Today a wide cross section of the population bears tattoos, from fashion models to known criminals and gang members. The designs are as varied as the people who wear them; names of loved ones are popular, as are symbols denoting membership of a group. Tattoos may be done just for fun, or they may have a more sinister connotation; for instance, prisoners have sometimes been tattooed with numbers, especially in concentration camps. Some elderly people may bear tattoos relating to experience in the Holocaust.

When a pathologist carries out an **autopsy**, he or she will look for and record tattoos in the same way as for any other **body marks** that could be identifying, like scars or birthmarks. The location and nature of the tattoo are the identifying features. A tattoo is made by inserting dyes or inks into piercings created by a needle. One approach to identifying the body is to extract a tiny amount of the dye and subject it to laboratory analysis. The pigments can be identified by techniques such as atomic absorption **spectro-**

scopy or **thin layer chromatography** and may be traceable back to a specific tattoo artist. Black pigments may contain carbon, reds mercuric chloride, and greens potassium dichromate.

Tattoos are valuable identification marks because they tend to be permanent. They can be removed, but they do not fade, and they persist even if the outer layer of skin has perished. The color may, however, change with exposure to the sun. Typically, blue pigment may turn black or purple.

When it comes to identifying a corpse, family members may be aware of the existence of a tattoo and this can be used as a distinguishing mark even if the body itself has been dismembered or otherwise mutilated. In one famous case, dating back from 1935, two fishermen caught a shark off the coast of Sydney, Australia, and took it to a local aquarium where the animal proceeded to disgorge a human arm. The limb appeared to have been severed by a knife, seeming to rule out a shark attack as the **cause of death**. It looked, rather, as if the corpse had been dismembered and disposed of at sea. The arm also bore a distinctive tattoo of two boxers squaring up for a fight. This led to the identification of the victim as James Smith, an ex-boxer with a criminal past. His wife recognized the tattoo, and **fingerprint evidence** confirmed the identity. Suspects were arrested, but the defense argued that an arm alone was insufficient evidence to convict, even if it did carry a tattoo and fingerprints. The case became known as the Shark Arm Murder.

Statistics show that people with anti-social personality disorder are often involved in crime, and they are also more likely to bear a tattoo than the rest of the population. The reason for this is unknown, but the tattoo can be a useful way of identifying these people. Indeed, this may be why criminals on parole sometimes can be identified through their tattoos if they run into more trouble. Often an ex-convict will have a tattoo bearing his name, his street name, or the name of a loved one. If he carries a gun, he may reveal this through a tattoo of the weapon. Wearing a tattoo may be a part of gang and criminal culture. For some people, the tattoo is an important part of belonging and of intimidating others. Certain gangs have distinctive tattoos. In California, the CALGANG database stores data on gang tattoos. This is a useful resource for the investigator who finds a tattoo on a corpse suspected of being the victim of a gangland killing or similar incident.

In Florida, a database has recently been created which includes around 372,000 tattoo records. All of these have been found on examination of criminals

Although usually obtained for cultural reasons, tattoos serve as identifying features for the body. © HENRY DILTZ/CORBIS

serving sentences in the state's prisons. Any investigator discovering a tattoo on a suspect or body can now utilize this database to try to find an identifying match. On its own, a tattoo may be insufficient evidence of identity, but it can be crucial when placed in the context of the whole investigation.

SEE ALSO Identification; Profiling.

Karen T. Taylor

1952–
AMERICAN
FORENSIC ARTIST

During the last two decades of the twentieth century, Karen T. Taylor worked as a forensic artist for at the Texas Department of Public Safety (DPS). In that position, she reconstructed facial features of the dead and drew composite sketches of criminals. As one of only thirty certified professional forensic

artists at that time, Taylor became internationally renowned for her facial reconstruction skills. Her work helped capture numerous criminals within the United States.

Taylor, born and raised in Texas, developed an early aptitude for sketching faces. She attended the University of Texas's School of Fine Arts and the Chelsea School of Fine Art in London. While in England, she worked as a portrait sculptor for Madame Tussaud's Wax Museum. Returning to Texas, Taylor found a job as an illustrator for the DPS; when detectives discovered her talent for drawing realistic facial sketches, she transitioned into the role of full-time forensic artist.

While working for the DPS, Taylor developed successful interviewing skills and produced incredibly accurate and detailed sketches. These sketches led to the arrests of many suspects accused of rape and **murder**. In order to develop her facial reconstruction skills, Taylor studied the techniques of Betty Pat Gatliff, an Oklahoma forensic sculptor considered a pioneer in the field. Taylor later used these facial reconstruction abilities to help identify missing persons and work on documentaries, studies, and other projects.

Throughout her career, Taylor served as a forensic art instructor at the **FBI** Academy and other international universities, medical schools, and law enforcement academies. She is also the author of *Forensic Art and Illustration*, which is considered an important text in the field of forensic art. Her artwork has been featured on numerous television programs, including *America's Most Wanted*. In addition, a character on the popular television drama *CSI:* was based on Taylor and her work.

In 1999, Taylor retired from the Texas Department of Public Safety. She continues to work as a forensic artist, but also works on fine art commissions from her studio in Austin. In 2002 she became the first woman to win the John A. Dondero Award from the **International Association for Identification**.

SEE ALSO Composite drawing; Identification; Television shows.

Technology and forensic science

Forensic science is a rapidly growing discipline and the tools available to forensic researchers are also evolving quickly. Painstaking protocols for

DNA collection, extraction, quantification, amplification, detection, and analysis have now been replaced by commercially available kits, high-throughput instrumentation, and computer algorithms. With these technologies, forensic scientists have the tools in hand to fortify databases and solve even the most complicated crimes.

There are several steps involved in the process of DNA analysis. These are collection, extraction, quantification, amplification, detection, and analysis. Each step can be accomplished by different methods and can encounter complications. In order to accurately determine a profile from a DNA sample and ensure it is admissible in a court of law, the process must be documented and the protocols followed appropriately.

Sample collection is the first step of **processing** a forensic sample for DNA analysis. Because contamination can instantly ruin a sample, the investigator at the scene must make cautious efforts not to touch any part of the sample. For example, a **blood** spot found on an article of clothing at the scene of a crime is easily contaminated with the investigator's DNA if it is picked up by a non-gloved hand. Therefore, forensic investigators and police at crime scenes wear gloves and immediately deposit samples in sealed bags or containers. Scene of crime samples can be in myriad of forms: hair found at the scene, an article of clothing, a piece of chewing gum, or the end of a cigarette, for example. All of these are collected, placed in sterile containers, and brought to the forensic laboratory for investigation.

Samples collected for reference databases are more straightforward than scene-of-crime samples. Reference samples are collected from the offender once he or she is arrested or found guilty. Whether or not a sample can be taken before the alleged perpetrator is convicted in court depends on the country and even the state in which the crime was committed. The most common means of **reference sample** collection is by buccal swab. This method involves using a sterile swab to wipe the inside of the subject's mouth. DNA is later isolated from the cheek cells attached to the swab. Other methods include drawing blood from the individual and storing it on an FTA® card. These are thick pieces of specialized, sterile paper on which a drop of blood can be absorbed and the DNA can be isolated later. Regardless of the method of collection, all samples are taken to the laboratory for further processing.

When a forensic investigator obtains a sample from which DNA must be analyzed, DNA must first be extracted from the sample. This is the case with either a scene-of-crime sample or a reference database sample. In the case of the latter, DNA extraction is much easier. Commercially available protocols exist for isolating DNA from buccal swabs or FTA® cards. Similarly, many companies now offer kits for the extraction of more complex scene of crime samples. Specialized protocols are available to isolate DNA from trace samples such as cigarette butts or blue jeans. DNA extraction kits are based on one of several different methods. The most basic means is an extraction using phenol-chloroform or alcohol precipitation. These methods are the most common in homemade methods. Kits are also available that use ion exchange resins or silica-based columns to isolate and purify the DNA. One of the newest techniques for DNA isolation involves the use of magnetic beads and specialized buffers. By adjusting the ionic charge of the environment surrounding the sample, DNA will stick to the magnetic beads and can be exposed to a series of buffers to remove contaminants.

A variety of manufacturers are now producing automated machines to aid in the extraction of DNA from forensic samples. Automated systems are available for all different types of chemistries, columns, and magnetic-bead-based extractions described above. There are many benefits to automated DNA extraction; it involves less hands-on time by technicians and thus, has a lower likelihood of contamination or human error with the protocol. Also, automated systems can be very simple and do not require that the laboratory staff be highly trained and specialized. Finally, the use of automated extraction allows for the processing of many more samples a day than manual methods, which can be quite time consuming.

Once the DNA is extracted and quantified, it must be amplified by **PCR (polymerase chain reaction)**. The **PCR** method involves three steps: denaturing, annealing, and extension, which are performed in an instrument called a thermalcycler. In more detail, DNA is placed in a reaction tube containing buffers, primers, nucleotides and an enzyme known as Taq polymerase. During the denaturing step, the mixture is subjected to high temperatures so that the double strands of DNA separate. Next, the temperature is lowered to one that allows for annealing of the specific primers to their sequence counterparts on the DNA of the sample. Finally, the temperature in the thermalcycler changes to the optimal temperature for the enzyme Taq polymerase, which extends the regions of DNA between the primers by adding the nucleotides, thus making a copy. The same reaction repeats over many cycles of these three steps resulting in an exponential amplification of the regions between the primers.

The forensic researcher chooses primers for specific sequences of the genome that show regions around the **gene** sequences that are common amongst individuals. The result of the PCR reaction is then copies of the sequences that differ in the regions between the primers. Several different companies now offer kits that contain all the necessary reagents to amplify STR profiles. Specific kits are even available to amplify only male DNA. The kits also include standards, or specific fragments of DNA of known size to determine the length of each gene sequence. This is important, as the length of the gene sequence is what differs among individuals. The number of repeats in the sequence determines its length. Accumulation of the various repeat regions provides a profile that is specific to a particular person.

In the detection step, the forensic researcher visualizes the DNA. The sequences of the amplified DNA are visualized on a gel that allows for the determination of the number of repeats in the sequence regions. The fluorescent dyes included in some kits help to visualize the sequences. Contemporary forensic scientists tend to use nucleic acid analyzers and automated sequencers for detection of DNA sequences. These automated methods remove the potential subjectivity of the analysis if performed by manual means. The DNA sequences are then entered into a computer and software is used to calculate and store the sequences. Then, sequences of the reference sample or scene-of-crime sample are compared via software programs to other gene sequence profiles in the database. Forensic scientists look for matches to assist them with their investigation.

Automation is commonplace in today's forensic laboratory for the amplification, detection, and analysis steps, as well. Most laboratories performing DNA analysis are equipped with a variety of instruments including extraction systems, thermalcyclers, nucleic acid analyzers, and gene analysis software. What was once was a complex manual process taking days can be accomplished with instruments in only a few hours. Automated methods must be validated, similar to manual methods, to ensure they meet the standards and guidelines set forth by the governing bodies in forensic science, such as **Interpol** or the Federal Bureau of Investigation.

Following collection, the processes of DNA extraction, quantification, amplification, detection, and analysis can be performed with almost no intervention of the forensic scientist. Automation has revolutionized the forensic laboratory to almost a high-tech factory. With the aid of automated systems, forensic scientists are not only processing their current case samples, but also chipping away at the large backlog of reference samples. DNA databases are building up at a rapid pace, which will ensure that investigators have the best chance of finding a match and solving a crime.

SEE ALSO DNA; DNA databanks; DNA fingerprint; DNA isolation methods; DNA profiling; Electrophoresis; European Network of Forensic Science Institutes; Interpol; Nucleic Acid Analyzer (HANAA); PCR (polymerase chain reaction); STR (short tandem repeat) analysis; Trace evidence.

Ludwig Karl Teichmann
1823–1895
POLISH
ANATOMIST

Ludwig Karl Teichmann was a Polish anatomist and physician who made an enduring contribution to **forensic science** with his discovery of the Teichmann test for **hemoglobin**. Also called the Teichmann crystal, this is a test that is used on dried stains to determine whether or not **blood** is present. Dr. Teichmann made his forensic discovery in 1853. His microcrystalline test remains in use today as a means of identifying whether or not dried stains at a crime scene, on clothing or other fabric, or elsewhere at the site of a forensic investigation contain (human) blood.

Teichmann attended medical school in Gottingen, Germany. After completion of his studies, he remained at the university as an anatomy professor. In 1853, Teichmann published a scientific paper in which he described the crystallization of several **organic compounds** contained in human blood. Within his research paper, he explained a process by which microscopic crystals of hemin could be prepared. Hemin is a substance made up of reddish brown, microscopic, prismatic crystals; it is formed from dried blood by the action of common salt and strong acetic acid (the substance in vinegar that gives it a distinctive odor and pungent taste).

Blood begins to dry after 3–5 minutes of exposure to air, and drips or spatters (blood that is not in large quantities, like pooled blood) typically form crusts quite quickly. Dried blood can readily be confused with other substances, both organic and inorganic, at a crime scene. That is why, when a black, brown, brownish-black, or very dark red substance is found at a crime scene, it is necessary to determine whether or not it is actually blood. The Teichmann test is a presumptive test for blood; it is used strictly to screen for the presence or absence of blood. A positive result from a crystalline test is an indication to go ahead and use other tests to confirm.

SEE ALSO Blood spatter; Bloodstain evidence; Cast-off blood; Crime scene investigation; Criminalistics.

Telephone caller identification (caller ID)

Electronic and digital information that is generated in the normal course of electronic communication can be valuable in the forensic tracing of the course of events in an accident or crime, and in the **identification** of a victim or assailant.

Caller identification, or caller ID, permits the receiver of a call to identify the caller's location. Available since the early 1990s, it has enhanced the sense of privacy enjoyed by people in their homes, and has also greatly reduced the number of prank calls, as well as calls made with threatening or criminal intent.

In the late 1980s and 1990s, telephone companies made such technology available. A caller ID box, or a caller ID unit built into a phone, simply reads the computerized information for the incoming call, assuming it is coming from a listed number. Calls from an unlisted number register as "Unknown Caller" or "Private Caller." Available on internal private branch exchange (PBX) telephone systems during the 1980s, caller ID gained use by businesses offering toll-free numbers in 1988. By 2005, over 50% of homes nationwide had caller ID.

SEE ALSO Dial tone decoder.

Telephone recording system

Electronic and digital information is a part of everyday communication. Recording or recovery of this information can be vital in the forensic investigation of an accident or crime, and in the **identification** of a victim or assailant. Telephone conversations can be easily recorded and can provide a wealth of information to a forensic scientist.

A telephone recording system can be as simple as a handheld phone receiver with an analogue (non-computerized, non-digital) recorder. In such a situation, the act of recording is hard to hide. On the other hand, some telephone recording systems are so seamless that the individual being recorded would not know he or she was being recorded someone unless informed them. For this reason, some states require that the person being recorded be informed of this fact, and many states require that the recorder emit a regular beep or other sound to serve as a reminder of the ongoing recording.

Consumers today are able to buy telephone recording systems that hook into the telephone line just as an answering machine would. Such systems, which retail from under $100, make it possible to begin recording as soon as the receiver is lifted. Twelve states require two-party notification, meaning that both participants in a recorded conversation must be informed of the fact that they are being recorded.

Digital systems are capable of saving a recorded call in a digital audio format, as a .wav file, making it possible for a user to e-mail a recording of a conversation.

SEE ALSO Tape analysis; Telephone tap detector.

Telephone tap detector

Telephone conversations can be monitored and recorded. Law enforcement personnel may even, with court permission, tap a phone to acquire information that can potentially be useful in a prosecution. But technology can also thwart this effort. When a telephone tap is suspected, an individual can acquire technology to detect the monitoring device.

A telephone tap detector aids communication security by providing electronic recognition of attempts to intercept a call through wiretapping or listening devices. Telephone tapping is, at least in certain particulars, an exact science, and tap detection technology must likewise be efficient to counteract those efforts. With telephone tapping no longer an extremely infrequent aspect of daily life, tap detectors have become a popular item among security-conscious consumers.

In tapping into a phone line, surveillance personnel use technology akin to that which an electrician might apply in attempting to siphon power from an electric line. However, whereas an electric wire attached to a circuit receives a regular supply of power, a telephone tap cannot maintain constant access to a telephone line, or it would be too easy to detect. Instead, the tap "seizes" the telephone line as a call is coming in.

The tap is most likely to engage between the first and third ring of an incoming call, and from that point onward, assuming all conditions are reasonably favorable for surveillance, the tap remains in effect for the duration of the call. A telephone tap detector recognizes this seizure of the phone line, and provides further verification once the call concludes. Depending on the number and timing of disconnection reactions after the receiver is reengaged, a good tap detector (consumer models sell for several hundred dollars) can determine whether wiretapping equipment is in the process of disengaging from the phone line.

SEE ALSO Telephone caller identification (caller ID).

Television shows

Since television's infancy, crime dramas, especially police procedurals, have been perennial favorites among viewers. Such shows typically focus on police detectives as they investigate the scene of a crime, gather clues, sift through suspects, and eventually bring the perpetrator to justice, either in court or at the end of a gun. At the center of many of these dramas are the mean streets of a big city, with its stew of suspects and complex motivations, as in the 1970s hit *The Streets of San Francisco*. Co-starring are the detectives themselves: strong, swift of foot, sure of shot, blessed with infallible instincts. The role that forensics is likely to play in these shows, though, is likely to be only a passing one. A detective orders a **ballistics** test run on a bullet removed from a murder victim. A subordinate finds a bit of fiber, a hair, or a suspicious cigarette butt, and the lead detective barks, "Run that down to trace!," the lab in the bowels of police headquarters where technicians examine **trace evidence** and read its story. In the past, though, those technicians rarely emerged from anonymity. Science was not considered as interesting to viewers as shootouts, car chases, or dramatic interrogations of suspects.

When science made an occasional appearance in past shows, it was generally in the figure of the **coroner**, whose bailiwick was where science and crime investigation intersected. From 1976 to 1983,

for example, veteran actor Jack Klugman starred as the title character in 147 episodes of *Quincy, M.E.* (viewers never learned his first name). As chief **medical examiner**, Quincy served as the catalyst behind crime investigations, teasing clues out of bodies that less intrepid investigators would have overlooked. The show broke ground for its relatively high level of realism. Its forensic consultant had been a scientist in the Los Angeles Medical Examiners office, and his on-screen role as a technician enabled him to operate complex equipment rather than trying to teach actors to do it. One episode of the show, in which Quincy used bite marks to identify a killer, was credited with helping solve a rape case in the Midwest after a nurse, having watched the episode, photographed bite marks on a victim.

By the late 1990s and early 2000s, though, a change had taken place. Many television crime shows had replaced gruff, street-smart detectives with teams of polished forensic lab scientists—the result, according to some observers, of America's fascination with the televised O. J. Simpson murder trial, with its dramatic testimony about **DNA**, **blood spatter**, and other forensic **evidence**. Sweaty interrogation rooms and the litter of coffee cups in stakeout cars had given way to smartly appointed labs and the clutter of pipettes and gas chromatographs, and the neatly pressed lab coat had replaced the rumpled suit.

The flagship of this new crop of shows was the CBS hit *CSI: Crime Scene Investigation*, launched in 2000 under the direction of Jerry Bruckheimer and starring William Petersen as the brooding, scholarly Gil Grissom and Marg Helgenberger as his female counterpart, ex-stripper Catherine Willows. While the show explores the human drama of its cast of characters, always at the center is the forensic evidence, which infallibly guides police to the wrongdoers.

In an episode aired on February 17, 2005, for example, the team is called to a Las Vegas mansion where a casino mogul is lying dead, having fallen, jumped, or been pushed from a second-story balcony. The team takes careful note of the crime scene: no **tire tracks**, no **cast-off blood**, the head's position relative to the pool of **blood** suggesting that the body had been moved, a suspicious oil leak in the driveway, greasy palm prints on the balcony ledge, and the floor of the upstairs study. Examination of the body back at the lab finds no drugs in the blood but eventually turns up LSD in the victim's urine and, bizarrely, breast milk in his stomach. Attention focuses on the man's wife, whose bloody shoes were found in the trash. Comparison of the shape of the shoes with the pattern of blood on the ground near the victim's head suggests that the wife stood nearby and watched her husband die. Further, the investigators examine the hard drive on the home's electronic security system, which recorded the time when doors were opened, including the garage door. By recreating the timeline of events, the investigators determine that after arriving home, pulling into the garage, and finding her husband on the ground, the wife waited an hour before calling 911. Eventually, the team pieces together what happened: that the disturbed husband engaged in elaborate infantile fantasies (the palm prints were left by baby lotion) and that a woman he forced into the role of nursemaid administered the LSD, which caused him to hurl himself off the balcony. The wife, her eye on his estate, was happy to allow him to die.

CSI became so successful, often the highest rated show for the week, that it became a franchise with two spin-offs: the hip, sun-bronzed *CSI: Miami* and the darker and moodier *CSI: NY*. In 2003 CBS also premiered *NCIS* (Naval Criminal Investigative Service), in which lead investigator Jethro Gibbs, played by heartthrob Mark Harmon, relies heavily on the scientific expertise of his medical examiner, quirky Renaissance man "Ducky" Mallard, and Abby, an uninhibited, tattooed forensic specialist who dresses in Goth clothing. By then, the roster of shows with prominent forensic themes, including both dramas and documentaries, was growing almost exponentially. On cable television, the Court TV channel had four shows: *I, Detective; Body of Evidence; Extreme Evidence;* and the network's signature series, *Forensic Files*. The Learning Channel had *Medical Detectives*. The Discovery channel featured *The New Detectives: Case Studies in Forensic Science, The Prosecutors: In Pursuit of Justice, The FBI Files,* and *The Justice Files,* and on the Discovery Health channel was *Dr. G.: Medical Examiner*. On A&E (Arts and Entertainment) were *Cold Case Files, Investigative Reports,* and *American Justice*. NBC had *Law and Order: Special Victims Unit* and *Crossing Jordan*, the latter with a technician nicknamed "Bug" who was often called on to bring his knowledge of **entomology** to bear on murder cases. What all of these shows had in common, to a greater or lesser extent, was the prominent place they gave to such forensic themes as fiber analysis, blood samples, blood spatter, DNA analysis, fingerprinting, shoeprint **casting**, and handwriting analysis—all

with the help of a panoply of high-tech gadgetry that became the envy of real forensic labs around the country.

In August 2002, Court TV capitalized on the popularity of these shows by airing a bundle of programs under the title "Forensics Week." Included were five new episodes of *Forensics Files*, during which viewers could "join the investigation" by logging on to the network's website and entering interactive, virtual forensics labs, including rooms devoted to **computer forensics** and linguistic forensics. Additionally, "Forensics Week" included two documentaries, one documenting an unsolved 1973 case that was reopened in 1995 and solved through new forensic techniques, the other documenting a three-year murder investigation solved with the help of FBI profilers and a handwriting expert. That week, too, Court TV's Mobile Investigation Unit (MIU), a traveling forensic lab, wrapped up a 20-city tour at the Children's Museum in Manhattan. The lab allowed visitors to take part in a "caper scene" and solve a crime using fingerprints, **handwriting analysis**, and fiber analysis.

Purists objected to technical and procedural flaws in such shows as *CSI*. They note, for example, the tendency of the shows to enhance drama by having investigators work in the dark, when in reality investigators set up floodlights to illuminate crime scenes. But science educators were delighted with the public's new fascination with forensics on television. Colleges and universities in the United States and around the world saw sharp increases in the number of students taking courses in such subjects as forensic **pathology**. In 2004 The College of New Jersey launched a 10-year, $2.2 million effort to develop a **criminology** and **forensic science** program, fueled in large part by the popularity of forensic television. Singer Britney Spears was quoted as saying that she was growing tired of her status as a pop icon and, because of such shows as *CSI*, wanted to pursue a career in forensic science.

One of the most tangible effects of the interest in forensic television was its usefulness for educators in making science more accessible to students. In connection with the MIU's stop at the Children's Museum, Court TV announced the kickoff of its Forensics in the Classroom (FIC) program. Developed in partnership with the **American Academy of Forensic Sciences** and the National Science Teachers Association, FIC bridged the gap between scientific theory and applications in the real world by requiring students to gather data, think logically about the connections between data and explanations, analyze

Actors David Anders, George Eads, and Marg Helgenberger on an episode of *CSI: Crime Scene Investigation*. CBS/LANDOV

hypotheses, and communicate results, all goals of the science classroom. Teachers could download classroom units and lesson plans, complete with lab activities that take students step-by-step through the scientific investigation of a pretend crime. In *The Cafeteria Caper*, students use DNA, hair, and blood analysis and conduct an enzyme test to determine who was responsible for an act of school vandalism. *It's Magic* uses handwriting analysis, a pH test, and paper **chromatography** to solve a "dognapping" case. *The Car That Swims* uses footprint casting to expose a girl's false statements about a car found in a river. *Renters Beware* requires students to conduct a flame test, a Kastle-Meyer test, and **fingerprint** analysis to uncover a plot involving a money-hungry landlord with a mysterious chemistry lab.

SEE ALSO American Academy of Forensic Sciences; Bite analysis; Blood spatter; Careers in forensic science; Casting; Cast-off blood; Chromatography; Coroner; Crime scene investigation; Hair analysis; Handwriting analysis; Medical examiner; Simpson (O. J.) murder trial; Trace evidence.

Terrorism, biological SEE Bioterrorism

Test controls SEE Control samples

Thanatology

Thanatology is the science that studies the events surrounding death, as well as the social, legal, and psychological aspects of death. The term thanatology originates from the Greek *thanatos*, meaning death and *logos*, for study or discourse. Thanatologists may study the cause of deaths, legal implications of death such as the rights and destiny of the remains or requirements for **autopsy**, and social aspects surrounding death. Grief, customs surrounding burial and remembrance, and other social attitudes about death are frequent subjects of interest for thanatologists.

From the forensic point of view, causes of death may be due to natural causes, such as from lethal disease or advanced age), accidental causes, such as falls, plain crashes, fires, drowning, or **automobile accidents**, criminal actions, such as **murder**, neglect, malpractice, or other irresponsible acts by third parties, and finally, suicide. Thanatology also overlaps forensics when it focuses on the changes that occur in the body in the period near death and afterwards.

Some social issues explored by thanatologists, such as euthanasia (the merciful induction of death to stop suffering) and abortion (termination of a pregnancy) are subject to much ethical and legal controversy. These issues are legal in some countries, while considered a crime in other countries. In Brazil, for instance, although outright euthanasia is illegal, patients have the right to refuse medical treatment and artificial life supporting procedures, if they sign a legal statement in advance while of sound mind.

Rights over the corpse of the deceased is also determined by law in most developed countries, as well as burial, cremation, and embalming requirements. Clinical autopsies are generally required in cases of unexplained or violent death, suspicion of suicide, drug overdose, or when requested by the family of the deceased due to suspicion of medical error or when confirmation of certain diseases is sought.

The thanatology community is usually composed of a variety of health professionals including psychiatrists and other physicians such as forensic pathologists, advanced practice nurses, and veterinarians, along with sociologists and psychologists.

SEE ALSO Assassination; Autopsy; Body marks; Coroner; Death, cause of; Death, mechanism of; Decomposition; Drowning (signs of); Entomology; Ethical issues; Exhumation; Fluids; Medical examiner; Parasitology; Pathogens; Pathology; Saliva; Semen and sperm; Serology; Skeletal analysis; Time of death; Toxicology.

Thin layer chromatography

A central part of many forensic investigations is the analysis of materials that are recovered from the scene of the investigation. A mainstay technique used to separate and identify individual components in a mixture of compounds is **chromatography**.

One type of chromatography that is relevant in **forensic science** is thin layer chromatography (TLC). TLC is a type of liquid chromatography that can separate chemical compounds of differing struc-

ture based on the rate at which they move through a support under defined conditions.

TLC is useful in detecting chemicals of forensic concern, including chemical weapons, **explosives**, and **illicit drugs**. Advances in TLC technology, largely driven by the efforts to quell terrorism, have benefited forensic science. As one example, the Forensic Service Center of Lawrence Livermore National Laboratory has designed a computerized and portable TLC machine that can be taken to the field, and which has the ability to analyze 20 samples at a time. Analysis can be completed within 30 minutes. This allows an analysis that previously required a dedicated laboratory to be done at the scene.

The current TLC technology was introduced by Justus Kirchner in 1951. From its beginning, the technique was an inexpensive, reliable, fast, and easy to perform means of distinguishing different compounds from each other. The method was qualitative—it showed the presence of a compound but not how much of the compound was present. In the late 1960s, TLC was refined so that it could reliably measure the amounts of compounds. In other words, the technique became quantitative. Further refinement reduced the thickness of the support material and increased the amount of the separating material that could be packed into the support. In High Performance TLC (HPTLC) the resolution of chemically similar compounds is better than with conventional TLC, and less sample is required. HPTLC requires specialized analysis equipment, and so is still not as popular or widespread as conventional TLC.

In TLC a solution of the sample is added to a layer of support material (i.e., grains of silica or alumina) that has been spread out and dried on a sheet of material such as glass. The support is known as the plate. The sample is added as a spot at one end of the plate. The plate is then put into a sealed chamber that contains a shallow pool of chemicals (the solvent), which is just enough to wet the bottom of the plate. As the solvent moves up through the plate support layer by capillary action, the sample is dragged along. The different chemical constituents of the sample do not move at the same speed, however, and will become physically separated from one another. The positions of the various sample constituents and their chemical identities are determined by physical methods (i.e., ultraviolet light) or by the addition of other chemical sprays that react with the sample constituents.

SEE ALSO Analytical instrumentation; Toxicology.

Time of death

The determination of time of death is of crucial importance for forensic investigators, especially when they are gathering **evidence** that can support or deny the stated actions of suspects in a crime. The time elapsed from the moment of death until a corpse is discovered is also known as the postmortem interval, or PMI.

Both the time of death and the postmortem interval cannot be determined with 100% accuracy, particularly when a body is found in advanced state of **decomposition** or is recovered from fire, water, or ice. Therefore, time of death and PMI are given as estimates, and can vary from hours to days, or from months to years, depending on each particular case.

Evidence for estimating time of death includes **physical evidence** present in the corpse (postmortem changes, presence of insects, etc.), environmental evidence such as location where the body was found (indoors, outdoors, buried, burned, in water, etc.), and other evidence found at the crime scene (a stopped wrist watch due to a blow or impact, an answering machine record, a 911 call, phone calls received or made around the time of the assault, etc.), and finally, the historical evidence (habits and daily routine of the victim, relationships, existence of enemies, etc). The knowledge of the internal sequential changes a dead body undergoes in relation to the variations on the rate of their occurrence due to ambient temperature, humidity, and the presence of insects or other predators are all considered when estimating the time of death.

The classical method of estimating time of death is the rate method, which measures postmortem (after death) stages and the types of transformation a body undergoes such as cooling rates (algor mortis), stiffening (**rigor mortis**), initiation and duration, postmortem **lividity** (discoloration stains), degree of putrefaction, **adipocere** (body fat saponification), and maceration (tissue softening due to the presence of liquid). Not all these stages take place in a single cadaver. Adipocere, for instance, is not common in most male adult corpses. It occurs most often in women or obese adult individuals and children, requiring enough humidity or the presence of water to take place. The process of maceration occurs at known rates in fetuses that died in the womb. Stomach contents can reveal the stage of digestion of the last meal at the time of death. The time of onset and rates of each postmortem transformative event are also subjected to variations originated by existing chronic diseases, types of medication, and individual metabolic characteristics. These variables are known as endogenous factors. For example, if the deceased individual was taking **antibiotics** at the time of death, the internal process of bacterial-mediated putrefaction may be delayed beyond the normal observed rates, thus masking the real PMI.

Algor mortis, or the process of body cooling, is a useful parameter for PMI estimation during the first 24 hours after death, as the internal body temperature drops at known rates. However, these rates are valid only in cool or temperate climates because hot summer seasons or tropical temperatures slow down the loss of heat and, in some regions, can even raise postmortem temperatures due to rapid putrefaction through bacterial activity inside the digestive tract. Algor mortis rates are measured with a thermometer or through the use of a multiple-probe thermometer that measures the cooling rate of the brain, liver, and rectum. Other variables interfering with postmortem cooling rates include the size of the body, amount of subcutaneous (under the skin) adipose (fatty) tissue, existence of clothing and coverings, air currents and humidity, and the medium where the body remained after death (such as inside a closed car, under water, on ice or snow, or inside a metallic container).

Rigor mortis, or postmortem stiffening and contraction of all muscles, usually occurs three or more hours after death and can last for approximately 36–48 hours in temperate climates and about 9–12 hours in tropical temperatures. If a murderer moves a body before rigor mortis (RM), the new position will be "frozen" during RM, not the original one that would have characterized the pattern of the body falling at the crime scene. Therefore, the position a body shows during rigor mortis cannot be assumed as the position in which the victim was at the moment of death. The rigor mortis phase is not the best time for the pathologist to determine the **cause of death**, because several changes take place in the internal muscles, such as the heart and the ocular muscles, which can be misleading. For example, rigor mortis dilates the myocardial (heart) muscles, giving it the appearance of cardiac hypertrophy (enlarged heart). Contraction of the iris muscles also dilates the pupils during rigor mortis.

The factors that interfere with the onset and duration of rigor mortis are temperature, existing antemortem pathologies, age, body muscular mass, and the degree of muscular activity immediately before death. Higher temperatures shorten the time till the onset of rigor mortis and its time of duration. A strong fight or lengthy physical effort before death causes an earlier onset and shorter duration of rigor mortis. Children and older adults have also earlier rigor mortis than younger adults. Generalized infections, or long, debilitating diseases also produce earlier onsets and shorter periods of rigor mortis, whereas extensive antemortem bleeding or death due to asphyxia delays rigor mortis onset.

Livor mortis, or postmortem lividity, is characterized by the reddish/purple discoloration of the skin, sometimes with a pink border, in consequence of the lack of the arterial pressure that counteracts the gravitational force. Therefore, when blood circulation ceases, the blood is gradually deposited in the lower internal vessels and in the lower parts of the body, with the signs of livor mortis usually appearing within the first hour after death. However, in many cases it can appear 2–3 hours after death, and is usually fixed after about 12 hours. Livor mortis rates of appearance are delayed by severe anemia and starvation, but can be present before death in individuals slowly dying from circulatory insufficiency.

Postmortem decomposition or putrefaction consists of the destruction of soft tissues, usually starting internally through the action of microorganisms present in the stomach and bowel and in the nasal pharyngeal pathways. Open wounds also provide access to bacteria from the environment to the body. Obesity accelerates the putrefaction process, as well as infectious conditions, congestive cardiac failure, or when edema (swelling with fluid) is present. Conversely, extensive external bleeding during death or severe dehydration delays the putrefaction onset. As mentioned before, temperatures may accelerate or delay putrefaction onset and rates. Gases derived from the putrefaction process are used to estimate time of death, known as the Brouardel method. According to this approach, in the first postmortem 24 hours, abdominal gases are not flammable; between the second and the fourth day they are flammable; from the fifth day on, they are not flammable again. Putrefaction stains start to form on the abdominal skin around 24–36 hours after death in temperate climates and in 12–18 hours in tropical regions. These stains are green and gradually appear all over the body between the third and the fifth day after death. As the blood undergoes putrefaction, crystal blades are formed in fragmented or clustered patterns, crisscrossed and colorless. These crystals start forming after the third day and can remain in the blood up to 35 days. Determining time of death by observing blood crystals is known as the Westernhoffer-Rocha-Valverde method, and was first applied in forensic **medicine** by the Brazilian forensic pathologists Martinho da Rocha and Belmiro Valverde.

The first postmortem transformative event, known as autolysis, consists of spontaneous self-destruction of tissues by enzymes present in the cells without bacterial interference. One of the byproducts of autolysis is the building up of potassium ions concentrations known as vitreous humor potassium (VHP), and occurs during the first 20 postmortem hours. The quantitative analysis of the concentration rates of VHP is one of the methods for PMI estimation, which yields the best results when combined with other measurements.

Postmortem tissue survival rates constitute another PMI estimation method. Different types of tissues lose their vital properties in different moments of the postmortem interval. For instance **sperm** cells show mobility for about 36 hours after death. Muscles react to electrical or mechanical stimuli for a postmortem interval of six hours, and pupils can be dilated with atropine until four hours after death. Leukocytes, the white blood cells, die at the following PMI rates: 8% during the first 5 hours; 58% within 30 hours; and 95% within 70 hours.

Corpses exposed to outdoor environments attract insects with different behavioral habits and life cycles. Another modern technique utilized in time of death estimation involves forensic **entomology**. Forensic entomology utilizes insects on or surrounding the body, as well as their eggs and larvae, to estimate the amount of time a body has been dead and left in a certain environment. Entomology is useful as a forensic tool because the life cycles of insects are both well known and predictable. In addition, the succession of colonization of a corpse by insects occurs in temporally specific waves of different species.

Once a person or animal has died, insects that have access to the corpse colonize it very rapidly. The succession of inhabitants in terms of species and life cycle stage is clearly understood. This succession can then be used to determine several aspects of the crime. These include post-mortem interval, location of the murder, where the body was stored, and whether or not it had been moved.

The first insects to approach and colonize a dead body are usually species of blowfly (*Diptera: Calliphoridae*) or the flesh fly (*Sarcophagidae*). These holometabolous insects quickly deposit their eggs on an exposed corpse, and maggots, the larval form, are often found feeding on dead bodies. A forensic entomologist would be able, with the use of a microscope, to identify the stage of a blowfly larva. There are three larval stages, called instars, and by looking closely at the mandibles (mouthparts), genitalia, and spiracles (holes and tubes for gas exchange) the

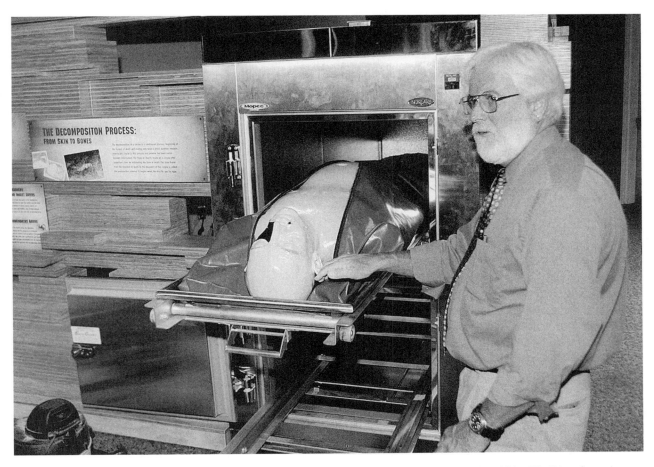

Professor Lee Goff shows a dummy in a morgue crypt display for the Science Museum of Minnesota's exhibit: CSI: Crime Scene Insects. The types of insects and stages of their development on a body can help determine the time since death. AP/WIDE WORLD PHOTOS. REPRODUCED BY PERMISSION.

entomologist can differentiate not only the species of the larvae, but also determine whether it is a first, second, or third instar.

The maggots then mature to the pupal form, which is often found deposited around the body. Forensic entomologists are cautious in scouring the region surrounding a corpse for the inactive pupae. However, if care is not taken by an investigator at a crime scene, the pupa can often be overlooked as it resembles rodent droppings. Once the insect has matured to an adult form, it emerges from the pupae. Empty pupal cases found in the vicinity of a body can also yield clues.

Beetles are generally the next insects to colonize a corpse. Carrion beetles of the order *Coleoptera* also undergo holometabolous development. Compared to the maggot larvae of flies, which are similar among species, the larval forms of beetle species are very different. In contrast to blowfly larvae, all beetle larvae also have legs, so the two orders of insect larvae are immediately differentiated by their appearance. Beetle larvae can be fat, slender, hairy, and a variety of colors from white to dark brown and black.

Forensic entomologists have been instrumental in solving homicide cases in recent years. Not only can they determine the approximate time of death from the succession of adult insects, larvae, and pupae found on the corpse, but they can also provide information such as if the body was moved. For example, if a body is found indoors, but colonized with insects typically found in a wooded outdoor location, the forensic entomologist would infer that the body had been moved.

In addition, bloodstains found at the scene of a crime can yield clues or confound police. Bloodstains could have been recently deposited, or possibly been there for a period of time from events unrelated to the crime under investigation. New and innovative techniques are now being used to establish time of death and age of bloodstains. These new techniques help forensic scientists and criminal investigators reconstruct more representative crime scenes and more precisely determine time of death.

When the suspected perpetrator of a crime is a relative or friend, crime scene analysis and reconstruction is much more complex. When the crime was committed in the relative or friend's home, it is difficult for investigators to separate evidence temporally since it is likely that the victim was in the environment previous to the crime. For example, if a woman murders her husband in their home, there may be small traces of blood in the house. However, this blood may have been present well before the crime and be totally independent of the events of the crime. Although forensic **DNA** analysis of the stain would easily identify to whom the blood belongs, this analysis would not provide any clues as to when the stain occurred. Similarly, a bit of blood found in an automobile could suggest a body was transported in a car. If the victim of the crime was a family member of the car's owner, how can it be determined if this blood came from a scratch before the crime was committed? Determination of the temporal events surrounding the deposition of a blood sample could prove crucial to solving a crime.

Often, characteristics of the blood protein **hemoglobin** such as color and solubility are used as an estimation of bloodstain age. These techniques have their drawbacks, however, as it is often necessary to determine the species from which the blood originated, and often the size of the stain affects the analysis. One new technique which shows potential for forensic analysis of bloodstain age utilizes RNA (ribonucleic acid) in the bloodstain. Although messenger RNA (mRNA) is easily degraded, researchers have found that highly abundant mRNA is detectable over six months following blood deposition. Furthermore, if **PCR** (ploymerase chain reaction, a DNA amplifying technique) is performed using species-specific primers, one can easily tell the species from which the blood originated.

The three different type of RNA—mRNA, transfer RNA (tRNA), and ribosomal RNA (rRNA)—are known to decay at different rates. Researchers have recently shown that using a ratio of mRNA of a highly abundant **gene** to that of rRNA, it is possible to determine the age of a bloodstain, because the degradation of the ribosomal RNA is much slower. Forensic scientists first isolate RNA from the bloodstain, then use real-time RT-PCR (reverse-transcriptase polymerase chain reaction) techniques to make DNA copies of the RNA. Real-time PCR provides an amplified DNA copy of the RNA, but still maintains a ratio of the amount of transcript in the reaction at the start of the reaction to that of the RNA at the end. By using primers specific to the RNAs of interest, only those are selectively amplified. Thus, it is possible to compare amounts of two different amplified DNAs that reflect the relative composition of those RNAs in the initial sample.

Although both RNA analysis and forensic entomology are relatively new techniques, they have great possibility for **crime scene investigation**. Forensic entomology has already proven useful in a variety of cases and, with more basic research, it is only a matter of time before RNA techniques prove equally as useful. As forensic techniques become more and more advanced, criminal investigations will be solved more rapidly and with even greater accuracy.

SEE ALSO Adipocere; Asphyxiation (signs of); Autopsy; Body marks; Crime scene reconstruction; Death, cause of; Death, mechanism of; Decomposition; DNA fingerprint; Drowning (signs of); Entomology; Hanging (signs of); Lividity; Mummies; Pathology; Rigor mortis; STR (short tandem repeat) analysis; Toxicological analysis.

Tire tracks

Tire tracks are the impressions left by tires on the surface onto which a vehicle drove. Not all tires and all surfaces will leave tire tracks. If the surface is soft or semi-soft, such as mud, dirt, or snow, the tire will leave an imprint under the weight of the vehicle. If the surface is hard, such as road pavement, the tire might still leave a trace, if dirt or dust was present. As with other traces such as fingerprints or **shoeprints**, tire tracks are extremely important in forensic investigations. They enable **identification** of the vehicle that left them. Tire tracks are usually found in road accident scenes or in the access and escape routes of other crime scenes.

Tires are made of semi-hard rubber and are characterized by class and individual characteristics. Class characteristics include size and general patterns. Individual characteristics include regular wear and tear as well as accidental cuts or holes. These characteristics may be reproduced in the tracks left by the tire, depending on the surface and the circumstances under which the track occurred.

When tire tracks are present at a crime scene or in the immediate vicinity, one must properly observe and record them. First, they need to be photographed

An aerial view shows skid marks leading from the end of the runway to a building where a corporate jet crashed after failing to take off from Teterboro Airport in Teterboro, New Jersey, on February 2, 2005. AP/WIDE WORLD PHOTOS. REPRODUCED BY PERMISSION.

at a 90-degree angle. This allows for a permanent record of their class and individual characteristics. Then, the tracks are carefully measured. Not only it is important to note the width, but also the circumference of the tire, if the lengths permit it. In addition, if multiple tire tracks from the different wheels of the vehicle are present, it is important to make as many measurements as possible in order to determine the toe (the distance between the front of the tires and the rear of the tires on the same axle) and turning radius of the vehicle. Finally, if the tracks are present in relief, it is also possible to make a cast from it. Usually, plaster of Paris is used and, if the whole track cannot be cast, the most pertinent spot is cast.

Once the general size and pattern of the track is determined, it is possible to consult a database of tires to determine the brand and model of the tire that left the impression. In addition, there are also databases that list which tires are installed from the

factory on which vehicles. Finally, with the dimensions of the vehicle, it is also possible to determine which vehicle could have left the tracks.

Recent advances in technology and research allow for the characterization of tire tracks by chemical analysis of the rubber. Based on **Locard's Exchange Principle**, if a tire leaves rubber residues on the surface, as is the case with skid marks, crime scene investigators can collect these traces and compare them with the tires from a suspected vehicle. The result of this analysis is not as powerful as having individual characteristics that will identify the exact tire, but it adds one more piece of information to the investigation.

SEE ALSO Accident reconstruction; Automobile accidents; Casting; Locard's exchange principle.

Toolmarks

A toolmark is defined as the impression left by the contact of a tool (or a similar object) onto a surface. When the tool or object contacts the surface with sufficient force to create an indentation, the pattern of the tool is permanently reproduced onto that surface. Toolmarks examination is an important discipline of **criminalistics**. Its goal is to establish a link between a toolmark and the tool that created it. Such links are crucial in forensic sciences, as tools are often used in criminal activities, particularly in burglaries, and can help to identify a criminal. For example, when a burglar uses a pry bar to force entry into a house, the marks left by the tool on the door frame are direct **evidence** of the presence of that tool for that particular use at the crime scene. If the tool is found with, or near, a suspect, it permits the establishment of a link between the suspect and the crime scene. Thus, the recognition and collection of toolmarks at the crime scene and their examination at the laboratory are paramount.

Toolmarks bear two kinds of characteristics: class and individual. The class characteristics of a toolmark include the type of impression, its general shape, and its general dimensions. Class characteristics typically allow the examiner to determine what type of tool created the impression and how the mark was created. Conversely, they do not permit for the **identification** of the exact tool that created the impression. This means that if only class characteristics are available on a toolmark, it will not be possible to distinguish which tool, among a series of similar tools, made the impression. Individual characteristics, also called accidental characteristics, are the striations and small particularities exhibited by the tool that are individual to one unique tool. They consist of small, commonly microscopic, indentations, ridges, and irregularities present on the tool itself. For example, the tip of a screwdriver is never perfectly flat, but shows small ridges along its edge. These are created by the history of the tool such as its use and misuse, its cleaning, and its maintenance. These characteristics are the only ones that permit a formal identification. If such characteristics are present in the toolmark, it is possible to identify the actual individual tool that created the impression, even among a series of identical tools.

There are two main types of toolmarks that can be distinguished: slipped and molded impressions. The slipped impression occurs as the tool drags or slides across the surface. The resulting toolmark is a series of striations running parallel to each other following the direction of the drag. For example, such impressions are created by slipping a key across the door of a vehicle, by cutting with a knife (not used in a sawing motion) through a given material, or by cutting an electrical wire using a pair of lineman's pliers. The molded impressions are the result of the contact of a tool onto a surface with no lateral motion (no drag nor slip). The resulting toolmarks are a three-dimensional mold of the part of the tool that contacted the surface. Examples of such impressions are the leverage of a door from its frame with a pry bar, or the serial number stamped onto a firearm's barrel. Some toolmarks are made of a combination of molded and slipped impressions.

Toolmark examination is a term that includes a wide variety of impressions that are not necessarily directly related to tools but that are created via the same fashion and are, therefore, examined with the same techniques. A clear example is the impression left by a firearm's barrel onto a bullet or by the firearm onto the cartridge. These are a specialized category of toolmarks. Other examples include the impressions left by human teeth or even the impressions left by shoes or tires. Very often, the toolmark examiner is the person responsible for examining and rendering expert opinions on such impression's identifications.

The examination of toolmarks is conducted in different phases. First, the toolmark is observed, measured, and described. Second, a photograph perpendicular to the toolmark, is taken. This provides a permanent record of the class and some individual characteristics of the toolmark. Then, if the support onto which the toolmark is located cannot be collected as evidence, a cast of the toolmark is made.

This cast is usually made with polymeric dental paste. When a tool is discovered and its class characteristics match the ones exhibited by the toolmark, the comparison process is started. Usually, the tool is observed and photographed. Then, comparison toolmarks are made with the tool on a soft material so that extra marks are not created on the tool. A **comparison microscope** is used to perform the comparison process. The incriminated toolmark is placed on the left side of the microscope and the comparison mark on the right side. If a match exists between the individual characteristics, the common origin between the incriminated toolmark and the tool is established.

SEE ALSO Casting; Impression evidence; Microscope, comparison.

Toxicological analysis

An important facet of a forensic investigation can be the analytical examination of **fluids** such as **blood** and urine for the presence of compounds that are not normally present. These can include excessive levels of prescription drugs, **illicit drugs**, and toxic compounds. The latter can be naturally occurring inorganic or microbial **toxins** or can be synthetic in origin.

Toxicological analysis is concerned with over 150 different compounds, depending on the circumstances of the crime or accident, and the observations of the physical appearance of the victim or suspect. As just a few examples, these include stimulants (amphetamine, caffeine, cocaine), alkaloids and amines (dextromethorphan, ephedrine, quinine), narcotics and analgesics (codeine, morphine), hallucinogens (LSD, PCP), antidepressants, sedatives (**barbiturates**), tranquilizers, marijuana, and amyl nitrate.

Toxicological analysis is done in several different ways, depending on the target compound. Typically, the fluids that are of forensic interest are blood and urine. At a crime or accident scene, or even later, collection of the fluid is all that is necessary. The actual analysis is done in a dedicated laboratory using sophisticated equipment and trained personnel.

Collection for analysis needs to be done under controlled conditions using collection reservoirs especially designed for the purpose. For example, collection of a urine sample in a non-sterile container without a lid could result in contamination of the urine and would be grounds for subsequent legal inadmissibility of the results. Fortunately, protocols for sample collection and transport are relatively easy to observe.

Toxicological analysis is geared towards the detection of the presence of a compound (qualitative analysis) rather than determining the amount that is present (quantitative analysis). Other than alcohol, determining the actual amount of a compound is of little value. For many illicit drugs, there are really no beneficial levels. Thus, for example, merely demonstrating the presence of marijuana or cocaine is sufficient.

Often, a toxic or illicit compound is present in blood or urine along with other substances. To identify the target compound, it must be physically separated from the other compounds.

One tried and true method of physical separation is **chromatography**. In the various forms of chromatography, compounds are separated from one another based on their tendency to prefer either a solid material that is packed in the volume of the chromatography column (the stationary phase) or the fluid or gas that percolates through or over the stationary phase (the mobile phase).

There may be several compounds in a sample that show a preference for the stationary or mobile phases. By tailoring the chemistry of the stationary phase (commonly by judicious selection of the stationary phase material and the composition of the chemical side groups that protrude from the material or the thin coating of fluid that chemically clings to the solid) and the composition of the mobile fluid, different compounds will move through the column at different speeds.

Sample molecules can move through the matrix passively, under the force of gravity or via capillary action as liquid is drawn upwards into chromatographic paper, or can involve the use of a pump to drive the sample through the matrix at high pressure.

As the fluid emerges from the chromatographic column, it is collected in defined amounts. Thus, the separated compounds in the mobile phase will be collected in different reservoirs for their subsequent analysis.

The compounds that have been more tenaciously retained in the solid material in the column can then be chemically driven off of the material by the addition of fluid that differs in chemistry from that present initially. This step is known as elution. Elution can be tailored so that the compounds are released at different times.

In gas chromatography, the mobile phase is an inert gas such as helium, while in liquid chromatography this phase consists of a liquid. The latter form of chromatography ranges in sophistication from the dipping of one end of a strip chromatographic paper in liquid, with the separation of compounds occurring as the liquid moves upward through the paper via capillary action, to high-performance liquid chromatography (HPLC), in which compounds are powered through the matrix at high pressure.

Ion exchange chromatography is also useful in forensic **toxicology**. This relies on the net charge (the balance of positive charges and negative charges) of the target molecule. If a compound has an overall net negative charge, it will be retained more so by a positively charged material than by a negatively charged matrix. The opposite is true for a compound that has a positive net charge.

Chromatography can be combined with mass spectrometry to reveal very detailed information about the separated compounds. For example, the use of mass spectrometry can reveal the molecular weight of each separated compound. When two mass spectrometers are connected in series (tandem mass spectrometry), the arrangement of amino acid build blocks of the separated proteins can be determined, as can the types of fatty acids that comprise a lipid sample.

Other detection methods include the absorption of ultraviolet radiation by the sample molecules (evident by a change in absorbance on a plotted graph), the different refraction of light by different molecules (which can be quantified as a refractive index), and the reaction of certain sample chemical groups with light that results in the emission of light of a different wavelength (**fluorescence**).

A different, and very efficient and economical, way to separate various proteins in blood and urine is **electrophoresis**. The technique is based on the migration of charged molecules in a solution in response to an electric field. The differing rates at which proteins migrate depends on the strength of the electric field, the protein's net charge, the size and shape of the protein molecules, and on the properties of the support matrix through which the molecules move.

The support matrix is typically paper, cellulose acetate, starch gel, agarose (which is purified from various species of seaweed), or polyacrylamide gel. The latter two are used most commonly.

Agarose and polyacrylamide are prepared as molten suspensions, which are poured into a mold. As

Ukranian President Viktor Yushchenko photographed in March 2002, left, and December, 2004, right. Toxicological analysis found the mysterious illness that scarred Yushchenko's face was caused by dioxin poisoning. **AP/WIDE WORLD PHOTOS. REPRODUCED BY PERMISSION.**

the suspension cools, a gel forms. Depending on the concentration of the agarose or polyacrylamide, the gel will contain spaces that vary in size. Thus, agarose and polyacrylamide gel electrophoresis provide ways of separating different protein species and even nucleic acid fragments based on their different sizes.

By the inclusion of the appropriate controls, nucleic acid electrophoresis can even reveal the sequence of nucleotide building blocks that make up deoxyribonucleic acid (**DNA**). Indeed, prior to the advent of computer technology and **gene** sequencers, the determination of DNA sequences was routinely done this way.

In electrophoresis, the separated compounds will typically form "bands" in the gel, which can be detected using special stains. As well, since under some electrophoretic conditions regions on the separated proteins can retain their ability to react with antibodies, the latter can bind to the protein. Then, tagging the bound **antibody** with a fluorescent probe allows a specific protein to be detected fluorescently.

More recently, the technique of capillary electrophoresis has proved useful in toxicologal analysis. Instead of a gel, compounds move through a tube of extremely small diameter (the capillary). The charge on the capillary wall retards the motion of the compounds to varying degrees.

Capillary electrophoresis is quite efficient; compounds that are very similar in character can be separated this way. As well, very small sample volumes are used and the separation is completed very quickly.

When the target compound is a protein, the molecule can be distinguished from other proteins by antibodies that have been formed in response. Generically, this approach is known as antibody capture. The binding of an antibody to its corresponding **antigen** can cause formation of a complex that becomes so large that it precipitates out of solution or suspension. Even more sophisticated applications of antibodies are available. For example, antibodies can be bound to magnetic particles. Once binding of the antibody-magnetic particle complex to a protein has occurred, the protein can be magnetically separated from other proteins in the mixture.

No matter what the nature of the toxicological analysis procedure, all are conducted using standard protocols and with the inclusion of the appropriate controls to ensure that the equipment is operating properly, that what is supposed to be detected is indeed being detected, and that extraneous or interfering compounds are excluded from detection.

These rigorous quality control procedures helps strengthen the validity and legal admissibility of the results of the toxicological analysis.

SEE ALSO Analytical instrumentation; Antibody; Biosensor technologies; Chromatography; Fourier transform infrared spectrophotometer (FTIR); Gas chromatograph-mass spectrometer; Pathogens; Spores; Thin layer chromatography.

Toxicology

Since **forensic science** is often concerned with determining the basis of death, investigations frequently are concerned with the influence and effects of **toxins**.

The science of toxicology is concerned with the adverse effects of chemicals on biological systems and includes the study of poisons, their detection, action, and counteractions. Toxicologists today generally use the techniques of analytical chemistry to detect and identify foreign chemicals in the body, with a particular emphasis on toxic or hazardous substances. Toxins can be simple metal ions or more complex, inorganic and organic chemicals, as well as compounds derived from bacteria or fungi and animal-produced substances such as venoms. Poisons can range in their effects from a low-level debilitation to a near instantaneous death. Many drugs used to counter diseases can also be poisons at higher concentrations.

One of the most significant historical figures in the development of the science of toxicology was the Swiss physician and alchemist, Paracelsus (1493–1541). He realized that there was a need for proper experimentation in the field of chemical therapeutics and distinguished between the therapeutic and toxic properties of substances, recognizing that they are indistinguishable except by dose. Paracelsus realized that it is not possible to categorize chemicals as either safe or toxic and laid the foundations for a key principle in toxicology known as the dose-response relationship.

There is a graded dose-response relationship in individuals and a quantal dose-response relationship in a population. The quantal "all or none" dose-response is used to determine the median lethal dose (LDm), which estimates what percentage of the population would be affected by a dose increase. Estimation of LDm involves the use of at least two different animal species and doses of the chemical under test are administered by at least two different routes. Initially, most of the test animals die within 14 days. Subacute exposure is then tested for a period of 90 days and long-term exposure testing takes a further 6 months to 2 years. Mathematical extrapolation is used to generalize results from animal testing to human risk incidence.

Another significant figure in toxicology was Spanish physician Matthieu Joseph Bonaventure Orfila (1787–1853) who contributed to the specialty known as forensic toxicology. He devised methods of detecting poisonous substances and therefore provided the means of proving when criminal poisoning had taken place. After Orfila, toxicology developed further to include the study of mechanisms of poison action.

Forensic toxicology involves the use of toxicological methods for legal purposes. There is a considerable overlap between forensic and clinical toxicology, **criminology**, forensic **psychology**, drug testing, environmental toxicology, **pathology**, pharmacology, sports medicine, and veterinary toxicology. The work of a forensic toxicologist generally falls into three main categories: **identification** of drugs such as heroin, cocaine, cannabis; detection of drugs and poisons in body **fluids**, tissues, and organs; and measuring of alcohol in **blood** or urine samples. Results of the laboratory procedures must then be interpreted and are often used as **evidence** in legal cases.

A forensic toxicologist is normally given preserved samples of body fluids, stomach contents, and organ parts along with a coroner's report containing information on symptoms and postmortem data. Specimens are generally divided into acidic and basic fractions for drug extraction from tissue or fluid. As an example, most of the barbiturate drugs are acid-soluble while most of the amphetamine drugs are base-soluble. After preliminary acid-base procedures, tissue or fluid samples are subjected to further laboratory tests consisting of screening tests and confirmation testing. Screening tests allow the processing of many specimens for a wide range of toxins in a short time and any positive indications from the screens are then verified with a confirmation test.

Various screening and confirmatory laboratory tests are used in **toxicological analysis**. There are three general types of screening tests. Firstly, physical aspects of a substance such as boiling point, melting point, density, and refractive index can be determined. Secondly, the substance can be crystallized, which can give a wealth of structural information. Thirdly, chemical spot testing can be done. Here, a substance is treated with a chemical reagent to produce crystals. Fourthly, thin layer or gas **chromatography** can be used to separate individual chemical components of a mixture.

Confirmatory tests generally involve mass spectrometry in combination with gas chromatography. Every toxin has a characteristic mass spectrum that identifies it absolutely.

Drug analysis in tissue samples can be very complicated and a substance under analysis must be subjected to rigorous tests with no margin for error. A range of screening tests employing color reactions exist for the detection of illegal drugs. Some commonly used color tests include the Marquis test for opium, Duqunois-Levine test for marijuana, Van Urk test for LSD, Scott test for cocaine, and the Dillie-Koppanyi test for **barbiturates**.

The challenges of modern science call on clinical and forensic toxicologists to expand their services. They are now encouraged to engage in research and development to meet a number of changing needs. Modern molecular biology has opened up a number of interesting possibilities for toxicologists. For example, genotyping for interpretation of potential toxic drug interactions and criminality testing is becoming a field of great interest. With the emergence of pharmacogenetics, genotyping may enhance rational drug therapy for better patient care, and may explain unexpected adverse or fatal drug reactions in postmortem analysis.

SEE ALSO Aflatoxin; Anthrax, investigation of the 2001 murders; Biological warfare, advanced diagnostics; Forensic science; Thin layer chromatography.

Toxicology, specialty areas

Broadly speaking, poisons are substances that cause harmful effects when they are introduced to living organisms. **Toxicology** is the systematic study of poisons. There are many different ways in which toxicology can be approached.

Interest in poisons, and their practical relevance to humans, goes back to antiquity. No doubt the earliest of humans recognized the effects of poisons in the form of animal venom or poisonous plants. Many poisons were included in the medical writings of ancient Egypt in the Ebers Papyrus (the oldest preserved medical document, written about 1552 B.C.), and by the time Greek **culture** had risen to prominence, the systematic study of poisons and their uses in everyday life had become fairly well developed. It was common practice throughout the ages for rulers and leaders to employ a cupbearer to taste their wine and food to avert threats of poisonings. Focus on toxicology has increased in recent years because of concerns for environmental pollutants and worries over toxic food additives. This resulted in the creation of the Environmental Protection Agency in 1970, and the Toxic Substances Control Act in 1976, which requires all uses of new chemicals be reported to the EPA prior to their use.

Forensic toxicology is a combination of analytical chemistry and general principles of toxicology. This is a branch of **medicine** that focuses on medical **evidence** of poisoning, and tries to establish the extent to which poisons were involved in human deaths. Forensic toxicology is in many ways a kind of detective work that assembles the subtle clues found in the tissues of the body during **autopsy**.

Clinical toxicology is the study of diseases and disease states caused by exposure to **toxins**. This differs from forensic toxicology in that it is most often a study of the living, rather than only the dead. It often involves a study of toxicokinetics, the study of how the levels of toxicants and their metabolites change over time, the time that it takes to eliminate toxicants after exposure, and ways in which the toxic effects of various poisons can be reduced in persons who have been exposed, or how elimination of the toxicant can be increased.

Descriptive toxicology is concerned directly with toxicity testing. In descriptive toxicology, the toxic properties of chemical agents are systematically studied for various endpoints using a variety of different organisms. At what point does a chemical agent cause death to 50% of the animals under study? To what extent are various agents irritating to the eyes? How frequent are birth defects in the offspring when mothers are exposed during pregnancy? Descriptive toxicology is an attempt to characterize the toxic potential of various agents in a wide array of systems.

Mechanistic toxicology is the study of the many mechanisms by which toxins exert their effects on living systems. This is the identification of the targets to which toxins may bind, the tracking of the toxin as it is absorbed and distributed throughout the body, and the process as it is metabolized and altered by the body. This includes study of the stepwise manner in which toxicants enter the system, find their targets, and make incremental changes on the natural system. Mechanistic toxicology also involves the study of how these agents are metabolized and excreted after exposure has occurred.

Regulatory toxicology is the translation of laboratory testing data into policies concerning the applications and uses of chemicals in society, and the limits of allowable exposure in various settings. The regulatory toxicologist compares the toxicity profile with other known toxicants and tries to establish standards for allowable limits that are consistent with other agents with similar effects. Regulatory toxicology is the primary basis for laws that limit exposures for people and for the environment.

Biochemical toxicology is the study of the interactions toxicants have within living systems. Many of the aspects of mechanistic toxicology are found in the study of biochemical toxicology. What are the portals of entry into the living system? How is the agent distributed and metabolized once it is taken in? How does toxicity vary by age, sex, diet, and during pregnancy? What are the sites of action of the toxicant? How is the toxicant eventually metabolized and eliminated?

It wasn't very long ago that lakes, rivers, and oceans were considered to be a nearly infinite in size; the atmosphere an infinitely large reservoir of air; and the ground a nearly endless reserve for solids. Consequently, wastes from manufacturing or daily living were dumped into the ocean, released through smokestacks into the air, or buried into landfills without concern for the long-term consequences. Rachel Carson's book *Silent Spring*, published in 1962, served as a powerful warning that continuing these practices would lead to a progressive erosion of many different ecosystems. The area of environmental toxicology arose to a high level of social concern for the study of the impact of toxic agents on the environment, and the fate of toxicants released into various ecosystems.

Pollutants in the air that can have sweeping consequences in human health and in various ecosystems have been long recognized as a problem in society. Environmental toxicology studies of the air can include the types and sources of airborne pollutants, acute and chronic health effects of various pollutants in the air, transport of particulate and gaseous pollutants in air, changes in the ozone layer resulting from natural and man-made pollutants, chemical and photochemical transformations and reactions, and monitoring of toxicant levels over time. Similarly, environmental toxicology studies of soil and water follow many of the same kinds of issues and problems seen with air pollutants.

Teratology is the study of the effect of toxicants on the developing embryo when the mother is exposed during pregnancy. Teratogens are agents that are capable of causing birth defects when exposure occurs during pregnancy. Embryonic and fetal growth and development begins at the time of conception, and continues on for a period of approximately 9 months. This is a time of remarkable growth, and a unique period of development of body tissues, organs, and structures.

For teratogens, the timing of exposure is a key consideration. The two-week period from conception until implantation into the uterus is generally regarded as an all-or-none period where toxins will either cause pregnancy failure altogether, or have no effect at all. As pregnancy proceeds from this point, many changes are taking place. The embryo starts off as a single cell, but very quickly grows and becomes highly organized, first with the development of specific tissues, followed by development of many different organs and body structures. Toxins that might not be very harmful in adults or children could disrupt these unique events during embryonic or fetal development. Because the various stages of development are carefully timed, it becomes essential to know the timing of exposures to various potential teratogens in assessing their safety. As in most other areas of toxicology, the amount of the toxicant reaching the target tissue is another important variable. As prescription drug exposures are fairly well defined both for dose and for timing, most of the reliable data on potential teratogens is associated with prescription drug use. **Illicit drugs**, and other environmental exposures are harder to track, and it is often difficult to establish the safety or risk associated with these kinds of agents. True teratogens generally leave a distinctive pattern of specific birth defects following exposure at a specified critical time during pregnancy. Exposures at times outside of the critical time period often have no toxic effects on the developing baby.

Genetic toxicology is the study of the effects of chemicals and other environmental agents that can cause mutations or cancer. Agents that cause cancer are called carcinogens, and those that cause genetic mutations are called mutagens. Agents that cause

chromosome breaks and rearrangements are called clastogens.

The Delaney Clause prohibits the use of any chemical intended for use in food in the United States that is found to induce cancer when ingested by humans or animals. Every new chemical that is proposed for use in foodstuffs therefore undergoes extensive testing to evaluate its carcinogenic potential, and all drugs and candidate drugs are subjected to similar scrutiny.

There are a number of approaches used to investigate the carcinogenic potential of chemicals. One method is to expose laboratory animals such as mice, rats, or dogs to a range of doses of a drug or chemical for the duration of their lives, and to compare their rates of cancer with control animals that are not exposed. A true carcinogen will generally show a significant difference in cancer rates between animals that are exposed compared with those that are not, and usually there is a higher rate of cancer in animals receiving higher doses compared with those receiving lower doses.

Other tests for cancer causing potential are focused on cells grown in culture. In these tests, the endpoint is usually not cancer, but some other physiological or biochemical change known to be associated with cancer such as breaks in **DNA**, chemical modifications of DNA, or a wide variety of other biochemical changes. Testing, such as the Ames test, may involve bacterial cells. Yeast, insect, rodent, and human cells may be utilized in different assays. These tests are relatively inexpensive compared to long-term animal exposure studies. Most often these tests are used to screen for carcinogens to avoid long-term whole animal studies, or are used to support the apparent safety of agents that test negative in long-term studies.

SEE ALSO Air and water purity; Animal evidence; Botulinum toxin; Death, cause of; FDA (United States Food and Drug Administration); Toxicological analysis; Toxins.

Toxins

Toxins are harmful compounds that are produced and released by a variety of microorganisms and other organisms. Toxins can be fast-acting and, because they are already pre-formed, do not require the growth of a microorganism in the host. The illness and death that result from exposure to a variety of toxins make their detection a central part of **forensic science**.

Toxins are the main disease-causing factor for a number of bacteria. Some examples include *Corynebacterium diphtheriae* (diptheria), *Vibrio cholerae* (cholera), *Bacillus anthracis* (**anthrax**), *Clostridium botulinum* (botulism), certain strains of ***Escherichia coli*** (hemolytic uremic syndrome), and *Staphylococcus aureus* (toxic shock syndrome).

Certain species of these bacteria are of particular concern in biological warfare and biological terrorism. As the events of 2001 in the United States demonstrated, powdered preparations of *Bacillus anthracis* **spores** were easily delivered to a target through the mail. The dispersal of the spores in the air and the inhalation of the spores can cause a form of anthrax that develops quickly and, without treatment, is almost always fatal. The bacteria in the genus *Clostridium* also form spores. Additionally, during the 1990s, a strain of *Staphylococcus aureus* emerged that is resistant to almost all known **antibiotics**.

Bacterial toxins have a wide variety of activity. Some toxins damage the cell walls of host cells, either by dissolving the wall or by chemically punching holes through the wall. Examples of such toxins are the alpha toxin of *Clostridium perfringens*, hemolysin of *Escherichia coli*, and streptokinase of *Streptococcus pyogenes*. The damage to the host cells allows the bacteria to spread rapidly through the host. This can cause an overwhelming infection.

Other bacterial toxins kill host cells by stopping the manufacture of protein in host cells, or by degrading the proteins. Examples of protein blockers include exotoxin A of *Pseudomonas aeruginosa* and the Shiga toxins produced by both *Escherichia coli* and *Shigella dysenteriae*. Protein degrading toxins include those produced by *Bacillus anthracis* and *Clostridium botulinum*

Still other toxins stimulate an immune response of the host that is so strong that it can damage the host. The toxic shock syndrome associated with *Staphylococcus aureus* results from a host hyperimmune response to three of the bacterial proteins.

Other microorganisms also produce toxins. Marine microorganisms called dinoflagellates can produce toxins when they grow in species of shellfish. Eating the toxic shellfish can cause serious illness.

Some species of mold produce **aflatoxin**. *Aspergillus flavus* and *Aspergillus parasiticus* are aflatoxin-producing molds. The toxin is especially a concern when potatoes are contaminated. Ingestion of the contaminated potatoes can cause serious, even fatal illness.

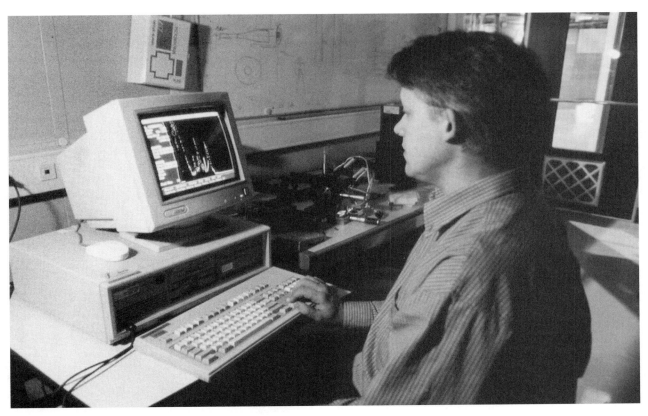

In 1994, French researchers ran tests using two strands of Napoleon's hair to rule out possible intentional poisoning of the French ruler. Napoleon did have elevated levels of arsenic in his hair, but not enough to cause his death. © FREDERIC PITCHAL/CORBIS SYGMA

Ricin is a toxin that is produced by the castor bean. It is the third most deadly toxin that is known, after the toxins produced by *Clostridium botulinum* and *Clostridium tetani*. The symptoms of ricin toxin include nausea, muscle spasms, severe lung damage, and convulsions. These symptoms appear within hours, and, without treatment, death from pulmonary failure can result within three days. There is no vaccine or antidote for ricin toxin.

Some toxins that are capable of causing much harm are also a source of protection. Because of its potency, a toxin cannot be used protectively in its unaltered form. Toxins can be altered, however, so that they do not produce the undesirable effects, but still stimulate the **immune system** to produce antibodies to a critical part of the toxin molecule. The weakened version of a toxin is called a toxoid.

The anthrax vaccine that is currently licensed for use contains two toxoids in addition to other immune stimulating molecules. The immune response will produce antibodies to the two toxins of the anthrax bacterium.

SEE ALSO Aflatoxin; Biosensor technologies; Botulinum toxin; Food supply; Pathogens; Thin layer chromatography.

Trace evidence

The scene of a crime often yields a large amount of trace **evidence** that has come from contact between the perpetrator and his or her surroundings. The importance of collecting and analyzing trace evidence comes from Edmond **Locard's Exchange Principle**, which states that every contact leaves a trace. That is, criminals leave something of themselves, such as hair or clothes **fibers**, behind at the crime scene, and they also take something away with them from their contact with people and objects there. Often criminals are not aware of this, because traces of contact evidence are, by their very nature, difficult to detect with the naked eye. It is precisely this property that makes trace evidence so valuable to the forensic investigator. Try as he might, the perpetrator cannot clear away all forms of trace evidence from the crime scene.

The most common forms of trace evidence are bloodstains, hair, textile fibers, paint, and **glass** fragments. The forensic scientist will be on the lookout for microscopic particles collected from the scene of the crime, to distinguish what is part of that environment and what is linked to the crime that took place there.

At the scene of a crime, the investigators will make an initial assessment that will tell them where to start looking for trace evidence. For instance, if a window has been broken, this might be a good source for textile fibers belonging to the perpetrator that might be matched in an examination of the clothing worn by a suspect. The investigator can probably work with a minute amount of trace evidence, given the power and sensitivity of modern analysis techniques. However, the investigator will be interested in how much material might be available for analysis. Rough surfaces will capture more trace evidence than smooth ones will, for example.

The persistence of the trace evidence is also an issue. Small particles persist longer than larger particles, as do those with irregular surfaces like broken glass or with rough surfaces like wool fibers. Trace evidence landing on a rough surface stays longer than that on a smooth surface. If a suspect's garments are worn between committing a crime and its investigation, there is a high chance that any trace evidence on the clothing may be lost.

However, material forming a smear on the surface through contact persists for longer than particle contact. This applies to **blood** or paint that might be found on a suspect's clothing. Washing may remove it, but otherwise it is more likely to be detected than particulate evidence, which can be brushed off.

Forensic scientists have a range of techniques for detecting invisible trace evidence. Much depends upon the contrast between the trace evidence and its background. Deeply dyed fibers are clearly easier to detect than pale ones, for example. One of the simplest methods of recovering trace evidence is to shake an item into a test container. This works for collecting glass and paint from garments. Some particulate trace evidence will not be dislodged by shaking but can be collected by brushing with a new toothbrush or paintbrush. Taping trace evidence can also be useful in the case of fibers and hairs. Strips of clear sticky tape are applied to surfaces like garments, car seats, and window ledges to pick up any trace evidence that might have been deposited there. Other methods of collection are vacuuming, swabbing, and hand picking.

In a 2001 murder trial in Texas, a senior trace evidence analyst for the Institute of Forensic Sciences shows the direction from which bullets hit a police officer. AP/WIDE WORLD PHOTOS. REPRODUCED BY PERMISSION.

There are many different techniques in use for the comparison and characterization of trace evidence, depending on its nature. The physical and chemical properties of glass fragments can easily be measured and compared with **control samples**. Textile fibers are often found at the scene of a crime. Typically, these are tiny, broken, and fragmented fibers that are not usually visible to the naked eye. Tapings of these fibers are usually first examined under a low power microscope. Further analysis involves a number of techniques such as **thin layer chromatography** or infrared **spectroscopy**.

Paint is another important kind of trace evidence. It is particularly important in the case of hit and run accidents, where fragments of paint might have been transferred to a victim's clothes or to another vehicle. If a match can be made between paint chips and the missing flakes of paint using microscopy, then a suspect may be either eliminated or convicted.

Hairs collected from the scene of a crime can also be a significant source of trace evidence. The inner layer, known as the cortex, is where the pigment granules lie, and this determines the color of the hair. However, on its own this kind of evidence is not really individualizing. If the hair has fresh roots, however, it may be a source of blood grouping or **DNA profiling**, in which case it may well establish identity. Other sources of trace evidence that can prove significant include: oils and waxes, as found in car accidents; soil, which may be trodden in all types of crime; and invisible bloodstains, which can be visualized with **luminol**. Taking care of the trace evidence may be the key to the investigator helping secure the right result in a crime investigation.

SEE ALSO Crime scene investigation; Hair analysis; Paint analysis.

Training

As a rule, the training for a forensic scientist involves the attainment of at minimum, a bachelor's (four year college or university degree) in criminal justice, biology, chemistry or the physical sciences, **psychology** (or one of the behavioral or social sciences), or forensic technology. Many colleges and universities have begun to offer degrees in **forensic science**, with concentrations in areas such as **toxicology**, **pathology**, or **criminalistics**. Many forensic scientists choose to pursue a master's or doctoral degree in their specialty area. In the United States, there are currently no mandatory requirements for specific licensure in forensics. Most forensic scientists, however, choose to obtain professional certification or accreditation from one or more of the nationally recognized forensic specialty boards, such as the Forensic Toxicologist Certification Board, the Association of Forensic Document Examiners, the American Board of Medicolegal Death Investigators, the American Board of Forensic Odontology, the American Board of Forensic Document Examiners, the American Board of Forensic Anthropology, the American Board of Criminalistics, and the American Board of Forensic Sciences.

The activities of forensic scientists all stem from the concept of using science in its myriad forms to attempt to answer questions regarding the who, what, where, when, why, and how of crime—for all avenues of the law enforcement and legal justice systems. During the investigation of a crime, or at a crime scene, they may identify and collect samples, package and preserve **evidence**, photograph and measure, sketch, draw, and model, estimate timing, stage, and reconstruct events, and help to develop a literal and psychological picture of the crime and its perpetrator.

In laboratory settings, forensic scientists examine **blood**, fingerprints, fiber, clothing, **serum** and tissue, **saliva**, **semen**, and other substances that may contain **DNA** or other physiological identifiers in order to create a unique physiological profile. They assess weapons, drugs, paint, and other materials for their relationship to the criminal event. Forensic scientists examine decomposed or fragmented human remains and build models of their likenesses in order to facilitate **identification**; they gather and synthesize physical and behavioral evidence to create offender psychological profiles; they examine and identify **questioned documents**; they construct, conduct and analyze polygraph, galvanic skin response, and other physiological tests; they conduct forensic psychological and psychiatric assessments and evaluations for both criminal identification and culpability (fitness to stand trial, competency, criminal responsibility, assessments relating to the sentencing process, etc.). Part of the job of a forensic scientist is to document, analyze, interpret, and report findings and the measures used to achieve them, for the criminal justice and legal systems. Forensic scientists are often called to courtrooms as **expert witnesses**.

Forensic scientists may work in the field at crime scene investigations. They may also be employed in the private sector, state, federal, or military crime or toxicology labs, in law enforcement agencies, at hospitals and other emergency or trauma centers, in universities or training academies, at medical examiner's or coroner's offices, or at private forensic science consulting firms.

In addition to careers within the legal, criminal justice or law enforcement systems, a small sample of specialty areas within forensic science include: **forensic nursing** (may work in many areas of forensic science, from emergency wound and trauma care to coroner's offices, to **crime scene investigation**, to victim and offender counseling to consultation to expert witness work); forensic **psychiatry** and forensic psychology (can run the gamut from psychological **profiling** to psychodiagnostics to competency and culpability assessments and evaluations to psychological autopsies to expert witness testimony); criminalistics (the analysis, comparison, identification, and interpretation of **physical evidence**); crime scene investigation (all aspects of documenting, identifying, collecting, preserving and transporting evidence from the location of occurrence); document examination (all aspects of identification and authentication of handwritten, typed, printed, and electronic documents); forensic engineering (crash, blast, accident, and structural failure analysis); forensic anthropology (using physical anthropology techniques to locate, recover and identify human, and sometimes, animal remains, and to reconstruct models or likeness from decayed, decomposed or fragmented remains); forensic **entomology** (estimating **time of death**, or time since death, and studying corpse decay and **decomposition** via analysis of insect populations and insect larvae); forensic linguistics (studying the legal aspects of written and spoken communication, evaluating confessions and the results of **interrogation**, courtroom use of linguistics, etc.); forensic **photography** (use of **cameras** for recording all possible aspects of a crime scene, from all available angles, in order to create a minutely detailed pictorial documentation of the event); and forensic odontology (examination of the teeth of corpses for the purposes of identification; making casts and models of bite marks on victims and at crime scenes in order to identify the person who inflicted the bite).

No matter what the area of specialty, the objective of a forensic scientist is to apply the rules and methodology of science to the criminal justice and legal systems. Forensic scientists may do their jobs anywhere from actual crime scenes to laboratory settings, to hospitals, to medical examiner's offices, to computers, to consulting offices, to courtrooms and beyond. They may be employed by local, state, military, or federal law enforcement or criminal justice systems. They may be trained in criminal justice or in the physical, biological, social or behavioral sciences. They may come from other fields of undergraduate work and then pursue graduate training and specialization in forensics, or they may have academic training specifically in the forensic sciences. They may begin in law enforcement or criminal justice, and then pursue academic training in forensic science. The occupational world of the forensic professional is ever expanding, and will continue to keep pace with advances in science and technology.

SEE ALSO Archaeology; Autopsy; Casting; Crime scene investigation; Identification; Medical examiner; Photogrammetry.

Trajectory

The trajectory of a bullet is the path of flight it follows from being fired to reaching its target. In cases of shootings that claim a victim as their target,

Bullet trajectory of one of the assassin's bullets that killed U.S. president John F. Kennedy, included as an exhibit for the Warren Commission in 1964. © CORBIS

the forensic specialist will want to try to work out the trajectory of the bullet as part of the **crime scene reconstruction**. The science of investigating projectile motion is known as **ballistics** and involves equations that can be used to work out a trajectory.

When the trigger of a gun is pulled, it sets off an explosion in the shell of the bullet. Chemical energy is converted into kinetic energy, and the bullet leaves the gun at a high velocity. At this point it is subject to the forces of gravity and air resistance, which make it travel in a roughly parabolic path. The range of the trajectory is the total distance the bullet travels in a horizontal direction, that is, the distance between the gun and its target.

When analyzing the trajectory of a bullet, ballistics investigators divide it up into three parts. First, there is the short journey the bullet makes from where the firing pin strikes it to the point where it leaves the gun. Then there is the journey it makes towards its target, which may last anything from a fraction of a second to several seconds. Finally, the bullet gives up its kinetic energy as it travels through its target. The bullet may end up lodged in a victim's body or, if it has sufficient kinetic energy, it may emerge on the other side, creating an exit wound as well as an entry wound. Sometimes a bullet will ricochet, that is, deviate from its trajectory because of an impact with an object. It can still hit someone but the shot would not have been aimed directly at the victim, which may be an important piece of **evidence**.

The main task of the ballistics specialist is to work out the range of a bullet's trajectory. When a bullet leaves a gun, it carries various gases with it that often form a tattoo-like pattern on the victim's skin. The extent and spread of this pattern is often revealing about the range between the perpetrator and the victim. The investigator will often try to reproduce the pattern by firing the weapon, if it is available, or a similar one at blank targets in a laboratory situation. Knowing the range can help establish where a perpetrator was standing and may either contradict or corroborate witness statements. The range can also help determine whether a fatal shooting was homicide or suicide.

SEE ALSO Ballistics; Bullet track; Gunshot residue.

Transfer evidence

Transfer **evidence** is defined as any evidential substance or particle such as **blood**, **fluids**, hairs, **fibers**, paint, and skin that is exchanged between an assailant and the victim or the scene of the crime. Such evidence can transfer either from the criminal to the victim or from the victim to the criminal. It can also be transferred into or out of the crime scene. This transfer often occurs when forcible contact occurs between persons, vehicles, or objects. For example, when **glass** fragments from one automobile are found on another vehicle, an exchange of transfer evidence has occurred. Different forms of transfer evidence can be small foreign materials such as food particles carried by the perpetrator to the crime scene and left behind, or identifying materials such as the victim's hairs or skin particles carried away from the scene on clothing. Other small particles of transfer evidence may lodge in the hair or under fingernails, or in some other way attach themselves to persons key to the criminal investigation.

An important forensic principle that involves transfer evidence is the **Locard's exchange principle**. Proposed in 1910 by Dr. **Edmond Locard**, the principle states that whenever there is contact between two objects (whether either are a living thing or not), there is a transfer of material between them. It is therefore the responsibility of forensic experts to find that transfer evidence, however difficult it may be to locate.

Transfer evidence often plays a critical role in hit-and-run accidents involving a pedestrian hit by a driver. When investigators locate the wrongdoer and his vehicle, it is common to find blood, pieces of clothing, and skin from the victim on the vehicle and pieces of paint or broken glass on the victim that has been transferred from the driver's vehicle.

The principal investigative value of transfer evidence is its ability to be traced. When it is found on a suspect it connects the suspect with the scene of the alleged crime or with the alleged victim. A suspect, who carries away fragments, small materials, or tissues that are clearly identifiable with the victim, can be definitely associated with a particular crime when such transfer evidence is found. Victims who scratch an assailant often lodge minute skin cells, clothing fibers, and other materials from the assailant's body and clothing under their fingernails. These materials can be retrieved by forensic investigators and used as evidence against the alleged criminal.

SEE ALSO Cast-off blood; Hair analysis; Locard's exchange principle; Paint analysis.

Tree ring analysis SEE Dendrochronology

Trials, civil (U.S. law)

Civil law is also referred to as procedural law; it is the system of legal jurisprudence providing the means and methods by which individuals may legally engage with one another in order to formally address disagreements, and enforce the right of the individual to ask for redress of wrongs (materially or by other means). Civil law provides an efficient, formal, systematic, and impartial means of dispute resolution in a public courtroom setting. The goal of a civil trial is to discern the truth of an event by employing and examining the best possible **evidence**. Civil procedures set forth the requirements for conducting a civil trial, and include laws of evidence to set guidelines for the presentation of witnesses, means of appropriate documentation, and presentation of items of evidence.

The highest Court in America, the United States Supreme Court, has judicial oversight in all matters pertaining to court proceedings, and it stipulates that all procedural rules in the legal system must be consistent with the tenets set forth in the U. S. Constitution, particularly as regards the due processes clauses specified in the Fifth and Fourteenth Amendments. Due process means that everyone in a civil action is entitled to have his/her story heard in an impartial manner.

The American judicial system is said to be an adversarial one, that is, a system in which the lawsuit occurs between the individuals engaged in the disagreement (or, more accurately, their attorneys). The attorneys are responsible for the case and evidentiary presentations, and the judge acts to guarantee the objectivity and fair outcome of the trial. In American civil trials, the judge is an active participant in the trial, examining the evidence and inquiring as to the factual presentations in the case.

Before the start of a jury trial, civil proceedings involve a number of pre-trial pleadings before a professional judge, who makes decisions as to the factual and evidentiary presentations in the case. This pretrial hearing period is then followed by the commencement of the jury trial. In the American civil trial system, juries are composed of lay people, not specially trained to act as officers of the court. As such, they need to have the facts of the case presented in a manner, and at a level of comprehension, that they can understand. They are available only for limited periods of time, as jury summonses pull individuals away from their normal daily business. As a result, trials are conducted in an intensive, focused fashion over the shortest possible period of time in which the evidence can be fairly presented and witnesses can offer their testimony (expert and otherwise). All evidence to be presented must be made available before the start of the trial; it is assembled and offered during the discovery phase of the proceedings. If new evidence is uncovered after the start of a trial, it may necessitate another hearing.

In civil law proceedings, the jury hears the evidence, convenes to make a decision based on presentation of fact, and offers a recommendation based on their conclusions to the judge. The judge makes all decisions regarding matters of law.

In order to be a party to a lawsuit (either plaintiff or defendant), the individual must have the capacity and legal standing to sue another person (or another group of individuals). Minor children and those judged to be mentally incompetent to participate in a lawsuit must be represented by a law guardian who can act on their behalf, and in their best interests.

Those who are directly affected by the outcome of a case are called the parties to an action, and they are generally the only ones bound by its outcome. However, there are situations in which a large group of individuals may be impacted by a specific controversy. In those cases, a class-action lawsuit may be the result. This is a situation in which a smaller number of individuals sue a corporation or a system in order to justify the right to legal relief of a much larger group. All parties to the class action are bound by the outcome. Recent examples of such class actions include an action in which a small group of individuals affected by the leakage of silicone breast implants represented the entire population of individuals who had experienced complications subsequent to silicone breast implants made by a specific manufacturer. All received financial damages as a result of the finding on behalf of the plaintiffs in the suit. In a much smaller example, a group of inmates in a maximum security penitentiary in the state of New Mexico filed a class action suit on behalf of all inmates in maximum and super maximum security facilities in the state regarding the conditions of their confinement, and their experienced limited access to mental health services. As a result of a negotiated agreement, all inmates received greater access to mental health services and improved living conditions, among other benefits.

Lawsuits often take several years for successful resolution. Because of this, the civil legal system provides for the imposition of provisional remedies in order to ensure that the outcome does not become superfluous by the time the case is decided in the courts. Provisional remedies constitute a sort of guarantee to the plaintiff that any obtained future judgment against the defendant will be meaningful. Provisional remedies are generally given if it is the opinion of the court that the plaintiff has a strong factual case, and is likely to garner a positive outcome. Some remedies ensure that the funds required to satisfy an eventual judgment, or to pay court costs, will remain available until the conclusion of the trial. In this case, the funds or real property involved may be "attached" by the court: an officer of the court will seize the funds or property in question and hold them until the conclusion of the case.

A lawsuit is generally divided into two phases, the pleading stage and the trial stage. At the pleading stage, the parties give notice of their claims, defenses, and proposed evidence. At the trial stage, their legal counsel presents their cases of fact before the jury. This is typically accomplished by the production and promulgation of material evidence, and the spoken (sometimes written or videotaped) testimony of witnesses and subject matter experts.

The pleading portion of the case involves the presentation of the formal written documents by which the parties make their claims. Pleadings specify the nature of the argument, they state each part's understanding of the facts of the case, they clarify the issues to be decided, and they provide a permanent record of the outcome and decisions in the case.

A civil jury trial is only mandated when there are disputes as to matters of fact. When cases can be adjudicated based strictly on matters of law, the party concerned can request permission to make a motion to the court to either dismiss the case or to request a summary judgment that can be issued immediately by a sitting judge.

Quite often, a pretrial conference or pretrial hearing is held in which the judge will either try to settle the case out of court, or try to narrow the focus of the issues to be presented at trial. As the civil trial process is so protracted in the United States, there is a great effort made to settle cases without having to go to trial. Generally, one party will make a motion, in an effort to resolve the dispute. When this occurs, both parties appear before a judge who receives all paperwork from each party specific to the motion. No witnesses are heard at motions, and the attorneys each present their specific arguments. In the matter of a request for a summary judgment, the judge is asked to decide whether there exists a matter of material dispute, or whether the preponderance of evidence is on one side of the case. If there is a material issue of dispute, the motion will be denied and the case will proceed eventually to trial. If the finding is the former, the judge can issue a final, legally binding, judgment.

During a civil trial, the attorneys for each party (plaintiff and defendant) make opening statements to the jury in which they specify what they believe to be the central issues of the case, and outline what they plan to prove in matters of fact during the course of the trial. The plaintiff's case is presented first: witnesses are called, questioned and cross-examined by the attorney for the defendant. When the plaintiff's case presentation has been concluded, the defense attorney will call and question his/her witnesses, who can then be cross-examined by the attorney for the plaintiff.

After all witnesses have given their testimony and been examined, and all evidence has been offered and explained, the attorneys for each side make closing arguments to the jury, in which they again present their interpretation of the case facts and the meaning of the evidence as it most positively impacts their client. The judge then instructs the jury on the applicable law. The jury retires to convene for private deliberation on the outcome of the factual case. When it reaches a verdict, the jury returns to the courtroom and the verdict is read in open court.

SEE ALSO Evidence; *Frye* standard; Trials, criminal (U.S. law); Trials, international.

Trials, criminal (U.S. law)

Criminal trials in the United States are governed by criminal law, defined as the body of law charged with the definition of criminal offenses, and the regulation of apprehension, charging, and trial of suspected individuals. Criminal law delineates penalties and specifies appropriate and applicable means and modes of treatment for convicted offenders.

Criminal law refers to offenses committed against the general public, even though the victim of the crime may be a single individual. It is distinguished from civil or tort law in that they (civil and tort law) refer to offenses constituting private injuries. Historically, criminal law has taken the approach that crime is morally, as well as legally, wrong. As a result, amends must be made and retribution for the offense must be exacted through the use of the criminal trial and penalty systems, in a proportion appropriate to the magnitude of the criminal act and the degree of culpability of the perpetrator. More modern views of criminal law have taken the perspective that it ought to serve as a deterrent to the commission of crime. As the tenets of the social and behavioral sciences have been progressively incorporated into the rubric of criminal justice, the concepts of rehabilitation of the criminal offender, and the need for protection of the public welfare have arisen. Among the goals of the criminal legal system are prevention, early intervention, and active deterrence from development and expression of criminal behaviors.

Although American criminal law was derived from English common law, it has some important differences. Primary among the differences is the principle that a person may not be tried for an offense unless it is specified in the statutory code of the state. In all American state systems, there is a rule that judicial proceedings must be fair and impartial, that the rights of the accused, as well as the accuser, must not be violated, and that society must be protected. Individuals have the right to be safe in their environments.

Criminal law is comprised of (1) definitions of the types of punishable offenses; (2) the standardized system for classifying crimes, by severity of general harm inflicted, as misdemeanors or felonies; (3) the specifications applied to the judgment of crime that indicate specific provisions or mitigations for criminal legislation, such as insanity, degree of mental illness (often utilized by the terminology of "guilty, but mentally ill"), necessity, and self-defense; and (4) guidelines for determining national jurisdiction over crimes with an international aspect, such as crimes committed on American soil by foreign nationals, crimes committed by Americans who are located in other countries, and crimes committed on aircraft or maritime vessels located in international waters.

The framework for the procedure and practice of criminal law is embedded in the principle of legality. First, it states that crimes can only be defined in the context of a law prohibiting a specific behavior. If there is no law against a particular act, its occurrence is not a crime. Second, criminal statutes must be rigorously adhered to; they must be construed fairly and consistently, with little or no ambiguity as to their interpretation. Third, and quite importantly, laws may not be applied retroactively; a person may not be tried according to a law enacted after the commission of the crime. Fourth, the language of the law, and the wording of criminal statutes, must be clear, direct, and unambiguous: individuals should be able to clearly understand the concept of violation of specific laws, as well as the potential penalties associated with the possible infraction. Lastly, a person may not generally be tried for the same offense twice (this is also referred to as double jeopardy). In the federal system of the United States, a person may be tried for the same crime in different judicial systems; that is, a person can be subject to both a criminal and a civil trial for a single offense. The principle of the statute of limitations provides the maximum amount of time that can elapse between the commission of a crime and the trial associated with it: generally speaking, the amount of time that may elapse between arrest and indictment and the commencement of the criminal trial can vary according to the seriousness of the offense. In the United States, there is no statute of limitations imposed on crimes considered to be the most heinous, including capital felonies (**felony** crimes punishable by death).

The principle of legal jurisdiction refers to the capacity of a court in a specific geographic region or, in the case of international crime, a country to take valid legal action. Many countries assert jurisdiction over the acts of their nationals even when they are in other countries, and refuse to turn over their citizens to law enforcement agencies in other countries in which their nationals are accused of the commission of a crime or crimes. American nationals who commit crimes in other countries may only be extradited if that is authorized or required by a valid treaty with the affected country.

In the United States, within-country jurisdiction is typically limited to criminal acts occurring in part, or in entirety, within the geographic boundaries of a single state. Historically, if a crime was committed that crossed territorial lines, such as a person in one state throwing an incendiary device across state lines and causing an explosion in a building on the other side of the state line, only the state with the explosion might be considered to have jurisdiction. In modern legal practice, many states have enacted statutes allowing them to extend their jurisdictional boundaries to encompass offenses in which the relevant conduct, or the relevant result, or any part of it, occurred in the specific state. Federal statutes give jurisdiction to United States courts in cases of forgery of ship's papers, bribery of an American official, acts of treason, enticing to commit desertion from the service of the United States military, crimes committed on vessels registered to the United States or on American aircraft flying over international airspace, and similar acts, whether or not those acts actually occurred within the geographic boundaries of the U.S.

There are two mandatory components of an act that lead to definition of a crime. It must be a voluntary action or voluntary omission of an action (legal term: *actus reus*); and it must be accompanied by a specific mental state, referred to as the guilty mind (legal term: ***mens rea***). There are four types of guilty mental state: acting negligently, recklessly, knowingly, or purposely.

The critical defining feature of the act is its volitional nature. A person may not be held criminally responsible for an act committed when they could not exert voluntary control of their behavior, for example, a crime occurring during a seizure or when the individual is in a state of altered unconsciousness not induced by ingestion of illegal substances. In order to be held criminally responsible for committing an act, the perpetrator must act in some way so as to cause its occurrence; it must be possible to establish a cause and effect relationship between the outcome of the act and the individual accused of perpetrating it. An individual may also be held criminally liable for failure to commit an action when he or she was legally responsible for doing so. For example, parents may be criminally prosecuted for failure to meet their obligation to provide food and water for their children.

There are some criminal offenses for which an individual can be charged without demonstrable evidence of a guilty mental state; one of these is statutory rape. An individual need not be aware that the child is below the age of legal consent in order to be prosecuted. Others fall into the category of public welfare offenses, involving such acts as those which endanger public health or safety.

United States criminal law makes a distinction between the concept of ignorance of the facts (in other words, a mistake) and ignorance of the law. In the former, a person is not held liable if he or she unwittingly commits an infraction such as inadvertently picking up the suitcase of another person from a luggage carousel at the airport when it is identical in appearance to his or her own. It is not theft if the baggage was taken without the intention to steal, but rather as a result of the person taking the item believing it to be his or her own personal property. Conversely, being unaware of the text of the law does not excuse a person from prosecution for violating it. It is a commonly held doctrine that criminal acts should be recognized as immoral, societally unacceptable, or harmful by any reasonable adult.

The issue of criminal responsibility has remained controversial in the American criminal system. Historically, a person was not charged with criminal responsibility if he or she either lacked substantial capacity to appreciate the criminality of his or her conduct or to be able to exercise volitional control over conforming his or her behavior to the extent required by law. The more modern interpretation of the principle looks more strictly at the ability to appreciate the distinction between right and wrong and leaves out the segment on ability to exert control over one's behavior.

The criminal system considers four degrees of participation in a crime. A principal in the first degree is one who commits a crime alone; a principal in the second degree is one who acts to aid the principal in the first degree and is present when the crime occurs; an accessory before the fact is one who instigates, counsels the perpetrator, or encourages the commission of the crime; and an accessory after the fact is a person who receives, conceals, or otherwise assists someone known to have committed a crime, in an effort to obstruct justice from being served. A conspiracy is when two or more individuals agree to act together in order to commit a crime.

Finally, there is the issue of effectiveness of punishment as a deterrent to the commission of

A forensic scientist identifies a .45 pistol during testimony in the trial of convicted sniper John Allen Muhammad, convicted of capital murder for his role in sniper attacks that killed 10 people and terrorized the Washington, DC area in 2002. © DAVE ELLIS/ POOL/CORBIS

future crimes. There is little evidence to suggest that this is an effective paradigm. If the most likely predictor of future behavior is past behavior, criminals who have already been convicted, or who have served prison terms, are more likely to commit future crimes than those who have never done so. Justice system statistics suggest that the degree of punishment is not a deterrent, in that lenient and stringent penalties appear to be equally effective (or ineffective) at preventing recidivism (repeat criminal behavior). Brief sentences are often considered particularly ineffective in that they remove the offender from providing for his or her family for long enough to lose employment but allow enough time to acclimate to being a convict and foster ostracizing from society upon release, yet they are not necessarily long enough to provide benefit from any sort of rehabilitation program. Long-term sentences are tantamount to institutionalization, and encourage complete indoctrination into the prison culture. Forensic psychiatric studies show that the most positive results occur when the principle of least restrictive means is employed; incarcerated individuals are given as much freedom for personal growth as possible within the confines of the penal system and are made to accept personal responsibility for their well-being by means of treatment, employment, education, job training, etc., in order to facilitate a productive transition back into society upon release.

SEE ALSO Criminal responsibility, historical concepts; *Mens rea*; Misdemeanor; Trials, civil (U.S law); Trials, international.

Trials, international

The European Union (EU) consists of a group of twenty-five (25) member and four (4) candidate countries that have established centralized ways of working together; central among these is international law enforcement. Europol is the international law enforcement organization for the European Union. It oversees international management of criminal intelligence, with stated goals of crime amelioration and prevention. Europol supports the underlying law enforcement agencies of each of the member states, and facilitates international cooperation.

The current member states of the European Union are Austria, Belgium, Cyprus, the Czech Republic, Denmark, Estonia, Finland, France, Germany, Greece, Hungary, Ireland, Italy, Latvia, Lithuania, Luxembourg, Malta, Poland, Portugal, Slovakia, Slovenia, Spain, Sweden, The Netherlands, and the United Kingdom. The candidate countries are Bulgaria, Croatia, Romania, and Turkey. Current research and statistics compiled by the International Criminal Police Organization (**Interpol**) suggest that crime among European Union nations has generally decreased during the past several years; this is thought to be due to both improvements in crime investigation methods brought about by advances in **forensic science** and to increasing international legal cooperation.

Exemplary of the increased spirit of international cooperation is an EU-funded program called CTOSE (cyber tools online search for **evidence**); this is an emerging best-practice model for the collection, analysis, storage, reporting, and presentation of electronic evidence. The EU members utilize state of the art forensic scientific methods, such as **DNA identification** and analysis; chemical, biological, biochemical, propellant, and explosive **trace evidence** analysis, and chemical component identification; and assaying, analysis, and identification of human bodily **fluids**, to solve and prosecute violent crimes. They also employ emerging information communication technologies (ICT) to solve and prosecute cybercrime, a burgeoning, and exceedingly expensive, concern worldwide.

An international concern in the prosecution of violent crime has been the lack of standardization of methods used for **DNA profiling**; this dilemma is being resolved by a project designed to standardize DNA profiling techniques in the EU (STADNAP). DNA profiling and analysis, because of its considerable expense, is not readily affordable for every nation in the EU. Consequently, the science of **ear print analysis** has been gaining a measure of popularity in international forensic science. In addition to the economic concerns, ear print analysis/identification is considered (relatively) incontrovertible in the justice system; it is virtually impossible to tamper with and equally difficult to accidentally introduce at a crime scene.

The European Union funds projects for the forensic scientific development and advancement of ear print analysis, called FEARID. The FEARID projects are considered another means of creating international standardization for the collection, analysis, interpretation, presentation, and legal system utilization of forensic scientific evidence. FEARID is setting the stage for a worldwide database for the collection and storage of individual ear print data.

Another international program spearheaded by the EU concerns explosive trace analysis (ETA). When a bomb explodes, residue remains in the form of unreacted explosive, propellants, accelerants, or other evidentiary materials. Minute amounts of trace materials can be collected, chemically isolated, and identified. These identified materials can be compared to those collected from suspects or known terrorist groups, and utilized as evidence in international trials.

In 2000, a new international currency was launched, called the euro. In anticipation, Europol expected a surge of counterfeit Euro coins and paper notes. An international decision was made to create a failsafe system consisting of distinctive watermarks, machine-readable properties, special fiber content resulting in identifiable (yet extremely difficult to reproduce) tactile qualities, and a foil hologram. The EU launched the Eurodetector project, targeted not only at uncovering counterfeiters, but also at providing an affordable system for authenticating and counting money.

Because humans have become progressively more mobile during the past century, it has become increasingly important for international police, criminal justice, and legal system authorities to become proficient at identifying even the most miniscule bits of evidence, whether they be paint, **glass**, solvents, or resins, soil, trace **minerals** from toxicological specimens, or bullet or weapon fragments. Until recently, there was little standardization among forensic chemical or biological laboratories; this made international (and sometimes interjurisdictional) comparisons virtually impossible. The EU created an expert working group of more than a dozen forensic science laboratories spanning Europe, the United States, and Australia for a project called Nite-Crime (Natural isotopes and trace elements in **criminalistics** and environmental forensics) designed to develop advanced mass spectroscopy-related chemical analysis techniques for identifying the components of extremely minute fragments in inert materials and unequivocally linking suspects to crime scenes.

Another international use for evolving mass **spectroscopy** techniques is in solving homicides in which the victim has been transported from one location to another. Forensic scientists sample traces of mineral debris on the victim's body or clothing, and compare them against samples removed from both sites in order to ascertain that the victim was at both locations. Mass spectroscopy procedures combining different methods of chemical elemental separation with **laser** ablation techniques requiring only scant samples are facilitated by the Nite-Crime project and have successfully provided proof of victim location and transportation between sites.

In 1999 the European Union committed to the creation of a cooperative network of national law enforcement authorities responsible for crime prevention. This laid the groundwork for the creation of the European Crime Prevention Network in 2001 and underscores the EU's commitment to a uniform and integrated approach to the investigation, solution, and prosecution of international crimes. Forensic scientific criminal investigations are at the cornerstone of Europol's intelligence efforts. With increasing terrorist threats, coupled with the very real concern of nuclear proliferation, a new market for international trafficking has been created—that of international transport of nuclear materials. This has, in turn, spawned a new field—international nuclear forensic science.

As information technologies continue to explode worldwide, the concept of international security, whether in individual homes, at the workplace, or online, has become progressively more difficult to effect. Because each nation varies in the level of sophistication of its information technology systems, there has been little international coherence; this is especially problematic as information technology (Internet) and cybercrime is propagated across the globe virtually instantaneously. Worldwide problems require worldwide solutions and the EU enacted a

Council Framework Decision on "Attacks against information systems" in 2002, which was designed to promote global cooperation and thereby improve cross-border and cross-continent information security.

The Forensic Science Service, an affiliate of the ENFSI (**European Network of Forensic Science Institutes**), provides support to law enforcement and criminal justice systems worldwide. It is a UK-based organization providing services internationally, designed to partner with worldwide criminal justice systems in order to diminish criminal activity. In addition to its worldwide criminal investigation capabilities, FSS advises (and provides oversight for) global government agencies on best practice approaches to the construction and equipping of forensic science facilities; they also maintain FORS, a worldwide forensic science literature database. In addition, FSS provides on-site expert **training** in cutting edge equipment and emerging technologies for forensic laboratories. The FSS offers worldwide forensic expert/expert witness support to the criminal justice system; some examples drawn from international trial transcripts follow.

This example involves FSS's use of familial DNA searching, resulting in the world's first successful prosecution using this technique. Nineteen-year-old Craig Harman had spent the evening of March 20, 2003 drinking with a friend. On their way home, the pair decided to attempt to steal a car (a Renault Clio). Their attempt at hotwiring the vehicle was unsuccessful, so they each decided to take a brick from a neighboring garden and throw it at oncoming traffic (they were about to cross a footbridge over the M3 in Surrey, UK). As they crossed the bridge, Mr. Harman and his companion tossed their bricks at oncoming traffic. One brick broke through the windshield of a truck driven by Michael Little from Essex; the other nearly hit another car.

The brick struck Mr. Little on the chest, causing heart failure and death. Forensic scientific examination of the brick that caused Michael Little's death yielded a mixed DNA profile for the victim and another person. A full DNA profile was obtained from **blood** found on the nearby Renault Clio. A highly sensitive technique called DNA Low Copy Number was utilized; it revealed that the partial profile obtained from the brick matched the full DNA profile found on the Renault Clio, linking the two crimes. The full profile was run against the UK National DNA Database (NDNAD) without uncovering a match. The ethnic markers elicited form the DNA profile indicated that the suspect was a Caucasian male; crime scene details suggested a perpetrator less than 35 years of age. The nature of the crime indicated a likelihood that he was a local resident, so the Surrey Police force conducted an intelligence-led DNA screen of 350 individuals (volunteers) from the surrounding area; again, no match. A groundbreaking decision to use familial searching was made, in an effort to uncover a suspect by searching NDNAD for persons who most closely matched the unknown DNA profile. The search parameters were narrowed to Caucasian males below the age of 35 who lived in the geographic areas adjacent to the crime. This method yielded a list of 25 names; the closest profile matched 16 of 20 parameters, indicating that it belonged to a close biological relative of the perpetrator. This data provided a direct link to Craig Harman; he was interrogated and he supplied a DNA sample. When it was analyzed, the sample exactly matched the one from the brick at the crime scene. Craig Harman went to trial and was convicted of **manslaughter**.

In 1981, a fourteen-year-old girl was raped, beaten, and strangled after being attacked while en route from her home to band practice in Hampshire, UK. There was a massive investigation at the time of the incident, but no suspect was found. A single microscopic slide containing biological evidence collected from the victim by the FSS was intentionally saved, in hopes that DNA evidence processing techniques would eventually be perfected for use with very small samples. In 1999, the FSS perfected their use of DNA Low Copy Number (DNA LCN) technology. Using this method, they were able to obtain a full DNA profile of the perpetrator by using evidence obtained from the victim's clothing. They ran the profile against the NDNAD, and it came up with a "hit" in 2001, when it matched that of Tony Jasinsky. Forensic scientists then removed the 20-year-old slide from FSS archives and attempted to extract a DNA profile, endeavoring to develop a closer link to Jasinsky. They successfully obtained a full profile, which matched that from the victim's clothing, as well as one obtained directly from Jasinsky. When the **murder** was committed, Tony Jasinsky was employed at the local Army barracks as a cook. Tony Jasinsky went to trial, was convicted for Marion Crofts' beating, rape, and murder, and received a life sentence in May of 2002.

Antonio Imiela was sentenced to life in prison after being convicted of a series of rapes committed over a one-year period. This most critical evidence in the case came from DNA and **fibers**. In November of 2001, a 10-year-old female was abducted from outside a community center in Kent (UK). She was taken to a nearby wooded area, where she was assaulted and raped. A full DNA profile was obtained from the victim

and the crime scene, but it failed to match anyone listed on the NDNAD. Eight months later, another attack occurred in an area geographically unrelated to the first; a 30-year-old woman was beaten and raped while out walking. Using the DNA Low Copy Number technique, a partial profile of the perpetrator was obtained; it matched the profile from the first rape. Three further rapes, each geographically distant from the last, occurred. In October of 2002, a 14-year-old girl was raped; she was able to give local authorities a sufficiently detailed description so as to enable them to create a composite picture of her assailant. The picture was widely circulated to the media. An anonymous caller contacted Crimestoppers, and directed the authorities to Imiela. Imiela gave a DNA sample to police detectives; two days later he kidnapped and sexually assaulted another 10-year-old girl. Imiela was arrested in December of 2002, as a result of DNA matching between samples obtained from the first crime scene and from the suspect.

FSS forensic scientists examined Imiela's clothing, and extracted a number of different brightly colored unusual fibers from it that hadn't come from the clothing itself. The fibers were sufficient in number so as to make the hypothesis that they might have come from the clothing of his victims via secondary transfer plausible (fibers from the clothing worn by the perpetrator being transferred to clothing that came into contact with the suspect's clothing; that is, the clothing of the victims). Over a period of several months, FSS forensic scientists were able to match these fibers, ranging from a single fiber in one case to numerous fibers of different types for the victim who had been in Imiela's car. In addition, a DNA profile matching the last 10-year-old victim was obtained from two hairs found in Imiela's car. Therefore, there was a transfer of fibers in one direction and DNA transfer the other way.

Ultimately, fiber evidence was recovered in all eight sexual assaults. Together with the DNA profile, there was sufficient forensic evidence to provide extremely strong material proof that Imiela was the assailant. He was ultimately convicted of seven rapes, one count of kidnapping, a sexual assault, and attempted rape of a 10-year-old girl. He was given seven life sentences.

SEE ALSO Accelerant; Artificial fibers; Cold case; Cold hit; Counterfeit currency, technology and the manufacture of; DNA databanks; Gas chromatograph-mass spectrometer; Inorganic compounds; Laser ablation-inductively coupled plasma mass spectrometry; Method of operation (M.O.).

Louis C. Tripoli

**AMERICAN
PHYSICIAN**

Louis C. Tripoli is both a physician and a forensic scientist. When not on active duty with the United States Navy (he was called up in August 2004 and deployed to duty in Iraq as a public health expert with the U.S. Marine 4th Civil Affairs Group), he is the Senior Vice President of Correctional Medical Services (CMS), the Chairman of the Correctional Medical Institute, an Adjunct Professor of Medicine at the Johns Hopkins University, Division of Infectious Diseases, and an Adjunct Professor at St. Louis University's School of Public Health. In addition to being Board Certified in internal medicine, he holds a certificate in forensic medicine from the American College of Forensic Examiners.

Tripoli is the Vice President of Medical Affairs and Chief Medical Officer for the Correctional Medicine Institute, a non-profit charitable educational organization dedicated to the advancement of medical care in correctional settings. He is committed to this premise, both as a forensic scientist and as a physician, because it is his contention that correctional healthcare is a growing specialty, dedicated to a population characterized by uniquely complex medical (and biopsychosocial) needs. As a forensic scientist, he understands that the majority of incarcerated individuals will eventually be released and returned to the community; by positively impacting inmate healthcare, it is also possible to improve public health and the health of the larger community.

Tripoli was born in Oklahoma and raised in Washington, Pennsylvania. The son of Charles and Rita Tripoli, he is one of twelve children, four of whom were adopted from other countries. Tripoli graduated from Harvard University and from medical school at the University of Pittsburgh.

His family has always strongly valued public service, and his father, a family medicine practitioner, has been a participant in numerous international medical missions. While in Iraq, Tripoli called upon his parents to come to Iraq to assist him in facilitating an international medical mission, in which he arranged for an infant with severe hemangiomas on her face (benign tumors of small blood vessels that can cause deformities and impinge on vital structures) to be brought to the USA for life-saving surgical intervention.

Tripoli was a contributing author to *Forensic Aspects of Chemical and Biological Terrorism*, published in 2004. This text is written particularly for professionals concerned with the interplay of forensics and public health and safety, particularly as they would be impacted by either the threat or the actuality of biochemical terrorism.

SEE ALSO Anthrax; Bacterial biology; Biological warfare, advanced diagnostics; Biological weapons, genetic identification; Chemical and biological detection technologies.

Truth serum

Part of a forensic investigation can involve interviewing or even interrogating someone to determine the course of events. An individual may not always be forthcoming with information. In such cases, one option can be to solicit information chemically.

Truth serum is a term given to a number of different sedative or hypnotic drugs that are used to induce a person to tell the truth. Truth serums are a misnomer. While they do cause a person to become uninhibited and talkative, they do not guarantee the veracity of the subject. Although inhibitions are generally reduced, persons under the influence of truth serums are still able to lie and even tend to fantasize. Courts have ruled that information obtained from narcoanalysis is inadmissible.

As well, the drugs are not truly serums. Nonetheless, once used, the term became ingrained.

In 1943 J. Stephen Horsley published a book in which he described a novel psychotherapeutic method, which he coined narcoanalysis. By chance, he observed that people who were under the influence of narcotics were uninhibited, talkative, and answered all questions that were asked of them. A **narcotic** is a drug that dulls the senses, relieves pain, and induces sleep. Persons who were under the influence of narcotics entered a hypnotic-like state and spoke freely about anxieties or painful memories. Once the drug effect had worn off, the person had no recollection of what he or she said. Narcoanalysis has since been used to assist in the diagnosis of several different psychiatric conditions.

Narcoanalysis is not used in the United States as an **interrogation** method. The Federal Bureau of Investigation (**FBI**) and other federal law enforcement agencies object to the use of truth drugs, preferring instead to use psychological methods to extract information from suspects or prisoners. The

United Nations considers the use of truth drugs to be physical abuse and, therefore, a form of torture.

The issue was revisited in 2002, when some authorities, including former Central Intelligence Agency and FBI chief William Webster, frustrated by the lack of forthcoming information from suspected al Qaeda and Taliban members held at the U.S. prison in Guantanamo Bay, Cuba, advocated administering narcoanalysis drugs to uncooperative captives. United States Secretary of Defense Donald Rumsfeld asserted that narcoanalysis was not used by United States military and intelligence personnel, but suggested that other countries have made use of the technique in the interrogation of suspected terrorists.

Two of the most commonly used truth serums are members of the barbiturate drug class. **Barbiturates** are sedatives and hypnotics that are created from barbituric acid. They are divided into classes according to the duration of sedation: ultrashort, short, intermediate, and long. Ultrashort-acting barbiturates are used as anesthetics whereas long-acting ones are used to treat convulsions (anticonvulsive). Barbiturates are controlled substances due to their high potential for abuse and for addictive behavior.

Sodium pentothal (pentothal sodium, thiopental, thiopentone) is an ultrashort-acting barbiturate, meaning that sedation only lasts for a few minutes. Sodium pentothal slows down the heart rate, lowers blood pressure, and slows down (depresses) the brain and spinal cord (central nervous system) activity. Sedation occurs in less than one minute after injection. It is used as a general anesthetic for procedures of short duration, for induction of anesthesia given before other anesthetic drugs, as a supplement to regional anesthesia (such as a spinal block), as an anticonvulsive, and for narcoanalysis.

Sodium amytal (amobarbital, amylobarbitone, Amytal) is an intermediate-acting barbiturate. Sedation occurs in one hour or longer and lasts for 10 to 12 hours. Sodium amytal depresses the central nervous system. It is used as a sedative, hypnotic, and anticonvulsive and for narcoanalysis. When sodium amytal is used for narcoanalysis it may be called an "Amytal interview."

Scopolamine (hyoscine) is an anticholinergic alkaloid drug that is obtained from certain plants. Anticholinergic drugs block the impulses that pass through certain nerves. Scopolamine affects the autonomic nervous system and is used as a sedative, to prevent motion sickness, to treat eye lens muscle

paralysis (cycloplegic), and to dilate the pupil (mydriatic).

SEE ALSO Nervous system overview; Polygraphs; Psychotropic drugs.

Tularemia

One aspect of **forensic science** is concerned with the investigation of an illness, outbreak, or death that is thought to be caused by a microorganism. Some microbes are exceptionally more adept at initiating disease than others. A good example of this is the microbe responsible for tularemia.

Tularemia is a plague-like disease caused by the Gram-negative bacterium *Francisella tularensis*. The organism is transferred to man from animals (i.e., a zoonosis) such as rodents, voles, mice, squirrels, and rabbits. Reflecting the natural origin of the disease, tularemia is also known as rabbit fever. Indeed, the rabbit is the most common source of the disease. Transfer of the bacterium via contaminated water and vegetation is possible as well.

The disease can easily spread from the environmental source to humans (although direct person-to-person contact has not been documented). This contagiousness and the potential high death rate among those who contract the disease made the bacterium an attractive bioweapon. Both the Japanese and Western armies experimented with *Francisella tularensis* during World War II. Experiments during and after that war established the devastating effect that aerial dispersion of the bacteria could exact on a population.

Tularemia naturally occurs over much of North America and Europe. In the United States, the disease is predominant in south-central and western states such as Missouri, Arkansas, Oklahoma, South Dakota, and Montana. The disease almost always occurs in rural regions. The animal reservoirs of the bacterium become infected typically by a bite from a blood-feeding tick, fly, or mosquito.

Francisella tularensis does not form a spore. Nevertheless, it can survive for protracted periods of time in environments such as cold water, moist hay, soil, and decomposing carcasses.

The number of cases of tularemia in the world is not known, since accurate statistics have not been kept and illnesses attributable to the bacterium go unreported. In the United States, the number of cases used to be high. In the 1950s thousands of people were infected each year. This number has dropped considerably, to less than 200 each year. Those who are infected now tend to be those who are exposed to the organism in its rural habitat (e.g., hunters, trappers, farmers, and butchers).

Humans can acquire the infection through breaks in the skin and mucous membranes, by ingesting contaminated water, or by inhaling the organism. An obligatory step in the establishment of an infection is the invasion of host cells. A prime target of invasion is the immune cell known as a macrophage. Infections can initially become established in the lymph nodes, lungs, spleen, liver, and kidney. As these infections become more established, the microbe can spread to tissues throughout the body.

Symptoms of tularemia vary depending on the route of entry. Handling an infected animal or carcass can produce a slow-growing ulcer at the point of initial contact and swollen lymph nodes. When inhaled, the symptoms include the sudden development of a headache with accompanying high fever, chills, body aches (particularly in the lower back), and fatigue. Ingestion of the organism produces a sore throat, abdominal pain, diarrhea, and vomiting. Other symptoms can include eye infection and the formation of skin ulcers. Some people also develop pneumonia-like chest pain. An especially severe pneumonia develops from the inhalation of one type of the organism, which is designated as *Francisella tularensis* biovar *tularensis* (type A). The pneumonia can progress to respiratory failure and death. The symptoms typically tend to appear three to five days after entry of the microbe into the body.

The infection responds to antibiotic treatment and recovery can be complete within a few weeks. Recovery produces a long-term immunity to re-infection. Some people experience a lingering impairment in the ability to perform physical tasks. If left untreated, tularemia can persist for weeks, even months, and can be fatal. The severe form of tularemia can kill up to 60% of those who are infected if treatment is not given.

A vaccine consisting of a living, but weakened form of the bacterium is available for tularemia. To date it has been administered only to those who are routinely exposed to the bacterium (e.g., researchers). This is because the potential risks of the vaccine are statistically greater than the risk of acquiring the infection.

SEE ALSO Bacterial biology; Bioterrorism; Vaccines.

Typewriter and printer analysis

Criminals may type a document like a ransom note or a threatening letter in the mistaken belief that, unlike handwriting, typed script cannot be readily identified. However, the forensic document examiner may well be able to extract some valuable **evidence** from a typed document. The advent of modern office technology has brought about some important changes in this kind of work. Most documents today are produced on modern **laser** printers and photocopiers that are difficult to distinguish from one another. Manual typewriters are much more individual as machines and the investigator can glean far more information from a manually typed document than from a printed document.

While it is unusual to find a manual typewriter in a modern office, some people still keep these machines for personal use. They are also still found in some developing countries. Therefore, the forensic examination of typewritten documents can still be important. A manual typewriter has many moving parts that tend to deteriorate over time and introduce tiny faults into a printed document. The document examiner looks for these faults when trying to tie a document to a particular machine that may already be available as an item of evidence, perhaps having been found at a suspect's address.

Typewriters produce letters with standard typefaces, but the size, shape, and styling of the letters may vary with the make and model of the machine. There are databases with identifying information on the letters produced by different typewriters and a comparison may be informative. If a suspect machine is present, the investigator will use it to produce a comparison document to see how closely it resembles the questioned document. He or she will try to reproduce the conditions, such as paper, age of the typewriter ribbon, and so on, that were used to produce the original. A side-by-side visual comparison of the two documents may be sufficient to decide whether they have been produced by the same machine.

Manual typewriters in which the individual characters are fixed to the end of a type bar can produce a number of individual characteristics, such as misaligned or damaged letters, as the letters begin to age. There may also be subtle variations in the pressure applied to the page by different keys which will show up as differences in how heavily inked the letters are. The investigator will also look for tiny variations in the spacing between the letters.

Italian police officers display seized counterfeit Iraqi dinar and U.S. $100 banknotes at a central police station in Rome in 2003. The seized counterfeit currency was elaborately detailed and printed on a high-quality printer. © REUTERS/CORBIS

Electric typewriters are more modern than manual machines and the letters are produced with either a daisy wheel or a golf ball. The most important feature of these two elements, from a forensic point of view, is that they start to deteriorate with increased use. Faults develop which are transferred to the typing on the paper and the examiner may be able to detect tiny flaws within the print. These same flaws will show up in a comparison document produced with the same machine and so can be used to help identify it.

Typewriter ribbons can be quite informative to the document examiner. The letters are stamped out on the paper as an image of the ink of the ribbon. Therefore the ribbon may bear an image of some of the letters and words of the document. The roller or platen of the typewriter may also contain information, because an image of the text may have been transferred to it. Tiny imperfections in the roller may also be transferred onto the document. Analysis of carbon paper, used to create copies, and correction papers may also reveal fragments of text from the document under investigation.

In most offices and homes, typewriters have now been replaced by printers. The first printers, which are not much seen now, were dot matrix printers. These were then superseded by ink jet and laser printers. It is relatively easy to determine whether a document was produced with a dot matrix, ink jet, or laser printer. Beyond this, however, it can be very hard to distinguish one make and model of printer from another. Printers are mass produced and they have fewer moving parts than typewriters which makes it hard to extract much identifying evidence that can tie a document to a particular machine. However, there may be tiny scratches on the drum of a laser printer which may be transferred onto the document.

Sometimes the investigator wants to determine whether a document is an original or a photocopy. Modern photocopiers have much the same mechanism as a laser printer. Minute faults on the camera lens, drum, or other part of the mechanism may be transferred onto the document. Similarly, specks of dust on the glass sheet where the paper to be copied is placed may transfer so called "trash marks" onto the copy. In this way, it might be possible to match a copy to a particular photocopier.

It was reported in late 2004 that, in an effort to assist governments trying to combat crimes such as counterfeiting, some color laser printer and copier manufacturing companies, such as Xerox, have begun utilizing technology that prints faint information, including the serial number of the machine, on every document it prints in small yellow dots that are virtually invisible to the naked eye. Though this technology is useful to those trying to combat crime, it also has privacy ramifications.

SEE ALSO Document forgery; Ink analysis.

Ultraviolet light analysis

Ultraviolet (UV) light technologies are used for multiple purposes in forensic investigations, including authenticating paintings and other fine art, authenticating signatures, analyzing **questioned documents**, illuminating latent fingerprints at crime scenes and **trace evidence** on clothing, analyzing ink stains, and revealing residual stains of body **fluids**.

Ultraviolet light analysis and other optical examination techniques are recommended by the Federal Bureau of Investigation guidelines as the first choice to examine biologically contaminated **evidence**. This is because ultraviolet analysis is not destructive. It allows precise images and preliminary **identification** of the evidence before other analytical methods, such as **luminol** or washing solutions, are applied.

Body fluids such as **saliva**, **semen**, vaginal fluids, urine, and perspiration give off fluorescent light when illuminated by a source of ultraviolet light, which is a very efficient method for detecting such stains in a crime scene or in objects collected from the scene, such as clothing, towels, bed sheets, or decorative items. Even dried stains become fluorescent under UV light.

Forensic technicians also use UV light technologies, such as ultraviolet monochromators or optical **spectroscopy**, to detect the presence of illegal or controlled substances or their residues in unidentified samples, or to determine how many types of ink or pens were used in a forged document.

Ultraviolet reflectance spectrography generates images from ultraviolet radiation in a technique known as RUVIS. This technique allows the detection of latent fingerprints on nonporous surfaces without dusting or chemical treatment as well as of those previously treated with superglue fumes (cyanoacrylate vapor). RUVIS produces clear detailed images that can be either photographed or filmed, depending on the equipment in use. The RUVIS technique basically consists of the generation of UV light by an external source, which is focused on the surface containing latent prints. The UV light is diffusely reflected from the **fingerprint** residues on the nonporous surface toward an optical filter and passes through an objective lens into an image intensifier that converts it into visible light, thus producing the fingerprint image. Latent fingerprints are those that are invisible to the naked eye and must be detected by optical devices before being photographed. For forensic purposes, all technical data involving the picture is also recorded, such as the type of camera, lens, film, shutter speed, camera position, angle, and distance from the object. These records ensure the reproducibility of the image by independent analysts, thus preventing accusations of image manipulation to force a print match.

SEE ALSO Alternate light source analysis; Isotopic analysis; Laser; Luminol; Monochromatic light.

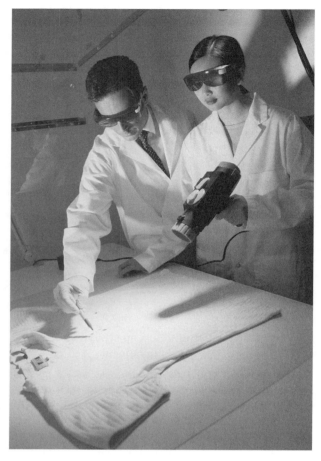

Forensic scientists using an ultraviolet light source to examine a piece of clothing. © JIM CRAIGMYLE/CORBIS

Unabomber case and trial

On April 13, 1996, Theodore (Ted) Kaczynski was arrested at his tiny cabin in the woods outside Lincoln, Montana. The arrest brought to a close a nearly 18-year-long manhunt for an elusive figure known as the Unabomber. By the time the manhunt ended, the **FBI**, the U.S. Postal Service, the Bureau of Alcohol, Tobacco, and Firearms (**ATF**), and even the U.S. Forestry Service had amassed thousands of volumes of information, including some 9,000 **evidence** photos, in connection with a series of explosive devices, mostly mail bombs, that killed three people and injured many others. On January 22, 1998, Kaczynski pled guilty to these crimes and began serving a life sentence in a Colorado prison. Thus ended the career of a troubled man who had entered Harvard at age 16, completed his master's and Ph.D. by age 25, and taught mathematics for two years at the University of California at Berkeley before dropping out to live primarily off the land, his distrust of technology

festering and growing until it erupted in criminal action.

The Unabomber case began on May 25, 1978, when a Northwestern University professor became suspicious of a parcel that had been returned to him by the postal service but that he had never mailed. He called campus security, and when a campus police officer opened the package, it exploded in his hand, although he suffered only slight injuries. The university contacted the ATF, which began that day to compile what would become a lengthy forensic record of the bomber's handiwork. The bomb was the work of an amateur, made from items that could be found in a home workshop. It consisted of a 9-inch-long piece of metal pipe filled with explosive powders. The triggering device was primitive, a nail held by rubber bands that was intended to strike match heads when the box was opened. The box was made of wood, as were the plugs at the ends of the pipe.

On May 9, 1979, a Northwestern University graduate student escaped serious injury when he opened a cigar box that exploded. This bomb was more sophisticated than the first, for the bomber had replaced the nail and rubber band trigger mechanism with a battery-operated filament wire that ignited the **explosives**. Again, the bomb consisted of common items: tape, wires, a fishing line, a lamp cord, and wooden dowels. On November 15, 1979, a bomb triggered by an altimeter began to smolder in the cargo hold of an American Airlines flight 444. The bomb did not explode because instead of explosives it contained barium nitrate, a powder often used to create green smoke in fireworks. On June 10, 1980, when the president of United Airlines opened a book he had received in the mail, he was injured when a bomb in its hollowed-out pages exploded. This bomb differed from the earlier ones because it had a "signature," the initials FC punched into the metal, which authorities would later learn stood for Freedom Club. At this point the FBI coined the term UnAbom to refer to the targets so far: *Uni*versities and *A*irlines *Bom*bings.

The Unabomber laid low for 16 months, until October 8, 1981, when a bomb found on the campus of the University of Utah was disarmed before it did any damage. In May 1982, a secretary at Vanderbilt University was seriously injured when she opened a package containing a bomb that the postal service was to have returned (like the first bomb) to an electrical engineering professor at Utah's Brigham Young University. Two months later, on July 2, an engineering professor at Berkeley was seriously injured after he

The building belonging to Theodore Kaczynski (also known as the Unabomber) is delivered to the site of his trial. Forensic investigators discovered evidence of bombmaking materials inside the hut. © CORBIS SYGMA

lifted the handle on a strange piece of equipment in a faculty lounge, triggering an explosion.

Again, there was a hiatus, almost three years. Then on May 15, 1985, a Berkeley graduate student was seriously injured in a computer lab when he opened a three-ring binder that exploded. Forensics showed that the bomber had graduated to more lethal explosives, a mix of ammonium nitrate and aluminum powder. The bomb's shrapnel consisted of tacks, nails, and bits of lead. Stamped on the end seal of the bomb's pipe were the initials FC. Less than a month later, on June 13, a similar bomb showed up at a Boeing plant in Auburn, Washington. A mailroom clerk thought that the package looked suspicious and called the authorities, who dismantled the bomb, where again they found the FC logo. Just two days later, on June 15, a psychology professor at the University of Michigan and his assistant were injured when the latter triggered an explosion when he opened a book the professor had received in the mail. The first death occurred on December 11, 1985, when the owner of a computer store in Sacramento, California, noticed in the parking lot a block of wood with nails protruding from it. When he picked it up, it exploded with enormous force. Forensic examina-

tion showed that the bomb consisted of three 10-inch pipes filled with potassium sulfate, potassium chloride, ammonium nitrate, and aluminum powder. Again, the shrapnel consisted of sharp chunks of metal, nails, and splinters.

At this point, authorities were no closer to catching the bomber than they had been in 1978, but a significant clue emerged in February 1987, when a secretary at a Salt Lake City, Utah, computer firm spotted a stranger loitering outside. From her description, sketch artists created the now-famous sketch of a man wearing a hooded sweatshirt and aviator sunglasses thought to be the Unabomber, who had placed in a block of wood in the parking lot a bomb that seriously injured the company's vice president. Forensics showed that the Unabomber was continuing to hone his skills, for this bomb contained a new, more sensitive triggering device.

The bombings then stopped for six years. They returned with new force in June 1993. On June 22, a geneticist at the University of California at San Francisco was seriously injured when he opened a wooden box inside a padded envelope he had received in the mail. A similar package mailed on the same date, June 18, arrived at the office of a Yale

University computer science professor on June 23. Again, when he opened the box, roughly the size of a shoebox, it exploded with devastating force. That same day, the world received its first communication from the Unabomber in the form of a letter to the editor of the *New York Times* in which he took responsibility for the two most recent bombings, identified FC as the initials of Freedom Club, and promised further communications in the future.

Authorities were scrambling to solve the case, and the UNABOM task force, made up of the FBI, the ATF, and the U.S. Postal Service, was born. The task force, though, could not prevent two further lethal bombs. On December 10, 1994, an advertising executive thought mistakenly to have had a hand in trying to refurbish the image of Exxon after the *Exxon Valdez* oil spill disaster was killed when he opened a package at his home. Again, the FC logo was found in the rubble, along with the remains of a wooden box. Then on April 24, 1995, the president of the California Forestry Association was killed when he opened a package addressed to his predecessor.

In time, the identity of the Unabomber would be discovered less through clues found at the crime scenes than through clues contained in his own writing. In 1995, he sent rambling and insulting letters to various scientists. In them he warned the recipients to abandon their research, making clear his opposition to modern science and technology. The most important of these letters was the one he wrote to the *New York Times*, threatening further violence and claiming that both the bomb-making expertise and membership of the Freedom Club were growing. He also attempted to strike a startling deal: He would stop his activities if the *Times* or some other well-known newspaper published his 35,000-word "Manifesto."

The *Times* and the *Washington Post* consulted with the FBI before deciding to publish the manifesto, a lengthy rant against progress, the Industrial Revolution, and modern technology. The authorities hoped that if the manifesto was published, someone would recognize the ideas or the writing style and come forward with information about the author's identity. They were correct, for David Kaczynski read the Manifesto and concluded that its likely author was his older brother Ted. David asked a private investigator to compare samples of Ted's writing with the manifesto. The investigator in turn took the samples to linguistic specialists, who agreed that the same person wrote the manifesto and the writing samples.

Six weeks later, Ted Kaczynski was arrested. His Montana cabin was a treasure trove of evidence, containing over 700 items that amounted to a small bomb factory and thousands of pages of his journal. During nearly two years of legal maneuvering, his attorneys hoped to enter an insanity plea, but Kaczynski refused to be examined by psychologists. He relented only after he petitioned the court to represent himself and the court ruled that it would agree only if he was found psychologically fit to do so. Facing unassailable forensic evidence and a possible death penalty, Kaczynski pled guilty to the charges.

SEE ALSO ATF (United States Bureau of Alcohol, Tobacco, and Firearms); Bomb (explosion) investigations; Handwriting analysis.

Uncertainty analysis in forensic science

Many decisions within **forensic science** are made in the face of uncertainties. As the world becomes increasingly complex, and along with it the complexity of crimes and their investigations, there is an escalating need by forensic scientists to provide more and better statistical information in order to more effectively fight criminals. One of the major tasks confronting the forensic science community is to carefully plan so that the quantity and quality of information obtained will meet the requirements to solve crime and convict criminals. However, any mathematical value that is calculated to estimate an actual value involves an uncertainty. Although uncertainty exists with regard to the quantity and quality of information, it can be minimized by using critical thinking, objectivity, and systematic measurement and examination of the facts.

Uncertainty with regards to mathematical statistics is the estimated amount or percentage by which an observed or calculated value may differ from the actual value. In other words, the uncertainty of a calculated result is a measure of the accurateness (or goodness) to the actual value. Without such a comparative measure, it would be impossible to judge the fitness (or goodness) of the value as a basis for making informed decisions relating to forensic science. For example, in the investigation of a drug bust, a forensic chemist might find from his chemical analysis of a white powder that $35.0 \pm 1.0\%$ of the contents of the tested powder is the **narcotic** drug cocaine. The plus-or-minus ($\pm$) one percent value (which is sometimes called a margin of error) is the uncertainty associated with the chemist's result; that is, the actual value could vary from 34.0–36.0% of cocaine, or one percent on either side of the value 35.

In this particular case, the chemist is wise to account for the fact that the equipment and instruments used to measure the concentration of cocaine in the tested powder are not perfectly accurate, so uncertainty arises in the measured value. Thus, uncertainty analysis in the field of forensic science, or in any other field for that matter, involves the procedures, methods, and tools of systematically accounting for every factor contributing to such uncertainties. It covers a wide range of topics that include probability and statistical variables, mathematical relationships and equations, and design and sensitivity of experiments.

The forensic purpose of uncertainty analysis is to evaluate the result of a particular measurement, in a particular laboratory, at a particular time; and as a consequence of knowing that such measurements are not totally accurate, to assign assumptions and approximations to those results. The most widely accepted and commonly used statistical approach to modeling uncertainty is probability theory, which is the branch of mathematics that deals with measuring or determining quantitatively the likelihood that an experiment or event will have a particular outcome.

A common probability measure used to calculate uncertainty is called the confidence interval, which is based on multiple runs of the same analysis. Thus, a confidence interval is a range around a measurement that shows how precise the measurement has been made. For instance, the forensic chemist who found out that $35.0 \pm 1.0\%$ of the tested substance is cocaine might also report that after repeated laboratory analysis of the substance there is a 95% certainty that the concentration of cocaine within the tested substance lies between 34.0 and 36.0 percent. The level of significance—in this case 95%—is a statistical term for defining how confident a measurement is contained within the confidence interval. In this case, the chemist is 95% confident that the actual concentration of cocaine (within the tested sample) lies between 34.0 and 36.0%. There are other confidence intervals based on different levels of significance, such as 90% or 99%. With a 95% confidence interval, the chemist has a 5% chance of being wrong (and a 95% change of being correct); with a 90% confidence interval, a 10% chance of being wrong; and with a 99% confidence interval, a 1% chance of being wrong.

Evaluation of uncertainty is becoming more important within forensic science. Forensic test laboratories are increasingly required to include uncertainty analyses in measurement results through quality management standards such as the ISO 9000 series (where ISO is the common short name for the International Organization for Standardization, the world's largest developer of standards). Several organizations, such as the National Conference of Standards Laboratories and the International Standards Organization are currently investigating ways to standardize and simplify the approach to uncertainty analysis within forensic science.

SEE ALSO Forensic science; Quality control of forensic evidence; Statistical interpretation of evidence.

United States Army Medical Research Institute of Infectious Diseases (USAMRIID)

Forensic science is carried out by civilian and military personnel. The aims can be different. While civilian law enforcement officers are typically concerned with the investigation of an illness outbreak, accident, or death, the military's concern can be on the use of chemical and biological agents as weapons.

For biological agents, one important driving factor behind military forensic science is vaccine development. In the United States, the principal laboratory for research into the medical aspects of biological warfare is the United States Army Medical Research Institute of Infectious Diseases (USAMRIID).

The facility is operated by the Department of Defense and serves mainly to develop **vaccines** to infectious diseases, other treatments such as drugs, and tests to detect and identify disease-causing microorganisms.

While developed for use in the laboratory, USAMRIID is mandated to explore the use of the treatments and tests in the real world of the battlefield. The research conducted at USAMRIID is defensive in nature. Infectious microbes are investigated only to develop means of protecting soldiers from the use of the microbes by opposition forces during a conflict. Investigations can thus focus on unraveling the course of events of an illness outbreak or use of a biological agent, and thererfore are forensic in nature.

The infectious disease research expertise at USAMRIID is also utilized to develop strategies and **training** programs regarding medical defense against infectious microorganisms. For example, the agency regularly updates and publishes a handbook that details the various medical defenses against biological warfare or terrorism. This handbook, now in its fourth edition, is available to the public.

While some of the research conducted at USAMRIID is classified, other research findings of the resident civilian and military scientists are used to benefit the larger public community. USAMRIID and its counterpart U.S. Army Medical Research Institute of Chemical Diseases (USAMRICD) trains more than 550 military medical personnel each year on biological and chemical defense measures. Furthermore, over 40,000 military and civilian medical professionals have attended an annual course on the medical management of biological casualties from 1999 to 2002.

The Office of the Surgeon General of the Army established USAMRIID on January 27, 1969. The facility replaced the U.S. Army Medical Unit (USAMU), which had been operating at the Fort Detrick, Maryland location since 1956. The USAMU had a mandate to conduct research into the offensive use of biological and chemical weapons. This research was stopped by U.S. President Richard Nixon in 1969. In 1971 and 1972, the stockpiled biological weapons were destroyed.

The defensive research that USAMU had been conducting, such as vaccine development, was continued by USAMRIID. In 1971 the facility was reassigned to the U.S. Army Medical Research and Development Command. Also in 1971, the centerpiece laboratory was completed. Construction of the high laboratory, which was designed to house and study highly infectious and dangerous microorganisms, cost $14 million.

Laboratories have a rating system with respect to the types of microbes that can safely be studied. There are four levels possible. A typical university research lab with no specialized safety features (i.e., fume hood, biological safely cabinet, filtering of exhausted air) is a Biosafety Level 1. Progression to a higher level requires more stringent safety and biological controls. A Biosafety Level 4 laboratory is the only laboratory that can safely handle microbes such as the **Ebola virus**, *Bacillus anthracis* (the cause of **anthrax**), the Marburg virus, and hantavirus.

USAMRIID has a 10,000 square foot Biosafety Level 4 facility and 50,000 square feet of Biosafety Level 3. It is the largest high-level containment facility in the United States and is one of only three such units. The others are at the **Centers for Disease Control and Prevention** in Atlanta, Georgia, and San Antonio, Texas. A fourth level 4 laboratory is planned for the Rocky Mountain Lab in Hamilton, Montana.

Entry to the Level 4 area requires passage through several checkpoints and the keying in of a security code that is issued only after the person has been successfully vaccinated against the microorganism under study. All work in the level 4 lab is conducted in a pressurized and ventilated suit. Air for breathing is passed into the suit through a hose and is filtered so as to be free of microorganisms.

The USAMRIID facility also contains a Biosafety Level 4 patient ward. The ward can house people who have been infected during a disease outbreak or researchers who have been accidentally exposed to an infectious microbe. This ward was used in 1982 to care for two researchers from the Centers for Disease Control and Prevention who were exposed to rat blood contaminated with the virus that causes Lassa fever. The two researchers, along with three others thought to have been exposed to the virus, remained in the containment ward until they were determined to be free of infection.

Equipment is also available that allows the Biosafety Level 4 conditions to be mimicked in the field. Thus, an infected person can be isolated at the site of an outbreak and transported back to Fort Detrick for medical treatment and study of the infection.

The research staff at USAMRIID numbers over 500 and includes physicians, microbiologists, molecular biologists, virologists, pathologists, and veterinarians. Among the support staff who assist the researchers are laboratory technicians who have volunteered to be test subjects during clinical trials of vaccines and drugs.

USAMRIID scientists have the ability to rapidly identify approximately 85 infectious microorganisms. Work is underway to develop protection against 40 of the microbes. Vaccines are in various stages of development for 10 of the microbes including the highly infectious anthrax bacterium, and the Ebola and Marburg viruses.

Researchers and support staff can also respond to disease outbreaks. On short notice, forensic teams can journey to the site of the infection to begin an investigation. This response is often conducted in conjunction with forensic personnel from the Centers for Disease Control and Prevention.

One well-known USAMRIID response occurred in 1989, when an outbreak of an Ebola virus occurred at a primate holding facility in nearby Reston,

Virginia. Some personnel even became infected with the virus, which was later determined to be a different variety from that which causes hemorrhagic Ebola fever in humans. The response of the USAMRIID personnel was subsequently detailed in best-selling books and inspired popular movies.

In the fall of 2001, several letters containing anthrax **spores** were sent to various locations in the eastern United States via the United States Postal Service. **Sequencing** of the genetic material from the spores determined that the source of the anthrax was a strain of the microbe that had been developed in the USAMRIID labs in the 1980s. Whether the bacteria actually used in the incidents came from USAMRIID or from another lab that acquired the bacteria from USAMRIID has not yet been established.

SEE ALSO Anthrax; Ebola virus; Pathogens; Vaccines.

Urban legends and myths SEE
Pseudoscience and forensics

U.S. Supreme Court (rulings on forensic evidence)

Throughout the twentieth century, the court system wrestled with the issue of whether the testimony of forensic experts was a valid form of **evidence**. The essential problem was that modern science moves at a brisker pace than the judicial system. As new scientific techniques with applicability to forensics emerged, the courts often had no precedents on which to accept or reject them. Today, for example, the validity of fingerprint identification, with its axiom that the fingerprints of no two persons are alike, is largely taken for granted. But a century ago the courts were not so sure, for there was little research to buttress such a claim. At the opposite end of the twentieth century came DNA evidence, with statistical claims about the uniqueness of a person's genetic markers left behind at crime scenes in the form of blood, semen, skin cells, or hair. While justice plods, science sprints, often leaving the court system struggling to catch up as it tries to answer fundamental questions about the validity of scientific testimony and how to distinguish the claims of science from those of pseudoscience.

The United States Supreme Court has decided very few cases that directly bear on the admissibility of forensic testimony. Rather than addressing the issue of the validity of any particular branch of **forensic science**, the Court has limited itself to establishing ground rules for forensic testimony. Currently, it does so through the **Federal Rules of Evidence**, a set of broad principles used in federal trials. Most state courts have adopted these rules as well. The Federal Rules govern a number of issues pertaining to the relevance of evidence, but the key rule for forensic scientists is Rule 702, "Testimony by Experts," which applies to the testimony of any forensic scientist called to the witness stand: "If scientific, technical, or other specialized knowledge will assist the trier of fact to understand the evidence or to determine a fact in issue, a witness qualified as an expert by knowledge, skill, experience, **training**, or education, may testify thereto in the form of an opinion or otherwise, if (1) the testimony is based upon sufficient facts or data, (2) the testimony is the product of reliable principles and methods, and (3) the witness has applied the principles and methods reliably to the facts of the case."

The Court entered the arena of forensic science in a 1923 case, *Frye v. United States*. Frye had been convicted of second-degree **murder**. His lawyer wanted to offer the testimony of a scientist who had conducted a systolic blood pressure deception test, today called a lie-detector or polygraph test, to demonstrate that his client was telling the truth. The trial court refused to admit the testimony, and the defendant appealed. In a remarkably brief and pointed decision, the Supreme Court affirmed the ruling of the lower court, famously stating: "Just when a scientific principle or discovery crosses the line between the experimental and demonstrable states is difficult to define. Somewhere in this twilight zone the evidential force of the principle must be recognized, and while courts will go a long way in admitting expert testimony deduced from a well-recognized scientific principle or discovery, the thing from which the deduction is made must be sufficiently established to have gained general acceptance in the particular field in which it belongs." In the Court's view, the systolic blood pressure deception test had "not yet gained such standing and scientific recognition."

Thus was born the so-called *Frye* standard, used in the years that followed by various lower courts to rule on the admissibility of such forensic tools as voiceprints, neutron activation, **gunshot residue** tests, bite mark comparisons, and blood grouping tests. The fundamental principle was "general acceptance in the particular field," making the scientific community itself the arbiter of whether a technique or procedure passed scientific muster. In a key case affirming the Frye standard in 1974, a U.S. Court of Appeals wrote in *United States v. Addison* that the standard "assures that those most qualified to assess the general validity of a scientific method will have the determinative voice." Thus, the Frye standard remained a well-settled principle for 70 years.

By the 1990s, though, the *Frye* standard was coming under pressure, largely because in 1975 the Federal Rules of Evidence were enacted, and nowhere did they mention the "general acceptance" test of *Frye*. The rules seemingly cleared the way for admitting scientific testimony based on new knowledge that had not necessarily gained general acceptance in the scientific community. Uncertainty over the question of whether the Federal Rules superceded the *Frye* standard had come to a head in 1993 when the Supreme Court heard the case of *Daubert v. Merrell Dow Pharmaceuticals*.

The case involved two children with serious birth defects. Daubert contended that the defects were caused by a Merrell Dow drug the mother had taken during pregnancy. He wanted to offer the scientific testimony of eight experts who had conducted animal studies and chemical structure analyses on the drug and concluded that it could cause birth defects. The company responded with published scientific epidemiological studies showing that the drug was not a risk factor for birth defects. The trial court, citing *Frye*, agreed with the company and ruled that the methods employed by the plaintiff's experts did not meet the standard of "general acceptance" under *Frye*. The Court of Appeals affirmed the trial court's ruling, but the U.S. Supreme Court reversed the Court of Appeals.

In its opinion, the Court undertook a detailed examination of whether the Federal Rules of Evidence superceded *Frye*. It concluded that *Frye's* 'general acceptance' is not a necessary precondition to the admissibility of scientific evidence" and that the Federal Rules "assign to the trial judge the task of ensuring that an expert's testimony both rests on a reliable foundation and is relevant to the task at hand." To guide the trial judge, the Court offered a flexible four-pronged test based on whether the theory or technique has been "tested"; whether it has been subjected to "peer review," usually through a peer-reviewed publication, so that the scientific community can detect flaws; what its "known or potential rate of error" is; and its "acceptability" in the relevant scientific community. Accordingly, the more stringent *Daubert* (pronounced "Dough-BEAR") standard replaced the earlier Frye standard. Judges,

not the scientific community, were to determine reliability and relevance.

The Daubert standard came into play in a 1997 case, *General Electric Co. et al. v. Joiner*. After he was diagnosed with lung cancer, Joiner sued General Electric and Monsanto. He proffered expert testimony that the cancer was caused by his exposure to workplace chemicals the companies manufactured. The trial court ruled in favor of the companies' motion to exclude the testimony, saying that the testimony did not rise above "subjective belief or unsupported speculation." The Court of Appeals reversed the trial court, but the Supreme Court concluded that the trial court had acted appropriately under *Daubert* and that in failing to defer to the trial court's judgment that there was "too great an analytical gap between the data and the opinion" in the animal studies on which Joiner's expert testimony was based; the Court of Appeals had overstepped its boundaries. In other words, the trial court judge had exercised his proper role under the Daubert standard by acting as a "gatekeeper" for expert scientific testimony.

It remained for the Court to determine whether the *Daubert* standard applied just to "scientific" testimony or to any other type of technical, skill-based, or experience-based knowledge on which expert testimony is based. It did so in *Kumho Tire Co., Ltd., et al. v. Carmichael et al.* in 1999. Carmichael was driving a vehicle on which a tire blew out. When the vehicle overturned, one passenger died and others were injured. Carmichael sued the tire manufacturer, offering the testimony of a tire failure analyst who concluded that the tire blew out because of a manufacturing defect. Kumho moved to have the testimony excluded on the grounds that the expert's methodology failed to satisfy the requirements of Rule 702 of the Federal Rules of Evidence. The trial court granted the motion, ruling that the expert's testimony failed the four-pronged test outlined in *Daubert*. In reversing the trial court, the Court of Appeals ruled that the *Daubert* standard applied only to scientific testimony. While the Supreme Court reversed the Court of Appeals, agreeing with the trial court that the tire expert's procedures failed the *Daubert* standard, the Court explicitly stated that "The *Daubert* factors may apply to the testimony of engineers and other experts who are not scientists" and that "The *Daubert* 'gatekeeping' obligation applies not only to 'scientific' testimony, but to all expert testimony. Rule 702 does not distinguish between 'scientific' knowledge and 'technical' or 'other specialized' knowledge, but makes clear that any such knowledge might become the subject of expert testimony."

Since 1993, the *Daubert* standard, as fortified by *Kumho Tire*, has raised the question of whether any form of widely accepted forensic testimony can be challenged. In January 2002, for example, influential Philadelphia judge Louis H. Pollock caused consternation in the law enforcement community when he ruled that fingerprint analysis failed the Daubert standard, though in March 2002, he reversed himself. The likelihood remains that further *Daubert* challenges to forensic science will be mounted.

SEE ALSO Expert witnesses; Federal Rules of Evidence; *Frye* standard.

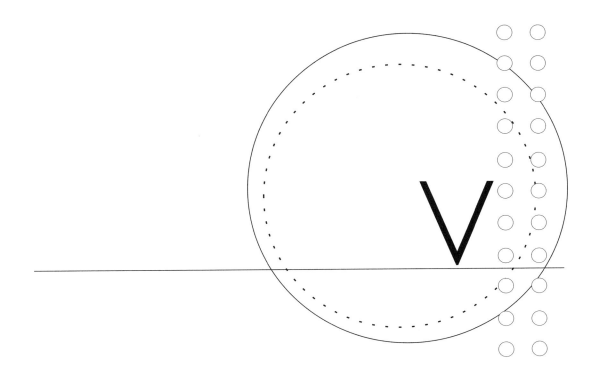

Vaccines

Investigations of the circumstances surrounding an illness outbreak can be a valuable means of determining how an infection is spread, its natural reservoirs, and in identifying subpopulations that display immunity to the infection. These forensic investigations can aid in the development of protective measures. Principle among protective measures are vaccines.

A vaccine is a medical preparation given to a person to provide immunity from a disease. Vaccines use a variety of different substances ranging from dead microorganisms to genetically engineered antigens to defend the body against potentially harmful antigens. Effective vaccines change the **immune system** by promoting the development of antibodies that can quickly and effectively attack disease causing microorganisms or viruses when they enter the body, preventing disease development.

The development of vaccines against diseases including polio, **smallpox**, tetanus, and measles is considered among the great accomplishments of medical science. Researchers are continually attempting to develop new vaccinations against other diseases. In particular, vigorous research into vaccines for acquired immune deficiency syndrome (AIDS), some cancer, severe acute respiratory syndrome (SARS), and avian influenza is currently underway.

The first successful vaccine was developed from cowpox as a treatment for smallpox. Coined by Louis Pasteur (1822–1895), the etymology of the term vaccine reflects this achievement. It is taken from the Latin for cow (*vacca*) and the word vaccinia, the virus that causes cowpox.

This first effective vaccine developed treated smallpox, a virulent disease that killed thousands of its victims and left thousands of others disfigured. In one of the first forms of inoculation, ancient Chinese people developed a snuff made from powdered smallpox scabs that was blown into the nostrils of uninfected individuals. Some individuals died from the therapy; however, in most cases, the mild infection produced offered protection from later, more serious infection.

In the late 1600s, European peasants employed a similar method of immunizing themselves against smallpox. In a practice referred to as "buying the smallpox," peasants in Poland, Scotland, and Denmark reportedly injected the smallpox virus under the skin to obtain immunity.

Lady Mary Wortley Montagu, the wife of the British ambassador to Turkey, brought information on immunization back to Europe in the early 1700s. Montague reported that the Turks injected a preparation of small pox scabs into the veins of susceptible individuals. Those injected generally developed a mild case of smallpox from which they recovered rapidly. Montague convinced King George I to allow trials of the technique on inmates in Newgate Prison. Although some individuals died after receiving the injections, the trials were successful enough that variolation, or the direct injection of smallpox, became accepted medical practice. Variolation also was credited with protecting United States soldiers from smallpox during the Revolutionary War.

Edward Jenner (1749–1823), an English country physician, observed that people who were in contact with cows often developed cowpox, which caused pox sores but was not life threatening. Those people never developed smallpox. In 1796 Jenner tested the hypothesis that cowpox could be used to protect humans against smallpox. He injected a healthy eight-year-old boy with cowpox obtained from a milkmaid's sore. The boy was moderately ill and recovered. Jenner then injected the boy twice with the smallpox virus, and the boy did not get sick.

Modern knowledge of the immune system suggests that the virus that causes cowpox is similar enough to the virus that causes smallpox that the vaccine simulated an immune response to smallpox. Exposure to cowpox **antigen** stimulated the boy's immune system, producing cells that attacked the original antigen as well as the smallpox antigen. The vaccine also conditioned the immune system to produce antibodies more quickly and more efficiently against future infection by smallpox.

During the two centuries since its development, the smallpox vaccine gained popularity, protecting millions from contracting the disease. In 1979, following a major cooperative effort between nations and several international organizations, world health authorities declared smallpox the only infectious disease to be eradicated from the planet.

In 1885 Louis Pasteur (1822–1895) saved the life of Joseph Meister, a nine year old who had been attacked by a rabid dog. Pasteur's series of experimental rabies vaccinations on the boy proved the effectiveness of the new vaccine.

Pasteur's rabies vaccine, the first human vaccine created in a laboratory, was made of an extract gathered from the spinal cords of rabies-infected rabbits. The live virus was weakened by drying over potash. The new vaccination was far from perfect, causing occasional fatalities and temporary paralysis. Individuals had to be injected 14 to 21 times.

The rabies vaccine has been refined many times. In the 1950s, a vaccine grown in duck embryos replaced the use of live virus, and in 1980, a vaccine developed in cultured human cells was produced. In 1998, the newest vaccine technology—genetically engineered vaccines—was applied to rabies. The new DNA vaccine cost a fraction of the regular vaccine. While only a few people die of rabies each year in the United States, more than 40,000 die worldwide,

particularly in Asia and Africa. The less expensive vaccine will make vaccination far more available to people in less developed nations.

In the early 1900s polio was extremely virulent in the United States. At the peak of the epidemic, in 1952, polio killed 3,000 Americans, and 58,000 new cases of polio were reported.

In 1955 Jonas Salk (1914–1995) developed a vaccine for poliomyelitis. The Salk vaccine, a killed virus type, contained the three types of poliovirus that had been identified in the 1940s. In the first year the vaccine was distributed, dozens of cases of polio were reported in individuals who had received the vaccine or had contact with individuals who had been vaccinated. This resulted from an impure batch of vaccine that had not been completely inactivated. By the end of the incident, more than 200 cases had developed and 11 people had died.

In 1961, an oral polio vaccine developed by Albert B. Sabin (1906–1993) was licensed in the United States. The Sabin vaccine, which uses weakened, live polio viruses, quickly overtook the Salk vaccine in popularity in the United States, and is currently administered to all healthy children. Because it is taken orally, the Sabin vaccine is more convenient and less expensive to administer than the Salk vaccine.

Advocates of the Salk vaccine, which is still used extensively in Canada and many other countries, contend that it is safer than the Sabin oral vaccine. No individuals have developed polio from the Salk vaccine since the 1955 incident. In contrast, the Sabin vaccine has a very small, but significant, rate of complications, including the development of polio. However, there has not been one new case of polio in the United States since 1975, or in the Western Hemisphere since 1991. Although polio has not been completely eradicated, there were only 144 confirmed cases worldwide in 1999.

Developing a vaccine against the influenza virus is problematic because the viruses that cause the flu constantly evolve. Scientists grapple with predicting what particular influenza strain will predominate in a given year. When the prediction is accurate, the vaccine is effective. When they are not, the vaccine is often of little help. However, the flu shot has had enough success that pediatricians are now recommending the vaccine for children older than six months.

Since the emergence of AIDS in the early 1980s, research for a treatment for the disease has resulted in clinical trials for more than 25 experimental vaccines.

These range from whole-inactivated viruses to genetically engineered types. Some have focused on a therapeutic approach to help infected individuals to fend off further illness by stimulating components of the immune system. Others have genetically engineered a protein on the surface of HIV to prompt immune response against the virus; and yet others attempted to protect uninfected individuals. The challenges in developing a protective vaccine include the fact that HIV appears to have multiple viral strains and mutates quickly.

In January, 1999, a promising study was reported in *Science* magazine of a new AIDS vaccine created by injecting a healthy cell with DNA from a protein in the AIDS virus that is involved in the infection process. This cell was then injected with genetic material from cells involved in the immune response. Once injected into the individual, this vaccine "catches the AIDS virus in the act," exposing it to the immune system and triggering an immune response. This discovery offers considerable hope for development of an effective vaccine. As of 2005, a vaccine for AIDS had not been proven in clinical trials.

Stimulating the immune system is considered key by many researchers seeking a vaccine for cancer. Currently numerous clinical trials for cancer vaccines are in progress, with researchers developing experimental vaccines against cancer of the breast, colon, and lung, among others. Promising studies of vaccines made from the patient's own tumor cells and genetically engineered vaccines have been reported. Other experimental techniques attempt to penetrate the body in ways that could stimulate vigorous immune responses. These include using bacteria or viruses, both known to efficiently circulate through the body, as carriers of vaccine antigens. These bacteria or viruses could be treated or engineered to make them incapable of causing illness.

The classic methods for producing vaccines use biological products obtained directly from a virus or a bacteria. Depending on the vaccination, the virus or bacteria is either used in a weakened form, as in the Sabin oral polio vaccine; killed, as in the Salk polio vaccine; or taken apart so that a piece of the microorganism can be used. For example, the vaccine for *Streptococcus pneumoniae*, which causes pneumonia, uses bacterial polysaccharides, carbohydrates found in bacteria which contain large numbers of monosaccharides, a simple sugar. The different methods for producing vaccines vary in safety and efficiency. In general, vaccines that use live bacterial or viral products are extremely effective when they work, but carry a greater risk of causing disease. This is most threatening to individuals whose immune systems are weakened, such as individuals with leukemia. Children with leukemia are advised not to take the oral polio vaccine because they are at greater risk of developing the disease. Vaccines which do not include a live virus or bacteria tend to be safer, but their protection may not be as great.

The classical types of vaccines are all limited in their dependence on biological products, which often must be kept cold, may have a limited life, and can be difficult to produce. The development of recombinant vaccines—those using chromosomal parts (or DNA) from a different organism—has generated hope for a new generation of man-made vaccines. The hepatitis B vaccine, one of the first recombinant vaccines to be approved for human use, is made using recombinant yeast cells genetically engineered to include the **gene** coding for the hepatitis B antigen. Because the vaccine contains the antigen, it is capable of stimulating **antibody** production against hepatitis B without the risk that live hepatitis B vaccine carries by introducing the virus into the blood stream.

As medical knowledge has increased—particularly in the field of DNA vaccines—researchers are working toward developing new vaccines for cancer, melanoma, AIDS, influenza, and numerous others illnesses. Since 1980, many improved vaccines have been approved, including several genetically engineered (recombinant) types which first developed during an experiment in 1990. These recombinant vaccines involve the use of so-called "naked DNA." Microscopic portions of a viruses's DNA are injected into the patient. The patient's own cells then adopt that DNA, which is then duplicated when the cell divides, becoming part of each new cell. Researchers have reported success using this method in laboratory trials against influenza and malaria. These DNA vaccines work from inside the cell, not just from the cell's surface, as other vaccines do, allowing a stronger cell-mediated fight against the disease. Also, because the influenza virus constantly changes its surface proteins, the immune system or vaccines cannot change quickly enough to fight each new strain. However, DNA vaccines work on a core protein, which researchers believe should not be affected by these surface changes.

The measles epidemic of 1989 was a graphic display of the failure of many Americans to be properly immunized. A total of 18,000 people were infected, including 41 children who died after developing measles, an infectious, viral illness whose complications include pneumonia and encephalitis. The epidemic was particularly troubling because an effective, safe vaccine against measles has been widely distributed in the United States since the late 1960s. By 1991, the number of new measles cases had started to decrease, but health officials warned that measles remained a threat.

SEE ALSO Pathogens; United States Army Medical Research Institute of Infectious Diseases (USAMRIID).

Variola virus

Variola virus (or *variola major*) is the virus that causes **smallpox**. The virus is one of the members of the poxvirus group (*Poxviridae*) and it is one of the most complicated animal viruses. The variola virus is extremely virulent and is among the most dangerous of all the potential biological weapons.

The variola virus particle is shaped like a biconcave (concave on both sides) brick about 200 to 400 nm (nanometers) long. Its inner compartment contains a highly compressed double strand of deoxyribonucleic acid as well as about 100 proteins and 10 viral enzymes. The enzymes are used in nucleic acid replication.

The variola virus attaches to membrane receptors on the exterior of the host cell. The exact mechanisms involved in the binding to and penetration of the host membrane are not known. As it enters the cell, however, the virus loses its exterior membrane coat. Once inside the cell, the interior membrane layer is removed and the virus's proteins, enzymes, and **DNA** are released into the cytoplasm of the host cell where viral replication and assembly takes place. The production of variola virus by the host cell usually results in host cell death.

Variola virus infects only humans and can be easily transmitted from person to person via the air. Inhalation of only a few virus particles is sufficient to establish an infection. Transmission of the virus is also possible if items such as contaminated linen are handled. The common symptoms of smallpox include chills, high fever, extreme tiredness, headache, backache, vomiting, sore throat with a cough, and sores on mucus membranes and on the skin. As the sores burst and release pus, the afflicted person can experience great pain. Males and females of all ages are equally susceptible to infection. Prior to smallpox eradication approximately one third of patients died—usually within a period of two to three weeks following appearance of symptoms.

The origin of the variola virus in not clear. However, the similarity of the virus and cowpox virus

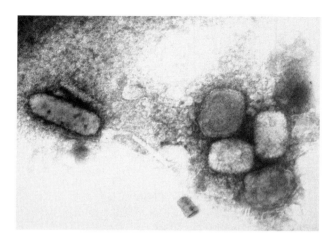

A micrograph shows the variola virus, the virus that causes smallpox, a potentially fatal disease which is preventable by vaccination. © CDC/PHIL/CORBIS

has prompted the suggestion that the variola virus is a mutated version of the cowpox virus. The mutation likely allowed the virus to infect humans. If such a mutation did occur, then it is possible that when early humans became more agricultural and less nomadic, there may have been selective pressure for the cowpox virus to adapt the capability to infect humans.

Vaccination to prevent infection by the variola virus was established in the 1700s. English socialite and public health advocate Lady Mary Wortley Montagu popularized the practice of injection with the pus obtained from smallpox sores as a protection against the disease. This technique became known as variolation. Late in the same century, Edward Jenner successfully prevented the occurrence of smallpox by an injection of pus from cowpox sores. This was the first vaccination. Vaccination against smallpox has been very successful; the variola virus is the only pathogenic virus that has been eliminated from the natural environment. Routine vaccination against smallpox was discontinued in the 1970s and considered globally eradicated in 1980. The last recorded case of naturally occurring smallpox infection was in 1977 in Somalia, Africa.

SEE ALSO Ebola virus; Pathogens; Smallpox.

Video evidence

The use of surveillance **cameras** and **closed-circuit television (CCTV)** for security and crime prevention has been growing in recent years. Shopping malls, car parks, offices, airports, and many other

Video evidence of the theft of a Picasso masterpiece from a London gallery in 1997. © BEN GOTT/CORBIS SYGMA

public and private places are often fitted with such systems, which means that an increasing number of crimes are now being caught on camera. Such cameras are often small and very discreet, so the perpetrators have no idea that they and their actions are being recorded. Video images relating to a crime can be used in court as **evidence**, but effective forensic video analysis is a specialized and highly technical task.

When collecting video evidence, the investigators must take as much care as they would in collecting any other form of evidence. Videotapes can readily be wiped or recorded over, so the first task is to preserve the evidence from a camera by preventing this. For analog video evidence, the record tab must be removed or moved to a saved position. For digital video evidence, write protection has to be in place. The **chain of custody** of the evidence, from collecting the tape from the camera to its receipt in the **processing** lab, must be carefully adhered to, because questions may be asked in court about whether the video evidence could have been tampered with. Storage should be in a climate-controlled

room, because extremes of temperature can damage a video tape.

The images from a surveillance camera or closed-circuit TV system are often blurred, grainy, and of low resolution. Lighting conditions, tape wear, and deficiencies in the camera system all contribute to poor quality pictures. Enhancing such images, without altering them, is challenging. The effort may, however, be well worthwhile if a crucial car number plate or a suspect may thereby be identified.

The video analysis lab will contain a monitor that can produce large images from the tape, a playback deck, a printer, and equipment that can digitize the signal from the original tape so that it can be processed by a computer. Before any analysis is actually carried out, the integrity of the tape should be reviewed and careful notes made of any damage. The video evidence must be protected throughout from external hazards such as magnetic fields or static electric charges that may harm it. It is also important not to over-play the tape, as this can also impair its quality.

There are various software packages that can enhance an image from a video camera and present them either as video tape, still images, or prints for the court. There are many image formats that can be used to do this work, but one of the most popular is the tagged image file format (.tif file). Everything the forensic video analysis technician does to the image must be carefully recorded, because this is sure to be questioned in court. Computer images can be readily manipulated and so everything that has been done to the evidence must be accounted for so that its integrity is preserved.

If a suspect has been detained, video evidence can be used to help identify them. They can be taken back to the original location of the camera and re-recorded standing or walking in the same position. This second image can be compared with the original and an **identification** or an elimination can often be usefully made. The original image can also be used to give an idea of the actual height and size of a suspect.

Video evidence played an important role in the investigation of the **murder** of two-year-old James Bulger in Liverpool, England, in 1993. A surveillance camera in a shopping mall clearly shows the child being separated from his mother and then being led to his death by the two boys who were later convicted of the killing. The tape was repeatedly shown on television and its poignancy has helped fix this especially tragic case in the memory of the British public. In another case, video footage from cameras in a West London shopping mall was intensively studied by police to solve the doorstep shooting of TV presenter Jill Dando in 1999. Although the key suspect did not appear in these images, they were a powerful aid to reconstruction of the crime as they provided sharp, clear images of much of the last hour of Miss Dando's life. Another famous piece of video evidence is the recording of Diana, Princess of Wales, leaving a hotel in Paris just minutes before the car accident that was to end her life in 1997.

SEE ALSO Digital imaging.

Eugène-François Vidocq

7/24/1775–4/30/1857
FRENCH
POLICE DETECTIVE

In the first half of the nineteenth century, French police detective Eugène-François Vidocq turned crime fighting into a scientific endeavor by using record-keeping, ballistic science, and shoe impres-sions to apprehend criminals. Vidocq's dramatic success in reducing the French crime rate helped to popularize **forensic science** methods. He served as the model for many fictional detectives, including Arthur Conan Doyle's Sherlock Holmes.

Vidocq was born in Arras, France, the first child of a baker and his wife. Notoriously weak for the ladies from an early age, Vidocq killed a man in a duel over a woman in 1790. The teenager escaped imprisonment only because the judge in the case permitted him to join the army. He subsequently served with distinction before returning home on leave in 1795 and discovering his unfaithful wife with another man.

Vidocq then deserted from the army and joined a band of card sharks. Arrested and jailed, he forged a pardon for a prisoner with a family and was caught. Vidocq escaped and joined a band of smugglers, but again was arrested because he lacked identity papers. In 1798 Vidocq was sentenced to serve eight years in the galleys, special prisons for hardened criminals who were required to wear leg and arm chains at all times and to don leaded boots whenever they left their cells. Vidocq escaped and, upon being caught, was sent to the brutal prison of La Force.

Facing a likely slow death, Vidocq offered his services as a police spy in 1809. He won the confidence of the authorities under circumstances never explained, and went to work for the Criminal Division of the Paris Prefecture of Police. In October 1812, Vidocq founded and became the first chief of the Brigade de la Sûreté or security police.

With the Sûreté, Vidocq established a plain-clothes bureau that would concentrate exclusively on the investigation and detection of non-political crimes. Its membership would be composed of men familiar with the methods and techniques of criminals. To aid his investigators, Vidocq established more than 60,000 files that identified the aliases, appearances, all previous convictions, and methods of operation of every robber, thief, forger, and confidence artist. He may have been the first police official to realize that criminals often gave themselves away by the repeated use of identifiable techniques.

In order to gather information, Vidocq used informants. Often, he donned a disguise to infiltrate criminal gathering places and acquire information, usually portraying "Jean-Louis," a sixty-year-old criminal merchant from the province of Brittany, complete with a distinctive accent, gray hair, drooping mustache, and old-fashioned pre-Revolutionary clothes.

François-Eugène Vidocq, French adventurer and detective.
© BETTMANN/CORBIS

Vidocq reasoned that most criminals were careless and succeeded only because the authorities' methods were even more undisciplined. He argued that the detective who won convictions did so because he saw and listened, then utilized anything he learned that was out of the ordinary. Accordingly, Vidocq would visit the scene of a crime to look for indicators about the perpetrator and to join in the initial search for **evidence**. He matched boots to footprints, physically taking the boots from a suspect and placing them in the soil indentation (the technology did not exist then to make impressions). He later became the first to make plaster-of-paris casts of foot and shoe impressions. Vidocq took bullets and physically placed them in the barrel of a pistol to make a primitive **ballistics** examination in 1822.

To halt forgers, Vidocq used his own money to hire chemists to develop indelible ink and unalterable bond paper. He also utilized the new technique of **handwriting analysis**. Although Vidocq recognized the value of fingerprints, he never found an ink suitable for fingerprinting and, as a result, never pursued this method of **identification**.

Vidocq's success in solving the crimes that befuddled the uniformed police did not endear him to police authorities. Pugnacious and passionate, he left the government in 1827 because of a political dispute. His memoirs, published in 1829 and highly embellished, gave Vidocq an international reputation as the world's greatest detective.

Vidocq returned to office from 1830 to 1833, before resigning because of his advanced age and his third wife's failing health. In 1834, he founded the first of the modern detective agencies, Les Bureau des Renseignements, aimed at professional and business people who did not trust the competency of the police to solve crimes. He died of a stroke in Paris, having spent much of his money on efforts to rehabilitate criminals and charm women.

SEE ALSO Crime scene investigation; Handwriting analysis.

Viral biology

Virology is the discipline of microbiology that is concerned with the study of viruses. Knowledge of the basics of viral biology, viral reproduction (viral replication), and the ability to identify potential virus-related pathologies are increasingly important skills for some forensic scientists. There are a number of different viruses that challenge the human **immune system** and that may produce disease in humans. Although virologists are the scientists most directly concerned with viral biology, with the rise of terrorism and global health issues such as the evolving H5N1 influenza (commonly called bird flu), forensic scientists now find that their work overlaps interests in **epidemiology** and/or national security.

Viruses are essentially nonliving repositories of nucleic acid that require the presence of a living prokaryotic cell (where **DNA** is present in the cytoplasm) or eukaryotic cell (where DNA is present within the nucleus) for the replication of the nucleic acid. They can exist in a variety of hosts. Viruses can infect animals (including humans), plants, fungi, birds, aquatic organisms, protozoa, bacteria, and insects. Some viruses are able to infect several of these hosts, while other viruses are exclusive to one host.

Viral replication refers to the means by which virus particles make new copies of themselves. All viruses share the need for a host in order to replicate their deoxyribonucleic acid (DNA) or ribonucleic acid (RNA). The virus commandeers the host's existing molecules for the nucleic acid replication process. There are a number of different viruses. The differences include the disease symptoms they cause, their antigenic composition, type of nucleic acid residing in the virus particle, the way the nucleic acid is arranged, the shape of the virus, and the fate of the replicated DNA. These differences are used to classify the viruses and have often been the basis on which the various types of viruses were named.

The classification of viruses operates by use of the same structure that governs the **classification of bacteria**. The International Committee on Taxonomy of Viruses established the viral classification scheme in 1966. From the broadest to the narrowest level of classification, the viral scheme is: Order, Family, Subfamily, Genus, Species, and Strain/type. To use an example, the virus that was responsible for an outbreak of Ebola hemorrhagic fever in a region of Africa called Kikwit is classified as Order Mononegavirales, Family Filoviridae, Genus *Filovirus*, and Species *Ebola Zaire*.

In the viral classification scheme, all families end in the suffix *viridae*, for example Picornaviridae. Genera have the suffix *virus*. In the family Picornaviridae there are five genera: enterovirus, cardiovirus, rhinovirus, apthovirus, and hepatovirus. The names of the genera typically derive from the preferred location of the virus in the body (for those viral genera that infect humans). As examples, rhinovirus is localized in the nasal and throat passages, and hepatovirus is localized in the liver. Finally, within each genera there can be several species.

As noted above, there are a number of criteria by which members of one grouping of viruses can be distinguished from those in another group. For the purposes of classification, however, three criteria are paramount. These criteria are the host organism or organisms that the virus utilizes, the shape of the virus particle, and the type and arrangement of the viral nucleic acid.

An important means of classifying viruses concerns the type and arrangement of nucleic acid in the virus particle. Some viruses have two strands of DNA, analogous to the double helix of DNA that is present in prokaryotes such as bacteria and in eukaryotic cells. Some viruses, such as the Adenoviruses, replicate in the nucleus of the host using the replication machinery of the host. Other viruses, such as the Poxviruses, do not integrate in the host genome, but replicate in the cytoplasm of the host. Another example of a double-stranded DNA virus is the Herpesviruses. Other viruses only have a single strand of DNA such as the Parvoviruses, which can replicate

their DNA in the host's nucleus. The replication involves the formation of what is termed as a negative-sense strand of DNA, a blueprint for the subsequent formation of the RNA and DNA used to manufacture the new virus particles.

The genome of other viruses, such as Reoviruses and Birnaviruses, is comprised of double-stranded RNA. Portions of the RNA function independently in the production of a number of so-called messenger RNAs, each of which produces a protein that is used in the production of new viruses. Other viruses contain a single strand of RNA. In some of the single-stranded RNA viruses, such as Picornaviruses, Togaviruses, and the Hepatitis A virus, the RNA is read in a direction that is termed "+ sense." The sense strand is used to make the protein products that form the new virus particles. Other single-stranded RNA viruses contain what is termed a negative-sense strand. Examples are the Orthomyxoviruses and the Rhabdoviruses. The negative strand is the blueprint for the formation of the messenger RNAs that are required for production of the various viral proteins.

Still another group of viruses have + sense RNA that contains the code for a DNA intermediate. The intermediate is used to manufacture the RNA that is eventually packaged into the new virus particles. The main example is the Retroviruses (the Human Immunodeficiency Viruses belong here). Finally, a group of viruses consist of double-stranded DNA that contains the code for an RNA intermediate. An example is the Hepadnaviruses.

One aspect of virology is the identification of viruses. Often, the diagnosis of a viral illness relies, at least initially, on the visual detection of the virus. Samples are prepared for electron microscopy using a technique called negative staining, which highlights surface detail of the virus particles. For this analysis, the shape of the virus is an important feature.

Any particular virus will have an attached shape. For example, viruses that specifically infect bacteria, the so-called bacteriophages, look similar to the Apollo lunar-landing spacecraft. A head region containing the nucleic acid is supported on a number of spider-like legs. Upon encountering a suitable bacterial surface, the virus acts like a syringe, to introduce the nucleic acid into the cytoplasm of the bacterium.

Other viruses have different shapes. These include spheres, ovals, worm-like forms, and even pleomorphic (irregular) arrangements. Some viruses, such as the influenza virus, have projections sticking out from the surface of the virus. These are crucial to the infectious process. As new species of eukaryotic and prokaryotic organisms are discovered, no doubt the list of viral species will continue to grow.

Viruses cannot replicate by themselves. They require the participation of the replication equipment of the host cell that they infect in order to replicate. The molecular means by which this replication takes place varies, depending upon the type of virus. Viral replication can be divided into three phases: initiation, replication, and release.

The initiation phase occurs when the virus particle attaches to the surface of the host cell, penetrates into the cell, and undergoes a process known as uncoating, where the viral genetic material is released from the virus into the host cell's cytoplasm. The attachment typically involves the recognition of some host surface molecules by a corresponding molecule on the surface of the virus. These two molecules can associate tightly with one another, binding the virus particle to the surface. A well-studied example is the haemagglutinin receptor of the influenzae virus. The receptors of many other viruses have also been characterized.

A virus particle may have more than one receptor molecule, to permit the recognition of different host molecules, or of different regions of a single host molecule. The molecules on the host surface that are recognized tend to be those that are known as glycoproteins. For example, the human immunodeficiency virus recognizes a host glycoprotein called CD4. Cells lacking CD4 cannot, for example, bind the HIV particle.

In the replication, or synthetic, phase the viral genetic material is converted to deoxyribonucleic acid (DNA) if the material originally present in the viral particle is ribonucleic acid (RNA). This so-called reverse transcription process needs to occur in retroviruses, such as HIV. The DNA is imported into the host nucleus where the production of new DNA, RNA, and protein can occur. The replication phase varies greatly from virus type to virus type. However, in general, proteins are manufactured to ensure that: the cell's replication machinery is harnessed to permit replication of the viral genetic material; the replication of the genetic material does indeed occur; and the newly made material is properly packaged into new virus particles.

Replication of the viral material can be a complicated process, with different stretches of the genetic material being transcribed simultaneously with some of these **gene** products required for the transcription of other viral genes. Also, replication can occur along a straight stretch of DNA, or when the DNA is circular (the so-called "rolling circle" form). RNA-containing viruses must also undergo a reverse transcription from DNA to RNA prior to packaging of the genetic material into the new virus particles.

In the final stage, the viral particles are assembled and exit the host cell. The assembly process can involve helper proteins, made by the virus or the host.

Release of viruses can occur by a process called budding. A membrane "bleb" containing the virus particle is formed at the surface of the cell and is pinched off. For herpes virus this is in fact how the viral membrane is acquired. In other words, the viral membrane is a host-derived membrane. Other viruses, such as bacteriophage, may burst the host cell, spewing out the many progeny virus particles. But many viruses do not adopt such a host destructive process, as it limits the time of an infection due to destruction of the host cells needed for future replication.

Although precise mechanisms vary, viruses cause disease by infecting a host cell and commandeering the host cell's synthetic capabilities to produce more viruses. The newly made viruses then leave the host cell, sometimes killing it in the process, and proceed to infect other cells within the host. Because viruses invade cells, drug therapies have not yet been designed to kill viruses, although some have been developed to inhibit their growth. The human immune system is the main defense against a viral disease.

Bacterial viruses, called bacteriophages, infect a variety of bacteria, such as *Escherichia coli*, a bacteria commonly found in the human digestive tract. Animal viruses cause a variety of fatal diseases. Acquired immune deficiency syndrome (AIDS) is caused by the human immunodeficiency virus (HIV); hepatitis and rabies are viral diseases; and hemorrhagic fevers, which are characterized by severe internal bleeding, are caused by filoviruses. Other animal viruses cause some of the most common human diseases. Often, these diseases strike in childhood. Measles, mumps, and chickenpox are viral diseases. The common cold and influenza are also caused by viruses. Finally, some viruses can cause cancer and tumors. One such virus, human T-cell leukemia virus (HTLV), was only recently discovered and its role in the development of a particular kind of leukemia is still being clarified.

Edward Jenner (1749–1823) is credited with developing the first successful vaccine against a viral disease, with his vaccine for **smallpox**. A vaccine works by eliciting an immune response. During this immune response, specific immune cells, called memory cells, are produced that remain in the body long after the foreign microbe present in a vaccine has been destroyed. When the body again encounters the same kind of microbe, the memory cells quickly destroy the microbe. **Vaccines** contain either a live, altered version of a virus or bacteria, or they contain only parts of a virus or bacteria, enough to elicit an immune response.

In 1797, Jenner developed his smallpox vaccine by taking infected material from a cowpox lesion on the hand of a milkmaid. Cowpox was a common disease of the era, transmitted through contact with an infected cow. Unlike smallpox, however, cowpox is a much milder disease. Using the cowpox pus, he inoculated an eight-year-old boy. Jenner continued his vaccination efforts through his lifetime. Until 1976, children were routinely vaccinated with the smallpox vaccine, called vaccinia. Reactions to the introduction of the vaccine ranged from a mild fever to severe complications, including (although very rarely) death. In 1977, when the last naturally occurring case of smallpox appeared and the global eradication of smallpox was complete, vaccinia vaccinations for children were discontinued, although vaccinia continues to be used as a carrier for recombinant DNA techniques. In these techniques, foreign DNA is inserted in cells. Efforts to produce a vaccine for HIV, for instance, have used vaccinia as the vehicle that carries specific parts of HIV.

SEE ALSO Bacterial biology; Careers in forensic science; Ebola virus; Pathogens; Vaccines; Variola virus.

Rudolf Ludwig Carl Virchow

10/13/1821–9/5/1902
GERMAN
PATHOLOGIST, PHYSICIAN

Rudolf Carl Virchow was the founder of the school of cellular **pathology**, which forms the basis of modern pathology. Pathologists examine tissues and organs to identify and study the effects of disease upon the body. Forensic pathologists examine tissues and organs for legal purposes and crime solving, such as determining the **cause of death**, and documenting disease processes or bodily injuries.

Virchow, an only child, was born in a small rural town in Germany. His early interest in the natural sciences and broad humanistic training helped him

get high marks throughout school. In 1839, his outstanding scholarly abilities earned him a military fellowship to study **medicine** at the Freidrich-Wilhelms Institute in Berlin, Germany. Virchow had the opportunity to study under Johannes Müller, who encouraged many German physicians to use experimental laboratory methods in their medical studies. Gaining experience in experimental laboratory and diagnostic methods, Virchow received his medical degree in 1843 from the University of Berlin and went on to become company surgeon at the Charité Hospital in Berlin.

As a young scientist, Virchow became a powerful speaker for the new generation of German physicians. He viewed medical progress as coming from three main sources: clinical observations, including examination of the patient; animal experimentation to test methods and drugs; and pathological anatomy, especially at the microscopic level. He also insisted that life was the sum of physical and chemical actions and essentially the expression of cell activity. Although these views caused some older physicians to condemn Virchow, he received his medical license in 1846.

Two years later, Virchow was sent to Prussia to treat victims of a typhus epidemic. Seeing the desperate condition of the Polish minority, he recommended sweeping educational and economic reform and political freedom. From that point on, he argued that to provide any benefit for the sick, one must treat the ills of society. Acting on his convictions, Virchow fought in the uprisings of 1848 and became a member of the Berlin Democratic Congress. Unfortunately, his strong political and social conscience cost him his university post. Virchow finally left Berlin for the more liberal atmosphere of the University of Würzburg.

It was at Würzburg that Virchow embarked on his highest level of scientific achievement—his development of cellular pathology. In 1855, Virchow published his journal article on cellular pathology. "*Omnis cellula e cellula,*" he wrote, meaning all cells arise from cells. Essentially, his article generalized the concept of cell theory and modernized the entire medical field. The cell became the fundamental living unit in both healthy and diseased tissue. He used the microscope to bring the study of disease down to a more fundamental level; disease occurred because healthy living cells were altered or disturbed. In 1859, Virchow's book *Cell Pathology* became a classic textbook that would influence generations of physicians. Although Virchow's work carries lasting significance, Virchow rejected the germ theory developed

Rudolf Virchow looking through a magnifying glass.
© BETTMANN/CORBIS

by Louis Pasteur, arguing instead that diseased tissue resulted from the breakdown of order within cells and not from the invasion of a foreign body. Scientists have since discovered that disease results from both circumstances.

SEE ALSO Autopsy; Pathology.

Virus SEE Viral biology

Virus, computer SEE Computer virus

Visible microspectrophotometry

Visible microspectrophotometry is a very useful tool in the forensic analysis of many kinds of **trace evidence**. It combines a microscope with a spectrophotometer so that the light absorption properties of a very small sample can be recorded. The technique is particularly valuable in the investigation of hair, textile **fibers**, and paint, which are typically of microscopic dimensions. A fiber, for instance, may have a diameter of only around 20 micrometers.

The chemical bonds within the molecular components of trace **evidence** interact with light in a characteristic manner. They will absorb, transmit, or reflect specific frequencies of visible light. When human eyes see a piece of cloth as blue, for example, this means that although white light falls upon the material, all the color frequencies making it up except blue are absorbed by the dye molecules in the material. It is therefore the blue frequencies of light that are reflected back. A yellow fiber contains different dye molecules, which reflect back only yellow frequencies. Visible spectrophotometry is a more sophisticated and highly accurate way of recording exactly what color an object is.

When an opaque or translucent item of trace evidence is inserted into the visible microspectrophotometer, it is exposed to a range of visible frequencies. The frequencies where it reflects, absorbs, or transmits, depending on the mode of the instrument, are recorded at a detector as a spectrum, or fingerprint, of that material. Comparisons can be made with materials whose visible spectra are held in reference databases. It is also possible to compare a piece of trace evidence with a control sample. A textile fiber found at the scene of the crime can be compared with one found on a suspect's clothing, for instance. If their visible spectra are identical, then they likely come from the same source. The same is true of hairs and paint flakes. Visible microspectrophotometry is also a useful and non-destructive way of analyzing colored inks in the investigation of **questioned documents**.

SEE ALSO Micro-fourier transform infrared spectrometry; Spectroscopy.

Voice alteration, electronic

In most cases, voice alteration technologies are employed to obscure an individual's identity. This can complicate the forensic **identification** of the individual. Forensic specialists who examine spoken or written materials in relation to legal matters and crimes are known as forensic stylists or forensic linguists. Forensic linguists frequently deal with **evidence** containing altered voices. Crude voice alteration can be achieved by physical training. Actors and singers, for example, can train their voices so that the speech or song "projects" to all areas of the theater. Also, accents can be learned and mimicked with reasonable accuracy.

In this natural process the vocal cords function as the source of the sounds and the vocal tract functions as the filter that can alter the frequency and cadence of the speech. The results is the rising and falling tones and intensity of spoken words.

However, the use of electronic technology can achieve accurate vocal alterations that are not otherwise possible. For example, vocal cords can be trained to be able to adopt different pitches—that is, to be capable of vibrating at different frequencies, to produce sounds that have different tones. However, electronic alterations of pitch can widen the vocal deceptions that are possible. For example, a man's voice can be altered to sound convincingly like a woman's.

The alteration of pitch can also be deliberately done electronically by detecting the frequency pattern of the speaker, and of the particular phrase being spoken. On a screen, the pattern appears as a series of waves and troughs. The arrangement of the waves and troughs is characteristic to the word being spoken. For example, the word "cat" will produce a different pattern than the word "invisible." By applying an electronic filter (or "window"; actually one or more mathematical equations, or algorithms) to the frequency pattern, waves and troughs can be selectively eliminated or shifted up and down to produce a different frequency. An experienced technician or sophisticated software program can alter a word so as to change the sound of the word (i.e., a higher or lower tone) without distorting the sound of the word. Thus, the altered speech is still recognizable and interpretable, but can sound like it is being spoken by another person.

Electronic voice alteration can be subtle or extreme. The latter is associated with the almost incomprehensible voices of anonymous witnesses. This type of voice alteration is actually a voice disguise. The intention is not to mimic a voice, but to scramble the voice patterns to make the speaker impossible to identify.

There are several different electronic means of voice alteration. One type is known as speech inversion. Here, the frequency signal is in effect turned inside out around a designated frequency. Put another way, the parts of the speech that are "high" are made to sound "low," and visa versa.

A voice can also be electronically jumbled, so that it sounds like gibberish. But **codes** assigned to sections of the speech allow the listener (who has the electronic codes) to put the words back in their proper order.

Another means of electronic voice alteration is known as speech encryption. Here, speech is digitized and the digital signal manipulated to make the text of the speech unrecognizable to the listeners ear. But the speech can be decoded, or decrypted, at the receiving end to yield the original recognizable speech.

Hardware and software voice encryption systems are available. Machines connected to a telephone can alter a person's speech during the telephone conversation. Anyone eavesdropping on the conversation would be incapable of understanding what was being said. However, a legitimate listener, having a machine on his or her phone, would be capable of decrypting the conversation.

The United States government and military uses a telephone conversation scrambling software program and hardware called Secure Telephone Unit, Generation III (STU III).

Scrambling digital electronic information in relation to time can also accomplish voice alteration. An example includes the delay of information. While an effective means of altering a voice, the method can produce an echo, and so is unpleasantly distracting to listen to.

SEE ALSO Linguistics, forensic stylistics; Telephone recording system; Telephone tap detector.

Voice analysis

Voice analysis was first used in World War II for military intelligence purposes. Its use in forensic investigation dates back to the 1960s and relies on the fact that each person's voice has a unique quality that can be recorded as a voiceprint, rather like a fingerprint, on an instrument called a sound spectrograph. Suspects knowingly or unknowingly leave recordings of the voices on the telephone, voice mail, answering machines, or hidden tape recorders, and these samples can be used as **evidence**. Forensic voice analysis has been used in a wide range of criminal cases such as **murder**, rape, drug dealing, bomb threats, and terrorism.

Each person's voice is different because the anatomy of the vocal cords, vocal cavity, and oral and nasal cavities is specific to the individual. Added to that, each person coordinates the muscles of the lips, tongue, soft palate, and jaw differently to produce words. The teeth also have an impact in the way speech is formed. The body's voice-producing apparatus is like an organ pipe producing notes, a tube in which sound waves vibrate, producing sounds which can readily be recorded.

The sound spectrograph records a voiceprint in terms of the frequencies and intensities of the sounds made by an individual while speaking. A good mimic may sound like the person they are imitating, but the voiceprint will be quite different. Of course, a person's voice changes with age, but the voiceprint remains distinctive.

Voiceprint samples may be obtained through covert police operations, such as by investigators wearing hidden microphones or putting surveillance equipment on a suspect's phone. As with fingerprints and **shoeprints**, samples for comparison can be taken from a suspect, by court order if necessary. The investigator will ask them to speak the same words as those that were recorded on the voice evidence that has been collected. This may be a 911 call from a murderer or a bomb threat call. There is always the possibility that the suspect will try to disguise his or her voice, but the voiceprint expert will probably be able to allow for this.

The investigator has two complementary ways of making an **identification** through voice analysis. First, he or she will listen to the evidence sample and the sample taken from the suspect, comparing accent, speech habits, breath patterns, and inflections. Then a comparison of the corresponding voiceprints is made. There is no international standard for the minimum number of points of identity needed in this comparison, but ten to twenty speech sounds that correspond are often taken as good proof of identification.

It has been argued that voiceprints may not be as individual as fingerprints. Certainly the technology for analysis is probably not as well developed. However, in one analysis of 2,000 cases by the Federal Bureau of Investigation, the error rate in both false identification and false elimination of suspects was found to be very low.

Voice identification played a key role in the investigation of the crimes of Peter Sutcliffe, the so-called Yorkshire Ripper, who murdered several women in the North of England in the late 1970s. Tapes purporting to be from the Ripper were sent to the police team involved in the case, taunting them for their lack of success in catching him. Voice analysis was at first inconclusive, but it now looks as if the tapes were probably the work of a hoaxer.

Voice analysis has also been applied to the investigation of tapes said to be made by Osama bin Laden, the world's most-wanted terrorist. Since the terror attacks in New York and Washington on September 11, 2001, bin Laden has apparently issued a number of video and audiotapes. Corresponding words on the tapes, like "America," can be compared, but the voiceprints do not match exactly because the same person will never say a word in exactly the same way each time. If there is enough similarity, however, an identification can be made even if it is tentative, especially if there is other evidence. Of course, bin Laden speaks in Arabic, but there is software to handle this and other languages. It may be significant that the most recent utterances by bin Laden have been by audio rather than video tape, raising the possibility that he has been dead for some time and the tape has been made by someone else hoping to raise the morale of al Qaeda. The tape is of poor quality and difficult for analysts to work with. It is unlikely, however, that a mimic could fool a voice analysis expert, even under these conditions. Yet there is the possibility that the tape has been created from previous ones that feature bin Laden's real voice, with new information pasted in to update it. The final possibility is that the tape has been made by one of his sons; parents and children tend to sound similar and may give similar voiceprints. The identification of bin Laden looks as if it will be an ongoing challenge to the forensic voice analysts.

SEE ALSO Linguistics, forensic stylistics.

August Vollmer

3/7/1876–11/4/1955
AMERICAN
POLICE CHIEF

August Vollmer was a pioneer in the science of forensic investigations. The founder of "professional policing," he was born in New Orleans, Louisiana, on March 7, 1876. Vollmer held a variety of jobs in his early years, including firefighting, a coal and feed business, a private in the military, and a mail carrier. In 1905, he became the town marshal of Berkeley, California, and by 1909 he was made the chief of police for Berkeley.

In the wake of years of police corruption and brutality throughout the United States, Vollmer sought to increase the professionalism of police. During his tenure as police chief, Vollmer began to revamp the Berkeley Police Department by making changes that would transform policing across the nation. Vollmer instituted police **training**, advocated using college-educated officers, and promoted the use of new technology for fighting crime such as fingerprinting, polygraph machines, and crime laboratories. In addition, Vollmer equipped the Berkeley Police Department with radio communication and in 1914 established the first automobile patrol in the United States.

Vollmer was elected as the president of the California Police Chiefs Association in 1907, and in 1922 he became the president of the International Association of Chiefs of Police. During his tenure as president, Vollmer suggested changes for policing nationwide. Many suggestions mirrored the policies and programs Vollmer instituted in Berkeley, such as increased use of technology and science and providing training for police. Vollmer also advocated using female officers more frequently and encouraged universities to increase their study of human behavior. Vollmer also contended that the goal of policing should be crime prevention. Throughout his life, both before and after retirement, Vollmer assisted police departments outside of Berkeley in improving their policing strategies. Vollmer helped revamp the San Diego Police Department, and completed several surveys of local police departments throughout the United States, including Los Angeles, Chicago, Detroit, Kansas City, Minneapolis, Santa Barbara, Piedmont, Syracuse, Dallas, and Portland. The surveys were used to help departments consider ways to reconstruct their police departments. Drawing on these surveys, Vollmer also authored a "Report on Police" for the Wickersham Commission in 1931.

In conjunction with his emphasis on the importance of education in policing, Vollmer taught police administration courses during the summer at the University of California. Additionally, he took leave as Police Chief of Berkeley from 1929–1931 and taught courses at the University of Chicago. When Vollmer retired as chief in 1931, he took on a position as a professor of police administration at the University of California Political Science Department where he continued to teach until 1937. During his years at the University of California, he wrote *Crime and the State Police* in 1935 and the *Police and Modern Society* in 1936. Vollmer also helped develop **criminology** courses at the university.

After retiring from his position at the University of California in 1937, he continued to play an active role in the field of criminal justice by founding the American Society of Criminology, and in 1941 served as its president. He also collaborated with Alfred E.

Parker in 1937 to write *Crime, Crooks and Cops*, and in 1949 he authored *The Criminal*. After a long and successful career in policing and criminal justice, August Vollmer took his own life on November 4, 1955, at the age of 79.

SEE ALSO Criminology; Fingerprint; Literature, forensic science in; Polygraphs.

Juan Vucetich
7/20/1858–1/25/1925
CROATIAN
POLICE OFFICIAL

Juan (Josip) Vucetich was a Croatian-born Argentinean anthropologist and police official who pioneered the use of fingerprinting. In 1882, at the age of 24, he left his birthplace of Lesina and immigrated to Argentina. He was one of the front-runners of scientific dactyloscopy (**identification** by fingerprints).

Fingerprints were already used on clay tablets for business transactions in ancient Babylon and more recently in the fourteenth century for identification purposes. But in 1788 J. C. Mayers recognized that friction ridges are unique. Until 1890, however, the technology used for individualization was the anthropometric method designed by the French criminalist **Alphonse Bertillon** (1853–1914), based on the size of body, head, and limbs.

In the 1880s Argentine police considered it necessary to create a department that would take care of identifying individuals and commissioned doctor Augusto P. Drago to study the method established by the Bertillon. Subsequently, the Police of the City of Buenos Aires created a division dedicated to anthropometric identification. While Drago was establishing anthropometric identification in Buenos Aires, Vucetich was investigating fingerprints in the nearby La Plata Office of Identification and Statistics.

Inspired by an article from the French *Revue Scientifique* that reported on the English scientist Francis Galton's (1822–1911) experiments with fingerprints and their potential use in identification, Vucetich started to collect impressions of all ten fingers to include with the anthropometric measurements he took from arrested men. His intense study led him to confirm that fingerprints could be classified by groups. In 1891 Vucetich devised his own **fingerprint** classification method by means of impressions. He also invented the necessary elements to obtain the best possible quality of fingerprints and implemented every resource to systematize the method. It wasn't until 1894, however, that his superiors were convinced that **anthropometry** measurements were not necessary in addition to full sets of fingerprint records. By this time Vucetich had refined his classification system and was able to categorize a large number of fingerprint cards into small groups that were easily searched.

Vucetich's new recognition procedure of the classification system was originally called Icnofalangometría or Galtonean method and was later changed to dactiloscopy at the suggestion of another fingerprint pioneer, Francisco Latzina. It consisted of 101 types of fingerprints that Vucetich personally had classified based on Galton's incomplete taxonomy. On September 1, 1891, Vucetich's method began to be applied officially for the individualization of 23 felons, and in March 1892 Vucetich opened the first fingerprint bureau at San Nicholas, Buenos Aires.

Within a short time of the bureau being set up, the first conviction by means of fingerprint **evidence** in a **murder** trial was obtained. In June 1892 a colleague of Vucetich's, Inspector Eduardo Alvarez, took digital impressions from a crime scene at Necochea. Eventually, Vucetich was able to identify Francisca Rojas, who had murdered her two sons and cut her own throat in an attempt to blame a neighboring ranch worker. Rojas's bloody print was left on a door post of her hut, taken to the fingerprint bureau for comparison with the inked fingerprint impressions of the ranch worker, and eventually proved Rojas's identity as the murderer.

The insight obtained by the police department through Vucetich's simple and efficient fingerprinting identification method encouraged the government to widen the filiations procedure and in 1900 the first identification cards were issued. Argentinean police adopted Vucetich's method of fingerprinting classification and it was widely spread to police forces all over the world for being scientifically efficient and superior to the existing methods.

Vucetich published all his methods, theories, and findings, which eventually were translated in the book *General Instructions for the Anthropometric System and Digital Impressions*. His work *Dactiloscopía Comparada* (Comparative Dactyloscopy) came out in 1904 and is considered to be his masterpiece, which led him to receive awards and honors from around the world.

Juan Vucetich created the most flawless system of fingerprint classification and is credited as being the first person to use a **latent fingerprint** to solve a crime. His work and perseverance went beyond his commitment. He made investigational trips to India and China trying to find out the origins of identification by fingerprints, and he attended scientific congresses and published numerous books based on his findings.

While Juan Vucetich's system is still used in most Spanish countries, William Henry's system of fingerprint classification, which was officially adopted by Scotland Yard as their identification system in 1901, continues to be in use in the United States and in Europe. A majority of the identification bureaus around the world use either the Vucetich or the Henry classification system. International organizations such as **Interpol** now use both methods.

Juan Vucetich died in the city of Dolores, province of Buenos Aires. He donated his files and his library to the Faculty of Judicial and Social Sciences of the National University of La Plata, which served to create the museum that bears his name. In the honor of Vucetic, La Plata Police Academy has been named "Escuela de policia Juan Vucetic."

SEE ALSO Anthropology; Anthropometry; Fingerprint; Interpol.

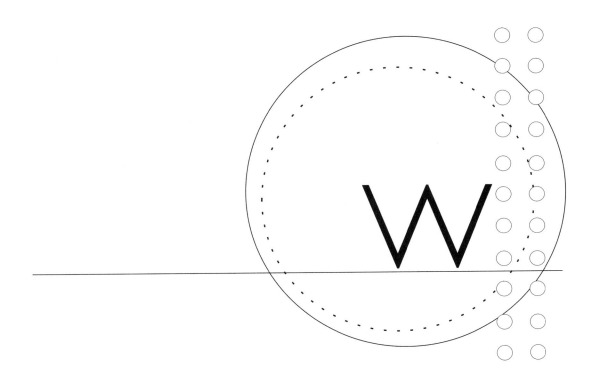

Charles E. Waite

1865–1926
AMERICAN
FORENSIC SCIENTIST

Forensic scientist Charles E. Waite was involved in a number of landmark advancements in the science of **ballistics** over the course of his career. He was the first person to compile a catalog of information on **firearms**, and was part of the group of scientists who adapted the **comparison microscope** for use in ballistics comparison. Waite also was a co-founder of the Bureau of Forensic Ballistics.

During the 1910s Waite was working as a special investigator for the New York Attorney General's office. It was at this point that he became involved in a case that would prove pivotal to his career. In 1915, an illiterate farmer in rural New York was accused of a double **murder**. Investigators hired a firearms expert who claimed that the bullets used in the murders matched the gun found in the farmer's house. Stielow, the farmer, was convicted to the murders and sentenced to death. However, the New York governor requested a reinvestigation of the case, and Waite was assigned to the job. He worked with microscopy expert Max Poser to examine the fatal bullets along with bullets test fired from Stielow's gun, studying the bullets with **microscopes**. They ultimately determined that Stielow's gun could not have been used in the murders. The man was pardoned and released.

Waite's experience with the Stielow case inspired him to look into developing a scientific system of cataloging ballistics information in order to prevent future mistakes. For a number of years he collected data, visited firearms manufacturers, and traveled around the United States and Europe. Waite, with the help of Calvin Goddard, created a database of information that was the first of its kind in the area of ballistics.

In 1925 Waite and fellow scientists Calvin Goddard, Phillip O. Gravelle, and John H. Fisher opened the Bureau of Forensic Ballistics in New York, New York. Their goal was to offer firearms **identification** services to agencies across the U.S. About this same time, Waite and the group also adapted the comparison microscope so that it could be used for bullet comparison. This capability made it much easier for examiners to identify matching bullet striations.

SEE ALSO Ballistic fingerprints.

War crimes trials

War crimes are offenses against the laws of engagement of war, such as killing or mistreating civilians or prisoners of war. After World War II (1939–1945), the principle of punishing those involved in war crimes became established although it is a concept that is still evolving in many ways. Suspects are tried by their own civilian or military courts or by international tribunals. Such trials have now been extended to cover genocide and crimes against humanity. Currently many war crimes trials, which tend to be very lengthy complex affairs, are ongoing or planned, such as the one that hears the charges against Saddam Hussein and his followers in Iraq. The first war crimes trials relied mainly on witness statements and documentary **evidence**. In more recent times, however, **forensic science** has begun to play a more important role in the prosecution of war crimes.

The Nuremberg Trials of 1945 tried many Nazi leaders, including Hermann Goering and Joachim von Ribbentrop, and were conducted by a tribunal consisting of representatives from Britain, the United States, the U.S.S.R., and France. German dictator Adolf Hitler (1889–1945) escaped trial by committing suicide shortly before the end of the war. Japanese war criminals from World War II were also tried by a tribunal in Tokyo. Large amounts of evidence were brought to bear, showing the extermination of civilians, especially Jews, mistreatment and **murder** of prisoners of war, looting, and the use of slave labor during the war years.

Nuremberg established a precedent and a model from which lessons could be drawn. Later, several Americans were tried for crimes committed in the Vietnam War and, in the 1990s, the United Nations set up a tribunal in The Hague to gather evidence for prosecutions against those accused of atrocities in the break-up of Yugoslavia. The highest-ranking official to be tried by this court is former Yugoslavian President Slobodan Milosevic, whose trial began in 2002. In the year 2000, rape, which was very common in the Yugoslav conflict, was established as a war crime. Meanwhile another tribunal in Tanzania has been investigating the Hutu massacres of the Tutsis in Rwanda in 1994, and one in Sierra Leone is trying those accused of atrocities during that country's civil war of the 1990s. In 1998, the United Nations General Assembly voted for a permanent international court for trying war crimes. The judges of the International Criminal Court, based in The Hague, were sworn in in 2003, and charged with trying war crimes, genocide, and crimes against humanity.

Modern war crimes trials depend upon witness statements, documentary evidence, and forensic evidence. Much of the forensic work carried out in places such as Bosnia, Afghanistan, and Iraq has involved the investigation of mass graves. This kind of work is very different for the forensic scientist compared to what is required in routine crime investigations. However, the principles of collecting, preserving, and analyzing evidence remain the same, although they are more difficult to achieve. Many places where atrocities have been committed in the recent past are still unsafe, and the investigative agencies must consider the safety of their personnel. There may be logistic problems in transport and in setting up laboratory space and equipment. The investigators attempt to work with local people and take care to respect their customs. There is also no guarantee that the crime scene, most likely a mass grave, has been kept secure and evidence preserved since the atrocities were committed.

An important part of the forensic work done in war crime investigations is **identification** of people who have disappeared during a conflict. Not only does this provide key trial evidence, but it also brings some comfort and closure to the loved ones of those who have gone. Identified remains can then be given a proper burial. However, there is often a conflict between the needs of the trial and the needs of families. The former require evidence of the scale of the war crime rather than the establishment of the identity of each victim. The family wants to know what happened to the individual.

Establishing identity begins with a physical description of the missing person provided by a close relative or friend. This includes details about the person's physical appearance such as height, hair color, teeth, tattoos, scars, as well as about items they may have been carrying or wearing at the time of their disappearance, such as jewelry, eyeglasses, shoes, and clothing.

Bodies and remains are then exhumed from the mass grave, usually by forensic archaeologists and forensic anthropologists. Documents found on a body may provide a lead for identification. Postmortem (after death) and antemortem (around the **time of death**) data can then be compared. Sometimes photographs of clothing worn by the deceased can be identified by the family. In the modern era, **DNA** analysis can provide confirmation of identity but this is a very expensive way of investigating a mass killing. Teeth and bones survive long after other tissues have decomposed and may yield DNA that can be compared to that of relatives. Such identity investigations are always, necessarily, incomplete. Not all of the bodies originally present in a mass grave will be recovered on **exhumation**, and not all of these will be identified. Around 30,000 people were missing in Bosnia by the time the conflict there was resolved in 1995. Since then, about 15,000 bodies have been recovered, of which 9,000 have been identified. DNA analysis contributed to identification in around 3,000 cases. The same has been found in the investigation

At an identification center in Tuzla, 2002, a forensic expert takes samples from a bone for future identification of one of almost 3,500 dead Bosnians. Former Yugoslav leader Slobodan Milosevic was charged with crimes against humanity. © REUTERS/CORBIS

of war crimes in Rwanda where the sheer scale of the killings, half- to three-quarters of a million people, makes a full forensic examination almost impossible. It is possible that forensic science may never uncover the full horror of some war atrocities.

The above approach has been adopted by the International Forensics Program for the Physicians for Human Rights group during its investigation of the 1995 massacre of Srebrenica in Bosnia and has led to the identification of many of the victims. The investigators have exhumed over 400 bodies; many had bullet wounds in the **skull** and ligatures around the wrists, important **physical evidence** for a war crimes trial. The Program has carried out similar investigations in many countries around the world including Afghanistan, Israel, Kosovo, and Rwanda.

Other evidence from a mass grave may be important to a war crimes trial. The investigators will try to establish if the victims belonged to a particular religious or ethnic group. This can help define whether the perpetrators are guilty of genocide, the targeting of a specific group in society for

destruction. The team will also try to establish patterns in the killing, whether the same methods were used at different sites and whether the killers tried to cover their tracks and destroy evidence. By building a picture of what happened at the various scenes, the investigators may also try to establish if a crime against humanity has been committed. This encompasses a wide range of acts: mass murder, enslavement, deportation, rape, and torture committed on a large scale against civilians. Documentary evidence of planning of such crimes may be found which can back up these forensic findings.

Lessons learned from other forensic investigations of war crimes and crimes against humanity may now be put to work in Iraq. As of April 2005, more than 250 mass graves have been discovered in the country since the removal of Saddam in 2003. Evidence from these sites will be vital in his trial and is also eagerly awaited by Iraqis wanting to know what happened to their loved ones. However, there are huge challenges for the investigators. Saddam's atrocities occurred over a 30-year period and many, if not most, of the corpses will now be badly decomposed. Victims were often transported over hundreds of miles for **interrogation** and execution, so a geographical link to help in identification is unlikely. Much documentation, which could have provided valuable evidence, has been destroyed or looted. Furthermore, 24-hour security, essential once a forensic investigation is underway, cannot currently be guaranteed at the sites.

The graves themselves have been located either by survivors of the massacres, or by witnesses. In some cases, people have just come across shallow graves. Some Iraqis, wanting to investigate the possible fate of disappeared relatives, started to investigate the graves themselves, but in a disorganized manner that was likely to destroy evidence. Many have since been persuaded to await a professional forensic investigation. While there are moves afoot to set this program in motion, there are huge difficulties involved. The medico-legal system in Iraq is in chaos, because of the war and ongoing conflict. Iraq has many forensic pathologists, but no forensic anthropologists. There is also a tradition of using **circumstantial evidence** such as documents found on the body, or clothing, for identification rather than dental records or x-rays. There are opportunities for international collaborations to provide support and **training** to Iraqi forensic scientists. First, however, the basic needs of the discipline need to be attended to. Work has begun on two mass graves, but there is an ongoing problem in protecting the sites to preserve the evidence.

SEE ALSO Anthropology; Archaeology; Disappeared children of Argentina; DNA mixtures, forensic interpretation of mass graves; Identification of war victims in Croatia and Bosnia.

War forensics

Modern forensic techniques for human **identification** as well as **crime scene investigation** protocols are also applied to the investigation of war crimes, aiding with assessing and characterizing the burden of proof against individuals before both national and international courts. Forensic techniques are essential in gathering **physical evidence** for the indictment, arrest, and prosecution of war criminals, and to the localization and identification of people who disappeared in times of war. The Hague Conventions of 1899 and 1907 established the Laws and Customs of War, and defined which breaches of these laws should be qualified and punished as war crimes. The use of poisonous weapons, wanton destruction of cities without military necessity, attacks on religious and cultural institutions, attacks of undefended civilian communities, and looting of public or private property are among war crimes defined by the Hague Conventions.

The International Military Tribunal, created in 1945, further defined war crimes in its Nuremberg Charter as any violations of the laws or customs of war, such as executions of captured military personnel or civilians without a judicial process, **murder** or ill-treatment of prisoners of war, deportation of civilians from occupied territories, looting of public and private property, killing of hostages, and any kind of devastation unjustified as military strategic necessity. The Geneva Conventions of 1949, which codified the International Humanitarian Law, included for the first time a list of serious offenses in times of war for which individual offenders should be criminally accountable. The Geneva Conventions also described the ethics to be followed by all military forces of signatory countries in relation to the 1) wounded and sick on land; 2) wounded and sick at sea; 3) prisoners of war; and 4) civilians in the occupied territories. The Geneva Convention also described other serious offenses liable for punishment under international law, including torture or inhuman treatment, unethical medical experimentation on prisoners, willful killings, willful inflicting of unnecessary suffering, slave labor, deprivation or injury to body or health, the extensive destruction or the unlawful arbitrary appropriation of property not justified by military necessity, forcing a prisoner of war or a civilian to serve in the forces of a hostile army, denial of a fair and regular trial to prisoners of war or civilians, and the taking of hostages.

In 1977, the protections of the Geneva Convention were extended to include violence against or wanton attack of civilians in non-defended communities, the transfer of an occupying power or of part of its population to an occupied territory, unjustified delays in the repatriation of prisoners of war, attacks to historic monuments, and perfidious (false) use of the Red Cross or Red Crescent emblems. The protocol also determined that states must prosecute or extradite to other states willing to prosecute, individuals accused of war crimes, and of crimes against humanity. The implication of the International Laws and Customs of War is to empower each signatory state with the legal right to search, arrest, and prosecute individuals indicted as war criminals (e.g., for crimes committed in the context of war).

Additional protocols in 1977 defined the rules for internal armed conflicts or civil wars, but did not offer provisions for criminal liability under the international law, leaving it to local jurisdictions. The crimes described for civil wars are: murder, torture, mutilation, rape, enforced prostitution, indecent assault, summary executions, collective punishments, looting, outrages upon personal dignity, and violence to life and person.

Crimes Against Humanity (CAH) were first defined in the Hague Convention of 1907, consisting of those acts that breached the Law of Humanity but are not limited to the context of war between nations. The provisions of CAH state that all signatory states have the duty to prosecute or to extradite offenders under such indictment, regardless of where the crime was committed. The Hague Convention also established that no one is immune from criminal liability, including heads of states. For instance, the trials against the Chilean dictator Augusto Pinochet were first held in Spain, although the crimes were committed in Chile, during his military regime. Claims of obedience to superior orders or political offense exception are inadmissible under the Laws of Humanity. The Crimes Against Humanity were established for the first time as international law by the International Military Tribunal in the Nuremberg Charter of 1945.

Although in some instances, Crimes Against Humanity overlap in their description with the Geneva Convention definition of War Crimes, as in the cases of genocide and other war crimes, they are not restricted alone to either times of war, or to the war crime definition of genocide. CAH provides criminal liability for cases in which atrocities are committed without the intent to destroy in whole or in part a given population and also targets any group committing widespread or systematic violations. Recent examples of such violations are those committed by the Hutus in Rwanda in 2002 and those underway, beginning in 2003, in East Congo by Rwandan Hutu militias against Congolese women and children. Such violations include rape and torture of women and children, sex enslavement, looting, and massacres of defenseless Congolese rural communities.

The challenges met by forensic investigators to gather **evidence** in zones of conflict are numerous, as illustrated by the Balkan conflicts of the last two decades. Primary crime scenes and graves were destroyed by the perpetrators, and human remains or body parts were scattered or transferred to secondary mass graves. Identification of victims and forensic corroboration of testimonial reports is complex and ongoing. Many locations containing mass graves are mined and difficult for investigators to access. Local authorities often create obstacles or impede gathering evidence by international investigators, especially in areas of Serbia.

An international team of forensic experts organized by Physicians for Human Rights (PHR) and working under the United Nations War Crimes Commission began the **exhumation** of two mass graves at Ovcara, near the city of Vukovar, Serbia. In spite of the fact that the forensic team had a written permit from Serbian authorities from Knin, local Serbian authorities in Vukovar passed a resolution through the Regional Council to ban the exhumation. The first evidence collected (three male skeletons) showed that the remains were of Croats and some ballistic studies were already underway when the local ban occurred. The information gave the International Criminal Tribunal for the Former Yugoslavia legal argument to commit to guarding the gravesites until 1996, when experts were able to return. However, land mines were planted by Serbian militias in the surrounding areas, which had to be localized and removed before the exhumation work was resumed. Two hundred bodies were then found, and identification proved that they were all Croat patients of the Vukovar Hospital, executed by bullets to the head. The expert team consisted of 33 pathologists, 24 forensic anthropologists, forensic photographers, x-ray and fluoroscope experts, evidence technicians, electricians, drivers, translators, and local workers.

Mass grave excavation starts with a previous assessment of its boundaries and the gathering of surface evidence, such as bullet cases, signs of tools or machinery used to dig the grave, scattered rags, or personal belongings in the adjacent bushes or woods, etc. The surface of the grave is then mapped, marked and photographed, and (in rainy seasons) trenches are dug around its boundaries to drain the water. Layers of soil are then carefully removed, until the first bodies are exposed and photographed before being removed for **autopsy** and **pathology** analysis. The outer bodies are usually more skeletonized than those underneath them, or those closer to the center of the grave, because body **fluids** and moisture that concentrate in these areas do favor **adipocere** formation or body fat saponification. In the case of the Vukovar Hospital patients, investigators found, even after five years, well-preserved remains with flesh and skin displaying tattoos, along with recognizable faces.

As a standard procedure, corpses are photographed in the position they were found inside the grave, before being carefully moved to reveal, for instance, if their hands were tied behind their backs. The victims were then photographed again after removal from the gravesite. If bullets are found inside the grave, they are also photographed and collected for identification. When the death was not due to shooting but poisoning, gassing, hanging, beating, or other cause, autopsy and laboratorial tests are performed to determine the *causa mortis* (**cause of death**). Several different *causa mortis* have been identified in remains of the same mass grave. In many mass graves, babies have been found in the arms of their mothers.

In Croatia and Bosnia, between 25–70% of the bodies found in mass graves were of women and children. Among those mass graves investigated by the United Nations War Crimes Commission, at Sirsca, 150 bodies were found, at Lazette 130, in Kibuye 500, and in Vukovar 200. Mass graves have also been exhumed in Rwanda, Argentina, Brazil, Iraqi, Kurdistan, Ethiopia, Mexico, Guatemala, and in several parts of Eastern Europe. The forensic evidence they yield has instrumented trials in several local and international tribunals in support of witnesses, testimony, and helped to indict war criminals and those accused of crimes against humanity.

To make a case of genocide, for instance, investigators and prosecutors have to supply evidence that a given religious or ethnic group was systematically persecuted and executed, such as the case of Jews and Roma people in World War II (1939–1945) or the Bosnian Muslims and Kosovars in the Balkans in the early 1990s. The Third and Fourth Geneva Conventions require the proper identification, registration, and burial of victims of war in individual graves. However, dead combatants are sometimes temporarily buried in collective graves by their comrades to be later recovered and transported. This does not constitute a crime. The United Nations Resolution 3074 of 1973 instructs all states to cooperate with war crime investigations, and to facilitate the safe access of forensic teams to suspicious sites. Nevertheless, much still must be done to empower international institutions and tribunals to chase and prosecute war criminals, and to enforce international law.

Forensic science is also used to identify the remains of soldiers. The remains of unidentified American soldiers from World War I, World War II, and the Korean conflict lie in honored tombs at Arlington National Cemetery. In 1973, Congress

United States Army engineers use highly sensitive metal detectors to search for the remains of GIs missing in action (MIA) between Tay Ninh and the Vietnam-Cambodia border. © STEVE RAYMER/ CORBIS

authorized the creation of a tomb for an unknown soldier from the Vietnam conflict. Yet internment of the remains of a soldier was delayed until 1984, as authorities awaited additional information about the circumstances of death of the potential unknown soldier. A single set of remains classified as "unknown" was finally interred in 1984, but was exhumed in 1998 when it was believed that the use of mitochondrial **DNA** testing could lead to identification of the soldier. He was finally identified as Air Force 1st Lt. Michael Joseph Blassie, a pilot who was shot down near An Loc, Vietnam, in 1972. To date, no other set of remains has been classified as "unknown," and the sarcophagus at Arlington remains empty.

SEE ALSO Adipocere; Anthropology; Archaeology; Autopsy; Ballistics; Exhumation; Pathology; Skeletal analysis; War crimes trials.

August von Wassermann

2/21/1866–3/16/1925
GERMAN
BACTERIOLOGIST

August von Wassermann discovered a **blood serum** test that enabled physicians to determine if a patient has syphilis, a potentially lethal disease which, in some persons, has a long latency period during which no symptoms are detectable.

Wassermann was born in Bamberg, Germany to Dora (Bauer) and Angelo Wassermann, a banker. Wassermann received his secondary education in Bamberg and studied **medicine** at several German and Austrian universities. Wassermann married Alice von Taussig in 1895 and the couple eventually had two sons. He received his M.D. degree in 1888 at the University of Strasbourg. In 1890, Wassermann began work at the Institute for Infectious Diseases in Berlin, which was directed by the famous bacteriologist Robert Koch.

Although Wassermann did important work on tetanus, cholera, diphtheria, and tuberculosis, he is best known for his discovery of a blood serum test (now called the Wassermann test) that showed if a patient was infected with syphilis. The bacterium that causes syphilis, *Treponema pallidum*, can lay dormant in a person's body for many years, even a lifetime, without ever manifesting overt symptoms. Syphilis can be spread by sexual intercourse or from a pregnant mother to her fetus. Therefore, people who are infected with the bacterium need to be identified, so they can be treated and do not spread the disease unintentionally.

In 1906, Wassermann and Albert Neisser developed a syphilis test for the blood serum of patients. Serum is the pale yellow fluid that is one of the constituents of blood. People with syphilis produce a specific **antibody**, which is a molecule in the blood serum produced by the body's **immune system** to attack the syphilis bacterium. When a patient's blood serum with the syphilis antibody is introduced into a mixture of beef heart extract, animal blood serum, and washed red blood cells, the patient's antibody combines with parts of the mixture to create visible clumps of cells, which demonstrate the presence of the antibody and thus, the presence of the syphilis bacterium. Wassermann's test helped doctors detect syphilis in babies and adults in order to treat the disease more effectively at an earlier stage in its development. The Wassermann test is a useful, inexpensive screening procedure. However, if positive, it must be confirmed with a more specific blood test.

From 1903 to 1909, in collaboration with Wilhelm Kolle, Wassermann wrote the six-volume *Handbuch der pathogenen Mikroorganismen*, a book detailing disease-producing microorganisms. Wassermann was named the director of the department of experimental therapy at the Kaiser-Wilhelm Institute in Berlin in 1913. In 1924, he was diagnosed with kidney disease, and he died in Berlin the following year. Wassermann continued to direct the department of experimental therapy up until his death.

SEE ALSO Serology.

Water contamination

In a forensic examination, a prime task is to discern the primary cause of illness or death. In some instances, a gunshot wound for example, the cause may be readily apparent; in other cases, such as those involving contaminated food or water, there may be no visual signs of the **cause of death**. Knowledge of the nature of the contamination is essential for the forensic examiner.

Water is known as the universal solvent. This means that a great many compounds will dissolve in water. Still others that do not dissolve can become suspended in water, or, if immiscible (incapable of mixing, i.e., gasoline and alcohol), can partition in the immediate vicinity of water.

Many of these compounds can be nutrients for a variety of microbiological life forms. Other microbes may be more dormant in the water, but still capable of growing when exposed to a more nutrient-rich environment. In the latter case, the water becomes the conduit between the organism's natural habitat and humans.

Water contamination is a concern, since the organisms present can cause disease. Typically, these pathogenic organisms are normally residents of the intestinal tract of warm-blooded animals, including humans. Examples include Salmonella, Shigella and Vibrio. In addition, certain types of the intestinal bacterium ***Escherichia coli*** can cause infections. A particularly noxious form of *E. coli* designated O157:H7 can be devastating. O157:H7 contamination of the municipal water supply of Walkerton, Ontario, Canada, in the summer of 2000 sickened over 2,000 people and killed seven others. The intestinal tract also contains viruses (i.e., rotavirus, enterovirus, and coxsackievirus) that can contaminate water and cause disease.

A number of protozoan microorganisms can contaminate water. The two most prominent are members of the genera Giardia and Cryptosporidium. These microorganisms normally live in the intestinal tract of animals such as beaver and deer. The increasing

Emergency drinking water arrives to aid Walkerton, Ontario, residents whose water supply was contaminated in 2000. After five people died, forensic evidence obtained form both the victims and the water supply showed contamination with the *E-coli* bacteria.
© REUTERS/CORBIS

contamination of water by these protozoans reflects the increasing encroachment of urban areas on wilderness.

Municipal drinking water is usually treated to minimize the risk of the contamination of the water with the above microbes. The benefits of water treatment have been reaped for millennia. Thousands of years ago, it was known that the storage of drinking water in metal jugs preserved the water's quality due to the antibacterial effects of the metal ions (although this property was not known until centuries later). Similarly, the protection of water quality by the boiling of the water, which kills the noxious microorganism, has long been known. "Boil water orders" are still routinely issued in municipalities when the water quality is suspect.

Water that is obtained from wells is often protected from contamination by the natural filtering action of the soil and rocky underlayers that the water percolates down through. However, if a well cover or internal casing is broken, then the well water can be directly contaminated.

Surface water supplies are especially prone to contamination, from run-off and the deposition of feces in the water from birds and animals. Surface water that is used as the drinking water supply for an individual or a community should be rigorously treated to ensure that microorganisms, debris, and chemicals have been removed prior to use of the water.

One popular treatment is chlorination. Addition of antibacterial disinfectant compounds, particularly chlorine or derivatives of chlorine, to water has been practiced for over a century. Other treatments that kill bacteria include the use of a gas called ozone and shining ultraviolet light through the water to disrupt the bacterial genetic material. The refinement of filters now allows even viruses to be excluded from filter-treated water.

The killing of the protozoan microorganisms has proved to be challenging, as both Giardia and Cryptosporidium form dormant and chemically resistant structures called cysts during their life cycles. The cyst forms are resistant to chlorine and can pass

Members of Greenpeace take water samples from a canal in the industrial area of Santiago, October 17, 2001. Greenpeace claims that every citizen has the right to know what pollutants industries are pumping into the waters. © REUTERS/CORBIS

through the filters typically used in water treatment plants. Contamination of the water supply of Milwaukee, Wisconsin, with Cryptosporidium in 1993 sickened over 400,000 people and killed at least 47 people.

Water contamination can also involve **inorganic compounds**. Gasoline, oil, pesticides, and other noxious chemicals can also contaminate water. These can be especially insidious, since, unlike microorganisms, they can persist in the water for a long time.

Until relatively recently, water contamination was an accidental occurrence. However, particularly since the domestic terrorist attacks of September, 11, 2001, the vulnerability of water supplies to deliberate sabotage has been recognized.

Pathogenic microorganisms or the toxic by-products of the organisms can be added to water. Drinking the contaminated water can be fatal. While this form of **bioterrorism** is unlikely in a municipal

water supply, because the quantities of microorganisms and **toxins** that would be needed, contamination of an individual well is entirely possible.

Descriptions of symptoms including diarrhea, vomiting, headache, or muscle ache can alert a forensic investigator to the possibility of a contamination event.

SEE ALSO Bioterrorism; *Escherichia coli*; Pathogens.

Weapon size SEE Caliber

Weapons and ammunition, examination and identification
SEE Ballistics

Dr. Cyril H. Wecht

3/20/1931–
AMERICAN
PHYSICIAN

As of 2005, Cyril Harrison Wecht served as the **coroner** for Allegheny County, Pennsylvania. Formerly the Chairman of the Department of Pathology at Saint Francis Central Hospital in Pittsburgh, Wecht also serves as the President of its medical staff and is actively involved as a medical-legal and **forensic science** consultant, author, and lecturer.

Cyril Harrison Wecht was born in Pittsburgh, Pennsylvania. He attended high school in Pittsburgh (1943–1948, Highest Honors, Valedictorian) and studied at the University of Pittsburgh (1948–1952, B.S.) and the University of Buffalo School of Medicine (1952–1954). Wecht received his medical degree from the University of Pittsburgh School of Medicine (1956). He studied at the University of Pittsburgh School of Law (1957–1959), received his law degree from the University of Maryland School of Law (1962), and his Juris Doctor degree from the University of Pittsburgh School of Law (1962).

Wecht served as chief forensic pathologist from 1966 to 1970 and as Coroner of Allegheny County from 1970 to 1980. After 16 years away from the post, Wecht reclaimed the role of Allegheny County Coroner in 1996.

He is certified by the American Board of Pathology in anatomic, clinical, and forensic pathology, and is also a Fellow of the College of American Pathologists and the American Society of Clinical Pathologists.

Wecht is a Clinical Professor at the University of Pittsburgh Schools of Medicine, Dental Medicine, and Graduate School of Public Health, and holds positions as an Adjunct Professor at the Duquesne University School of Law, School of Pharmacy, and School of Health Sciences.

He has served as President of the American College of Legal Medicine, the **American Academy of Forensic Sciences**, and served as Chairman of the Board of Trustees of the American Board of Legal Medicine and the American College of Legal Medicine Foundation.

Wecht has lectured at numerous medical, law, and other graduate schools, as well as many colleges and universities, and numerous professional organizations and governmental agencies, including Harvard Law School, Yale Medical School, the FBI Academy, and the Medical Division of the CIA.

The author of more than 500 **professional publications**, Wecht is also an editorial board member of more than 20 national and international medico-legal and forensic scientific publications; editor of the five-volume set *Forensic Sciences*; co-editor of the two three-volume sets *Handling Soft Tissue Injury Cases* as well as *Preparing and Winning Medical Negligence Cases*.

Wecht has organized and conducted postgraduate medico-legal seminars in more than fifty countries throughout the world in his capacity as Director of the Pittsburgh Institute of Legal Medicine. He has performed approximately 15,000 autopsies and has supervised, reviewed, or has been consulted on about 35,000 additional postmortem examinations.

Wecht has testified in more than 1,000 civil, criminal, and workers compensation cases in state and federal courts in more than 30 states and several foreign countries.

As an expert in forensic medicine, Wecht has appeared as a frequent guest on numerous national television and radio shows, discussing various medico-legal and forensic scientific issues, including medical malpractice; alcohol and drug abuse; the assassinations of President John F. Kennedy, Senator Robert F. Kennedy, and Reverend Martin Luther King; the death of Elvis Presley; the Sheppard, O.J. Simpson, JonBenet Ramsey, and Diallo cases; the Chandra Levy death investigation; and Laci Peterson homicide.

His expertise has also been utilized in high profile cases involving Mary Jo Kopechne, Sunny von Bulow, Jean Harris, Dr. Jeffrey McDonald, the Waco Branch Davidian fire, and Vincent Foster. A comprehensive study of these cases are discussed from the perspective of Wecht's own professional involvement in his books.

Wecht has received numerous awards and honors from various educational, professional, community, and governmental organizations, including County Detectives' Association of Pennsylvania, Deputy Sheriffs' Association of Pennsylvania, Vectors, New York Society of Forensic Sciences, American College of Legal Medicine, National Junior Chamber of Commerce, and the American Legion. He has been invited as a Distinguished Professor to lecture in several foreign countries, and is an Honorary Life Member of the National Academies of Legal Medicine of France, Spain, Belgium, Yugoslavia, Mexico, Columbia, and Brazil.

SEE ALSO FBI (United States Federal Bureau of Investigation); Kennedy assassination; Pathology; Simpson (O. J.) murder trial.

Michael Welner

FORENSIC PSYCHIATRIST

Michael Welner, founder and chairman of The Forensic Panel (a national forensic consultation group), is a clinical associate professor of psychiatry at New York University School of Medicine, and an adjunct professor of law at Duquesne University.

In 1996, he launched *The Forensic Echo*, a practitioner written forensic journal designed to combine cutting edge technology in **forensic science** with expert commentary, case studies, and investigative reportage.

Early in his career as a forensic psychiatrist, Welner recognized the need for a different approach to forensic examination than was typically provided by so-called "hired gun" experts. He held that the way to fair and precise assessment of criminal culpability (or the lack thereof) was to institute a peer-reviewed system for thorough, accurate, objective forensic assessments. This led to the creation of The Forensic Panel in 1998. The Panel's headquarters is in New York City; it is the first, and only, peer-reviewed expert forensic consultation practice in the United States. The peer-review process is this: members conduct their assessments and synthesize their findings. They then present their conclusions to renowned, expert peers through the use of a formal protocol intended to minimize examiner bias and maximize examiner objectivity.

Welner's goal, that of scientific neutrality in the criminal sentencing (and in all aspects of the law enforcement system) process, is achieved within the context of his nationally acclaimed Forensic Panel: to bring depth of understanding, diligence, extensive use of scientific methodology, and objectivity to the process of forensic examination.

More recently, Michael Welner has self-funded The Depravity Scale Project, the end product of which is the Depravity Scale, leading to a forensic definition of the concept of evil. The Scale is an historical assessment tool designed to codify definition of such concepts as "atrocious, cruel, heinous, depraved, and vile" in order to ensure fair and consistent application of the their use during criminal sentencing.

The American Psychiatric Institute publicly recognized Welner for excellence in medical education in 1997, and noted that his consistent innovations in clinical practice have had far-reaching beneficial effects on the practice and the profession of forensic psychiatry. Michael Welner is a frequent consultant to the court system throughout the nation.

SEE ALSO American Academy of Forensic Sciences; Careers in forensic science; Criminal profiling; Expert witnesses; Psychological profile.

Wendy's chili finger

In March 2005, a woman claimed to have found part of a severed finger in a bowl of chili at a Wendy's restaurant in San Jose, California. The woman claimed to have discovered the finger (actually two sections of finger tissue) after eating a portion of the chili containing the severed tissue. The woman alleged to have put a portion of the finger tissue in her mouth and then spat it out. After vomiting, she notified restaurant employees, who then called the police. A **medical examiner** identified the tissue as part of a human finger.

The charges and claims generated far reaching and intense negative publicity for the third largest U.S. hamburger chain; sales dropped nationwide.

After a forensic investigation that included analysis of every step in the food production chain and "trace-back" analysis of elements discovered in the finger tissue, authorities suspected that the initial complaint was a fraud intended to intimidate the restaurant chain into a potentially lucrative financial settlement for the initial complainant.

Forensic trace element analysis showed that the finger had not been cooked with the ingredients in the chili, and therefore, must have been placed in the chili after it was cooked.

Ultimately, the woman who claimed to have found the finger was arrested, initially on one count of grand theft stemming from an unrelated real estate transaction and on one count of attempted grand theft for the allegations made against the Wendy's restaurant. The woman's long history of suing large corporations, along with claims against other restaurant chains, cast doubt on her claim with investigators. As of April 2005, the resolution of larceny charges against the woman remained pending.

Initially started as a public health investigation, the case was soon turned over to criminal forensic investigators. Along with the official investigation, the Wendy's chain hired their own team of detectives and forensic experts to test and verify the integrity of their **food supply** and processing. The chain also offered an award eventually boosted to $100,000 for information about the origin of the finger.

By mid-May 2005, the finger had been identified as that from an associate of Ayala's husband, who had lost the digit in an industrial accident in December 2004.

SEE ALSO Food supply.

Charles H. Wick

AMERICAN
RESEARCH PHYSICAL SCIENTIST

Charles H. Wick, team leader of the Edgewood Chemical Biological Center (ECBC), is a physical scientist who has made significant contributions to **forensic science**. Although his 30–year professional career has spanned both the public sector and the military, his better-known work in the area of forensic science has occurred in concert with the Department of Defense (DOD).

After earning four degrees from the University of Washington, Wick worked in the private sector (civilian occupations) for twelve years, leading to a patent, numerous publications, and international recognition among his colleagues.

In 1983, Wick joined the Vulnerability/Lethality Division of the United States Army Ballistic Research Laboratory, where he quickly achieved recognition as a team leader and principal investigator. It was at this point that he made one of his first major contributions to forensic science and to the field of antiterrorism; his team was the first to utilize current technology to model sub-lethal chemical, biological, and nuclear agents. This achievement was beneficial to all areas of the Department of Defense, as well as to the North Atlantic Treaty Organization (NATO), and gained Wick international acclaim as an authority on individual performance for operations conducted on a nuclear, biological, and chemical (NBC) battlefield.

During his career in the United States Army, Wick rose to the rank of Lieutenant Colonel in the Chemical Corps. He was a Unit Commander for twelve years, a staff officer for six years (he was an ARCOM Staff Chemical Officer for two rotations), Deputy Program Director Biological Defense Systems, and retired from the position of Commander of the 485th Chemical Battalion in April of 1999.

Wick has continued to work for the DOD as a civilian at ECBC. His most notable achievement, and one which earned him the Department of the Army Research and Development Award for Technical Excellence and a Federal Laboratory Consortium

Technology Transfer Award in 2002, was his involvement in the invention of the Integrated Virus Detection System (IVDS), a fast-acting, highly portable, user-friendly, extremely accurate and efficient system for detecting the presence of, screening, identifying, and characterizing viruses. The IVDS can detect and identify the full spectrum of known, unknown, and mutated viruses, from AIDS to foot and mouth disease, to West Nile Virus, and beyond. This system is compact, portable, and does not rely upon elaborate chemistry.

Throughout his career, Wick has made lasting and important contributions to forensic science and to the field of antiterrorism. He has written more than forty-five civilian and military publications and has received myriad awards and citations, including twenty-five decorations and awards for military and community service, two United States Army Achievement Medals for Civilian Service, the Commander's Award for Civilian Service, and the Technical Cooperation Achievement Award.

SEE ALSO Air and water purity, forensic tests; Analytical instrumentation; Chemical and biological detection technologies; Chemical warfare; Ebola virus.

Alexander S. Wiener

AMERICAN
PHYSICIAN

In 1940 Alexander Wiener and **Karl Landsteiner** discovered the Rhesus, or Rh, factor in **blood** group typing, during the course of a series of scientific experiments. The two scientists injected guinea pigs and rabbits with the red blood cells of rhesus monkeys, and discovered that the experimental animals produced an **antibody** that agglutinated (caused the red blood cells to clump together) the rhesus red cells. In addition, they discovered that the antibody in the rabbits and guinea pigs' **serum** also agglutinated blood samples equivalent to approximately 85% of the human population. The percentage rate was later found to correspond to approximately 85% of the Caucasian population and an even larger percentage of the Black and Asian populations.

The agglutination meant that blood cells of the members of the 85% population group contained the same factor as did the rhesus monkeys. Their blood was termed Rh positive (Rh+), and the blood of the remaining 15% was termed Rh negative (Rh−). The Rh antibody reaction was, by its nature, acquired and not present at birth; that is, red blood cells of

Rh+ individuals needed to be exposed to those of Rh− individuals in order for there to be an antibody reaction. The presence or absence of the Rh factor is of particular forensic importance in cases of disputed paternity, blood type and grouping inheritance, and genetic control. In everyday life, the presence or lack of the Rh factor has no bearing on health. It is only when the two blood types are mingled in an Rh-negative individual that problems ensue, since the Rh factor acts as an **antigen** in Rh− persons, causing the production of antibodies.

Wiener hypothesized that Rh **gene** inheritance occurred in the form of a single gene on a single DNA locus. Since blood type and presence or absence of the Rh factor are genetic traits that are easy to test, and the blood type of an individual is related to parental blood types, blood group typing may be used legally to establish paternity.

It has become understood, since Wiener and Landsteiner's discovery of the Rhesus factor in 1940, that the Rh system is far more complex than the presence or absence of a single factor. There are now known to be three genes that combine to create Rhesus antigens (C, D, and E), all of which are encoded on a single **chromosome** (chromosome 1). There are two possible alleles at each locus: C or c, D or d, and E or e. One haplotype which contains c/C, d/D, and e/E is inherited from each parent. The resulting Rhesus type of the individual depends on which genotype they inherit. If a person inherits at least one of the C, D, or E antigens, they are Rh+. If they inherit two sets of cde genes, they will be Rh−.

Wiener made a lasting contribution to **forensic science** in his discovery and advancement of the concept of the Rhesus factor. By using blood typing and blood grouping technologies, it has become increasingly possible to identify unique individuals, whether suspects or victims, from among the entire population of humans.

SEE ALSO Antibody; Antigen; Chromosome; DNA; Paternity evidence.

Wildlife forensics

Wildlife forensics is a relatively new field of criminal investigation. Its goals are to use scientific procedures to examine, identify, and compare **evidence** from crime scenes, and to link this evidence with a suspect and a victim, which is specifically an animal. Killing wild animals that are protected from hunting by laws, also called poaching, is one of the most serious crimes investigated by wildlife forensic

Confiscated luxury items made from animals on the endangered species list are stored by the U.S. Fish and Wildlife Service in Ashland, Oregon. © **GALEN ROWELL/CORBIS.**

scientists. Other crimes against wildlife include buying and selling protected animals and buying and selling products made from protected animals.

The international organization that monitors trade in wild animals and plants is the Convention on International Trade in Endangered Species of Wild Fauna and Flora (CITES), which was established in 1963 and, as of 2004, includes 167 member countries. In the United States, the Endangered Species Act, which was authorized in 1973, protects endangered and threatened species and the U.S. Department of Fish and Wildlife has the authority to prosecute violations against protected species. Trent University in Ontario, Canada houses one of the largest wildlife **DNA** forensics departments in North America, incorporating an extremely active research facility.

The types of evidence analyzed by a wildlife forensics lab include any part of an animal including **blood** and tissue samples, carcasses, hair, teeth, bones, claws, talons, tusks, hides, fur, feathers, or

Wildlife rangers stack elephant ivory at Kenya Wildlife Headquarters during planning conference for Convention on International Trade in Endangered Species, Nairobi, Kenya. KHALIL SENOSI/AP WIDE WORLD PHOTOS. REPRODUCED BY PERMISSION.

stomach contents. Wildlife forensic scientists may also investigate materials used to kill or harm animals, such as poisons, pesticides, projectiles, and weapons. Products that are made from animals are also of interest, including leather goods and medicines, especially those from Asia.

One of the most critical problems facing wildlife forensic scientists is identifying a particular species from crime scene evidence. For example, wildlife forensic scientists may have to distinguish if a piece of leather on a watchband is made from a protected animal, like an elephant or a zebra, or if it comes from a non-protected animal, like a cow or a horse. They must be able to determine if a medicinal powder contains the pulverized remains of a protected animal, like a rhinoceros, a tiger, or coral. They must be able to differentiate between the roe of protected fish from farm-raised caviar.

A variety of scientific techniques allow wildlife forensic scientists to answer these types of questions. Techniques similar to those used in a police crime lab are used to identify and analyze parts of animals as well as bullets, shot casings, paint chips, soil, and **fibers** found at the crime scene. Experts in fingerprinting, **ballistics**, soil analysis, and hair comparisons examine evidence visually and with microscopic techniques.

Pathologists examine carcasses for wounds in order to determine how the animal died and to distinguish natural death from human killing. Experts in the morphology, or the form, of animals can identify the species, and sometimes subspecies, of animals found at crime scenes. They can often determine the age and sex of animals as well as the time-since-death by careful observations of feathers, skulls and skeletons. Chemists may be asked to identify poisons and pesticides, characterize the contents of Asian medicines, and provide species **identification**, when possible. Molecular biologists use protein and DNA analyses to provide information about the identity of a sample. Genetics can be particularly useful when the sample is very small or unidentifiable from its morphology. Some answers that genetic tests may provide include identification of species, characterization of the familial relationships between animals, and evaluation of two different samples in order to determine if they originated from the same individual. In addition, geneticists may be able to provide environmental information about an animal.

Examples of criminal cases in which wildlife forensics have been used are extensive, but a few examples illustrate the importance of this field. A large proportion of the cases in the United States involve trafficking in fake caviar or caviar that is illegal to import. One man, who owned a caviar company in New York, sold the eggs of the American paddlefish, a protected species that lives in the Tennessee and Mississippi rivers, as caviar. DNA testing by wildlife forensic scientists verified that the roe was not Russian Sevruga, as labeled, but from the paddlefish. He was sentenced to two years in jail and fined $100,000. His company was additionally fined $110,000. In Wyoming, six carcasses of pronghorn antelope were discovered in a pit. The heads were removed, but no meat was taken. After a suspect was apprehended, wildlife forensic scientists were able to match DNA from the skulls of antelope in his custody to the DNA in the carcasses. The man was fined, served time in jail and his hunting license was suspended. In 1991, the sale of wild red drum (a fish) was banned in the state of Texas, however farm-raised red drum may still be sold legally. Using chemical assays to distinguish between the types of fats found in wild and farm-raised red drum, forensic scientists were able to identify the origin of red drum in the marketplace. Eventually, poaching rings were infiltrated and violators prosecuted in court. In 1998, an Iowa hunter returned from a safari to Africa with the **skull** of a brown hyena that he had shot. The brown hyena is an endangered species and after the man bragged about his kill, local wildlife agents seized the skull. Wildlife experts used morphology, comparing the skull to a series of hyena skulls, to identify the skull as illegal. The hunter was fined and his hunting license was revoked worldwide.

SEE ALSO DNA banks for endangered animals; DNA fingerprint; Fingerprint; Hair analysis; Paint analysis; Pathology; Soils.

Wine authenticity

Counterfeiting of wine has occurred for centuries, but since the 1990s both rumors of counterfeit wines and cases of fraud associated with wine increased drastically. Some believe that wine counterfeiting is a multi-million dollar industry associated with organized crime. Both the **FBI** and Scotland Yard have investigated cases of crime fraud. Industry experts estimate that about 5% of all wine sold is counterfeited.

A variety of testing methods can be used to ensure the authenticity of wine. Along with more traditional methods of inspection, chemical assays such as stable isotope analysis, **chromatography**, mineral content analysis, and **DNA** fingerprinting are being used by various wineries. A novel method that incorporates unique DNA codes into the label of wine bottles is also used to avoid counterfeiting.

Wine fraud occurs in many different forms. Often counterfeiters target the more expensive and older wines. Not only are sales of these wines financially profitable, but few people are familiar with the labels and other markings on these bottles so the fraud is harder to detect. Auctioneers and resellers sell expensive wines in large quantities, so the contents of a bottle or a case can be tampered with without anyone noticing for some time. One of the easiest scams involves replacing the contents of a case of expensive wine with bottles of less expensive wine. The cases are sold at auction houses without ever being opened and then stored for years in warehouses before being sold again. By the time someone decides to verify the contents, the counterfeiter is removed from the crime by both time and by layers of transaction.

Another common type of fraud involves replacing the contents of an expensive bottle of wine with a wine of a lesser quality. Using a two-pronged wine opener, corks can be removed and replaced with little damage. Capsules, which are the metal or plastic coverings sealing the corks in the bottle, can also be replicated and replaced. Recipes for duplicating expensive wines using inexpensive ingredients are known to experienced sommeliers (wine stewards) as well as counterfeiters. For example, blending a 1960 Pétrus with a Pomerol can mimic a 1961 Pétrus, which is one of the most expensive wines sold and usually costs more than ten times as much as the 1960. Other types of altering the contents of a wine bottle include adding sugar or other flavorings, and watering down the contents.

Blending was at the heart of a series of scandals in the Burgundy region of France in 2001. Several chateaux (vineyards) were blending burgundies with table wines from other regions of France, which is illegal. The winemakers involved confessed to making more than 10,000 cases of fraudulent wine during a ten-year period. Some of the wine was sold for as much as 300% profit.

Relabeling bottles of a less expensive wine with labels of a more expensive vintage is another common scam. In 2002 customs agents in China seized approximately 700 bottles of a wine that usually sells for $200 that had been relabeled as 1982 Chateau Lafite Rothschild, which sells for more than $5,700. The gang of counterfeiters had been selling the bottles for approximately $1,100 each.

In 1998 a wine auctioneer in Australia noticed that the bar code on some bottles of 1990 Penfolds Grange on the auction block were printed in black while genuine bottles have the code printed in red. Further investigation revealed that the labels had been forged and there were at least ten discrepancies between the original and the fake. One of the discrepancies included the misspelling of the word "pour" for "poor." Penfolds Grange 1990 is one of Australia's top wines and was named Wine of the Year by The Wine Spectator magazine in 1995. In 2005 it sells for more than $400 a bottle.

In 2000 a large wine fraud ring was broken up in Tuscany. More than 20,000 bottles of fake Tenuta San Guido 1994 and 1995 Sassicaia were discovered. Sassicaia is one of Italy's top wine producers known for its Super Tuscan. When the storage cellars of the gang were raided, another six million bottles of fake Chianti were seized. The police were alerted when a customer became suspicious that the price for the wine was too low. The counterfeiters tried to convince the customer that the original sale of the wine had fallen through and so they needed to sell it at a special price. Twelve people were arrested in connection with the incident.

A variety of techniques are used to determine the authenticity of wine. Traditional techniques involve careful observation of the bottle, its labels and its contents. This requires familiarity with both the wine and experience detecting counterfeits. Novel techniques of authentication rely on biochemical methods including stable isotope analysis, chromatography, mineral content analysis, and DNA fingerprinting.

General observation of the parts of the wine bottle and experience with wines are fundamental to the detection of counterfeit wines. The type of **glass** used to make the bottle should be consistent with the time period. Glass making has changed throughout the years and the type and manufacture of glass used should reflect these changes. The capsule should be consistent in color and markings with other examples from the same vintage. The corks should also be inspected. Since 1970, corks have been printed with the correct vintage and brand. Prior to 1970, casks were often shipped to resellers, who corked bottles themselves, so they may have printed their own corks. Labels may show damage such as peeling and staining, especially in older wines stored in the proper humid conditions. When old wines have labels in perfect condition, it may be a sign of relabeling. Spelling errors and font changes are key indicators of fraud. Wines that are imported into the

United States have strip labels that show the name of the importer. These should also be consistent with the wine.

As grapes grow, they incorporate atoms of hydrogen, carbon, nitrogen and oxygen from their environment into proteins and carbohydrates. Each of these elements exists in more than one form called stable isotopes. Stable isotopes have the same number of protons and electrons but different numbers of neutrons. For example, carbon has two stable isotopes: one of them has 12 neutrons in the nucleus and the other has 13. The stable isotopes of carbon are referred to as ^{12}C and ^{13}C, respectively. About 98.9% of all carbon is ^{12}C, while 1.1% is ^{13}C, however these ratios change depending on geographic region and weather conditions. Nuclear magnetic resonance (NMR) is used to measure the stable isotope ratios of hydrogen in the alcohol of wines. Isotopic ratio mass spectrometry (IRMS) is used to measure the stable isotope ratios of carbon and oxygen.

Grapes grown in different regions during different years have different ratios of stable isotopes and these ratios remain constant when the grapes are processed into wine. The European Union houses a database containing the stable isotope ratios from all of its wine growing regions measured each year. Determination of stable isotope ratios from a bottle of wine can be compared to the values in the database in order to determine the origin of the grapes used to make the wine.

Chromatography is a technique that involves separating the components of a mixture, such as wine. An extremely sensitive form of chromatography, high-pressure liquid chromatography (HPLC) can measure the relative quantities of the pigments, called anthocyanins, which give wine its red color. The ratio of two particular forms of anthocyanin is often used as an indicator of the type of grape used to make the wine. Evidence shows that the ratio of these two forms of anthocyanin is determined by the genetic composition of the grapes and therefore indicates the type of grape used to make the wine. However, some chemists believe that concentrations of anthocyanin in wine are affected by processing. They have found that length of fermentation, exposure to varying temperatures and the addition of enzymes, can affect the anthocyanin ratios.

When grapes grow, they incorporate small amounts of metals from the soil into their skin and pulp. These metals are called trace metals and they include aluminum, calcium, copper, iron, potassium, magnesium, strontium, and zinc, among others. The concentration of these metals varies from location to

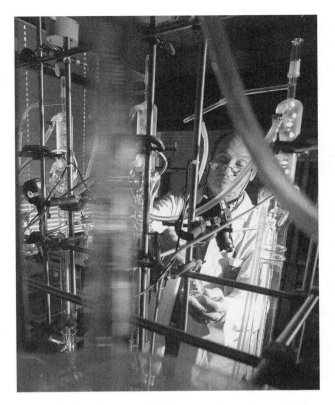

Testing wine in order to establish the properties on the product's identity card. © DUNG VO TRUNG/CORBIS SYGMA

location and so the concentrations of these metals incorporated into grapes varies depending on where they are grown.

In 2004 researchers from the University of Seville, Spain, developed a method to identify the trace metal composition of sparkling wines. They used atomic spectrophotometers to determine the elemental composition of the wine based on patterns of absorption of electromagnetic waves. Samples of cava from Spain and champagne from France were compared. The two wines are made using identical processes, but the regions from which the grapes originate differ. As a result, the trace mineral content also differs. For example, the ratio of strontium to zinc was always greater than 1 in cava and always less than 1 in champagne. The researchers showed that using the concentrations of 16 different trace **minerals**, they could identify the regional identity of the wine with perfect accuracy.

In the late 1990s a group of researchers from the University of California, Davis, developed a method to identify wine-grapes based on their genetic characteristics. They identified 17 different regions of DNA that varied greatly between different grape vari-

eties. Collaborating with a research team from Montpellier, France, they assembled a database of genetic profiles for 300 different wine-grape varieties. In 2005, the database was expanded to include the more than 2,500 varieties of wine-grapes in existence.

Beginning in 2005 the research group in Montpellier began developing methods to perform DNA fingerprinting on wine. Using techniques similar to those used to study DNA from **mummies**, they believe that they will be able to extract and purify enough DNA from wine to compare it to the database of grape-wine genetic markers. Some scientists are skeptical of the technique however. Wine-grapes are heavily processed during the wine making process and the DNA may be too damaged to analyze.

In 2001 an Australian wine company, BRL Hardy, began labeling their wine with ink laced with DNA as a security measure against tampering. The technology was developed by a company called DNA Technologies for use in labeling souvenirs from the 2000 Sydney Olympics. DNA Technologies extracted DNA from one of BRL Hardy's 125-year-old grape vines. A segment of the vine DNA is then coated with a protective protein and imbedded into the neck label of the wine. Along with the DNA, optical taggants that emit unique spectral signatures in the presence of the proper excitation wavelengths are incorporated into the label. A handheld electronic scanner can then be used to test for the presence of the DNA label. BRL Hardy believes that the technology will discourage counterfeiting of its wines.

SEE ALSO Analytical instrumentation; DNA fingerprint; DNA sequences, unique; Fluorescence; Soils.

World Trade Center, 1993 terrorist attack

The World Trade Center (WTC) bombing of 1993 has since been overshadowed by the attack that brought the twin towers down on September 11, 2001. Yet, at the time it occurred, the attack loomed as large on the American landscape as the towers themselves once did on the Manhattan skyline. The attack killed six people and injured more than one thousand.

The law enforcement response to the tragedy involved a massive forensic investigation designed to determine the cause of the blast, the identities of

FBI and ATF agents entering the World Trade Center parking garage in New York after the 1993 bombing. © REUTERS/CORBIS

those responsible and, ultimately, to ascertain why, although Trade Tower One sustained a great deal of damage, it did not collapse. The forensic sleuthing involved the detailed examination of the blast scene, physical and chemical analyses of samples, and **forensic accounting** to trace a paper trail that led to the suspects.

At 12:18 P.M. on Friday, February 26, 1993, an explosion rocked the second level of the parking basement beneath Trade Tower One. The explosive material, as forensic investigators would later determine in their chemical analyses of samples retrieved at the site, was somewhere between 1,200 and 1,500 pounds (544–680 kg) of urea nitrate, a homemade fertilizer-based explosive.

The blast ripped open a crater 150 feet (46 meters) in diameter and 5 floors deep, rupturing sewer and water mains and cutting off electricity.

Over the hours that followed, more than 50,000 people were evacuated from the Trade Center complex.

The first forensic analysis team to arrive was from the Federal Bureau of Investigation (**FBI**). The bureau brought in two examiners from the FBI Laboratory Explosives Unit. Over the week that followed, a team of more than 300 law-enforcement officers (including forensic specialists) from various agencies throughout the country would sift through some 2,500 cubic yards of debris weighing more than 6,800 tons.

At the same time that this forensic investigation began, government authorities rushed to protect against physical, chemical, and biological hazards associated with the blast. The explosion had exposed raw sewage, asbestos, mineral wool, acid, and fumes from automobiles. Meanwhile, small electrical fires burned, and pieces of concrete and sharp metal hung threateningly from distended beams.

On Saturday, authorities installed seismographic equipment, cleared the area, and conducted a test run of an empty subway train. The results showed that with a few adjustments, the area could be rendered safe for the operation of the Port Authority Transportation system (PATH) on Monday, thus preventing a virtual shutdown of lower Manhattan. The Environmental Protection Agency and the Occupational Safety and Health Administration began taking steps to clean up biological and chemical debris.

Meanwhile, the forensic investigation expanded, with two chemists each from the FBI, **ATF** (Bureau of Alcohol, Tobacco, and Firearms), and the New York Police Department collecting and studying residue from the blast area. In the course of this work, investigators found a key piece of **evidence**: a 300-pound (136-kg) fragment of a vehicle that, based on the damage it had sustained, must have been at the epicenter of the blast. Sewage contamination had rendered it unusable for residue analysis, but recovery of a vehicle identification number allowed the vehicle to be traced.

Authorities traced the vehicle to a Ryder truck rental facility in Jersey City, New Jersey, where it had been reported stolen. On Monday, while FBI special agents were at the Jersey City facility to interview personnel there, a Ryder clerk received a call from a man identified as Mohammed Salameh. The latter demanded the return of his $400 deposit for the van in question, and the Ryder clerk arranged for him to return and collect the deposit on March 4, 1993. When Salameh arrived, he was arrested.

A search of Salameh's belongings led investigators to Nidal Ayyad, a chemist working for the Allied Signal Corporation in New Jersey. Forensic accounting of toll records and receipts helped lead to a safe house in Jersey City, New Jersey, where authorities found traces of nitroglycerine and urea nitrate. They also uncovered evidence that Salameh and Ayyad had obtained three tanks of compressed hydrogen gas. In the course of searching a storage room rented by Salameh, investigators found large caches of urea, sulfuric acid, and other chemicals commonly used in making bombs. On March 3, the *New York Times* received a letter that claimed responsibility for the bombing. A subsequent forensic investigation of **DNA** samples matched Ayyad with the **saliva** on the envelope flap.

A forensic investigation was conducted to examine how such a massive blast failed to collapse the tower. The consensus opinion is that the location of the explosion, on the second level of the underground parking lot, acted to diffuse the intensity of the explosion. When the concrete floor of that level ruptured, much of the force of the blast was directed downward into the lower levels of the parking garage.

SEE ALSO Architecture and structural analysis; Bomb (explosion) investigations; Bomb damage, forensic assessment; Explosives; September 11, 2001, terrorist attacks (forensic investigations of).

World Trade Center, 2001 attack upon SEE September 11, 2001, terrorist attacks (forensic investigations of)

Theodore George Wormley

4/1/1826–1/2/1897
AMERICAN
MICROCHEMIST

Over the course of his career, Theodore G. Wormley became known as distinguished microchemist and toxicologist, frequently writing, teaching, and consulting on the subjects of chemistry, poisons, **toxicology**, and **medicine** to local, national, and international audiences. He spent more than forty years teaching at universities in Ohio and Pennsylvania, and also worked as a chemist for the state of Ohio. Wormley is the author of the 1867 *The Micro Chemistry of Poisons*, a book that became known as a standard on the subject at that time.

Wormley was born in Wormleysburg, Pennsylvania, in 1826. He attended Dickinson College, where his interest in science and mathematics grew. To pursue these interests, Wormley left Dickinson to attend Philadelphia Medical College, where he earned a medical degree in 1849. He then opened his own medical practice in Columbus, Ohio.

Within just a few years of opening his own practice, Wormley also began working as a professor. He was hired as a professor of chemistry and natural sciences at Capitol University in Columbus, a position he held for thirteen years. During the same time, Wormley took on a second professorship, teaching chemistry and toxicology at Starling Medical College. He left Starling in 1877 to take the position of professor of chemistry and toxicology at the University of Pennsylvania, a position he held until his death. And while Wormley was teaching students the intricacies of chemistry and toxicology, he also spent a great deal of time studying and researching the topics of poisons and chemicals. Wormley's expertise on these subjects made him a frequent consultant and witness on criminal cases and trials.

In addition to his work as an educator, Wormley also held a number of positions within the Ohio state government. In 1867, he was appointed as the state gas commissioner of Ohio, and in 1869 he became the state chemist of the Ohio Geological Survey. In that role Wormley developed chemical methods to analyze coal, iron ores, clays, **soils**, slags, and limestone.

Wormley was also a prolific writer, publishing articles and books about chemistry, medicine, and toxicology. His best-known work is *The Micro Chemistry of Poisons*, published in 1867. In the book Wormley discusses the chemical compositions of poisons. His wife drew many of the accompanying illustrations.

SEE ALSO Poison and antidote actions; Toxins.

Wound assessment

The assessment of wounds is an important part of both an **autopsy** and the medical examination of a living victim. The **medical examiner** will make a careful note of each wound and its location on the body. Wounds, or injuries, are generally classified as being due to either blunt force or sharp force trauma. Blunt force would be applied by weapons which do not have a cutting edge, such as baseball bats, clubs, or fists, while sharp force trauma comes, as the name suggests, from weapons such as knives.

An abrasion or scrape is the mildest kind of wound caused by blunt force trauma. It involves only the epidermis, or outer layer of the skin, and bleeds little, if at all. A contusion or bruise involves leakage of **blood** from tiny vessels in the deeper layers of the skin. A laceration is a form of blunt force trauma in which the skin is actually broken.

When it comes to sharp force trauma, the examiner distinguishes between incised wounds and stab wounds. The former are wider than they are deep. Stab wounds are deeper than they are wide and often lead to significant blood loss.

It is not just the nature of the wounds on a victim but their pattern that may be significant. Contusions and lacerations widely scattered over the arms, legs, and torso may be indicative of torture or struggle. If the victim tries to defend himself, there may be wounds on their arms and hands. **Hesitation wounds** are common in cases of suicide. These are small nicks and cuts inflicted, typically on the wrists, as someone tries to get up the courage to make a fatal cut.

Should a potential murder weapon like a knife or gun be available, the examiner will try to determine whether it was capable of making the wounds being assessed. In the case of a fractured **skull** caused by a blunt instrument, x rays of the injury can be very useful to see if the injury maps onto the dimensions of the weapon.

SEE ALSO Body marks.

Wounds, defensive SEE Defensive wounds

Brian Wraxall

12/6/1943–
AMERICAN
FORENSIC SEROLOGIST

Forensic serologist Brian G.D. Wraxall is widely recognized as the co-developer in 1966, along with Brian J. Culliford, of the immunoelectrophoretic technique for haptoglobin typing in bloodstains. Wraxall is also credited, along with **Mark Stolorow**, with developing the **multisystem method** for the parallel testing of isoenzyme systems in 1978. During that same year, the team of Wraxall and Stolorow were also recognized as the first forensic scientists to develop methods for typing **blood serum** proteins. Currently, Wraxall is the executive director of the Serological Research Institute in California, a company that provides consultation, laboratory analysis, and court testimony to the **forensic science** community.

Wraxall grew up in England during the middle part of the twentieth century where from 1958 to 1962 he attended King Edward VI Grammar School in the town of Totnes in Devon County. (The school later became known as King Edward VI College.) Even at this young age, Wraxall was interested in biology and chemistry, receiving school certificates in both subjects. Beginning in 1962, he worked as a laboratory chemist for Western Countries Brick Company in Torquay, Devon, and later as a senior scientific officer for the Metropolitan Police Laboratory in London, England. During this twelve-year period, Wraxall specialized in **serology**, where he delved into the research and development of **electrophoresis** methods that specifically involved blood enzymes and proteins in body **fluids** and bloodstains. In 1966, Wraxall and Culliford developed a technique of immunoelectrophoresis for haptoglobin typing in bloodstains. At this time, Wraxall and Culliford published the paper "Haptoglobin Types in Dried Bloodstains" in *Nature*, which was followed by additional scientific papers over the next few years.

In 1969, Wraxall received a higher national certificate in applied biology—specializing in biochemistry, microbiology, and physiology—from the Borough Polytechnic College in London, England. Eight years later, in 1977, Wraxall began working as a consultant for the Bloodstain Analysis project (funded by the Law Enforcement Assistance Administration) for Beckman Instruments and The Aerospace Corporation. One year later, Wraxall and Stolorow developed a Bloodstain Analysis System (BAS), or the multisystem method, for simultaneously testing generic (**identification**) markers—such as ACP1 (acid phosphatase 1, soluble), ADA (adenosine deaminase), AK (adenylate kinase), EsD (esterase D), GloI (glyoxalase I), and PGM (phosphoglucomutase)—using one of three different electrophoretic trials. The BAS method resulted in the efficient identification of genetic characteristics (or phenotypes) of organisms with respect to their environment when only a very small amount of materials are available as **evidence** in criminal cases. As a result, Wraxall introduced, along with other scientists, the paper "Final Report: Bloodstain Analysis System" (The Aerospace Corporation, September 1978).

At this same time, Wraxall and Stolorow also developed methods for typing blood serum proteins such as Hp (haptoglobin) and Gc (glycoprotein C). As a result, the pair published the paper "An Efficient Method to Eliminate Streaking in the Electrophoretic Analysis of Haptoglobin in Bloodstains" in the *Journal of Forensic Science*.

In 1978, Wraxall became employed for the Serological Research Institute (SERI) located in Richmond, California, first as a technical leader and later as its chief forensic serologist. SERI is a non-for-profit corporation that has served the legal and forensic sciences communities since 1978 with a number of support services. Wraxall is currently the executive director of the Serological Research Institute, where he coordinates the work of providing forensic, serological, and **DNA** analysis services. During his years with SERI he

has taught various **training** courses that involve: identification and typing of biological evidence in such specific topics as bloodstain analysis; electrophoresis; **semen** identification and analysis; genotyping of immunoglobulins (Ig), heavy chain (GM) and light chain (KM) allotypes; and DNA (deoxyribonucleic acid) typing.

Also while employed with SERI, Wraxall attended the University of California at Berkeley where he studied molecular biology in 1990. Later, in 2002, Wraxall graduated from Hamilton University—located in Evanston, Wyoming—with a bachelor's of science degree in biological sciences.

For most of his professional career, Wraxall has worked as a consultant with respect to expert testimony for both the prosecution and the defense sides of courtroom cases involving both civil and criminal matters. In preparation for these court cases and in direct testimony during these cases, Wraxall lent his proficiency in forensic serology throughout various U.S. courts involving the examination and explanation of biological evidence. His expertise covers a broad range of case material involving the presence of **trace evidence** such as the phenotyping of bloodstains in polymorphic systems (involving antigens, enzymes, and proteins); the phenotyping of stains of body fluids; and the extraction and analysis of DNA from hairs, bodily fluids, and skeletal materials.

Wraxall has published numerous scientific papers from 1967 to the present day including "Use of Prostate-Specific Antigen (PSA) to Measure Semen Exposure Resulting from Male Condom Failures: Implications for Contraceptive Efficacy and the Prevention of Sexually Transmitted Disease" in *Contraception* (2003). He has also presented various papers throughout his career including "Advances on DNA in Forensic Testing" for the Legal Secretaries 2nd Quarterly Conference (Modesto, California, 2003) and "Roles of Markers in Forensics" for the Evaluation of Markers of Intercourse in Trials of Vaginal Barriers (Conrad, Washington, D.C., 2003).

SEE ALSO Bloodstain evidence; DNA; DNA sequences, unique; Mitochondrial DNA analysis; Mitochondrial DNA typing; Multisystem method; Paternity evidence; RFLP (restriction fragment length polymorphism).

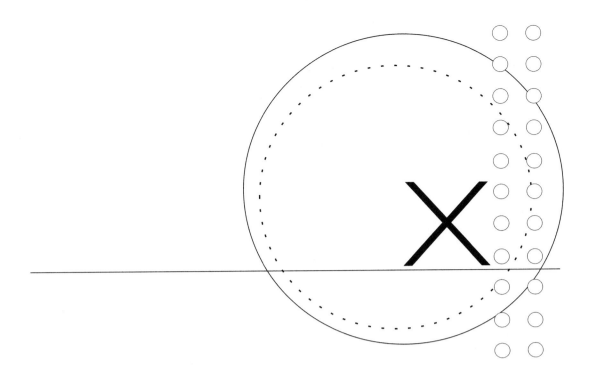

Xylotomy

Xylotomy is the cutting of thin sections of wood specimens for microscopic examination. Wood splinters, chips, or fragments can be important items of **trace evidence** in some crimes. Typically, the forensic botanist will cut the sections from the wood sample with a very sharp knife mounted on a jig called a microtome. The sections are then stained so that features such as cells and grain direction can be seen under the high-powered microscope.

It is not always possible to identify a tree species from this kind of fragment examination. However, comparison with known samples will give an idea of the type of timber involved. If a suspect has used a piece of wood to assault someone, the suspect's clothing may carry splinters. The forensic investigator can compare these splinters with the weapon to try to make an association. Similarly, doors and windows may be damaged on entering or leaving a crime scene. Splinters found on the suspect's clothes can be compared with samples from the entry and exit sites of the scene.

Wood analysis played a crucial part in one famous case, the kidnapping and **murder** of the infant son of aviator Charles Lindbergh from his New Jersey home in 1932. The ransom note left at the scene suggested the kidnapper was poorly educated and of German descent. This was not much to go on, given there were no fingerprints on the note. However, a homemade wooden ladder was left at the scene and had been used to gain access to the child's nursery. Arthur Koehler, an expert in wood and wood products, examined the ladder and determined it was made of Ponderosa pine, North Carolina pine, birch, and fir. He suggested that the fir section was actually a piece of flooring. Microscopic examination revealed marks made by a planing machine. Planed wood samples from mills around the country were compared to the ladder samples. The timber was tracked down to a company in the Bronx. Lindbergh had paid out a ransom and bills with the corresponding serial numbers also turned up in this location, narrowing down the search for the kidnapper.

Bruno Richard Hauptmann, a carpenter of German descent, was later arrested in connection with the crime. Examination of his home revealed a missing floorboard and nail holes corresponding to those in the piece of fir used in the ladder. The final piece of incriminating **evidence** was the presence of a wood plane which made smoothing marks matching those found on the ladder.

SEE ALSO Dendrochronology; Lindbergh kidnapping and murder.

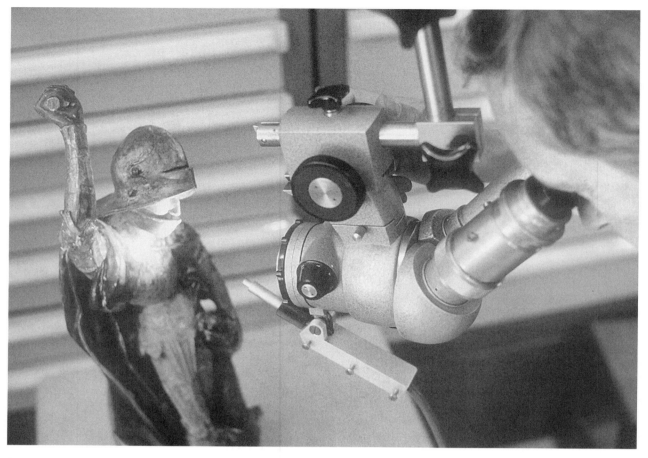

A conservator inspects a small 15th century wooden statue at the Louvre laboratories in Paris, France.
© ANNEBICQUE BERNARD/CORBIS SYGMA

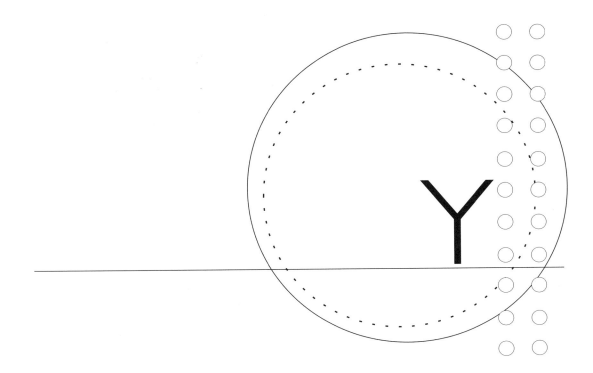

Y chromosome analysis

In the human, there are normally 46 chromosomes, two sex chromosomes and 22 **chromosome** pairs for which one copy is inherited from each parent at conception. The sex chromosomes are called the X and the Y chromosome. Everyone needs at least one X chromosome to survive. Females normally have two X chromosomes whereas males typically have one X and one Y chromosome. In the absence of a Y chromosome, babies will develop as females. When the Y chromosome is present, they will develop as males.

The Y chromosome is different from all of the other chromosomes in a couple of different ways. First, it contains the fewest number of genes of any chromosome, far fewer than chromosome 21, the next smallest chromosome. Second, the vast majority of the Y chromosome is composed of heterochro-matin, a form of **DNA** that does not contain functional genes. Third, the genes that are present on the Y chromosome are critically important in sexual development.

As only males have a Y chromosome, and the presence of the Y chromosome determines male sexual development, the pattern of inheritance is that fathers uniformly transmit the Y chromosome to their sons at conception, and never to their daughters. This allows a tracing of inheritance patterns for genes and other markers on the Y chromosome from father to son down through many generations.

Because the Y chromosome has so much non-coding DNA, there are many different DNA sequence variants that may be identified on the Y chromosome. These non-coding DNA sequences have a very high rate of mutation, and many potentially informative short tandem repeat (STR) sequences that permit a detailed study of paternity and other forensic testing based on DNA sequences.

The Y chromosome has a distinctive pattern of **fluorescence** (light emission) naturally and also when using certain organic dyes. These properties can be exploited in various ways to identify the presence of **semen** based on natural fluorescence, or to identify Y-bearing **sperm** and separate them from X-bearing sperm. Furthermore, chromosomal analysis for the sex chromosomes can be used to predict the sex of a baby prenatally. As of 2005, it is not considered ethical to use chromosome analysis prenatally to facilitate sex selection for parents who desire either a boy or a girl unless there is a sex-linked genetic disease risk.

SEE ALSO Fluorescence; Sex determination; STR (short tandem repeat) analysis.

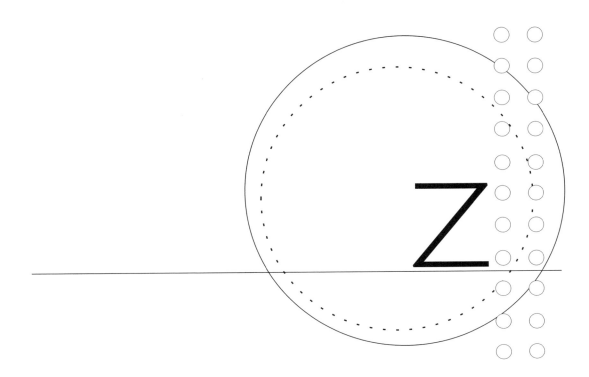

Frits Zernike

7/16/1888–3/10/1966
DUTCH
PHYSICIST

Frits Zernike was a pioneer in **forensic science**; his invention of the phase-contrast microscope enabled scientists to study living tissue samples under magnification for the first time. Zernike won the 1953 Nobel Prize in physics for his invention.

Zernike's background in statistical mathematics and thermodynamics was responsible for his groundbreaking discovery. A conventional microscope utilizes ordinary light, and under these instruments living tissues, particularly transparent ones, are not visible unless stained. Yet staining usually kills the specimen or produces artifacts that are impossible to differentiate from the specimen. The phase-contrast technique can reveal variations in opacity as well as variations in the thickness of transparent objects.

Born on July 16, 1888, in Amsterdam, Zernike was the son of two mathematicians, Carl Frederick August Zernike and Antje Dieperink Zernike. Early in life he was recognized for his mathematical abilities. He received both his B.S. and his Ph.D. in physics from the University of Amsterdam, and he worked at an astronomy laboratory while pursuing his graduate studies. His doctoral thesis, "Critical Opalescence, Theoretical and Experimental," quickly established him as a leader in his field.

In 1915 he was appointed lecturer in theoretical physics at the University of Groningen. In 1920, he was promoted to professor, where he remained for the rest of his career.

It was while working in the field of astronomy that Zernike first discovered the advantages of phase-contrast techniques. Irregularities on the surfaces of the curved mirrors of telescopes were a common problem at that time; these mirrors sometimes produced "ghost" images and Zernike hypothesized that they were caused by out-of-phase wavelengths. If he could somehow bring direct and diffracted images back into phase, perhaps these aberrations would disappear. He developed a glass plate with tiny grooves etched in it to be placed in the focal plane of the telescope; he called this a phase plate. His experiment worked: when looking through the phase plate, the out-of-phase areas became clearly visible. Zernike published these findings in 1934, and by 1935 he was applying these same principles to **microscopes**, which he knew had optical problems that were similar to telescopes.

Although the practical applications of Zernike's findings seem obvious now, it was some years before he could find a manufacturer for a phase-contrast microscope. He first approached the German company, Carl Zeiss, in 1932. Finally, in 1941, Carl Zeiss agreed to produce the instrument. But it was not until American troops arrived in Germany in 1945 and discovered photomicrographs taken by a phase-contrast microscope that

Zernike's instrument received worldwide attention. When he won the Nobel Prize in 1953, the phase-contrast microscope was cited as being a key to insights into cancer research.

Though the phase-contrast microscope is considered his crowning achievement, Zernike is also known for other work. Early in his career he invented the Zernike galvanometer, an instrument used to detect and measure small electrical currents. The Zernike polynomials are a method he developed regarding the wave theory of light, and are widely used by mathematicians. He also made many improvements in infrared and ultraviolet **spectroscopy**, as well as in the construction of the electromagnet.

Although Zernike stayed at his alma mater for his entire career, he was a visiting professor of physics at the Johns Hopkins University in Baltimore in 1948. In 1950 he was elected to the Royal Microscopical Society of London, and he was presented with the Rumford Medal of the British Royal Society in 1952.

Zernike married Dora van Bommel van Vloten in 1929. The couple had two children; his wife died in 1944. In 1954, Zernike married L. Koperberg-Baanders. He retired in 1958 and died in Groningen on March 10, 1966.

SEE ALSO Microscopes; Spectroscopy.

Zoonoses

Zoonoses are diseases of microbiological origin that can be transmitted from animals to people. The causes of the diseases can be bacteria, viruses, parasites, and fungi.

As of 2005, the best scientific evidence available suggested that the cornonavirus responsible for severe acute respiratory syndrome (SARS) was originally transmitted from animal hosts. Also, the avian flu, which until 2004 was resident in poultry, has caused a number of human deaths and now appears able to be transmitted both from poultry to felines and, ominously in terms of a global epidemic, from human to human.

Zoonoses are relevant for humans because of their species-jumping ability. Because many germs that can transfer from species to species are found in domestic animals and birds, agricultural workers and those in food processing plants are at risk. From a research standpoint, zoonotic diseases are interesting as they result from organisms that can live in a host innocuously while producing disease upon entry into a different host environment.

Humans can develop zoonotic diseases in different ways, depending upon the microorganism. Entry through a cut in the skin can occur with some bacteria. Inhalation of bacteria, viruses, and fungi is also a common method of transmission. As well, the ingestion of improperly cooked food or inadequately treated water that has been contaminated with the fecal material from animals or birds presents another route of disease transmission.

A classic historical example of a zoonotic disease is yellow fever. The construction of the Panama Canal took humans into the previously unexplored regions of the Central American jungle, where mosquitoes ferried the yellow fever virus from monkeys to man. When mosquitoes fed upon an infected monkey (the disease's natural host), the virus passed into the mosquito (the vector), which in turn, infected humans with their bite. Only after mosquito prevention measures were employed about 1910, with techniques such as the use of mosquito netting to cover tents and water supplies, were efforts successful in carving the canal through the jungle.

A number of bacterial zoonotic diseases are known. A few examples are **Tularemia**, which is caused by *Francisella tulerensis*, Leptospirosis (*Leptospiras spp.*), Lyme disease (*Borrelia burgdorferi*), Chlaydiosis (*Chlamydia psittaci*), Salmonellosis (*Salmonella spp.*), Brucellosis (*Brucella melitensis, suis*, and *abortus*, Q-fever (*Coxiella burnetti*), and Campylobacteriosis (*Campylobacter jejuni*).

Zoonoses produced by fungi include Aspergillosis (*Aspergillus fumigatus*). Well-known viral zoonoses include rabies and encephalitis. The microorganisms called Chlamydia cause a pneumonia-like disease called psittacosis.

Within the past two decades two protozoan zoonoses have emerged. These are Giardia (also commonly known as "beaver fever"), which is caused by *Giardia lamblia* and Cryptosporidium, which is caused by *Cryptosporidium parvum*. These protozoans reside in many vertebrates, particularly those associated with wilderness areas. The increasing encroachment of human habitations with wilderness is bringing the animals, and their resident microbial flora, into closer contact with people.

Cows at a farm in Washington state are quarantined after another cow at the farm is found infected with bovine spongiform encephalopathy (BSE), better known as "mad cow" disease. Authorities tracked the infected cow to a source in Canada.
© KEVIN P. CASEY/CORBIS

Similarly, human encroachment is thought to be the cause for the emergence of devastatingly fatal viral hemorrhagic fevers, such as Ebola, Marburg, and Rift Valley fever. While the origin of these agents is not definitively known, zoonotic transmission is virtually assumed.

Outbreaks of "mad cow" disease (bovine spongiform encephalopathy or BSE) among cattle in the United Kingdom in the 1990s (the latest being in 2001) has established a probable zoonotic link between these animals and humans, involving the disease causing entities known as **prions**. While the story is not fully resolved, the current evidence supports the transmission of the prion agent of mad cow disease to humans, where the similar brain degeneration disease is known as variant Creutzfeld-Jacob disease.

The increasing incidence of these and other zoonotic diseases has been linked to the increased ease of global travel. Microorganisms are more globally portable than ever before. This, combined with the innate ability of microbes to adapt to new environments, has created new combinations of microorganism and susceptible human populations.

SEE ALSO Centers for Disease Control and Prevention (CDC); Mad cow disease investigation; Pathogens.

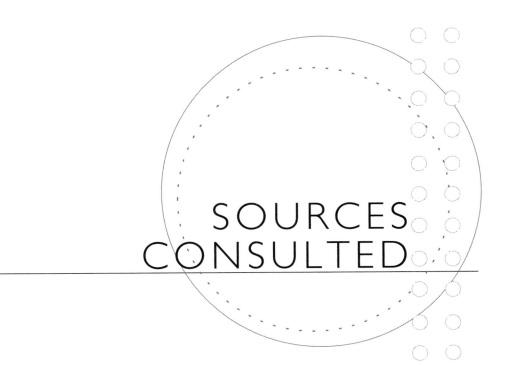

SOURCES CONSULTED

Books

Aitken, C.G.G., and D. A. Stoney, eds. *The Use of Statistics in Forensic Science*. New York: E. Horwood, 1991.

Aitken, C.G.G., and Franco Taroni. *Statistics and the Evaluation of Evidence for Forensic Scientists*. Chichester: Wiley, 2004.

Allan, Tony. *The Troubles in Northern Ireland*. Heinemann Library, 2004.

Amirall, Jose R., and Kenneth G. Furton. *Analysis and Interpretation of Fire Scene Evidence*. Boca Raton, FL: CRC Press, 2004.

Aretha, David. *Steroids and Other Performance-Enhancing Drugs*. Berkeley Heights: Enslow Publishers, 2005.

Ashbaugh, D. R. *Quantitative-Qualitative Friction Ridge Analysis: An Introduction to Basic and Advanced Ridgeology*. Boca Raton, FL: CRC Press, 2000.

Ausubel, Frederick M., et al. *Current Protocols in Molecular Biology*. New York: John Wiley & Sons, 2005.

Barberm, Jacqueline. *Fingerprinting (Great Explorations in Math and Science)*. Berkeley: University of California Press, 2000.

Barnett, Peter D. *Ethics in Forensic Science: Professional Standards for the Practice of Criminalistics*. Boca Raton, FL: CRC Press, 2001.

Bartlet, John G., et al. *2004 Pocket Book of Infectious Disease Therapy*. 12th ed. Philadelphia, PA: Lippincott Williams & Wilkins, 2004.

Bartlet, John G., et al. *A Guide to Primary Care of People with HIV/AIDS*. Rockville, MD: Department of Health and Human Services, Health Resources and Services Administration HIV/AIDS Bureau, 2004.

Bartlet, John G., et al. *Bioterrorism and Public Health: An Internet Resource Guide*. Princeton, NJ: eMedguides.com, Inc.; Montvale, NJ: Thomson/Physicians' Desk Reference, 2002.

————. *The Guide to Living with HIV Infection*. Baltimore, MD: Johns Hopkins University Press, 2001.

Bass, Bill, and Jon Jefferson. *Death's Acre: Inside the Legendary Body Farm*. London: Time Warner Books, 2004.

Beavin, Colin. *Fingerprints: The Origins of Crime Detection and the Murder Case that Launched Forensic Science*. New York: Hyperion, 2001.

Bevel, Tom, and Ross M. Gardner. *Bloodstain Pattern Analysis*. Boca Raton, FL: CRC Press, 2001.

Bhushan, Vikas *First Aid for the USMLE Step 1: 2005*. New York: McGraw-Hill, 2004.

Block, E. B. *Science vs. Crime: The Evolution of the Police Lab*. Cragmont Publications, San Francisco, 1979.

————. *The Wizard of Berkeley*. Coward-McCann, New York, 1958.

Bodziak, W. J. *Footwear Impression Evidence*. New York: Elsevier, 1999.

Brach, Raymond M., and Patrick F. Dunn *Uncertainty Analysis for Forensic Science*. Tucson, AR: Lawyers & Judges Publishing Company, 2004.

British Medical Association. *Drugs in Sport: The Pressure to Perform*. London: BMJ Press, 2002.

Brodie, Fawn. *Thomas Jefferson: An Intimate History*. New York: Norton, 1974.

Brown, Michael F. *Criminal Investigation: Law and Practice*, 2nd ed. Boston: Butterworth-Heinemann, 2001.

Byrd, Mike. *Crime Scene Evidence: A Guide to the Recovery and Collection of Physical Evidence*. Wildmar: Staggs Publishing, 2001.

Caddy, Brian, ed. *Forensic Examination of Glass and Paint: Analysis and Interpretation.* New York: Taylor & Francis, 2001.

Campbell, Andrea. *Forensic Science: Evidence, Clues, and Investigation.* Philadelphia: Chelsea House Publishers, 2000.

Cassidy, M. J. *Footwear Identification.* Ottawa: Public Relations Branch of the Royal Canadian Mounted Police, 1980.

Cole, Michael D. *The Analysis of Controlled Substances (Analytical Techniques in the Sciences).* New York: John Wiley & Sons, 2003.

Cole, Simon A. *Suspect Identities: A History of Fingerprinting and Criminal Investigation.* Boston: Harvard University Press, 2002.

Cooper, Cynthia L., and Sam Reese Sheppard. *Mockery of Justice: The True Story of the Sheppard Murder Case.* Boston: Northeastern University Press, 1995.

Cotchett, Joseph W., and Fulton Haight. *California Courtroom Evidence.* 4th ed. Carlsbad, CA: Parker Publications Division, 1995.

Culliford, Bryan J. *The Examination and Typing of Bloodstains in the Crime Laboratory.* Washington: National Institute of Law Enforcement and Criminal Justice, 1971.

Cuthbert, C. R. M. *Science and the Detection of Crime.* London: Hutchinson, 1958.

Dabney, Virginius. *The Jefferson Scandals: A Rebuttal.* New York: Dodd, Mead, 1981.

Daeid, Niamh Nic. *Fire Investigation.* Boca Raton, FL: CRC Press, 2004.

Davies, Geoffrey. *Forensic Science.* 2nd ed., rev. and expanded. Washington, DC: American Chemical Society, 1986.

DeForest, P. H. Lee, and R. Gaensslen. *Forensic Science: An Introduction to Criminalistics.* New York: McGraw Hill, 1983.

Department of Defense. *21st Century Complete Guide to U.S. Coast Guard Marine Accident Reports on Ships and Boats from 1947 to 1999.* Washington, DC: Progressive Management, 2002.

Di Maio, Vincent J. M., and Dominick J. Di Maio. *Forensic Pathology.* 2nd ed. Boca Raton, FL: CRC Press, 2001.

Eckert, W. G. *Introduction to Forensic Sciences.* Boca Raton, FL: CRC Press, 1997.

Eckert, W. G., and S. H. James. *Interpretation of Bloodstain Evidence at Crime Scenes.* Boca Raton, FL: CRC Press, 1989.

Evett, I. W., and B. S. Weir. *Interpreting DNA Evidence.* Sunderland, MA: Sinauer Associates, Inc., 1998.

Fairman, David L. *Legal Alchemy.* New York: W. H. Freeman, 1999.

Faith, Nicholas. *Blaze: The Forensics of Fire.* New York: St. Martin's Press, 2000.

Fenton, John. *Toxicology: A Case-Oriented Approach.* Boca Raton, FL: CRC Press, 2001.

Ferllini Timms, Roxana. *Silent Witness: How Forensic Anthropology Is Used to Solve the World's Toughest Crimes.* Willowdale, Ontario; Buffalo, NY: Firefly Books Ltd., 2002.

Finkelstein, Michael O. *Statistics for Lawyers.* 2nd ed. New York: Springer, 2001.

Fisher, Barry A. J. *Techniques of Crime Scene Investigation.* 7th ed. Boca Raton, FL: CRC Press, 2004.

Gaensslen, R. E. *Sourcebook in Forensic Serology.* Washington, DC: U.S. Government Printing Office, 1983.

———. *Sourcebook in Forensic Serology, Unit IX: Translations of Selected Contributions to the Original Literature of Medicolegal Examination of Blood and Body Fluids.* Washington, DC: U.S Dept. of Justice, National Institute of Justice, 1983.

Galton, F. *Finger Prints.* London: Macmillan, 1892.

Garrity, George, ed. *Bergey's Manual of Systematic Bacteriology: Volume 2: The Proteobacteria.* New York: Plenum Press, 2005.

Gastwirth, Joseph L., ed. *Statistical Science in the Courtroom.* New York: Springer, 2000.

Geberth, V. J. *Practical Homicide Investigation: Tactics, Procedures and Forensic Techniques.* Boca Raton, FL: CRC Press, 1996.

Genge, Ngaire. *The Forensic Casebook: The Science of Crime Scene Investigation.* New York: Ballantine Books, 2002.

Gerber, Samuel M., and R. Saferstein. *More Chemistry and Crime: From Marsh Arsenic Test to DNA Profile.* Washington, DC: American Chemical Society, 1997.

Goddard, K. W. *Crime Scene Investigation.* Reston, VA: Reston Publishing Company, 1977.

Goldstein, Dennis. *Polarized Light (Optical Engineering).* New York: Marcel Dekker, 2003.

Grant, J. *Science for the Prosecution.* London: Chapman & Hall, 1941.

Griffiths, Anthony J. F. *An Introduction to Genetic Analysis.* 5th ed. New York: W. H. Freeman and Company, 1993.

Gurstelle, William. *Backyard Ballistics.* Chicago: Chicago Review Press, 2001.

Hamilton, Charles. *The Hitler Diaries: Fakes That Fooled the World.* Lexington: University Press of Kentucky, 1991.

Harris, Robert. *Selling Hitler.* New York: Pantheon, 1986.

Hatcher, Julian Sommerville. *Firearms Investigation.* Harrisburg, PA: Stackpole Co., 1957.

Hazelwood, Loren F. *Can't Live Without It: The Story of Hemoglobin in Sickness and in Health.* Huntington: Nova Publishers, 2001.

Hibbs, Alan R. *Confocal Microscopy for Biologists.* New York: Plenum Press, 2005.

Hofstadter, D. R. *Gödel, Escher, Bach: An Eternal Golden Braid.* New York: Basic Books Inc., 1979.

Hollas, J. Michael. *Modern Spectroscopy*. New York: John Wiley & Sons, 2004.

Homewood, S. L., D. L. Oleksow, and W. L. Leaver. *Questioned Document Evidence in Forensic Evidence*. California District Attorneys Association, 1999.

Houlihan, Barry. *Dying to Win: Doping in Sport and the Development of Anti-Doping Policy*. Strasbourg: Council of Europe Publishing, 1999.

Inman, Keith, and Norah Rudin. *Principles and Practice of Criminalistics: The Profession of Forensic Science*. Boca Raton, FL: CRC Press, 2001.

Jackson, Andrew R. W., and Julie M. Jackson. *Forensic Science*. Harlow, England; New York: Pearson Prentice Hall, 2004.

James, Stuart H., and William G. Eckert. *Interpretation of Bloodstain Evidence at Crime Scenes*. CRC Press, 1999.

James, Stuart H., and Jon J. Nordby, eds. *Forensic Science: An Introduction to Scientific and Investigative Techniques*. Boca Raton, FL: CRC Press, 2003.

Jeffreys, Harold, Sir. *Theory of Probability*. 3rd ed. New York: Oxford University Press, 1983.

Jones, Leland V., and E. Caroline Gabard. *Scientific Investigation and Physical Evidence; Handbook for Investigators*. Springfield, IL: C. C. Thomas, 1959.

Kind, Stuart S., and Overman, Michael. *Science against Crime*. Garden City, NY: Doubleday, 1972.

Kirk, P. L. *Crime Investigation*. Malabar, FL: Krieger Publishing Co., 1974.

Kirsch, Andrea, and Rustin S. Levenson. *Seeing through Paintings: Physical Examination in Art Historical Studies*. New York: Yale University Press, 2000.

Komarinski, Peter. *Automated Fingerprint Identification Systems*. Amsterdam, The Netherlands; Boston, MA: Elsevier Academic, 2005.

Lee, Henry C. *Physical Evidence in Forensic Science*. Tucson, AZ: Lawyers & Judges Pub. Co., 2000.

Lee, Henry C., and Robert Gaensslen. *Advances in Fingerprint Technology*. 2nd ed. Boca Raton, FL: CRC, 2001.

Lee, Henry C., and Howard A. Harris. *Physical Evidence in Forensic Science*. Tucson, AZ: Lawyers & Judges Pub. Co., 2000.

Lee, Henry C., and Jerry Labriola. *Famous Crimes Revisited*. Southbury, CT: Publishing Directions, 2001.

Lee, Henry C., and Thomas W. O'Neil. *Cracking More Cases: The Forensic Science of Solving Crimes*. Amherst, NY: Prometheus Books, 2004.

Lee, Henry C., Timothy Palmach, and Marilyn T. Miller. *Henry Lee's Crime Scene Handbook*. San Diego, CA; London: Academic Press, 2001.

Lenehan, Pat. *Anabolic Steroids and Other Performance Enhancing Drugs*. Boca Raton, FL: CRC Press, 2003.

Levine, Barry, ed. *Principles of Forensic Toxicology*. Washington, DC: AACC press, 2003.

Lewin, Benjamin. *Genes VI*. Oxford; New York: Oxford University Press, 1997.

Locard, Edmond. *L'Enquete Criminelle et les Methodes Scientifique*. Paris: Ernest Flammarion, 1923.

———. *Manuel de Tachnique Policiere*. Paris: Payot, 1923.

———. *Traité de Criminalistique*. Lyon: J. Desvigne, 1931.

Lodish, Harvey, et al. *Molecular Cell Biology*. New York: W. H. Freeman & Co., 2000.

Loftus, Elizabeth F. *Eyewitness Testimony*. Cambridge, MA: Harvard University Press, 1996.

Lyle, D. P. *Forensics for Dummies*. Hoboken, NJ: Wiley, 2004.

Lyman, Michael D. *Criminal Investigation: The Art and the Science*. 4th ed. Upper Saddle River, NJ: Pearson/Prentice Hall, 2005.

Markov, Georgi. *The Truth That Killed*. London: Weidenfeld and Nicolson, 1983.

McKenzie, Shirlyn B. *Clinical Laboratory Hematology*. Upper Saddle River, New York: Pearson Education, 2003.

Mycek, Mary Julia, Richard A. Harvey, and Pamela C. Champe. *Pharmacology*. 2nd ed. New York: Lippincott Williams & Wilkins, 2000.

May, Luke S. *Crime's Nemesis*. New York: Macmillan, 1936.

Mays, Larry W. *Water Supply Systems Security*. New York: McGraw-Hill Professional, 2004.

Meyers, Charles. *Silent Evidence: Firearms Forensic Ballistics and Toolmarks: Cases from Forensic Science*. Boone, NC: Parkway Publishers, 2004.

Saks, Michael J., et al. *Admissibility of Scientific Evidence*. Westlaw, 2004.

Michel, Lou, and Dan Herbeck. *American Terrorist: Timothy McVeigh and the Oklahoma City Bombing*. New York: ReganBooks, 2001.

Morn, Frank. *Foundations of Criminal Investigation*. Durham, NC: Carolina Academic Press, 2000.

Murphy, Douglas B. *Fundamentals of Light Microscopy and Electronic Imaging*. New York: Wiley-Liss, 2001.

Nickell, Joe, and John Fischer. *Crime Science: Methods of Forensic Detection*. Lexington: University Press of Kentucky, 1999.

Nordby, Jon J. *Dead Reckoning: The Art of Forensic Detection*. Boca Raton, FL: CRC Press, 2000.

O'Brien, Joanne. *A Matter of Minutes: The Enduring Legacy of Bloody Sunday*. Dublin, Ireland: Wolfhound Press, 2002.

Olson, Kent R. *Poisoning & Drug Overdose*. New York: McGraw-Hill Professional, 2003.

Owen, David. *Hidden Evidence: Forty True Crimes and How Forensic Science Helped Solve Them*. Buffalo, NY: Firefly Books, 2000.

Parker, James N., and Philip M. Parker, eds. *Asphyxiation: A Medical Dictionary, Bibliography, and Annotated Research Guide*. San Diego: Icon Health Publications, 2004.

Parker, James N., and Philip M. Parker, eds. *Barbiturates: A Medical Dictionary, Bibliography, and Annotated Research Guide*. San Diego: Icon Health Publications, 2004.

Pringle, Peter. *Those Are Real Bullets: Bloody Sunday, Derry, 1972*. New York: Grove Press, 2001.

Ramsland, Katherine M. *The Science Of Cold Case Files*. New York: Berkley Boulevard Books, 2004.

Ramsland, Katherine M. *The Forensic Science of CSI*. New York: Berkley Boulevard Books, 2001.

Redmayne, Mike. *Expert Evidence and Criminal Justice*. Oxford, England; New York, NY: Oxford University Press, 2001.

Redsicker, David R. *The Practical Methodology of Forensic Photography*. 2nd ed. Boca Raton, FL: CRC Press, 2000.

Rendell, Kenneth W. *Forging History: The Detection of Fake Letters and Documents*. Norman: University of Oklahoma Press, 1994.

Robertson, Bernard, and G. A. Vignaux. *Interpreting Evidence*. Chichester; New York: John Wiley & Sons, 1995.

Rollins, Barbara B., and Michael Dahl. *Ballistics (Forensic Crime Solvers)*. Mankato, MN: Capstone Press, 2004.

Rouessac, Francis, and Annick Rouessac. *Chemical Analysis: Modern Instrumentation Methods and Techniques*. New York: Wiley, 2000.

Saferstein, Richard. *Criminalistics: An Introduction to Forensic Science*. 7th ed. Upper Saddle River, NJ: Prentice-Hall, 2001.

Saks, Michael J., et al. *Admissibility of Scientific Evidence*. Westlaw, 2004.

Schwoeble, A. J., and David E. Exline. *Current Methods in Forensic Gunshot Residue Analysis*. Boca Raton, FL: CRC Press, 2000.

Shepherd, Richard. *Simpson's Forensic Medicine*. New York: Arnold, 2003.

Smith, Brian C. *Quantitative Spectroscopy: Theory and Practice*. Burlington: Academic Press, 2002.

Smith, Frederick P. *Handbook of Forensic Drug Analysis*. Amsterdam; Boston: Elsevier Academic Press, 2004.

Society of Automotive Engineers. *Airbag Technology 2002*. Warrendale, PA: Society of Automotive Engineers, 2002.

Steinberg, Martin H. *Disorders of Hemoglobin: Genetics, Pathophysiology and Clinical Management*. Cambridge: Cambridge University Press, 2001.

Struthers, J. Keith, and Roger P. Westran. *Clinical Bacteriology*. Washington, DC: ASM Press, 2003.

Sunshine, Irving. *Was It a Poisoning?: Forensic Toxicologists Searching for Answers*. Washington, DC: AACC Press, 2001.

Taft, Stanley W., and James W. Mayer. *The Science of Paintings*. New York: Springer, 2000.

Thygerson, Alton L. *CPR: Cardiopulmonary Resuscitation and First Aid for Choking*. Sudbury: Jones & Bartlett Publishers, 2001.

Tobin, William A. *Comparative Bullet Lead Analysis: A Case Study in Flawed Forensics*. Westlaw, 2004.

Trestrail, John H. *Criminal Poisoning: Investigational Guide for Law Enforcement, Toxicology, Forensic Scientists, and Attorneys*. Totowa, NJ: Humana Press, 2000.

Walsh, Dermot P. J. *Bloody Sunday and the Rule of Law in Northern Ireland*. Macmillan Press, 2000.

Warlow, Tom. *Firearms, the Law and Forensic Ballistics*, . 2nd ed. Boca Raton, FL: CRC Press, 2004.

Wecht, Cyril H. *Forensic Science and the Law: Investigative Evidence in Criminal and Civil Cases*. Boca Raton, FL: CRC Press, 2005.

White, P. C. *Crime Scene to Court: The Essentials of Forensic Science*. Cambridge: Royal Society of Chemistry, 2004.

Wonder, Anita Y. *Blood Dynamics*. Burlington: Academic Press, 2001.

Woodward, John D., Jr., Nicholas M. Orlans, and Peter T. Higgins. *Biometrics*. New York: McGraw-Hill/Osborne, 2003.

Yeatts, Tabatha. *Forensics: Solving the Crime*. Minneapolis, MN: Oliver Press, 2001.

Periodicals

Allard, J. E., and Kenneth G. Wiggins. "The evidential value of fabric car seats and car seat covers." *Journal of the Forensic Science Society*. 27(2), 93-101, 1987.

Almirall, Jose. "The Importance of Standards in Forensic Science." *Standardization News*. April 1, 1995.

Apuzzo, Matt. "Connecticut to Simulate Chemical Attack." *Government CustomWire*. July 23, 2004.

Arrillaga, Pauline. "New Evidence Points to Man's Suicide." *Rocky Mountain News*. February 1, 1998.

Banta, Bob. "Artists Shining Light on Crimes." *Austin American-Statesman*. September 22, 1997.

Biasotti, A. "A statistical study of the individual characteristics of fired bullets." *Journal of the Forensic Science Society*. 4(1), 133-40, 1959.

Bryant, Vaughn. "Book Review—Flora of the Shroud of Turin." *Palynos*. June, 2000.

Budowle, B., et al. "Forensics and mitochondrial DNA: applications, debates, and foundations." *Annual Review of Genomics and Human Genetics*. no. 4 (2003): 119-41.

Cain, Steve. "Examining Questionable Documents." *South Florida Investigators Association Journal*. May, 2000.

Ceccaldi, P. F. "From crime to evidence." *International Police Journal* 1974.

Chivers, C. J. "Beslan militants were drug-dependent, forensic study shows." *The New York Times*. October 18, 2004.

Cole, S. "What counts for identity? The historical origins of the methodology of latent fingerprint identification." *Science in Context*. 12(1), 139, 1999.

———. "Witnessing identification: latent fingerprinting evidence and expert knowledge." *Social Studies of Science*. 28(5-6), 687, 1998.

Committee on Child Abuse and Neglect. "Shaken baby syndrome: Rotational Cranial Injuries-Technical Report." *American Academy of Pediatrics.* 2001;108:206-10.

Cook, R., et al. "A hierarchy of propositions: deciding which level to address in casework." *Science & Justice.* 38(4), 231-239. 1998b.

———. "A model for case assessment and interpretation." *Science & Justice.* 38(3), 151-156. 1998a.

Cordiner, S. J., P. Stringer, and P. D. Wilson, "Fiber diameter and the transfer of wool fiber." *Journal of the Forensic Science Society.* 25(6), 425-426, 1985.

Coxon, A., Grieve, M., and Dunlop, J. "A method of assessing the fibre shedding potential of fabrics." *Journal of the Forensic Science Society.* 32(2), 151-158, 1992.

Critchlow, Donald T. "Book review of Coping with Sickness: Medicine, Law, and Human Rights—Historical Perspectives." *Isis.* June, 2002.

Curran, J. M., C. M. Triggs, and J. S. Buckleton. "Sampling in forensic comparison problems." *Science & Justice.* 38(2), 101-107, 1998.

Dalrymple, Brian. "Serendipitous Sleuthing." *Canadian Chemical News.* October, 2001.

Dubowski, Kurt. "Sidney Kaye: Internationally Renowned Forensic Toxicologist." *American Journal of Forensic Medicine and Pathology.* June, 1985.

Evett, I. "Expert evidence and forensic misconceptions of the nature of exact science." *Journal of the Forensic Science Society.* 23, 35, 1983.

Evett, I. "What is the probability that this blood came from that person? A meaningful question?" *Nature.* 22, 605, 1880.

Fish, Raymond. "Effects of Stun Guns and Tazers." *The Lancet.* September 1, 2001.

Fletcher, Martin." Dead Men Do Tell Tales." *The Times (London).* January 27, 1992.

Fregeau C. J., K. L. Bowen, and R. M. Fourney. "Validation of Highly Polymorphic Fluorescent Multiplex Short Tandem Repeat Systems Using Two Generations of DNA Sequencers." *Journal of Forensic Science.* 44(1), 133, 1999.

Fregeau, C. J., and R. M. Fourney. "DNA typing with fluorescently tagged short tandem repeats: a sensitive and accurate approach to human identification." *Biotechniques.* 15 (1) 1993.

Furton, K. G., Y. L. Hsu, and M. D. Cole. "What educational background do crime laboratory directors require from applicants?" *Journal of Forensic Science.* 44(1): 128-132, 1999.

Galton, F. "Personal Identification and Description II." *Nature.* 38, 201-202, 1888.

Gaudette, B. D. "A supplementary discussion of probabilities and human hair comparisons." *Journal of Forensic Science.* 27 (2) 279-289, 1982.

———. "Some further thoughts on probabilities and human hair comparisons." *Journal of Forensic Science.* 23, 758, 1978.

Gerchman, Liddy. "Shrouded in Mystery: The Turin Debate." *Odyssey.* December, 2000.

Green, Sara Jean. "Mason's Blood Was in Car, DNA Expert Testifies in Kirkland." *Seattle Times.* May 21, 2003.

Grice, Gordon. "Crime Seen." *Popular Science.* 2004.

Grieve, M. C., T. W. Biermann. "The population of coloured textile fibres on outdoor surfaces." *Science & Justice.* 37(4), 231-239, 1997.

Gross, A. M., K. A. Harris, and G. L. Kaldun. "The effect of luminol on presumptive tests and DNA analysis using the polymerase chain reaction." *Journal of Forensic Science.* 44(4), 837, 1999.

Hanlon, Michael. "The Finger of Fate." *Daily Mail (London).* January 14, 2002.

Hesman, Tina. "Forensic Sleuths Swap Tips and Tales of Crime Solving." *St. Louis Post-Dispatch.* August 26, 2004.

Hoang, Son. "Forensic Scientist Uses Blood to Solve Crime." *America's Intelligence Wire.* February 1, 2005.

Hollon, T. "Reforming Criminal Law, Exposing Junk Forensic Science." *The Scientist.* no.15 (2001).

Holohan, Meghan. "For the People: Bruce Dixon." *University of Pittsburgh Alumni Magazine.* February, 2004.

Home, J. M., and R. J. Dudley. "A summary of data obtained from a collection of fibres from casework materials." *Journal of the Forensic Science Society.* 20, 253-261, 1980.

Horrocks, M., S. A. Coulson, and K. A. J. Walsh. "Forensic Palynology: Variation in the Pollen Content of Soil On Shoes and in Shoeprints in Soil." *Journal of Forensic Science.* 44 (1) 119-122, 1999.

Huffine, E., B. Crews, K. Bomberger, A. D. Sinbo. "Mass identification of persons missing from the break-up of the former Yugoslavia: Structure, Function, and Role of the International commission on missing persons." *Croatian Medical Journal.* 42(3):271-275, 2001.

Inbau, Fred E. "Firearms Identification—Ballistics." *Journal of Criminal Law and Criminology.* Summer, 1999.

Israel National Police. "International Symposium on Fingerprint Detection and Identification." *Journal of Forensic Identification.* 45, 578-84, 1995.

Jeffreys, A. J., V. Wilson, and S. L. Thein. "Individual-specific 'fingerprints' of human DNA." *Nature.* 316(4), 76, 1985.

Judis, John B. "Loathing in Las Vegas." *The New Republic.* July 15, 1996.

Kahler, K., J. Haber, H. P. Seidel. "Reanimating the dead: Reconstruction of expressive faces from skull data." *ACM TOG (SIGGRAPH conference proceedings).* no. 3: 554-561, 2003.

Kalia, R. K., et al. "Role of ultrafine microstructures in dynamic fracture in nanophase silicon nitride." *Physical Review Letters.* 78, 2144-2147, 1997.

Kaplan, Allison. "His Old-Fashioned Microscope Helps Him See Who's Guilty." *Daily Herald.* June 25, 1998.

Kaye, Sidney. "The Rebirth and Blooming of Forensic Medicine." *American Journal of Forensic Medicine and Pathology.* December, 1992.

Kidd, C. B. M., and J. Robertson. "The transfer of textile fibers during simulated contacts." *Journal of the Forensic Science Society*. 22(3), 301-308, 1982.

————. "The persistence of textile fibers transferred during simulated contacts." *Journal of the Forensic Science Society* 22(4), 353-360, 1982.

Kingston, C. R., and P. L. Kirk. "Historical development and evaluation of the 12 point rule." *International Criminal Police Review*. 186, 62-69, 1965.

Kirk, P. L. "The ontogeny of criminalistics." *Journal of Criminal Law, Criminology, and Police Science*. 54, 235-238, 1963.

Koehler, A. "Techniques used in tracing of the Lindbergh kidnapping ladder." *Police Science*. 27(5), 1937.

Lewis, Mark. "Author Undertakes Cold Case Sleuthing." *Tampa Tribune*. February 27, 2005.

Lewis, Paul. "Walter McCrone, Debunker of Legends, Is Dead at 86." *New York Times*. July 26, 2002.

Locard, E. "Dust and its analysis." *Police*. J. 1, 177, 1928.

Locard, E. "The analysis of dust traces, Part I-III." *The American Journal of Police Science*. 1, 276, 401, 496, 1930.

May, L. S. "The identification of knives, tools and instruments, a positive science." *American Police Journal*. 1, 246, 1930.

Metinko, Chris. "Richmond, Va., Lab's DNA Work Vital." *Contra Costa Times*. August 13, 2000.

Mladek, Klaus. "Radical Play." *Germanic Review*. Summer 2003.

Moore, Evan. "How Do You Determine Identity When a Victim's Body Is Decomposed or Damaged Beyond Recognition?" *Houston Chronicle*. May 2, 2004.

Mullis, K. B., et al. "Specific enzymatic amplification of DNA in vitro: The polymerase chain reaction." *Cold Spring Harbor Symposium on Quantitative Biology*. 51, 263-273, 1986.

Naess, A. "Book review." *New Scientist*. August, 1998.

Neyman, J., and E. S. Pearson. "On the use and interpretation of certain test criteria for purposes of statistical inference." *Biometrika*. 20, 174-240, 263-294, 1928.

R .G. Nichols. "Firearm and toolmark identification criteria: a review of the literature." *Journal of Forensic Science*. 42(3), 466-474, 1997.

Nickell, Joe. "Pollens on the 'Shroud'." *Skeptical Inquirer*. Summer, 1994.

Nickell, Joe. "Scandals and Follies of the 'Holy Shroud'." *Skeptical Inquirer*. September, 2001.

Nordby, J. J. "Can we believe what we see, if we see what we believe?—Expert disagreement." *Journal of Forensic Science*. 37(4) 1115-1124, 1992.

O'Brien, Sue. "Speculation not a Journalistic Tool." *Denver Post*. January 12, 1997.

Palmer, R., and V. Chinherende. "A target fiber study using cinema and car seats as recipient items." *Journal of Forensic Science*. 41, 802-803, 1996.

Parybyk, A. E., and R. J. Lokan. "A study of the numerical distribution of fibers transferred from blended fabrics." *Journal of the Forensic Science Society*. 26(1), 61-68, 1986.

Porter, Dorothy. "Book review of The Trials of Masculinity: Policing Sexual Boundaries 1870-1930." *Canadian Journal of History*. December, 1999.

Primorac, D., et al. "Identification of war victims from mass graves in Croatia, Bosnia, and Herzegovina by use of standard forensic methods and DNA testing." *Journal of Forensic Science*. (41) 1996.

Riley, Michael. "Tales from the Crypt." *Time*. September 14, 1992.

Robertson, J., and A. K. Lloyd. "Observations on redistribution of textile fibers." *Journal of the Forensic Science Society*. 24(1), 3-7, 1984.

Roux, C., and P. Margot. "An attempt to assess the relevance of textile fibres recovered from car seats." *Science & Justice*. 37(4), 225-230, 1997.

Saiki, R. K., et al. "Enzymatic amplification of beta-globin genomic sequences and restriction site analysis for diagnosis of sickle cell anemia." *Science*. 230, 1350, 1985.

Sampson, William. "How to Get Latent Prints from Human Skin." *Evidence Technology*. May/June 2004.

Scanlon, Lisa. "Fingerprinting's Finger-Pointing Past." *Technology Review*. June, 2003.

Schlatter, Katherine. "Identifying Tsunami Vicitms." *The Scientist Daily News*. January 7, 2005.

Shannon, C. E. "A mathematical theory of communication." *Bell System Technical Journal*. 27, 379-423, 623-656, 1948.

Siegel, J. A. "The appropriate educational background for entry level forensic scientists: a survey of practitioners." *Journal of Forensic Science*. 33:1065-8, 1988.

Smith, W. C., R. Kinney, and D. Departee. "Latent Fingerprints—A Forensic Approach." *Journal of Forensic Identification*. 43(6) 563-570, 1993.

Specter, Michael. "Do Fingerpints Lie?" *New Yorker*. May 27, 2002.

Stoney, D. A. "A medical model for criminalistics education." *Journal of Forensic Science*. 33 (4), 1086-94, 1988.

————. "Criminalistics in the new millennium." *The CACNews*. 1st Quarter, 2000.

————. "Evaluation of associative evidence: choosing the relevant question." *Journal of the Forensic Science Society*. 24, 472-482, 1984.

————. "What made us ever think we could individualize using statistics?" *Journal of the Forensic Science Society* 3(2), 197-199, 1991.

Stoney, D. A., and J. I. Thornton. "A Critical analysis of quantitative fingerprint individuality models."*Journal of Forensic Science*. 31(4), 1187-1216, 1986a.

————. "A method for the description of minutia pairs in epidermal ridge patterns." *Journal of Forensic Science*. 31(4), 1217-1234, 1986b.

————. "A systematic study of epidermal ridge minutiae." *Journal of Forensic Science*. 32(5), 1182-1203, 1987.

Takatori, T. "Investigations on the mechanism of adipocere formation and its relation to other biochemical reactions." *Journal of Forensic Sciences.* 2001.

Taroni, F. "Probalistic reasoning in the law. Part 2: assessment of probabilities and explanation of the value of trace evidence other than DNA." *Science & Justice.* 38, 179-188.

Taroni, F., C. Champod, and P. Margot. "Forerunners of Bayesianism in early forensic science." *Jurimetrics.* 38; 183-200.

Technical Working Group on DNA Analysis Methods. "Guidelines for a Quality Assurance Program for DNA Analysis." *Crime Laboratory Digest* 22 (2), 21-43.

Thompson, W. C., and E. L. Schumann. "Interpretation of statistical evidence in criminal trials: The prosecutor's fallacy and the defense attorney's fallacy." *Law and Human Behavior.* 11, 167-187, 1987.

Thornton, J. I. "The DNA statistical paradigm vs. everything else." *Journal of Forensic Science.* 42(4) 758, 1997.

———. "Ensembles of class characteristics in physical evidence examination." *Journal of Forensic Science.* 31 (2) 501-503, 1986.

———. "The snowflake paradigm." *Journal of Forensic Science.* 31 (2) 399-406, 1986.

Toupin, Laurie. "It's Elementary, My Dear Watson…If You Have a Microscope." *Odyssey.* January, 2004.

Watling, R. J. "Laser ablation ICP-MS as an investigational tool for insurance fraud, forensic science and forensic archaeology." *Winter Conference on Plasma Spectrochemistry.* Pau, France, 49-50 (1999).

———. "Novel applications of Laser Ablation Inductively Coupled Plasma Mass Spectrometry (LA-ICP-MS) in the field of Forensic Science and Forensic Archaeology." *Spectroscopy.* (1999) 14(6), 16-34.

Watling, R. J., B. F. Lynch, and D. Herring. "Use of Laser Ablation Inductively Coupled Plasma Mass Spectrometry for Fingerprinting Scene of Crime Evidence." *Journal of Analytical Atomic Spectrometry.* February 1997, Vol. 12 (195-203).

Other

A&E Interactive Television Networks. "Cold Case Files." http://www.aetv.com/tv/shows/coldcasefiles/ (accessed February 18, 2005.)

Abramowitz, Mortimer, et al. "Polarized Light Microscopy." http://www.olympusmicro.com/primer/lightand color/polarization.html (accessed March 3, 2005.)

American Academy of Family Physicians. "Injuries Can Offer Clues." April 1998. http://www.aafp.org/fpr/980400fr/2.html (accessed March 31, 2005.)

American Board of Criminalistics (ABC). "GKE Examination Philosophy." http://www.criminalistics.com/ABC/abc002.htm (accessed April 1, 2005.)

American Board of Medicolegal Death Investigators, Inc. "American Board of Medicolegal Death Investigators, Inc." GKE Examination Philosophy. (accessed March 24, 2005.)

Associated Press. "The Unabomber Case." January 22, 1998. http://www.unabombertrial.com/archive/1998/012298.07.html (accessed March 13, 2005.)

Australian Broadcasting Corporation. " Bali bombing website." http://abc.net.au/news/indepth/default.htm (accessed March 11, 2005.)

Australian Museum Online. "Decomposition—Body Changes." 2003. http://www.deathonline.net/decomposition/body_changes/grave_wax.htm (accessed January 18, 2005.)

Australian Museum Online. "When the heart stops beating." 2003. http://www.deathonline.net/decomposition/decomposition/index.htm (accessed January 18, 2005.)

Bahrke, Michael S., and Charles E. Yesalis. "The Future of Performance-Enhancing Substances in Sport." http://www.physsportsmed.com/issues/2002/11_02/guested.htm (accessed March 5, 2005.)

Bartel, Nick. "Medieval Medicine, Health and Hygiene." November 2003. http://www.sfusd.k12.ca.us/schwww/sch618/Medicine/Medicine_and_Health.html (accessed March 13, 2005.)

BBCNews. "Agony goes on for Beslan relatives." http://bbcnews.co.uk/1/hi/world/europe/3636304.stm.htm (accessed March 13, 2005.)

———. "Beslan searches for its missing." http://newswww.bbc.net.uk/1/hi/world/europe/3635520.stm.htm (accessed March 03, 2005.)

———. "The forensics of investigating war crimes." http://news.bbc.co.uk/1/hi/world/europe/259995.stm.htm (accessed March 03, 2005.)

Bieber, Frederick R. "Science and Technology of Forensic DNA Profiling: Current Use and Future Directions." http://www.ksg.harvard.edu/dnabook/bieber.doc (accessed February 10, 2005.)

Biohazard News. "John G. Bartlett: Infectious Disease Expert on U.S. Bioterrorism Preparedness." April 30, 2001. http://www.biohazardnews.net/int_bartlett.shtml (accessed February 13, 2005.)

Bonsor, Kevin. "How Facial Recognition Systems Work." 1998-2005. http://people.howstuffworks.com/facial-recognition.htm/printable (accessed March 13, 2005.)

Bowen, Richard. "Salivary Glands and Saliva." http://arbl.cvmbs.colostate.edu/hbooks/pathphys/digestion/pregastric/salivary.html (accessed March 6, 2005.)

Bureau of Alcohol, Tobacco, Firearms and Explosives, U.S. Department of the Treasury. "National Integrated Ballistics Information Network." http://www.atf.gov/nibin/ (accessed February 23, 2005.)

———. "The Missing Link: Ballistics Technology That Helps Solve Crimes." http://www.atf.gov/nibin/missing/index.htm (accessed February 23, 2005.)

Capital Defense Network. "Successful Cases: Supreme Court (Incompetency to Stand Trial)." http://www.capdefnet.org/hat/contents/constitutional_issues/incompetencys_to_stand_trial/incompetency_to_stand_trial_rightframe.htm (accessed March 23, 2005.)

CBSNews. "Investigators: Forensic Animation." http://cbsnews.com/stories/2002/10/25/48hours/main526999.shtml (accessed January 28, 2005.)

Center for Forensic Studies. "Fluorescence in Criminalistics: Fingerprints and Other Trace Evidence." http://www.phys.ttu.edu/~menzel/workshop_info.html (accessed March 12, 2005.)

CNN trial transcripts. "United States of America v. Terry Nichols." 1997. http://europe.cnn.com/US/9703/okc.trial/transcripts/ (accessed March 23, 2005.)

———. "People v. Simpson." http://www.cnn.com/US/OJ/trial/ (accessed March 1, 2005.)

CNN.com. "DNA bid to solve Columbus riddle." http://archives.cnn.com/2002/WORLD/europe/06/11/columbus (accessed March 12 2005.)

CODIS. "Standards for Forensic DNA Testing Laboratories." http://fbi.gov/hq/lab/codis/forensic.htm (accessed March 12, 2005.)

Columbia University. "Henry Pelouze DeForest." http://library.cpmc.columbia.edu/hsl/arch/psdbrecord.cfm?RecordNum=3547 (accessed March 30, 2005.)

Computer Crime Research Center. ""Combating Computer Crime." January 10, 2005. http://www.crimeresearch.org/articles/trenton1 (accessed February 28 2005.)

Council of Europe. "The European Convention on Human Rights." http://www.hri.org/docs/ECHR50.html (accessed February 23, 2005.)

Court TV. The Crime Library. "DNA in Court." http://www.crimelibrary.com/criminal_mind/forensics/dna/6.html?sect=21 (accessed February 28, 2005.)

———. "Forensic Voiceprints." http://www.crimelibrary.com/criminal_mind/forensics/voiceprints/1.html?sect=21 (accessed March 20, 2005.)

———. "The Horror Ends." http://www.crimelibrary.com/ (accessed March 7, 2005.)

———. "The Pressure is On." http://www.crimelibrary.com/ (accessed April 7, 2005.)

———. "The Professor-Explorer." http://www.crimelibrary.com/ (accessed April 4, 2005.)

———. "The Science of Lies: From the Polygraph to Brain Fingerprinting and Beyond." http://www.courttv.com/ (accessed March 7, 2005.)

Crime Library. "Age Progression." http://www.crimelibrary.com/criminal_mind/fornensics/art/6.html?sect=21 (accessed April 2, 2005.)

———. "Professional Opinions." http://www.crimelibrary.com/notorius_murders/famous/bimion/opinion (accessed February 20, 2005.)

———. "Serology." http://www.crimelibrary.com/criminal_mind/forensics/serology/3.html?sect=21 (accessed May 5, 2005.)

———. "The Reconstruction of a Face." http://www.crimelibrary.com?criminal_mind/forensics/art/5.html?sect=21 (accessed April 1, 2005.)

Dartmouth College Chance Team, J. Laurie Snell, Peter Doyle, Joan Garfield, Tom Moore, Bill Peterson, and Ngambal Shah. Chance News. "Toward a Firm Foundation for Statistical Interpretation." http://www.dartmouth.edu/~chance/teaching_aids/books_articles/DNAtyping/node6.html (accessed March 7, 2005.)

Deedrick, Douglas W. "Hairs, Fibers, Crime and Evidence." http://www.fbi.gov/hq/lab/fsc/backissu/july2000/deedric3.htm (accessed March 28, 2005.)

Doyle, Jeffrey Scott. "Gunshot Residue." http://www.firearmsid.com/A_distanceGSR.htm (accessed March 29, 2005.)

Duquesne University School of Law. "Solving the Great American Murder Mystery." http://www.jfk.duq.edu/biostarrs.html (accessed April 4, 2005.)

The Family Violence and Sexual Assault Institute "Family Violence and Sexual Assault." http://www.fvsai.org/ (accessed March 24, 2005.)

Federal Bureau of Investigation, U.S. Department of Justice. "Integrated Automated Fingerprint Identification System of IAFIS: What is it?" http://www.fbi.gov/hq/cjisd/iafis.htm (accessed February 19, 2005.)

———. "Biography of J. Edgar Hoover." http://www.fbi.gov/ (accessed March 29, 2005.)

———. "CODIS: Combined DNA Index System." http://www.fbi.gov/hq/lab/codis/index1.htm (accessed February 18, 2005.)

———. "FBI Laboratory: Latent Print Unit." October 2000. http://www.fbi.gov/hq/lab/org/lpu.htm (accessed February 24, 2005.)

———. "Integrated Automated Fingerprint Identification System." August 20, 2004. http://www.fbi.gov/hq/cjisd/iafis.htm (accessed January 16, 2005.)

———. "National DNA Index System." http://www.fbi.gov/hq/lab/codis/national.htm (accessed February 18, 2005.)

———. "Violent Crimes and Major Offenders Section." http://www.iir.com/nygc/youthGangDoc/7_justice3.htm (accessed March 30, 2005.)

Federal Bureau of Investigation, Forensic Science Research Unit. "Firearms and Toolmarks in the FBI Laboratory." Forensic Science Communications. http://www.fbi.gov/hq/lab/fsc/backissu/april2000/schehl2.htm (accessed February 23, 2005.)

Federal Bureau of Investigation's Criminal Justice Information Section. "NCIC: National Crime Information Center." http://www.fbi.gov/hq/cjisd/ncic.htm (accessed March 21, 2005.)

Fiatal, Robert A. "DNA Testing and the Frye Standard." http://www.totse.com/en/law/justice_for_all/dnatest.html (accessed March 30, 2005.)

The Fingerprint Society. http://www.fpsociety.org.uk/ (accessed February 24, 2005.)

Firearms Tactical Institute. "Wound Ballistics." http://www.firearmstactical.com/wound.htm (accessed January 28, 2005.)

Fong, Jason. "Erythropoietin Abuse and Detection in Athletes." http//www.sportsmed.info/articles/epo.html (accessed March 5, 2005.)

Forensic Art Service. "Composite Drawing." http://www.forensicartist.com/composite.html (accessed February 27 2005.)

Forensic Artist. "Composite Art and Police Drawing." http://www.forartist.com/forensic/composite (accessed February 27 2005.)

Forensic Geology. "Overview of Services; Raymond C. Murray resume." http://www.forensicgeology.net/ (accessed March 29, 2005.)

Forensic Handbooks Online. "Biography of David Ashbaugh, Overview of Quantitative-Qualitative Friction Ridge Analysis." http://www.forensicnetbase.com/ (accessed April 8, 2005.)

Forensic Science. "What is a Forensic Scientist?" http://www.forensic-science.com (accessed February 28, 2005.)

Forensic Science Associates. "Edward Blake Curriculum Vitae." http://www.fsalab.com (accessed February 7, 2005.)

Forensic Science Service. "Welcome to the Forensic Science Service." http://www.forensic.gov.uk/forensic_t/index.htm (accessed March 21, 2005.)

Forensic Technology, Inc. "Home Webpage of Forensic Technology, Inc." http://www.fti-ibis.com/en/index.asp (accessed February 23, 2005.)

The Franklin Institute. "Lifeblood." http://sln.fi.edu/biosci/blood/blood.html (accessed January 26, 2005.)

Freudenrich, Craig. "How Performance-Enhancing Drugs Work." http://health.howstuffworks.com/athletic-drug-test.htm (accessed March 4, 2005.)

Frey, Regina. "Gas Laws Save Lives: The Chemistry Behind Airbags." http://www.chemistry.wustl.edu/~edudev/LabTutorials/Airbags/airbags.html (accessed January 28, 2005.)

George Washington University. "A Short History of Forensic Sciences."http://www.gwu.edu/~forensic/ (accessed March 29, 2005.)

———. "GW Law Profiles: James E. Starrs." http://www.law.gwu/edu/ (accessed April 4, 2005.)

German, Ed. "The History of Fingerprints." http://www.onin.com/fp/fphistory.html (accessed April 4, 2005.)

———. "Automated Fingerprint Identification Systems (AFIS)." December 12, 2004. http://onin.com/fp/afis/afis.html (accessed January 16, 2005.)

Goll-McGee, Barbara, et al. "Forensic Nursing Process: An Evaluation of Forensic Patients in the Clinical Environment." *Forensic Nursing.* http://www.forensicnursemag.com/articles/371lifedeath.html (accessed March 31, 2005.)

Government of Canada. "Computer Age Progression." http://www.ourmissingchlidren.ca/en/about/age.html (accessed April 2, 2005.)

Guillong, Marcel. "Laser Ablation Inductively Coupled Plasma Mass Spectrometry: Laser ablation system developments and investigations on elemental fractionation." March 3, 2004. http://e-collection.ethbib.ethz.ch/ecol-pool/diss/abstracts/p15437.pdf (accessed February 24, 2005.)

Harvard University. "An Overview of Hemoglobin." http://sickle.bwh.harvard.edu/hemoglobin.html (accessed Febraury 20, 2005.)

Houck, Max M. "Statistics and Trace Evidence: The Tyranny of Numbers." *Forensic Science Communications.* October 1999. http://www.au.af.mil/au/awc/awcgate/fbi/houck.htm (accessed March 7, 2005.)

How Stuff Works. "How Airbags Work." http://auto.howstuffworks.com/airbag.htm (accessed January 28, 2005.)

———. "How Breathalyzers Work." http://science.howstuffworks.com/breathlayzer.htm (accessed Febraury 22, 2005.)

Human Rights Watch. "Iraq. The Forensic Evidence." http://www.hrw.org/reports/2004/iraq1104/4.htm (accessed March 20, 2005.)

Indiana University. "Indiana University Center for Studies of Law in Action: The Borkenstein Course." http://www.indiana.edu/~lawactn/ (accessed February 18, 2005.)

Institute for the Research into Organized and Ritual Violence. "The Forensics of Sacrifice." *Anthropoetics.* Fall 2003/Winter 2004. http://www.anthropoetics.ucla.edu/ap0902/sacrifice.htm (accessed April 3, 2005.)

Institute of Mineralogy, University of Wrzburg. "Laser Ablation (LA-ICPMS) at the Institute of Mineralogy, University of Wrzburg." http://www.uni-wuerzburg.de/mineralogie/icpms/icpms.html#ablation (accessed February 24, 2005.)

International Association for Identification. "Home Web Page of International Association for Identification." February 1, 2005. http://www.theiai.org/ (accessed February 8, 2005.)

International Association for Property and Evidence. "Biography of Nancy E. Masters." http://www.iape.org/bios/masters/ (accessed February 7, 2005.)

The International Council on Alcohol, Drugs & Traffic Safety. "ICADTS Home Page." http://www.icadts.org/ (accessed February 18, 2005.)

Interpol. "Genocide, War Crimes, and Crimes Against Humanity." http://www.interpol.int/public/crimesagainsthumanity/default.asp (accessed March 01, 2005.)

———. "Interpol's Operational response to the tsunami disaster." http://interpol.int/public/asiandisaster/synopsis20050126.htm (accessed March 03, 2005.)

Johns Hopkins Medicine. "Home Web Page of Johns Hopkins Medicine." http://www.hopkinsmedicine.org/index.html (accessed February 8, 2005.)

KidsHealth. "What's Spit?". http://kidshealth.org/kid/talk/yucky/spit.html (accessed March 6, 2005.)

Kime, J. W. "Marine Casualty Report: Capsizing and sinking of the mobile offshore drilling unit Rowan Gorilla I in the Atlantic Ocean on 15 December 1988." http://www.uscg.mil/hq/g-m/moa/boards/rowangorilla.pdf (accessed January 27, 2005.)

Lang, J. S., and N. A. Beer. "Voyage data recorders in marine accident investigations." http://www.ntsb.gov/events/symp_rec/proceedings/authors/lang.htm (accessed Januray 26, 2005.)

Latent-prints.com. "Latent prints: A forensic fingerprint impression evidence discussion site." February 15, 2005. http://www.latent-prints.com/ (accessed February 24, 2005.)

Lederman, Peter H., and Gilbert Snowden. "DWI Field Sobriety Testing." http://www.nj-dwi.com/sobriety-1.htm (accessed March 8, 2005.)

Legal Information Institute, Cornell Law School. "Federal Rules of Evidence." 1999. http://www.law.cornell.edu/rules/fre/overview.html (accessed March 29, 2005.)

Materials Evaluation and Engineering, Inc. "Energy Dispersive Spectroscopy: Description of Technique." http://www.mee-inc.com/eds.html (accessed March 9, 2005.)

McCrone Research Institute. "About the Institute." http://www.mcri.org/ (accessed March 24, 2005.)

McFarland, P. "Guide to the Henry deForest Papers, 1898-1947." http://rmc.library.cornell.edu/EAD/htmldocs/RMM03214.html (accessed March 31, 2005.)

MedicineNet. "Hemoglobin." http://www.medicinenet.com/hemoglobin/article.htm (accessed February 20, 2005.)

Medline Plus (U.S. National Library of Medicine and National Institutes of Health). "Carbon Monoxide Poisoning." http://www.nlm.nih.gov/medlineplus/carbonmonoxidepoisoning.html (accessed March 24, 2005.)

Monroe County, New York, Office of the Conflict Defender. "Misdemeanor Indictment." http://www.mcacp.org/issue14.htm (accessed February 22, 2005.)

National Center on Shaken Baby Syndrome. "All about SBS: Physical Signs/Symptoms." http://www.dontshake.com/Subject.aspx?CategoryID=12 (accessed March 24, 2005.)

National Exchange Club Foundation. "Babies are fragile. Please don't shake a child (National Shaken Baby Syndrome Campaign)." http://www.preventchildabuse.com/shaken.htm (accessed March 24, 2005.)

National Forensic Science Technology Center (NFSTC). http://www.nfstc.org/ (accessed March 25, 2005.)

National Institute for Truth Verification. "The History and Evolution of Lie Detection." http://www.cvsa1.com/ (accessed March 7, 2005.)

National Institute of Justice—Publications and Products. "Using DNA to Solve Cold Cases." October 1, 2002. http://www.ojp.usdoj.gov/nij/pubs-sum/194197.htm (accessed February 18, 2005.)

National Institute of Neurological Disorders and Stroke. "NINDS Shaken Baby Syndrome Information Page." March 9, 2005. http://www.ninds.nih.gov/disorders/shakenbaby/shakenbaby.htm (accessed March 24, 2005.)

National Institute on Drug Abuse (NIDA)—Research Report Series. "MDMA Abuse (Ecstasy)." December 2004. http://www.erowid.org/psychoactives/law/law_fed_sched.shtml (accessed January 18, 2005.)

National Transportation Safety Board. http://www.ntsb.gov (accessed February 12, 2005.)

The National Women's Health Information Center (4woman.gov). "Sexual Assault." http://www.4woman.gov/faq/sexualassault.htm (accessed March 24, 2005.)

New York State Division of Criminal Justice Services. http://criminaljustice.state.ny.us/ (accessed March 10, 2005.)

Peterson, Richard N. "Setting the standard for expert witness testimony." http://www.aaos.org/wordhtml/bulletin/oct04/fline2.htm (accessed March 29, 2005.)

Physicians for Human Rights. "Medical Group Announces First Identification of Victims of Srebrenica Massacre." July 16, 1997. http://www.phrusa.org/research/forensics/bosnia/forid.html (accessed March 22, 2005.)

Piquepaille, Roland. "3D Biometric Facial Recognition Comes To UK." November 26, 2004. http://www.primidi.com/2004/11/26.html (accessed March 13, 2005.)

Pissarenko, Dimitri. "Eigenface-based facial recognition." February 13, 2003. http://openbio.sourceforge.net/resources/eigenfaces/eigenfaces-html/facesOptions.html (accessed March 13, 2005.)

Police Academy Alumni Association. January 8, 2005. http://www.cspaaa.com/ (accessed February 7, 2005.)

Protocol online. "DNA extraction and Purification." 1999–2004. http://www.protocol-online.org/prot/Molecular_Biology/DNA/DNA_Extraction___Purification/index.html (accessed March 13, 2005.)

Rensselaer Polytechnic Institute. "Chromatography." http://www.rpi.edu/dept/chem-eng/Biotech-Environ/CHROMO/chromintro.html (accessed April 3, 2005.)

Ridges and Furrows. "Early Fingerprint Pioneers." http://www.ridgesandfurrows.homestead.com (accessed February 28, 2005.)

———. "Significant Dates and Events." http://www.ridgesandfurrows.homestead.com (accessed April 8, 2005.)

Robinson, Philip C., and Michael W. Davidson. "Introduction to Polarized Light Microscopy." http://www.microscopyu.com/articles/polarized/polarizedintro.html (accessed March 3, 2005.)

Roche Diagnostics. "Innovating Health Information." February 7, 2005. http://www.roche-diagnostics.com/ (accessed February 8, 2005.)

RxMed. "Lilly Glucose Enzymatic Test Strip Diagnostic Aid." http://rxmed.com/b.main/b2.pharmaceutical/b2.1.monographs/CPS-%20Monographs/CPS%20(accessed General%20Monographs-%20T)/TES.htm (accessed March 27, 2005.)

Scottish Criminal Record Office. "History of Fingerprints—A Time Line." http://www.scro.police.uk/fingerprint_history.htm (accessed February 28, 2005.)

Shaken Baby Syndrome Defense. "Shaken Baby Syndrome: A Tutorial and Review of the Literature." http://www.sbsdefense.com/SBS%20101.htm (accessed March 24, 2005.)

SMC Business Councils. "Southwestern PA Conference on Emergency Preparedness & Disaster Planning." http://www.smc.org/ (accessed February 21, 2005.)

Society of Forensic Ink Analysts. "Introduction." http://www.sofia-ink.org/ (accessed March 9, 2005.)

Southern California Association of Fingerprint Officers. "Effective and Cost Efficient Catalyst." March 1994. http://www.scafo.org/ (accessed February 21, 2005.)

Sponberg, Eric W. "Forensic Naval Architecture." http://www.sponbergyachtdesign.com/Forensic.htm (accessed January 26, 2005.)

Technology Review Online. "The Voice of Osama bin Laden." January 23, 2004. http://muller.lbl.gov/Tressays/24-Voice_of_Osama.htm (accessed March 20, 2005.)

The Thin Blue Line. "Forensic Serology—Bloodstain Pattern Analysis." http://www.policesw.com/info/forensic/ (accessed April 4, 2005.)

Triplett, Michele. "Fingerprint Terms." http://www.fprints.nwlean.net/sl.htm (accessed February 21, 2005.)

Trueman, C. "A history of medicine." 2002. http://www.historylearningsite.co.uk/history_of_medicine.htm (accessed March 13, 2005.)

University of California. "Obituary of Paul Kirk." http://dynaweb.oac.cdlib.org:8088/dynaweb/ (accessed March 24, 2005.)

University of Cape Town. "SDS Polyacrylamide Gel Electrophoresis (accessed SDS-PAGE)." http://www.mcb.uct.ac.za/sdspage.html (accessed April 3, 2005.)

University of Dundee, Department of Forensic Medicine. "Undergraduate Teaching Materials." http://www.dundee.ac.uk/forensicmedicine/ugmaterials.htm (accessed February 13, 2005.)

———. "Wounds." http://www.dundee.ac.uk/forensicmedicine/llb/woundsdjp.htm (accessed April 3, 2005.)

University of Pennsylvania Law School. "Uniform Rules of Evidence." 1998. http://www.law.upenn.edu/bll/ulc/fnact99/ure88.html. (accessed February 15, 2005.)

University of Pittsburgh Medical Center. "Center for Biosecurity of UPMC." http://www.upmc-biosecurity.org/ (accessed February 8, 2005.)

University of Virginia. "DNA fingerprinting using VNTRs." August 25, 1999. http://www.people.virginia.edu/~rjh9u/vntr1.html (accessed January 25, 2005.)

The University of Utah, Genetic Science Learning Center. "How to Extract DNA from Anything Living." 2005. http://gslc.genetics.utah.edu/units/activities/extraction/ (accessed March 13, 2005.)

U.S. Congress, Office of Technology Assessment. "Chapter 4: DNA as Evidence from Genetic Witness: Forensic Uses of DNA Tests." http://www.wws.princeton.edu/cgi-bin/byteserv.prl/~ota/disk2/1990/9021/902106.PDF (accessed February 28, 2005.)

U.S. Department of Justice, Drug Enforcement Administration. "Description of Federal Controlled Substances—Schedules I–V." June 2004. http://www.erowid.org/psychoactives/law/law_fed_sched.shtml (accessed January 18, 2005.)

U.S. Department of Transportation. "Introduction to Standardized Field Sobriety Test." http://www.nhtsa.dot.gov/people/injury/alcohol/SFST/introduction.htm#1%20Development%20and%20Validation (accessed March 8, 2005.)

USConstitution.net. "The U.S. Constitution Online." http://www.usconstitution.net/const.html#A1Sec9 (accessed March 23, 2005.)

WebMD. "Complete Blood Count (CBC)." http://my.webmd.com/hw/health_guide_atoz/hw4260.asp (accessed January 27, 2005.)

Weeks, Eric. "How does a confocal microscope work?" http://www.physics.emory.edu/~weeks/confocal/ (accessed January 26, 2005.)

Weintraub, Arlene. "Can Drug-Busters Beat New Steroids?". http://www.businessweek.com/magazine/content/04_24/b3887096_mz018.htm (accessed March 4, 2005.)

West Virginia University College of Law. "Competency to Stand Trial." http://myweb.wvnet.edu/~jelkins/lawpsy04/competence.html (accessed March 23, 2005.)

WhyFiles. "Virtually Framed, or Animatedly Exonerated?" http://whyfiles.org/014forensic/computer_animation.html (accessed January 28, 2005.)

Wired News. "Tsunami tests limits of forensics." http://www.wired.com/news/medtech/0,1286,66184 2,00.html?tw=wn_story_page_next1.htm (accessed March 03, 2005.)

HISTORICAL CHRONOLOGY

c.1980 B.C. Egyptian pharaoh Amenemhet I is targeted as one of the first recorded victims of political assassination.

1500 B.C. In Babylon, fingerprints are pressed onto clay tablets of business contracts.

c.480 B.C. Demaratus of Sparta uses an early form of secret writing, concealing a message on a wooden tablet covered with wax, to warn his countrymen of invasion by the Persian empire.

c.300 B.C. *Arthasastra*, an ancient Indian manual on politics, discusses mining, metallurgy, medicine, pyrotechnics, poisons, and fermented liquors.

c.618 In China during the T'ang dynasty (618–906 A.D.) fingerprints mark divorce decrees and business documents.

c.1600 Chemists invent invisible inks, and the rebirth of complex mathematics revives encryption and code methods long dormant since Antiquity. Later, during the Scientific Revolution and the Enlightenment, telescopes and magnifying glasses are developed.

1609 In France, François Demelle publishes a book on the techniques of document analysis.

1679 The *Habeas Corpus* Act is formally passed by English Parliament.

1681 Publication of Jean Mabillon's *De Re Diplomatica*, which outlines the science of diplomatics, a precursor of questioned document examination.

c.1684 British physician Nehimiah Grew describes the shapes of ridges on the ends of the fingers in a treatise.

c.1686 As part of a general study of human skin, Italian anatomist Marcello Malpighi, an anatomy professor at the University of Bologna, describes the patterns of the ridges on the fingertips. Malpighi does not suggest that fingerprints can be used for unique identification of individuals.

1703 Although concepts of disease are primitive, in an act of biological warfare, Sir Jeffrey Amherst, commander-in-chief of British forces in North America, suggests grinding the scabs of smallpox pustules into blankets intended for Native American tribes known to trade with the French.

1789 Congress passes the Judiciary Act, which establishes the federal justice system and creates the Office of the Attorney General, as well as the U.S. Marshal Service.

1790 France introduces the metric system.

1802 John Dalton introduces modern atomic theory into the science of chemistry.

1817 German pharmacist Frederick Serturner announces the extraction of morphine from opium.

1818 Augustin Jean Fresnel (1788–1827), French physicist, publishes his *Mémoire sur la diffraction de la lumière* in which he demonstrates the ability of a transverse wave theory of light to account for such phenomena as reflection, refraction, polarization, interference, and diffraction patterns.

1828 Friedrich Wöhler synthesizes urea. This is generally regarded as the first organic chemical produced in the laboratory, and an important step in disproving the idea that only living organisms can produce organic compounds. Work by Wöhler and others establishes the foundations of organic chemistry and biochemistry.

1828 Luigi Rolando (1773–1831), Italian anatomist, achieves the first synthetic electrical stimulation of the brain.

1836 Toxicological evidence (related to arsenic poisoning) is first used in a trial (in the U.K.).

1839 Semen and sperm characteristics are defined by microscopic examination.

1839 Theodore Schwann extends the theory of cells to include animals and helps establish the basic unity of the two great kingdoms of life. He publishes *Microscopical Researches into the Accordance in the Structure and Growth of Animals and Plants*, in which he asserts that all living things are made up of cells, and that each cell contains certain essential components. He also coins the term "metabolism" to describe the overall chemical changes that take place in living tissues.

1840 Friedrich Gustav Jacob Henle publishes the first histology textbook, *General Anatomy*. This work includes the first modern discussion of the germ theory of communicable diseases.

1843 Charles-Frédéric Gerhardt (1816–1856), French chemist, simplifies chemical formula-writing, so that water becomes H_2O instead of the previous H_4O_2.

1857 Louis Pasteur demonstrates that lactic acid fermentation is caused by a living organism. Between 1857 and 1880, he performs a series of experiments that refute the doctrine of spontaneous generation. He also introduces vaccines for fowl cholera, anthrax, and rabies, based on attenuated strains of viruses and bacteria.

1858 Rudolf Ludwig Karl Virchow publishes his landmark paper "Cellular Pathology" and establishes the field of cellular pathology.

Virchow asserts that all cells arise from preexisting cells (*Omnis cellula e cellula*). He argues that the cell is the ultimate locus of all disease.

1862 Dutch scientist J. Van Deen develops a presumptive blood test.

1862 Department of Agriculture establishes the Bureau of Chemistry, the organizational forerunner of the Food and Drug Administration.

1864 First photographic plates made for the purpose of identification of criminals and questioned documents.

1865 The United States Secret Service is established to interdict counterfeit currency and its manufacturers.

1867 Secret Service responsibilities broadened to include "detecting persons perpetrating frauds against the government."

1870 Lambert Adolphe Jacques Quetelet shows the importance of statistical analysis for biologists and provides the foundations of biometry.

1872 Ferdinand Julius Cohn publishes the first of four papers entitled "Research on Bacteria," which establishes the foundation of bacteriology as a distinct field. He systematically divides bacteria into genera and species.

1876 Robert Koch publishes a paper on anthrax that implicates a bacterium as the cause of the disease, validating the germ theory of disease.

1877 Microscopic delineation of palm prints.

1877 Congress passes legislation prohibiting the counterfeiting of any coin, gold, or silver bar.

1878 Charles–Emanuel Sedillot introduces the term "microbe." The term becomes widely used as a term for a pathogenic bacterium.

1879 German pathologist Rudolf Ludwig Karl Virchow studies and characterizes hair.

c.1880 Two Englishmen working abroad notice that fingerprints are unique to individuals. Sir William Herschel, a British Magistrate working in India, uses the impressions of fingers of local businessmen to validate contracts. As Herschel collects these fingerprints, he notices that no two are alike. In Japan, British physician Henry Faulds studies fingerprints he finds on ancient pottery. He documents their individual patterns and develops a method for categorizing them. His work is published in the journal *Nature*.

1880 Louis Pasteur develops a method of weakening a microbial pathogen of chicken, and uses the term "attenuated" to describe the weakened microbe.

1882 Sir Francis Galton publishes a book titled *Fingerprints*, that proves that fingerprints do not change during a person's lifetime. He also develops a set of characteristics called minutia that can be used to identify fingerprints. These characteristics, also called Galton's Details, are still used in modern forensics.

1882 The German bacteriologist Robert Koch (1843–1910) discovers the tubercle bacillus and enunciates "Koch's postulates," which define the classic method of preserving, documenting, and studying bacteria.

1883 French police worker Alphonse Bertillon links criminal behavior to body measurement (anthropometry).

1887 Arthur Conan Doyle publishes first Sherlock Holmes story.

1889 In 1899 and 1900, Sir Edward Richard Henry improves on Galton's classification system, allowing forensics experts to handle larger numbers of fingerprints in their filing systems. Henry's system remains one of the most common systems used.

1892 Argentinean police worker Juan Vucetich advances the fingerprint classification system. Vucetich identifies a woman who murdered her own sons by finding her bloody print on the doorpost.

1898 In Germany, Paul Jesrich compares bullets using photomicrographs.

1900 Friedrich Ernst Dorn (1848-1916), a German physicist, demonstrates that the newly discovered radium gives off a gas as well as producing radioactive radiation. This proves to be the first demonstrable evidence that in the radioactive process, one element is actually transmuted into another.

1900 Karl Landsteiner discovers the blood-agglutination phenomenon and the four major blood types in humans.

1901 In England and Wales, fingerprints are incorporated into the criminal investigation system.

1903 The New York State Prison system begins systematically fingerprinting criminals.

1904 The St. Louis Police department uses fingerprint identification during the World's Fair.

1904 Oskar and Rudolf Adler develop a benzidine-based presumptive test for blood.

1908 Formal beginning of the Bureau of Investigation (BOI) that became the FBI in 1935.

1911 Fritz Pregl (1869–1930), an Austrian chemist, first introduces organic microanalysis. He invents analytic methods that make it possible to determine the empirical formula of an organic compound from just a few milligrams of the substance.

1912 Joseph Thomson develops a forerunner of mass spectrometry and separation of isotopes.

1913 In Paris, Victor Balthazard identifies bullet marking classifications and techniques.

1915 The International Association for Criminal Identification, a precursor of the International Association for Identification (IAI), is founded, with founder Harry H. Caldwell as its presiding officer.

1915 Germany uses poison gas at the Battle of Ypres.

1916 Vacuums are used to collect trace evidence.

1918 Edmond Locard advances 12 point fingerprint matching scheme.

Oct 28, 1919 Congress passes the National Motor Vehicle Theft Act, also known as the Dyer Act. This act authorizes the Bureau of Investigation to investigate auto thefts that cross state lines.

1921 William Marston develops first modern polygraph.

1921 Twenty-six year old J. Edgar Hoover named Assistant Director of BOI.

1922 White House police force created at request of President Warren G. Harding. Ultimately this will become the uniformed division of the United States Secret Service.

1924 United States consolidates fingerprint files in the Identification Division of the Federal Bureau of Investigation. By 1946, there are more than 100 million fingerprint cards in their files. Eventually this collection of cards becomes the Automated Fingerprint Identification System, or AFIS, and in 1999 it becomes IAFIS.

1924 Los Angeles Police Chief Vollmer establishes the first U.S. police crime laboratory.

1924 J. Edgar Hoover designated Director of the BOI.

1924 BOI establishes an Identification Division after Congress authorized "the exchange of identification records with officers of the cities, counties, and states."

1925 Johannes Hans Berger (1873–1941), German neurologist, records the first human electroencephalogram (EEG).

1925 Special Agent Edwin C. Shanahan becomes the first BOI agent killed in the line of duty.

1930 *American Journal of Police Science* begins publication.

1930 United States Food, Drug, and Insecticide Administration is renamed Food and Drug Administration (FDA).

1930 U.S. Treasury Department creates Bureau of Narcotics, which will remain the principal anti-drug agency of the federal government until the late 1960s.

1930 Primitive anthrax vaccine developed.

1932 Federal Bureau of Investigation (FBI) crime laboratory established.

1932 The Bureau of Investigation starts the international exchange of fingerprint data with friendly foreign governments. Halted as war approaches, the program is not re-instituted until after World War II.

1932 In response to the Lindbergh kidnapping case and other high profile cases, the Federal Kidnapping Act is passed to authorize BOI to investigate kidnappings perpetrated across state borders.

1934 U.S. Congress passes National Firearms Act.

1935 The Federal Bureau of Narcotics, forerunner of the modern Drug Enforcement Administration (DEA), began a campaign that portrayed marijuana as a drug that led users to drug addiction, violence, and insanity. The government produced films such as *Marihuana* (1935), *Reefer Madness* (1936), and *Assassin of Youth* (1937).

Jul 1, 1935 The BOI officially becomes the Federal Bureau of Investigation (FBI).

1941 Researchers publish studies of voiceprint identification.

1941 Arnold O. Beckman, American physicist and inventor, invents the spectrophotometer. This instrument measures light at the electron level and can be used for many kinds of chemical analysis.

1942 Formation of the American Society of Questioned Document Examiners

1942 Alcohol Tax Unit (ATU) formed and given responsibility for enforcing the Firearms Act.

1946 R. R. Race advances Kell blood group system.

1950 Duffy blood group system advanced.

1950 American Academy of Forensic Science (AAFS) established.

1950 Puerto Rican nationalists attempt to assassinate President Harry S Truman. As a result of this incident, in which a United States Secret Service (USSS) agent is killed, Congress greatly expands the duties of USSS.

1950 The FBI initiates the Ten Most Wanted Fugitives Program in May in order to draw national attention to dangerous criminals who have avoided capture.

1951 Kidd blood grouping system advanced.

1953 James D. Watson and Francis H. C. Crick publish two landmark papers in the journal *Nature*. The papers are entitled "Molecular structure of nucleic acids: a structure for deoxyribose nucleic acid" and "Genetic implications of the structure of deoxyribonucleic acid." Watson and Crick propose a double helical model for DNA and call attention to the genetic implications of their model. Their model is based, in part, on the x-ray crystallographic work of Rosalind Franklin and the biochemical work of Erwin Chargaff. Their model explains how the genetic material is transmitted.

1954 Indiana State Police Captain R. F. Borkenstein invents Breathalyzer®.

1958 International Association for Identification establishes the John A. Dondero Memorial Award, first awarded to FBI Director J. Edgar Hoover.

1959 The microchip, forerunner of the microprocessor, is invented.

Nov 22, 1963 Lee Harvey Oswald assassinates President John F. Kennedy in Dallas, Texas.

1966 The Naval Investigative Service, predecessor of the Naval Criminal Investigative Service, formed as an office within the Office of Naval Intelligence.

1967 National Crime Information Center created by U.S. Federal Bureau of Investigation.

1968 U.S. anti-drug agencies in the Treasury and Health, Education, and Welfare departments merge to form the Bureau of Narcotics and Dangerous Drugs under the Justice Department.

1968 The National Institute of Justice established under the authority of the Omnibus Crime Control and Safe Streets Act to provide independent, evidence-based tools to assist state and local law enforcement.

Apr 4, 1968 James Earl Ray assassinates Dr. Martin Luther King, Jr. in Memphis, Tennessee. The FBI opens a special investigation based on the violation of Dr. King's civil rights so that federal jurisdiction in the matter could be established.

Jun 5, 1968 Senator Robert F. Kennedy is assassinated by Sirhan B. Sirhan.

1968 As a result of Senator Robert F. Kennedy's assassination, Congress authorizes protection of major Presidential and Vice Presidential candidates and nominees.

1969 Microprocessor developed.

1969 Defense Department Advanced Research Projects Agency (ARPA) establishes ARPANET, a forerunner to the Internet.

1970 Forensic odontology division of the American Academy of Forensic Sciences created.

1970 United States Congress passes Controlled Substance Act (CSA).

1970 The Consolidated Federal Law Enforcement Training Center, a bureau of the Department of the Treasury, is established as an organization to provide training for all federal law-enforcement personnel. Today known as the Federal Law Enforcement Training Center, it is now part of the Department for Homeland Security.

1970 Congress approves the Organized Crime Control Act of 1970 in October. This law contains a section known as the Racketeer Influenced and Corrupt Organization Act or RICO. RICO becomes an effective tool in convicting members of organized criminal enterprises.

1971 B. J. Culliford publishes *The Examination and Typing of Bloodstains in the Crime Laboratory.*

1972 Recombinant technology emerges as one of the most powerful techniques of molecular biology. Scientists are able to splice together pieces of DNA to form recombinant genes. As the potential uses, therapeutic and industrial, become increasingly clear, scientists and venture capitalists establish biotechnology companies.

1972 The ATF Division of IRS becomes a separate Treasury bureau, the Bureau of Alcohol, Tobacco, and Firearms.

1974 Scanning electron microscopy with electron dispersive x rays (SEMEDX) used to identify gunshot residue.

1975 The Federal Rules of Evidence enacted.

1977 Forensic scientists begin to use Fourier transform infrared spectrophotometer.

1977 FBI advances Automated Fingerprint Identification System (AFIS).

1981 First corpse donated for study received at the Body Farm.

1982 In January, federal law enforcement reorganization gives Drug Enforcement Administration (DEA) and Federal Bureau of Investigation (FBI) concurrent jurisdiction in drug-related criminal matters.

1982 The FDA issues regulations for tamper-resistant packaging after seven people die in Chicago from ingesting Tylenol capsules laced with cyanide. The following year, the federal Anti-Tampering Act was passed, making it a crime to tamper with packaged consumer products.

1984 Crime-fighting efforts bolstered by the Sentencing Reform Act, which stiffens prison sentences, requiring mandatory terms for certain crimes and abolishing federal parole; and by the Victims of Crime Act. Throughout the 1980s, numerous national and community-based organizations are formed to provide support to victims of rape, spousal abuse, drunk driving, and other crimes.

1984 Congress enacts legislation making the fraudulent use of credit and debit cards a federal violation.

1984 The United States Department of Energy (DOE), Office of Health and Environmental Research, U.S. Department of Energy (OHER, now Office of Biological and Environmental Research), and the International Commission for Protection Against Environmental Mutagens and Carcinogens (ICPEMC) cosponsor the Alta, Utah, conference, which highlights the growing role of recombinant DNA technologies. OTA incorporates the proceedings of the meeting into a report acknowledging the value of deciphering the human genome.

1984 President Ronald Reagan issues a directive giving the NSA responsibility of maintaining security of government computers.

1985 Alec Jeffreys develops "genetic fingerprinting," a method of using DNA polymorphisms (unique sequences of DNA) to identify individuals. The method, which is subsequently used in paternity, immigration, and murder cases, is generally referred to as "DNA fingerprinting."

1985 Kary Mullis, who was working at Cetus Corporation, develops the polymerase chain reaction (PCR), a new method of amplifying DNA. This technique quickly becomes one of the most powerful tools of molecular biology. Cetus patents PCR and sells the patent to Hoffman-LaRoche, Inc. in 1991.

1985 The Global Positioning System (GPS) becomes operational.

1986 First use of PCR-based forensic DNA analysis in the United States. Henry Erlich confirms that two autopsy samples came from the same person in the case *Pennsylvania v. Pestinikas.*

1986 DNA is first used to solve a crime as Alec Jeffreys uses DNA profiling evidence to identify Colin Pitchfork as a murderer.

1986 Computer Fraud and Abuse Act enacted, defining federal computer crimes.

1986 U.S. intelligence community establishes Intelligence Community Staff Committee on MASINT (measurement and signatures intelligence) to oversee all relevant activities.

1987 Based on RFLP analysis, DNA profiling is introduced into a U.S. criminal trial.

1987 Congress passes the Computer Security Act, which makes unclassified computing systems the responsibility of the National Institute of Standards and Technology (NIST) and not the NSA with regard to technology standards development.

1987 The idea to use patterns of the iris of the eye as an identification marker was patented, along with the algorithms necessary for iris identification.

1988 International Association for Identification establishes peer-reviewed publication: *Journal of Forensic Identification.*

1988 Loss of Pan Am Flight 103 over Lockerbie, Scotland.

1988 The Human Genome Organization (HUGO) is established by scientists in order to coordinate international efforts to sequence the human genome.

1988 The federal Polygraph Protection Act prohibits employers from using polygraphs for employment screening.

1991 Forensic Science Service (U.K.) established as an executive agency of the Home Office of the U.K. government.

1992 National Crime Information Center consolidates with the FBI's Criminal Justice Information Services division.

1992 Naval Criminal Investigative Service formed as an entity separate from the Office of Naval Intelligence.

1993 A U.S. federal court relaxes *Frye* standard for admission of scientific evidence (*Daubert et al. v. Merrell Dow.*

Feb 26, 1993 The World Trade Center in New York City is badly damaged when a car bomb planted by Islamic terrorists explodes in an underground garage. The bomb leaves six people dead and 1,000 injured. The men carrying out the attack were followers of Umar Abd al-Rahman, an Egyptian cleric who preached in the New York City area.

1993 After a 51-day siege by the Bureau of Alcohol, Tobacco, and Firearms, a federal team assaults a compound held by the Branch Davidians, a religious sect charged with hoarding illegal weapons. The Branch Davidians allegedly set the buildings on fire, killing 76 people, including cult leader David Koresh.

1994 DNA Identification Act of 1994 authorizes establishment of NDIS.

1994 The Genetic Privacy Act, the first United States Human Genome Project legislative product, proposes regulation of the collection, analysis, storage, and use of DNA samples and genetic information obtained from them. These rules were endorsed by the ELSI Working Group.

1995 Forensic Science Service (U.K.) established the world's first national criminal intelligence DNA database, the National DNA Database.

1995 A study by the Rand Corporation finds that every dollar spent in drug treatment saves society seven dollars in crime, policing, incarceration, and health services.

Apr 19, 1995 A car bomb explodes outside the Alfred P. Murrah Federal office building in Oklahoma City, Oklahoma, collapsing walls and floors, killing 169 people, including 19 children and one person who died in the rescue effort. Timothy McVeigh and Terry Nichols are later convicted in the anti-government plot to avenge the Branch Davidian standoff in Waco, Tex., exactly two years earlier.

1996 The Forensic Science Service (U.K.) merges with the Metropolitan Police Laboratory, London, England.

1996 First computerized searches of the AFIS fingerprint database.

1996 First use of mitochondrial DNA typing evidence in a U.S. trial (*Tennessee v. Ware*).

1997 The National Center for Human Genome Research (NCHGR) at the National Institutes of Health becomes the National Human Genome Research Institute (NHGRI).

Dec 8, 1997 The FBI announces its new National DNA Index System (NDIS) allowing forensic science laboratories to link serial violent crimes to each other and to known sex offenders through the electronic exchange of DNA profiles.

1998 NDIS becomes operational.

1998 FBI and ATF agree to pursue joint development of one system, using only IBIS, and create the National Integrated Ballistics Information Network.

1998 DNA analyses of semen stains on a dress worn by Monica Lewinsky were found to match DNA from a blood sample taken from President Clinton.

1998 DNA fingerprinting used to identify remains of Russian Imperial Romanov family.

1999 The FBI teams with federal, state, and local criminal investigation departments to establish IAFIS, the Integrated Automated Fingerprint Identification System. This facility electronically stores the fingerprints and criminal history information of more than 47 million individuals.

1999 Osama bin Laden is added to the FBI's "Ten Most Wanted Fugitives" list in June, in connection with the U.S. Embassy bombings in East Africa.

Jun 23, 1999 FBI personnel travel to Kosovo to assist in the collection of evidence and the examination of forensic materials in support of the prosecution of Slobodan Milosevic and others before the International Criminal Tribunal for the former Yugoslavia.

2000 Debut of the CBS television series *CSI: Crime Scene Investigation*.

Sep 11, 2001 Islamist terrorists mount a coordinated terrorist attack on New York and Washington. The World Trade Center Towers are destroyed, killing nearly 3,000 people. In Washington, a plane slams into the Pentagon, but passengers aboard another hijacked airliner, aware of the other terrorist attacks, fight back. During the struggle for the aircraft, it crashes into a Pennsylvania field, thwarting the terrorist's plans to crash the plane into either the U.S. Capital or White House, but killing all on board.

2001 The FBI dedicates 7,000 of its 11,000 Special Agents and thousands of FBI support personnel to the PENTTBOM investigation. "PENTTBOM" is short for Pentagon, Twin Towers Bombing.

2001 Letters containing a powdered form of *Bacillus anthracis*, the bacteria that causes anthrax, are mailed by an unknown terrorist or terrorist group (foreign or domestic) to government representatives, members of the news media, and others in the United States. One letter is postmarked to a U.S. senator on October 8, resulting in closure of the Hart Senate building and other government offices and postal facilities. More than 20 cases and five deaths are eventually attributed to the terrorist attack.

Oct 18, 2001 In conjunction with the U. S. Post Office, the FBI offers a reward of $1,000,000 for information leading to the arrest of the person who mailed letters contaminated with anthrax to media organizations and congressional offices.

Oct 26, 2001   President George W. Bush signs the Patriot Act into law, giving the FBI and CIA broader investigatory powers and allowing them to share with one another confidential information about suspected terrorists. Under the act, both agencies can conduct residential searches without a warrant and without the presence of the suspect. The act also allows immediate seizure of personal records. The provisions are not limited to investigating suspected terrorists, but may be used in any criminal investigation related to terrorism. The Patriot Act also grants the FBI and CIA greater latitude in using computer tracking devices to gain access to Internet and phone records. Forensic science becomes more entwined with National Security interests.

2001   Enough closed-circuit television cameras (CCTV) are installed in public places in Britain that, on an average day in any large British city, security experts calculate that a person will have over 300 opportunities to be captured on CCTV during the course of normal daily activities.

2002   Cable television network Court TV launches its Forensics in the Classroom program.

Jan 24, 2003   The Office of Homeland Security becomes the Department of Homeland Security.

2004   Total number of DNA profiles in the FBI NDIS database reaches 2,132,470; the total number of forensic profiles is 93,956, and the total number of convicted offender profiles is 2,038,470.

GENERAL INDEX

Bold page numbers refer to the main entry on the subject. Page numbers in italics refer to illustrations.

5′-monophosphate dehydrogenase (IMPDH), 1:81

A

AAFS. *See* American Academy of Forensic Science

AAIB (Air Accidents Investigation Branch) (United Kingdom), 1:13, 15, 16

Abbe, Ernst, 2:456

ABC (American Broadcasting Corporation), 1:31

Abdominal dissection, in autopsies, 1:57

Abdominal region (Anatomy), 1:*21*, 22

Abduction (Anatomy), 1:22

Abduction of children. *See* Missing children

Abdullah (King of Jordan), 1:48

ABO blood types
absorption-elution test, 2:621
blood transfusions and, 1:37
discovery of, 1:347
isoantibodies and, 1:390
secretor phenotype, 2:602–603
testing for, 2:610–611

ABP (Academy of Behavioral Profiling), 2:555–556

Abrasions, 1:97

Abru, Elly, 1:327

Absence epilepsy, 1:258

Absorbents for decontamination, 1:199

Absorption chromatography, 1:141

Absorption-elution blood tests, 2:621

Abstracting services (Journals), 2:552

Abuelas de Plaza de Mayo (Argentina), 1:207

Academic journals, 2:551–553

Academy of Behavioral Profiling (ABP), 2:555–556

Accelerants, 1:**1,** 313
found in fire debris, 1:297–298
gas chromatography on, 1:430
pattern evidence from, 2:523

Accessories to a crime, defined, 2:691

Accident investigations
chemical releases, 1:135–136
fires, 1:1, 297–299, *299*
at sea, 1:**1–2**
See also Aircraft accidents; Automobile accidents

Accident reconstruction, 1:**2–4**
3-D laser stations, 1:409
animation in, 1:26–27, 163
filament analysis, 1:291
SMAC program, 1:163–164
World Trade Towers structural analysis, 1:38–39, *39*

Accidental deaths
vs. suicide, 2:654, 655, 656
number of, 1:196

Accidental pathogens, 2:517

Accountability, criminal. *See* Criminal responsibility

Accounting, forensic, 1:**309–310**

Accreditation
forensic professionals, 2:685
laboratories, 2:569, 577

Accumulated degree days (ADDs), 1:98

Acetylcholine, 2:484

Acetylcholinesterase, 2:479–480

Acid-base indicators, 1:**376–377**

Acid phosphatase, 2:603

Acoustic resonance detection technique, 1:133

Acoustic waves, 1:250

Acquired resistance to antibacterial agents, 1:66

Acquittal of criminal responsibility, 2:449–450

Acrylic paint analysis, 1:42, 44

ACTH (Adrenocorticotrophic hormone), 2:527

Action heroes (Films), 1:292–293

Active metal detectors, 2:450

Actus reus principle, 1:412, 2:690

Adaptation (Bacteria), 1:65–66

Addiction. *See* Substance abuse

Addison, United States v. (1974), 2:708

ADDs (Accumulated degree days), 1:98

Adduction (Anatomy), 1:22

Adenosine triphosphate (ATP), rigor mortis and, 2:584

Adhesive tape
fracture matching, 1:316
tape lift evidence collection, 1:317, 2:684

Adipocere, 1:**4–5,** 198

Adjudication of authorship, 1:423

Adleman, Leonard, 1:190

Admissibility of evidence, state *vs.* federal rules, 1:147–148

Admission-seeking inteviews (Fraud), 1:310

Adrenocorticotrophic hormone (ACTH), 2:527

Adsorbents for decontamination, 1:199

E

Incidence rate (Epidemiology), 1:256

Incisions for autopsies, 1:56–57

Independent Safety Board Act of 1975, 2:487

Indicators, acid-base, 1:**376–377**

Indirect transmission of pathogens, 2:516

Individual evidence
defined, 1:264
tools, 2:675–676

Inductive criminal profiling, 2:553–554

Inductively coupled plasma-optical emission spectroscopy (ICP-OES), 1:115, 2:639

Inelastic electrons, 2:599

Infants
cocaine-addicted babies, 2:*447*
decomposition of newborns, 1:197
shaken baby syndrome, 2:**616–617**

Infectious diseases
detection, 1:81
electrophoresis research on, 1:250
epidemiological methods, 1:255–258
immunoglobulin G and, 1:35
from prions, 2:545–546
saliva tests, 2:595
USAMRIID work, 2:705–707
See also Bacterial infections;
Viruses (Biological)

Inferior (Anatomical term), 1:20, *21*

Inflation systems (Airbags), 1:12–13

Influenza vaccines, 2:712

Information technology security. *See*
Computer crime/computer security

Infrared analysis
artificial fibers, 1:45
for artwork identification, 1:43, 44
detection devices, 1:**377–378,** 2:486
Fourier transform infrared spectrophotometry, 1:**314–315,** 2:454
spectroscopy, 2:638–639, 640

Infrared radiation, 1:248

Inhalants (Drugs), 1:373

Inhalation anthrax, defined, 1:28, 31
See also Anthrax

Inhalation tularemia, 2:697

Inherent resistance to antibacterial agents, 1:65

Inhibitors (Catalysts), 1:129

Initiation stage (Viral replication), 2:719

Injuries
antemortem, 1:**27–28**
automobile accidents, 1:54
blunt, 1:**97,** 2:746
from bullets, 1:70–71, 116
driving, 1:**239–240**
photography of, 2:534
See also Wounds

Ink
for currency, 1:175, 409
DNA markers, 2:635–636, 637, 743
invisible, 2:602

Ink analysis, 1:**378–379**
at FBI Crime Lab, 1:281
Hitler diaries, 1:349
Richard Brunelle work, 1:111
stolen money, 1:409

Inmates. *See* Prisoners

Innocence Projects, 1:215–217

Innocence Protection Act of 2003, 1:219

Inorganic compounds, 1:**379–380**

Inquests, 1:174

Insanity, criminal responsibility and, 2:449–450, 560

Insects, 1:**253–254,** *254*
biological weapon identification, 1:87
role in body decomposition, 1:98, 2:622–623
succession of, on bodies, 2:672–673, *673*

Instars (Larvae), 2:672–673

Institute for Law and Justice (Alexandria, Virginia), 1:215

Institute of Forensic Research (Poland), 1:381

Institute of Zoology (United Kingdom), 1:212

Institutes of forensic science, 1:**380–381**

Instrumentation, 1:**19–20**
See also Laboratory analysis

Insulin-like growth factor (IGF-1), 2:645

Insurance Committee for Arson Control (ICAC), 1:41

Insurance fraud, 1:40, 2:459–460

Integrated Automated Fingerprint Identification System (IAFIS), 1:**381–382,** *382,* 412

Integrated Ballistics Identification System (IBIS), 1:53, 241, **382–383**

Integrated Virus Detection System (IVDS), 2:738

Integrative medicine, 2:448

Integumentary system. *See* Skin

Interferograms, 1:315

Internal fraud, 1:309–310

Internal Revenue Service (IRS), 1:52, 53

Internal trajectories (Bullets), 1:116

International Association for Identification (IAI), 1:**384–385**

International Association of Forensic Nurses (IAFN), 1:310

International Biometric Industry Association (IBIA), 1:84

International Civil Aviation Organization (ICAO), 1:13

International Commission on Missing Persons (ICMP), 1:225, 369

International Council of Museums (ICOM), 1:353

International Council on Alcohol, Drugs and Traffic Safety (ICADTS), 1:105

International Criminal Police Commission (ICPC), 1:386

International Criminal Police Organization (ICPO-Interpol). *See* Interpol

International Criminal Tribunal for the former Yugoslavia (ICTY), 1:369, 2:731

International Environmental Sample Archive (IESA), 1:255

International Laws and Customs of War, 2:730–731

International Military Tribunal, 1:351, 2:730, 731

International Olympic Committee (IOC), 2:643, 644

International Organization for Standardization, 2:567–568, 705

International programs and cases, 2:**692–694**

International Society for Infectious Diseases, 1:258

Internet
online journals, 2:552–553
for tracking and tracing, 1:**385–386**
usage of, as evidence, 1:159

Internet Journal of Forensic Medicine and Toxicology, 2:553

Interpol, 1:380, **386–387,** *387*
DNA Monitoring Group, 1:219, 2:646
tsunami victim identification, 1:366
U.S. National Central Bureau, 1:**387–388**

Interrogation, 1:**388–390,** *389,* 2:564–565, 695–696
See also Polygraph machines

Interstate crime, FBI history and, 1:284

Interviews *vs.* interrogation, 1:388

Intoxilyzers, 1:110

Intranets, 1:162

Intravariability (Glass samples), 1:333

Introns, 1:143, 220

Inversion (Anatomy), 1:22

Investigative Support Unit (FBI), 1:237–238

Invisible ink, 2:602

Involuntary manslaughter, 2:472

IOC (International Olympic Committee), 2:643, 644

Ion channel biosensor technologies, 1:86

Ion exchange chromatography, 1:142, 223, 2:677

Ion mobility spectroscopy, 1:11, 102

Ionizing radiation
defined, 2:573
detection methods, 2:489
postal mail, 2:435–436

IRA (Irish Republican Army), 1:271, 2:*451*

Iran, nerve agent use by Iraq, 2:480

Iraq
1988 attack on Kurds, 1:137
interrogation cell, 1:*389*
mass graves, 2:729–730
nerve agent use, 2:480
satellite images of mass graves, 2:579
See also Persian Gulf Wars (1991 and 2003)

Ireland, William Henry, 2:569–570

Iris scans, 1:82, *83*, 84

Irish Republican Army (IRA), 1:271, 2:*451*

Irregular bones, defined, 2:623

IRS (Internal Revenue Service), 1:52, 53

ISO 9000 quality standards, 2:567–568, 705

Isoantibodies, 1:**390–391**

Isotopic analysis, 1:**391**, 2:742

Israelite Jews (Cohen Modal Haplotype), 1:6, 7

Istanbul University Institute of Forensic Sciences (Turkey), 1:381

Italy
2003 explosion in Rome, 1:270
casting of human remains, 1:*128*
counterfeit currency, 2:*698*
wine fraud, 2:742

Ivanov, Pavel, 2:588

IVDS (Integrated Virus Detection System), 2:738

Ivory, illegal, 2:*740*

J

"Jack the Ripper" murder case, 1:*171*, 172, 338, *404*

James, P. D., 1:293

Japan
ancient fingerprints, 1:279
Pokemon-induced seizures, 1:258
Superglue fuming discovery, 2:441, 656
Tokyo subway poisoning of 1995, 1:8, 9, 51, 2:*596*
Training Institute of Forensic Science, 1:380
World War II bomb-carrying balloons, 1:328

Japanese Society of Legal Medicine, 2:552

Jasinsky, Tony, 2:694

Jefferson, Field, 1:393, 394

Jefferson, Randolph, 1:394

Jefferson, Thomas (Paternity issue), 1:**393–394**, *394*

Jeffreys, Alec John, 1:216, 220, 224–225, 232, **394–395**

Jenkins, United States v. (1997), 1:115

Jenner, Edward, 1:375, 2:627, 712, 714, 719–720

Jennings, Thomas, 1:296

Jewish people
African Lemba tribe and, 1:6–7
crime scene cleaning ritual, 1:*177*
See also Holocaust

Jk antigens, 1:403

Johannsen, Wilhelm, 1:324

John Paul II (Pope), 1:48

Johnson, Lyndon B., 1:399

Johnson, Robert, 1:60

Johnson, Sally, 1:272

Joiner, General Electric v. (1997), 1:286, 2:708

Jordan, Michael, 2:635

Journal of Forensic Sciences, 2:551

Journals, professional, 2:**551–553**

Judicial precedents, 1:145

Jung, Karl, 2:563

Jurisdiction principle, 2:690

Jurisprudence, common law, 1:145

Justice for All Act of 2004, 1:219, 2:652

Juvenile delinquency
arson, 1:40
Chicago study, 1:187
gang violence, 1:322–323

K

Kaczynski, David, 2:704

Kaczynski, Theodore (Unabomber), 1:272, 2:**702–704**, *703*

Kafka, Franz, 1:334

Kansas highway accident, 1:*55*

Karyotypes, 1:143–144

Kasai, Kentaro, 1:**397**

Kassem, Abdul Karim, 1:50

Kastle-Meyer color tests, 2:610

Katyn Forest Massacre (World War II), 1:329

Katzmann, Frederic G., 2:592

Kaye, Sidney, 1:**398**

Keeler, Leonard, 1:**398–399**

Keep, Nathan Cooley, 2:494

Kell blood system, 2:467

Kendall, Edward, 1:376

Kennedy, John F., 1:48, **399–401**, *401*
Baden examination of, 1:67–68

bullet analysis, 1:*115*, *122*, *400*, 2:*686*

Kennedy, Robert, 1:48

Kennewick Man (Washington State), 1:**402**

Kent, Debbie, 1:117

Kenya (Illegal ivory), 2:*740*

Keratin, 1:383

Ketamine, 1:372

KeyHole surveillance satellites, 2:580

Keys (Ciphers), 1:150, 152, 190, 201

Keystroke recorders (Computer), 1:**162–163**

KGB (Soviet intelligence agency), 1:49, 50, 2:583

Kidd blood grouping system, 1:**403**

Kidnapping of children. *See* Missing children

Kihlstrom, John F., 1:277

Kikwit, Zaire (Ebola virus outbreak), 1:*245*

Kimball, Spencer W., 1:356

Kinealy, "Big Jim," 1:418

Kinetic energy (Collisions), 1:3

King, David, 2:542

King, Leslie, 1:356

King, Martin Luther, Jr., 1:48

King, Mary-Claire, 1:207

King Lear (Shakespeare) forgery, 2:569–570

Kingston, C. R., 1:403

Kirchner, Justus, 2:670

Kirk, Paul Leland, 1:184, **403–404**

Kirkpatrick, Jeanne, 1:235

Kitasato, Shibasaburo, 1:375

Klaas, Polly, 1:297

Klinger, R., 1:347

Klugman, Jack, 2:667

Knives
as assassination weapons, 1:51
forensic information from, 1:405
wounds from, 1:201–202, *404*, **404–405**

Knots, analysis of, 1:**405**

Known-plaintext cryptanalysis, 1:152

Known samples. *See* Control samples

Koehler, Arthur, 1:421, 2:749

Kostov, Vladimir, 2:439

Kotsev, Vasil, 2:439

Kujau, Konrad, 1:348, 349–350, 2:571

Kulikovsky, Tikhon, 2:588

Kumho Tire v. Carmichael (1999), 1:286, 2:708

Kursk (Russian nuclear submarine), 1:*75*

L

La Cantrella (Assassination agent), 1:49

LA-ICPMS (Laser ablation-inductively coupled plasma mass spectrometry), 1:**410–411,** *411*

Laboratory analysis
air plumes, 1:11
air/water purity, 1:9–10
art forgeries, 1:42
automobile accidents, 1:3
bombs, 1:104
control samples, 1:**170–171,** 2:583–584
pollen, 2:540–541
reference samples, 2:**577,** 664
sea-going accidents, 1:2
tampered products, 2:549
video evidence, 2:715–716
See also Crime laboratories

Lacassagne, Alexandre, 1:**407**

Lacerations (Blunt injuries), 1:97

Laënnec, René-Théophile-Hyacinthe, 1:188

Lafarge, Marie, 2:440

Lag phase of bacteria cultures, 1:62

Lambert, Marcelle, 1:71

Lamp filaments, 1:**290–291**

Land Remote Sensing Policy Act of 1992, 2:597

Lander, Eric, 1:261

Landsat surveillance satellites, 2:579, 597

Landsteiner, Karl, 1:90–91, 375, **407–408,** 2:582

LANs (Local area networks), 1:162

Larson, John, 1:398, 2:541

Laser ablation-inductively coupled plasma mass spectrometry (LA-ICPMS), 1:**410–411,** *411*

Laser desorption mass spectrometry (LDMS), 1:409

Laser technology, 1:**408–410,** *410*
confocal microscopy, 1:169
fingerprint analysis, 1:193
microphone bugs, 1:114
radars, 1:409

Latent fingerprints, 1:**411–412,** *412*
development of, 1:295, 318–319
environmental effects on, 2:595
single latent prints, 1:53
Superglue fuming method, 2:441–442, **656–657**

Latent Print Unit (FBI Crime Lab), 1:281

Latent shoeprints, 2:617

Lateral (Anatomical term), 1:20, *21*

Lateral rotations (Anatomy), 1:22

Latin terms in forensics, 1:**412–413**

Laubach, Karl, 2:544, 545

Law Enforcement Training Center, Federal (FLETC), 1:**413–414**

Law of the Sea, 1:74

Lawrence Livermore National Laboratory, 1:199, 418, 2:670

Lawyers, as forensics career option, 1:126

Lay witnesses, 1:287

Laybourne, Roxie C., 1:**414–415**

LDIS (Local DNA Identification System), 1:152

LDm (Median lethal dose), 2:679

LDMS (Laser desorption mass spectrometry), 1:409

Leach, Kimberley, 1:117

Lead
bullet analysis, 1:114–116, 2:639–640
paint analysis, 1:44

Leahy, Patrick, 1:9

Lecter, Hannibal (Fictional character), 1:293

Lee, Henry C., 1:181, **415–416,** 2:620

Lee, Manfred B., 1:292, 426

Lee, Philip, 1:30

Lee, Wen Ho, 2:541

Leeuwenhoek, Antony van, 1:64, 2:456

Lefaucheux, Casimir, 1:299

Legal jurisdiction principle, 2:690

Legal Medicine, 2:552

Legal responsibility. *See* Criminal responsibility

Legality principle, 2:690

Lemba tribe (Africa), 1:**6–7**

Lenses (Camera), 1:122

Lesions, 1:97

Less-lethal weapons technology, 1:**416–417**

Letelier, Orlando, 1:157

Lethal Weapon (Film), 1:292

Letter bombs. *See* Unabomber case

Leukotriene B4 (LTB4), 1:28

Levine, Philip, 1:408, **417–418**

Levite Jews (Cohen Modal Haplotype), 1:6, 7

Levy, Harlan, 2:620

Levy, Lisa, 1:117

Lewis blood group system, 2:467

Leydig cells, 2:613

Leyshon, Mabel, 2:585

L-Gel (Decontaminating agent), 1:199, **418**

LH (Luteinizing hormone), 2:526

Lichtenberg figures (Lightning strikes), 1:247

Lie detectors. *See* Brain wave scanners; Polygraph machines

Lifting of fingerprints, 1:295

Ligatures, 1:341, **405**

Light bulb filaments, 1:**290–291**

Light firearms, defined, 1:300

Light sources for analysis, alternate. *See* Alternate light source analysis

Lightning strikes, 1:246–247

Lincoln, Abraham, 1:48, 285, **418–420**

Lincoln, Robert, 1:419

Lindbergh baby kidnapping and murder case, 1:339, *340,* **420–422,** *421, 422*

Lindley, Fleetwood, 1:419

Line quality (Handwriting analysis), 1:339

Linguistics, 1:**422–423**
See also Speech patterns

Linkage groups (Genetics), 1:325

Linker DNA, 1:144

Linnaeus, Carolus, 2:657

Liquid mobile phase chromatography, 1:141, 229, 2:670

Liquid putrefaction, 1:197

List, John, 1:76

Literature, 1:**423–426**
See also specific literary characters and authors

Little, Michael, 2:693–694

Live vaccines, 2:712, 713

Lividity, 1:**426–427,** 2:672

Living forensics, 1:**427**

Lloyd, Eddie Joe, 1:*217*

Local area networks (LANs), 1:162

Local DNA Identification System (LDIS), 1:152

Locard, Edmond, 1:184, **427–428,** 2:633

Locard's exchange principle, 1:179, 209, 264, **428–429,** 2:683, **687**

Locard's Tripartite Rule (Fingerprints), 1:71

Lock-picking, 1:**429**

Lockerbie, Scotland (Pan Am Flight 103 crash of 1988), 1:15–16, *101,* 272

Logarithmic phase of bacteria cultures, 1:62

Logic bombs, 1:165

Lollia Paulina, 2:494

Lombroso, Cesare, 1:33–34, 186, 2:541

London, England (Soccer fans mishap), 1:*149*

London Agreement of 1945 (United Kingdom), 1:351

Long, Huey, 1:48

Long, John, 1:*123*

Long, Robert, 1:138, 139

Long bones, 1:330, 331, 2:623, *624*

Loops (Fingerprints), 1:295, 2:583, *584*

September 11, 2001, terrorist attacks, 2:**603–606,** *604, 605*
  DNA identification of victims, 1:153, 2:652
  geospatial image, 1:*330*
  World Trade Towers structural analysis, 1:37–39, *39*
  See also Anthrax letters incident of 2001

Septicemia, 1:64–65

Sequencing (DNA), 1:*230*, 2:**606–607,** 665

Serbia (Mass grave exhumation), 2:731

Serial killers, 2:**607–609**
  CAPTURE program, 1:111
  criminal profiling, 1:181–182
  film portrayal, 1:293
  origin of term, 2:580
  See also specific people

Serial offenders, geographic profiling, 1:326–327, 331
  See also Signatures of criminals

Serology, 2:521, **609–611**

SERRS (Surface enhanced resonance Raman spectroscopy), 2:571

Sertoli cells, 2:613

Serum, 1:36, 2:610, **611–612**

Sesamoid bones, defined, 2:623

Sex chromosomes, 1:143, 2:613–614, 751

Sex determination, 1:32, 33, 2:**612–614**

Sexual assault
  as contact crime, 1:170
  date rape drug, 1:372
  evidence kits, 2:527–528, 575–576, *576*
  nursing specialists, 1:118, 310, 311

Sexual dimorphisms, 2:**614–615**
  bones, 2:502–503, 625
  cranial volume, 1:34
  mastoid process, 1:33

Sexual Homicide Exchange (SHE), 1:110–111

Sexual homicides, 1:110–111, 2:616

Sexual predators, 2:**616**

SFC (Supercritical Fluid Chromatography), 1:141

Sfiri, Xenia, 2:588

SFSTs (Standardized Field Sobriety Tests), 2:631

SGEMPs (Systems-generated electromagnetic pulses), 2:574

Shadowcrew identity theft case, 1:166

Shaken baby syndrome, 2:**616–617**

Shamir, Adi, 1:190

Shark Arm Murder, 2:662

SHE (Sexual Homicide Exchange), 1:110–111

Sheppard, Marilyn, 1:172

Sheppard, Sam, 1:172, 403

Sherlock Holmes (Fictional character). *See* Holmes, Sherlock

Ship accidents, 1:1–2

Shipman, Harold, 1:341, 2:609

Shoeprints, 2:**617**
  2-D *vs.* 3-D impressions, 1:376
  early work on, 2:717
  as physical evidence, 2:535–536

Short bones, 2:623, *624*

Short tandem repeat (STR) analysis, 2:**653**
  CODIS profiles, 1:153, 218–219
  commercial kits, 1:155
  disappeared children of Argentina, 1:207–208
  early work on, 1:232
  laser technologies, 1:409–410
  vs. VNTR analysis, 1:221, 227–228
  Y chromosomes, 2:751

Shotgun DNA sequencing, 2:607

Shotgun wounds, rule of sixes, 2:588–589

"Shoulder surfing" identity theft, 1:370

Shoulder weapons (Firearms), 1:300

Shredding of documents, 1:234

Shroud of Turin, 1:24–25, 317, 2:443

Sickert, Walter, 1:172

Sickle cell anemia, 1:344, 2:582

Side-by-side comparison, 2:**537–538**

The Sign of Four (Doyle), 1:424

Signal amplification DNA recognition, 1:229

Signature forgeries, 1:340

Signatures of criminals
  film portrayal, 1:293
  method of operation and, 1:182, 2:453
  Unabomber case, 2:702, 703, 704

The Silence of the Lambs (Film), 1:293

Silencers, 2:**617–618**

Silent Spring (Carson), 2:681

Silicon Valley Regional Computer Forensics Lab (Menlo Park, California), 1:*151, 158, 165*

Simpson, Nicole Brown, 1:146, 2:618, 619

Simpson, O. J., murder trial, 2:**618–620**
  alleged digital image tampering, 1:207
  circumstantial evidence, 1:146
  civil *vs.* criminal trials, 1:147, 2:649
  DNA typing, 1:95, 2:618–620
  evidence handling, 2:*569*

Simpson Tacoma Kraft Pulp Mill (Tacoma, Washington), 1:*10*

Simulation. *See* Computer modeling

Simulation Model of Automobile Collisions (SMAC), 1:163–164

Single bullet theory (Kennedy assassination), 1:399–400

Single latent fingerprints, 1:53

Single nucleotide polymorphisms (SNPs), 1:233, 2:652

Sinus prints, 2:**620–621**

Siracusa, Vittorio, 2:**621**

Sister chromatids, 1:144

Sixes, Rule of, 2:**588–589**

Size-exclusion chromatography, 1:142

Skeletal analysis, 2:**621–623**
  anthropometric techniques, 1:33
  sinus prints, 2:620–621
  x rays, 2:503, 504

Skeletal system, 2:500, **623–625,** *624*

Skeletonization, 1:197–198

Skeletons
  fossilization, 2:660, 661
  Kennewick Man, 1:402
  Millennium Ancestor, 2:*503*
  See also Human remains; Skulls

Skidding (Vehicle accidents), 1:3

Skilling, John, 2:605

"Skimming" (Credit card fraud), 1:370

Skin, 1:**383–384,** 2:500
  airbag residue irritants, 1:13
  lividity, 1:**426–427**
  See also Friction ridge skin

Skulls, 2:*624,* **626–627**
  anthropological techniques, 1:32
  autopsy work, 1:57
  facial reconstruction, 1:276, 2:622, 627
  from ritual killing, 2:*587*
  sinus prints, 2:**620–621**

Slaughter, Karin, 1:425

Slide agglutination tests, 1:61–62

Slipped tool impressions, 2:676

SMAC (Simulation Model of Automobile Collisions), 1:163–164

Smallpox, 2:**627–628,** *628*
  as biological weapon, 1:87
  vaccines, 1:375, 2:627–628, 711–712, 719–720
  variola virus, 2:**714**

Smart identification cards, 1:*85*

Smells. *See* Odors

SMERSH assassination squad, 1:50–51

Smith, David L., 1:168, 2:437

Smith, James, 2:662

Smith, Ron, 2:**628–629**

Smith, Theobald, 1:375

Smuggling of drugs, internally, 1:*265*

Sniffers (Bomb detection devices), 1:102

Sniper shootings of 2002 (Washington, D.C.). *See* Washington, D.C. sniper shootings of 2002

Snow, Sue, 2:550

Snowball the cat, 2:**629**

SNPs (Single nucleotide polymorphisms), 1:233, 2:652

Soba, Masato, 2:441

Sobriety testing, 2:**630–632,** *631*
See also Breathalyzers

Soccer fans mishap (London, England), 1:*149*

Social and ethical issues, 1:**261–262**
criminal profiling, 2:554–556
definition of crime, 1:184–185
DNA evidence, 1:214, **218–219**
privacy, 1:114, 218–219, 2:**546–548,** 666
quality control in labs, 2:568, 569
thanatology, 2:**669–670**

Social contract and crime, 1:185

Social determinism, 1:186–187

Social theories of crime, 1:184–187

Sociopathic personality disorder. *See* Antisocial personality disorder

Socrates, 1:49

Soda-lime glass, 1:332

Söderman, Harry, 1:184, 428, 2:456, **633–634**

Sodium azide, in airbags, 1:12–13

Sodium pentothal, as truth serum, 2:564–565, 696

SOE (Special Operations Executive) (United Kingdom), 1:51

Software
automobile accident simulation, 1:163–164
geographic profiling, 1:326–327
GIS, 1:331–332
image rendering, 2:461, *462*
See also Computer crime/computer security

Soils, 2:**634–635**
forensic botany and, 1:106
grave exhumation and, 1:268
Popp, Georg work, 2:544–545
provenance concept and, 1:328

Solar Sunrise hacking incidents, 1:160

Soldiers, identification of remains, 2:732

Solid-phase microextraction, 1:314

Solid state flight data recorders, 1:304–305

Solids, spectroscopy of, 1:253, 315

Solubility and decontamination, 1:199–200

Soman nerve agent, 2:480

Somatic nervous system, 2:481

Sorbents for decontamination, 1:199

Sorensen, Paul S., 2:478

Sound-based detection technologies, 1:133

Source-region electromagnetic pulses (SREMPs), 2:574

South African Lemba tribe, 1:6–7

Southeast Asia tsunami of 2004. *See* Tsunami of 2004 (Southeast Asia)

Southern blots (Electrophoresis), 1:252

Souvenirs
counterfeit sports memorabilia, 2:**635–637**
of crimes, 1:182, 2:609

Souviron, Richard, 1:117

Soviet Union
forgeries, 1:235
KGB, 1:49, 50, 2:583
Moscow Declaration, 1:351
See also Russia

Space images. *See* Satellite images

Space shuttle accidents, 1:4

Spade, Sam (Fictional character), 1:292

Spain
ice storm of 2000, 2:*453*
Madrid train bombing of 2004, 1:272–273
wine analysis, 2:743

Spatter analysis of blood. *See* Blood spatter analysis

Specht, Walter, 2:**637–638**

Special Operations Executive (SOE) (United Kingdom), 1:51

Special Photographic Unit (FBI Crime Lab), 1:282

Species differentiation, 1:231, 2:582

Specificity of biomarkers, 1:430–431

Specter, Arlen, 1:399

Spectral signatures, 2:636, 743

Spectrophotometry, 1:314–315, 2:454, 743

Spectroscopy, 2:499, **638–642**
for air plume analysis, 1:11
artificial fibers, 1:45
flame analysis, 1:303–304
ICP-OES, 1:115, 2:639
ion mobility, 1:11, 102
laser technologies, 1:409
nuclear, 2:**490–491**
See also Gas chromatography-mass spectroscopy

Speech patterns
analysis of, 2:660, 722–723
linguistics and, 1:422–423
sobriety testing, 2:630
voice alteration, 2:721, 722

Speeding vehicles, laser calculation, 1:409

Sperm, 2:**603**
aspermia, 1:**46–47**
DNA analysis, 1:223, 409–410
microscopic analysis, 1:76

Sphenoid fontanel, 2:626

Spinning (Artificial fibers), 1:45

Spite-motivated arson, 1:40

Spontaneous mummification, 2:470–472

Spores, 2:510–511, **642–643,** *643*

Sports
memorabilia counterfeiting, 2:**635–637**
performance-enhancing drugs, 2:525–527, 643–646, *645*

Sporulation, 2:642–643

SPOT (Satellite pour l'Observation de la Terre) (France), 2:597

Spree killers, defined, 2:608

SQL Slammer virus, 1:167

SREMPs (Source-region electromagnetic pulses), 2:574

SRY (Sex-determining region of the Y chromosome) gene, 2:613

St. Louis Art Museum, 1:44

St. Mary's Church (Luebeck, Germany), 1:*42*

St. Valentine's Day Massacre of 1929 (Chicago), 1:333

Stabbing wounds, 1:201–202, 2:565, 746

Stachybotrys chartarum poisoning, 1:9

Staging of crimes. *See* Crime scene staging

Stagnant hypoxia, 1:360

Stalin, Josef, 1:329

Standard anatomical position, 1:20

Standardized Field Sobriety Tests (SFSTs), 2:631

Standards (Handwriting specimens), 1:339

Standards in forensic science, 2:**646–647**
digital encryption, 1:152
ENFSI support, 1:263
FBI Crime Lab, 1:282
profiling practices, 2:555–556
uncertainty analysis, 2:705
See also Quality control of evidence

Staphylococcus species, 1:35, 307

Starer-type infrared detection devices, 1:378

Starling, Clarice (Fictional character), 1:293

Starrs, James, 1:262, 2:*647*, **647**

Stas, Jean Servais, 2:**648**

State DNA Identification System (SDIS), 1:152

State of Texas, Doyle v. (1954), 2:494

State Rules of Evidence, 1:147–148, 2:**649**
See also Federal Rules of Evidence

Stationary phase of bacteria cultures, 1:62

Stationary phases (Chromatography), 1:141, 142

Statistical methods, 2:**650–651**
paternity testing, 2:514–515
uncertainty analysis, 2:**704–705**

Temperature
  effect on bacteria cultures, 1:62
  hypothermia and, 1:359
  role in body decomposition, 1:98
  spore survival, 2:642
  weather patterns, 2:452–453

Template-based facial recognition methods, 1:276

Temporal events and time of death, 2:674

Ten-print fingerprints, 1:53

Tentative wounds, 1:347

Teratogens, 2:681

Terminal trajectories (Bullets), 1:116

Terrorism
  building structural analysis and, 1:37–38
  driving injuries from, 1:239–240
  drug abuse and, 1:363
  FBI work on, 1:282
  See also Bioterrorism; Oklahoma City bombing of 1995; Pan Am Flight 103 crash of 1988; September 11, 2001 terrorist attacks

Tertiary injuries, 1:240

Testes, 1:46

Testimony
  civil court, 1:147
  lay witnesses, 1:287
  See also Expert witnesses

Testosterone, 2:527

Teten, Howard, 2:553, 580

Teterboro Airport, New Jersey plane crash, 2:675

Tetrahydrocannabinol (THC), 1:371

Tetramers, 1:153

Thailand
  pet cockroach craze, 1:254
  tsunami victims, 1:198, 295, 368

Thalassemia, 1:344

Thallium poisoning, 2:459–460

Thanatology, 2:669–670

THC (Tetrahydrocannabinol), 1:371

The Hague (Netherlands)
  war conventions, 2:730, 731
  war crimes tribunals, 2:728

Thermal plumes, 1:11

Thermoluminescent dosimeters (TLDs), 1:236–237

Thin layer chromatography (TLC), 2:670
  defined, 1:141
  ink analysis, 1:379
  organic compound analysis, 2:499

Thomas, W. I., 1:186

Thompson, J. C., 1:419

Thomson, Sir J. J., 1:323

Thoracic region (Anatomy), 1:21, 22

Three-dimensional facial recognition methods, 1:276

Three-dimensional glasses, 2:539

Three-dimensional mapping laser equipment, 1:409

Thrust weapons, 1:51

Thumb knives, 1:51

Tibial (Anatomical term), 1:22

Time of death, 2:671–674, 673
  insects used to establish, 1:253–254
  tree ring analysis and, 1:204
  See also Body Farm

Tires
  blow-out, 1:3, 2:708
  tracks, 2:674–675, 675

Tiselius, Arne, 1:251

Titration (Acid-base indicators), 1:377

TLC. See Thin layer chromatography

TLDs (Thermoluminescent dosimeters), 1:236–237

Todorov, Vladimir, 2:439

Tokyo, Japan (Subway poisoning of 1995), 1:8, 9, 51, 2:596

Toledo, Alejandro, 2:514

Tollund Man mummy, 2:471

Tones (Dial tone decoders), 1:204–205

Tools
  fracture matching, 1:316
  impression evidence, 2:675–676
  lock-picking, 1:429

Topographic features affecting weather, 2:452

Torture, 1:389, 2:696

Toxic Substances Control Act of 1976, 2:680

Toxicity, defined, 2:538

Toxicodendrol, 2:538

Toxicology, 2:676–680, 678
  career options, 1:126, 2:679–681
  cocaine-addicted newborn baby, 2:447
  specialty areas, 2:680–682

Toxins, 2:682–683
  aflatoxins, 1:5–6, 2:682
  antidotes, 2:538
  E. coli, 1:261
  research on, 1:375
  ricin, 2:582
  See also Botulinum toxin; Poisons

Toxoids, 2:683

Toxoplasmosis, 2:512–513

Trace evidence, 1:264–265, 2:683–685, 684
  alternate light source analysis, 1:17
  bombs, 1:103–104
  building materials, 1:114
  collection, 1:78, 179–180, 2:684
  cross contamination, 1:187–188
  See also specific types of evidence

Tracing and tracking via Internet, 1:385–386

Tracing (Handwriting forgery), 1:340

Traditional Chinese medicine, 2:447–448

Traffic accidents. See Automobile accidents

Train accidents
  Amtrak Sunset Limited derailment of 1993, 2:488
  Madrid train bombing of 2004, 1:272–273
  suicide vs. homicide, 2:656

Training. See Education and training

Training Institute of Forensic Science (Japan), 1:380

Trajectories. See Bullet tracks

Transactions, non-reputable, 1:190

Transcription (RNA), 1:143

Transfection (Bacteria), 1:63

Transfer evidence, 2:687

Transfer RNA, 2:674

Transformation (Bacteria), 1:63

Transition interval (Acid-base indicators), 1:377

Transitions, atomic, 2:466

Transmission electron microscopy, 2:456–457

Transplant rejection, 1:36

Transportation Security Administration (TSA), 1:59–60

Transversal psychiatric evaluations, 2:560

Transverse planes (Anatomy), 1:21, 22

Trapped air plume samples, 1:11

Trees
  dendrochronology, 1:42, 202–204, 203
  xylotomy, 2:749, 750

Trenton, New Jersey postal facility (Anthrax incident), 1:31

The Trial (Kafka), 1:334

Trials. See Civil court systems; Criminal trials

Triangle of fraud, 1:309

Trichology. See Hair analysis

Trichomonas vaginalis (Parasite), 2:512

Triploidy, 1:143

Tripoli, Louis C., 2:695

tRNA, 2:674

Trojan horse viruses (Computers), 1:163, 166, 167

Trophies (Serial killings), 2:609

Truck bombs (Oklahoma City bombing of 1995), 2:496

Truman, Harry S, 1:48

Truth Control Tests (TCTs), 2:544

Truth serum, 2:564–565, 695–696

TSA (Transportation Security Administration), 1:59–60

Tsunami of 2004 (Southeast Asia), 1:**366–368**, *367, 368*
  decomposed body, 1:*198*
  fingerprint scan, 1:*295*

Tularemia, 2:**696–697**

Tungsten, in lamp filaments, 1:290–291

Turin, Italy (Shroud of Turin), 1:24–25, 317, 2:443

Turkey X disease, 1:6

The Turner Diaries (Macdonald), 2:496

Tutankhamen mummy, 1:23, *24*

Two-dimensional facial recognition methods, 1:276

Two-part codes, 1:151

Tylenol cyanide poisoning of 1982, 2:549, *550*

Typewriter analysis, 2:**697–698**

Typing of blood. *See* Blood typing

U

UCR (Uniform Crime Report), 1:39, 41

Uhlenhunth, Paul, 2:610

Ulnar (Anatomical term), 1:22

Ultra-high-pressure (UHP) sterilization, 2:436

Ultrasonography, 1:330, 374

Ultraviolet light, 2:**701**, *702*
  artwork identification, 1:43, 44
  defined, 1:248
  postal mail sanitization, 2:436

Ultraviolet spectroscopy, 2:640, 701

Unabomber case, 1:272, 2:**702–704**, *703*

Uncertainty analysis, 2:**704–705**

Underdrawings, in artwork identification, 1:43, 44

UNESCO (United Nations Educational, Scientific and Cultural Organization), 1:353

Uniform Crime Report (UCR), 1:39, 41

Uninterruptible power supplies (UPSs), 1:162

United Kingdom
  fingerprint cases, 1:296
  history of criminal responsibility, 2:449
  London Agreement of 1945, 1:351
  mad cow disease, 2:434–435, 755
  pub bombings, 1:271
  ritual killing in London, 2:586
  soccer fans mishap, 1:*149*

United Nations Convention on the Law of the Sea of 1982, 1:74

United Nations Educational, Scientific and Cultural Organization (UNESCO), 1:353

United States Army Medical Research Institute of Infectious Diseases (USAMRIID), 2:**705–707**

United States Army Medical Unit (USAMU), 2:706

United States government agencies. *See specific agency names*

United States National Central Bureau (USNCB) (Interpol), 1:**387–388**

United States Postal Service (USPS)
  mail sanitization, 2:435–436
  ricin letter, 2:*583*
  UNABOM task force, 2:704
  See also Anthrax letters incident of 2001

United States Supreme Court, 2:687, **707–709**

United States v. Addison (1974), 2:708

United States v. Jenkins (1997), 1:115

United States v. Piccinonna (1989), 2:544

United States v. Prime (2002), 1:340

United States v. Saelee (2001), 1:340, 2:558

United States v. Scarfo (2001), 1:163

University of Nottingham (United Kingdom), 1:212

University of Tennessee Anthropology Research Facility. *See* Body Farm

University of Trent (Ontario, Canada), 1:213

Unsolved cases. *See* Cold cases

Upper extremities (Anatomy), 1:*21*, 22

UPSs (Uninterruptible power supplies), 1:162

Uranium powder, 2:*489*

Urinary system, 2:500

Urine tests
  orthotolidine solution, 2:501
  performance-enhancing drugs, 2:527, 645–646

U.S. government agencies. *See specific agency names*

USA Today, 1:261

USAMRIID (United States Army Medical Research Institute of Infectious Diseases), 2:**705–707**

USCSB (Chemical Safety and Hazard Investigation Board), 1:**135–136**

USNCB (United States National Central Bureau) (Interpol), 1:**387–388**

USPS. *See* United States Postal Service

UV light. *See* Ultraviolet light

V

V series nerve agents, 1:138, 2:480

Vaccines, 2:**711–714**
  anthrax, 1:29, 2:683
  for bacteria groups, 1:88
  development of, 1:375
  smallpox, 1:375, 2:627–628, 711–712, 714, 719–720
  USAMRIID work, 2:705–707

Vacher, Joseph, 1:407

Vagal inhibition, 1:341

Values. *See* Social and ethical issues

ValuJet Flight 592 crash, cockpit voice recorder, 1:*305*

"Vampire Boy Killer," 2:585

"Vampire of Sacramento," 2:562, 586

Vampirism, 2:585

Van Zandt, Clinton R., 2:496

Vandalism-motivated arson, 1:40

Vanzetti, Bartolomeo, 1:333, 2:**591–593**, *593*

Variable number tandem repeats (VNTR), 1:221, 224–225, 227–228, 397

Variant CJD. *See* Creutzfeldt-Jakob disease

Variola virus. *See* Smallpox

Variolation, 2:711–712, 714

Varnish layer analysis, in art forgeries, 1:43

Vass, Arpad, 1:98

vCJD. *See* Creutzfeldt-Jakob disease (CJD)

Vectors (Disease transmission), 2:516, 517

Vehicle accidents. *See* Automobile accidents

Ventral (Anatomical term), 1:20, *21*

Verdicts (Medical examiners), 2:444–445

Vernam ciphers, 1:189

Vertebral column, 2:*624*, 625

Vesuvius, Mount (Casting of human remains), 1:*128*

VH-IWJ Westwind 1124 aircraft accident of 1985 (Sydney, Australia), 1:15

Vibrational spectroscopy. *See* Raman spectroscopy

VICAP (Violent Criminal Apprehension Program), 2:554, 580

Victimology, 1:182, 2:561, 609

Video Motion Detectors (VMDs), 1:148–149

Videos. *See* Closed-circuit television; Surveillance cameras

Vidocq, Eugène-François, 2:**716–717**, *717*

Vietnam War, identification of soldier remains, 2:732

Vinland map, 2:443

Violent Criminal Apprehension Program (VICAP), 2:554, 580

Violent gangs, defined, 1:322

Viral replication, 2:717–718, 719

Virchow, Rudolf Ludwig, 2:**720–721**, *721*

Virchow autopsy method, 1:57